SOMETHING ABOUT THE AUTHOR

ISSN 0276-816X

SOMETHING ABOUT THE AUTHOR

**Facts and Pictures about Authors
and Illustrators of Books for Young People**

EDITED BY
DONNA OLENDORF

VOLUME 66

 **Gale Research Inc.** · *DETROIT* · *LONDON*

STAFF

Editor: Donna Olendorf

Associate Editor: James F. Kamp

Senior Editor: Hal May

Sketchwriters: Marilyn K. Basel, Barbara Carlisle Bigelow, Elizabeth A. Des Chenes, Janice E. Drane, Kevin S. Hile, Katherine Huebl, Denise E. Kasinec, Thomas Kozikowski, Sharon Malinowski, Margaret Mazurkiewicz, Carol DeKane Nagel, Julia M. Rubiner, Mary K. Ruby, Edward G. Scheff, Neil R. Schlager, Kenneth R. Shepherd, Diane Telgen, Arlene True, Polly A. Vedder, and Thomas Wiloch

Research Manager: Victoria B. Cariappa

Research Supervisor: Mary Rose Bonk

Editorial Associates: Jane A. Cousins, Andrew Guy Malonis, and Norma Sawaya

Editorial Assistants: Mike Avolio, Patricia Bowen, Reginald A. Carlton, Clare Collins, Catherine A. Coulson, Theodore J. Dumbrigue, Shirley Gates, Sharon McGilvray, and Tracy Head Turbett

Production Manager: Mary Beth Trimper

External Production Assistant: Shanna P. Heilveil

Art Director: Arthur Chartow

Keyliner: C. J. Jonik

The paper used in this publication meets the minimum requirements of American National Standard for Information Sciences—Permanence Paper for Printed Library Materials, ANSI Z39.48-1984. ∞™

Copyright © 1991
Gale Research Inc.
835 Penobscot Bldg.
Detroit, MI 48226-4094

Library of Congress Catalog Card Number 72-27107

ISBN 0-8103-2276-5
ISSN 0276-816X

Printed in the United States

Published simultaneously in the United Kingdom
by Gale Research International Limited
(An affiliated company of Gale Research Inc.)

Contents

Introduction ix   **Acknowledgments xi**

A

Asch, Frank 1946- 1

Atheling, William, Jr.
See Blish, James (Benjamin) 21

Atwater, Florence (Hasseltine Carroll)
1896-1979 11

Atwater, Richard (Tupper) 1892-1948 11

Austin, Margot 1909(?)-1990
Obituary Notice 12

Azaid
See Zaidenberg, Arthur 243

B

Baker, Pamela J. 1947- 13

Baum, L. Frank
See Thompson, Ruth Plumly 212

BB
See Watkins-Pitchford, Denys James 222

Bellairs, John (A.) 1938-1991
Obituary Notice 13

Berman, Paul (Lawrence) 1949- 13

Birdseye, Tom 1951- 14

Blanc, Esther Silverstein 1913- 14

Blegvad, Erik 1923- 15

Blegvad, Lenore 1926- 20

Blish, James (Benjamin) 1921-1975 21

Blishen, Edward 1920- 22

Botsford, Ward 1927- 26

Bradford, Barbara Taylor 1933- 27

Briggs, Raymond (Redvers) 1934- 28

Butterworth, Oliver 1915-1990
Obituary Notice 34

C

Caine, Geoffrey
See Walker, Robert W(ayne) 218

Camps, Luis 1928- 34

Carter, Angela 1940- 35

Causley, Charles (Stanley) 1917- 36

Chartier, Normand L. 1945- 39

Cooper, Ilene 41

Cosby, Bill
See Cosby, William Henry, Jr. 41

Cosby, William Henry, Jr. 1937- 41

Cuffari, Richard 1925-1978 47

Cunliffe, Marcus (Falkner) 1922-1990
Obituary Notice 51

D

d'Aulaire, Edgar Parin 1898-1986 51

d'Aulaire, Ingri (Mortenson Parin)
1904-1980 54

de Bono, Edward 1933- 55

Demi
See Hitz, Demi 128

Denton, Kady MacDonald 57

Downey, Fairfax D(avis) 1893-1990
Obituary Notice 57

Durell, Ann 1930- 57

E

Ekwensi, C. O. D.
See Ekwensi, Cyprian (Odiatu Duaka) 57

Ekwensi, Cyprian (Odiatu Duaka) 1921- 57

Emecheta, (Florence Onye) Buchi 1944- 59

Essrig, Harry 1912- 60

F

Ferguson, Sarah (Margaret) 1959- 60

Fiammenghi, Gioia 1929- 62

Fischler, Shirley (Walton) 64

Fischler, Stan(ley I.) 64

Fisk, Pauline 1948- 66

Fleishman, Seymour 1918- 68

Francis, Charles
  See Holme, Bryan 130

Frankel, Alona 1937- 69

Freeman, Sarah (Caroline) 1940- 70

Fry, Christopher 1907- 71

G

Galdone, Paul 1907(?)-1986 77

Galloway, Priscilla 1930- 83

Gerrold, David 1944- 85

Gibson, William 1914- 87

Godkin, Celia (Marilyn) 1948- 90

Goodall, John S(trickland) 1908- 91

Greene, Carol 19(?)- 93

Gregorich, Barbara 1943- 95

Grifalconi, Ann 1929- 97

Gruber, Terry (deRoy) 1953- 107

H

Haertling, Peter 1933- 108

Hale, Glenn
  See Walker, Robert W(ayne) 218

Hale, Kathleen 1898- 111

Hall, Willis 1929- 120

Hamilton, (John) Alan 1943- 121

Haugen, Tormod 1945- 121

Heller, Ruth M. 1924- 123

Hill, Eric 1927- 125

Hitz, Demi 1942- 128

Holme, Bryan 1913-1990
  Obituary Notice 130

J

Jaffee, Al(lan) 1921- 130

Janger, Kathleen N. 1940- 133

Jennings, Elizabeth (Joan) 1926- 133

Jordan, Lee
  See Scholefield, Alan 199

K

Kesey, Ken (Elton) 1935- 135

King, Larry L. 1929- 137

Kliban, B(ernard) 1935-1990
  Obituary Notice 138

Knoepfle, John (Ignatius) 1923- 138

Krasne, Betty
  See Levine, Betty K(rasne) 150

Kroll, Steven 1941- 142

L

Laverty, Donald
  See Blish, James (Benjamin) 21

Lebrun, Claude 1929- 145

Levin, Ira 1929- 146

Levine, Betty K(rasne) 1933- 150

Lifton, Robert Jay 1926- 151

Lyons, Marcus
  See Blish, James (Benjamin) 21

M

MacDougal, John
  See Blish, James (Benjamin) 21

Maeterlinck, Maurice 1862-1949 154

Marsden, John 1950- 161

Marsh, Dave 1950- 162

McGrath, Thomas (Matthew) 1916-1990
  Obituary Notice 164

Mendez, Raymond A. 1947- 164

Merlin, Arthur
  See Blish, James (Benjamin) 21

Mitton, Jacqueline 1948- 165

Mitton, Simon 1946- 166

Morris, Chris(topher Crosby) 1946- 166

Morris, Janet (Ellen) 1946- 168

Morrison, Bill 1935- 169

N

Naylor, Phyllis
  See Naylor, Phyllis Reynolds 170

Naylor, Phyllis Reynolds 1933- 170

Nichol, B(arrie) P(hillip) 1944-1988 176

Nickless, Will 1902-1979(?) 178

O

Olds, Elizabeth 1896-1991
  Obituary Notice 179

P

Peebles, Anne
  See Galloway, Priscilla 83

Penrose, Gordon 1925- 179

Prelutsky, Jack 1940- 180

Prescott, Casey
  See Morris, Chris(topher Crosby) 166

Prichard, Katharine Susannah 1883-1969 184

Provost, Gary (Richard) 1944- 186

Purdy, Carol 1943- 186

Pyle, Katharine 1863-1938 187

R

Reeder, Carolyn 1937- 188

Renaud, Bernadette 1945- 188

Rhyne, Nancy 1926- 190

Riq
  See Atwater, Richard (Tupper) 11

Robertson, Stephen
  See Walker, Robert W(ayne) 218

S

Sanderson, Irma 1912- 190

Sarah, Duchess of York
  See Ferguson, Sarah (Margaret) 60

Schaefer, Jack (Warner) 1907-1991 192

Schatell, Brian 194

Schoenherr, John (Carl) 1935- 194

Scholefield, A. T.
  See Scholefield, Alan 199

Scholefield, Alan 1931- 199

Schroeder, Alan 1961- 200

Segal, Lore (Groszmann) 1928- 200

Seton, Anya 1904(?)-1990
  Obituary Notice 204

Spillane, Frank Morrison 1918- 204

Spillane, Mickey
  See Spillane, Frank Morrison 204

Steel, Danielle (Fernande) 1947- 205

Stephens, Alice Barber 1858-1932 207

Stryker, Daniel
  See Morris, Chris(topher Crosby) 166

T

Tamminga, Frederick William 1934- 209

Thompson, Ruth Plumly 1891-1976 212

Tippett, James S(terling) 1885-1958 214

Tong, Gary S. 1942- 215

Torley, Luke
  See Blish, James (Benjamin) 21

Traherne, Michael
  See Watkins-Pitchford, Denys James 222

W

Walker, Lou Ann 1952- 216

Walker, Robert W(ayne) 1948- 218

Watkins, Peter 1934- 221

Watkins-Pitchford, Denys James 1905-1990
  Obituary Notice 222

Watterson, Bill 1958- 222

Wesley, Mary 1912- 227

Williams, Garth (Montgomery) 1912- 228

Williams, Karen Lynn 1952- 235

Willius, T. F.
  See Tamminga, Frederick William 209

Wohlberg, Meg 1905-1990
  Obituary Notice 235

Wooding, Sharon
  See Wooding, Sharon L(ouise) 235

Wooding, Sharon L(ouise) 1943- 235

Wrightson, (Alice) Patricia 1921- 238

Z

Zaidenberg, Arthur 1908(?)-1990
  Obituary Notice 243

Zed, Dr.
See Penrose, Gordon 179

Zwerger, Lisbeth 1954- 244

Introduction

Something about the Author (SATA) is an ongoing reference series that deals with the lives and works of authors and illustrators of children's books. *SATA* includes not only well-known authors and illustrators whose books are widely read, but also those less prominent people whose works are just coming to be recognized. This series is often the only readily available information source for emerging writers or artists. You'll find *SATA* informative and entertaining whether you are a student, a librarian, an English teacher, a parent, or simply an adult who enjoys children's literature for its own sake.

What's Inside SATA

SATA provides detailed information about authors and illustrators who span the full time range of children's literature, from early figures like John Newbery and L. Frank Baum to contemporary figures like Judy Blume and Richard Peck. Authors in the series represent primarily English-speaking countries, particularly the United States, Canada, and the United Kingdom. Also included, however, are authors from around the world whose works are available in English translation. The writings represented in *SATA* include those created intentionally for children and young adults as well as those written for a general audience and known to interest younger readers. These writings cover the entire spectrum of children's literature, including picture books, humor, folk and fairy tales, animal stories, mystery and adventure, science fiction and fantasy, historical fiction, poetry and nonsense verse, drama, biography, and nonfiction.

Obituaries are also included in *SATA* and are intended not only as death notices but as concise views of people's lives and work. Additionally, each edition features newly revised and updated entries for a selection of *SATA* listees who remain of interest to today's readers and who have been active enough to require extensive revision of their earlier biographies.

Two Convenient Indexes

In response to suggestions from librarians, *SATA* indexes no longer appear in each volume, but are included in alternate (odd-numbered) volumes of the series, beginning with Volume 57.

SATA continues to include two indexes that cumulate with each alternate volume: the Illustrations Index, arranged by the name of the illustrator, gives the number of the volume and page where the illustrator's work appears in the current volume as well as all preceding volumes in the series; the Author Index gives the number of the volume in which a person's Biographical Sketch or Obituary appears in the current volume as well as all preceding volumes in the series.

These indexes also include references to authors and illustrators who appear in Gale's *Yesterday's Authors of Books for Children, Children's Literature Review*, and the *Something about the Author Autobiography Series*.

Easy-to-Use Entry Format

Whether you're already familiar with the *SATA* series or just getting acquainted, you will want to be aware of the kind of information that an entry provides. In every *SATA* entry the editors attempt to give as complete a picture of the person's life and work as possible. A typical entry in *SATA* includes the following clearly labeled information sections:

● *PERSONAL:* date and place of birth and death, parents' names and occupations, name of spouse, date of marriage, and names of children, educational institutions attended, degrees received, religious and political affiliations.

● *ADDRESSES:* complete home, office, and agent's address.

● *CAREER:* name of employer, position, and dates for each career post; military service.

● *MEMBER:* memberships and offices held in professional and civic organizations.

● *AWARDS, HONORS:* literary and professional awards received.

● *WRITINGS:* title-by-title chronological bibliography of books written and/or illustrated, listed by genre when known; lists of other notable publications, such as plays, screenplays, and periodical contributions.

● *WORK IN PROGRESS:* description of projects in progress.

● *SIDELIGHTS:* a biographical portrait of the author's development, either directly from the person—and often written specifically for the *SATA* entry—or gathered from diaries, letters, interviews, or other published sources.

● *FOR MORE INFORMATION SEE:* references for further reading.

● *EXTENSIVE ILLUSTRATIONS:* photographs, movie stills, manuscript samples, book covers, and other interesting visual materials supplement the text.

How a SATA Entry Is Compiled

A *SATA* entry progresses through a series of steps. If the biographee is living, the *SATA* editors try to secure information directly from him or her through a questionnaire. From the information that the biographee supplies, the editors prepare an entry, filling in any essential missing details with research and/or telephone interviews. When necessary, the author or illustrator is sent a copy of the entry to check for accuracy and completeness.

If the biographee is deceased or cannot be reached by questionnaire, the *SATA* editors examine a wide variety of published sources to gather information for an entry. Biographical and bibliographic sources are consulted, as are book reviews, feature articles, published interviews, and material sometimes obtained from the biographee's family, publishers, agent, or other associates.

We Welcome Your Suggestions

We invite you to examine the entire *SATA* series, starting with this volume. Please write and tell us if we can make *SATA* even more helpful to you. Send comments and suggestions to: The Editor, *Something about the Author*, Gale Research Inc., 835 Penobscot Bldg., Detroit, Michigan 48226.

Acknowledgments

Grateful acknowledgment is made to the following publishers, authors, and artists whose works appear in this volume.

FRANK ASCH. Illustration by Frank Asch from his *Rebecka.* Harper & Row, Publishers, 1972. Copyright (c) 1972 by Frank Asch. Reprinted by permission of HarperCollins Publishers,Inc./ Illustration by Frank Asch from his *Moon Bear.* Charles Scribner's Sons, 1978. Copyright (c) 1978 by Frank Asch. Reprinted with permission of Charles Scribner's Sons, an imprint of Macmillan Publishing Company./ Illustration from *Turtle Tale,* by Frank Asch. Dial, 1978. Copyright (c) 1978 by Frank Asch. Used by permission of Dial Books for Young Readers, a division of Penguin Books USA Inc./ Jacket by Frank Asch from his *Mooncake.* Copyright (c) 1983 by Frank Asch. Used by permission of Prentice-Hall, a division of Simon & Schuster, Englewood Cliffs, NJ./ Jacket by Frank Asch from his *Bear Shadow.* Copyright (c) 1985 by Frank Asch. Used by permission of Prentice-Hall, a division of Simon & Schuster, Englewood Cliffs, NJ./ Illustration by Frank Asch and Vladimir Vagin from their *Here Comes the Cat.* Scholastic, 1989. Reprinted by permission of Scholastic, Inc./ Photograph courtesy of Frank Asch.

RICHARD ATWATER. Illustration from *Mr. Popper's Penguins,* by Richard and Florence Atwater. Little, Brown and Company, 1938. Copyright 1938 by Richard and Florence Atwater. Illustration by Robert Lawson. Reprinted by permission of Little, Brown and Company.

PAUL BERMAN. Illustration by Paul Berman from his *Make-Believe: A How-to Book.* Atheneum, 1982. Copyright (c) 1982 by Paul Berman. Reprinted with the permission of Atheneum Publishers, an imprint of Macmillan Publishing Company.

ESTHER SILVERSTEIN BLANC. Photograph courtesy of Esther Silverstein Blanc.

ERIK BLEGVAD. Illustration by Erik Blegvad from *The Gammage Cup,* by Carol Kendall. Harcourt Brace Jovanovich, 1959. Copyright (c) 1959 and renewed 1987 by Carol Kendall. Reprinted by permission of Harcourt Brace Jovanovich, Inc./ Illustration by Erik Blegvad from *The Five Pennies,* by Barbara Brenner. Knopf, 1964. Copyright (c) 1964 by Barbara Brenner and Erik Blegvad. Reprinted by permission of Alfred A. Knopf, Inc./ Illustration by Erik Blegvad from *The Finches' Fabulous Furnace,* by Roger Drury Wolcott. Little, Brown, 1971. Reprinted by permission of Little, Brown and Company./ Jacket of *This Little Pig-A-Wig: And Other Rhymes about Pigs,* chosen by Lenore Blegvad. Copyright (c) 1982 by Erik Blegvad. Illustrations by Erik Blegvad. Reprinted with the permission of Margaret K. McElderry Books, an imprint of Macmillan Publishing Company./ Jacket of *The Parrot in the Garret: And Other Rhymes about Dwellings,* chosen by Lenore Blegvad. Copyright (c) 1982 by Erik Blegvad. Illustration by Erik Blegvad. Reprinted with the permission of Margaret K. McElderry Books, an imprint of Macmillan Publishing Company./ Photograph courtesy of Eric Blegvad.

EDWARD BLISHEN. Illustration by Brian Wildsmith from *The Oxford Book of Poetry for Children,* by Edward Blishen. Franklin Watts, 1964. Reprinted by permission of the publisher./ Photograph courtesy of Edward Blishen.

BARBARA TAYLOR BRADFORD. Photograph courtesy of Barbara Taylor Bradford.

RAYMOND BRIGGS. Illustration by Raymond Briggs from his *Father Christmas.* Coward-McCann, Inc., 1973. Text and illustrations copyright (c) 1973 by Raymond Briggs. Reprinted by permission of Coward, McCann & Geoghegan, Inc./ Illustration by Raymond Briggs from his *The Snowman.* Random House, 1978. Copyright (c) 1978 by Raymond Briggs. Reprinted by permission of Random House, Inc./ Illustration by Raymond Briggs from his *The Tin-Pot Foreign General and the Old Iron Woman.* Little, Brown, 1984. Reprinted by permission of Little, Brown and Company./ Photograph courtesy of Raymond Briggs./ Scene from *When the Wind Blows,* photograph by Donald Cooper.

LUIS CAMPS. Illustration by Luis Camps from *Les Farfeluches font des achats en 314 mots,* by d'Alain Gree. Casterman Publishers, 1977. Copyright (c) 1977 by Casterman Publishers. Reprinted by permission of Casterman Publishers./ Photograph courtesy of Luis Camps.

ANGELA CARTER. Photograph (c) Jerry Bauer.

CHARLES CAUSLEY. Illustration from *Figgie Hobbin,* by Charles Causley. Text copyright (c) 1973 by Charles Causley. Illustrations copyright (c) 1973 by Trina Schart Hyman. Reprinted with permission of Trina Schart Hyman./ Photograph by Nicholas Elder, courtesy of Charles Causley.

JOHN GOODALL. Jacket illustration by John Goodall from his ***Paddy to the Rescue.*** Copyright (c) 1985 by John S. Goodall. Reprinted with the permission of Margaret K. McElderry Books, an imprint of Macmillan Publishing Company./ Illustration from ***The Story of the Seashore,*** by John S. Goodall. Margaret K. McElderry Books, 1990. Copyright (c) 1990 by John S. Goodall. Reprinted with permission of Margaret K. McElderry Books, an imprint of Macmillan Publishing Company./ Photograph by F. Futcher & Son.

BARBARA GREGORICH. Cover of ***The Gum on the Drum,*** by Barbara Gregorich. Copyright (c) 1984 by School Zone Publishing. Illustrations by John Sandford. Reprinted by permission of School Zone Publishing Company./ Cover of ***Nine Men Chase A Hen,*** by Barbara Gregorich. Copyright (c) 1984 by School Zone Publishing. Illustrations by John Sandford. Reprinted by permission of School Zone Publishing Company./ Photograph courtesy of Barbara Gregorich.

ANN GRIFALCONI. Illustration by Ann Grifalconi from ***Everett Anderson's Goodbye,*** by Lucille Clifton. Holt, 1983. Copyright (c) 1983 by Lucille Clifton. Illustrations copyright (c) 1983 by Ann Grifalconi. Reprinted by permission of Henry Holt and Company, Inc./ Illustrations from ***The Village of Round and Square Houses,*** by Ann Grifalconi. Little, Brown and Company, 1986. Copyright (c) 1986 by Ann Grifalconi. Reprinted by permission of Little, Brown and Company./ Illustrations from ***Darkness and the Butterfly,*** by Ann Grifalconi. Little, Brown and Company, 1987. Copyright (c) 1987 by Ann Grifalconi. Reprinted by permission of Little, Brown and Company./ Photograph by Walter Meyers.

PETER HAERTLING. Jacket of ***Crutches,*** by Peter Haertling. Jacket illustration copyright (c) 1988 by Wendell Minor. Reprinted by permission of William Morrow and Company, Inc./ Jacket of ***Old John,*** by Peter Haertling. Jacket illustration copyright (c) 1990 by Ted Lewin. Reprinted by permission of William Morrow and Company, Inc.

KATHLEEN HALE. Illustration by Kathleen Hale from her ***Orlando the Marmalade Cat: A Camping Holiday,*** by Kathleen Hale. Frederick Warne & Co., 1990. Copyright (c) Kathleen Hale, 1938, 1959, 1990. Reproduced by permission of Frederick Warne and Co./ Illustration by Kathleen Hale from her ***Orlando's Night Out.*** Frederick Warne & Co., 1991. Copyright (c) 1941, 1991, by Kathleen Hale. Reprinted by permission of Frederick Warne and Co./ Photographs courtesy of Kathleen Hale.

TORMOD HAUGEN. Jacket of ***The Night Birds,*** by Tormod Haugen. Delacorte Press, 1982. Copyright (c) Gyldendal Norsk Forlag A/S 1975. Translation copyright (c) 1982 by Dell Publishing Co., Inc. Jacket design by Jordan Brener. Jacket illustration copyright (c) 1982 by Stan Skardinski. Reprinted by permission of Delacorte Press/Seymour Laurence.

RUTH HELLER. Illustration by Ruth Heller from her ***Animals Born Alive and Well.*** Grosset & Dunlap, 1987. Copyright (c) 1982 by Ruth Heller. Reprinted by permission of Grosset & Dunlap./ Photograph courtesy of Ruth Heller.

ERIC HILL. Illustrations by Eric Hill from his ***Where's Spot?,*** G.P. Putnam's Sons, 1987. Copyright (c) 1980 by Eric Hill. Copyright (c) 1987 sign language translation by G.P. Putnam's Sons. Sign Language drawings by Jan Skrobisz. Reprinted by permission of G.P. Putnam's Sons./ Illustrations from ***How Many Opposites Do You Know?,*** by Eric Hill. Price Stern Sloan, Inc. 1984. Copyright (c) 1984 text and illustrations by Eric Hill. Reprinted by permission of the publisher./ Photograph courtesy of Eric Hill.

DEMI HITZ. Illustration by Demi Hitz from her ***Demi's Count the Animals 1 2 3.*** Grosset & Dunlap, 1990. Copyright (c) 1986 by Demi. Reprinted by permission of Grosset & Dunlap, Inc./ Illustration by Demi Hitz from her ***The Empty Pot.*** Holt, 1990. Copyright (c) 1991 by Demi. Reprinted by permission of Henry Holt and Company, Inc.

AL JAFFEE. Illustrations by Al Jaffee from his ***Snappy Answers to Stupid Questions, No. 7.*** Warner Books, 1989. Copyright (c) 1989 by Al Jaffee and E.C. Publications, Inc. Reprinted by permission of E.C. Publications, Inc.

KEN KESEY. Photograph by Brian Lanker.

JOHN KNOEPFLE. Cover of ***Dogs and Cats and Things Like That,*** by John Knoepfle. McGraw-Hill, 1971. Cover art by Paul Galdone. Illustrations (c) 1971 by Paul Galdone. Reproduced with permission./ Photograph from ***Our Street Feels Good,*** by John Knoepfle. McGraw-Hill, 1972. Photographs (c) 1972 by Bonnie Unsworth. Reproduced by permission of Bonnie Unsworth./ Cover of ***Poems from The Sangamon,*** by John Knoepfle. University of Illinois Press, 1985. Copyright (c) 1985 by John Knoepfle. Cover photograph by Larry Kanfer. Reprinted by permission of The Larry Kanfer Gallery, P.O. Box 6555, Champaign, IL 61826-6555, (217) 398-2000./ Photograph courtesy of Sangamon State University, Media Services.

STEVEN KROLL. Jacket of ***Branigan's Cat and the Halloween Ghost,*** by Steven Kroll. Holiday House, 1990. Text copyright (c) 1990 by Steven Kroll. Illustrations copyright (c) 1990 by Carolyn Ewing. Reprinted by permission of the publisher./ Cover of ***Gone Fishing,*** by Steven Kroll. Crown, 1990. Copyright (c) 1990 by Steven Kroll. Illustrations copyright (c) 1990 by Harvey Stevenson. Reprinted by permission of Crown Publishers, Inc./ Jacket of ***Princess Abigail and***

MARY WESLEY. Photograph (c) Jerry Bauer.

GARTH WILLIAMS. Illustration by Garth Williams from *Flossie and Bossie,* by Era LeGallienne. Harper, 1948. Reprinted by permission of HarperCollins Publishers, Inc./ Illustration by Garth Williams from *Charlotte's Web,* by E.B. White. Harper & Row, Publishers, 1952. Copyright (c) 1952 by E.B. White. Reprinted by permission of HarperCollins Publishers, Inc./ Illustration by Garth Williams from *Little House in the Big Woods,* by Laura Ingalls Wilder. Harper & Row, Publishers, 1953. Text Copyright (c) 1932 by Laura Ingalls Wilder. Illustrations Copyright (c) 1953 by Garth Williams. Reprinted by permission of HarperCollins Publishers, Inc./ Illustration by Garth Williams from his *The Rabbits' Wedding.* Harper & Row, Publishers, 1958. Copyright (c) 1958 by Garth Williams. Reprinted by permission of HarperCollins Publishers, Inc./ Illustration by Garth Williams from *Stuart Little,* by E.B. White. Harper & Row, Publishers, 1973. Copyright (c) 1945 by E.B. White. Text copyright renewed (c) 1973 by E.B. White. Illustrations copyright renewed (c) 1973 by Garth Williams. Reprinted by permission of HarperCollins Publishers, Inc./ Illustration from *Ride a Purple Pelican,* by Garth Williams. Greenwillow, 1986. Illustrations by Jack Prelutsky. Reprinted by permission of Greenwillow Books, a division of William Morrow and Company, Inc./ Photograph by Vern Torongo.

SHARON L. WOODING. Illustration by Sharon L. Wooding from her *Arthur's Christmas Wish.* Atheneum, 1986. Copyright (c) 1986 by Sharon Wooding. Reprinted with the permission of Atheneum Publishers, an imprint of Macmillan Publishing Company./ Photograph courtesy of Sharon Wooding.

PATRICIA WRIGHTSON. Jacket of *The Ice Is Coming,* by Patricia Wrightson. Atheneum, 1977. Copyright (c) 1977 by Patricia Wrightson. Jacket painting by Victor Mays. Reprinted by permission of Margaret K. McElderry Books, an imprint of Macmillan Publishing Company./ Jacket of *The Dark Bright Water,* by Patricia Wrightson. Atheneum, 1978. Copyright (c) 1978 by Patricia Wrightson. Jacket painting by Victor Mays. Reprinted with permission of Margaret K. McElderry Books, a division of Macmillan Publishing Company./ Illustration from *Night Outside,* by Patricia Wrightson. Margaret K. McElderry Books, 1979. Text Copyright (c) 1979 by Patricia Wrightson. Illustrations copyright (c) 1985 by Beth Peck. Reprinted with permission of Margaret K. McElderry Books, an imprint of Macmillan Publishing Company./ Jacket of *Journey behind the Wind,* by Patricia Wrightson. Atheneum, 1981. Copyright (c) 1981 by Patricia Wrightson. Jacket painting by Victor Mays. Reprinted by permission of Margaret K. McElderry Books, an imprint of Macmillan Publishing Company./ Cover by Robert Roennfeldt from *A Little Fear,* by Patricia Wrightson. Puffin Books, 1983. Copyright (c) 1983 by Patricia Wrightson. Reproduced by permission of Random Century Group Ltd. In Canada by Penguin Books Australia Ltd./ Cover by Stephen Marchesi from *The Nargun and the Stars,* by Patricia Wrightson. Copyright (c) Viking Penguin Inc., 1988. Reproduced by permission of Random Century Group Ltd. In Canada by Penguin Books Australia Ltd./ Photograph courtesy of Patricia Wrightson.

LISBETH ZWERGER. Illustration by Lisbeth Zwerger from *The Gift of the Magi,* by O. Henry. Picture Books Studio, 1982. Copyright (c) 1982 by Neugebauer Press USA Inc. Reprinted by permission of the publisher./ Illustration by Lisbeth Zwerger from *A Christmas Carol,* by Charles Dickens. Picture Books Studio, 1988. Copyright (c) 1988 by Neugebauer Press. Reprinted by permission of the publisher./ Photograph by Nancy Gorbics.

something about the author

ASCH, Frank 1946-

PERSONAL: Born August 6, 1946, in Somerville, NJ; son of John (a truck driver) and Margaret (Giasullo) Asch; married wife, Janani (a teacher); children: Devin. *Education:* Attended Rutgers University and Pratt Institute, both during 1960s; Cooper Union, B.F.A., 1969; trained as a Montessori teacher.

ADDRESSES: Home—Spruce Knob Rd., Middletown Springs, VT 05757.

CAREER: Author and illustrator of children's books, 1968—. Teacher in a public grammar school in Gondia Maharastra, India, 1972, and in a Montessori school in Edison, NJ, 1975; performer and producer with wife, Janani Asch, as the "Belly Buttons" children's theater troupe, during mid-1970s; New England Center for Contemporary Art, Brooklyn, CT, artist in residence, during late 1970s. Leads workshops in art and storytelling.

AWARDS, HONORS: Citations for a Brooklyn Art Book for Children from the Brooklyn Public Library and Brooklyn Museum of Art, 1970 and 1971; Award for Children's Book Illustration from American Graphic Illustrators Association, 1972; citation for Notable Children's Book of the Year from American Library Association, 1978; citations for an Outstanding Book of the Year for Children from the *New York Times,* 1979 and 1982; with Vladimir Vagin, shared the Soviet National Book Award, 1990, for *Here Comes the Cat!*

FRANK ASCH

WRITINGS:

SHORT FICTION FOR CHILDREN, ILLUSTRATIONS BY F. ASCH, EXCEPT AS INDICATED

George's Store, McGraw, 1968.
Linda, McGraw, 1969.
Elvira Everything, Harper, 1970.
The Blue Balloon, McGraw, 1971.
Yellow, Yellow, illustrations by Mark Alan Stamaty, McGraw, 1971.

I Met a Penguin, McGraw, 1972.

Rebecka, Harper, 1972.

In the Eye of the Teddy, Harper, 1973.

Gia and the One Hundred Dollars Worth of Bubble Gum, McGraw, 1974.

Good Lemonade, illustrations by Marie Zimmerman, F. Watts, 1976.

Monkey Face (Junior Literary Guild selection), Parents' Magazine Press, 1977.

City Sandwich (poems), Greenwillow, 1978.

MacGoose's Grocery, illustrations by James Marshall, Dial, 1978.

Moon Bear, Scribner, 1978.

Sand Cake (Junior Literary Guild selection), Parents' Magazine Press, 1978.

Turtle Tale (Junior Literary Guild selection), Dial, 1978.

Country Pie (poems), Greenwillow, 1979.

Little Devil's A, B, C (reader), Scribner, 1979.

Little Devil's 1, 2, 3 (reader), Scribner, 1979.

Popcorn, Parents' Magazine Press, 1979.

(With wife, Jan Asch) *Running with Rachel,* photographs by J. Asch and Robert Michael Buslow, Dial, 1979.

The Last Puppy, Prentice-Hall, 1980.

Starbaby, Scribner, 1980.

Goodnight Horsey, Prentice-Hall, 1981.

Just Like Daddy, Prentice-Hall, 1981.

Bread and Honey, Parents' Magazine Press, 1982.

Happy Birthday Moon, Prentice-Hall, 1982.

Milk and Cookies, Parents' Magazine Press, 1982.

Moon Cake (Book-of-the-Month Club selection), Prentice-Hall, 1983.

Moongame, Prentice-Hall, 1984.

Pearl's Promise (novel), Delacorte, 1984.

Skyfire, Prentice-Hall, 1984.

Bear Shadow (Junior Literary Guild selection), Prentice-Hall, 1985.

Bear's Bargain (Junior Literary Guild selection), Prentice-Hall, 1985.

I Can Blink, Kids Can Press, 1985.

I Can Roar, Kids Can Press, 1985.

Goodbye House (Junior Literary Guild selection), Prentice-Hall, 1986.

Pearl's Pirates (novel), Delacorte, 1987.

Oats and Wild Apples, Holiday House, 1988.

Baby in the Box, Holiday House, 1989.

(With Vladimir Vagin) *Here Comes the Cat!,* illustrations by Asch and Vagin, Scholastic, 1989.

Journey to Terezor (science-fiction novel), Holiday House, 1989.

Flags of the United Nations Sticker Book, Scholastic, 1990.

Contributor of articles to periodicals, including *Dragon Lode.* Books available in translation in several languages, including Danish, German, Japanese, Spanish, Swedish, and Russian.

In *Rebecka,* a boy feels so devoted to his dog that he's taken aback when a girl moves in next door and wants to play house. (From *Rebecka,* written and illustrated by Frank Asch).

ADAPTATIONS: Happy Birthday Moon has been adapted for videocassette, Simon & Schuster, 1988; *Here Comes the Cat!* is being adapted for a film in the Soviet Union.

WORK IN PROGRESS: Dear Brother, another joint project with Vladimir Vagin, publication expected in 1992; *Hands around Lincoln School,* a children's novel, publication expected in 1992; *Moondance,* a new "Bear Book"; *The Flower Fairy;* and *The Sandbox Geni.*

SIDELIGHTS: Frank Asch's lighthearted, perceptive fables have won the hearts of children and the admiration of adults. In a series of stories—including his highly popular Bear Books—Asch has expressed his own insights into the nature of life in a manner simple enough for a small child to understand and enjoy. His concerns have blossomed into such groundbreaking projects as *Here Comes the Cat!,* a playful cat-and-mouse story that is also a parable about world peace. Created by Asch and Soviet artist Vladimir Vagin, it is the first children's book to spring from a partnership between citizens of the Soviet Union and the United States.

Asch grew up in Bridgewater, New Jersey—a suburb today, but a part of the countryside when he was a child in the late 1940s and 1950s. "I had a brook next to where I lived where I could catch frogs, and I could always wander around," he recalled in an interview with *Something about the Author* (*SATA*). Across the road, "my grandfather had a small farm with cows, chickens, and a horse and wagon that we used to pick up hay. So when I was little I was able to ride on the haywagon and stuff like that. When I got a little older, I enjoyed being able to go into the forest and sit in a tree—I remember calling it my 'thinking tree.' I would sit in the tree and think, and I would have the solace of being with nature."

The Asches were a working-class family: John and Margaret Asch met in a factory where they were both weavers. The parents didn't press their son to be a "high achiever," and that had its advantages: "I got a sense of freedom, in that I was allowed to be a kid," Asch recalled. "My father didn't read me stories from a book," the author continued, "but he liked to talk about what he did that day on the job and all the characters he worked with. I also had an uncle who was a kind of character. He was outside the mainstream. I enjoyed hanging out around him because he really enjoyed kids and made them feel special. He had a knack for entertaining kids—he was kind of a big kid himself. He had a tremendous imagination and I was inspired being around him." The uncle, a carpenter and an avid collector of odds and ends, built a store for one of his friends that carried "a little bit of everything." Years later, the episode inspired Asch's first published book—*George's Store*—about a shopkeeper who loves to buy and sell things and who can guess what his customers want as soon as they walk in the door.

Asch, who both writes and illustrates his books, told *SATA* that he started to like both kinds of work at about the same time. "In grade school, I noticed that I really didn't care who helped me finish my math or history homework, but anything that had to do with writing I wanted to do on my own. What I wrote was an expression of my personality and not of somebody else's books." By high school, Asch had written a play, a hundred-page poem, and a philosophical treatise titled "Concerning the Nature of Dream Existence." "It was a crazy, philosophical idea put into a kind of science-fiction context," he recalled. "It was based on the principle that since life was an illusion, dreams were probably more important

than reality because dreams were freer, and we really ought to spend most of our time dreaming." Meanwhile, "I read a lot of adult literature, half of which I didn't understand"—hefty philosophical novelists such as Leo Tolstoy, Fyodor Dostoevsky, and Franz Kafka—"which in a way is very appropriate for an adolescent mind." By contrast, as an adult, Asch often finds himself reading children's books.

As a small child, Asch reported, "I never really thought I could draw. I grew up in the era of sputnik"—the first orbiting spacecraft—"and I was very interested in science." The young Asch thought that his older brother, who was taking draftsmanship in high school, was the artist of the family. But in the eighth grade Asch met a special teacher, art instructor Desmond MacLean, who helped him to appreciate his own potential. "I'll never forget one day when I walked into the art room, and he had displayed my drawings on the bulletin board with the label 'One Man Show.' I began to shift my identity from future scientist to someday artist." MacLean "also had a film club," Asch added, "so there were a lot of opportunities for me to grow in a way that wasn't just *visual* but was *interdisciplinary.*" In other words, along with drawing, "literature was important, movies were important."

Using words and pictures together soon came naturally to Asch. "I started doing cartoons and greeting cards," he recalled. "I remember when I was just thirteen or fourteen making my first children's book for my sister, to commemorate the birthday of her first baby. It was a gift that I wrote and illustrated for her." Even though "it seemed totally outside the realm of possibility that I could be an artist or a writer," Asch said, "nothing else was of interest. It was like an impossible dream: no one around was telling me it would be possible; no one was saying I could survive." Except Desmond MacLean. "He said to me one day, 'Well, you're going to art school, aren't you?' It just totally hit me by surprise, like—'Gosh, somebody thinks I could be an artist?' That really encouraged me."

Asch went to art school in New York City for several years during the 1960s: first to the Pratt Institute, and then to the Cooper Union. "I went looking for an experience," he told *SATA.* For a child of the countryside, part of the experience was learning to cope with a city. More importantly, Asch hoped for "more varied and in-depth interaction with the art world." Going to art school "was a mixed experience," he eventually decided. "It was disillusioning in a way, because I began to see that my particular talent had to do with the interaction of words and the visual world, and I had a pure fine arts program at the time. There really weren't any classes in children's books, for example. I had one book-design course and that really stimulated me a lot, but there was very little interdisciplinary study—nothing, really, that fit my particular talents. I was constantly frustrated. Rather than do one painting I would do ten of them in a row and hang them on a wall, almost as if they were pages in a book. The instructors thought it was interesting, but it didn't really fit with what they were comfortable teaching. I felt like a round peg in a square hole." By graduation time, "I felt held back," Asch reported. "I wanted to be involved and be a participant of life rather than a student of life. It felt like I had gotten in the first two or three years what I needed to get out of the experience, and the last year or so was simply redundant. I stayed to get the degree because I was unsure of my future and didn't know whether I would need it or not."

Among Asch's key experiences as an art student was his discovery of children's author Maurice Sendak. Shortly

Tucked safely inside his shell,
Turtle waited for Fox to go away.

(From *Turtle Tale*, written and illustrated by Frank Asch.)

before Asch entered art school in the mid-1960s, Sendak published the award-winning book *Where the Wild Things Are,* which many believe brought new life to children's literature. In the book Sendak was startlingly honest about showing the inner feelings of a child. The story begins when a young boy is sent to bed without supper for dressing in a wolf costume and misbehaving, as if he were a "wild thing." As the boy sits angrily in his room, the furniture seems to turn into a forest and he imagines himself king of all the "wild things" there. Then his daydream ends, and he is glad to find that his mother has forgiven him and brought dinner up to his room. Sendak illustrated the book with wildly imaginative line drawings. "*Where the Wild Things Are* was the first children's book that I put on a level with the painting and the other art that I had been studying," Asch recalled. "It opened up the

possibility of children's books as art and not just entertainment. It opened up the possibility of doing children's book *art,* of being a children's book *creator.* It had the depth that being a painter had in my mind."

While auditing some classes at Rutgers University, Asch met another special teacher—art professor Billé Pritchard —whom he described as "one of the most extraordinary instructors, and men, that I ever met." Pritchard gave Asch new inspiration by helping him to see "what levels of intricacy were possible" in art. "Even though I went five years to art school," Asch continued, "he became the person I kept going back to for more in-depth instruction. He was not only a great artist but a great teacher. I am still digesting his gems of guidance some thirty years later, and using the input that he gave to me when I was twenty years old." As Asch entered the 1990s he still met with Pritchard—as a colleague, now.

When Asch graduated from art school with a bachelor's degree in painting in 1969, he had already published *George's Store.* The book was praised by reviewers, including Stanley Mack of the *New York Times Book Review,* who hailed its "originality," "spontaneity," and "wit." Only twenty-two years old at the time, Asch found his sudden success "very intimidating and disruptive," as he noted in his *SATA* interview. "Part of me was really unsettled as to just what I was going to do with my life—I wasn't even sure that children's literature was something I wanted to continue." Sometimes, Asch recalled, he told himself, "Well, I'm going to be a painter, and I'll just do these children's books for a while because it'll be a way to bankroll my painting." But at other times, the whole experience seemed "a total fluke—it's just going to all disappear tomorrow and I'll never be able to write another book." Moreover, as with many young Americans in the 1960s, Asch found himself questioning the spiritual consequences of success. It seemed like "something that was out to get me rather than something that I could use to advance who I was," he explained, "so my reaction was to be very cautious rather than go full speed into this *career.* I went out to San Francisco to live in an ashram [Hindu religious retreat] as soon as I got out of art school. Then I went to India for a while. I was trying to save my soul from the evil meatgrinder of success."

In India Asch became a teacher in a public grammar school. Back in the United States, he studied more formally to teach small children. "I did the training and I only taught for about one year," Asch recalled. "I realized that I really wasn't a good teacher in the sense that I had a lot of patience for teaching kids the nuts and bolts of reading. I was more interested in making environments for them to play in and telling stories. I was a terrible teacher but I was interested in having fun with the kids." With his wife Jan, who was also a teacher, Asch formed a traveling children's theater troupe called the "Belly Buttons." They went through New Jersey, New York, and Connecticut performing stories for children in schools and libraries.

Along the way, Asch came to terms with his success as a children's author. He found that writing stories for children could add meaning to his own life. "My work has been a real lifesaver for me," Asch told *SATA.* "It's been an important thing, a kind of salvation. It's given me a place to do my exploring of who I am. And I think people feel nurtured by that. Kids feel nurtured by that." Many of his books, Asch suggested, are "like notebooks of my own inner explorations and conclusions that I've drawn about how things work." To succeed, such books require a delicate mix of emotions. "The challenge," he confided, "has always been to seek some kind of truth, but not get lost in a heavy, moralistic, self-defeating work." Reviewers praise Asch's ability to tell meaningful stories that are graced with a light, whimsical sense of humor.

Two early examples of Asch's special talent are *Rebecka* (1972) and *Turtle Tale* (1978). *Rebecka,* Asch told *SATA,* is a humorous story about the meaning of love. The real Rebecka "was a very special dog that would guard my bicycle. I liked my dog because it would seem to prefer my company over the company of adults, and that made me feel special." In Asch's book, a boy feels so devoted to his dog Rebecka that he's taken aback when a girl moves next door and wants to play house. The girl seems like an intruder on the friendship between dog and boy. In a wild, silly fantasy the boy imagines what it would be like to be married to his dog, and decides, for obvious reasons, that it's totally impossible. The story ends happily the next day: "All day we played house together," the boy says. "I was the daddy, the girl from next door was the mommy, and Rebecka was the dog." In Asch's last picture of the three together, there is a tiny book entitled "How to Love." *Rebecka,* wrote Elaine McDonald in *Library Journal,* "sensitively depicts the wanderings of a child's thoughts as he solves a problem."

Turtle Tale was one of Asch's first books to be honored as a Junior Literary Guild selection. The idea for the story, he told the Guild, came when he was thinking about his own life and the need to be open to the world while still keeping a sense of security. As he pondered the problem, "I developed a turtle-like image of myself," he continued. "So *Turtle Tale* is really an attempt to share the universal aspect of my own inner emotional drama." The book begins as Turtle gets hit on the head by an apple. He decides to stay safe by *always* keeping his head in his shell. Then, of course, he bumps into things, falls down hills, and can't eat. So he decides to keep his head *out* all the time, gets doused in a storm, and is then approached by a hungry fox. "Maybe it's best," Turtle concludes, "if I keep my head out sometimes and sometimes pull it in." As he finishes talking, Turtle hides his head again and the fox's teeth clunk harmlessly against his shell. Then the fox leaves, the clouds part, and Turtle comes out to enjoy the sun. "Even very young children can fully appreciate this tale because it is brief, basic, and comprehensible," wrote Mary B. Nickerson in *School Library Journal.* "Older children will find it amusing and true." The meaning of love and the nature of fear, Asch told *SATA,* are both recurring themes in his books.

At first glance, the style Asch used to illustrate his books seems to have changed a great deal during the six years between *Rebecka* and *Turtle Tale.* Like many books Asch created when he was starting out in the early 1970s, *Rebecka* is basically in black and white. Its line drawings sometimes use fantastically intricate loops and squiggles, a technique that reviewers praised for its joyous energy and which seemed to be an Asch trademark. *Turtle Tale,* by contrast, is in color, and the pictures use very simple shapes and lines. Carefully balanced, simple shapes—and a rainbow of subtly varied, harmonious colors—have seemed, since the late 1970s, to be the new Asch trademark.

The change, Asch told *SATA,* doesn't really represent a change in his own attitude, but a change in what publishers would let him do as an artist. "I would have worked in color earlier on," Asch recalled in his *SATA* interview, "but in the late '60s and early '70s in the publishing industry, color was something that authors and illustrators weren't given off the bat—they had to prove themselves. And I had proved myself to be very successful in black and white. So publishers were reluctant to move me into color, because it was a lot less expensive to make black-and-white books and they had other illustrators who weren't as successful in black and white. So I kind of had to fight my way up into color. Twice I had to leave a publisher because they refused to give me full color for my books. It was a matter of breaking out of a stereotype that had developed around my work."

Basically, Asch explained, his black-and-white pictures and his color pictures have much in common. "Everyone makes a big contrast between the intricate black-and-white style and the color," he said. "But if you look at the intricate black and white, you'll see a lot of very basic shapes." All those squiggles are usually part of a larger, simpler shape—like

Frank Asch's popular "Bear" series features a blend of fantasy and reality that delights the very young. (Cover illustration from *Bear Shadow,* written and illustrated by Asch.)

hundreds of blades of grass in a broad, flat lawn. "The intricate lines are really a kind of coloration. When I got color, I didn't need to create color with textures anymore—I could just use color—so what was left was the simple shapes. It was mostly publishers giving me real color that allowed me to phase out the 'colorful' black-and-white treatment that I was involved with."

The *way* Asch draws his pictures, he suggested in his *SATA* interview, helps him to tell his stories. If a story coaxes a child to think about an important issue in life—such as dealing with fear, or the nature of love—the pictures need to be simple and reassuring. "Painting the polka dots on the bow tie just didn't feel appropriate," he observed, since the pic-

tures are for "a kid trying to figure out what's going on in reality, and getting down to the nuts and bolts." Such pictures, Asch explained, should say: "Okay, we're going to see something interesting, and it's *not* going to be scary. There's nothing creepy or crawly happening in the corner. It's safe." The calm style of the pictures "sets a mood for the kind of *exploration* that the story is about." A *Kirkus Reviews* article about *Turtle Tale* seems to summarize Asch's approach: "[Asch's] simple color pictures . . . make the lesson clear and the fun part of the lesson."

Asch has continued his explorations into the nature of life in his popular series of Bear Books. One of the first titles in the series is *Moon Bear,* in which a bear is so in love with the

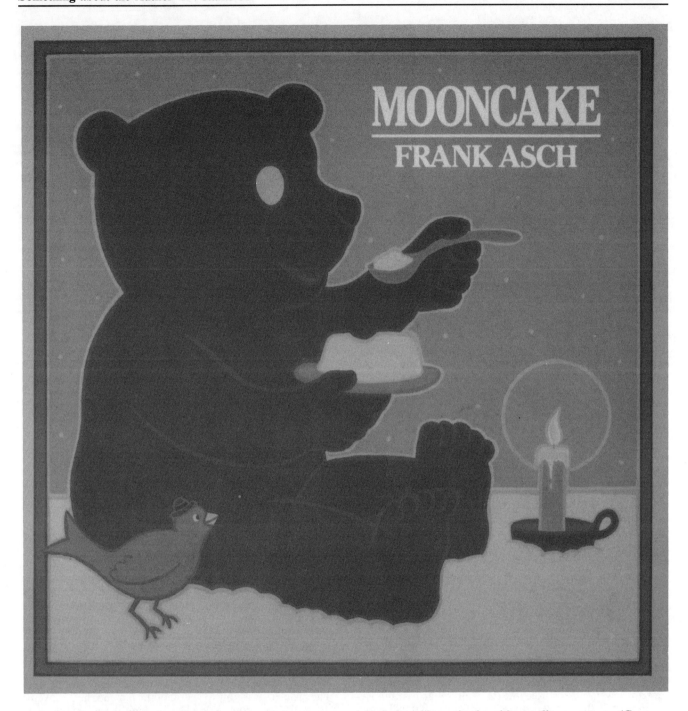

Asch selected a bear for the series because bears are upright human-like animals with a solitary nature. (Cover illustration from *Mooncake,* written and illustrated by Asch.)

moon that he lets his imagination run away with him. As the story begins, Bear notices that the full moon is slowly becoming a thin crescent, so he imagines that the moon needs more food. Going hungry, he leaves his honey out for the moon at night, and birds eat the honey while he is asleep. When the moon becomes full again, Bear is convinced that he has saved the moon by feeding it. Finally a little bird explains to Bear that the moon doesn't need his help. Bear becomes sad, thinking he has no one to love, but eventually he realizes that the birds still need him. Exploring the nature of imagination, Asch told *SATA,* is another recurring element in his books. For adults, "trying to grasp what's real and what's not real is an intellectual quest"—a matter for philosophers. "At the same time," Asch continued, "a kid is involved with the question, but for them it's incredibly tangible." They're "new beings on the planet," he explained, and "they can't really distinguish between dreams and reality."

The Bear Books have dealt with many other issues as well. In *Goodbye House,* a bear family comes to terms with moving away from their home by going from room to room and saying goodbye to all the memories the house seems to contain. "A friend of mine actually did what the bears do," Asch told *SATA.* "He took his kid around and said goodbye to all the rooms. That's the person the book is dedicated to." In *Bear Shadow,* Bear decides that he doesn't like his shadow and foolishly tries to run away from it, bury it, and even nail it to the ground. Eventually he finds a way to get along with it.

That book, Asch said, "really relates to the whole concept of coming to peace with yourself."

Why a bear? "I think using an animal in a story has to do with every animal having a particular essence or quality," Asch observed. "The bear is an upright, human-like animal." Also, he continued, "the bear is a solitary animal. Bear doesn't interact with a lot of characters, so he wouldn't be a gregarious animal like a monkey." And Asch has a personal fondness for bears.

After *Goodbye House* appeared in 1986, Asch stopped publishing Bear Books for a few years. But he assured *SATA*—and Bear fans everywhere—that the bears weren't saying goodbye forever. "I think it'll be an ongoing series," he said, "but I'm doing them when they happen. I'm trying to be very respectful and not capitalize on them." The books are important to Asch. "I look at them sometimes and I go: 'Oh, gosh! That's really good, that's really *special.*' And that's what keeps me going." *Moondance,* a new entry in the series, was under way in the early 1990s.

At the end of the 1970s, about the time that the Bear Books first appeared, Asch and his wife had a son, Devin. Soon thereafter, they settled in rural Vermont. With a streak of self-reliance, the Asches built their own house and joined with neighboring parents who were schooling their children at home. The parents adopted specialties and took turns leading workshops for the children. Not surprisingly, Asch introduced the kids to art. "I organized a fathers' group when they were very young," he told *SATA.* "We would get together with the kids as fathers and make things for them and do things with them. We made sleds out of cardboard boxes, we made spaceships, and things like that." Later on, he continued, "I had a puppet club with the kids. I got them involved with the whole process of making the puppet set, making the puppets, writing the scripts, and performing, and I actually took them around to various schools and libraries and they got paid for it. And then they went to Canada on a trip. Now they're doing their own puppet shows as a group and they've totally taken it over. The oldest is fifteen and the youngest is eleven, so they're old enough to do it themselves. I'm helping a little, but mostly from the sidelines."

As Devin and the other children got older, Asch seemed to follow them by writing his first full-length children's novels, beginning with the mouse adventures *Pearl's Promise* and *Pearl's Pirates* and going on to the science-fiction novel *Journey to Terezor* and the book *Hands around Lincoln School.* Did Devin influence the move? "Well, not in any conscious way," Asch told *SATA,* "although it's almost uncanny that the age levels are increasing." Basically, he recalled, "I saw picture books and I thought, I can do that! and so I did it. And then I saw some E. B. White"—author of such classic children's novels as *Charlotte's Web* and *Stuart Little*—"and I said, Well, I can do that, and so I did that." He continued: "What I'm noticing now is that when I go back and forth, one kind of writing nourishes the other. The experience I've gained in picture books is sometimes a real detriment—you have to work on a different level when you're doing children's novels—but it can also be helpful. And then when I do picture books, I find that the character and dialogue ability that I've become comfortable with through the longer books bleeds into the picture books. So they're cross-fertilizing one another in a very interesting way."

Meanwhile, Asch found new ways of remaining in contact with the world of early childhood. "Now that my son is getting older, I don't necessarily have that stimulus in my immediate environment," he observed, "but I still have the kid that I was." Over the years, Asch has investigated meditation and a variety of theories about the human personality, "all geared to spanning the time that's passed since I was a little kid, and being able to communicate with the entity that I was then." He is particularly interested in the idea that every adult retains within themselves an "inner child": "Since time is an illusion," he explained, "who you were is just as much a reality as who you are." During meditation, Asch said, "I go back into my past, interact with my child, and tell him stories. The energy generated from that process bleeds over into my other work."

Along with love and fear and imagination, Asch had another major interest that he wanted to explore in his work: peace. "I was trying for *years* to write a book about peace for kids," he told *SATA.* "A lot of the Bear Books were in a sense dealing with that theme, like *Bear Shadow*—he gets aggressive toward his shadow, then makes peace with himself." And Bear finds solace in the beauty of nature, much as the young Asch did in his "thinking tree." Asch was especially concerned about peace because he grew up during the 1950s, when the United States and the Soviet Union seemed poised on the brink of nuclear war and schoolchildren were taught how to hide under their desks in case the bombs began to fall. "I knew from the time that I was a small child that my entire world existed on a banana peel which was ready to slide into oblivion at the push of a button," he wrote in an article for *Dragon Lode* magazine. Art teacher Desmond MacLean, whose Quaker religion counseled peace, introduced Asch to the peace movement. "I was one of the few kids in school who refused to take cover during civil-defense air raid drills," Asch told *SATA,* and he "got in trouble with the school administration over things like that." He added, "I don't know if you would say I was a total pacifist, but I was drawn to the philosophy of pacifism." Asch went on to join the Congress of Racial Equality (CORE) and met its guiding spirit, James Farmer, who was a pioneer of nonviolent protest.

For all of his concern, Asch found it surprisingly difficult to discuss peace directly in his books. "I wanted to write a book that reflected [the danger of war] and the incredible fears it engenders," he wrote in *Dragon Lode.* "But I also wanted to write a book that would project a credible vision of hope and peace. I kept searching for characters and a plot that would fit my objective. I wrote some pretty odd stories . . . , none of them publishable. One was about a world made of bubbles. The hero was a bubble prince who found a pin made of steel. The problem was how to get rid of the pin once he discovered its destructive potential. Even burying it was neither convincing nor reassuring."

"Then," Asch told *SATA,* "I got the idea—Well, maybe if I worked on a book with a Soviet, whatever we did would have some kind of credibility, because it would not just be a book *about* peace, but a *model* of peace." So in 1986 he went to a Soviet-American conference on children's books and art, which happened to be held within driving distance of his Vermont home. His first moments at the conference were a shock: he found himself in a room full of Soviet delegates who could speak only Russian, and the translators were all busy running the meeting. "More or less thrown back on myself, I began to get strange thoughts," he reported in *Dragon Lode.* "In spite of my peaceful intentions, every negative stereotype I ever encountered about Soviets came crawling out of my subconscious." He wondered if some of the delegates could be spies, sent to keep watch over the others. Eventually Asch

One night Bear looked up into the sky and
for the first time he really saw the moon.
It was love at first sight.

(From *Moon Bear,* written and illustrated by Frank Asch.)

found a translator and made his general proposal for a
Soviet-American children's book. The idea was accepted
with enthusiasm. "By the end of the symposium," he continued in *Dragon Lode,* "my stereotypes and most of my para-
noia had been dissipated and dissolved."

When the conference ended, Asch had a promising book
project. But he still didn't know which Soviet he would work
with on the book, or even what it would be about. A few days
later, the basic storyline for *Here Comes the Cat!* came to him
in a dream. *Here Comes the Cat!* begins when a mouse spies
the outline of a cat appearing from behind the hills. By riding
on everything from a bicycle to a balloon, the mouse warns
other mice for miles around that a cat is approaching. The
title of the book—the mouse's warning—is almost the only
phrase spoken; it appears again and again, written in both
English and Russian. The mice assemble in town, gasping as
the shadow of the cat looms over them. But the cat turns out
to be a friend, smiling and pulling a wagonload of cheese. The
mice give the cat some milk and brush its fur, and as the book
ends, a mouse is riding the cat's back as the two head off into
the sunlight. The story, Asch realized, was a reflection of his
own groundless fears at the book conference—and the warm
feelings that replaced them. It would be an ideal book for a
Soviet and an American to create together.

The Soviets had returned home, so Asch brought his idea to
one of the organizers of the conference. She showed him a
large collection of work by Soviet illustrators, out of which he
chose Vladimir Vagin as his foreign partner. "I was particularly struck by his vibrant sense of color," Asch wrote in
Dragon Lode. Vagin was eager to work with Asch, so the two
began a unique round-the-world collaboration to make *Here
Comes the Cat!* a reality. Asch set the storyline and sent Vagin
the simplest possible sketch for each picture. Then the two

men would send more elaborate sketches back and forth,
along with messages that had to be translated—neither man
understood the other's language. Finally Vagin would apply
his vivid, intricate colors to the finished sketch. When *Here
Comes the Cat!* was completed, it was published jointly in the
United States and the Soviet Union and was a bestseller in
both countries. The authors—who were only able to meet as
friends three years after they began their work—toured New
York and Moscow together, were seen nationwide on both
Soviet and American television, and received the 1990 Soviet
National Book Award.

"I like collaborating with Mr. Vagin because, first of all,
there's a meaning behind it. We're maintaining a little bridge
between nations," said Asch in his *SATA* interview. "Above
and beyond that, I just find him to be a delightful person. He
can understand what I'm trying to say in a rough sketch" and
bring the idea to fruition "in an ideal way." Vagin, Asch
declared, "is like a little genie: I say I want a yard of gold and
he weaves it for me. I can't think of another illustrator in the
United States, or anywhere, that I'd feel as comfortable with.
It's very strange, because I didn't really know this when I
picked him. It was very serendipitous. I've never worked with
someone who was so tuned in to what my intentions are."

After the success of *Here Comes the Cat!,* Asch and Vagin
promptly began a second children's book, to be known as
Dear Brother. "Mr. Vagin got more involved in the writing
this time," Asch told *SATA,* "in that we actually exchanged
letters from the Soviet Union and the United States, back and
forth. The book is about a country mouse and a city mouse
exchanging letters. So he would write a letter and I would
write a letter, and that was part of pretending to be city and
country mice." Then Vagin took an extended vacation to
Vermont, where he could work with Asch on the illustrations.

Here Comes the Cat! **was the first children's book written and illustrated by both an American and a Soviet—Frank Asch and Vladimir Vagin.**

With his peace book published and other interesting projects on the way, Asch faces the future with optimism. Such good feelings, he told *SATA,* are a gift from children. "The things that children like are the things that are enjoyable to be involved with," he observed. "Children draw out of me the most interesting, the most humorous ideas, and the least negative aspects of myself." As he grew up in the 1950s, Asch suggested, he was part of an era of "doom and gloom" and "fear of atomic destruction." If tomorrow holds the promise of a better world, he contended, then working with children is a special privilege, because it enables an adult to be a part of that better world. "The messages, the themes, that children elicit from me in my work, I feel, is really a kind of energy that's coming from the light, bright future—the future where the earth *doesn't* get blown up or drown in its own pollution," Asch declared. "By working with and for children, I'm able to savor the positive, lighter energies of a successful, positive reality."

WORKS CITED:

Asch, Frank, *Rebecka,* Harper, 1972.
Asch, telephone interview with Thomas Kozikowski for *Something about the Author,* March 14, 1991.
Asch, *Turtle Tale,* Dial, 1978.
Asch, "Writing *Here Comes the Cat,*" *Dragon Lode,* winter, 1991, pp. 1-4.
Mack, Stanley, review of *George's Store, New York Times Book Review,* March 2, 1969, p. 30.
McDonald, Elaine T., review of *Rebecka, Library Journal,* November 15, 1972, p. 3792.
Nickerson, Mary B., review of *Turtle Tale, School Library Journal,* December, 1978, p. 42.
Review of *Turtle Tale, Junior Literary Guild,* September, 1978.
Review of *Turtle Tale, Kirkus Reviews,* January 1, 1979, p. 1.

FOR MORE INFORMATION SEE:

BOOKS

Sendak, Maurice, *Where the Wild Things Are,* Harper, 1963.

PERIODICALS

Bulletin of the Center for Children's Books, April, 1979; September, 1979; July, 1987.
Horn Book, February, 1979; February, 1981; August, 1982; October, 1983; April, 1984; March, 1985; July, 1985.
Junior Literary Guild, March, 1977; March, 1979; April, 1986.
Kirkus Reviews, July 1, 1973; May 1, 1974; August 15, 1978; December 1, 1978; May 15, 1987; February 1, 1989.
Library Journal, April 15, 1969; November 15, 1969; October 15, 1970; January 15, 1973; October 15, 1973.
Newsweek, December 4, 1989.
New Yorker, December 6, 1982.
New York Times Book Review, February 1, 1970; December 6, 1970; May 5, 1974; December 10, 1978; June 4, 1989.
Publishers Weekly, August 18, 1969; October 9, 1972; March 18, 1974; March 7, 1977; September 18, 1978; December 4, 1978; April 16, 1979; April 18, 1980; August 8, 1980; June 11, 1982; April 29, 1983; June 1, 1984; December 13, 1985; December 23, 1988; April 28, 1989; February 22, 1991.
School Library Journal, November, 1978; December, 1978; April, 1979; September, 1979; May, 1982; November, 1982; April, 1984; August, 1985; September, 1986; August, 1988; April, 1989.
Times Literary Supplement, January 6, 1989.
Washington Post Book World, November 12, 1978.
Wilson Library Bulletin, March, 1979.

Sketch by Thomas Kozikowski

ATHELING, William, Jr.
See BLISH, James (Benjamin)

*　　*　　*

ATWATER, Florence (Hasseltine Carroll) 1896-1979

PERSONAL: Born September 13, 1896; died August 23, 1979; married Richard Atwater (a writer), 1921; children: Doris, Carroll (daughter). *Education:* University of Chicago, B.A., M.A. in French Literature.

CAREER: High-school teacher of English, French and Latin. Partially rewrote *Mr. Popper's Penguins* after her husband's stroke in 1934. See *Sidelights* below.

AWARDS, HONORS: Newbery Honor Book from the American Library Association, 1939, Young Reader's Choice Award from the Pacific Northwest Library Association, 1941, and Lewis Carroll Shelf Award, 1958, all for *Mr. Popper's Penguins.*

WRITINGS:

(With husband, Richard Atwater), *Mr. Popper's Penguins* (juvenile), illustrated by Robert Lawson, Little, Brown, 1938, 50th anniversary edition, 1988.

SIDELIGHTS: "Anyone who can follow the antics in *Mr. Popper's Penguins . . .* without at least a twinge of jealousy, not to mention a chortle or two, is definitely an odd bird," declares Karen Jameyson in *Horn Book.* "Fifty years after its inception Richard and Florence Atwater's minor masterpiece of tomfoolery continues to tickle readers' funny bones."

Carroll Atwater Bishop, the Atwaters' daughter, told *Something about the Author,* "My father had a stroke in 1934. He did improve, but never recovered the ability to write. *Mr. Popper* was a completely written children's book before his stroke, and I may say both my sister and I adored the first version, which was more of a fantasy—Mr. Popper drew the first penguin on the mirror in shaving soap and he came to life, for instance. After the stroke my mother tried all kinds of ways to rescue the family fortunes—we're talking Great Depression here, though my father had been able to keep working and writing up to 1934—did some writing of her own (published some things in the *New Yorker* and the *Atlantic*), got an M.A. in French (thesis on *The Song of Roland*), got *three* Chicago teachers' certificates—one in English, one in French, one in Latin—and submitted *Mr. Popper* in its original form to two publishers, both of whom turned it down. "She then rewrote it," Ms. Bishop continues, "removing the fantasy—she would probably have called it whimsy—and brought it down to earth. (Mothers are famous for this.) Thus both the beginning and the end are her contribution. So, as I remember, is a good deal of the *tone* of the Popper marriage."

See also the sketch in this volume on Richard Atwater.

WORKS CITED:

Jameyson, Karen, "A Second Look: *Mr. Popper's Penguins,*" *Horn Book,* March/April, 1988, pp. 186-87.

FOR MORE INFORMATION SEE:

BOOKS

Fuller, Muriel, editor, *More Junior Authors,* H. W. Wilson, 1963.

*　　*　　*

ATWATER, Richard (Tupper) 1892-1948 (Riq)

PERSONAL: Born Frederick Mund Atwater on December 29, 1892, in Chicago, IL; name legally changed in 1913; died August 21, 1948, in Downey, WI: son of Clarence and May (maiden name, Marks) Atwater; married Florence Hasseltine Carroll (a writer), 1921; children: Doris, Carroll (daughter). *Education:* University of Chicago, B.A. (with honors), 1910, graduate study until 1917.

CAREER: Writer. Worked at various jobs, including instructor in Greek at the University of Chicago, Chicago, IL, columnist for the *Evening Post,* in Chicago, IL, and for the *Daily News,* Chicago, IL. Also book editor and columnist for other newspapers. *Military service:* Served in the U.S. Army, 1918-1919.

AWARDS, HONORS: Newbery Honor Book from the American Library Association, 1939, Young Reader's Choice Award from the Pacific Northwest Library Association, 1941, and Lewis Carroll Shelf Award, 1958, all for *Mr. Popper's Penguins.*

WRITINGS:

(Under pseudonym Riq) *Rickety Rimes of Riq* (verse), Ballou, 1925.
(Translator) Procopius of Caesarea, *Secret History of Procopius,* Covici-Friede, 1927, new edition, University of Michigan Press, 1961.
Doris and the Trolls (juvenile), illustrated by John Gee, Rand McNally, 1931.
The King's Sneezes (operetta), H. T. FitzSimons Co., 1933.
(With wife, Florence Atwater) *Mr. Popper's Penguins* (juvenile), illustrated by Robert Lawson, Little, Brown, 1938, 50th anniversary edition, 1988.

Also author of humor column under pseudonym Riq for the *Evening Post,* Chicago, IL, and the *Chicago Daily News.*

ADAPTATIONS: "Mr. Popper's Penguins" (listening cassette; read-along cassette; record; filmstrip with cassette), Miller-Brody, 1975, (sound filmstrip), Pied Piper Productions, 1979, (videocassette) Random House, 1985. *Mr. Popper's Penguins* is also available as a talking book and in braille.

SIDELIGHTS: Richard Atwater's second and last children's book, *Mr. Popper's Penguins,* was a Newbery Honor Book in 1939. The story is about a house painter who receives penguins as a gift and keeps them in the family refrigerator. Elizabeth Rider Montgomery in *The Story behind Modern Books,* called it "an amusing story. . . . Because of its very absurdity, the book is entrancing, and its matter-of-fact style adds to its charm. In fact, it is hard to tell whether the story owes its popularity more to the humor of its situation or to the simple way it is told."

A Newbery Honor Book in 1939, *Mr. Popper's Penguins* is about the adventures of a house painter who receives penguins as a gift. (Illustration by Robert Lawson from *Mr. Popper's Penguins,* by Florence and Richard Atwater.)

The idea for *Mr. Popper's Penguins* came to Atwater after attending a film about the first Byrd Antarctic Expedition with his wife and two daughters. Although he had great interest in his idea, his story did not satisfy him. After Atwater suffered a debilitating stroke in 1934, his wife, Florence, rewrote the manuscript, changing the first few chapters and the final chapters, and leaving the middle chapters as they were. *Mr. Popper's Penguins* was published in 1938 and was an immediate success. It has been enjoyed by children and their parents ever since.

Atwater died at the V. A. Hospital in Wood (Greater Milwaukee), Wisconsin, on August 21, 1948. He was fifty-six years old.

Mr. Popper's Penguins has been translated into Dutch, German, Catalan, Danish, French, Polish, Spanish, Swedish, Hebrew, Afrikaans, Thai, Japanese, and Korean.

See also the sketch in this volume on Florence Atwater.

WORKS CITED:

Montgomery, Elizabeth Rider, *The Story behind Modern Books,* Dodd, 1949.

FOR MORE INFORMATION SEE:

BOOKS

Burke, W. J., and Will D. Howe, *American Authors and Books, 1640 to the Present Day,* 3rd revised edition, Crown, 1972.

Fuller, Muriel, editor, *More Junior Authors,* H. W. Wilson, 1963.

Kirkpatrick, D. L., editor, *Twentieth-Century Children's Writers,* St. Martin's, 1978, 2nd edition, 1983.

Robinski, Jim, compiler, *Newbery and Caldecott Medalists and Honor Book Winners,* Libraries Unlimited, 1982.

PERIODICALS

New York Times, October 23, 1938.

*   *   *

AUSTIN, Margot 1909(?)-1990

OBITUARY NOTICE—See index for *SATA* sketch: Born c. 1909, in Portland, OR; died of heart failure, June 25, 1990, in New Fairfield, CT. Illustrator and author. Austin was known for her self-illustrated children's books, including *Moxie and Hanty and Bunty, Once Upon a Springtime, Peter Churchmouse, Gabriel Churchkitten,* and *Trumpet.* She also illustrated editions of nursery rhyme collections, including *Mother Goose Rhymes.*

OBITUARIES AND OTHER SOURCES:

PERIODICALS

New York Times, June 26, 1990.

*   *   *

AZAID
See ZAIDENBERG, Arthur

*   *   *

BAKER, Pamela J. 1947-

PERSONAL: Born June 23, 1947, in Buffalo, NY; daughter of James Eugene, Jr. (a dentist) and Marjorie Jean (a homemaker; maiden name, Schenk) Decker; married David Lee Baker (a dentist), June 27, 1970; children: Katherine Jean. *Education:* University of Wales, University College of Swansea, B.Sc., 1969; Bates College, B.S., 1970; State University of New York at Buffalo, M.A., 1978, Ph.D. candidate, 1982—.

ADDRESSES: Home—R.F.D. 2, Box 987, Norway, ME 04260. *Office*—Department of Biology, Bates College, Lewiston, ME 04240.

CAREER: Medical University of South Carolina, Charleston, research assistant in microbiology, 1973-74; State University of New York at Buffalo, research assistant in oral microbiology, 1974-82; Bates College, Lewiston, ME, research associate in biology, 1982—.

MEMBER: International Association for Dental Research, American Society for Microbiology, New York Academy of Sciences.

WRITINGS:

My First Book of Sign, illustrated by Patricia Bellan Gillen, Kendall Green, 1986.

Contributor to scientific journals.

WORK IN PROGRESS: Research on antibodies and neutrophils in host defense against periodontal disease.

SIDELIGHTS: Pamela J. Baker commented: "My motivation for writing *My First Book of Sign* was the experience of parenting a deaf child. As I explain in the book, our daughter's diagnosis at age fifteen months as profoundly hearing impaired was rather upsetting. However, through learning sign language and meeting deaf people, we learned all the positive aspects of deafness. There were no sign language books available for babies, and I hoped to fill that gap and to help other parents realize that deafness is not a devastating experience."

*   *   *

BAUM, L. Frank
See THOMPSON, Ruth Plumly

BB
See WATKINS-PITCHFORD, Denys James

*   *   *

BELLAIRS, John (A.) 1938-1991

OBITUARY NOTICE—See index for *SATA* sketch: Born January 17, 1938, in Marshall, MI; died of cardiovascular disease, March 8, 1991, in Haverhill, MA. Educator and author. Bellairs wrote fourteen fantasy, horror, and mystery novels for children, including the award-winning *House with a Clock in Its Walls.* His work is well regarded for its humor, imagination, atmosphere, and avoidance of sentimentality. At the beginning of his career, from 1963 to 1971, Bellairs supported himself by teaching English at colleges in Minnesota, Illinois, and Massachusetts. His first three books appeared during this period. Among his later novels are *The Figure in the Shadows, The Curse of the Blue Figurine, The Spell of the Sorcerer's Skull, The Eyes of the Killer Robot, Chessmen of Doom,* and *The Lamp from the Warlock's Tomb.*

OBITUARIES AND OTHER SOURCES:

PERIODICALS

New York Times, March 14, 1991.
Washington Post, March 15, 1991.

*   *   *

BERMAN, Paul (Lawrence) 1949-

PERSONAL: Born September 29, 1949, in White Plains, NY; son of Alan (a businessman) and Hannah (an artist; maiden name, Rubman) Berman; married Margaret Kaye (a writer-illustrator). *Education:* Columbia University, B.A., 1971, M.A., 1974. *Politics:* Socialist. *Religion:* "Judeo-Whitmanian."

ADDRESSES: Home—471 Columbus Ave., New York, NY 10024. *Office*—*Village Voice,* 842 Broadway, New York, NY 10003. *Agent*—Charlotte Sheedy Literary Agency, Inc., 145 West 86th St., New York, NY 10024.

CAREER: Brooklyn College, Brooklyn, NY, instructor in Western civilization, 1973-74; WGBH-TV, Boston, MA, researcher in labor history, 1975-76; *Harper's* (magazine), New York City, editorial assistant, 1977-79; *Village Voice,* New York City, columnist, 1980—. Worked as trombonist in various bands, 1967-70, and 1977-81.

MEMBER: National Writers Union, National Book Critics' Circle.

WRITINGS:

Quotations from the Anarchists, Praeger, 1972.
(Self-illustrated) *Make-Believe Empire: A How-to Book* (juvenile), Atheneum, 1982.

Paul Berman's self-illustrated children's book, *Make-Believe Empire*, was published in 1982.

Also author of a screenplay for a documentary film. Drama critic, *Nation,* 1984-86. Contributor to magazines and newspapers, including *New Republic, New York Times Book Review, Vanity Fair, Parnassus: Poetry in Review, Dissent, Harper's, Mother Jones,* and *Village Voice.*

WORK IN PROGRESS: A book on literary radicalism; *The Plazas of Masaya,* about the Sandinista Revolution.

SIDELIGHTS: Paul Berman once commented: "My interests are literature and politics, especially the 'bloody crossroads' where they intersect. I enjoy trying to define the political imagination that animates serious writers, and the book I am working on does this with various Americans from Emerson to the present.

"I also write about the theatre and, from time to time, when I become sufficiently indignant, political topics of the day. I have had great success with dull essays on Marxism and am slowly putting together a series of essays describing the progress of the American left. I enjoy writing for children and hope to do more of it in the belief that children need better written, more intelligent books than they usually get.

"I once wrote a screenplay for a documentary film on anarchism, which was produced, and though working with film people was less than delightful, I might like to do more of that anyway."

FOR MORE INFORMATION SEE:

PERIODICALS

Commentary, January, 1982.

New Republic, December 23, 1981; January 31, 1983.
School Library Journal, May, 1982.
Village Voice, July 4, 1981.

*   *   *

BIRDSEYE, Tom 1951-

PERSONAL: Born July 13, 1951, in Durham, NC; son of Irving (a minister) and Mary Hughes (a librarian; maiden name, Carmichael) Birdseye; married Debbie Holsclaw (a teacher), May 18, 1974; children: Kelsey, Amy. *Education:* Attended University of Kentucky, 1969-72; Western Kentucky University, B.A. (mass communications), 1974, B.A. (elementary education), 1977.

ADDRESSES: Home and office—Sagle, ID. *Agent*—Jean V. Naggar, 216 East Seventy-fifth St., New York, NY 10021.

CAREER: Elementary schoolteacher in Lincoln City, OR, and Sandpoint, ID, 1977-82; free-lance writer, 1984—. English teacher in Japan.

MEMBER: Society of Children's Book Writers.

AWARDS, HONORS: Children's Choice Book Award from International Reading Association, 1989, for *Air Mail to the Moon.*

WRITINGS:

FOR CHILDREN

I'm Going to Be Famous, Holiday House, 1986.
Air Mail to the Moon, Holiday House, 1986.
A Song of Stars, Holiday House, 1990.
Tucker, Holiday House, 1990.

WORK IN PROGRESS: Two adult novels, *One Silk Thread* and *While Echoes Dance;* a children's novel, *Cowboy Arlo and the Harbor Street Lot War;* picture books; research for an adult novel involving the discovery of a box of sermons left in an attic.

SIDELIGHTS: Tom Birdseye commented: "I am a latecomer to the field of writing, having only recently discovered the wealth of 'daily life' material passing before my eyes. Stories, I now find, are at their best when they are about the small increments of growth we humans achieve, as opposed to the grandiose leaps that mark history. I focus on these little steps and try to find the humor even in the toughest of trials. Then I work stubbornly until I've done my best."

*   *   *

BLANC, Esther Silverstein 1913-

PERSONAL: Born in 1913, in Goshen County, WY; daughter of Simon (a tailor) and Gazella Silverstein; married Richard Blanc (a biologist and statistician), January 25, 1941 (died 1986); children: Robert, Michael, Paul. *Education:* University of California, San Francisco, R.N., 1934, M.S.N., 1960, Ph.D., 1972, University of Rochester, B.S., 1947. *Politics:* Left. *Religion:* Jewish. *Hobbies and other interests:* History of science (biology), music, art, sociology, history of medicine, collecting antiques and books.

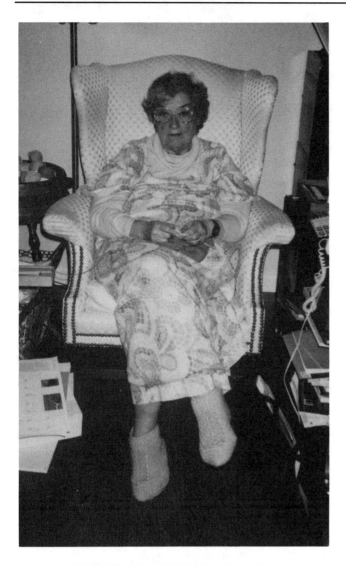

ESTHER SILVERSTEIN BLANC

ADDRESSES: Home—1464 Sixth Ave., San Francisco, CA 94122. *Agent*—Ruth Gottstein, Volcano, CA 95689.

CAREER: Formerly a nurse.

AWARDS, HONORS: Jewish National Book Award, Jewish Library Association Award, and Bay Area Book Award, all 1990, all for *Berchick: My Mother's Horse.*

WRITINGS:

Berchick: My Mother's Horse, illustrated by Tennessee Dixon, Volcano Press, 1989.

WORK IN PROGRESS: Two stories for children, *A Union Suit for a Small Chicken* and *Moko and His Friends;* a play, *Pieces of War.*

SIDELIGHTS: In *Berchick: My Mother's Horse,* Esther Silverstein Blanc writes about an orphaned colt who becomes a family's pet. When the family must move from its ranch into the city and tries to auction the horse, the horse keeps returning. The mother, to whom the horse is deeply attached, finally convinces it to ride off into freedom. According to

Karen Litton in *School Library Journal,* the novel is "a low-key story of change, acceptance, and growth, moving in its restraint and simplicity." Regarding *Berchick* as "more than an appealing tale for horse fanciers," Ellen Mandel continues in *Booklist,* that "this unusual story of an Old World Jewish family and its thoroughbred pet leads readers to explore immigrants' roles in settling the West."

WORKS CITED:

Mandel, Ellen, *Booklist,* September 1, 1989, p. 66.
Litton, Karen, *School Library Journal,* November, 1989, p. 74.

*   *   *

BLEGVAD, Erik 1923-

PERSONAL: Born March 3, 1923, in Copenhagen, Denmark; immigrated to France, 1947; immigrated to United States, 1951; immigrated to England, 1966; immigrated again to United States, 1986; son of Harald (a marine biologist for the Danish government) and Anna (a homemaker; maiden name, Claudi-Hansen) Blegvad; married Lenore Hochman (a painter and writer), September 12, 1950; children: Peter, Kristoffer. *Education:* Attended Copenhagen School of Arts and Crafts, 1941-44. *Politics:* None. *Religion:* None.

ADDRESSES: Home and office—Mountain Spring Farms, Wardsboro, VT 05355; 3 Place Capitaine Vincent, 06190 Roquebrune Cap Martin, Alpes Maritimes, France.

ERIC BLEGVAD

CAREER: Artist and illustrator. Employed in an advertising agency in Copenhagen, Denmark, during the end of World War II; free-lance artist in London, 1947; free-lance artist for book and magazine publishers in Paris, 1947-51; illustrator of children's books, 1951—. *Exhibitions:* "Fifty Years of Illustration: Eric Blegvad," presented by Duncan of Jordanstone College of Art, Dundee, Scotland, 1991; Blegvad's works have also been featured in several exhibitions of the American Institute of Graphic Arts. *Military service:* Royal Danish Air Force, interpreter with the British forces in Germany, 1945-47.

AWARDS, HONORS: The Gammage Cup was listed as a notable book of 1959, American Library Association; *The Tenth Good Thing about Barney, The Narrow Passage, Polly's Tiger,* and *May I Visit?* were listed among the Children's Books of the Year, Child Study Association of America, 1972, 1973, 1974, and 1976, respectively; *Mushroom Center Disaster* and *The Winter Bear* were Children's Book Showcase Titles, 1975 and 1976, respectively; *This Little Pig-a-Wig: And Other Rhymes about Pigs* was listed as one of the ten best illustrated books of 1978, *New York Times; Self-Portrait: Erik Blegvad* was listed among *Horn Book*'s honor list of books of 1979.

WRITINGS:

ILLUSTRATOR

E. Prunier, *Madame Prunier's Fiskekogebog,* Fonss Forlag (Copenhagen), 1947.
Dore Ogrizek, *Les Pays Nordiques,* Editions Ode (Paris), 1950.
Thomas Franklin Galt, *Story of Peace and War,* Crowell, 1952.
Julie F. Batchelor and Claudia De Lys, *Superstitious: Here's Why!,* Harcourt, 1954.
Bob Brown, *The Complete Book of Cheese,* Random House, 1955.
Lee Kingman, *Village Band Mystery,* Doubleday, 1956.
Lillian Pohlman, *Myrtle Albertina's Secret,* Coward, 1956.
B. J. Chute, *Greenwillow,* Dutton, 1956.
Dan Wickenden, *Amazing Vacation,* Harcourt, 1956.
Edward Anthony, *Oddity Land,* Doubleday, 1957.
Mary Norton, *Bed-Knob and Broomstick,* Harcourt, 1957.
Jean Fritz, *Late Spring,* Coward-McCann, 1957.
(And translator) Hans Christian Andersen, *The Swineherd,* Harcourt, 1958.
L. Kingman, *Flivver,* Doubleday, 1958.
L. Pohlman, *Myrtle Albertina's Song,* Coward, 1958.
B. J. Chute, *Journey to Christmas,* Dutton, 1958.
(And translator) H. C. Andersen, *The Emperor's New Clothes,* Harcourt, 1959.
Isabella Holt, *The Adventures of Rinaldo,* Little, Brown, 1959.
Carol Kendall, *The Gammage Cup,* Harcourt, 1959.
Betty Miles, *Having a Friend,* Knopf, 1959.
Margaret Otto, *The Little Old Train,* Knopf, 1960.
Robert Paul Smith, *Jack Mack,* Coward-McCann, 1960.
Millicent Selsam, *Plenty of Fish,* Harper, 1960.
Seymour Reit, *Where's Willie?,* Artists and Writers Press, 1961.
Ronna Jaffe, *The Last of the Wizards,* Simon & Schuster, 1961.
Myra Cohn Livingston, *I'm Hiding,* Harcourt, 1961.
Marjorie Winslow, *Mud Pies and Other Recipes,* Macmillan, 1961.
Jane Langton, *The Diamond in the Window,* Harper, 1962.
M. C. Livingston, *See What I Found,* Harcourt, 1962.

Walter the Earl thrust his sword into the air. "Sound the trumpets! Advance the host! Death to the invaders!" (From *The Gammage Cup,* by Carol Kendall, illustrated by Eric Blegvad.)

Miska Miles, *Dusty and the Fiddlers,* Little, Brown, 1962.
Jean Stafford, *Elephi,* Farrar, Straus, 1962.
Leonard Wibberley, *The Ballad of the Pilgrim Cat,* Ives & Washbourne, 1962.
Margaret Rudkin, *The Pepperidge Farm Cook Book,* Atheneum, 1963.
Barbara Brenner, *The Five Pennies,* Knopf, 1963.
Felice Holman, *Elisabeth the Bird Watcher,* Macmillan, 1963.
M. C. Livingston, *I'm Not Me,* Harcourt, 1963.
Richard Webber Jackson, *A Year Is a Window,* Doubleday, 1963.
Helen Taylor, *A Time to Recall,* Norton, 1963.
M. Miles, *Pony in the Schoolhouse,* Little Brown, 1964.
F. Holman, *Elisabeth the Treasure Hunter,* Macmillan, 1964.
M. C. Livingston, *Happy Birthday!,* Harcourt, 1964.
William Allingham, *The Dirty Old Man,* Prentice-Hall, 1965.
F. Holman, *Elisabeth and the Marsh Mystery,* Macmillan, 1966.
M. C. Livingston, *I'm Waiting,* Harcourt, 1966.
Doris Orgel, *The Good-Byes of Magnus Marmalade,* Putnam, 1966.
Sally Clithero, editor, *Beginning-to-Read Poetry,* Follett, 1967.
J. Langton, *The Swing in the Summer House,* Harper, 1967.
D. Orgel, *Phoebe and the Prince,* Putnam, 1969.
Max Steele, *The Cat and the Coffee Drinkers,* Harper, 1969.
Monica Stirling, *The Cat from Nowhere,* Harcourt, 1969.
Janice Udry, *Emily's Autumn,* Albert Whitman, 1969.
E. Nesbit, *The Conscience Pudding,* Coward-McCann, 1970.

Margery Sharp, *Miss Bianca in the Orient*, Heinemann, 1970.

Alvin R. Tresselt, *Bonnie Bess: The Weathervane Horse*, Parents' Magazine Press, 1970.

J. Langton, *The Astonishing Stereoscope*, Harper, 1971.

Judith Viorst, *The Tenth Good Thing about Barney*, Atheneum, 1971.

M. Sharp, *Miss Bianca in the Antarctic*, Little, Brown, 1971.

Roger Drury Wolcott, *The Finches' Fabulous Furnace*, Little, Brown, 1971.

O. Henry, *The Gift of the Magi*, Hawthorn, 1971.

M. Sharp, *Miss Bianca and the Bridesmaid*, Little, Brown, 1972.

E. Nesbit, *The Complete Book of Dragons*, Macmillan, 1973.

Mark Taylor, *The Wind's Child*, Atheneum, 1973.

Oliver Butterworth, *The Narrow Passage*, Little, Brown, 1973.

N. M. Bodecker, *The Mushroom Center Disaster*, Atheneum, 1974.

Ruth Craft, *The Winter Bear*, Collins, 1974, Atheneum, 1975.

Joan Phipson, *Polly's Tiger*, Dutton, 1974.

Jan Wahl, *The Five in the Forest*, Follett, 1974.

Jean O'Connell, *The Dollhouse Caper*, Crowell, 1976.

Charlotte Zolotow, *May I Visit?*, Harper, 1976.

Nancy Dingman Watson, *Blueberries Lavender*, Addison-Wesley, 1977.

J. Wahl, *The Pleasant Fieldmouse Storybook*, Prentice-Hall, 1977.

J. Wahl, *Pleasant Fieldmouse Valentine Trick*, Windmill, 1977.

"I need some meat," thought Nicky. "When I get my animal, I will have to feed him." (From *The Five Pennies*, by Barbara Brenner, illustrated by Erik Blegvad.)

(And reteller) *Burnie's Hill: A Traditional Rhyme*, Atheneum, 1977.

C. Zolotow, *Someone New*, Harper, 1978.

Robert Louis Stevenson, *A Child's Garden of Verses*, Random House, 1978.

Gail Mack, *Yesterday's Snowman*, Pantheon, 1978.

Andrew Lang, *The Yellow Fairy Book*, Kestrel Books, 1979.

(And reteller) *The Three Little Pigs*, Atheneum, 1979.

Rare Treasures from Grimm: Fifteen Little-Known Tales, compiled and translated by Ralph Manheim, Doubleday, 1981.

Mary Stolz, *Cat Walk*, Harper, 1983.

J. Wahl, *Peter and the Troll Baby*, Golden Press, 1984.

Jane L. Curry, *Little, Little Sister*, Macmillan, 1989.

C. Zolotow, *I Like to Be Little*, Harper, 1990.

N. M. Bodecker, *Water Pennies* (poems), Margaret K. McElderry, 1991.

ILLUSTRATOR; WRITTEN BY WIFE, LENORE BLEGVAD

Mr. Jensen and Cat, Harcourt, 1965.

One Is for the Sun, Harcourt, 1968.

The Great Hamster Hunt, Harcourt, 1969.

Moon-Watch Summer, Harcourt, 1972.

Anna Banana and Me, Atheneum, 1985, Macmillan, 1987.

This Is Me, Random House, 1986.

Rainy Day Kate, Macmillan, 1987.

ILLUSTRATOR; EDITED BY L. BLEGVAD

Mittens for Kittens: And Other Nursery Rhymes about Cats, Atheneum, 1974.

Hark! Hark! The Dogs Do Bark: And Other Rhymes about Dogs, Atheneum, 1975.

This Little Pig-a-Wig: And Other Rhymes about Pigs, Atheneum, 1978.

The Parrot in the Garret: And Other Rhymes about Dwellings, Atheneum, 1982.

OTHER

Self-Portrait: Erik Blegvad, Addison-Wesley, 1978.

Also illustrator of *Rare Treasures from Grimm*, translated by Ralph Manheim, Doubleday; and several works on fishing written by his father, Harald Blegvad. Contributor to periodicals in France, including *France Soir, Elle*, and *Femina*, and the United States, including *Esquire, Reader's Digest, Sports Illustrated, Life, American Heritage, McCall's, Saturday Evening Post*, and the *Woman's Day* serialization of Mary Norton's *The Borrowers* and *The Magic Bed Knob*.

WORK IN PROGRESS: Translating and illustrating a book of eight to twelve fairy tales by Hans Christian Andersen.

SIDELIGHTS: Eric Blegvad is a distinguished artist who has illustrated nearly one hundred books for children. A Danish national, Blegvad has lived and worked in England, France, and the United States during his career, which spans six decades. His drawings can be found in several notable books, such as *The Emperor's New Clothes* by Hans Christian Andersen, *The Tenth Good Thing about Barney* by Judith Viorst, and *The Winter Bear* by Ruth Craft. He has also successfully collaborated with his wife, Lenore Blegvad, on numerous children's books, including *This Little Pig-a-Wig* and *Anna Banana and Me*. The recipient of several awards and honors, Blegvad is a talented artist whose drawings favorably compare to works by the famed illustrator of Winnie-the-Pooh: "Working in black and white line or tinted drawings, Erik Blegvad carries on a tradition we have associated with Ernest Shepard," according to *Illustrators of Chil-*

In the morning, Ashfield was a strange sight. People who waked early and looked out the window rubbed their eyes and pinched themselves. Snow? It couldn't be. Yet it did look like snow. (From *The Finches' Fabulous Furnace,* by Roger Drury Wolcott, illustrated by Erik Blegvad.)

dren's Books, 1957-1966. "His decorations and illustrations on a small scale are very accessible to a child and provide the comfort of the known without ever sinking into the mannered or the banal."

Born on March 3, 1923, Blegvad spent his early years living in Copenhagen, Denmark, and traveling abroad. Visiting foreign countries greatly inspired the young artist. "When I was still a school boy I would go abroad with my family or sometimes by myself," Blegvad recalled in an interview for *Something about the Author* (*SATA*). "I suppose coming to places like Italy or London, where I saw things that I had never seen before, had an influence on me. I think the idea of taking a child outside his own environment opens his eyes to all sorts of things, especially if you come from a small bourgeois town like Copenhagen or from a flat country like Denmark. I was fascinated to see the mountains south of Munich, Germany, or the bright colors of London—like the red buses or the beautiful lettering on tube stations. These things had a visual impact that perhaps helped me decide to become an illustrator."

During these early years Blegvad was an avid reader. He began a lifelong interest in the works of Hans Christian Andersen, the nineteenth-century Danish author of such fairy tales as "The Princess and the Pea" and "The Ugly Duckling." The young Blegvad also read newspapers and was thrilled by the illustrators whose drawings appeared in the Sunday paper. "The color supplements on Sunday were usually full of drawings by our best commercial artists. The term 'commercial artist' I may use a little bit loosely here, but these were people who made their living doing posters, book

jackets, and book illustrations. They actually became our heroes. We looked for their drawings every Sunday."

Blegvad started drawing in childhood and received his formal training when he went to Copenhagen School of Arts and Crafts from 1941 until 1944. At that time German troops occupied Denmark. "Studying art during the German occupation had a sort of hothouse effect," Blegvad told *SATA*. "There was very little talk about politics at the school, and yet it was impossible not to be aware of what was going on. I think an awful lot of excuses for not having finished your homework came up because 'the war' and the Germans, 'the filthy Germans,' had prevented you from doing your work."

Although he did not excel in his studies, Blegvad learned some useful techniques in art school. "There was a rumor that the only reason I graduated was because I had been arrested by the Gestapo and that the school did not want to see somebody who had been arrested also fail his exams. I was not a very good student. But I did learn some valuable things. I really learned how to observe more clearly than I think people who did not have art training might. It wasn't as if I had been blind before, but art classes did open my eyes to a lot of things I might otherwise have just walked by."

Blegvad also made a lasting friendship in art school: "The friendship I enjoyed with N. M. Bodecker began with our first meeting in the art school in Copenhagen in February of 1941 and lasted until he died in Hancock, New Hampshire, in February of 1988. We shared a studio for a number of years in Westport, Connecticut, until my family and I moved to London in 1966. We collaborated on, among other projects, a series of soup labels for Pepperidge Farm. I have recently

Illustrator Erik Blegvad derives great enjoyment from working with his wife, Lenore, on books such as *This Little Pig-a-Wig*. (Cover illustration by Erik Blegvad.)

just finished illustrating his posthumous collection of poems, *Water Pennies.* It was a sobering experience, reminding me at every step how sublimely his own drawings complemented his wonderful poems."

When Germany was defeated in 1945 Blegvad signed up with the Royal Danish Air Force, hoping to realize a childhood dream of becoming a pilot: "I was always crazy about airplanes, completely mad about aviation." Instead of flying, however, Blegvad was assigned to serve as a translator with the British forces. Still, the assignment provided an opportunity for travel. "There was something about the occupation which had the effect of making you feel that you would never get out to see the world as you were meant to. So as soon as I saw an opportunity to join with the British forces, I volunteered for that and I came to Germany and worked for them. Towns like Hamburg and Hanover were completely ravaged, a dreadful part of the industrialized northwest of Germany. It was a pretty gruesome sight, but on the other hand we were so full of thoughts of revenge that I don't remember feeling particularly sorry for anybody."

After completing his military service in 1947, Blegvad moved to Paris to begin working as an illustrator. It was an important career move, though he initially had trouble adjusting to the city. "I remember hating Paris. I came during a very hot summer, and I couldn't speak a word of French. I couldn't understand what they were saying to me. I was very shocked that they didn't understand English, which was the first and only international tongue I had apart from German. I took it for granted that such an enlightened populace as the people of Paris would certainly have learned English at school, but, as many people have discovered, that was not the case.

"When I came to Paris the jobs that I managed to get were not very easy to land or very well paid to begin with. There were very few of them, so my life sort of fell into an extremely frugal, almost poverty-stricken routine. Then I landed a job with a very famous lady in Paris publishing, Madame Helene Lazareff, who had been in New York during the war with her family. She had been working for *Harper's Bazaar,* and she and her husband Pierre came back from New York when Paris was liberated. He became the editor of that enormous concern called Paris Presse, and she created a very famous ladies' weekly called *Elle.* When I showed her my drawings, she fell in love with them, and she gave me all the work I could handle. My fortune was actually made right there in Paris in April of 1948. The city is now my very favorite, perhaps because I speak and understand French."

While in Paris Blegvad also met American painter Lenore Hochman, and the two were married in 1950. A year later they moved to America, where Blegvad began illustrating books for dozens of children's authors. Though he clearly enjoys working with various writers, some of his most pleasurable work has come from projects involving Lenore. He described their working relationship in his *SATA* interview. "Usually Lenore comes up with the idea in the beginning. She might say, 'let's see, you like to draw such and such a thing, I think I'll try and get something on that subject.' Her very first book was about Copenhagen. I remember that at the time I was homesick for Copenhagen, so it was nice to sit and draw those drawings. I also like to draw animals. So my wife came up with the idea of having these series of nursery rhymes, because she knew I liked to draw cats and dogs and pigs." First appearing in the mid-1970s, the series includes *Mittens for Kittens, Hark! Hark! The Dogs Do Bark, This Little Pig-a-Wig,* and *The Parrot in the Garret.*

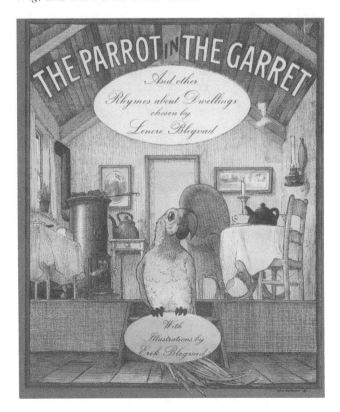

The last in the series of four books by the Blegvads that feature traditional English rhymes. (Cover illustration from *The Parrot in the Garret,* written by Lenore Blegvad, illustrated by Erik Blegvad.)

Over the years Blegvad has gained a reputation for producing richly detailed pen-and-ink drawings. Composed of carefully drawn lines, his pictures feature people and animals that are clearly defined without appearing stiff. While he also works with watercolors, Blegvad prefers pen and ink. "It's obvious that I feel most at home when I have a bottle of ink, a nib, a holder, and a rag to wipe the nib with," Blegvad remarked in his *SATA* interview. "Those are more or less the tools that I feel most at home with. I don't know why that should be. I suppose a pencil would be a very natural tool also, but I never fell in love with that. I think I smudge it too much. I like to see the illustration with my hand resting on the paper when I draw. I have friends who can draw from the shoulder or the elbow, but I'm used to drawing from the wrist, more or less. I don't have that lovely free-and-easy swing my wife has on her canvas. I can't do that. I more or less sit around and scratch my drawings with a movement from the wrist."

As he "scratches" out his drawings, Blegvad has a goal in mind: "It would be nice if my illustration could give a graphically satisfying pleasure to the person who is watching it. I hardly ever worry about whether it's a grown-up or child who has to see it. That doesn't seem to matter much to me. I'm a little worried about drawing simply for children and complicatedly for adults, as if children couldn't quite see or couldn't quite enjoy something that was a little sophisticated. I know it's sometimes an argument between myself and editors. They're afraid I'm going to show something which might upset a child or frighten a child or puzzle too much. I don't think that's my own worry so much.

"I think the text should be the most important element and the picture should be the complement. I never became a real 'gung ho' picture book artist where there are just a few lines of text and this enormous picture in full color. I prefer the other imbalance, where the text is the dominating part and the drawing is just a suggestion of what you're reading. It also looks so nice on the page when there is a column of text and then the drawing."

With nearly one hundred books to his credit, Blegvad has covered a wide range of subjects. He likes diversity and is comfortable drawing almost anything. "I actually enjoy illustrating almost any subject you can imagine. It's a rich and varied world. I don't really have many preferences: I like drawing the sea and the ships as much as I like drawing the farm, the animals, the aircraft, the harbor, and the town. They all seem to me to be enjoyable subjects."

Toward the end of his interview for *SATA*, Blegvad reflected on his long and prosperous career as a free-lance illustrator. "I think it's the best possible life one could lead, and you don't have to just sit at home and do it. I didn't have to stay in Copenhagen. It must be one of the nicest jobs there is to be a commercial artist and to be a free-lance illustrator. I can't really imagine anything nicer."

WORKS CITED:

Blegvad, Erik, telephone interview with James F. Kamp for *Something about the Author,* March 5, 1991.
Illustrators of Children's Books, 1957-1966, Horn Book, 1968, p. 3.

FOR MORE INFORMATION SEE:

PERIODICALS

American Artist, September, 1961.

Sketch by James F. Kamp

*   *   *

BLEGVAD, Lenore 1926-

PERSONAL: Born May 8, 1926, in New York, NY; daughter of Julius C. (a mechanical engineer) and Ruth (a teacher; maiden name, Huebschman) Hochman; married Eric Blegvad (an illustrator), September 12, 1950; children: Peter, Kristoffer. *Education:* Vassar College, B.A., 1947.

ADDRESSES: Home—Mountain Spring Farms, Wardsboro, VT 05355; 3 Place Capitaine Vincent, 06190 Roquebrune Cap Martin, Alpes Maritimes, France.

CAREER: Painter and writer.

WRITINGS:

ALL ILLUSTRATED BY HUSBAND, ERIC BLEGVAD

Mr. Jensen and Cat, Harcourt, 1965.
One Is for the Sun, Harcourt, 1968.
The Great Hamster Hunt, Harcourt, 1969.
Moon-Watch Summer, Harcourt, 1972.
(Editor) *Mittens for Kittens: And Other Nursery Rhymes about Cats,* Atheneum, 1974.
(Editor) *Hark! Hark! The Dogs Do Bark: And Other Rhymes about Dogs,* Atheneum, 1975.
(Editor) *This Little Pig-a-Wig: And Other Rhymes about Pigs,* Atheneum, 1978.
(Editor) *The Parrot in the Garret: And Other Rhymes about Dwellings,* Atheneum, 1982.
Anna Banana and Me, Atheneum, 1985, Macmillan, 1987.
This Is Me, Random House, 1986.
Rainy Day Kate, Macmillan, 1987.

WORK IN PROGRESS: A self-illustrated grandmother/grandchildren book.

SIDELIGHTS: Lenore Blegvad told *SATA:* "I have divided my time between writing and painting for many years—all my life in fact. I drew from the time I was very young, and I seem to remember writing a miniature book on the joys of chicken pox when I was not much older. These two interests were reinforced and encouraged at my beloved Walden School in New York and later at Vassar College as well as at various art schools in New York and Paris. Which one of these activities I do at any given moment is dictated by a number of things: mood, inspiration, location. (We live part of the year in Vermont and part in the South of France, and we often visit our children and grandchildren in London.) I find the creative effort for each equally arduous and absorbing while the change from one occupation to the other brings new insights every time. Somehow this suits me to perfection."

BLISH, James (Benjamin) 1921-1975
(William Atheling, Jr., Marcus Lyons, Arthur Merlin, Luke Torley, pseudonyms; Donald Laverty, John MacDougal, joint pseudonyms)

PERSONAL: Born May 23, 1921, in East Orange, NJ; died of cancer, July 30 (one source says 29), 1975, in Henley-on-Thames, England; son of Asa Rhodes and Dorothea (Schneewind) Blish; married Mildred Virginia Kidd Emden, May 23, 1947 (divorced, 1963); married Judith Ann Lawrence, November 7, 1964; children: (first marriage) Elisabeth, Charles Benjamin. *Education:* Rutgers University, B.Sc., 1942; attended Columbia University, 1945-46. *Hobbies and other interests:* Music, astronomy, and flying.

ADDRESSES: Agent—Robert P. Mills Ltd., 156 East Fifty-second St., New York, NY 10022.

CAREER: Trade newspaper editor, New York City, 1947-51; public relations counsel in New York City and Washington, DC, 1951-69; writer. *Military service:* U.S. Army, medical laboratory technician, 1942-44.

MEMBER: Science Fiction Writers of America (vice president, 1966-68), American Rocket Society, British Interplanetary Society, Society of Authors, James Branch Cabell Society, History of Science Society, Association of Lunar and Planetary Observers, Authors League, Civil Air Patrol.

AWARDS, HONORS: Hugo Award for best science fiction novel, 1958, for *A Case of Conscience;* Eighteenth World Science Fiction Convention Guest of Honor, 1960.

WRITINGS:

Jack of Eagles (science fiction novel), Greenberg, 1952, published as *ESPer,* Avon, 1958.
(With Fritz Leiber and Fletcher Pratt) *Witches Three,* Twayne, 1952.
Sword of Xota, Galaxy, 1953.
The Warriors of Day (science fiction novel), Galaxy, 1953.
Earthman, Come Home (science fiction novel; also see below), Putnam, 1955.
The Frozen Year (novel), Ballantine, 1957, published in England as *The Fallen Star,* Faber, 1957.
The Seedling Stars (short stories), Gnome, 1957.
They Shall Have Stars (science fiction novel; also see below), Faber, 1957, also published as *Year 2018!,* Avon, 1957.
A Case of Conscience (science fiction novel), Ballantine, 1958.
The Triumph of Time (science fiction novel; also see below), Avon, 1958, published in England as *A Clash of Cymbals,* Faber, 1958.
VOR (science fiction novel), Avon, 1958.
(With Robert A. W. Lowndes) *The Duplicated Man* (science fiction novel), Avalon, 1959.
Galactic Cluster (short story collection), New American Library, 1959.
(With Poul Anderson and Thomas N. Scortia) *Get Out of My Sky,* edited by Leo Margulies, Fawcett, 1960.
So Close to Home (short story collection), Ballantine, 1961.
The Star Dwellers (science fiction novel for children), Putnam, 1961.
(With Virginia Kidd) *Titan's Daughter* (science fiction novel), Berkley Publishing, 1961.

A Life for the Stars (science fiction novel; also see below), Putnam, 1962.
The Night Shapes (novel), Ballantine, 1962.
Doctor Mirabilis: A Novel, Faber, 1964, revised edition, Dodd, 1971.
(Under pseudonym William Atheling, Jr.) *The Issue at Hand: Studies in Contemporary Magazine Science Fiction,* Advent, 1964, 2nd edition published as *More Issues at Hand: Critical Studies in Contemporary Science Fiction,* 1970.
Best Science Fiction Stories of James Blish, Faber, 1965, revised edition, 1973, published as *The Testament of Andros,* Hutchinson, 1977.
Cities in Flight (contains *Earthman, Come Home, They Shall Have Stars, The Triumph of Time,* and *A Life for the Stars*), Faber, 1965, Avon, 1966, revised edition, 1970.
Mission to the Heart Stars (science fiction novel for children), Putnam, 1965.
(Editor and author of introduction) *New Dreams This Morning,* Ballantine, 1966.
(With Norman L. Knight) *A Torrent of Faces* (science fiction novel), Doubleday, 1967.
(Adapter) *Star Trek* (novelizations of scripts from the National Broadcasting Company television series; also see below), Bantam, Volumes 1-11, 1967-75, Volume 12 (with wife, Judith A. Lawrence), 1977.
Welcome to Mars! (science fiction novel for children), Faber, 1967, Putnam, 1968.
Black Easter; or, Faust Aleph-Null (science fiction novel), Doubleday, 1968.
The Vanished Jet (science fiction novel for children), Weybright & Talley, 1968.
(With Robert Silverberg and Roger Zelazny) *Three for Tomorrow: Three Original Novellas of Science Fiction,* Meredith Press, 1969.
Anywhen (short story collection), Doubleday, 1970, revised edition, Faber, 1971.
(Editor) *Nebula Award Stories 5,* Doubleday, 1970.
Spock Must Die! (original novel; also see below), Bantam, 1970.
(Editor) *Thirteen O'Clock and Other Zero Hours: The "Cecil Corwin" Stories of C. M. Kornbluth,* Dell, 1970.
. . . And All the Stars a Stage (science fiction novel), Doubleday, 1971.
The Day after Judgment (science fiction novel), Doubleday, 1971.
Midsummer Century (science fiction novel), Doubleday, 1972.
The Quincunx of Time (science fiction novel), Dell, 1972.
The Star Trek Reader (contains *Star Trek,* Volumes 1-10, Volume 12, and *Spock Must Die!*), four volumes, Dutton, 1976-78.
The Best of James Blish, edited by Robert A. W. Lowndes, Ballantine, 1979.
The Tale That Wags the God, Advent, 1987.
The Devil's Day, Baen, 1990.

Also author of television scripts and motion picture screenplays. Contributor of short stories, articles, poetry, and criticism, occasionally under pseudonyms, to numerous magazines. Editor, *Vanguard Science Fiction,* 1958; co-editor, *Kalki: Studies in James Branch Cabell,* beginning in 1967.

WORK IN PROGRESS: A History of Witchcraft, Demonology and Magic; a study of the semantics of music; *The Sense of Music;* a science fiction novel.

SIDELIGHTS: Although James Blish was known to many readers for adapting *Star Trek* television scripts into book form, a *Times Literary Supplement* reviewer once referred to him as "one of the best five or six living writers of science fiction." Blish made a point of including actual scientific and technological detail in his works, for he felt that it was necessary for a science fiction writer to be as accurate as possible so that the reader would believe the story. He also, at least after writing *A Case of Conscience* in 1958, displayed an interest in religious topics, especially in Christianity's early struggles with satanic powers.

WORKS CITED:

Review of *The Seedling Stars, Times Literary Supplement,* September 21, 1967, p. 844.

FOR MORE INFORMATION SEE:

BOOKS

Contemporary Literary Criticism, Volume 14, Gale, 1980.
Dictionary of Literary Biography, Volume 8: *Twentieth-Century American Science Fiction Writers,* Gale, 1981.
Walker, Paul, editor, *Speaking of Science Fiction: The Paul Walker Interviews,* Luna, 1978.

PERIODICALS

Magazine of Fantasy and Science Fiction, April, 1972.
New York Herald Tribune Book Review, April 13, 1952.
Washington Post Book World, June 27, 1982.
Young Readers' Review, February, 1968.

OBITUARIES:

PERIODICALS

AB Bookman's Weekly, September 8, 1975.
New York Times, July 31, 1975.
Washington Post, August 1, 1975.

*   *   *

BLISHEN, Edward 1920-

PERSONAL: Born April 29, 1920, in Whetstone, Middlesex, England; son of William George (a civil servant) and Elizabeth Ann (Pye) Blishen; married Nancy Smith, November 4, 1948; children: Jonathan Edward, Nicholas Martin. *Education:* Educated in England. *Hobbies and other interests:* Walking, photography, listening to music.

ADDRESSES: Home—12 Bartrams Ln., Hadley Wood, Barnet, EN4 0EH England. *Agent*—Irene Josephy, 35 Craven St., Strand, London WC2, England.

CAREER: Employed in London, England, and vicinity, as journalist, 1937-40; preparatory schoolmaster, 1946-49; teacher in secondary school, 1950-59; University of York, Heslington, England, part-time lecturer in department of education, 1963-65; writer, 1965—. British Broadcasting Corporation (BBC-radio), broadcaster of radio programs, including "Writers' Club," "World of Books," "A Good Read," and "Meridian," 1959—. *Wartime service:* Essex and Hertfordshire War Agriculture Committee, manual laborer, 1941-46.

MEMBER: PEN (member of executive committee of English Center, 1962-66), Society of Authors.

AWARDS, HONORS: Oxford Book of Poetry for Children received a Kate Greenaway Medal Commendation from the British Library Association, 1963, and was selected as one of Child Study Association of America's children's books of the year, 1986; Kate Greenaway Medal Commendation and Carnegie Medal from the British Library Association, both 1971, both for *The God beneath the Sea;* Society of Authors Traveling Scholarship, 1979; J. R. Ackerley Prize for autobiography, English Center of International PEN, 1981, for *Shaky Relations.*

WRITINGS:

Roaring Boys, a Schoolmaster's Agony, Thames & Hudson, 1955.
Changing School: The Problems of Selection and Some Solutions, Council for Children's Welfare, 1959.
(Editor) *Junior Pears Encyclopaedia,* twenty-nine volumes, Pelham Books, 1961-89.
(Editor) *Education Today: The Existing Opportunities,* BBC Publications, 1963.
(Editor) *Oxford Book of Poetry for Children,* illustrated by Brian Wildsmith, Oxford University Press, 1963, F. Watts, 1964.
Town Story, illustrated by J.C. Armitage, Anthony Blond, 1964.
(Editor) *Miscellany,* six volumes, Oxford University Press, 1964-69.
(Editor) *Come Reading: A Book of Prose for Young Readers,* M. Joseph, 1968.
Hugh Lofting (monographs), Bodley Head, 1968.
(Editor) *Encyclopaedia of Education,* Anthony Blond, 1969, Philosophical Library, 1970.
This Right Soft Lot, Thames & Hudson, 1969.
The School That I'd Like, Penguin, 1969.
(With Leon Garfield) *The God beneath the Sea,* illustrated by Charles Keeping, Longmans, Green, 1970, Pantheon, 1971.
Have You Read This in Paperback?, National Book League, 1972.
A Cackhanded War, Thames & Hudson, 1972.
(With Garfield) *The Golden Shadow,* illustrated by Charles Keeping, Longman, 1973, Pantheon, 1973.
Uncommon Entrance, Thames & Hudson, 1974.
(Editor) *The Thorny Paradise: Writers on Writing for Children,* Penguin Books, 1975.
The Writer's Approach to the Novel, Harrap, 1976.
Sorry, Dad, Hamish Hamilton, 1978.
(Editor with Chris Cook) *Pears Guide to Today's World,* Pelham Books, 1979.
A Nest of Teachers, Hamish Hamilton, 1980.
Shaky Relations, Hamish Hamilton, 1981.
Lizzie Pye, Hamish Hamilton, 1982.
Donkey Work, Hamish Hamilton, 1983.
A Second Skin, Hamish Hamilton, 1984.
The Outside Contributor, Hamish Hamilton, 1986.
(Editor) *Robin Hood,* illustrated by Geoff Taylor, Knight, 1987.
The Disturbance Fee, Hamish Hamilton, 1988.
(Editor) *Science Fiction Stories,* Kingfisher Books, 1988.
(Editor with wife, Nancy Blishen) *Treasury of Stories for Six Year Olds,* Kingfisher Books, 1988.
(Editor with N. Blishen) *Treasury of Stories for Seven Year Olds,* Kingfisher Books, 1988.

"I look more and more like my father all the time, which worries me a great deal," Edward Blishen told *Something about the Author*.

(Editor with N. Blishen) *Treasury of Stories for Five Year Olds,* Kingfisher, Books, 1989.

Also selector of excerpts from Charles Dickens's novel *Bleak House,* with Leon Garfield, to accompany Mervyn Peake's book of illustrations titled *Sketches from Bleak House,* Methuen, 1984. Former editorial board member of *Forum.*

WORK IN PROGRESS: "My first attempt at fiction and another autobiography."

SIDELIGHTS: When British author Edward Blishen was a child, two of his favorite activities were reading and writing in his diary. His diaries would later become the basis of a volume of autobiographies in which he recalls various people and episodes of his life. The first book Blishen wrote, *Roaring Boys, a Schoolmaster's Agony,* describes how he began his job as a teacher. In an interview for *Something about the Author* (*SATA*) he remarked, "I drifted into teaching by mistake. I found I liked it, but was quite glad to get out of it in the end. I wrote this book about how difficult it was and was immediately taken to be an expert." The success of *Roaring Boys* convinced Blishen to give up teaching and return to his real love, writing. He explained: "I never thought of myself as anything else than a writer from the age of five onward." In addition to his autobiographies, Blishen has also collaborated on two children's books with his friend Leon Garfield

and edited encyclopedias and anthologies of literature for young readers.

Blishen, born in 1920, was the first child of his working class parents. Many of his early memories involve his mother and father, and they appear as characters in several of his autobiographies. He described them to *SATA:* "My mother was . . . *wholesome* is a good word for it. As a young woman, innocent and eager, she must have been very attractive, but very quickly in a poverty-stricken marriage with an unsatisfied husband she became oppressed and her good looks vanished. She lived in a very narrow world of the street and the next door neighbor and the people you met while shopping. My mother's only friends that I can think of were two women with whom she'd been in the service."

Although he admired his mother, the author had a love-hate relationship with his father. He explained, "When I was a small child I actually adored him. He was a very attractive and charming man." Yet, as Blishen grew older, he realized that his father was not always kind. He stated, "My father could be very cruel. He was an explosive, impatient man and a violent man when he needed to be. One reason for the life-long quarrel between us was that I was like my mother—hopelessly given to liking people and finding reasons for approving of them or for excusing them for being beastly. I remember my father saying to me once, 'You drive me up the wall. You've got a good word to say for everybody.' I really did drive him up the wall. I felt sorry for him."

Blishen believes that his father was strongly affected by his experiences as a soldier during World War I. "He spent about two years in the trenches. I don't think the experience determined his gloomy outlook on things, however, which was very much present before. But I've no doubt the war made things worse for him. He spoke very little about it. He did suffer from shell shock and my earliest memory of him—I'm not sure if I actually remember it or if I remember the effect of this—is as a man sitting in the corner of the kitchen sobbing. He had a breakdown, obviously the result of that terror men went through in the trenches—of being buried alive."

Blishen's other childhood memories involve radio and books. For a child growing up before television was invented, radio was an interesting source of information. Blishen told *SATA*, "Radio was part of the world of everybody growing up at the time. I always say I was educated, not really by school, but by Penguin and the BBC. In the early days I listened to almost everything. We had hardly any books at home; nobody read to us. I remember trying to interest my father in my comics and being terribly hurt because he wasn't. He didn't regard what a child read as something worth discussing, and was very cross about the literature I had accumulated." However, despite the lack of support from his parents, Blishen managed to read by borrowing books from his local library. "I read madly right from the very beginning—all sorts of things. I didn't understand the difference between adult and children's books. What I loved about books was that they switched your world from day to day. For a long time I read a book a day. I can remember walking up the road, bumping into lampposts and old ladies, trying to get the last chapter read so I could change the book at the library."

Additional opportunities to learn presented themselves when the author began to attend school at Green Road Elementary. Blishen recalled, "I very much enjoyed the primary school. I was an odiously bright boy, a prodigy and expected to do amazingly well. I was the boy who could write nice notes and got ten out of ten for composition. Doing compositions and things made me rather unpopular and I did worry about that somewhat." Because Blishen did so well in his studies, he received a scholarship when he was ten years old to go to grammar school and continue his education.

However, the new school was quite different from his elementary school. He declared, "Nobody made any attempt to ease our way from one way of life to another. It was a great leap to take. In 1930, I didn't understand anything about the whole business of going to grammar school. All I knew was that it separated you in a rather exciting way from your old friends. In fact, the grammar school made it perfectly clear that you should remain separated from your old friends. You were going to be made into gentlemen.

"Though my father was very pleased when I went to the grammar school, he very rapidly changed his mind because I began to drift away from home, and it acted as a divorce. I was bewildered by the impossibility of explaining the world of school at home, or indeed, explaining the world of home at school." Much of this tension was due to the fact that the author's parents had not received the same amount of education as their son. Blishen commented, "My mother was barely literate. My father left school at thirteen on the grounds that his mother was a widow and needed his support.

He was a bright and intelligent man. Had he been properly educated, heaven knows what he might have done."

At grammar school many of the author's fellow students were rich, and they made fun of the boys, including Blishen, who received scholarships because their families didn't have the money to pay for school. Although he remembered this as one of the negative aspects about school, Blishen remarked: "I'm glad I went there. I met at least two people who made it worthwhile, including Spencer Vaughan Thomas who was one of the staff. Spencer was a great bonus and I'm terribly glad to have gone to the school in order to have met him. The second important friend I met at the school was an Irishman, Gerald Murray. He was appointed to teach us mathematics. He did all sorts of good things, like taking me to the theatre."

When it was time for final examinations in grammar school, Blishen realized he had spent too much time reading and not enough time doing his school work. "I fooled about," he commented. "I was in such an hysterical state. I didn't read any of the set books for higher school certificate. I read furiously everything that wasn't in the syllabus. Finally, I turned up for the vital part of the Latin exam in the afternoon to find it had taken place in the morning. I was a contender for a state scholarship, but I didn't stand a chance. I didn't get a school certificate.

"I became a newspaper reporter after being thrown out of school. Mrs. Wright, who taught me the piano, knew of a vacancy on the *Muswell Hill Records,* one of the most awful weekly newspapers you can imagine. So I went and was accepted. They would have accepted anybody. I paid ten shillings for the privilege of working for them—a kind of apprenticeship. I learned nothing. I was reporting on everything from church bazaars, fires, concerts to police courts. I hated *Muswell Hill.*"

Blishen's reporting career was interrupted by the start of World War II. He remembers the fear that was created by this event. "At that time, in 1938, many of us were absolutely certain that the end of the world was about to come anyway. I still say that despite all the terrible political things that have happened in the world since, the 1930s still haunt me—it was a time when Germany seemed to be a madhouse. The most civilized nation in Europe was a lunatic asylum and the lunatics were in charge. I don't think anybody gets over a war. It's still the most haunting event of my own life—a great and horrible political event.

"I could see when war began there would be a tremendous impulse to join but that I mustn't. I mustn't be part of it—it was all wrong, it was terrible. All these men who had written about war afterward had deplored the whole thing. I became a conscientious objector. At the time I didn't know anybody else who was, but I was absolutely determined. There were two very strong and logically contradictory things going on inside me: an awareness of the appalling things that Adolf Hitler was doing and threatened, and certainly the knowledge that unless he was disposed of there was no future for the world at all, and, at the same time, this extraordinarily powerful pacifism which had grown up in me from literature. It was also part of my terror of aggression. To this day I'm horrified by quarrels and aggression of all kinds."

Even though Blishen was a conscientious objector who didn't think it was right to fight a war, he still had to serve his country in a nonmilitary role during World War II. He was sent to work as a laborer, first for the Essex War Agriculture Committee and later with the Hertfordshire War Agriculture

(From the *Oxford Book of Poetry for Children,* edited by Edward Blishen, illustrated by Brian Wildsmith.)

Committee. "I was completely unready for heavy manual work. I spent five and a half years with filthy, very scarred hands. When the war ended I had a general feeling that I'd like some sort of indoor occupation where you could keep your hands clean all the time. I really wanted to go back to reporting and writing. Writing was my life, really. I'd kept diaries and written little bits of stories and poems in my notebooks during the war, but I'd not published anything or tried to get anything published.

"A friend knew of a vacancy in a preparatory school in Hampstead. It wasn't my world. I wasn't trained as a teacher. The headmaster summoned me and I thought the interview was so dreadful that I was safe. To my amazement, I got a letter saying I would be very successful. I was untrained. I knew nothing. But I taught, and a dreadful teacher I was! This was a very high-flying school of brilliant kids, ages six to thirteen. I taught them English. I taught them mathematics, a subject I'd warned the headmaster I had no capacity to teach at all. I liked quite a lot of the children, but at the same time they filled me with terror. I never realized how difficult it was to maintain any kind of control.

"I taught in the end for about nine years in a desperate kind of school at the Archway, Islington, known locally as the 'dustbin.' I discovered the only resource I had as a teacher was that I knew about language. A colleague and I founded the first library in the school. One of the few miracles I ever observed in teaching was that if you opened a school library, the number of comics being read dropped. Certainly the existence and availability of books made it possible to say

that children didn't necessarily want to live entirely on comics." In creating this library, Blishen provided various types of literature, both good and bad. He believed that a child could not appreciate classic works without having lesser works for comparison. Blishen told *SATA,* "The whole business of evaluating and comparing one book with another—so that you actually do see in what respect one is good and the other is not—seems to me essential lessons that a collection of books should provide."

Even as he was teaching, Blishen continued to write. Often his short sketches about events that took place in his classroom appeared in the *Manchester Guardian* magazine. A publisher, having read these stories, asked Blishen if he would consider writing a book. The author recounted, "I never really expected any publisher to show any enthusiasm for a book from me. The fact that one had was the crowning moment of my life. There was no point in doing anything more! Certainly no point in risking the ruin of the whole thing by actually trying to write the book. So I did nothing." Then, another publisher asked Blishen to write a book. "They gave me an advance of fifty pounds—a fantastic sum of money then. It was terrifying. If they gave me fifty pounds, I must write the book. So I tried to write the book.

"I had the most appalling problems. First, I didn't know how to write a book. I had no idea what a book was. I'd read millions of them, but when it came to write one, I didn't know how to do it. So, I wrote the book about the school in which I was teaching. It describes the development of the teacher. It's full of recognizable persons. How I got away without a libel case, I've no idea, except that people would rather be libeled than left out. The people who are really angry are the people who can't find themselves in it." The book was titled *Roaring Boys, a Schoolmaster's Agony.* According to Blishen, "It became a modest best-seller. It felt astonishing to see it published. It's great, it's a lovely feeling. I can remember the first time I saw someone picking up a copy of my book in a book shop. He looked at it, sniffed, and put it down. It got very well reviewed, but I was cautious. I thought it was all probably an illusion and couldn't be sustained. I didn't try to write another book for fourteen years after that."

Blishen felt strained by trying to combine writing and teaching. "My wife bravely agreed to my suggestion that I give up teaching and try to do half-time writing and broadcasting and try to find part-time teaching. We had small children, so it was quite a thing to agree to. All my efforts to find part-time teaching didn't work, and after a few months, I found I didn't need it. I've been free-lance ever since. I've edited a children's encyclopedia for thirty years—we're just coming up to the thirtieth edition, which was part of the free-lancing activity that prevented me from writing books for those fourteen years. I edited a book called *The Thorny Paradise,* a collection of works by children's writers of the sixties. That was the golden age of children's writing." More recently, Blishen has collaborated with his wife Nancy to edit anthologies of children's literature. "We were simply invited to do it, and we did. It's a very pleasant task—reading as many stories as we can and recommending them to each other and making the final, quite difficult, choice."

Blishen also has written two children's books with his friend Leon Garfield. "All our friends counselled against our working together, pointing to a number of classical cases of persons who ceased to be good friends after collaboration. As it turned out, our friendship was strengthened by the experience. The first book we collaborated on was *The God beneath the Sea.* The idea for it came up in two ways. There was an idea that one of us should write an account of creation as seen through the eyes of the Greek myth makers. But before that, Leon and I had discussed what stories we'd heard or read when young that had the greatest impression upon us. We agreed that they were the Greek myths." *The God beneath the Sea* won a Carnegie Medal as the outstanding British children's book of the year. "It was the first time they had ever given it to two authors. They had only one medal, so I had to wait for mine."

In addition to writing, Blishen has also lectured about education and visited schools to talk to children about writing. He shared the advice he gives to young writers: "What I always say when I go into schools to talk about writing is 'Don't suppose that you have to scratch around desperately for something to write about. You're in the middle of stories the whole time, you're a hero or heroine of your own stories.' The other day I was talking at a school in East Grinstead to children who wanted to talk about writing. I was telling them that one of the most infamous things we do in school is to talk about 'correcting' the work you do. You write something and you 'correct' it. Correction has such a punitive, shamefaced feeling about it. It's not really correction. What you do is write something and then you improve it. You work on it, polish it, and change it. Once you've got something down on paper then you can begin the real work. I think that's how schools ought to look at it, rather than at this notion that you write something down and then you correct it. I love the business of working over the thing."

As for his own philosophy about his work, Blishen concluded: "I think the feeling that moves me as a writer more than anything is the notion that life is a gift. You are given this gift and it is awful not to respond. As Greek philosopher Aristotle said, 'The unexamined life is not worth living.' To me that sums everything up. I can't imagine what it is like not to write about life. I feel guilty now if I don't write down what happens."

WORKS CITED:

Blishen, Edward, interviews with Cathy Courtney for *Something about the Author,* conducted August 16, 1989; August 23, 1989; and November 22, 1989.

FOR MORE INFORMATION SEE:

PERIODICALS

Times (London), July 2, 1981; September 1, 1983; October 25, 1984.
Times Literary Supplement, March 21, 1980; October 15, 1982; January 18, 1985.

*   *   *

BOTSFORD, Ward 1927-

PERSONAL: Born June 22, 1927, in Titusville, PA; son of Harry (a writer) and Ruth (maiden name, Epstein) Botsford; married Lynn Kalsner (an executive), August 20, 1954; children: Diana Dru, Andrea Gwyn. *Education:* Attended The Juilliard School, 1947-48.

ADDRESSES: Home—Robin Hood Rd., Pound Ridge, NY 10576. *Agent*—Bob Brenner Associates, 31 Amherst Dr., New Rochelle, NY 10804. *Office*—Arabesque Recordings, 60 East 42nd St., New York, NY 10165.

CAREER: Vox Productions, Inc., New York City, vice-president, 1951-65; Caedmon (record company), member of staff, New York City, 1965—; Arabesque Recordings, New York City, owner, 1987—.

MEMBER: Sir Thomas Beecham Society (president).

AWARDS, HONORS: Grammy Award, 1980, for "Ages of Man," and 1981, for "Gertrude Stein, Gertrude Stein, Gertrude Stein."

WRITINGS:

Archaeology: Middle America, Doubleday, 1960.
Sir Thomas Beecham: A Critical Discography, Beecham Society, 1964.
(Adapter) *The Pirates of Penzance: The Story of the Gilbert and Sullivan Operetta,* illustrated by Edward Sorel, Random House, 1981.

Contributor of articles to periodicals, including *American Record Guide, New York Times,* and *Hi Fidelity.*

FOR MORE INFORMATION SEE:

PERIODICALS

Bulletin of the Center for Children's Books, January, 1982.
New York Times Book Review, February 14, 1982.
Publishers Weekly, December 4, 1981.
Washington Post Book World, November 8, 1981.

*   *   *

BRADFORD, Barbara Taylor 1933-

PERSONAL: Born May 10, 1933, in Leeds, Yorkshire, England; came to the United States in 1964; daughter of Winston (an industrial engineer) and Freda (a children's nurse; maiden name Walker) Taylor; married Robert Bradford (a movie and television producer), 1963. *Hobbies and other interests:* Collecting antiques, reading.

ADDRESSES: Office—450 Park Ave., New York, NY 10022.

CAREER: Writer. *Yorkshire Evening Post,* Yorkshire, England, reporter, 1949-51, women's editor, 1951-53; *Women's Own,* London, England, fashion editor, 1953-54; *London Evening News,* columnist, 1955-57; *London American,* London, women's editor and executive editor, 1959-62; National Design Center, New York, NY, editor, 1964-65; *Newsday,* Long Island, NY, syndicated columnist, 1968-70; columnist for *Chicago Tribune, New York Daily News,* and *Los Angeles Times* syndicates, 1970-81. Also served as feature writer for *Today* magazine in the United Kingdom.

MEMBER: Authors Guild (member of council), Authors League of America.

BARBARA TAYLOR BRADFORD

AWARDS, HONORS: Distinguished Editorial Award, National Society of Interior Designers, 1969; Dorothy Dawe Award, American Furniture Mart, 1970, 1971; National Press Award, 1971; Matrix Award, New York Women in Communications, 1985; honorary doctorate, Leeds University, 1990.

WRITINGS:

FOR CHILDREN

(Editor) *Children's Stories of the Bible from the Old Testament,* illustrations by Laszlo Matulay, Lion Press, 1966.
(Editor) *Children's Stories of Jesus from the New Testament,* illustrations by L. Matulay, Lion Press, 1966.
(Editor) Samuel Nisenson, *The Dictionary of 1001 Famous People: Outstanding Personages in the World of Science, the Arts, Music, and Literature,* Lion Press, 1966.
A Garland of Children's Verse (based on an original Czech edition entitled *Frantisek Halas Detem*), illustrations by Ota Janecek, Lion Press, 1968.
(Editor) *Childrens' Stories of the Bible from the Old and New Testament,* Crown, 1988.

NOVELS

A Woman of Substance (alternate selection of Doubleday Book Club and Literary Guild), Doubleday, 1979.
Voice of the Heart (main selection of Literary Guild and Doubleday Book Club), Doubleday, 1983.
Hold the Dream (main selection of Literary Guild and Doubleday Book Club; also see below), Doubleday, 1985.
Act of Will (main selection of Literary Guild and Doubleday Book Club), Doubleday, 1986.
To Be the Best (main selection of Literary Guild and Doubleday Book Club), Doubleday, 1988.
The Women in His Life (main selection of Literary Guild and Doubleday Book Club), Random House, 1990.

OTHER

The Complete Encyclopedia of Homemaking Ideas, Meredith Press, 1968.
How To Be the Perfect Wife: Etiquette to Please Him, Essandess, 1969.
How To Be the Perfect Wife: Entertaining to Please Him, Essandess, 1969.
How To Be the Perfect Wife: Fashions That Please Him, Essandess, c. 1970.
Easy Steps to Successful Decorating, Simon & Schuster, 1971.
How to Solve Your Decorating Problems, Simon & Schuster, 1976.
Decorating Ideas for Casual Living, Simon & Schuster, c. 1977.
Making Space Grow, Simon & Schuster, 1979.
Luxury Designs for Apartment Living, Doubleday, 1981.

Also author of screenplay for *Hold the Dream.*

ADAPTATIONS: A Woman of Substance, Voice of the Heart, Hold the Dream, and *To Be the Best* have been adapted as television miniseries; and *Act of Will* has been adapted for television in the United Kingdom.

WORK IN PROGRESS: Novel, as yet untitled, for Random House.

SIDELIGHTS: Barbara Taylor Bradford is best known for her novels about women of strength and character, wealth and love. She was born and raised in northern England, and her mother, a former children's nurse, introduced her to the world of books when she was very young. By the time she was twelve years old, she had read all the works of Charles Dickens and the Bronte sisters. She had also started to write stories of her own and had sold her first story, for ten shillings and sixpence, to a British children's magazine. Determined to become a writer, Bradford left school at sixteen to work as a typist at the *Yorkshire Evening Post.* She became a reporter, and was promoted to editor of the paper's women's page within two years, and two years after that she went to London as fashion editor of *Women's Own* magazine. She also worked at a number of other London periodicals, including *Today* magazine, the *London Evening News,* and the *London American.* In 1963, Bradford married an American movie producer and moved to the United States a year later, where she continued her career as a journalist. She became author of a syndicated column that covered lifestyle and interior decorating topics and wrote several books on interior design. As a sideline, she began experimenting with fiction, and *A Woman of Substance* became the first of her many bestsellers. Among her books for young readers, *A Garland of Children's Verse* earned praise in *Publishers Weekly* both for its selection of "gentle, rhythmic reflections of birds' flight and bedtime dreams," and the "magnificent" accompanying illustrations by Ota Janecek, which reminded a *Library Journal* reviewer of "Chinese watercolors."

WORKS CITED:

Library Journal, September 15, 1969, p. 3229.
Publishers Weekly, October 28, 1968, pp. 59-60.

FOR MORE INFORMATION SEE:

BOOKS

Bestsellers, Volume 89, number 1, Gale, 1989.
Contemporary Authors, Volume 89-92, Gale, 1980.

PERIODICALS

Writer, March, 1986.
Writers Digest, June, 1987.

*   *   *

BRIGGS, Raymond (Redvers) 1934-

PERSONAL: Born January 18, 1934, in London, England; son of Ernest Redvers (in milk delivery) and Ethel (Bowyer) Briggs; married Jean Taprell Clark (a painter), 1963 (died, 1973). *Education:* Attended Wimbledon School of Art, 1949-53; received National Diploma in Design, 1953; attended Slade School of Fine Art, 1955-57; University of London, D.F.A., 1957. *Politics:* "Green." *Religion:* "None—atheist." *Hobbies and other interests:* Reading, gardening, growing fruit, modern jazz, secondhand bookshops.

ADDRESSES: Home—Weston, Underhill Lane, Westmeston, Hassocks, Sussex BN6 8XG, England.

CAREER: Illustrator and author of books for children, 1957—. Brighton Polytechnic, Sussex, England, part-time lecturer in illustration, 1961-87; teacher at Slade School of Fine Art and Central Art School. Set designer and playwright. Member of British Campaign for Nuclear Disarmament, beginning 1982. *Military service:* British Army, 1953-55.

RAYMOND BRIGGS

MEMBER: Chartered Society of Designers (fellow), Society of Industrial Artists, Dairy Farmer's Association, Groucho Club.

AWARDS, HONORS: British Library Association Kate Greenaway Medal, commendation, 1964, for *Fee Fi Fo Fum,* winner, 1966, for *Mother Goose Treasury,* and 1973, for *Father Christmas,* and high commendation, 1978, for *The Snowman;* Spring Book Festival Picture Book honor, *Book World,* 1970, for *The Elephant and the Bad Baby;* Children's Book Showcase, Children's Book Council, 1974, for *Father Christmas;* Art Books for Children Citations, Brooklyn Museum and Brooklyn Public Library, 1975, for *Father Christmas,* and 1979, for *The Snowman;* Francis Williams Illustration Awards, Book Trust, 1977, for *Father Christmas,* and 1982, for *The Snowman; Boston Globe-Horn Book* Award for Illustration, Premio Critici in Erba from Bologna Book Fair, Lewis Carroll Shelf Award, and Dutch Silver Pen Award, all 1979, and *Redbook* Award, 1986, all for *The Snowman;* Other Award, Children's Rights Workshop, 1982, for *When the Wind Blows;* British Academy Award for best children's program—Drama, 1982, and Academy Award ("Oscar") nomination for best animated short film, 1982, both for *The Snowman;* most outstanding radio program, Broadcasting Press Guild, 1983, for *When the Wind Blows.*

WRITINGS:

SELF-ILLUSTRATED

The Strange House, Hamish Hamilton, 1961.

Instead of the usual jolly image of Saint Nick, *Father Christmas*, by Raymond Briggs, presents a grumbling but dutiful old fellow with very human shortcomings. (Illustrated by the author.)

Midnight Adventure, Hamish Hamilton, 1961.
Ring-a-Ring o' Roses (verse), Coward, 1962.
Sledges to the Rescue, Hamish Hamilton, 1963.
(Editor) *The White Land: A Picture Book of Traditional Rhymes and Verses,* Coward, 1963.
(Editor) *Fee Fi Fo Fum: A Picture Book of Nursery Rhymes,* Coward, 1964.
(Editor) *The Mother Goose Treasury,* Coward, 1966.
Jim and the Beanstalk, Coward, 1970.
Father Christmas, Coward, 1973.
Father Christmas Goes on Holiday, Coward, 1975.
Fungus the Bogeyman, Hamish Hamilton, 1977.
The Snowman, Random House, 1978.
Gentleman Jim, Hamish Hamilton, 1980.
When the Wind Blows, Schocken, 1982.
Fungus the Bogeyman Plop-up Book, Hamish Hamilton, 1982.
The Tin-Pot Foreign General and the Old Iron Woman, Little, Brown, 1984.
The Snowman Pop-up, Hamish Hamilton, 1986.
Unlucky Wally, Hamish Hamilton, 1987.
The Snowman Storybook, Random House, 1990.

Also author of *The Big Rocket,* 1962.

"SNOWMAN BOARD BOOKS"; SELF-ILLUSTRATED

Building the Snowman, Little, Brown, 1985.
Dressing Up, Little, Brown, 1985.
Walking in the Air, Little, Brown, 1985.
The Party, Little, Brown, 1985.

ILLUSTRATOR

(With others) Julian Sorell Huxley, *Wonderful World of Life,* Doubleday, 1958.
Ruth Manning-Sanders, *Peter and the Piskies,* Oxford University Press, 1958, Roy, 1966.
Alfred Leo Duggan, *Look at Castles,* Hamish Hamilton, 1960, published as *The Castle Book,* Pantheon, 1961.
Duggan, *Arches and Spires,* Hamish Hamilton, 1961, Pantheon, 1962.
Jacynth Hope-Simpson, editor, *The Hamish Hamilton Book of Myths and Legends,* Hamish Hamilton, 1964.
William Mayne, *Whistling Rufus,* Hamish Hamilton, 1964, Dutton, 1965.
Elfrida Vipont, *Stevie,* Hamish Hamilton, 1965.

Manning-Sanders, editor, *Hamish Hamilton Book of Magical Beasts,* Hamish Hamilton, 1965, published as *A Book of Magical Beasts,* T. Nelson, 1970.

James Aldridge, *The Flying 19,* Hamish Hamilton, 1966.

Mabel Esther Allan, *The Way over Windle,* Methuen, 1966.

Bruce Carter (pseudonym of Richard Alexander Hough), *Jimmy Murphy and the White Duesenberg,* Coward, 1968.

Carter, *Nuvolari and the Alfa Romeo,* Coward, 1968.

Nicholas Fisk, *Lindbergh: The Lone Flier,* Coward, 1968.

Fisk, *Richthofen: The Red Baron,* Coward, 1968.

Mayne, editor, *The Hamish Hamilton Book of Giants,* Hamish Hamilton, 1968, published as *William Mayne's Book of Giants,* Dutton, 1969.

Michael Brown, *Shackelton's Epic Voyage,* Coward, 1969.

Vipont, *The Elephant and the Bad Baby,* Coward, 1969.

Showell Styles, *First Up Everest,* Coward, 1969.

James Reeves, *Christmas Book,* Dutton, 1970.

Ian Serraillier, *The Tale of Three Landlubbers,* Hamish Hamilton, 1970, Coward, 1971.

Virginia Haviland, editor, *The Fairy Tale Treasury,* Coward, 1972.

Manning-Sanders, editor, *Festivals,* Heinemann, 1972, Dutton, 1973.

Reeves, *The Forbidden Forest,* Heinemann, 1973.

(With others) *All in a Day,* Philomel, 1986.

Also illustrator of a book of Cornish fairy stories for Oxford University Press, 1957, *The Wonderful Cornet,* by Barbara Ker Wilson, 1958, *Peter's Busy Day,* by A. Stephen Tring, 1959, and *William's Wild Day Out,* by Meriol Trevor, 1963.

ADAPTATIONS:

The Snowman (animated film), TV Cartoons, 1982.

When the Wind Blows (stage play; produced in London, England, 1983, Washington, DC, 1984, and New York, NY, 1988), Samuel French, 1983.

When the Wind Blows (radio play), British Broadcasting Corp., 1983.

Gentleman Jim (stage play), produced at Nottingham Playhouse, 1985.

When the Wind Blows (animated film), TV Cartoons/Meltdown Productions, 1987.

SIDELIGHTS: Raymond Briggs is an award-winning author and illustrator of popular books for children and dark, satirical works for adults. He has drawn hundreds of pictures for collections of traditional nursery rhymes and fairy tales, revisited old favorites like "Jack and the Beanstalk," and written his own stories. Briggs's *Fungus the Bogeyman* is a cartoon-style look at a repulsive yet humane imaginary world, full of filth and wordplay; *The Snowman* is a wordless story, poignant and more softly illustrated. *When the Wind Blows,* a devastating, understated cartoon-style work basically for adults, portrays a middle-aged working-class couple before, during, and after a nuclear war. The characters and settings in the books often reflect elements of Briggs's past.

Briggs had "an uneventful but happy childhood and home life," he told Lee Bennett Hopkins in *Books Are by People.* "My parents were happily married. Their faces turn up constantly in my illustrations but quite unconsciously. I hated school for there was too much emphasis on teamwork, competition, sports, science, and mathematics—all the opposite interests of an 'arty' type." Briggs was always drawing and as an only child was somewhat spoiled, so when at fifteen

he said he'd like to study art, his parents "weren't fussed that I didn't want to learn a useful trade," he recalled in a *Publishers Weekly* interview. The principal of the school he wanted to attend, however, was dismayed that Briggs wanted to be a cartoonist. "He said: 'Good God, boy, is that *all* you want to do?'" Briggs revealed in *Designer.* "He told me it wasn't an occupation for gentlemen. It was a great shock to realise that these things weren't respectable. So I changed to painting."

In his painting courses Briggs did a lot of figure drawing, which he said was "absolutely perfect training for an illustrator, in that you learnt about tone and colour, and figure composition in general." It was a very traditional art education, like that of Renaissance painters. Abstract art was not taught. Cartooning and illustration were scorned as "commercial." In *Designer* Briggs described what happened when his tutor found one of his illustrations: "He said, horrified: 'You're *not* doing this in school time, are you?'—almost as if I was spitting in church. 'No sir, certainly not. Good Lord.'" Briggs continued to practice illustration in his spare time anyway. Finally he decided that painting was not really his strength and was unprofitable as well, so he started accepting illustration assignments from publishers and advertising agencies.

"Out of all the work I did, I must have suited the children's book world best," Briggs remarked in *Designer,* "because that was the sort of work that increasingly came in. I didn't choose it; it chose me. I entered the field at a very good time, when there were some marvellous books being written and I was lucky enough to get some to illustrate." *The Mother Goose Treasury,* for which Briggs did nearly nine hundred pictures, was one example. Reviewers praised it for its completeness and for Briggs's exuberant illustrations, and he received the Kate Greenaway Medal for his work. But he found other books "appalling," he continued, "and it was this that made me start writing. I could see simple grammatical faults even, and felt that if publishers were willing to publish tripe like that, I couldn't do worse. I wrote two or three little stories, and showed the first one to the editor just to get his advice—to see if he thought I might ever write anything. To my absolute amazement he said he'd publish it. To me, that just showed the standard. I thought it was staggering that someone who knew nothing about writing could make a first attempt and have it published, just like that."

Father Christmas was one of Briggs's first original books to become widely popular. Instead of the usual jolly or saintly image of Saint Nick, Briggs presents a grumbling but dutiful old fellow with very human foibles. Not fond of winter, Father Christmas dreams of a beach holiday and complains about "blooming chimneys" and "blooming soot." Observed Briggs in *Junior Bookshelf,* "I think the character of Father Christmas is very much based on my father," who delivered milk early each morning. "The jobs are similar and they both grumble a lot in a fairly humorous way." Briggs also drew on his own past for details of Father Christmas's house and other aspects of his life—sometimes unconsciously. Often when he draws something, he says, "I recognise it when it appears on the paper and think 'Gosh, yes! That's how it was.'"

A few years after *Father Christmas* came *Fungus the Bogeyman,* Briggs's story about and descriptive guide to the mucky lives of Bogeys, who revel in filth and rise each night to frighten humans. Fungus is a happily married Bogey who wonders about the meaning of his life and wistfully dreams of

So the poor shepherds on the sad little island went on counting their sheep and eating them. They had mutton for breakfast, mutton for dinner and mutton for tea.

Three of them were killed in the battle, but no one was to blame.

In his children's book, *The Tin-Pot Foreign General and the Old Iron Woman,* **Raymond Briggs takes a look at the adult theme of war.** (Illustrated by the author.)

a day when Bogeys and humans can get along with each other. Oddly enough, this story too bears some resemblance to Briggs's life. Observed Suzanne Rahn in *The Lion and the Unicorn,* "Briggs . . . came from a working-class family, and one can see a similarity between his milkman-father and Fungus: both have a 'round' of houses to which they deliver their stock-in-trade while most of their customers are still sleeping." Briggs has suggested a more direct link between Fungus and himself. When Elaine Moss of *Signal* asked him whether the character was real, Briggs answered, "I'm noticing all my characters now are sad old men or, rather, sad middle-aged men, which is what I am probably."

The Snowman, published the year after *Fungus the Bogeyman,* is a very different book, but like the earlier story it also draws on Briggs's life. The artist used his own house and garden as the setting for his gentle, loving tale. Unlike *Fungus the Bogeyman,* it is a wholesome story, describing how a snowman comes to life and befriends the boy who made him. During a magical night the snowman shares the human world and the world of snow people with the boy. In the morning the boy sadly discovers that his friend has mostly melted away. Briggs conveyed the story completely without words, and for the first time he set aside the black pen and watercolor of cartoon-style work. Noting that people often said they liked his original pencil drawings better than his ink work, Briggs decided to use colored pencils for the book. "I wanted to avoid the abrupt change that takes place when a brutal black pen line is scratched on top of a quiet pencil drawing,"

he said when he accepted the *Boston Globe-Horn Book* Award for the book.

Originally published as a book for adults, *When the Wind Blows* is Briggs's cartoon-style comment on how unprepared ordinary people are to deal with nuclear war. Its two characters are a retired British husband and wife living in the country. They survived the bombing of England during World War II, and they ignorantly expect the next war to be much the same. They build a useless bomb shelter, following government guidelines, and cheerily go on with life after the bomb drops, wondering why the water is shut off and why nothing is on the radio. Briggs got the idea for the book when he saw a documentary on the effects of nuclear war. "I imagined what would actually happen if some ordinary people were told there would be war in three days' time," he told Bart Mills in a *Los Angeles Times* interview. Said Briggs: "I used to think the main threat facing us was the Russian menace. Now I think the main threat is nuclear weapons themselves." Several critics judged *When the Wind Blows* too grim for young readers, and Briggs agreed. "But we found it went into the children's bookshops and started selling there too, to my surprise," he said in a *Times Educational Supplement* interview with Richard North. It has also been recommended reading for high schools and junior high schools that have courses dealing with nuclear war.

Briggs does not aim his books specifically at children or at adults. "I just write and draw to please myself and feel it ought to please others," he said in *Publishers Weekly.* His

Raymond Briggs's wordless story of a snowman who comes to life and befriends the boy who made him, *The Snowman* is softly illustrated with colored pencils. (Illustrated by the author.)

Ken Jones and Patricia Routledge starred in the London stage adaptation of *When the Wind Blows*, Raymond Briggs's portrayal of a middle-aged working couple before, during, and after a nuclear war.

work appeals to all ages, in fact. His more adult-oriented books reach younger readers with their cartoon style, and the so-called children's books often discuss adult issues. Even nursery rhymes have adult aspects, Briggs observes. Many are actually "quite rude, quite tough, adult gutsy material about money and marriage and work and laziness and theft—not sweet innocent pink and blue baby stuff," he said in *Signal*. His own books fit this description in many ways. *Father Christmas* shows adult attitudes toward work and features a character who swears constantly, if mildly. *Fungus the Bogeyman* looks at human intolerance and philosophical ideas. *The Snowman* squarely faces the sorrow of losing a friend. "Each one I do is different," said Briggs in *Designer*. And despite his doubts about how they would be received, he remarked, "they've all sold like hot cakes."

WORKS CITED:

"Best Children's Book: Raymond Briggs 'The Snowman,'" *Designer*, October, 1982, pp. 8-9.

Briggs, Raymond, "That Blooming Book," *Junior Bookshelf*, August, 1974, pp. 195-96.

Briggs, "For Illustration: *The Snowman*" (acceptance speech for *Boston Globe-Horn Book* Award), *Horn Book*, February, 1980, p. 96.

Hopkins, Lee Bennett, *Books Are by People*, Citation Press, 1969, p. 24.

Mercier, Jean P., "PW Interviews: Raymond Briggs," *Publishers Weekly*, November 5, 1973, p. 12.

Mills, Bart, "Author! Author! Wind Blowing Raymond Briggs' Way," *Los Angeles Times*, November 10, 1982, Part V, p. 12.

Moss, Elaine, "Raymond Briggs: On British Attitudes to the Strip Cartoon and Children's-Book Illustration," *Signal*, January, 1979, pp. 28 and 31.

North, Richard, "Cartoon Apocalypse," *Times Educational Supplement*, June 11, 1982, p. 41.

Rahn, Suzanne, "Beneath the Surface with *Fungus the Bogeyman*," *The Lion and the Unicorn*, Volume 7/8, 1983-84, p. 12.

FOR MORE INFORMATION SEE:

BOOKS

Children's Literature Review, Volume 10, Gale, 1986.

Kilborn, Richard, *The Multi-Media Melting Pot: Marketing "When the Wind Blows*," Comedia, 1986.

Twentieth-Century Children's Writers, St. Martin's, 1983.

PERIODICALS

Animation, spring, 1988; winter, 1989.

Films and Filming, February, 1987.

Horn Book, December, 1966.

New York Times, September 14, 1982.

Observer (London), February 8, 1987.
Plays and Players, July, 1983.
Publishers Weekly, May 14, 1982.
Times (London), September 20, 1984; May 8, 1985; November 17, 1986; February 6, 1987.
Times Educational Supplement, November 18, 1977.
Times Literary Supplement, December 2, 1977; October 5, 1984.
Undercurrents, April, 1982.
Variety, April 27, 1983.
Washington Post, March 6, 1984.

* * *

BUTTERWORTH, Oliver 1915-1990

OBITUARY NOTICE—See index for *SATA* sketch: Born in 1915 in Hartford, CT; died of cancer, September 17, 1990, in West Hartford, CT. Educator and author. Butterworth was known for his children's books. He taught English at Hartford College for Women from the late 1940s to the late 1980s. Among his works are *The Enormous Egg,* which was adapted for both the stage and television; *The Trouble With Jenny's Ear; The Narrow Passage; The First Blueberry Pig; A Visit to the Big House;* and *Orrie's Run.*

OBITUARIES AND OTHER SOURCES:

BOOKS

The Writers Directory: 1988-1990, St. James Press, 1988.

PERIODICALS

Chicago Tribune, September 19, 1990.
Los Angeles Times, September 26, 1990.
New York Times, September 19, 1990.

* * *

CAINE, Geoffrey
See WALKER, Robert W(ayne)

* * *

CAMPS, Luis 1928-

PERSONAL: Born May 27, 1928 in Perpignan, France; son of Jose M. and Maria (maiden name, Juncadella) Camps Miro; married Lucienne Chauvet, July 19, 1951; children: Pierre. *Education:* Attended Estudio Camps Miro and Foment de les Arts Decoratives (Barcelona). *Religion:* Catholic.

ADDRESSES: Home—France.

CAREER: Free-lance illustrator and designer; art and publicity director. Has also worked as a designer and model maker for Dupuy-Compton, Paris.

ILLUSTRATOR:

(With Marc Berthier and Gerard Gree) Alain Gree, *Quarante-cinq jeux pour tout seul* (with record), Casterman, 1975.
A. Gree, *Filou, le raton laveur,* F. Nathan, 1984.

"LES FARFELUCHES" SERIES; WRITTEN BY A. GREE

Les Farfeluches a l'ecole, Casterman, 1973, translation published as *The Smashers at School,* Ward, Lock, 1974,

parallel English and Spanish text translation published as *At School,* Derrydale Books, 1986.
Les Farfeluches au marche, Casterman, 1973, translation published as *The Smashers Go to Market,* Ward, Lock, 1974.
Les Farfeluches au bord de la mer, Casterman, 1973, translation published as *The Smashers by the Sea,* Ward, Lock, 1974.
Les Farfeluches a la campagne, Casterman, 1973, translation published as *The Smashers in the Country,* Ward, Lock, 1974, parallel English and Spanish text translation published as *In the Country,* Derrydale Books, 1986.
Les Farfeluches a la maison, Casterman, 1973, parallel English and Spanish text translation published as *At Home,* Derrydale Books, 1986.
Les Farfeluches au cirque, Casterman, 1974.
Les Farfeluches sur la route, Casterman, 1974.
Les Farfeluches prennent le train, Casterman, 1974.
Les Farfeluches au zoo, Casterman, 1975.
Les Farfeluches en pleine action, Casterman, 1976.
Vrai ou faux?: Les Farfeluches en vacances (with record), Casterman, 1976.
Je reponds a tout avec les Farfeluches (with record), Casterman, 1977.
Les Farfeluches font des achats, Casterman, 1977.
Les Farfeluches choisissent un metier, Casterman, 1977.
Les Farfeluches aiment les animaux, Casterman, 1979, parallel English and Spanish text translation published as *Animal Fun,* Derrydale Books, 1986.
Les Farfeluches apprennent a compter, Larousse, 1981.
Les Farfeluches sur l'ocean, Casterman, 1981.
Les Farfeluches 1, 2, 3, qui dit vrait?, Casterman, 1981.
Les Farfeluches autour de monde, Casterman, 1982.

LUIS CAMPS

(From *Les Farfeluches font des achats,* by Alain Gree, illustrated by Luis Camps.)

Les Farfeluches jouent avec les couleurs, Casterman, 1986.
Les Farfeluches font un jardin, Casterman, 1987.

"LE LIVRE-JEUX" SERIES; WRITTEN BY A. GREE; ALL WITH GAMES

Le Livre-jeu de la foret, Casterman, 1970.
Le Livre-jeu de la maison, Casterman, 1971, translation published as *The Home,* Little, Brown, 1972.
Le Livre-jeux des animaux, Casterman, 1973, translation published as *Animals,* Ward, Lock, 1974, another translation published as *The All-Color Activity Book of Animals,* Little, Brown, 1974.
Le Livre-jeux des saisons, Casterman, 1974.
Le Livre-jeu de l'aeroport, Casterman, 1975.
Le Livre-jeux de la mer, Casterman, 1976.
Le Livre-jeux des quatre coins du monde, Casterman, 1978.

"LES AVENTURES DES POUSCALOUFS" SERIES; WRITTEN BY MONIQUE FARGE (PSEUDONYM OF A. GREE):

Les Aventures des Pouscaloufs par ici les souris!, Casterman, 1978.
Les Aventures vive les vacances!, Casterman, 1978.
Les Aventures a nous la neige!, Casterman, 1978.
Les Aventures toutes voiles dehors!, Casterman, 1978.
Les Aventures rien ne va plus!, Casterman, 1979.
Les Aventures en avant la musique!, Casterman, 1979.

*   *   *

CARTER, Angela 1940-

PERSONAL: Born May 7, 1940, in London, England; daughter of Hugh Alexander (a journalist) and Olive (Farthing) Stalker; married Paul Carter, September 10, 1960 (divorced, 1972). *Education:* University of Bristol, B.A., 1965. *Politics:* Left. *Religion:* None.

ADDRESSES: Home—5 Hay Hill, Bath BA1 5LZ, England. *Agent*—Deborah Rogers, 29 Goodge St., London, England.

CAREER: Novelist, short story writer, teacher, and critic. Journalist for newspapers in Croyden, Surrey, England, 1958-61.

AWARDS, HONORS: John Llewllyn Rhys Prize, 1968, for *The Magic Toyshop;* Somerset Maugham Award, 1969, for *Several Perceptions;* Cheltenham Literary Festival Award, 1979, for *The Bloody Chamber and Other Stories;* Kurt Maschler Award, 1982, for *Sleeping Beauty and Other Favorite Fairy Tales;* James Tait Black Memorial Prize, 1986, for *Nights at the Circus.*

WRITINGS:

JUVENILE

The Magic Toyshop, Heinemann, 1967, Simon & Schuster, 1968.
Miss Z, the Dark Young Lady, Simon & Schuster, 1970.
The Donkey Prince, Simon & Schuster, 1970.
(Translator) *Fairy Tales of Charles Perrault,* Gollancz, 1977.
Comic and Curious Cats, illustrated by Martin Leman, Crown, 1979.
(With Leslie Carter) *The Music People,* Hamish Hamilton, 1980.
Moonshadow, David & Charles, 1984.
(Editor) *Sleeping Beauty and Other Favorite Fairy Tales,* Schocken, 1984.

NOVELS

Shadow Dance, Heinemann, 1966, published as *Honeybuzzard,* Simon & Schuster, 1967.

ANGELA CARTER

Several Perceptions, Heinemann, 1968, Simon & Schuster, 1969.

Heroes and Villains, Heinemann, 1969, Simon & Schuster, 1970.

Love, Hart-Davis, 1971.

The Infernal Desire Machines of Doctor Hoffman, Hart-Davis, 1972, published as *The War of Dreams*, Harcourt, 1974.

Passion of New Eve, Harcourt, 1977.

War of Dreams, Avon, 1983.

Nights at the Circus, Viking, 1985.

Come Unto These Yellow Sands, Bloodaxe, 1985.

Saints and Strangers, Viking, 1986.

OTHER

Unicorn (poetry), Location Press, 1966.

Fireworks: Nine Profane Pieces, Quartet Books, 1974, published as *Fireworks: Nine Stories in Various Guises*, Harper, 1981.

The Bloody Chamber and Other Stories, Gollancz, 1979, Harper, 1980.

Nothing Sacred: Selected Journalism, Virago, 1982.

(With Neil Jordan) *The Company of Wolves* (screenplay), ITC Entertainment, 1985.

The Sadeian Woman: And the Ideology of Pornography, Pantheon, 1988.

The Magic Toyshop (screenplay; based on novel of same title), Granada Television Productions, 1989.

(Editor) *Wayward Girls and Wicked Women: An Anthology of Subversive Women*, Penguin, 1989.

Old Wives' Fairy Tale Book, Random House, 1990.

Also author of radio scripts for *Vampirella*, 1976; *Come Unto These Sands*, 1979; *Puss in Boots*, 1982. Contributor to periodicals, including *New Society* and *Vogue*.

SIDELIGHTS: Angela Carter was born on May 7, 1940, and grew up in South London. After passing the "11-plus" qualifying exam, Carter attended a local grammar school. Upon graduation, she embarked on a brief career in journalism. Carter got married in 1960 and, after nearly a four-year absence, started back to school at Bristol College.

While at Bristol, Carter concentrated on medieval literature, although her tastes outside the classroom were much broader. She had a special interest in French language and literature, especially the works of Rimbaud and Racine. Carter also studied psychology and anthropology, as well as social science. When she graduated, Carter remained in Bristol and became part of the city's bohemian culture.

Carter wrote her first novels while living in Bristol. These early works accentuated Carter's powerful imagination and gift for description. In novels such as *The Magic Toyshop*, Carter added a strong fantasy element to the plot line. After suffering some setbacks in her personal life, however, Carter began to critically examine the role of various myths in literature. As a result, works like *Heroes and Villains* contain not only fantastic elements, but complex themes and psychological overtones as well.

Carter's interest in mythology and fantasy has resulted in collections such as *The Bloody Chamber*, which includes adult retellings of fairy tales like *Snow White* and *Little Red Riding Hood*. She has also edited fairy tale collections for children, including *Sleeping Beauty and Other Fairy Tales* and *The Fairy Tales of Charles Perrault*.

FOR MORE INFORMATION SEE:

BOOKS

Contemporary Issues Criticism, Volume 1, Gale, 1982.

Contemporary Literary Criticism, Volume 5, Gale, 1976; Volume 41, 1987.

Dictionary of Literary Biography, Volume 14: *British Novelists Since 1960*, 2 parts, Gale, 1983.

PERIODICALS

Books and Bookmen, February, 1975.

Listener, May 20, 1971; September 26, 1974.

Literature and History, spring, 1984.

Los Angeles Times Book Review, March 16, 1980.

New Review, June/July, 1977.

New Statesman, July 8, 1968; November 14, 1969; August 16, 1974; March 25, 1977; May 25, 1979; October 18, 1985.

Saturday Review, February 18, 1967.

Spectator, March 26, 1977.

Times Literary Supplement, August 1, 1968; November 20, 1969; June 18, 1974; February 8, 1980; July 4, 1981; September 28, 1984; October 18, 1985.

Washington Post Book World, August 18, 1974; February 24, 1980; June 28, 1981; February 3, 1985.

* * *

CAUSLEY, Charles (Stanley) 1917-

PERSONAL: Born August 24, 1917, in Launceston, Cornwall, England; son of Charles Samuel and Laura Jane (Bartlett) Causley. *Education:* Attended Launceston College and Peterborough Training College.

ADDRESSES: Home—2 Cyprus Well, Launceston, Cornwall PL15 8BT, England. *Agent*—David Higham Associates Ltd., 5-8 Lower John St., Golden Square, London W1R 4HA, England.

CAREER: Writer; former teacher. Member of Poetry Panel of the Arts Council of Great Britain, 1962-65. *Military service:* Royal Navy, 1940-46.

MEMBER: Royal Society of Literature (fellow, 1958), Poetry Society of Great Britain (vice-president), West County Writers Association (vice-president).

AWARDS, HONORS: Traveling scholarships, Society of Authors, 1954 and 1966; Queen's Gold Medal for Poetry, 1967; Cholmondeley Award for poetry, 1971; Signal Poetry Award and Newyear Honours List for services to poetry, both 1986; Emil/Kurt Maschler Award, 1987, for *Jack the Treacle Eater;* Ingersoll/T. S. Eliot Award, 1990; Charity Randall Citation, International Poetry Forum, 1991. D.Litt., University of Exeter; M.A., Open University.

WRITINGS:

POEMS

Farewell, Aggie Weston, Hand and Flower Press, 1951, reprinted, Ditchling Press, 1987.

Survivor's Leave, Hand and Flower Press, 1953.

Union Street, preface by Edith Sitwell, Hart-Davis, 1957, Houghton, 1958.

CHARLES CAUSLEY

The Ballad of Charlotte Dymond (originally published in *Bryanston Miscellany*), illustrations by Lionel Miskin, privately printed, 1958.

Johnny Alleluia, Hart-Davis, 1961, Dufour, 1962.

(With George Barker and Martin Bell) *Penguin Modern Poets 3,* Penguin, 1962.

Underneath the Water, Macmillan, 1968.

Figure of 8: Narrative Poems, illustrations by Peter Whiteman, Macmillan, 1969.

Charles Causley and Kathleen Raine; Poems, Longmans, 1969.

Timothy Winters (poem set to music), music by Wallace Southam, Turret Books, 1970.

(With Laurie Lee) *Pergamon Poets X,* compiled by Evan Owen, Pergamon, 1970.

Figgie Hobbin: Poems for Children, illustrations by Pat Marriott, Macmillan, 1971, published as *Figgie Hobbin,* illustrations by Trina Schart Hyman, Walker & Co., 1973.

The Tail of the Trinosaur, illustrations by Jill Gardiner, Brockhampton Press, 1973.

Six Women, illustrations by Stanley Simmonds, Keepsake Press, 1973.

As I Went Down Zig Zag, illustrations by John Astrup, Warne, 1974.

Collected Poems, 1951-1975, David Godine, 1975.

The Hill of the Fairy Calf: The Legend of Knockshegowna, illustrations by Robine Cignett, Hodder & Stoughton, 1976.

Dick Whittington: A Story from England (juvenile), illustrations by Antony Maitland, Puffin, 1976.

Here We Go round the Round House, illustrations by Stanley Simmonds, New Broom Press, 1976.

The Animals' Carol, illustrations by Judith Horwood, Macmillan, 1978.

The Gift of a Lamb: A Shepherd's Tale of the First Christmas (verse play), music by Vera Gray, illustrations by Shirley Felts, Robson Books, 1978.

Three Heads Made of Gold (juvenile), illustrations by Pat Marriott, Robson Books, 1978.

The Last King of Cornwall (juvenile), illustrations by Krystyna Turska, Hodder & Stoughton, 1978.

(Translator) *Twenty-five Poems by Hamdija Demirovic,* illustrations by Petar Waldegg, Keepsake Press, 1980.

The Ballad of Aucassin and Nicolette (verse play), music by Stephen McNeff, Penguin, 1981.

(Author of introduction) S. Baring-Gould, *Cornwall,* Wildwood House, 1981.

(Translator) *Schondilie,* illustrations by Robert Tilling, New Broom Private Press, 1982.

Secret Destinations: New Poems, Macmillan, 1984.

(Translator) *King's Children* (German ballads), Midnag, 1986.

Twenty-one Poems, illustrations by Robert Tilling, Celandine Press, 1986.

Quack! Said the Billy-Goat (juvenile), illustrations by Barbara Firth, Harper, 1986.

Early in the Morning: A Collection of New Nursery Rhymes, music by Anthony Castro, illustrations by Michael Foreman, Viking Kestrel, 1986.

Early in the Morning (juvenile), Penguin, 1987.

Jack the Treacle Eater, illustrations by Charles Keeping, Macmillan Children's Books, 1987.

A Field of Vision: Poems, Macmillan, 1988.

Secret Destinations: Selected Poems, 1977-1988, David Godine, 1989.

The Young Man of Cuky: Poems for Children, illustrations by Michael Foreman, Macmillan Children's Books, 1991.

Bring in the Holly: Poems for Children, illustrations by Lisa Kopper, Frances Lincoln, 1991.

EDITOR

Peninsula: An Anthology of Verse from the West-Country, Macdonald, 1957.

(And author of introduction) *Dawn and Dusk: Poems of Our Time* (juvenile), illustrations by Gerald Wilkinson, Brockhampton, 1962, F. Watts, 1963, 2nd edition, Brockhampton, 1972.

(And author of introduction) *Rising Early: Story Poems and Ballads of the 20th Century,* Brockhampton, 1964, published as *Modern Ballads and Story Poems,* illustrations by Anne Netherwood, F. Watts, 1965.

(And author of introduction) *Modern Folk Ballads,* Studio Vista, 1966.

In the Music I Hear (poems by children), Arc Press, 1970.

(And author of introduction) *Oats and Beans and Barley* (poems by children), Arc Press, 1971.

(And author of introduction) Frances Bellerby, *Selected Poems,* Enitharmon Press, 1971.

(And author of introduction) *The Puffin Book of Magic Verse,* illustrations by Barbara Swiderska, Penguin, 1974.

The Puffin Book of Salt-Sea Verse, Penguin, 1978.

The Batsford Book of Story Poems for Children, Batsford, 1979.

The Sun, Dancing: Christian Verse, illustrations by Charles Keeping, Penguin, 1981.

OTHER

Runaway (one-act play), Curwen, 1936.

The Conquering Hero (one-act play), Schirmer, 1937.

Benedict (one-act play), Muller, 1938.

How Pleasant to Know Mrs. Lear: A Victorian Comedy, Muller, 1948.

Hands to Dance (short stories), Carroll & Nicholson, 1951, revised edition published as *Hands to Dance and Skylark,* Robson Books, 1979.

St. Martha and the Dragon (libretto), music by Phyllis Tate, Oxford University Press, 1977.

Jonah (libretto), music by William Mathias, Oxford University Press, 1990.

Also author of introduction to books, including *Those First Affections,* edited by Timothy Rogers, Routledge, 1979; *The Splendid Spur* by Sir Arthur Quiller-Couch, Anthony Mott, 1983; and *Poetry Please!: 100 Popular Poems from the BBC Radio 4 Program,* J. M. Dent, 1985.

Contributor to *Encounter, Harper's Bazaar, Ladies' Home Journal, Listener, London Magazine, New Statesman, Spectator, Observer, Outposts, Sunday Times* (London), *Times Literary Supplement, Transatlantic Review, Twentieth Century,* and other periodicals, and to anthologies of verse.

ADAPTATIONS: Recordings of poems, read by Causley, include: *Authopoetry,* Poets Lot Ltd.; *Here Today, The Jupiter Anthology of 20th Century English Poetry: Part III* (which he also edited), and *The Jupiter Book of Contemporary Ballads,* all Jupiter Recordings Ltd.; *The Poet Speaks, Record 8,* Argo Record Co. Ltd.; *Causley Reads Causley,* Sentinel, and *Secret Destinations!,* Sentinel. Poems and interviews have been recorded on tape for the British Council. A number of Causley's poems appear in the series "Poetry and Song," Argo, and in settings by folk-singers on a number of long-playing albums.

WORK IN PROGRESS: A new edition of *Collected Poems, 1951-1975,* bringing the work up to the present.

Wood! Wood! Logs of wood . . . (From *Figgie Hobbin* by Charles Causley, illustrations by Trina Schart Hyman.)

SIDELIGHTS: "Charles Causley has stood apart from the mainstream of contemporary poetry," observes Dana Gioia in the *Dictionary of Literary Biography.* "His work bears little relation to the most celebrated achievements of the modernist movement but refers back to older, more specifically English roots." Pointing to the influence of folk songs and ballads in his work, Gioia likens Causley to writers such as A. E. Housman, Thomas Hardy, Rudyard Kipling, Walter de la Mare, Robert Graves, and John Betjeman, and places him in "a conservative countertradition in English letters which stresses the fundamentally national nature of its poetry and the critical role of popular forms in its inspiration." Many critics consider him a prominent figure in the revitalization of the English ballad. Calling him "the most celebrated and accomplished living writer of ballads in the English language," Gioia believes that his achievements reach beyond a mastery of form to a "fundamental commitment to certain traditional virtues of English poetry—simplicity, clarity, grace, and compassion."

According to Gioia, becoming a writer was a childhood ambition for Causley, who started a novel at nine years of age, continued to experiment with literary genres throughout his formal education, and had three one-act plays published when he was barely out of his twenties. "During the same period Causley also played piano in a four-piece dance band," notes Gioia, "an experience which may have influenced his later predilection for writing poems in popular lyric forms such as the ballad." War, though, was perhaps the most important influence upon Causley, who served in the Royal Navy for six years during World War II. His first exposure to the consequences of war came when his father returned from France an invalid and died seven long years later from the effects of German mustard gas. According to Gioia, this experience plus the death of friends "proved decisive to his literary career, pulling him from prose and drama into poetry."

In 1976, Causley published his *Collected Poems, 1951-1975,* a volume that selects from seven of his earlier works, presenting several new poems as well. According to Gioia, the book "solidified Causley's reputation in England and broadened his audience in America," however, while the critics "admired the ease and openness of his work and praised his unwavering commitment to narrative poetry . . . they classified Causley as an accomplished minor poet, an engagingly eccentric antimodernist." Gioia points out, though, that much of the critical reception to Causley's work focuses on subjective appreciations of his work rather than critical discussions: "This situation has given many critics unfamiliar with his work the understandable impression that while it may be enjoyed, because of its simplicity, it does not bear serious analysis."

In *Poetry Today, 1960-1973,* Anthony Thwaite mentions the apparent simplicity of Causley's poems and comments: "There is in fact a great deal more art in Causley's work than may appear at first sight. . . . A Causley poem is instantly recognizable and always fresh." Much of Causley's work is written or appropriate for children. Asked to what extent he considers himself a children's poet, Causley indicated in an interview with Brian Merrick in *Children's Literature in Education:* "Oh I don't see these separately at all. What happened was that I didn't write a book of children's poems, or so-called children's poems, until 1970: until *Figgie Hobbin.* I'd written what I considered purely adult poems all my life until then, and I noticed that a lot of the poems up to that point were used in children's anthologies—as well as in adult anthologies. . . . I've always been very much influenced by the idea that the only difference between an adult poem and a children's poem is the *range* of the audience. I mean a children's poem is a poem that has to work for the adult and the child as well—at the same time—that's the only difference." According to Gioia, Causley's book of children's verse *Figgie Hobbin* "bears an illuminating relationship to Causley's 'adult' work. Although the poems in *Figgie Hobbin* are simple in structure and usually written from a child's perspective, they are almost indistinguishable from his other verse." Not only do the poems explore the same thematic concerns, says Gioia, "their clarity and grace epitomize the transparent style that he has striven for throughout his career." Upon the publication of *Figure of 8: Narrative Poems* as a children's book, Causley commented: "I'd hope, though, that the book wouldn't be read by children only—in writing such a book I think one should simply aim at widening the age-range of one's audience, and in the process try and avoid producing poetry and water. . . . In the event, one doesn't think about a possible audience at all when writing: only about the problem of getting the poem on the paper as close as possible to what's in one's head in a vague form. After the poem's written is the time to decide (if ever) what kind of audience it might reach."

Causley has traveled widely from Scapa Flow, off the northern coast of Scotland, to Sydney, Australia and New Zealand, and from Freetown, West Africa, to Rabaul, New Britain; he has visited many countries, including Italy, France, Germany, Spain, Portugal, Czechoslovakia, Yugoslavia, Poland, the U.S.S.R., Israel, Greece, Egypt, Macao, India, Malaysia, Sri Lanka, Canada, and the United States. He once said that one of the principal delights of travel was the intense pleasure he experienced on returning to his native Cornwall.

WORKS CITED:

Children's Literature in Education (interview with Brian Merrick), Volume 19, number 3, 1988, pp. 123-135.
Dictionary of Literary Biography, Volume 27: *Poets of Great Britain and Ireland, 1945-1960,* Gale, 1984, pp. 40-48.
Thwaite, Anthony, *Poetry Today, 1960-1973,* published for the British Council by Longmans, Green, 1973.

FOR MORE INFORMATION SEE:

BOOKS

Chambers, Harry, editor, *Causley at 70,* Peterloo Poets, 1987.
Contemporary Literary Criticism, Volume 7, Gale, 1977.
Currey, R. N., *Poets of the 1939-1945 War,* published for the British Council and National Book League by Longmans, Green, 1960.
Hanke, Michael, editor, *Poems for Charles Causley,* Enitharmon Press, 1982.
Jennings, Elizabeth, *Poetry Today,* published for the British Council and National Book League by Longmans, Green, 1961.
Merrick, Brian, *Talking with Charles Causley,* National Association for the Teaching of English, 1989.
Schmidt, Michael, *An Introduction to Fifty Modern British Poets,* Pan Books, 1979.

PERIODICALS

Books, January, 1970.
Books and Bookmen, April, 1971.
Chicago Review, summer, 1977.
Hudson Review, Volume 29, number 2, 1976, January, 1991.
London Magazine, November, 1968.
Manchester Guardian, January 15, 1965.
New Poetry, Number 45, 1979.
New Statesman, March 22, 1968.
New York Times Book Review, January 11, 1976.
PN Review 6, Volume 5, number 2, 1977.
Punch, March 27, 1968.
Saturday Review, February 7, 1976.
Signal, September, 1982.
Times Educational Supplement, November 17, 1972; May 4, 1990.
Times Literary Supplement, October 16, 1969.
Virginia Quarterly Review, Volume 52, number 3, 1976.

* * *

CHARTIER, Normand L. 1945-

PERSONAL: Surname is pronounced "shartee-*air*"; born September 23, 1945, in Danielson, CT; son of Gerard M. (a doctor) and L. Rubia (a homemaker; maiden name, Lavigne) Chartier; children: Molly Beth, Samuel Gerard, Matthew Luke. *Education:* Attended University of Connecticut, 1965-68. *Politics:* Independent. *Religion:* Christian. *Hobbies and other interests:* Carpentry, sports, birdwatching.

ADDRESSES: Home—317 Barstow Rd., Canterbury, CT 06331.

CAREER: Sargent Hardware, New Haven, CT, assistant art director and illustrator, 1968-70; free-lance filmstrip illustrator, 1970-74; Smith, Soos, Cheshire, CT, free-lance advertising artist, 1973-78; Masticure Products, Norwich, CT, art director, 1975-77; free-lance artist and illustrator of children's books, 1974—. Part-time owner of gallery at home. Member of Brooklyn Recreation Commission, 1980-83, and Brooklyn Board of Education, 1980-83. *Exhibitions:* West Village Gallery, Brooklyn, CT, 1985-86.

MEMBER: Mystic Art Association, Boothbay Region Art Association.

AWARDS, HONORS: Filmstrip of the Year citation from *Learning* magazine, 1974, for *The Voyages of Dr. Doolittle;* Children's Book of the Year citations from Child Study Association, 1974, for *Devin and Goliath* and 1979, for *Donkey Ysabel;* Children's Book of the Year citation from Library of Congress, 1979, for *Donkey Ysabel;* Children's Choice Award from International Reading Association, 1981, for *Oscar's Rotten Birthday,* 1982, for *Grover Goes to School,* and 1985, for *Bartholomew the Bossy;* Illustration Excellence citation from *Highlights* magazine, 1982, for "The Great Divide"; Excellence Award from Society of Illustrators, 1990, for *Silly Fred.*

ILLUSTRATOR:

Mary Blount Christian, *Devin and Goliath,* Addison Wesley, 1974.
Matt Christopher, *Jinx Glove,* Little, Brown, 1975.
Geda Bradley Mathews, *What Was That!,* Golden Press, 1975.
Children's Television Workshop, *Who Am I?,* Western, 1978.
Elizabeth Upham, *Little Brown Bear Loses His Clothes,* Platt & Munk, 1978.

Normand L. Chartier's self-portrait, done with a Rapidograph, which produces pictures by a form of radiation other than light.

Dorothy O. Van Woerkom, *Donkey Ysabel,* Macmillan, 1978.
Children's Television Workshop, *Big Bird's Rhyming Book* (pop-up book), Random House, 1979.
Judy Freudberg, *The Many Faces of Ernie,* Golden Press, 1979.
Emily Perl Kingsley, *The Sesame Street Pet Show,* Western, 1979.
Marjorie Weinman Sharmat, *Griselda's New Year* (Junior Literary Guild selection), Macmillan, 1979.
Patricia Thackray, *Amazing Mumford Forgets the Magic Words,* Golden Press, 1979.
Timothy Foote, *The Great Ringtail Garbage Caper,* Houghton, 1980.
Jocelyn Stevenson, *All about Bones,* Western, 1980.
Dan Elliot, *Oscar's Rotten Birthday,* Random House, 1981.
Elliot, *Grover Goes to School,* Random House, 1982.
Sandra Chartier, *Time for Bed, Sleepyheads,* Golden Press, 1983.
Jeffrey Moss and others, *The Songs of Sesame Street in Poems and Pictures,* Random House, 1983.
Stephanie Calmenson, *All Aboard the Goodnight Train,* Grosset & Dunlap, 1984.
Sharmat, *Bartholomew the Bossy,* Macmillan, 1984.
Elliott, *Grover Learns to Read,* Random House, 1985.
Jingle Bells, Simon & Schuster, 1986.
Sara Coleridge, *January Brings the Snow,* Simon & Schuster, 1987.
Deborah Hautzig, *Where Is My Skate?,* Random House, 1987.
Mike Thaler, *Pack 109,* Dutton, 1988.
Hautzig, *Grover's Lucky Jacket,* Random House, 1989.
Hautzig, *Happy Mother's Day!,* Random House, 1989.
Jingle Bells: Chubby Board Book, Simon & Schuster, 1989.
Millicent Selsam and Joyce Hunt, *Keep Looking!,* Macmillan, 1989.
Karen Wagner, *Silly Fred,* Macmillan, 1989.
Linda Hayward, *All Stuck Up,* Random House, 1990.
Pamela Kennedy, *A, B, C, Bunny,* edited by Janet Kobobel, Focus on the Family, 1990.

Kennedy, *All Mine, Bunny,* edited by Kobobel, Focus on the Family, 1990.
Kennedy, *Night, Night, Bunny,* edited by Kobobel, Focus on the Family, 1990.
Kennedy, *Oh, Oh, Bunny,* edited by Kobobel, Focus on the Family, 1990.
Kennedy, *One, Two, Three, Bunny,* edited by Kobobel, Focus on the Family, 1990.
Kennedy, *Red, Yellow, Blue, Bunny,* edited by Kobobel, Focus on the Family, 1990.
Over the River and Thro' the Woods, Simon & Schuster, 1990.
Christopher A. Myers and Lynne Born Myers, *McCrephy's Field,* Houghton, in press.

Contributor of illustrations to children's magazines, including *Sesame Street, Highlights, Humpty Dumpty, Cricket,* and *Ladybug.*

SIDELIGHTS: Normand L. Chartier told *SATA:* "I grew up in rural Connecticut, one of twelve children of my general-practitioner Dad and his support system (my Mom). I enjoyed drawing, sketching, and looking at children's books from a very early age. My fondest childhood memories were of being read children's stories. Not so much for the stories themselves, but for the wonderful pictures. That has never left me and my pictures kind of reflect the quality and feel from those books of the thirties, forties, and fifties.

"My family was very sports-minded and I participated in just about every sport available. In high school I won many honors, including all-conference in three sports and all-state in football. I went to college on a football scholarship, but after a serious neck injury curtailed my intentions of a sports career, I turned my focus to art and illustration.

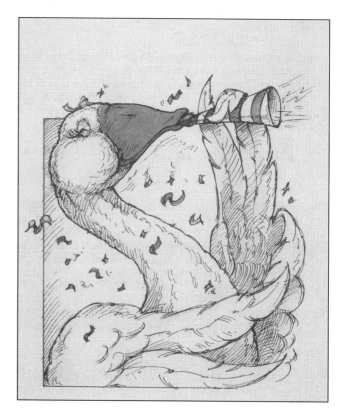

Griselda Goose blew her Happy New Year horn. (From *Griselda's New Year,* by Marjorie Weinman Sharmat, illustrated by Normand Chartier.)

"My art has two separate yet connected directions. One is art for children. In that capacity I have illustrated dozens of children's books and done numerous magazine pieces.

"The other is art for grown-up children in which I try to capture the beauty of simple settings. Many of my watercolor paintings were done from subjects in and around Cozy Harbor, Southport, Maine. I am especially lured by coastal Maine. I guess I sort of envy the classic simplicity that making one's living from fishing the sea represents.

"Therein lies the connection between the two idioms. I believe children are simple and unassuming creations of God and I try to infuse in my art for them a feeling for what is good and true. In my paintings for adults, I strive to remind myself as well as the observer that inherent within God's simple and unassuming creations is truth and goodness. It's almost a Shaker type of philosophy that I can't escape from or argue with that comes through in my art—that is, the more ornate, glitzed-up, or excessive a thing is, the further away from real beauty and truth it gets."

* * *

COOPER, Ilene

WRITINGS:

Susan B. Anthony, Watts, 1984.
The Winning of Miss Lynn Ryan, Morrow, 1987.
(Editor with Denise Wilms) *Guide to Non-Sexist Children's Books,* Volume II: *1976-1985,* Academy Chicago, 1987.
Queen of the Sixth Grade, Morrow, 1988.
Choosing Sides, Greenwillow, 1990.

* * *

COSBY, Bill
See COSBY, William Henry, Jr.

* * *

COSBY, William Henry, Jr. 1937-
(Bill Cosby)

PERSONAL: Born July 12, 1937, in Philadelphia, PA; son of William Henry (a U.S. Navy mess steward) and Anna (a domestic worker) Cosby; married Camille Hanks, January 25, 1964; children: Erika Ranee, Erinn Chalene, Ennis William, Ensa Camille, Evin Harrah. *Education:* Attended Temple University, 1961-62; University of Massachusetts, M.A., 1972, Ed.D., 1977.

ADDRESSES: Agent—The Brokaw Co., 9255 Sunset Blvd., Los Angeles, CA 90069.

CAREER: Comedian, actor, recording artist, writer, and producer. Performer in nightclubs, including The Cellar, Philadelphia, PA, Gaslight Cafe, New York City, Bitter End, New York City, and Hungry i, San Francisco, CA, 1962—; performer in television series for National Broadcasting Co. (NBC-TV), including *I Spy,* 1965-68, *The Bill Cosby Show,* 1969-71, and *The Cosby Show,* 1984—, for Columbia Broadcasting System (CBS-TV), *The New Bill Cosby Show,* 1972-73, and for American Broadcasting Co. (ABC-TV), *Cos,* 1976; actor in motion pictures, including *Hickey and Boggs,* 1972, *Man and Boy,* 1972, *Uptown Saturday Night,* 1974, *Let's Do It Again,* 1975, *Mother, Jugs, and Speed,* 1976, *A*

BILL COSBY

Piece of the Action, 1977, *California Suite,* 1978, *The Devil and Max Devlin,* 1981, *Bill Cosby Himself,* 1985, *Leonard Part VI,* 1987, and *Ghost Dad,* 1990; creator of animated children's programs *The Fat Albert Show* and *Fat Albert and the Cosby Kids,* both for CBS-TV, 1972-84. Also performer on *The Bill Cosby Radio Program,* television specials, *The First Bill Cosby Special* and *The Second Bill Cosby Special,* in animated feature *Aesop's Fables,* in *An Evening with Bill Cosby* at Radio City Music Hall, 1986, and in videocassette *Bill Cosby: 49,* sponsored by Kodak, 1987. Guest on Public Broadcasting Co. (PBS-TV) children's programs *Sesame Street* and *The Electric Company,* and NBC-TV's *Children's Theatre;* host of Picture Pages segment of CBS-TV's *Captain Kangaroo Wake Up.* Commercial spokesman for Jell-O Pudding (General Foods, Inc.), Coca-Cola Co., Ford Motor Co., Texas Instruments, E.F. Hutton, and Kodak Film.

President of Rhythm and Blues Hall of Fame, 1968. Member of Carnegie Commission for the Future of Public Broadcasting; member of board of directors of National Council on Crime and Delinquency, Mary Holmes College, and Ebony Showcase Theatre; member of board of trustees of Temple University; member of advisory board of Direction Sports; member of communications council at Howard University; member of steering committee of American Sickle Cell Foundation. *Military service:* U.S. Navy Medical Corps., 1956-60.

AWARDS, HONORS: Eight Grammy Awards for best comedy album from National Society of Recording Arts and Sciences, including 1964, for *Bill Cosby Is a Very Funny Fellow . . . Right!,* 1965, for *I Started Out as a Child,* 1966, for *To Russell, My Brother, Whom I Slept With;* Emmy Award for best actor in a dramatic series from Academy of Television Arts and Sciences, 1965-66, 1966-67, and 1967-68, for *I Spy;* named "most promising new male star" by *Fame* magazine, 1966; Emmy Award for television special, 1969, for *The First Bill Cosby Special;* Seal of Excellence from Children's Theatre Association, 1973; Ohio State University award, 1975, for *Fat Albert and the Cosby Kids;* NAACP Image Award, 1976; named "Star Presenter of 1978" by *Advertising Age;* Gold Award for Outstanding Children's Program from International Film and Television Festival, 1981, for *Fat Albert and the Cosby Kids;* Emmy Award for best comedy series, 1985, for *The Cosby Show;* honorary degree from Brown University; Golden Globe Award from Hollywood Foreign Press Association; four People's Choice Awards; voted "most believable celebrity endorser" three times in surveys by Video Storyboard Tests Inc.

WRITINGS:

UNDER NAME BILL COSBY

The Wit and Wisdom of Fat Albert, Windmill Books, 1973.
Bill Cosby's Personal Guide to Tennis Power; or, Don't Lower the Lob, Raise the Net, Random House, 1975.
(Contributor) Charlie Shedd, editor, *You Are Somebody Special,* McGraw, 1978, 2nd edition, 1982.
Fatherhood, Doubleday, 1986.
Time Flies, Doubleday, 1987.
(Author of foreword with Alvin Poussaint) Malcolm-Jamal Warner and Daniel Paisner, *Theo & Me: Growing Up Okay,* Dutton, 1988.
Love and Marriage, Doubleday, 1989.

Also author of *Fat Albert's Survival Kit.* Author of recordings, including *Bill Cosby Is a Very Funny Fellow ... Right!,* 1964, *I Started Out as Child,* 1965, *Why Is There Air?,* 1966, *Wonderfulness,* 1967, *Revenge,* 1967, *Russell, My Brother, Whom I Slept With,* 1969, *Bill Cosby Is Not Himself These Days, Rat Own, Rat Own, Rat Own,* 1976, *My Father Confused Me ... What Must I Do? What Must I Do?,* 1977, *Disco Bill,* 1977, *Bill's Best Friend,* 1978, and also *It's True, It's True, Bill Cosby Himself, 200 MPH, Silverthroat, Hooray for the Salvation Army Band, 8:15, 12:15, For Adults Only, Bill Cosby Talks to Kids about Drugs, Inside the Mind of Bill Cosby,* and *Where You Lay Your Head.*

TELEVISION/FILM PRODUCTIONS

Fat Albert and the Cosby Kids, Series 1, Barr Films, 1978.
Fat Albert and the Cosby Kids, Series 2, Barr Films, 1979.
Fat Albert and the Cosby Kids, Series 3, Barr Films, 1979.
Fat Albert and the Cosby Kids (three cartoon espisodes), HBO Home Video, 1978.
Fat Albert and the Cosby Kids, Cassette #4 (three cartoon episodes from the TV series), HBO Home Video, 1978.
Fat Albert and the Cosby Kids, Cassette #2 (two cartoon episodes), HBO Home Video, 1982.
Sinister Stranger, Tele-Story, 1984.
Fat Albert and the Cosby Kids, Cassette #3, HBO Home Video, 1984.
Kids and Alcohol Don't Mix! with Fat Albert and the Cosby Kids, Barr Films, 1985.
Do Your Job Right! with Fat Albert and the Cosby Kids, Barr Films, 1985.

SIDELIGHTS: Bill Cosby is a talented, popular, and hardworking entertainer. Considered a superstar in the areas of comedy, acting, recording, writing, and producing, Cosby has received much praise and admiration for the work he has done in the entertainment field. Cosby is recognized as a master storyteller with a great talent for making everyday and ordinary occurrences hilarious. Currently starring in the phenomenally successful television series, *The Cosby Show,*

Cosby has frequently and publicly credited his parents, wife, and family for inspiring and motivating him.

Cosby was born on July 12, 1937, in north Philadelphia, Pennsylvania, an area often referred to as "Germantown" or "The Jungle." His father, William Henry Cosby, Sr., was a welder and his mother, Anna Pearl Cosby, was a housekeeper who often worked twelve hours a day, leaving Bill in charge of his brothers—Russell, Robert, and James, who died at age six of rheumatic fever.

When Cosby was eight years old his father enlisted in the U.S. Navy. Serving as a mess steward on Navy vessel caused his father to be away from home for very long periods of time. As a result, Cosby's responsibility as the oldest male at home increased. In addition to caring for his younger brothers, Cosby shined shoes, was a stock boy at a local supermarket, and sold fruit before school to help supplement the family's income. But despite his efforts, the family's financial situation declined, forcing them to move from the family's home on Beechwood Street to smaller quarters on Steward Street and finally into the Richard Allen Homes, low-income housing known as "The Projects."

Cosby's mother was a tremendous influence on him. Although Mrs. Cosby had to work very long hours to support her family, she kept close tabs on her sons. She also did everything she could to provide a strong moral foundation for her sons, knowing that the neighborhood they grew up in was rough and dangerous. She regularly read the Bible and books by such authors as Mark Twain to her boys. "I think one of the most important things to understand is that my mother, as a domestic, worked 12 hours a day, and then she would do the laundry, and cook the meals and serve them and clean them up, and for this she got $7 a day," Cosby once recounted in the *Los Angeles Times.*

As a young boy, Cosby attended Mary Channing Wister Elementary School where he was captain of the baseball and track teams and president of his class. However, Cosby was more interested in sports and clowning than in studying. He enjoyed making his fellow students and friends laugh. Cosby noted in *Contemporary Authors New Revision Series:* "I always used to pay attention to things that other people didn't even think about. . . . I'd remember funny happenings, just little trivial things, and then tell stories about them later. I found I could make people laugh, and I enjoyed doing it because it gave me a sense of security. I thought that if people laughed at what you said, that meant they liked you." Perhaps this was the starting point of Cosby's very successful career as comedian, actor, recording artist, writer, and commercial spokesperson.

During this time sports was just as interesting to Cosby as clowning. "I lived sports the way few teenagers do today," Cosby fondly remembered in his book, *Time Flies.* "On a typical summer morning, I got up, washed my face, and skipped a hearty breakfast; and then I went out to meet my friends. I was clean and empty; but I was also full of a lust for all-day competition. . . . When I say all-day, I *mean* all-day: the boys and I played baseball, basketball, football, and stickball for eight or nine hours with no breaks. From time to time, one of our mothers would come down . . . and try to drag one of the members home for some forced feeding."

At Fitz-Simmons Junior High, Cosby remained active in sports and began acting in school plays. Although he was still a class clown and a sports nut, his teachers felt he was gifted

Bill Cosby did all the voice-overs in his popular cartoon series "Fat Albert and the Cosby Kids," for CBS-TV.

and Cosby was sent to Central High School, an academically tough school. While he excelled in sports and as a classroom joker, Cosby did not make an effort academically. He was unhappy at Central and decided to transfer to Germantown High School because it was less demanding.

In 1954, Cosby failed tenth grade and was told he would have to remain in the same class for another year. Cosby refused to repeat tenth grade and dropped out of school. He became an apprentice at a shoemaker's shop, then worked at an auto muffler factory. While he saw others take the fast and illegal way to earn a living, Cosby resisted the street lure of easy money. As he explained in *Bill Cosby: America's Most Famous Father,* "Even though certain things were open to me in the way of hanging out with the gang and that sort of acceptance, the thing that always turned me around and kept me from taking a pistol and holding up a store or jumping in and beating some old person on the street was that I could go to jail, and this would bring a great amount of shame on my mother and father."

Unable to find a good job he enjoyed, Cosby enlisted in the U.S. Navy. "I joined the Navy because my buddies had all joined the Air Force and I didn't want to be like everybody

else," he wrote in *Time Flies.* He was sent to Bethesda Naval Hospital in Maryland as a medical corpsman in a physical therapy unit. While in the service he realized how important an education was to his future and worked for and received a high school equivalency degree. "I met a lot of guys in the navy . . . who didn't have as much 'upstairs' as I knew I did, yet here they were struggling away for an education," Cosby remarked in *The Cosby Wit.* "I finally realized I was committing a sin—a *mental* sin."

When Cosby's term of service came to an end, he knew he wanted to continue his education so he accepted an offer of an athletic scholarship to Temple University in Philadelphia. He planned on becoming a physical education teacher. To earn extra money, Cosby took a part-time job waiting on tables and bartending in a comedy club. Occasionally he would get on stage and try out his jokes on the audience. Before long, Cosby was "bitten by the show business bug" and quit school during his sophomore year to pursue a career as a comedian.

Cosby's parents did not approve of his decision and repeatedly asked him to finish college. But he persevered and worked diligently at being a good comedian. Some of the

Bill Cosby and Sidney Poitier in a scene from their movie *Let's Do It Again*, produced by Warner Brothers in 1975.

comedians who impressed and influenced him were Buster Keaton, Charlie Chaplin, Jerry Lewis, Mel Brooks, Carl Reiner, Redd Foxx, Dick Gregory, Dave Gardner, Slappy White, Jonathan Winters, Bob Newhart, Lenny Bruce, and Buddy Hackett.

Cosby worked at comedy clubs in Philadelphia and before long was performing at clubs in other cities, including at the Gaslight Cafe in New York City and at numerous nightclubs in Las Vegas. In his early performances he occasionally used racial humor and stereotypes to get a laugh from the audience. But he soon came to see that this kind of humor did nothing to help stop racism. "Racial humor was about 35% of my act when I first started," Cosby confessed in *Time*. "But I realized that it was a crutch. . . . I don't think you can bring the races together by joking about the differences between them. I'd rather talk about the similarities, about what's universal in their experiences."

It was while he was in Washington, D.C., for a performance that he meet his future wife, Camille Hanks, then a student at the University of Maryland. Cosby explained their meeting in *Love and Marriage* in this way: "I began to perform at little nightclubs all along the East Coast. . . . The day I reached Washington, a friend named George Green asked me if I wanted to go out with a beautiful nineteen-year-old student from the University of Maryland named Camille Hanks, whose family lived in a fashionable suburb of Silver Springs."

Cosby fell head-over-heels in love with Camille and asked her to marry him on their second date. She was not as impressed with him as he was with her so she refused this first proposal. However, the couple continued to date and after a long-distance courtship, with Cosby on the road much of the time, Cosby and Camille Hanks were married on January 25, 1964.

Later that same year Cosby recorded and released his first comedy album, "Bill Cosby is a Very Funny Fellow . . . Right!" Cosby's special gift for storytelling combined with his knack for making commonplace happenings comical made this recording very popular and his audience of fans grew to include people who had never seen him perform in clubs or concert. The album sold extremely well, and was praised by many reviewers. It also won a Grammy for the "best comedy album of the year." Cosby's next six comedy albums were even more successful with each one also winning a Grammy. And all together, Cosby has won a total of eight Grammys for his comedy recordings. This makes Bill Cosby one of the more successful comedic recording artists ever.

In 1965, with his career as comedian and recording artist launched and flourishing, Cosby was asked to co-star with Robert Culp on the proposed television series, *I Spy*. Without any acting experience, he took the role of Alexander Scott, a Rhodes Scholar and C.I.A. agent posing as Culp's tennis trainer. This move made television history because Cosby would become the first black person to star in a major TV series. The show was an immediate hit with viewers and Cosby won an Emmy for his work on the series.

Cosby was receiving praise and recognition for his acting, but he was also criticized by some people for not being a more forceful role model for other blacks. He looked back on this period in this life in *The Cosby Wit:* "Because I was the first, the network and the advertisers were nervous about how I should act, on camera *and off.* . . . There were a dozen thin lines I was supposed to walk. I had to dress and talk like 'them,' or I was considered uneducated. But if I dressed or spoke too well, as in *better than,* then I was threatening—and that was no good. With all this, I still had to live with me in that role, making the character acceptable not just to white America but to me and to blacks everywhere."

Cosby explained further: "Suppose, as a kid, I wanted to grow up and be like Charlie Chaplin. That doesn't mean I want to grow up to be white. It means I want to be funny, to bump into a pole, to fall in love with a beautiful woman and be very clumsy about giving her a rose. But people want to force us into saying, 'Here is my blackness.' Well, I don't think anybody really learns anything from that. . . . I had an idol—Jackie Robinson. He made it happen for blacks in baseball by using his talents, never his rage, to express his blackness. I felt that if in my ball park I did my job as well as

Fatherhood, **Bill Cosby's lighthearted look at parenting, dominated national bestseller lists for several years running.**

Robinson did his, I would also therefore be moving us down the road a piece."

Television proved to be a comfortable home for Cosby. Cosby would go on to star in several television series, including *The Bill Cosby Show,* and his blockbuster hit, *The Cosby Show.* In *The Bill Cosby Show,* Cosby was cast in the role of Chet Kinkaid, a physical education teacher at Richard Allen Holmes High School. Cosby summed up his character in *Cosby* as "a human being: He makes mistakes, gets into trouble, and reflects quite frequently on the human condition. . . . What I'm really doing is a study of human behavior." In *The Cosby Show* Cosby plays the part of an obstetrician, Dr. Heathcliff Huxtable, the father of five lively children and husband of the lovely lawyer, Claire. The show follows the activities of the spirited family. "This is a show with a Black American family, but what's important in this show is that our family represents about 90 percent of all people out in the audience," Cosby stated in *Ebony.* We are family and the humor comes out of our attitudes toward each other and life in general. This show will work to show all Americans that if they really love *our* children, all children are the same the world over."

Both professionally and personally, Cosby began to reap the rewards from his hard work and success. Professionally, Cosby set up a number of corporations, including a television production company that has put together and produced several top-rated shows and a recording business that has ushered numerous hit albums onto bestselling charts. In his personal life, Cosby purchased a home in Beverly Hills and he and Camille started their family. The Cosbys have four daughters and one son—Erika Ranee, Erinn Chalene, Ennis William, Ensa Camille, and Evin Harrah. Asked why he named his children the way he did, Cosby once explained that the first letter "E" that their names all shared stood for excellence. He also commented in *Bill Cosby: America's Most Famous Father,* "My wife and I were just looking for odd names to give the children so they'd have an identification of their own instead of Tom Cosby, Roy Cosby, and so on."

While his family has often provided good comedic material, Cosby has taken his role as father very seriously. "I like children," Cosby declared in the preface of *Fatherhood.* "Nothing I've ever done has given me more joys and rewards than being a father to my five. In between these joys and rewards, of course, has come the natural strife of family life, the little tensions and conflicts that are part of trying to bring civilization to children. The more I have talked about such problems, the more I have found that all other parents had the very same ones and are relieved to hear me turning them into laughter."

Cosby was an early vocal opponent of drug abuse. On March 27, 1971, his television special "Bill Cosby Talks to Kids about Drugs" aired. In *Bill Cosby: Family Funny Man,* Cosby recalls that during the program he said: "The time spent acquiring a drug habit and kicking it is time you could have used to educate yourself. . . . Every person I have ever known who developed a bad habit spent most of the rest of his life trying to kick it, staying with it, or never using it forever." The TV special was followed later by an album of the same title.

While his television special on drugs introduced him to a younger audience, Cosby officially entered the world of children's television and entertainment when he developed the cartoon character Fat Albert. The perfect spokesman for

Cosby's views on how to handle childhood problems—acceptance, lying, stealing, and safety—Fat Albert could combine Cosby's desires to teach and to entertain. Fat Albert soon had his own show which premiered on CBS-TV. Later Cosby developed more characters and *Fat Albert and the Cosby Kids* was created. Cosby did all the voice-overs. The goal of these programs was to provide wholesome children's television that entertained while also addressing moral and ethical issues. He planned the show to be "so casual in its teaching, the children will never know they're being taught."

At the same time, Cosby's new adult show, *The New Bill Cosby Show* premiered. The program had a short-lived season and was canceled. But Cosby was undaunted, for he was about to achieve a lifetime dream: completing his education. Cosby began classes at the University of Massachusetts. He and his family moved to an old farm in Amherst. Camille renovated the farmhouse and Cosby worked on his various projects in show business and pursued a doctorate in education. And on May 19, 1977, Cosby was awarded an Ed.D. from the University of Massachusetts just a few months before his fortieth birthday.

One of the show business projects he began while working on his doctorate included acting in motion pictures. His first acting role in films was in *Hickey and Boggs* and Cosby would go on to star in ten additional movies. Once again Cosby received praise for his performance in a variety of pictures over the years, including *Hickey and Boggs, Man and Boy, Uptown Saturday Night, Let's Do It Again, Mother, Jugs, and Speed, A Piece of Action, California Suite, The Devil and Max Devlin, Bill Cosby Himself, Leonard Part VI,* and *Ghost Dad.*

In 1973, Cosby ventured into the world of publishing with the release of his first book, *The Wit and Wisdom of Fat Albert,* which was later followed by *Fat Albert's Survival Kit,* and *Bill Cosby's Personal Guide to Tennis Power, or Don't Lower the Lob, Raise the Net,* a humorous look at tennis. While these books were very well received by reviewers and the book buying public, Cosby hit bestseller lists with *Fatherhood, Time Flies,* and *Love and Marriage.* In these books, Cosby lovingly pokes fun at the ups and downs involved in everyday life as seen through his life experiences. After reading *Fatherhood,* Cathleen McGuigan noted in *Newsweek* that it "is like a prose version of a Cosby comedy performance—informal, commiserative anecdotes delivered in a sardonic style that's as likely to prompt a smile of recognition as a belly laugh." "Cosby has an extraordinarily keen ear for everyday speech and everyday event, and knows how to put just enough of a comic spin on it so that even as we laugh we know we are getting a glimpse of the truth," wrote Jonathan Yardley in the *Washington Post Book World.*

Another great triumph in Cosby's life and career occurred on September 20, 1984, when *The Cosby Show* premiered on NBC. A huge hit from the beginning, the show became number one after four weeks. Cosby created *The Cosby Show* because he was disturbed by the lack of good role models on television for blacks and he wanted to present a family-oriented comedy series featuring a loving, yet lively, black family. As Cosby said to Jane Hall of *People:* "I got tired of seeing TV shows that consist of a car crash, a gunman and a hooker talking to a black pimp.... It was cheaper to do a series than to throw out my family's six TV sets."

Yet despite the show's success, critics have complained that it doesn't reflect the majority black experience or discuss controversial issues such as interracial dating or poverty. Cosby

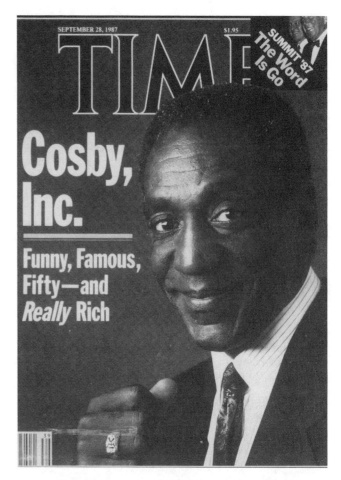

Bill Cosby was featured on the cover of *Time,* September 28, 1987.

told Hall: "Does it mean only white people have a lock on living together in a home where the father is a doctor and the mother is a lawyer and the children are constantly being told to study by their parents?... This is a black American family. If anybody has difficulty with that, it's their problem, not ours."

Cosby put a great deal of time and energy into making this series successful. He wanted to provide good, wholesome quality entertainment that families could watch and enjoy together. Cosby employed Harvard psychiatrist Dr. Alvin Poussaint as an adviser to assure that no stereotypes were portrayed. "I said to the writers I don't want sitcom jokes," Cosby remarked in Ronald L. Smith's *Cosby.* "I don't want jokes about behinds or breasts or pimples or characters saying 'Oh my God' every other line. What we want to deal with is human behavior. Save the wisecracks for *Webster* and *Diff'rent Strokes, Benson* and *Gimme a Break.* Save the leering for John Ritter and the plastic gags for the plastic yuppies on shows like *Night Court ....*"

Cosby also wanted his show to be as realistic as possible—to show a family living and loving together in the 1980s and 1990s. "If this was 1964, my wife could do the cooking and I could be the guy on the sofa who just says, 'Let your mother handle this,'" Cosby told his writing staff. "But today a lot of things have changed and I want the show to reflect those changes. A family where the father cooks, too, and pitches in with the kids, and where everyone has responsibilities.... I feel a great responsibility to make it as good and as real as I can. . . . All we're trying to show all America is that in a lot of ways behavior is the same all over. . . . Let's talk about the similarities, not the differences." Despite his intense involvement in writing, producing, and acting in the show, Cosby refused the Emmy Award and the Golden Globe Award in deference to the rest of the cast.

Realizing how fortunate he and his family are, Cosby and his wife, Camille have donated many hours and great sums of money to causes or institutions they believe in. One particular area that the couple has been most generous in is education. Just to name a few examples of their generosity, the couple has contributed $1.3 million to Fisk University, another $1.3 million, divided equally, to Central State, Howard, Florida A&M, and Shaw, four black colleges. They also donated $1.5 million to Meharry Medical College and Bethune-Cookman College and a whopping $20 million to Spelman College in Atlanta. Cosby discussed his thoughts concerning his gift to Spelman College with Robert E. Johnson in *Ebony*. He explained: "I'm not going to yell at anybody. . . . I'm just giving my philosophy that it appears that we have been taking the blues too seriously. We need to call a moratorium on the blues until we get some things in order. About 65 percent of all blues songs start out with the guy saying, 'I woke up this morning.' And from that point on, nothing is right the rest of the day. And everybody shakes their head and says, 'Yes.'"

Cosby continued: "The next thing we need to call a moratorium on is, 'Well, it's his world; I'm just in it.' Clearly, nothing with initiative is going to happen the rest of the day, or week, or month, or year. This $20 million gift to Spelman is manyfold, carrying many, many messages. Mostly, it is a gift to the world. I say that in all seriousness without standing on top of a soap box or anything."

In *The Cosby Wit,* Cosby offered this advice to young people: "What can young people, black and white, do to help improve relations? They can try to be as fair with each other as is humanly possible. That's the important thing: fair. Not what they think is fair, but what *is* fair. My one rule is to be true rather than funny."

WORKS CITED:

Adler, Bill, *The Cosby Wit: His Life and Humor,* Morrow, 1986, pp. 15, 78, 79-80, 81, 108, 120.
Contemporary Authors New Revision Series, Volume 27, Gale, 1989, pp. 112-114.
Cosby, Bill, *Fatherhood,* Doubleday, 1986, preface.
Cosby, Bill, *Time Flies,* Doubleday, 1987, pp. 11, 35-36, 127-29.
Cosby, Bill, *Love and Marriage,* Doubleday, 1989, p. 92.
Hall, Jane, "Bill Cosby Huffs and Puffs On and Off His Hit Sitcom, But His TV Kids Say Father Knows Best," *People,* December 10, 1984, pp. 141-149.
Haskins, Jim, *Bill Cosby: America's Most Famous Father,* Walker & Co., 1987, pp. 11, 22.
Johnson, Robert E., "Bill and Camille Cosby: First Family of Philanthropy," *Ebony,* May, 1989, p. 26.
Kettlecomp, *Bill Cosby: Family Funny Man,* Simon & Schuster, 1987, p. 111.
McGuigan, Cathleen, "Papa Cosby Knows Best," *Newsweek,* May 19, 1986, pp. 70-71.
Smith, Ronald D., *Cosby,* St. Martin's, 1986, pp. 90, 178.
Yardley, Jonathan, "Bill Cosby Knows Best," *Washington Post Book World,* April 27, 1986, p. 3.

Zoglin, Richard, "Cosby, Inc.," *Time,* September 28, 1987, pp. 56-60.

FOR MORE INFORMATION SEE:

BOOKS

Adams, Barbara J., *The Picture Life of Bill Cosby,* F. Watts, 1986.
Bestsellers '89, Gale, Issue 4, 1990.
Damerell, Reginald G., *Education's Smoking Guns,* Freundlich, 1985.
Johnson, Robert E., editor, "Bill Cosby in Words and Pictures," *Black Writers,* Gale, 1986.
Latham, Caroline, *Bill Cosby—For Real,* TOR Books, 1985.
Olson, James T., *Bill Cosby: Look Back in Laughter,* Creative Education, 1977.
Sheed, Charles, *You Are Somebody Special* (juvenile), Quest, 1978.
Woods, Harold and Geraldine Woods, *Bill Cosby: Making America Laugh and Learn* (juvenile), Dillon Press, 1983.

PERIODICALS

Daily News, April 16, 1989.
Ebony, February, 1988.
Ladies' Home Journal, January, 1988.

*   *   *

CUFFARI, Richard 1925-1978

PERSONAL: Born March 2, 1925, in Brooklyn, NY; died October 10, 1978, in Brooklyn, NY; married Phyllis Klie (an

RICHARD CUFFARI

artist), February 18, 1950; children: Richard, Ellen, William, David. *Education:* Attended Pratt Institute, 1946-49. *Hobbies and other interests:* Music, cooking, history.

ADDRESSES: Home and office—Brooklyn, NY.

CAREER: Painter and illustrator; worked for various art studios prior to 1968; free-lance book illustrator, 1968-1978. Parsons School of Design, instructor of book illustration, beginning in 1976. *Military service:* U.S. Army, 1943-46; served in Europe. *Exhibitions:* Works exhibited in New York City and in museums, including Contemporary Art Museum, Houston, TX, 1975. Works included in permanent collections, including Kerlan Collection of the University of Minnesota and Grummond Collection of the University of Southern Mississippi.

MEMBER: American Institute of Graphic Arts, Society of Illustrators.

AWARDS, HONORS: Citation of Merit from Society of Illustrators, 1967-68 and 1969-70; Lewis Carroll Shelf Award, 1970, for *Old Ben;* Christopher Award, 1973, for *This Star Shall Abide;* Children's Book Showcase citation from Children's Book Council, 1974, for *Escape from the Evil Prophecy,* and 1975, for *The Perilous Gard,* a Newbery honor book; American Institute of Graphic Arts included *The Endless Pavement* in its children's book show, 1973-74, and *Two That Were Tough* in its general book show, 1976.

ILLUSTRATOR:

Kenneth Grahame, *The Wind in the Willows,* Grosset, 1966.
Mildred W. Willard, *The Man Who Had to Invent a Flying Bicycle,* Stackpole, 1967.
Dorothy Aldis, *Nothing Is Impossible: The Story of Beatrix Potter* (Junior Literary Guild selection), Atheneum, 1969.
(With James MacDonald) Ralph E. Bailey, *Wagons Westward: The Story of Alexander Majors,* Morrow, 1969.
E. John Dewaard, *Plants and Animals in the Air,* Doubleday, 1969.
Richard B. Erno, *Billy Lightfoot,* Crown, 1969.
Cecilia Holland, *The Ghost on the Steppe,* Atheneum, 1969.
Robert C. Lee, *I Was a Teenage Hero,* McGraw, 1969.
A. M. Lightner, *The Walking Zoo of Darwin Dingle,* Putnam, 1969.
Alice Marriott, *Winter Telling Stories,* Crowell, 1969.
Walt Morey, *Angry Waters,* Dutton, 1969.
Richard O'Connor, *Tom Paine: Rebel with a Cause,* McGraw, 1969.
Lee Wyndham, *Florence Nightingale: Nurse to the World,* World Publishing, 1969.
Ewan Clarkson, *Halic: The Story of a Gray Seal,* Dutton, 1970.
Carla Greene, *Before the Dinosaurs,* Bobbs, 1970.
Greene, *Gregor Mendel,* Dial, 1970.
Miriam Gurko, *Indian America: The Black Hawk War,* Crowell, 1970.
Holland, *King's Road,* Atheneum, 1970.
Hans Konigsberger, *The Golden Keys,* Doubleday, 1970.
Robert Martin, *Yesterday's People,* Doubleday 1970.
Gunilla B. Norris, *The Top Step,* Atheneum, 1970.
Thomas B. Perera and Wallace Orlowsky, *Who Will Wash the River?,* Coward, 1970.

Gene Smith, *The Winner,* Cowles, 1970.
Jesse Stuart, *Old Ben,* McGraw, 1970.
Rosemary Weir, *The Lion and the Rose,* Farrar, Straus, 1970.
James Playsted Wood, *The People of Concord,* Seabury, 1970.
Herbert S. Zim and James R. Skelly, *Cargo Ships,* Morrow, 1970.
Edna Barth, *I'm Nobody, Who Are You: The Story of Emily Dickinson,* Seabury, 1971.
Barbara Corcoran, *This Is a Recording,* Atheneum, 1971.
Sylvia Louise Engdahl, *The Far Side of Evil,* Atheneum, 1971.
Constance Fecher, *The Link Boys,* Farrar, Straus, 1971.
Sophia H. Fenton, *Ancient Rome: A Book to Begin On,* Holt, 1971.
Robert Froman, *Hot and Cold and in Between,* Grosset, 1971.
Nancy Garden, *What Happened in Marston?,* Four Winds, 1971.
Mirra Ginsburg, editor and translator, *The Kaha Bird: Tales from the Steppes of Central Asia,* Crown, 1971.
Elizabeth S. Helfman, *The Bushmen and Their Stories,* Seabury, 1971.
John L. Hoke, *Ecology,* F. Watts, 1971.
Elizabeth Ladd, *The Indians on the Bonnet,* Morrow, 1971.
Harold S. Longman, *Andron and the Magician,* Seabury, 1971.
Perera and Orlowsky, *Who Will Clean the Air?,* Coward, 1971.
Kenneth Rudeen, *Jackie Robinson,* Crowell, 1971.
Eileen Thompson, *The Golden Coyote* (Junior Literary Guild selection), Simon & Schuster, 1971.
Mary Towne, *The Glass Room,* Farrar, Straus, 1971.
Joseph Claro, *I Can Predict the Future,* Lothrop, 1972.
Eth Clifford, *The Year of the Three-Legged Deer,* Houghton, 1972.
Engdahl, *This Star Shall Abide,* Atheneum, 1972.
Doris Portwood Evans, *Mr. Charley's Chopsticks,* Coward, 1972.
Roma Gans, *Water for Dinosaurs and You,* Crowell, 1972.
Helfman, *Maypoles and Wood Demons: The Meaning of Trees,* Seabury, 1972.
Ross E. Hutchins, *The Carpenter Bee,* Addison-Wesley, 1972.
Virginia Lee, *The Magic Moth,* Seabury, 1972.
Anne Molloy, *The Years before the Mayflower: The Pilgrims in Holland,* Hastings House, 1972.
Mary K. Phelan, *Mr. Lincoln's Inaugural Journey,* Crowell, 1972.
Franklin Russel, "Pond Trilogy," Volume I: *Datra the Muskrat,* Volume II: *Corvus the Crow,* Volume III: *Lotor the Raccoon,* Four Winds Press, 1972.
Julius Schwartz, *Magnify and Find Out Why,* McGraw, 1972.
Ronald Syme, *Jaurez: The Founder of Modern Mexico,* Morrow, 1972.
Irwin Touster and Richard Curtis, *The Perez Arson Mystery,* Dial, 1972.
Touster and Curtis, *The Runaway Bus Mystery,* Dial, 1972.
Martha Bacon, *In the Company of Clowns,* Little, Brown, 1973.
Betsy Byars, *The Winged Colt of Casa Mia,* Viking, 1973.
Vada F. Carlson, *John Wesley Powell: Conquest of the Canyon,* Harvey House, 1973.
Engdahl, *Beyond the Tomorrow Mountains,* Atheneum, 1973.
Dale Fife, *Ride the Crooked Wind* (Junior Literary Guild selection), Coward, 1973.
Wilma Pitchford Hays, *Little Yellow Fur: Homesteading in 1913,* Coward, 1973.
D. C. Ipsen, *Eye of the Whirlwind: The Story of John Scopes,* Addison-Wesley, 1973.

They caught a half-grown tiger and secured it in a box. (From *In Her Father's Footsteps*, by Bianca Bradbury, illustrated by Richard Cuffari.)

Jacqueline Jackson and William Perlmutter, *The Endless Pavement* (Junior Literary Guild selection), Seabury, 1973.

Lee Kingman, *Escape from the Evil Prophecy*, Houghton, 1973.

Meridel Le Sueur, *Conquistadores*, F. Watts, 1973.

Peggy Mann, *My Dad Lives in a Downtown Hotel*, Doubleday, 1973.

Robert Newman, *The Testing of Tertius*, Atheneum, 1973.

Andrew J. Offut, *The Galactic Rejects*, Lothrop, 1973.

Stella Pevsner, *Call Me Heller, That's My Name*, Seabury, 1973.

Edward R. Riccuti, *Dancers on the Beach: The Story of the Grunion*, Crowell, 1973.

Keith Robertson, *In Search of a Sandhill Crane*, Viking, 1973.

Rosemary Sutcliff, *The Capricorn Bracelet*, Walck, 1973.

Syme, *Fur Trader of the North: The Story of Pierre de la Verendrye*, Morrow, 1973.

Theodore Taylor, *Rebellion Town: Williamsburg, 1776*, Crowell, 1973.

Janet Townsend, *The Comic Book Mystery*, Pantheon, 1973.

R. Weir, *The Blood Royal*, Farrar, Straus, 1973.

Alice Wellman, *Small Boy Chuku*, Houghton, 1973.

Elizabeth Coatsworth, *All-of-a-Sudden Susan*, Macmillan, 1974.

Barbara Cohen, *Thank You, Jackie Robinson*, Lothrop, 1974.

Engdahl, *The Planet-Girded Suns*, Atheneum, 1974.

The Free Wheeling of Joshua Cobb, Farrar, Straus, 1974.

Daniel Jacobson, *The Hunters*, F. Watts, 1974.

Adrienne Jones, *So, Nothing Is Forever*, Houghton, 1974.

Norma Klein, *Confessions of an Only Child*, Pantheon, 1974.

F. N. Monjo, *Grand Papa and Ellen Aroon* (Junior Literary Guild selection), Holt, 1974.

Tunie Munson, *A Fistful of Sun*, Lothrop, 1974.

Norris, *Standing in the Magic* (Junior Literary Guild selection), Dutton, 1974.

Elizabeth M. Pope, *The Perilous Gard*, Houghton, 1974.

Syme, *John Charles Fremont: Last American Explorer*, Morrow, 1974.

Caroline Tapley, *John Come Down the Backstay*, Atheneum, 1974.

Taylor, *Teetoncey*, Doubleday, 1974.

Ester Wier, *The Hunting Trail*, Walck, 1974.

Jane Yolen, *Ring Out! A Book of Bells* (Junior Literary Guild selection), Seabury, 1974.

Melvin Berger, *Time after Time*, Coward, 1975.

Ruth Blair, *Van Ness, Mary's Monster*, Coward, 1975.

Betty Cavanna, *Ruffles and Drums*, Morrow, 1975.

Child Study Association of America, compiler, *Families Are Like That*, Crowell, 1975.

Peter Z. Cohen, *Bee*, Atheneum, 1975.

Doris Gates, *Mightiest of Mortals: Heracles*, Viking, 1975.

Cheryl Hoople, *The Heritage Sampler: A Book of Colonial Arts and Crafts*, Dial, 1975.

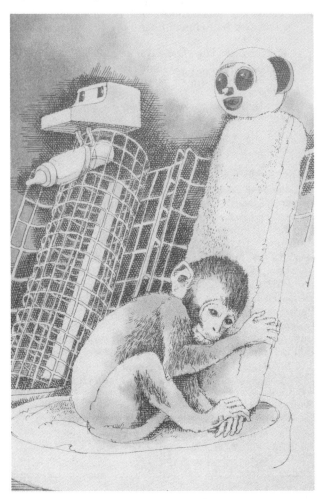

The softness of the mother is what causes the baby to love her. (From *Good and Bad Feelings*, by Mark L. Stein, illustrated by Richard Cuffari.)

Jacobson, *The Fisherman,* F. Watts, 1975.

J. J. McCoy, *A Sea of Troubles* (Junior Literary Guild selection), Clarion, 1975.

Lila Perl, *Slumps, Grunts, and Snickerdoodles: What Colonial America Ate and Why,* Clarion, 1975.

Taylor, *Teetoncey and Ben O'Neal,* Doubleday, 1975.

Bianca Bradbury, *In Her Father's Footsteps,* Houghton, 1976.

Robin Brancato, *Something Left to Lose,* Knopf, 1976.

Robert Burch, *Two That Were Tough,* Viking, 1976.

Byars, *The TV Kid,* Viking, 1976.

Frances Duncombe, *The Summer of the Burning,* Putnam, 1976.

Barbara Shook Hazen, *The Ups and Downs of Marvin,* Atheneum, 1976.

Janet Hickman, *The Stones,* Macmillan, 1976.

F. N. Monjo, *Zenas and the Saving Mill,* Coward, 1976.

Mindel Sitomer and others, *How Did Numbers Begin?,* Crowell, 1976.

Mark Stein, *Good and Bad Feelings,* Morrow, 1976.

Susan Terris, *No Boys Allowed,* Doubleday, 1976.

Herbert H. Wong and Matthew F. Vessel, *My Plant,* Addison-Wesley, 1976.

Bradbury, *I'm Vinny, I'm Me,* Houghton, 1977.

Ruth Goode, *People of the First Cities,* Macmillan, 1977.

Peggy Mann, *There Are Two Kinds of Terrible,* Doubleday, 1977.

The Melodeon, Doubleday, 1977.

Perl, *Hunter's Stew and Hangtown Fry: What Pioneer America Ate and Why* (Junior Literary Guild selection), Clarion, 1977.

P. K. Roche, *Dollhouse Magic: How to Make and Find Simple Dollhouse Furniture* (also illustrated with photographs by John Knott; Junior Literary Guild selection), Dial, 1977.

Wilda Ross, *The Rain Forest—What Lives There,* Coward, 1977.

Judith St. George, *The Shad Are Running,* Putnam, 1977.

Taylor, *The Odyssey of Ben O'Neal,* Doubleday, 1977.

Ruth Winter, *Scent Talk among Animals,* Lippincott, 1977.

Barth, *Balder and the Mistletoe: A Story for the Winter Holidays,* commentary by James Giblin, Clarion, 1978.

Esther W. Brady, *The Toad on Capitol Hill,* Crown, 1978.

Byars, *The Cartoonist,* Viking, 1978.

Martha O. Conn, *Crazy to Fly* (Junior Literary Guild selection), Atheneum, 1978.

Barbara Girion, *Joshua, the Czar, and the Chicken Bone Wish,* Scribner, 1978, published as *The Chicken Bone Wish,* Scholastic, 1982.

Hays, *Yellow Fur and Little Hawk,* Coward, 1978.

Barbara Ireson, editor, *The April Witch and Other Strange Tales,* Scribner, 1978.

Lucy Kavaler, *The Dangers of Noise,* Crowell, 1978.

Eda LeShan, *What's Going to Happen to Me? When Parents Separate or Divorce,* Four Winds Press, 1978.

Shirley R. Murphy, *The Flight of the Fox* (Junior Literary Guild selection), Atheneum, 1978.

Harry Sitomer and M. Sitomer, *Zero Is Not Nothing,* Crowell, 1978.

Leonard Wibberley, *Little League Family,* Doubleday, 1978.

Zim, *Caves and Life,* Morrow, 1978.

Brady, *Toliver's Secret,* Avon, 1979.

Hope Campbell, *A Peak beneath the Moon,* Four Winds Press, 1979.

June A. Hanson, *Summer of the Stallion,* Macmillan, 1979.

Susan Shreve, *Family Secrets: Five Very Important Stories,* Knopf, 1979.

Gurney Williams, *Ghosts and Poltergeists,* F. Watts, 1979.

The jacket art from *Family Secrets* is a composite drawing of Richard Cuffari's four children. (Cover illustration by Cuffari.)

Illustrator of additional works, including Mildred Lee's *Sycamore Year,* 1974, Rosemary Wells's *Leave Well Enough Alone,* 1977.

SIDELIGHTS: Richard Cuffari was a product of the working-class Brooklyn region of New York City, where he was born, grew up, and eventually raised a family of his own. He was a child during the lean years of the Great Depression of the 1930s, and as with many Americans, his experiences during that time were difficult ones. His immigrant parents both worked to provide money for the family, and young Cuffari spent many of his after-school hours taking care of a disabled relative. Cuffari was quick to show talent as an artist and won many awards by the time he was in high school. One happy day an uncle surprised him with an oil painting kit—a great luxury in such difficult times. When Cuffari graduated from high school in the early 1940s the Depression was over, but he and most young men of his generation had to serve their country as soldiers during World War II.

When the war ended Cuffari returned to Brooklyn to study at the Pratt Institute, where he met his future wife. After the couple married in 1950, he spent many years as a commercial artist before becoming a free-lance illustrator of children's books in the mid-1960s. Now his talents and his interests combined to give him a highly rewarding career. Drawing for children seemed to come readily to a man who enjoyed having four children of his own. Cuffari, moreover, had a strong interest in history and soon became a specialist in illustrating books set in earlier times, ranging from America in the 1700s to Iceland in the Middle Ages. He wanted his drawings to be as authentic as possible and collected his own library to assist his work. By the 1970s Cuffari's illustrations were featured in many important book shows, and he was remembered with admiration after he died in his native Brooklyn at the untimely age of fifty-three.

FOR MORE INFORMATION SEE:

BOOKS

Edna Barth, *Balder and the Mistletoe: A Story for the Winter Holidays,* commentary by James Giblin, Clarion, 1978.

OBITUARIES:

PERIODICALS

School Library Journal, December, 1978.

*   *   *

CUNLIFFE, Marcus (Falkner) 1922-1990

OBITUARY NOTICE—See index for *SATA* sketch: Born July 5, 1922, in England; died of leukemia, September 2, 1990, in Washington, DC. Historian, educator, and author. Cunliffe, a British-born scholar known for his contributions to American studies, was described in the London *Times* as "a true mid-Atlantic man. It would be hard to say if he was more English than eastern American." Between 1949 and 1980 Cunliffe taught at English universities in Manchester and Sussex, departing on occasion to serve as visiting professor at such American universities as Harvard and Michigan. He spent his last decade in the United States as University Professor at George Washington University. Cunliffe's expertise on American topics was first revealed during the 1950s when he published *The Literature of the United States* and *George Washington: Man and Monument.* Later works include *Soldiers and Civilians, American Presidents and the Presidency, The Ages of Man: From Sav-age to Sew-age,* and *In Search of America.* In addition, he joined R. B. Morris in writing a children's book titled *George Washington and the Making of a Nation.*

OBITUARIES AND OTHER SOURCES:

BOOKS

Who's Who, 142nd edition, St. Martin's, 1990.

PERIODICALS

Chicago Tribune, September 5, 1990; September 9, 1990.
Los Angeles Times, September 8, 1990.
New York Times, September 5, 1990.
Times (London), September 4, 1990.
Washington Post, September 5, 1990.

*   *   *

d'AULAIRE, Edgar Parin 1898-1986

PERSONAL: Surname is pronounced "doh-*lair*"; original surname Parin, took mother's maiden name as professional name; born September 30, 1898, in Munich, Germany; immigrated to United States, 1929, naturalized citizen, 1939; died May 1, 1986, in Georgetown, CT; son of Gino (a portrait painter) and Ella (an artist; maiden name, d'Aulaire) Parin;

married Ingri Mortenson (an artist and author), July 24, 1925 (died October 24, 1980); children: Per Ola, Nils Maarten. *Education:* Attended Technological Institute of Munich, 1917-19, Schule Hans Hofman, Munich, Germany, 1922-24, and art schools in Paris, France; pupil of Henri Matisse. *Hobbies and other interests:* Landscaping, forestry, and working a large farm.

ADDRESSES: Home—Lia Farm, 74 Mather Rd., Georgetown, CT 06829; (summer) South Royalton, VT 05068.

CAREER: Artist, lecturer, and author and illustrator of children's books. Worked as book illustrator in Germany, 1922-26; wrote and illustrated books in collaboration with wife, Ingri d'Aulaire, beginning in 1930. *Exhibitions:* Exhibited art in several countries, including Norway, France, Italy, Czechoslovakia, and United States.

MEMBER: Authors League of America.

AWARDS, HONORS: Children of the Soil: A Story of Scandinavia was a Newbery honor book, 1933; American Library Association's Caldecott Medal (jointly with wife) for best illustrated children's book, 1940, for *Abraham Lincoln;* award from Boys Club, 1953, for *Buffalo Bill;* Catholic Library Association Regina Medal, 1970, for "continued distinguished contribution to children's literature"; *D'Aulaires' Trolls* was selected by the *New York Times Book Review* as one of the outstanding books of 1972, and was a National Book Award finalist, 1973; nominated for Hans Christian Andersen Award, 1974.

WRITINGS:

AUTHOR AND ILLUSTRATOR WITH WIFE, INGRI d'AULAIRE; FOR JUVENILES

The Magic Rug, Doubleday, Doran, 1931.
Ola, Doubleday, Doran, 1932.
Ola and Blakken and Line, Sine, Trine, Doubleday, Doran, 1933, revised edition published as *The Terrible Troll-Bird,* Doubleday, 1976.
The Conquest of the Atlantic, Viking, 1933.
The Lord's Prayer, Doubleday, Doran, 1934.
Children of the Northlights, Viking, 1935, revised edition, 1963.
George Washington: A Biography for Children, Doubleday, Doran, 1936.
Abraham Lincoln, Doubleday, Doran, 1939, revised edition, Doubleday, 1957.
Animals Everywhere, Doubleday, Doran, 1940.
Leif the Lucky, Doubleday, Doran, 1941, revised edition, Doubleday, 1951.
The Star Spangled Banner, Doubleday, Doran, 1942.
Don't Count Your Chicks, Doubleday, Doran, 1943.
Wings for Per, Doubleday, Doran, 1943.
Too Big, Doubleday, Doran, 1945.
Pocahontas, Doubleday, 1946.
Nils, Doubleday, 1948.
Foxie, Doubleday, 1949, revised edition published as *Foxie the Singing Dog,* 1969.
Benjamin Franklin, Doubleday, 1950.
Buffalo Bill, Doubleday, 1952.
The Two Cars, Doubleday, 1955.
Columbus, Doubleday, 1955.
The Magic Meadow, Doubleday, 1958.
Ingri and Edgar Parin d'Aulaire's Book of Greek Myths, Doubleday, 1962.

EDGAR AND INGRI d'AULAIRE

Norse Gods and Giants, Doubleday, 1967, published as *D'Aulaires' Norse Gods and Giants,* 1986.
D'Aulaires' Trolls, Doubleday, 1972.

ILLUSTRATOR

John Matheson, *Needle in the Haystack,* Morrow, 1930.
Katie Seabrook, *Gao of the Ivory Coast,* Coward, 1930.
Dhan Gopal Mukerji, *Rama, the Hero of India,* Dutton, 1930.
Hanns H. Ewers, *Blood,* Heron Press, 1930.
Florence McClurg Everson and Howard Everson, *Coming of the Dragon Ships,* Dutton, 1931.
Nora Burglon, *Children of the Soil,* Doubleday, 1932.

Also illustrator of seventeen books in Germany, 1922-26, and of Dmitri Merejkowski's *Leonardo da Vinci,* 1931.

OTHER

(Translator and illustrator with I. d'Aulaire) Peter Christen Asbjoernsen and J. E. Moe, *East of the Sun and West of the Moon: Twenty-one Norwegian Folktales,* Viking, 1938.
(Contributor with I. d'Aulaire) Bertha Mahony Miller and Elinor Whitney Field, editors, *Caldecott Medal Books: 1938-1957,* Horn Book, 1957.

SIDELIGHTS: With his wife Ingri, Edgar d'Aulaire wrote and illustrated highly praised children's books and won the 1940 Caldecott Medal. Many of the couple's early books depict the scenery, myths, and folktales of Ingri's native Norway. In later books the artists proceeded to explore larger-than-life figures and heroes of their adopted country, the United States.

Edgar was born in 1898 in Munich, Germany, but grew up in Switzerland. His parents separated when he was six years old, and thereafter he lived alternately with his mother, an American artist, and his father, a well-known Italian painter. At an early age d'Aulaire observed his father's work and decided that he, too, wanted to be an artist.

To please his father d'Aulaire first studied architecture. He then began his art studies in Munich, where he met his future wife, Ingri. When the couple became engaged Edgar visited Norway to meet Ingri's large, hearty family and was inducted into their traditional thirty-mile ski trips. Opting for a modest wedding ceremony in 1925, the d'Aulaires used the money saved to travel to Paris and Florence to continue painting.

While in Europe Edgar illustrated books and exhibited his work in Paris, Berlin, Oslo, and Tunis. In 1929 he and his wife vacationed in the United States and liked the country so much they decided to immigrate, settling first in New York and later on a farm in Connecticut. Initially, the d'Aulaires desired to pursue their artistic careers separately from each other to prevent their marriage from interfering with their work. Edgar specialized in murals and Ingri in children's portraits. Acting on a suggestion from a librarian at the New York Public Library, they worked together on their first picture book for children, *The Magic Rug*, in 1931. With this book they found the perfect way to combine their talents. In describing their individual contributions to the books, Edgar once remarked that Ingri supplied the humor, and Ingri noted that Edgar provided the drama and directed the artistic work.

The next year the d'Aulaires published *Ola*, a popular book about the adventures of a young Norwegian boy during the course of a winter. The title character was so well-liked that they featured him in their next book, *Ola and Blakken and Line, Sine, Trine*, which tells how Ola shoots the giant bird belonging to the trolls of the mountains. In 1935 the d'Aulaires wrote and illustrated *Children of the Northlights*, focusing on a year in the life of two Lapp children. The book was considered the d'Aulaires' most beautifully illustrated, appreciated for its winter landscapes and close-up pictures of children. The pair went on to illustrate other highly regarded books on Scandinavian subjects, including *East of the Sun and West of the Moon*, a collection of Norwegian folk tales, and *Leif the Lucky*, the d'Aulaires' biography of Viking explorer Leif Eriksson.

Meanwhile the d'Aulaires began to shift their attention to the United States by creating books about American heroes. Among the first such efforts was *Abraham Lincoln*, which won the 1940 Caldecott Medal for illustration. Throughout the years the d'Aulaires lavished attention on characters dear to Americans in such books as *Pocahontas*, *Benjamin Franklin*, *Buffalo Bill*, and *Columbus*. Modern critics note that the

***Abraham Lincoln* won the 1939 Caldecott Medal for most distinguished American picture book.** (Text and illustrations by Ingri and Edgar Parin d'Aulaire.)

d'Aulaires tended to idealize America and its celebrated personalities. *Abraham Lincoln* was criticized for omitting the fact that Lincoln had been assassinated, and *Columbus* for depicting Christopher Columbus as a saintly figure. The d'Aulaires' book *The Star Spangled Banner* is now regarded as patriotic propaganda, although when it was published during World War II, its sentiments may have reflected the attitudes of most Americans. In his *Dictionary of Literary Biography* essay on the couple, Hugh Crago decided, "There can be no disputing the historical importance of the d'Aulaires in establishing the validity of the picture book as an art form.... It may well be, though, that they will ultimately be remembered for how well their style and their themes matched the view of America—and childhood—held by the Americans of their time."

In later years the d'Aulaires returned to their early interest in mythic subjects with *Ingri and Edgar Parin d'Aulaire's Book of Greek Myths, Norse Gods and Giants,* and *D'Aulaires' Trolls.* The couple received the Catholic Library Association's Regina Medal for "continued distinguished contribution to children's literature" in 1970.

WORKS CITED:

Crago, Hugh, "Ingri and Edgar Parin d'Aulaire," *Dictionary of Literary Biography,* Volume 22: *American Writers for Children, 1900-1960,* Gale, 1983, pp. 102-110.

FOR MORE INFORMATION SEE:

BOOKS

Children's Literature Review, Volume 21, Gale, 1990.
Fisher, Margery, *Matters of Fact: Aspects of Non-Fiction for Children,* Crowell, 1972.
Hopkins, Lee Bennett, *Books Are by People,* Citation, 1969.
MacCann, Donnarae, and Gloria Woodard, editors, *Cultural Conformity in Books for Children: Further Readings in Racism,* Scarecrow Press, 1977.
Miller, Bertha Mahony, and Elinor Whitney Field, editors, *Caldecott Medal Books: 1938-1957,* Horn Book, 1957.
Twentieth-Century Children's Writers, 2nd edition, St. Martin's, 1983.

PERIODICALS

Book World, January 14, 1968.
Children's Libraries Newsletter (Library Association of Australia), August, 1972.
Commonweal, April 6, 1934.
Cricket, November, 1976.
Horn Book, September-October, 1935; July-August, 1940; December, 1972.
Lion and the Unicorn, summer, 1980.
New York Herald Tribune, October 30, 1956.
New York Herald Tribune Books, October 16, 1932; September 8, 1935; November 15, 1936.
New York Times Book Review, September 27, 1931; October 9, 1932; December 10, 1933; March 25, 1934; October 6, 1935; September 10, 1972.
Washington Post Book World, November 5, 1972.

OBITUARIES:

PERIODICALS

Publishers Weekly, May 23, 1986.

d'AULAIRE, Ingri (Mortenson Parin) 1904-1980

PERSONAL: Surname is pronounced "doh-*lair*"; name originally Ingrid Maartenson; born December 27, 1904, in Kongsberg, Norway; immigrated to United States, 1929, naturalized citizen, 1939; died of cancer, October 24, 1980, in Wilton, CT; daughter of Per (a business executive) and Line (Sandsmark) Maartenson; married Edgar Parin d'Aulaire (an artist and author), July 24, 1925; children: Per Ola, Nils Maarten. *Education:* Attended Kongsberg Junior College, Institute of Arts and Crafts, Oslo, Norway; Hans Hofman School of Art, Munich, Germany; and Academie Scandinave, Academie Gauguin, and Academie Andre L'Hote, all Paris, France. *Hobbies and other interests:* Traveling, walking, skiing, gardening, cooking, playing with children, family.

ADDRESSES: Home—Lia Farm, 74 Mather Rd., Georgetown, CT 06829; (summer) South Royalton, VT 05068.

CAREER: Artist, lecturer, and author and illustrator of children's books; wrote and illustrated books in collaboration with husband, Edgar d'Aulaire, beginning in 1930.

MEMBER: Authors League of America, Scandinavian-American Foundation.

AWARDS, HONORS: American Library Association's Caldecott Medal (jointly with husband) for best illustrated children's book, 1940, for *Abraham Lincoln;* award from Boys Club, 1953, for *Buffalo Bill;* Catholic Library Association Regina Medal, 1970, for "continued distinguished contribution to children's literature"; *D'Aulaires' Trolls* was selected by the *New York Times Book Review* as one of the outstanding books of 1972, and was a National Book Award finalist, 1973; nominated for Hans Christian Andersen Award, 1974.

WRITINGS:

AUTHOR AND ILLUSTRATOR WITH HUSBAND, EDGAR PARIN d'AULAIRE; JUVENILES

The Magic Rug, Doubleday, Doran, 1931.
Ola, Doubleday, Doran, 1932.
Ola and Blakken and Line, Sine, Trine, Doubleday, Doran, 1933, revised edition published as *The Terrible Troll-Bird,* Doubleday, 1976.
The Conquest of the Atlantic, Viking, 1933.
The Lord's Prayer, Doubleday, Doran, 1934.
Children of the Northlights, Viking, 1935, revised edition, 1963.
George Washington: A Biography for Children, Doubleday, Doran, 1936.
Abraham Lincoln, Doubleday, Doran, 1939, revised edition, Doubleday, 1957.
Animals Everywhere, Doubleday, Doran, 1940.
Leif the Lucky, Doubleday, Doran, 1941, revised edition, Doubleday, 1951.
The Star Spangled Banner, Doubleday, Doran, 1942.
Don't Count Your Chicks, Doubleday, Doran, 1943.
Wings for Per, Doubleday, Doran, 1943.
Too Big, Doubleday, Doran, 1945.
Pocahontas, Doubleday, 1946.
Nils, Doubleday, 1948.
Foxie, Doubleday, 1949, revised edition published as *Foxie the Singing Dog,* 1969.

Benjamin Franklin, Doubleday, 1950.
Buffalo Bill, Doubleday, 1952.
The Two Cars, Doubleday, 1955.
Columbus, Doubleday, 1955.
The Magic Meadow, Doubleday, 1958.
Ingri and Edgar Parin d'Aulaire's Book of Greek Myths, Doubleday, 1962.
Norse Gods and Giants, Doubleday, 1967, published as *D'Aulaires' Norse Gods and Giants,* 1986.
D'Aulaires' Trolls, Doubleday, 1972.

OTHER

(Illustrator) Hans Aanrud, *Sidsel Longskirt: A Girl of Norway,* Winston, 1935.
(Illustrator) Hans Aanrud, *Solve Suntrap,* Winston, 1936.
(Translator and illustrator with husband, E. P. d'Aulaire) Peter Christen Asbjoernsen and J. E. Moe, *East of the Sun and West of the Moon: Twenty-one Norwegian Folktales,* Viking, 1938.
(Illustrator) Dikken Zwilgmeyer, *Johnny Blossom,* Pilgrim Press, 1948.
(Contributor with E. P. d'Aulaire) Bertha Mahony Miller and Elinor Whitney Field, editors, *Caldecott Medal Books: 1938-1957,* Horn Book, 1957.

SIDELIGHTS: Ingri d'Aulaire was an acclaimed author and illustrator of children's books, most of them created jointly with her husband, Edgar Parin d'Aulaire. Born in Kongsberg, Norway, the youngest in a large, funloving family, Ingri grew up enjoying the outdoors and reading and listening to traditional Scandinavian folktales and legends. The husband-and-wife team frequently drew on Ingri's childhood memories and familiarity with Nordic stories and scenery in their books, among them *Ola, Ola and Blakken and Line, Sine, Trine, Children of the Northlights, Leif the Lucky, Norse Gods and Giants,* and *D'Aulaires' Trolls.*

D'Aulaire knew as a young girl that she wanted to become an artist. When she was fifteen, the renowned Norwegian painter Harriet Backer viewed her drawings and encouraged her to pursue art as a career. D'Aulaire studied academics at Kongsberg Junior College, then attended the Arts and Crafts Institute in Oslo, the Hans Hofman School of Art in Munich, Germany, and art schools in Paris.

In Munich Ingri met her future husband and artistic partner, Edgar Parin d'Aulaire. After their marriage in 1925, they continued painting and studying in Paris, France. In 1929, after a vacation in the United States, the couple decided to make America their permanent home. They settled first in New York and later moved to rural Connecticut, where they ran a farm and collaborated on books for children.

The d'Aulaires' first book, *The Magic Rug,* was written at the suggestion of a librarian at the New York Public Library. Thereafter the couple worked together to produce numerous picture books, beginning with Scandinavian subjects and later focusing on American heroes. The couple received the Caldecott Medal in 1940 for illustrating *Abraham Lincoln,* their biography of America's Civil War president. In an article about the couple in *Caldecott Medal Books,* the pair commented on their respective contributions to their work; Ingri mentioned her husband's flair for drama and Edgar cited his wife's sense of humor. Ingri took a strong interest in children, initially concentrating in her artwork upon children's portraits, and critics credit her with the strong understanding of children evidenced in the d'Aulaires' books. Reviewers of *Children of the Northern Lights* attributed the fine landscapes and children's portraits to Ingri's particular talents.

One of the d'Aulaires' more popular books, *Ola,* relates the wintertime adventures of a Norwegian boy. "The first word that comes to mind for 'Ola' is ingratiating," a reviewer remarked in *New York Herald-Tribune Books* in 1932. "The d'Aulaires paint from full hearts and make friends thus for their Norway," the critic added. American children so liked the title character that the d'Aulaires included him in their next story, *Ola and Blakken and Line, Sine, Trine,* which tells how he shoots the giant bird belonging to the mountain trolls. When the d'Aulaires' first son was born, they thought the baby resembled the fictional character and named him Per Ola.

The d'Aulaires won high praise for their simple, childlike illustrations. Noting the youthful imagination in their artwork, *Commonweal* contributor G. N. Schuster remarked, "If youngsters could draw and color as well as the d'Aulaires, they themselves might make just such pictures." Critics also appreciated the couple's efforts to accurately portray different regions, from the Virginia of U.S. President George Washington to the prairie of Western showman Buffalo Bill. Avid campers and travelers, the d'Aulaires spent time in northern Africa, Europe, and the United States, and succeeded in capturing the scenery of these places in their illustrations.

WORKS CITED:

Commonweal, April 6, 1934, p. 642.
Miller, Bertha Mahony, and Elinor Whitney Field, editors, *Caldecott Medal Books, 1938-1957,* Horn Book, 1957, pp. 55-62.
New York Herald-Tribune Books, October 16, 1932, p. 7.

FOR MORE INFORMATION SEE:

BOOKS

Children's Literature Review, Volume 21, Gale, 1990.
Dictionary of Literary Biography, Volume 22: *American Writers for Children, 1900-1960,* Gale, 1983.
Fisher, Margery, *Matters of Fact: Aspects of Non-Fiction for Children,* Crowell, 1972.
Hopkins, Lee Bennett, *Books Are by People,* Citation, 1969.
MacCann, Donnarae, and Gloria Woodard, editors, *Cultural Conformity in Books for Children: Further Readings in Racism,* Scarecrow Press, 1977.

PERIODICALS

Book World, January 14, 1968.
Children's Libraries Newsletter (Library Association of Australia), August, 1972.
Cricket, November, 1976.
Horn Book, September-October, 1935; July-August, 1940; December, 1972.
Lion and the Unicorn, summer, 1980.
New York Herald Tribune, October 30, 1956.
New York Herald Tribune Books, September 8, 1935; November 15, 1936.
New York Times Book Review, September 27, 1931; October 9, 1932; December 10, 1933; March 25, 1934; October 6, 1935; September 10, 1972.
Washington Post Book World, November 5, 1972.

OBITUARIES:

PERIODICALS

New York Times, October 28, 1980.
Publishers Weekly, November 14, 1980.

*   *   *

de BONO, Edward 1933-

PERSONAL: Born May 19, 1933, in Malta; son of Joseph Edward (a physician) and Josephine (maiden name, Burns) de Bono. *Education:* Royal University of Malta, B.Sc., 1953, M.D., 1955; Oxford University, M.A., 1957, D.Phil., 1961; Cambridge University, Ph.D., 1963. *Hobbies and other interests:* Polo, canoeing (paddled 112 miles from Oxford to London non-stop while at Oxford University), and games design.

ADDRESSES: Home—11 Warkworth St., Cambridge, England. *Agent*—Michael Horniman, A. P. Watt, 26/28 Bedford Row, London WC1R 4HL, England.

CAREER: Oxford University, Oxford, England, research assistant, 1957-60, lecturer, 1960-61; University of London, London, England, lecturer, 1961-63; Cambridge University, Cambridge, England, assistant director of research, 1963—. Research associate, Harvard University, Cambridge, MA, 1965-66. Lecturer to industry and education groups on research cognitive processes. Inventor; designer of the L-game. Honorary director and founding member of Cognitive Research Trust.

MEMBER: Medical Research Society.

AWARDS, HONORS: Rhodes Scholar.

WRITINGS:

The Use of Lateral Thinking, J. Cape, 1967, published as *New Think: The Use of Lateral Thinking in the Generation of Ideas,* Basic Books, 1967.
The Five-Day Course in Thinking, Basic Books, 1967.
The Mechanism of Mind, Simon & Schuster, 1969.
Lateral Thinking: Creation Step by Step, Harper, 1970 (published in England as *Lateral Thinking: A Textbook of Creativity,* Ward, Lock, 1970).
The Dog Exercising Machine, J. Cape, 1970, Simon & Schuster, 1971.
(Editor) *Technology Today,* Routledge & Kegan Paul, 1971.
Lateral Thinking for Management: A Handbook of Creativity, American Management Association, 1971.
Practical Thinking: Four Ways to Be Right, Five Ways to Be Wrong, Five Ways to Understand, J. Cape, 1971.
Children Solve Problems, Penguin, 1972, Harper, 1974.
PO: A Device for Successful Thinking, Simon & Schuster, 1972 (published in England as *PO: Beyond Yes and No,* Penguin Education, 1973, reprinted, International Center for Creative Thinking, 1990).
Think Tank, Think Tank Corp., 1973.
(Editor) *Eureka: A History of Inventions,* Holt, 1974.
Teaching Thinking, Maurice Temple Smith, 1976.
The Greatest Thinkers, Putnam, 1976.
Wordpower: An Illustrated Dictionary of Vital Words, Harper, 1977.

EDWARD de BONO

The Case of the Disappearing Elephant (juvenile; illustrated by George Craig), Dent, 1977.
Opportunities: A Handbook of Business Opportunity Search, Associated Business Programmes (London), 1978.
The Happiness Purpose, Maurice Temple Smith, 1978.
Future Positive, Maurice Temple Smith, 1979.
Atlas of Management Thinking, Maurice Temple Smith, 1981.
De Bono's Thinking Course, B.B.C. Publications, 1982.
Learn-to-Think, Capra/New, 1982.
Tactics: The Art and Science of Success, Collins, 1985.
Conflicts: A Better Way to Resolve Them, Harrap, 1985.
Six Thinking Hats: An Essential Approach to Business Management from the Creator of Lateral Thinking, Penguin, 1985, published as *The Power of Focused Thinking: Six Thinking Hats,* International Center for Creative Thinking, 1990.
CoRT Thinking Program: CoRT 1-Breadth, Pergamon, 1987.
Letters to Thinkers: Further Thoughts on Lateral Thinking, Harrap, 1987.
De Bono's Thinking Course, Facts On File, 1988.
Masterthinker II: Six Thinking Hats, International Center for Creative Thinking, 1988.
Masterthinker, International Center for Creative Thinking, 1990.
Masterthinker's Handbook, International Center for Creative Thinking, 1990.

Also author of *Decision Mate,* International Center for Creative Thinking.

OTHER

The Greatest Thinkers (thirteen-part television series), WDR (Germany), 1980.
DeBono's Thinking Course (ten-part television series), British Broadcasting Corporation, 1982.
Sixty Minutes to Super Thinking (cassette recording), Audio Renaissance, 1988.

Also author of *How to Change Ideas: Your Own* (recording), J. Norton Publishers. Writer of television items and of feature stories for *Sunday Mirror, Telegraph Machine, Nova, Oz, Mind Alive, Science Journal, Sunday Times, Fashion,* and *Honey.* Contributor of articles to professional journals.

SIDELIGHTS: Edward de Bono is a medical doctor, philosopher, and student of thinking who has written many books on the subject for adults. He has identified two kinds of thinking: lateral thinking, which is careful and organized, and creative thinking, which is more spontaneous. *Lateral Thinking: A Textbook of Creativity* suggests ways in which people involved in business can improve their performance on the job by using creative thinking.

To show that children and adults use different kinds of thinking when solving problems, de Bono collected nearly two hundred drawings by children that reveal their different approaches to problem solving in the book *Children Solve Problems.* The children were asked to invent a sleep machine, a machine to weigh elephants, and systems for building a house and then a rocket quickly. They also were asked to think of ways to improve the human body and ways to help the police. The book compares how the children and the adults arrived at their solutions. The author feels that the kind of training most students receive in grade school discourages their creativity, which he thinks should be encouraged instead.

Writing in the *Library Journal,* Suzanne Hildenbrand comments that *Children Solve Problems* does not present a complete study of how people learn to think, but calls the drawings "quite charming." Critics also value de Bono's *The Case of the Disappearing Elephant,* illustrated by George Craig, and *Eureka: The History of Inventions* for their illustrations.

WORKS CITED:

Hildenbrand, Suzanne, review of *Children Solve Problems,* *Library Journal,* May 1, 1974, p. 1297.

FOR MORE INFORMATION SEE:

PERIODICALS

Realities (France), August, 1967.
Realities (United States), November, 1967.
Times Literary Supplement, March 30, 1973.

*   *   *

DEMI
  See HITZ, Demi

DENTON, Kady MacDonald

ADDRESSES: c/o McElderry Books, 866 Third Ave., New York, NY 10022.

CAREER: Children's book author and illustrator.

WRITINGS:

SELF-ILLUSTRATED CHILDREN'S BOOKS

The Picnic, E. P. Dutton, 1988.
Granny Is a Darling, Margaret K. McElderry, 1988.
Dorothy's Dream, Margaret K. McElderry, 1989.
The Christmas Boot, Little, Brown, 1990.
Janet's Horses, Walker, 1990.

ILLUSTRATOR

Pam Zinnemann-Hope, *Find Your Coat, Ned,* Margaret K. McElderry, 1987.
Hope, *Let's Play Ball, Ned,* Margaret. K. McElderry, 1987.
David Booth, editor, *Til All the Stars Have Fallen,* Kids Can Press, 1989.
Ann Pilling, *Before I Go to Sleep: A Collection of Bible Stories, Poems, and Prayers for Children,* Crown, 1990.

FOR MORE INFORMATION SEE:

PERIODICALS

Horn Book, January-February, 1991.

* * *

DOWNEY, Fairfax D(avis) 1893-1990

OBITUARY NOTICE—See index for *SATA* sketch: Born November 28, 1893, in Salt Lake City, UT; died May 30, 1990, in New Hampshire. Editor, journalist, poet, and author. Beginning his career as a journalist with the *Kansas City Star* and *New York Tribune,* Downey served in both world wars and later became known for his military histories and biographies. Among his books are *The Grande Turke: Suleyman the Magnificent* and *Burton, Arabian Nights Adventurer;* the children's historical novels *War Horse* and *Guns for General Washington;* and collections of light verse, including *Young Enough to Know Better.* Downey also edited volumes such as *My Kingdom for a Horse.*

OBITUARIES AND OTHER SOURCES:

BOOKS

International Authors and Writers Who's Who, 9th edition, [and] *International Who's Who in Poetry,* 6th edition, Melrose, 1982.
The Writers Directory: 1988-1990, St. James Press, 1988.

PERIODICALS

New York Times, June 6, 1990.

* * *

DURELL, Ann 1930-

PERSONAL: Born September 20, 1930, in Belleplain, NJ; daughter of Thomas J. and Marian (Dudley) Durrell; married James T. McCrory, May 8, 1982. *Education:* Mt. Hol-

yoke College, B.A., 1952; attended University of St. Andrews (Scotland). *Politics:* Democrat. *Religion:* Presbyterian.

CAREER: Junior Literary Guild, New York City, editor in chief, 1960-62; Holt, Rinehart & Winston, New York City, children's book editor, 1962-69; E. P. Dutton, Inc., New York City, publisher and vice president of children's books, 1969-87; editor at large, 1987—; writer.

MEMBER: American Library Association, Children's Book Council (president), National Council of Teachers of English.

WRITINGS:

Holly River Secret, illustrated by Ursula Koering, Doubleday, 1956.
My Heart's in the Highlands, Doubleday, 1958.
Lost Bear, Doubleday, 1959.

EDITOR

Just for Fun: A Collection of Original Humorous Stories, Dutton, 1977.
Mary Bruce Sharon, *Scenes from Childhood,* Dutton, 1978.
Judith M. Goldberger, *The Looking Glass Factor,* Dutton, 1979.
Delores Beckman, *My Own Private Sky,* Dutton, 1980.
Eleanor Cameron, *Beyond Silence,* Dutton, 1980.
Judy Malloy, *Bad Thad,* illustrated by Martha Alexander, Dutton, 1980.
Marjorie and Mitchell Sharmat, *The Day I Was Born,* illustrated by Diane Dawson, Dutton, 1980.
Jovial Bob Stine and Jane Stine, *The Sick of Being Sick Book,* illustrations by Carol Nicklaus, Dutton, 1980.
Nathan Zimelman, *Positively No Pets Allowed,* illustrated by Pamela Johnson, Dutton, 1980.
Robert L. Crowe, *Tyler Toad and the Thunder,* illustrated by Kay Chorao, Dutton, 1980.
Charlotte Herman, *My Mother Didn't Kiss Me Good-Night,* illustrated by Bruce Degan, Dutton, 1980.
Sydney Taylor, *Danny Loves a Holiday,* illustrated by Gail Owens, Dutton, 1980.
The Diane Goode Book of American Folk Tales and Songs, illustrated by Diane Goode, Dutton, 1989.
(With Marilyn Sachs) *The Big Book for Peace,* Dutton Children's Books, 1990.

* * *

EKWENSI, C. O. D.
See EKWENSI, Cyprian (Odiatu Duaka)

* * *

EKWENSI, Cyprian (Odiatu Duaka) 1921-
(C. O. D. Ekwensi)

PERSONAL: Born September 26, 1921, in Minna, Nigeria; son of Ogbuefi David Duaka and Uso Agnes Ekwensi; married Eunice Anyiwo; children: five. *Education:* Attended Achimota College, Ghana, and Ibadan University; received B.A.; further study at Chelsea School of Pharmacy, London, and University of Iowa, Iowa City. *Hobbies and other interests:* Hunting game, swimming, photography, motoring, and weightlifting.

ADDRESSES: Home—12 Hillview, Independence Layout, P.O. Box 317, Enugu, Nigeria.

CAREER: Novelist and writer of short stories and stories for children. Igbodi College, Lagos, Nigeria, lecturer in biology, chemistry, and English, 1947-49; School of Pharmacy, Lagos, lecturer in pharmacognosy and pharmaceutics, 1949-56; pharmacist superintendent for Nigerian Medical Services, 1956-57; head of features, Nigerian Broadcasting Corp., 1957-61; Federal Ministry of Information, Lagos, director of information, 1961-66; chairman of Bureau for External Publicity during Biafran secession, 1967-69, and director of an independent Biafran radio station; chemist for a plastics firm in Enugu, Nigeria; managing director of Star Printing & Publishing Co. (publishers of *Daily Star*), 1975-79; managing director of Niger Eagle Publishing Co., 1980-81; managing director of Ivory Trumpet Publishing Co., 1981-83. Owner of East Niger Chemists and East Niger Trading Company. Chairman of East Central State Library Board, 1972-75, and Hospitals Management Board, 1986. Newspaper consultant to *Weekly Trumpet* and *Daily News* of Anambra State and to *Weekly Eagle* of Imo State, 1980-83; consultant on information to the executive office of the president; consultant to Federal Ministry of Information; public relations consultant.

MEMBER: P.E.N., Society of Nigerian Authors, Pharmaceutical Society of Great Britain, Institute of Public Relations (London), Institute of Public Relations (Nigeria; fellow).

AWARDS, HONORS: Dag Hammarskjold International Prize for Literary Merit, 1969.

WRITINGS:

(Under name C. O. D. Ekwensi) *When Love Whispers* (novella), Tabansi Bookshop (Onitsha, Nigeria), 1947.
People of the City (novel), Andrew Dakers, 1954, Northwestern University Press, 1967, revised edition, Fawcett, 1969.
Jagua Nana (novel), Hutchinson, 1961, Fawcett, 1969, Heinemann, 1975.
Burning Grass (novel), Heinemann, 1962.
Beautiful Feathers (novel), Hutchinson, 1963.
The Rainmaker and Other Stories (short story collection), African Universities Press, 1965.
Lokotown and Other Stories (short story collection), Heinemann, 1966.
Iska, Hutchinson, 1966.
The Restless City and Christmas Gold, Heinemann, 1975.
Survive the Peace, Heinemann, 1976.
(Editor) *Festac Anthology of Nigerian Writing,* Festac, 1977.
Divided We Stand (novel), Fourth Dimension Publishers, 1980.
Motherless Baby (novella), Fourth Dimension Publishers, 1980.

Also author of *Jagua Nana's Daughter,* 1986, *For a Roll of Parchment,* 1987, and *Behind the Convent Wall,* 1987.

FOR YOUNG PEOPLE

(Under name C. O. D. Ekwensi) *Ikolo the Wrestler and Other Ibo Tales,* Thomas Nelson, 1947.
(Under name C. O. D. Ekwensi) *The Leopard's Claw,* Thomas Nelson, 1950.
The Drummer Boy, Cambridge University Press, 1960.

The Passport of Mallam Ilia, Cambridge University Press, 1960.
An African Night's Entertainment (folklore), African Universities Press, 1962.
Yaba Roundabout Murder (short novel), Tortoise Series Books (Lagos, Nigeria), 1962.
The Great Elephant-Bird, Thomas Nelson, 1965.
Juju Rock, African Universities Press, 1966.
The Boa Suitor, Thomas Nelson, 1966.
Trouble in Form Six, Cambridge University Press, 1966.
Coal Camp Boy, Longman, 1971.
Samankwe in the Strange Forest, Longman, 1973.
The Rainbow Tinted Scarf and Other Stories (collection), Evans Africa Library, 1975.
Samankwe and the Highway Robbers, Evans Africa Library, 1975.

OTHER

Writer of plays and scripts for BBC radio and television, Radio Nigeria, and other communication outlets. Contributor of stories, articles, and reviews to magazines and newspapers in Nigeria and England, including *West African Review,* London *Times, Black Orpheus, Flamingo,* and *Sunday Post.*

SIDELIGHTS: "Cyprian Ekwensi is the earliest and most prolific of the socially realistic Nigerian novelists," according to Martin Tucker in his *Africa in Modern Literature: A Survey of Contemporary Writing in English.* "His first writings were mythological fragments and folk tales. From these African materials he turned to the city and its urban problems, which he now feels are the major issues confronting his people." Reviewing Cyprian Ekwensi's *Beautiful Feathers* in *Critique: Studies in Modern Fiction,* John F. Povey writes: "Ekwensi is interesting because he is concerned with the present, with the violence of the new Lagos slums, the dishonesty of the new native politicians. Other Nigerian novelists have sought their material from the past, the history of missionaries and British administration as in Chinua Achebe's books, the schoolboy memoirs of Onuora Nzekwu. Ekwensi faces the difficult task of catching the present tone of Africa, changing at a speed that frighteningly destroys the old certainties. In describing this world, Ekwensi has gradually become a significant writer."

Ekwensi states that his life in government and quasi-government organizations like the Nigerian Broadcasting Corporation has prevented him from expressing any strong political opinions, but adds, "I am as much a nationalist as the heckler standing on the soap-box, with the added advantage of objectivity." During the late 1960s Biafran war, during which the eastern region of Biafra seceded temporarily from the rest of Nigeria, Ekwensi visited the United States more than once to help raise money for Biafra and to purchase radio equipment for the independent Biafran radio station of which he was director. He has also traveled in western Europe.

Several of Ekwensi's novels have been translated into other languages, including Russian, Italian, German, Serbo-Croatian, Danish, and French. His novellas have been used primarily in schools as supplementary readers.

WORKS CITED:

Critique: Studies in Modern Fiction, October, 1965.
Tucker, Martin, *Africa in Modern Literature: A Survey of Contemporary Writing in English,* Ungar, 1967.

FOR MORE INFORMATION SEE:

BOOKS

Contemporary Literary Criticism, Volume 4, Gale, 1975.

PERIODICALS

Books Abroad, autumn, 1967.
Times Literary Supplement, June 4, 1964.

*   *   *

EMECHETA, (Florence Onye) Buchi 1944-

PERSONAL: Born July 21, 1944, in Yaba, Lagos, Nigeria; daughter of Jeremy Nwabudike (a railway worker and molder) and Alice Ogbanje (Okwuekwu) Emecheta; married Sylvester Onwordi, 1960 (separated, 1966); children: Florence, Sylvester, Jake, Christy, Alice. *Education:* University of London, B.Sc. (with honors), 1972. *Religion:* Anglican. *Hobbies and other interests:* Gardening, attending the theatre, listening to music, reading.

ADDRESSES: Home—7 Briston Grove, Crouch End, London N8 9EX, England.

CAREER: British Museum, London, England, library officer, 1965-69; Inner London Education Authority, London, youth worker and sociologist, 1969-76; community worker, Camden, NJ, 1976-78. Writer and lecturer, 1972—. Visiting professor at several universities throughout the United States, including Pennsylvania State University, University of California, Los Angeles, and University of Illinois at Urbana-Champaign, 1979; senior resident fellow and visiting professor of English, University of Calabar, Nigeria, 1980-81; lecturer, Yale University, 1982, London University, 1982—; fellow, London University, 1986. Proprietor, Ogwugwu Afor Publishing Company, 1982-83. Member of Home Secretary's Advisory Council on Race, 1979—, and of Arts Council of Great Britain, 1982-83.

AWARDS, HONORS: Jock Campbell Award for literature by new or unregarded talent from Africa or the Caribbean, *New Statesman,* 1978; selected as the Best Black British Writer, 1978, and one of the Best British Young Writers, 1983.

WRITINGS:

In the Ditch, Barrie & Jenkins, 1972.
Second-Class Citizen (novel), Allison & Busby, 1974, Braziller, 1975.
The Bride Price: A Novel (paperback published as *The Bride Price: Young Ibo Girl's Love; Conflict of Family and Tradition*), Braziller, 1976.
The Slave Girl: A Novel, Braziller, 1977.
The Joys of Motherhood: A Novel, Braziller, 1979.
Destination Biafra: A Novel, Schocken, 1982.
Naira Power (novelette directed principally to Nigerian readers), Macmillan, 1982.
Double Yoke (novel), Schocken, 1982.
The Rape of Shavi (novel), Ogwugwu Afor, 1983, Braziller, 1985.
Adah's Story: A Novel, Allison & Busby, 1983.
Head above Water (autobiography), Ogwugwu Afor, 1984, Collins, 1986.
A Kind of Marriage (novelette), Macmillan, 1987.
The Family (novel), Braziller, 1990.

Gwendolen (novel), Collins, 1990.

JUVENILE

Titch the Cat (based on story by daughter, Alice Emecheta), Allison & Busby, 1979.
Nowhere to Play (based on story by daughter, Christy Emecheta), Schocken, 1980.
The Moonlight Bride, Oxford University Press in association with University Press, 1981.
The Wrestling Match, Oxford University Press in association with University Press, 1981, Braziller, 1983.
Family Bargain (publication for schools), British Broadcasting Corp., 1987.

OTHER

(Author of introduction and commentary) Maggie Murray, *Our Own Freedom* (book of photographs), Sheba Feminist (London), 1981.
A Kind of Marriage (teleplay; produced by BBC-TV), Macmillan (London), 1987.

Also author of teleplays *Tanya, a Black Woman,* produced by BBC-TV, and *The Juju Landlord.* Contributor to journals, including *New Statesman, Times Literary Supplement,* and *Guardian.*

SIDELIGHTS: Though she has lived in London since 1962, Buchi Emecheta has become one of Nigeria's most recognizable female writers. She enjoys particular popularity in Great Britain and has gathered an appreciative audience in America as well. Emecheta is best known for her historical novels set in Nigeria. Depicting the clash of cultures and the impact of Western values upon Nigeria's farming traditions and customs, Emecheta's work is strongly autobiographical. Many of her books concern the changing roles of African women: the sufferings they have for years endured as second-class citizens in a traditional, male-dominated society, and the recent opportunities for growth provided by Africa's new openness towards women. Most recently, Emecheta has begun writing children's books. Her first two, *Titch the Cat* and *Nowhere to Play,* are based on stories by two of her daughters.

Born to Ibo parents in the small village of Yaba, Nigeria, Emecheta related in a *Voice Literary Supplement* interview how her aunt sparked her interest in storytelling: "She was very old and almost blind, and she would gather the young children around her after dinner and tell stories to us. She would start with the 'new' children—those of us who came from the city—and say 'Oh yes, you, Buchi the daughter of Emecheta, whose great-grandfather murdered the first European that came to this place, whose grandparents did this, whose parents did that; now, you listen to my song.' Her song was a story. When she would finish the song she would pant and say 'Oh, and I have run all the way from the land of seven dead people to come and tell you the story.' And do you know when I was five I used to really believe my [aunt] had been there? Because I would see her with her stick, puffing, and everyone gathered around would say to her, 'Welcome.' I thought she was so clever to have come all that way to tell us her story. I thought to myself, 'No life could be more important than this.' So when people asked me what I wanted to do when I grew up I told them I wanted to be a story-teller—which is what I'm doing now."

Emecheta's early years were often filled with unhappiness. She was orphaned and lived with foster parents who often mistreated her. At sixteen, she wed a man to whom she had been contracted to marry since the age of eleven; and by the time she was twenty-two, Emecheta was the mother of two sons and three daughters. She followed her husband to London, where she endured poor living conditions, including one-room apartments without heat or hot water, to help finance his education. The marriage finally ended when her husband read and then burned the manuscript of her first book.

While she supported her five children on the meager income provided by public assistance and occasional cleaning jobs, Emecheta continued to write in the mornings before her children arose. Her early books recount the hardships she endured under the domination of her first husband. Emecheta told Bray, "When I sat down to write those books, I was so angry! But do you know, when I finished them, I was laughing. My husband was not a bad man. He was just a traditional man who could not accept the woman I had become."

Emecheta's works have continued to display Nigerian culture and to challenge the traditional African attitudes toward women. "My characters are not weak," she told Bray. "In my books, the women speak—even from the grave." No different are her more recent books for children, where Emecheta retains the strong female perspective evident in her adult novels. "What I am trying to do is get our profession back. Women are born storytellers. We keep the history. We are the true conservatives—we conserve things and we never forget. What I do is not clever or unusual. It is what my aunt and my grandmother did, and their mothers before them."

WORKS CITED:

Bray, Rosemary, "Nefertiti's New Clothes," *Voice Literary Supplement,* June, 1982, pp. 13-14.

FOR MORE INFORMATION SEE:

BOOKS

Contemporary Literary Criticism, Gale, Volume 14, 1980; Volume 28, 1984.
Emecheta, Buchi, *Head above Water* (autobiography), Ogwugwu Afor, 1984, Collins, 1986.
Zell, Hans M., and others, *A New Reader's Guide to African Literature,* 2nd revised and expanded edition, Holmes & Meier, 1983.

PERIODICALS

African Literature Today, Number 3, 1983.
Atlantic, May, 1976.
Black Scholar, November/December, 1985; March/April, 1986.
Library Journal, September 1, 1975; April 1, 1976; January 15, 1978; May 1, 1979.
Listener, July 19, 1979.
Los Angeles Times, October 16, 1983; March 6, 1985; January 16, 1990.
Ms., January, 1976; July, 1984; March, 1985.
New Statesman, June 25, 1976; October 14, 1977; June 2, 1978; April 27, 1979.
New Yorker, May 17, 1976; January 9, 1978; July 2, 1979; April 23, 1984; April 22, 1985.
New York Times, February 23, 1985; June 2, 1990.
New York Times Book Review, September 14, 1975; November 11, 1979; January 27, 1980; February 27, 1983; May 5, 1985; April 29, 1990.

Times Literary Supplement, August 11, 1972; January 31, 1975; June 11, 1976; February 26, 1982; February 3, 1984; February 27, 1987; April 20, 1990.
Washington Post Book World, May 13, 1979; April 12, 1981; September 5, 1982; September 25, 1983; March 30, 1985.
World Literature Today, spring, 1977; summer, 1977; spring, 1978; winter, 1979; spring, 1980; winter, 1983; autumn, 1984; winter, 1985.

* * *

ESSRIG, Harry 1912-

PERSONAL: Born August 16, 1912, in Safed, Palestine; immigrated to United States, 1920; son of Isaac and Hannah (maiden name, Trovitz) Essrig; married Rose Baskin, August 14, 1946; children: Miriam, Ronald. *Education:* Columbia University, B.S., 1932; Jewish Theological Seminary of America, teacher's certificate, 1934; Hebrew Union College, M.H.L., 1940; University of Michigan, Ph.D., 1957.

ADDRESSES: Home—1943 Westridge Terrace Rd., Los Angeles, CA. *Office*—11960 Sunset Blvd., Los Angeles, CA.

CAREER: Ordained rabbi, 1940; Hillel director, University of Chicago, Chicago, IL, 1940-42, Harvard University, Cambridge, MA, 1946-47, Massachusetts Institute of Technology, Cambridge, 1946-47; Temple Emanuel, Grand Rapids, MI, rabbi, 1947-64; University Synagogue, Los Angeles, CA, rabbi, 1964—. Visiting instructor in education, Hebrew Union College, 1948-50; director, Union of American Hebrew Congregations, Great lakes Council, 1955-59; psychotherapy and counseling intern, Merrill-Palmer Institute, 1962-64. *Military service:* U.S. Marine Corps, during World War II; assistant staff chaplain.

MEMBER: American Association of Marriage Counselors, American Psychological Association.

AWARDS, HONORS: D.D., Hebrew Union College, 1965.

WRITINGS:

The Rabbi's Corner: A Collection of Weekly Columns, 1956-1960, Temple Emmanuel, 1961.
(With Abraham Segal) *Israel Today* (juvenile; illustrated by Robert Sugar), Union of American Hebrew Congregations, 1964, 2nd revised edition, 1977.
(With A. Segal) *Israel: A Course on the Jewish State* (based on *Israel Today*), Union of American Hebrew Congregations, 1971.

Contributor to *One America,* 1962, and of articles to religious journals.

* * *

FERGUSON, Sarah (Margaret) 1959-
(Sarah, Duchess of York)

PERSONAL: Born October 15, 1959, in London, England; daughter of Ronald Ivor (in the military) and Susan Fitzherbert Wright Ferguson; married Prince Andrew (a naval officer), July 23, 1986; children: Beatrice, Eugenie. *Education:* Attended Queen's Secretarial College.

ADDRESSES: Home—Buckingham Palace, London SW1, England.

CAREER: Worked for various public relations and publishing firms in London, England.

WRITINGS:

Budgie the Little Helicopter, illustrated by John Richardson, Simon & Shuster, 1989.
Budgie at Bendick's Point, illustrated by John Richardson, Simon & Shuster, 1989.

SIDELIGHTS: As a girl growing up in the village of Sunninghill near Ascot, England, Sarah Ferguson never dreamed that she would eventually marry a prince and live in Buckingham Palace. On July 23, 1986, however, that's exactly what happened when Sarah wed Britain's Prince Andrew and became the Duchess of York in a ceremony televised around the world. Although she did not grow up in the limelight like her new husband, Sarah assumed her role as a royal bride with gusto, emerging as one of the most colorful and controversial members of England's royal family.

Sarah Ferguson and her sister Jane spent much of their childhood at Major Ferguson's family home, Dummer Down House. It was there that both girls took up riding and attended the Daneshill School at Basingstoke. The Fergusons' placid world was shattered in 1972 when Susan Ferguson ran off with Argentine polo player Hector Barrantes. As a result, Sarah and Jane were raised largely by their father. By

The Duchess of York, Sarah Ferguson, and her daughter Princess Beatrice.

all accounts, the girls maintained a happy and cheerful attitude throughout what was a difficult adolescent experience.

Major Ferguson eventually remarried, and Sarah warmly welcomed her stepmother Susan Deptford into the family. At the same time, Sarah attended Hurst Lodge, a boarding school near Ascot. While attending Hurst Lodge, Sarah was an average student who excelled at sports, especially swimming, riding, and tennis. Sarah's easy manner and sense of humor made her popular with her fellow students, who elected her head girl during her senior year.

After graduating from Hurst Lodge at age sixteen, Sarah visited her mother in Argentina. Upon her return, she enrolled in the Queen's Secretarial College in Kensington with her friend Charlotte Eden. During the nine-month course, Sarah took classes in typing, shorthand, bookkeeping and cooking, but graduated at the bottom of her class due to a strong interest in skiing, tennis, and parties.

The years following Sarah's graduation from Queen's College were full of traveling and odd jobs with a variety of London public relations firms and art galleries. Sarah also became part of the "Sloan Rangers" social set which included Diana Spencer (who would go on to marry Prince Charles and become the Princess of Wales in 1981). Sarah and Diana became good friends, and Sarah became a frequent guest at Buckingham Palace. In 1985, while working for a Swiss graphic arts publisher, Sarah was asked by Diana to be Prince Andrew's date during Royal Ascot Week. She accepted and had a wonderful time. More dates followed and, after a very secretive courtship, Andrew asked Sarah to marry him. She said yes and the two were married in a lavish ceremony in Westminster Abbey.

Marrying royalty did not stop Sarah from working. She continued to keep busy in the publishing field until the firm she worked for went out of business. Not content to be idle for long, Sarah became more involved with charities and royal duties. In 1988, she gave birth to her first child, Beatrice, all the while maintaining a busy schedule which included writing two children's books. About this time, Sarah came under attack from the press over her lifestyle and personal appearance. Sarah responded to the attacks with candor, defending her right to live her life as she saw fit.

Part of the criticism leveled at Sarah concerned the publication of *Budgie the Little Helicopter* and *Budgie at Bendick's Point.* The books sold well, both in England and abroad. Some critics attacked the stories, however, labelling them simplistic and full of stereotyped characters. Other critics claimed that the books only sold because a member of the royal family had written them. Once again, Sarah defied convention by giving interviews and appearing on television to defend her work. The results of her actions were mixed, and the press stepped up its attack on Sarah's behavior.

Since early 1990, Buckingham Palace has made a concerted effort to repair Sarah's tarnished image. She has made more public appearances and supported more charitable causes. Her popularity has been helped somewhat by the birth of a second daughter, Eugenie, in March of 1990. Always open about herself, Sarah concedes that she still has a lot to learn about being a royal. In an interview with Ingrid Seward of *Woman's Day,* Sarah stated: "I'm a newcomer. I try very hard to learn the right way and to do what is best for the family. . . . I think the main thing about everything we do . . .

Sarah Ferguson's courtship and marriage to Prince Andrew made her an international celebrity.

is to improve public awareness—whether it's charity work, helping the whales or helping the environment."

WORKS CITED:

Seward, Ingrid, "Fergie at 30," *Woman's Day,* October 24, 1989, p. 52.

FOR MORE INFORMATION SEE:

BOOKS

King, Norman, *Two Royal Women,* Wynwood, 1989.
Morton, Andrew, *Duchess: An Intimate Portrait of Sarah, Duchess of York,* Contemporary Books, 1988.
Warwick, Christopher, and Valerie Garner, *Their Royal Highnesses, The Duke and Duchess of York,* Sidgewick and Jackson, 1986.

PERIODICALS

Good Housekeeping, April, 1987.
Maclean's, July 24, 1989.
Majesty, February, 1990.
McCall's, June, 1986.
Newsweek, December 4, 1989.
People Weekly, August 4, 1986; November 20, 1989.
Redbook, September, 1989.
Woman's Day, October 24, 1989.

FIAMMENGHI, Gioia 1929-

PERSONAL: Given name is pronounced Joya, and surname Fya-men-gi (hard "g"); born September 29, 1929, in New York, NY; daughter of Luigi (a banker) and Jeanne (Elmo) Fiammenghi; married Guido Caputo (an industrialist), October 4, 1959; children: Jean-Guy, Marco, Giogio. *Education:* Parsons School of Design, graduate, 1950; also studied at Art Student's League of New York on and off for fifteen years. *Religion:* Roman Catholic.

ADDRESSES: 3 Avenue d'Alsace, Nice, Alpes-Martimes, France.

CAREER: Pettinella Advertising Agency, New York City, assistant art director, 1951-52; free-lance artist and book illustrator, 1951—. Fashion model for short time in earlier career; before going to Europe to live did advertising illustration, record covers, and book jackets for adult books. Work has been shown at several exhibitions in New York and at American consulate in Nice; drawings and sketches included in Kerlan collection at University of Minnesota and in collection of Alexis Dupont Library, Wilmington, DE.

AWARDS, HONORS: The Golden Doors was chosen by the *New York Times* as one of the hundred outstanding children's books, 1957, and *First Book of England* received the same honor in 1958; *Rimbles* was selected by American Institute of Graphic Arts as one of the fifty best designed books of 1961; Child Study Association of America's Best Books of the Year, 1965, included *Lizard Comes Down from the North* and *Little Raccoon and the Outside World.*

ILLUSTRATOR:

Loretta Marie Tyman, *Michael Mcgillicudy,* Abelard, 1951.
Rachel Learnard, *Lucky Pete,* Abelard, 1954.
Moritz A. Jagendorf, compiler, *The Priceless Cats, and Other Italian Folk Stories,* Vanguard, 1956.
Edward Fenton, *The Golden Doors,* Doubleday, 1957.
Lois Allen, *Mystery of the Blue Nets,* Coward, 1957.
Elizabeth F. Abell, reteller, *The First Book of Fairy Tales,* F. Watts, 1958.
Paul Gallico, *Mrs. Arris Goes to Paris,* Doubleday, 1958.
Noel Streatfield, *The First Book of England,* F. Watts, 1958.
Margaret E. Martignomi, compiler, *Every Child's Storybook: A Horn of Plenty of Good Reading for Boys and Girls,* F. Watts, 1959.
Lilian Moore, *Once Upon a Holiday* (stories and poems), Abingdon, 1959.
Guy H. Hansen, *Burrhead's Confessions,* Doubleday, 1960.
Patricia Evans, *Rimbles: A Book of Classic Children's Rhymes, Songs and Sayings,* Doubleday, 1961.
Irene Kampen, *Life without George* (autobiography), Doubleday, 1961.
Moore, *Once Upon a Season,* Abingdon, 1962.
Moore, *Little Raccoon and the Thing in the Pool,* McGraw, 1963.
Barbee O. Carlton, *Chester Jones,* Holt, 1963.
Susan Bartlett, *A Book to Begin On: Libraries,* Holt, 1964.
Lou Ann Gaeddert, *Noisy Nancy Norris,* Doubleday, 1964.
Moore, *Papa Albert,* Atheneum, 1964.
Gallico, *Mrs. Arris Goes to Parliament,* Doubleday, 1965 (published in England as *Mrs. Harris, M.P.,* Heinemann, 1965).
Moore, *Little Raccoon and the Outside World,* McGraw, 1965.

Gioia Fiammenghi and her husband, Guido Caputo.

Anita Hewett, *Lizard Comes Down from the North,* McGraw, 1965, adapted as *The Dragon from the North,* McGraw, 1965.

Scott Corbett, *The Cave above Delphi,* Holt, 1965.

Gallico, *The Day Jean-Pierre Went round the World,* Doubleday, 1965.

Mildred O. Knopf, *Around the World Cookbook for Young People,* Knopf, 1966.

Frederic Rossomondo and others, *Spending Money,* F. Watts, 1967.

Rossomondo and others, *Earning Money,* F. Watts, 1967.

Aileen Lucia Fisher, *Skip around the Year,* Crowell, 1967.

Ray Broekel, *Hugo the Huge,* Doubleday, 1968.

Phyllis R. Naylor, *Meet Murdock,* Follett, 1968.

Philip M. Sherlock, *The Iguana's Tale: Crick Crack Stories from the Caribbean,* Crowell, 1969.

Eleanor L. Clymer, *Belinda's New Spring Hat* (Junior Literary Guild selection), F. Watts, 1969.

Alex Rider, *When We Go to Market: Cuando vamos al mercado* (text in English and Spanish), Funk, 1969.

Gallico, *The Day Jean-Pierre Joined the Circus,* Heinemann, 1969.

Gaeddert, *Noisy Nancy and Nick,* Doubleday, 1970.

Barbara Ireson, compiler, *Puffin Book of Poetry,* Puffin, 1970.

Michael Bond, *Mr. Cram's Magic Bubbles,* Puffin, 1970.

Robert Froman, *Bigger and Smaller,* Crowell, 1971.

William C. McGraw, under pseudonym William Corbin, *The Day Willie Wasn't,* Coward, 1971.

Robert K. Smith, *Chocolate Fever,* new edition, Coward, 1972.

Moore, *Little Raccoon and No Trouble at All,* new edition, McGraw, 1972.

Shulamith Oppenheim, *A Trio for Grandpapa,* Crowell, 1974.

Carlo Collodi, *Pinocchio,* Puffin, 1974.

Moore, *Little Raccoon and Poems from the Woods,* McGraw, 1975.

Gallico, *The Day the Guinea Pig Talked,* Pan Books, 1975.

Gallico, *The Day Jean-Pierre Was Pignapped,* Pan Books, 1975.

Thom Roberts, *The Barn,* McGraw, 1975.

Robert Froman, *The Greatest Guessing Game: A Book About Dividing,* Crowell, 1978.

Miriam Cohen, *Born to Dance Samba,* Harper, 1984.

Elizabeth Bolton, *Secret of the Ghost Piano,* Troll Associates, 1985.

Susan Meyers, *P. J. Clover: The Case of the Missing Mouse,* Lodestar, 1985.

Adrian Robert, *My Grandma, the Witch,* Troll Associates, 1985.

Erica Frost, *A Kitten for Rosie,* Troll Associates, 1986.

Sharon Gordon, *Mike's First Haircut,* Troll Associates, 1987.

Thomas Rockwell, *How to Fight a Girl,* F. Watts, 1987.

Meyers, *P. J. Clover: The Case of the Borrowed Baby,* Lodestar, 1988.

Smith, *Chocolate Fever,* Putnam, 1989.

Susan Pearson, *The Boogeyman Caper,* Simon & Shuster, 1990.

Pearson, *The Campfire Ghosts,* Simon & Shuster, 1990.

Pearson, *Eagle-Eye Ernie Comes to Town,* Simon & Shuster, 1990.

Pearson, *The Tap Dance Mystery,* Simon & Shuster, 1990.

SIDELIGHTS: Gioia Fiammenghi grew up in a house full of artists. In an interview with *Something about the Author* (*SATA*), Fiammenghi recalled: "The arts were very important in my family when I was a child. Many members of my mother's family were artists and the tradition continues in one form or another. On my father's side is a well-known painter in Italy. Our family name comes from the Italian word Fiamminghi which means 'Flemish' (plural form). About five hundred years ago, my father's family went from Italy to Belgium to study painting."

As a child, Fiammenghi learned to express her creativity in many ways. She told *SATA:* "I started drawing very young and always knew I would do something in the arts. I used to sew outfits and costumes for a mannequin doll I had. I even stitched a tiny piece of my mother's fur coat for the doll. When I was about fifteen I started going to life classes at the Art Student's League. I continued going on and off until I came to live in Europe." After high school, Fiammenghi received a scholarship to the Parsons School of Design and, upon graduating, attended their European campus.

Fiammenghi's three sons carry on the family's artistic tradition. "When I am working on a drawing, I often ask the boys' opinion about it," Fiammenghi noted. She added: "I like to get a child's viewpoint. The two younger boys draw very well and we have gone sketching together. All three boys play the piano very well."

(From "Big/Little" in *Little Raccoon and Poems from the Woods,* by Lilian Moore, illustrated by Gioia Fiammenghi.)

When she is working on illustrations, Fiammenghi follows a fairly set routine. She commented to *SATA:* "When I have a job I must finish, I get up at five in the morning to work. I love the stillness of the household when everyone is asleep.... When I start a book I might just read it [the manuscript] and think about it for a couple of days. I do all the research I can to really get into the atmosphere of the story.... When I need models I ask my husband or children to pose for me.

Even when she is not working on new illustrations, Fiammenghi is never far from books. "I love to read and always have a book in my bag to read on the bus or in the offices," she told *SATA.* In her free time, Fiammenghi likes to cook, go antique shopping, play the piano, and dance.

WORKS CITED:

Something about the Author, Volume 9, Gale, 1976.

* * *

FISCHLER, Shirley (Walton)

PERSONAL: Married Stanley I. Fischler (a writer).

ADDRESSES: Home—520 West 110th St., New York, NY 10025.

CAREER: Author.

AWARDS, HONORS: Fischlers' Ice Hockey Encyclopedia was chosen one of New York Public Library's Books for the Teen Age, 1980.

WRITINGS:

WITH HUSBAND, STAN FISCHLER

Up from the Minor Leagues of Hockey, Cowles, 1971.
Fischlers' Hockey Encyclopedia, Crowell, 1975, revised edition published as *Fischlers' Ice Hockey Encyclopedia,* 1979.
The Best, Worst and Most Unusual in Sports, Crowell, 1977.
Everybody's Hockey Book, Scribner, 1983.
The Hockey Encyclopedia: The Complete Record of Professional Ice Hockey, Macmillan, 1983.
Breakaway '86: The Hockey Almanac, Collins, 1986.

FOR MORE INFORMATION SEE:

PERIODICALS

Quill and Quire, December, 1986.

* * *

FISCHLER, Stan(ley I.)

PERSONAL: Born in 1932; married Shirley Walton (a writer).

ADDRESSES: Home—520 West 110th St., New York, NY 10025.

CAREER: Sportswriter. Has held a variety of positions as broadcaster and journalist, including publicity writer for the

Stan Fischler (left) and Denis Potvin, coauthors of *Power on Ice*.

New York Rangers hockey team, sportswriter for *Journal-American*, New York correspondent for *Toronto Star*, and commentator for New York Islanders hockey team.

AWARDS, HONORS: Fischlers' *Ice Hockey Encyclopedia* was chosen one of New York Public Library's Books for the Teen Age, 1980.

WRITINGS:

Gordie Howe, Grosset, 1967, revised edition, 1973.
(With Rod Gilbert and Hal Bock) *Goal! My Life on Ice*, Hawthorn, 1968.
Bobby Orr and the Big, Bad Bruins, Dodd, 1969.
(With Richard Beddoes and Ira Gitler) *Hockey! The Story of the World's Fastest Sport*, Macmillan, 1969, third edition, 1973.
Stan Mikita: The Turbulent Career of a Hockey Superstar, Cowles, 1969.
(With Derek Sanderson) *I've Got to Be Me*, Dodd, 1970.
Strange But True Hockey Stories, Cowles, 1970.
The Burly Bruins: Hockey's Tempestuous Team (illustrated with photographs by Dan Baliotti), Prentice-Hall, 1971.
The Conquering Canadiens, Stanley Cup Champions (illustrated with photographs by D. Baliotti), Prentice-Hall of Canada, 1971, Prentice-Hall, 1972.
(With Maurice Richard) *The Flying Frenchmen: Hockey's Greatest Dynasty*, Hawthorn, 1971.
Go, Leafs, Go! The Toronto Hockey Story (illustrated with photographs by D. Baliotti), Prentice-Hall of Canada, 1971.
Heroes of Pro Hockey, Random House, 1971.
(With Brad Park) *Play the Man: Defenseman's Journal*, Dodd, 1971.

The Roaring Rangers and the Emile Francis Years (illustrated with photographs by D. Baliotti), Prentice-Hall, 1971.
(With wife, Shirley Fischler) *Up from the Minor Leagues of Hockey*, Cowles, 1971.
The Blazing North Stars (illustrated with photographs by D. Baliotti and Bob Rush), Prentice-Hall, 1972.
The Champion Bruins, Stanley Cup Winners (illustrated with photographs by D. Baliotti and B. Rush), Prentice-Hall, 1972.
Chicago's Black Hawks (illustrated with photographs by D. Baliotti and B. Rush), Prentice-Hall, 1972.
The Fast-Flying Wings (illustrated with photographs by D. Baliotti and B. Rush), Prentice-Hall, 1972.
Power Play! The Story of the Toronto Maple Leafs, Henry Regnery, 1972.
Saga of the St. Louis Blues (illustrated with photographs by Lew Portnoy and Bob Kolbrener), Prentice-Hall, 1972.
Hockey's Greatest Teams, Henry Regnery, 1973.
Phil Esposito, Grosset, 1973.
Slapshot!, Grosset, 1973.
Bobby Clarke and the Ferocious Flyers, Dodd, 1974.
The Buffalo Sabres: Swashbucklers of the Ice (illustrated with photographs by Melchior Di Giacomo and Joe Bongi, Jr.), Prentice-Hall, 1974.
Fire on Ice: Hockey's Superstars (illustrated with photographs by M. Di Giacomo), Prentice-Hall, 1974.
Hockey's Great Rivalries, Random House, 1974.
Hockey's Toughest Ten, Grosset, 1974.

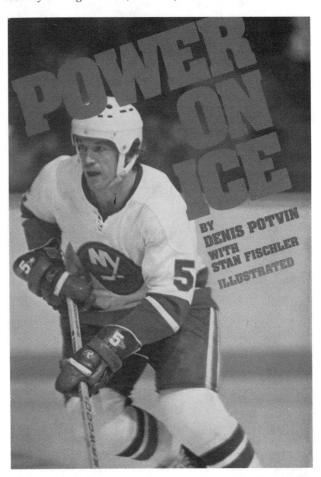

For a quarter-century, Stan Fischler, one of North America's foremost hockey writers, has been offering readers an inside look at this lightning-quick sport. (Dustjacket photo of Denis Potvin by Dan Baliotti.)

New York's Rangers: The Icemen Cometh (illustrated with photographs by M. Di Giacomo), Prentice-Hall, 1974.

The Philadelphia Flyers: Supermen of the Ice, Prentice-Hall, 1974.

(With Shirley Fischler) *Fischlers' Hockey Encyclopedia,* Crowell, 1975, revised edition published as *Fischlers' Ice Hockey Encyclopedia,* 1979.

Slashing! Hockey's Most Knowledgeable Critic Tells What Should Be Done to Save the Game, Crowell, 1975.

The Scoring Punch, Grosset, 1975.

(With D. Baliotti) *This Is Hockey,* Prentice-Hall, 1975.

Make Way for the Leafs: Toronto's Comeback, Prentice-Hall of Canada, 1975, Prentice-Hall, 1976.

Speed and Style: The Montreal Canadiens, Prentice-Hall of Canada, 1975, Prentice-Hall, 1976.

Garry Unger and the Battling Blues, Dodd, 1976.

(With Marv Albert) *Marv Albert's Sports Quiz Book,* Grosset, 1976.

(Editor) *Those Were the Days: The Lore of Hockey by the Legends of the Game,* Dodd, 1976.

Uptown, Downtown: A Trip through Time on New York's Subways (illustrated by Ray Judd), Hawthorn, 1976.

The Triumphant Islanders: Hockey's New Dynasty (illustrated with photographs by JoAnne Kalish, Mecca, and Bereswill), Dodd, 1976.

(With Shirley Fischler) *The Best, Worst and Most Unusual in Sports,* Crowell, 1977.

(With Denis Potvin) *Power on Ice,* Harper, 1977.

(With Laura Stamm and Richard Friedman) *Power Skating the Hockey Way,* Hawthorn, 1977.

Kings of the Rink, Dodd, 1978.

More Stan Fischler's Sports Stumpers, Grosset, 1978.

Showdown! Baseball's Ultimate Confrontations, Grosset, 1978.

(With R. Friedman) *Getting into Pro Soccer,* F. Watts, 1979.

Moving Millions: An Inside Look at Mass Transit, Harper, 1979.

(With Bill Mazer) *The Amazin' Bill Mazer's Football Trivia Book,* Warner Books, 1981.

(With Dave Schultz) *The Hammer: Confessions of a Hockey Enforcer,* Summit Books, 1981.

The Great Gretzky, Morrow, 1982.

Hockey's One Hundred: A Personal Ranking of the Best Players in Hockey History, A & W, 1982.

The New Breed, Morrow, 1982.

(With Shirley Fischler) *Everybody's Hockey Book,* Scribner, 1983.

(With Don Cherry) *Grapes: A Vintage View of Hockey,* Prentice-Hall, 1983.

(With Shirley Fischler) *The Hockey Encyclopedia: The Complete Record of Professional Ice Hockey,* Macmillan, 1983.

Stan Fischler's Amazing Trivia from the World of Hockey, Penguin Books, 1983.

(With L. Stamm and R. Friedman) *Power Skating: A Pro Coach's Secrets,* Sterling, 1983.

Off Side: Hockey from the Inside, Methuen, 1986.

(With Shirley Fischler) *Breakaway '86: The Hockey Almanac,* Collins, 1986.

Edmonton Oilers, Creative Education, 1986.

Montreal Canadiens, Creative Education, 1986.

New York Islanders, Creative Education, 1986.

Toronto Maple Leafs, Creative Education, 1986.

(With Irving Rudd) *The Sporting Life: The Duke and Jackie, Pee Wee, Razor Phil, Ali, Mushky Jackson and Me,* St. Martin, 1990.

All New Hockey's One-Hundred, Wynwood Press, 1990.

Golden Ice, Wynwood Press, 1990.

Also author of *The Comeback Yankees, The Fabulous Rangers, Hockey Action,* and with Marv Albert, *Ranger Fever;* co-editor, *Action Sports Hockey.* Contributor of articles to newspapers and magazines, including *Sporting News, Hockey News, New York Times, Weekend, Toronto Star, Sports Illustrated, Sport,* and *Look.*

FOR MORE INFORMATION SEE:

PERIODICALS

Books in Canada, April, 1986.
Quill and Quire, December, 1986.

*   *   *

FISK, Pauline 1948-

PERSONAL: Born September 27, 1948, in London, England; daughter of Gordon and Millicent Fisk; married David Davies (an architect), February 12, 1972; children: Nathaniel, Nancy, Beulah, Idris, Grace. *Education:* Attended Wimbledon County School for Girls, 1959-66. *Religion:* Non-Conformist. *Hobbies and other interests:* Walking, reading, weaving.

ADDRESSES: Agent—Cecily Ware Literary Agents, John Spencer Square, Canonbury, London N1 2L3, England.

CAREER: Writer.

MEMBER: Society of Authors.

AWARDS, HONORS: Overall winner and winner of nine-to-eleven-year-old group for Smarties Prize for Children's Books from Book Trust (England), and shortlisted for Whitbread Award for Children's Books from Booksellers Association of Great Britain and Ireland, both 1990, both for *Midnight Blue.*

WRITINGS:

The Southern Hill (short stories), Lion, 1972.
Midnight Blue (novel for young people), Lion, 1990.
Telling the Sea (novel for young people), Lion, in press.

WORK IN PROGRESS: Lavender Castle, an animated television series, with fantasy artist Rodney Matthews, filmmaker Gerry Anderson, and composer and musician Rick Wakeman.

SIDELIGHTS: In 1990 Pauline Fisk won the most generous prize available to children's authors—the Smarties book award—for her first novel for young people, *Midnight Blue.* Fisk had been writing since she was a little girl; however, as she told *SATA,* "the births of my five children brought this to a halt for some time." Finally she made time to write *Midnight Blue* by working on the novel in the early hours of the morning.

Midnight Blue was hailed by the Smarties jury—and book critics as well—as a gripping example of the classic conflict between good and evil. "The story is, in every sense, marvellous," wrote a reviewer for *Junior Bookshelf.* "The magical elements in it are closely integrated. There is no contrivance, and the action evolves naturally out of the characters and their situation. The same might be said of a number of other

PAULINE FISK

stories, but what makes this one so very special is the telling."
A reviewer for the London *Sunday Times* declared:
"*Midnight Blue* is the kind of book that casts a life-long spell
over the imagination. It emerges as an original work which is
far greater than the sum of its parts."

Fisk also told *SATA:* "I began to write fiction and poetry at
the age of nine, giving up only after the publication of a book
of short stories in 1972, when my first child was born. It
seemed to me at that time that the obsessional drives of a
writer were incompatible with motherhood. I am now striv-
ing, after fifteen years away from it, to prove otherwise!
Midnight Blue was begun at the worst possible time, after the
birth of my fifth child, when I still had a toddler at home as
well. But the need to hear what increasingly felt like my 'lost
inner voice' was so strong that there was no gainsaying it.
Thankfully, now that all my children are at school, I don't
have to write at five in the morning anymore!

"Since I decided at the age of nine that I would be a writer,
there has never been another career that has attracted me. My
only interest when I left school at age eighteen was to
'discover the world' (as I put it then), aware of how limiting
my youth and experience were for a potential novelist! 'Discovering the world' found me living in central London,
opposite King's Cross Station in the red light district; in
Brixton in south London; and out in the wilds of Worces-
tershire in a laborer's cottage without running water of
electricity, two miles away from the nearest road. It found me

working for as disparate employers as the Boys' Brigade (an
alternative organization to the Boy Scouts) and J. P.
Donleavy, the author, in southern Ireland. I worked for the
Spastics' Society in London, helping to organize fundraising
events, and as an assistant in a social services department,
where my discoveries about the nature of the society in which
I lived came as something of a shock. 'Discovering the world'
in the heady 1960s and early 1970s also meant making some
(limited as I see them now, but major as they seemed at the
time) discoveries about myself. Those were exciting times,
whatever anybody thinks of them now! Of everything I've
done, the career of motherhood has been the one that has
been the one that has called from me more wit, intelligence,
and stamina than any other. It continually turns my whole
life upside down, and in it I've 'discovered more of life' than I
did in all the rest put together—and more about myself.

"My method of writing is less one of invention than of
discovering the story that's already inside me. I begin by
slinging down ideas indiscriminately, and then I work on
them to find the story that I know is in there somewhere. I feel
like a sculptor, hacking at stone or wood to get at the shape
that's hidden in it. Or like a composer writing music (I go over
what I'm writing again and again, mostly out loud, to make
sure that what I hear is what I'm meant to hear).

"The plot of *Midnight Blue* grew out of the description of a
smoke-filled balloon flight in the book *Nazca: The Flight of
the Condor I* by Jim Woodman and the Shropshire legend of

the Arthurian 'Wild Edric,' who is claimed to slumber beneath a range of hills known as the Stiperstones. The house on Highholly Hill is a (now ruined) farmhouse where my family lived while our own home was being rebuilt. I wrote about Shropshire, blending elements and places together, out of the sheer good sense of writing about what I know.

"I write for children, again, because they're what I know. I'm surrounded by them. They're the ones I want to entertain. I also write for children out of my own vivid memories of childhood, and my own often painful struggle to reach adulthood—to get out into the world at large. My childhood memories are of great frustration and despair. I sympathize with many of the struggles that children—often lonely, to all intents and purposes trapped by the circumstances of their lives—go through, and with many of their hopes and aspirations and fears, when they contemplate their approaching adult lives.

"I may not always write for children (I hope I'll have a go at all sorts of things) but I suspect that loneliness and weakness will be a recurring theme.

"The success of *Midnight Blue* has been very gratifying after a half-a-lifetime's wait to even begin. But I'm aware, despite everything, that this is still an apprenticeship; I've got so much to learn (in a sense I hope I *always* will have so much to learn). Graham Greene likened a first novel to a short, sharp sprint into which the runner puts all he's got, and everything after to the long-distance race.

"He's a particularly favorite writer, whose skills I admire, not least his ability to 'lift' a story out of the ordinary onto another plane. Bruce Chatwin and Sylvia Plath are favorite writers at the moment. Jack Clemo, George Herbert, and Bob Dylan are favorite poets too. The single book that has influenced me most is the Bible, both in its language and for the content and quality of its epic tale. It never fails to provoke, surprise, and stir me.

"Among children's writers, A. A. Milne has always been a favorite—I wouldn't be writing today without the stimulus of his character Winnie-the-Pooh—and Hans Christian Andersen and (dare I admit it?) *Enid Boynton!* Favorite children's books now are *The Homecoming* by Cynthia Voigt and *Goodnight, Mr. Tom* by Michelle Margorian.

"J. R. R. Tolkein's *Lord of the Rings* influenced me greatly in my younger days. And something he said is never far out of my mind now, as I struggle to write realistically for children—but with hope—about our difficult world: 'That on callow, lumpish, and selfish youth, sorrow and the shadow of death can bestow dignity and sometimes even wisdom.'"

WORKS CITED:

Review of *Midnight Blue, Junior Bookshelf,* December, 1990, p. 292.
Review of *Midnight Blue, Sunday Times* (London), April 8, 1990.

FOR MORE INFORMATION SEE:

PERIODICALS

Fear, April, 1991.
Horn Book Guide, January, 1990.
Publishers Weekly, November 30, 1990.

FLEISHMAN, Seymour 1918-

PERSONAL: Born January 29, 1918, in Chicago, IL; son of Nathan and Rose (Yaffee) Fleishman; married wife, September 7, 1946; children: Janet Fleishman, Susan Sheilds. *Education:* Attended School of the Art Institute of Chicago, 1935-41.

ADDRESSES: Home—5331 North Magnolia Ave., Chicago, IL 60640.

CAREER: Illustrator and author. Worked in promotional art department of Chicago *Sun,* 1945-48. *Military service:* U.S. Army, 1941-45; served in Australia and New Guinea.

WRITINGS:

AUTHOR AND ILLUSTRATOR OF CHILDREN'S BOOKS

Where's Kit?, Albert Whitman, 1962.
Four Cheers for Camping, Albert Whitman, 1963.
Gumbel, the Fire-Breathing Dragon, Harvey House, 1970.
Printcrafts for Fun and Profit, Albert Whitman, 1977.
Too Hot in Potzburg, Albert Whitman, 1981.

ILLUSTRATOR

Helen Lobdell, *Golden Conquest,* Houghton, 1953.
Marlin Perkins, *Marlin Perkins' Zoo Parade,* Rand McNally, 1954.
Jane Thayer, *The Puppy Who Wanted a Boy,* Morrow, 1958.
Thayer, *Gus Was a Friendly Ghost,* Morrow, 1962.
Thayer, *Quiet on Account of Dinosaur,* Morrow, 1964.
Thayer, *The Bunny in the Honeysuckle Patch,* Morrow, 1965.
Thayer, *The Part-Time Dog,* Morrow, 1965.
Mary Alice Jones, *Know Your Bible,* Rand McNally, 1965.
Margaret Davidson, *The Adventures of George Washington,* Four Winds, 1965.
William S. Haynie, *Headstart with Music,* Systems for Education, 1966.
Thayer, *The Lighthearted Wolf,* Morrow, 1966.
Thayer, *What's a Ghost Going to Do?,* Morrow, 1966.
Thayer, *The Cat That Joined the Club,* Morrow, 1967.
Muriel Novella Stanek, *One, Two, Three for Fun,* Albert Whitman, 1967.
Irma Black, *The Little Old Man Who Could Not Read,* Albert Whitman, 1968.
Thayer, *Little Mr. Greenthumb,* Morrow, 1968.
Thayer, *Curious, Furious Chipmunk,* Morrow, 1969.
Thayer, *Gus Was a Christmas Ghost,* Morrow, 1969.
Thayer, *I'm Not a Cat,* Morrow, 1970.
Black, *The Little Old Man Who Cooked and Cleaned,* Albert Whitman, 1970.
Carl Lamson Carmer, *The Boy Drummer of Vincennes,* Harvey House, 1972.
Florence Parry Heide, *The Mystery of the Missing Suitcase,* Albert Whitman, 1972.
F. P. Heide, *The Mystery of the Silver Tag,* Albert Whitman, 1972.
Thayer, *Gus and the Baby Ghost,* Morrow, 1972.
F. P. Heide, *The Hidden Box Mystery,* Albert Whitman, 1973.
F. P. Heide, *The Mystery at MacAdoo Zoo,* Albert Whitman, 1973.
David Johnstone, *People and Places,* Southwestern, 1973.
F. P. Heide, *The Mystery of the Melting Snowman,* Albert Whitman, 1974.
F. P. Heide, *The Mystery of the Whispering Voice,* Albert Whitman, 1974.

Thayer, *Gus Was a Mexican Ghost,* Morrow, 1974.
F. P. Heide, *The Mystery of the Bewitched Bookmobile,* Albert Whitman, 1975.
F. P. Heide, *The Mystery of the Vanishing Visitor,* Albert Whitman, 1975.
Anita Deyneka, *Alexi's Secret Mission,* David Cook, 1975.
Esther Loewen Vogt, *Turkey Red,* David Cook, 1975.
F. P. Heide, *The Mystery of the Lonely Lantern,* Albert Whitman, 1976.
Bettie Wilson Story, *The Other Side of the Tell,* David Cook, 1976.
F. P. Heide, *The Mystery at Keyhole Carnival,* Albert Whitman, 1977.
Edward G. Finnegan, *A Treasure House Book of Children's Bible Stories,* Consolidated Book Publishers, 1977.
F. P. Heide, *The Mystery of the Midnight Message,* Albert Whitman, 1977.
F. P. Heide, *The Mystery at Southport Cinema,* Albert Whitman, 1978.
Thayer, *Gus Was a Gorgeous Ghost,* Morrow, 1978.
Vogt, *Harvest Gold,* David Cook, 1978.
Sylvia Root Tester, *Magic Monsters around the Year,* Child's World, 1979.
F. P. Heide, *The Mystery of the Mummy's Mask,* Albert Whitman, 1979.
F. P. Heide, *The Mystery of the Forgotten Island,* Albert Whitman, 1980.
Sandra Ziegler, *Friends: A Handbook about Getting Along Together,* Child's World, 1980.
Penny S. Anderson, *The Big Storm,* Dandelion House, 1982.
Jill Kingdon, *The ABC Dinosaur Book,* Childrens Press, 1982.
F. P. Heide and Roxanne Heide, *The Mystery on Danger Road,* Albert Whitman, 1983.
Patricia Eastman, *Sometimes Things Change,* Childrens Press, 1983.
(Illustrator of reprint) Guernsey Van Riper, Jr., *Babe Ruth: One of Baseball's Greatest,* Bobbs-Merrill, 1983 (reprint of *Babe Ruth, Baseball Boy,* 1959).
Thayer, *Gus Loved His Happy Home,* Linnet Books, 1989.

*   *   *

FRANCIS, Charles
See HOLME, Bryan

*   *   *

FRANKEL, Alona 1937-

PERSONAL: Born June 27, 1937, in Cracow, Poland; immigrated to Israel, 1949; daughter of Solomon and Gusta (Gruber) Goldman; married Zygmunt Frankel (an engineer, writer, and painter), 1958; children: Ari Shlomo and Michael. *Education:* Avni Art Academy, Tel-Aviv, 1953-55.

ADDRESSES: 4 Nathan St., Ramat-Gan 52450, Israel.

CAREER: Graphic designer and illustrator since 1955; author and illustrator of children's books since 1975. Exhibitions in Israel and abroad. *Military service:* Israeli Air Force, Intelligence, sergeant, 1955-57.

AWARDS, HONORS: Children's Books Illustration Award from the Israel Museum, Jerusalem, 1979; Children's Books Award from the Israel Export Institute, 1975, 1977, 1979; International Board on Books for Young People Honor List,

ALONA FRANKEL

1982; *If Mother Were an Elephant* and *The Child's Prayer* were both exhibited at the Bologna International Children's Book Fair, 1985; Please Touch Book Award honorable mention from the Please Touch Museum for Children (PA), 1986, for *Hello, Clouds!*

WRITINGS:

JUVENILE; ALL SELF-ILLUSTRATED

Once Upon a Potty, Massada (Tel-Aviv), 1975, published in the United States as two books, *Once Upon a Potty: His,* Barron's Educational, 1980, and *Once Upon a Potty: Hers,* Barron's Educational, 1984.
The Family of Tiny White Elephants, Massada, 1978, Barron's Educational, 1980.
The Goodnight Book, Massada, 1979.
Let's Go from Head to Toe, Massada, 1979.
Angela, the Little Devil, Zmora Bitan (Tel-Aviv), 1979.
One, Two Three, What Can a Mushroom Be?, Zmora Bitan, 1980.
A Book to Eat By, Massada, 1980.
A True Story, Massada, 1981.
The Clothes We Wear, Massada, 1983.
The Moon Book, Zmora Bitan, 1983.
The Book of Numbers, Zmora Bitan, 1983.
The Book of Letters, Zmora Bitan, 1983.
The Princess of Dreams, Massada, 1984.
A Fairy Tale, Zmora Bitan, 1985.
There Is No One Like Mother, Am Oved (Tel-Aviv), 1985.
The Ship and the Island, Keter (Jerusalem), 1985.
The Princess and the Caterpillar, Keter, 1987.
A Lullaby, Israel Museum (Jerusalem), 1987.
One Day . . . (a book of numbers), Massada, 1990.
From Armadillo to Octopus (a book of the Hebrew alphabet), Massada, 1990.
The Book of Manners, Keter, 1990.

I Want My Mother, Keter, 1990.
"A Book to Babysit By," Steimatzky (Tel Aviv), 1991.

ILLUSTRATOR

Greer Fay Cashman, *Jewish Days and Holidays,* Massada Press, 1976, SBS, 1979.
Dalia Hardof Renberg, *Hello, Clouds!,* Harper, 1985.
Maggie Rennert, *I Love You,* Adama Books, 1987.

Also illustrator of Dvora Hacohen, editor, *The Child's Prayer,* Am Oved. Many of Frankel's books have been translated into other languages, including Spanish, Danish, Dutch, Norwegian, Swedish, German, Japanese, Yiddish, and Arabian.

WORK IN PROGRESS: The Moon over the Forest; writing and illustrating children's books.

SIDELIGHTS: Alona Frankel writes, "I spent the war years as a child [in Cracow, Poland] first in the Lvov ghetto with my parents; then alone in hiding in a small village; and finally with my parents in Lvov again. I have lived in Israel since 1949. After school, compulsory army service, and art studies, I married Zygmunt Frankel, an artist and writer. We have two sons, Ari, a composer, and Michael, a naval cadet.

"I have been drawing and painting ever since I can remember. My other great passion, ever since I learned to read (very early), has been literature and, in due time, this combination led to book illustration. Writing my own texts came later, when Michael was still a baby, and I made up and illustrated a story for him, *Once Upon a Potty.* It was published by Massada Ltd. in 1975, became an instant and lasting bestseller in Israel, and has since been translated into nine other languages. It is distributed in the States by Barron's Educational in book form, as a video cassette, and boxed with a doll based on the leading character and a miniature potty. This encouraged further books, some of them based on

Alona Frankel tries to please the child inside herself with her work. (Drawing from *Angela, the Little Devil,* written and illustrated by Alona Frankel.)

ideas which I had for a long time. To date, I have written and illustrated twenty-three children's books.

"I have also illustrated over twenty books by other poets and writers, including some major Israeli ones; designed book covers; illustrated magazine articles and stories; had three one-man exhibitions, including one at the Israel Museum in Jerusalem; participated in international exhibitions and books fairs, in the U.S., Italy, Israel, Egypt, and Japan; and have received several awards and prizes. I have occasionally lectured to audiences of children and on television and radio programs, and tutored at art academies, museums, and libraries.

"I always start a new book by writing the story, which may take from a few days to a few years, concentrating on the text only. When the text is finished, I let it rest for a while (sometimes quite long) and only then begin to work on the illustrations, presenting the book to the publisher in a completely finished form.

"During all the stages of my work I try very hard to keep open the channels to my own childhood and to please that particular child above all. I do not seek outside opinion, advice, or approval of educators, psychologists, publishers, parents, or even children. Otherwise, although children differ from grown-ups by their size, experience, and dependence, I give them full credit as judges of my books. I believe that my books reflect my liberal attitudes, the right to a freedom of choice, dislike of indoctrination, and a certain amount of anarchistic humor which, in my opinion, is the best—and sometimes the only—defense against the troubles that befall grown-ups and children alike.

"When illustrating a text, I try to make the style fit the subject and the mood of the book, which occasionally calls for a change of medium or technique (colored pencils, watercolor, gouache, acrylics on canvas, pastel, collage, and various mixed techniques). In spite of some occasional periods of hesitation and doubt, some short and some long, I am happy at my work, and am always proud and a little surprised when it is appreciated."

*   *   *

FREEMAN, Sarah (Caroline) 1940-

PERSONAL: Born December 12, 1940, in Newcastle, Staffordshire, England; daughter of Richard Herbert (an architect) and Jean (an architect; maiden name, Shufflebotham) Sheppard; married Michael Freeman (an analyst), 1965; children: Polly Antonia, Alexander Henry. *Education:* Somerville College, Oxford, M.A., 1961. *Politics:* Liberal.

ADDRESSES: Home and office—47 Onslow Gardens, London N10 3JY, England. *Agent*—Anthony Sheil Associates Ltd., 43 Doughty St., London WC1N 2LF, England.

CAREER: Penguin Books, London, England, member of editorial staff, c. 1961-63; *Architectural Design,* London, member of editorial staff, c. 1963-64; *Harper's Bazaar,* London, sub-editor, c. 1964-67; *Wine and Food,* London, managing editor, c. 1968; *Harpers,* arts editor, until 1972; writer, 1972—. Arts editor, *Queen,* until 1972; art director, Mary Somerville Art Trust.

MEMBER: Contemporary Art Society.

WRITINGS:

The Piccolo Picture Cook Book (juvenile), Pan Books, 1975.
Isabella and Sam, Gollancz, 1977.
Mutton and Oysters (self-illustrated), Gollancz, 1989.
The Student Cook Book (self-illustrated), Collins & Brown, 1990.

Contributor to magazines and newspapers.

WORK IN PROGRESS: Three books.

SIDELIGHTS: Sarah Freeman commented: "Although all the books I have published so far have been connected with food, it is the consumers even more than the food who fascinate me. *Mutton and Oysters,* initially a study of Victorian food, turned into a study of Victorian society (and our own).

"My life is an unresolved dichotomy between art and writing. My enjoyment of art (both active and passive) comes from my father, who supported up-and-coming artists in every way he could. Had it not been for shyness about encroaching on his territory, I would probably have become a painter.

"Until now, I have only attempted to combine my interests by illustrating my last two books. In the future, however, I hope to write one or more biographies of artists."

FOR MORE INFORMATION SEE:

PERIODICALS

Times Literary Supplement, December 22, 1989.

*   *   *

FRY, Christopher 1907-

PERSONAL: Name originally Christopher Harris; born December 18, 1907, in Bristol, England; son of Charles John (a builder and later a church reader) and Emma Marguerite Fry (Hammond) Harris; married Phyllis Marjorie Hart, December 3, 1936 (died, 1987); children: one son. *Education:* Attended Bedford Modern School, Bedford, England, 1918-26. *Religion:* Church of England.

ADDRESSES: Home—The Toft, East Dean, near Chichester, West Sussex PO18 0JA, England. *Agent*—Thelma Wax, ACTAC Ltd., 15 High St., Ramsbury, Wiltshire 5N8 2PA, England.

CAREER: Bedford Froebel Kindergarten, teacher, 1926-27; Citizen House, Bath, England, actor and office worker, 1927; Hazelwood Preparatory School, Limpsfield, Surrey, England, schoolmaster, 1928-31; secretary to H. Rodney Bennett, 1931-32; Tunbridge Wells Repertory Players, founding director, 1932-35; Dr. Barnardo's Homes, lecturer and editor of schools' magazines, 1934-39; Oxford Playhouse, director, 1940; Arts Theatre Club, London, England, director, 1945, staff dramatist, 1947. Visiting director, Oxford Playhouse, 1945-46. Composer. *Military service:* Noncombatant Corps, 1940-44.

MEMBER: Dramatists Guild, Royal Society of Literature (fellow), Garrick Club.

CHRISTOPHER FRY

AWARDS, HONORS: Shaw Prize Fund award, 1948, for *The Lady's Not for Burning;* William Foyle Poetry Prize, 1951, for *Venus Observed;* New York Drama Critics Circle Award, 1951, for *The Lady's Not for Burning,* 1952, for *Venus Observed,* and 1956, for *Tiger at the Gates;* Queen's Gold Medal for Poetry, 1962; Heinemann Award, Royal Society of Literature, 1962, for *Curtmantle: A Play;* D.A., 1966, and Honorary Fellow, 1988, Manchester Polytechnic; Writers Guild Best British Television Dramatization award nomination, 1971, for *The Tenant of Wildfell Hall;* D.Litt., Lambeth and Oxford University, 1988.

WRITINGS:

PLAYS

(With Monte Crick and F. Eyton) *She Shall Have Music,* first produced in London, England, 1934.
Open Door, first produced in London, England, 1936.
The Boy with a Cart: Cuthman, Saint of Sussex (also see below; first produced in Coleman's Hatch, Sussex, England, 1938; produced in the West End at Lyric Theatre, January 16, 1950), Oxford University Press, 1939, 2nd edition, Muller, 1956.
The Tower (pageant), first produced at Tewkesbury Festival, Tewkesbury, England, July 18, 1939.
Thursday's Child: A Pageant (first produced in London, 1939), Girl's Friendly Press (London), 1939.
A Phoenix Too Frequent (also see below; first produced in London at Mercury Theatre, April 25, 1946; produced on Broadway with *Freight,* 1950), Hollis & Carter, 1946, Oxford University Press, 1949.

The Firstborn (also see below; broadcast on radio, 1947; first produced at Gateway Theatre, Edinburgh, Scotland, September 6, 1948), Cambridge University Press, 1946.

The Lady's Not for Burning (also see below; first produced in London at Arts Theatre, March 10, 1948; produced in the West End, May 11, 1949, produced on Broadway at Royale Theatre, November 8, 1950), Oxford University Press, 1949, revised edition, 1973.

Thor, with Angels (also see below; first produced at Chapter House, Canterbury, England, June, 1948; produced in the West End at Lyric Theatre, September 27, 1951), H. J. Goulden, 1948, Oxford University Press, 1949.

Venus Observed (also see below; first produced in London at St. James Theatre, January 18, 1950; produced on Broadway at Century Theatre, February 13, 1952), Oxford University Press, 1950.

A Sleep of Prisoners (also see below; first produced in Oxford, England, at University Church, April 23, 1951; produced in London at St. Thomas's Church, May 15, 1951), Oxford University Press, 1951.

The Dark Is Light Enough: A Winter Comedy (also see below; first produced in the West End at Aldwych Theatre, April, 30, 1954; produced on Broadway at ANTA Theatre, February 23, 1955), Oxford University Press, 1954.

Curtmantle: A Play (also see below; first produced in Dutch in Tilburg, Netherlands, at Stadsschouwburg, March 1, 1961; produced in the West End at Aldwych Theatre, October 6, 1962), Oxford University Press, 1961.

A Yard of Sun: A Summer Comedy (first produced at Nottingham Playhouse, Nottingham, England, July 11, 1970; produced in the West End at Old Vic Theatre, August 10, 1970), Oxford University Press, 1970.

(Author of libretto) *Paradise Lost* (opera of John Milton's poem adapted by Penderecki; first produced in Chicago, 1978), Schott, 1978.

One Thing More; or, Caedmon Construed (first produced at Chelmsford Cathedral, England, 1986; broadcast on radio, 1986), King's College, 1986, Dramatists Play Service, 1987.

Also author of librettos for two operas for children by Michael Tippett: *Robert of Sicily,* first produced in 1938, and *Seven at a Stroke,* first produced in 1939. Author of *Youth of the Peregrines,* produced at Tunbridge Wells with premiere production of George Bernard Shaw's *Village Wooing.* Author of radio plays for *Children's Hour* series, 1939-40, and of *Rhineland Journey,* 1948.

SCREENPLAYS AND TELEPLAYS

The Queen Is Crowned (documentary), Universal, 1953.

(With Denis Cannan) *The Beggar's Opera,* British Lion, 1953.

Ben Hur, Metro-Goldwyn-Mayer, 1959.

Barabbas, Columbia, 1961.

(With Jonathan Griffin, Ivo Perilli, and Vittorio Bonicelli) *The Bible: In the Beginning,* Twentieth Century-Fox, 1966.

The Tenant of Wildfell Hall, BBC-TV, 1968.

The Brontes of Haworth (also see below; four teleplays; BBC-TV, 1973), published in two volumes, Davis-Poynter, 1975.

The Best of Enemies, BBC-TV, 1976.

Sister Dora, BBC-TV, 1977.

Star over Bethlehem, BBC-TV, 1981.

TRANSLATOR

(And adaptor from *L'Invitation au Chateau* by Jean Anouilh), *Ring round the Moon: A Charade with Music* (first produced in the West End at Globe Theatre, January 26, 1950), Oxford University Press, 1950.

The Canary (teleplay), British Broadcasting Corp. (BBC-TV), 1950.

(And adaptor) Jean Giraudoux, *Tiger at the Gates* (also see below; first produced in the West End at Apollo Theatre, October 3, 1955), Methuen, 1955, 2nd edition, 1961, Oxford University Press, 1956, produced as *The Trojan War Will Not Take Place* (London, 1983), Methuen, 1983.

(And adaptor) Anouilh, *The Lark* (first produced in the West End at Lyric Theatre, May 11, 1955), Methuen, 1955, Oxford University Press, 1956.

(And adaptor from *Pour Lucrece* by Giraudoux), *Duel of Angels* (also see below; first produced in the West End at Apollo Theatre, April 22, 1958; produced on Broadway at Helen Hayes Theatre, April 19, 1960), Methuen, 1958, Oxford University Press, 1959.

(And adaptor) Giraudoux, *Judith* (also see below; first produced in the West End at Her Majesty's Theatre, June 20, 1962), Methuen, 1962.

Sidonie Gabrielle Colette, *The Boy and the Magic,* Dobson, 1964, Putnam, 1965.

Henrik Ibsen, *Peer Gynt* (first produced at Chichester Festival Theatre, Chichester, England, May 13, 1970), Oxford University Press, 1970.

After being produced in 1938, *The Boy with a Cart* became Christopher Fry's first published play the following year.

Edmond Rostand, *Cyrano de Bergerac* (first produced at Chichester Festival Theatre, May 14, 1975), Oxford University Press, 1975.

OMNIBUS VOLUMES

Three Plays: The Firstborn; Thor, with Angels; A Sleep of Prisoners, Oxford University Press, 1960.

(Translator) Giraudoux, *Plays* (contains *Judith, Tiger at the Gates*, and *D of Angels*), Methuen, 1963.

Plays (contains *Thor, with Angels* and *The Lady's Not for Burning*), Oxfor University Press, 1969.

Plays (contains *The Boy with a Cart: Cuthman, Saint of Sussex, The Firstborn*, and *Venus Observed*), Oxford University Press, 1970.

Plays (contains *A Sleep of Prisoners, The Dark Is Light Enough*, and *Curtmantle*), Oxford University Press, 1971.

Selected Plays (contains *The Boy with a Cart: Cuthman, Saint of Sussex, A Phoenix Too Frequent, The Lady's Not for Burning, A Sleep of Prisoners, Curtmantle*), Oxford University Press, 1985.

(Translator with Timberlake Wertebaker) *Jean Anouilh: Five Plays*, Heinemann, 1986.

OTHER

(Contributor) Kaye Webb, editor, *An Experience of Critics and the Approach to Dramatic Criticism*, Perpetua, 1952, Oxford University Press, 1953.

(Contributor) Robert W. Corrigan, editor, *The Modern Theatre*, Macmillan, 1964.

The Boat That Mooed (juvenile fiction), Macmillan, 1965.

(Contributor) H. F. Rubinstein, editor, *The Drama Bedside Book*, Atheneum, 1966.

(With Jonathan Griffin) *The Bible: Original Screenplay*, Pocket Books, 1966.

Root and Sky (poetry from Fry's plays), Rampant Lions Press (Cambridge, England), 1975.

Can You Find Me: A Family History, Oxford University Press, 1978.

Death Is a Kind of Love (lecture; drawings by Charles E. Wadsworth), Tidal Press, 1979.

Charlie Hammond's Sketch Book, Oxford University Press, 1980.

Genius, Talent and Failure (lecture), King's College, 1987.

Looking for a Language (lecture), King's College, 1991.

Also author of libretto for cantata *Crown of the Year*, first produced in 1958. Contributor to anthology, *Representative Modern Plays: Ibsen to Tennessee Williams*, edited by Robert Warnock, Scott, Foresman, 1964. Contributor to *Theatre Arts* and *Plays and Players*.

Fry's plays have been translated into French, German, Spanish, Dutch, Norwegian, Finnish, Italian, Swedish, Danish, Greek, Serbo-Croat, Hungarian, Tamil, Portuguese, Flemish, Czech, Polish, and Albanian.

SIDELIGHTS: Christopher Fry is a distinguished English playwright noted for his dramas written in verse form. While many other playwrights during the mid-twentieth century were writing about the bleak realities of modern life, Fry chose to emphasize the wonder and mystery of life in his poetic plays. He first gained widespread attention during the late 1940s with *The Lady's Not for Burning*. Set in medieval times, this play involves a wealthy orphan who is accused of being a witch by the townspeople, who want her killed so they can inherit her belongings. According to Harold Hobson in *Drama*, "It is difficult to exaggerate the sense of freshness and

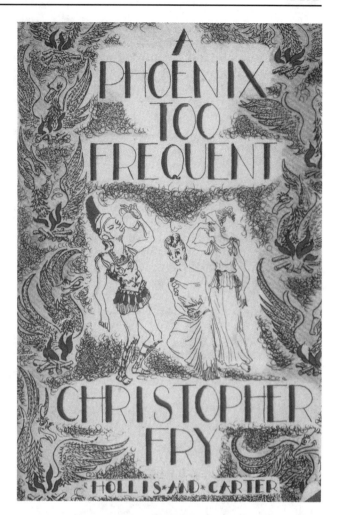

One of Christopher Fry's most successful early plays, *A Phoenix Too Frequent*, made its Broadway debut in 1950. (Cover illustration by Ronald Searle.)

excitement that swept through the theatrical world when *The Lady's Not for Burning* . . . [hit] the British stage." British audiences enjoyed most of Fry's later plays as well, many of which had religious or war themes and starred famous actors such as Laurence Olivier and Richard Burton. Fry is also a translator and the author of screenplays and teleplays, including *Ben-Hur* and *Barabbas*. In addition, he wrote radio plays for the *Children's Hour* series, which were broadcast between 1939 and 1940, and his book *Can You Find Me: A Family History* includes his childhood memoirs.

Christopher Harris (later known as Christopher Fry) was born on December 18, 1907, in Bristol, England. In *Can You Find Me*, Fry reflects on the first moments after his birth and the relatives that came before him: "So there I was, in a state of life, learning to focus on what was round me, knowing light and dark, exploring the differences between near and far, attuning to sound, distinguishing one sensation from another . . . , carrying within me who knows how much of the lives of the past, the attorneys, the churchmen, the Quakers (I hope), the bargemen, the shipwrights, the bishop who got into Johnson's *Lives*, the auctioneers, the blacksmith, the yeomen, the carpenters, whose existences meeting and begetting gave place to the term of consciousness which I call my own."

Fry's first few years were relatively uneventful. Things changed, however, when his father died when Fry was three. In an interview with Cathy Courtney for *Something about the Author,* Fry recalls how he was affected by his father's death: "I was very ill immediately afterwards, and my mother always said that it was due to my reaction to his death. The memory of my mother lying on the sofa crying is very vivid, but whether I understood what his dying really meant I don't know. I just took it that that was the state of affairs. I took each day as it came along."

As might be expected, family life was very different after Fry's father passed away. He had worked as a lay reader in a poor parish in Bristol, and the family did not have much money to live on. When he died, there was nothing. So for a short time the family of three (his mother, his older brother, and he) had to live with Fry's grandparents. Wanting a life of her own, his mother soon moved the family into a rented house in Bedford. They shared the house and living expenses with his invalid Aunt Ada. His mother kept so busy taking care of Aunt Ada that she "didn't really have much time," Fry told Courtney. "My mother was brought up as a girl never to do anything for herself, and she had to become this totally dedicated person who had no life of her own at all. She did it without complaint."

Religious themes are found in many of Christopher Fry's plays, including *A Sleep of Prisoners*. (Cover illustration by Ronald Searle.)

In *Can You Find Me* Fry notes that his mother's work habits and sense of self control caused her to hide her deep emotions most of the time. "My mother's devotion to duty had the weakness of never teaching us to help her in any way. We took her labours for granted. I saw her self-control break for a moment on only two occasions: once when I must have been more than usually exasperating, or she was more than usually tired. She suddenly chased me round the kitchen table as though to hit me, and as quickly regained her calm. And several years later when my brother, with acute appendicitis, was being taken to hospital in an ambulance. She had put on her hat and coat and was lacing up her boots. I tried to comfort her, and she bit my head off to stop herself from crying. She was over eighty before I saw her let her deep feelings break surface again."

Even with his father dead and mother busy with work, Fry was still able to enjoy himself by playing with friends. "I don't think I was a solitary child," he explained to Courtney. "There were all the children in the kindergarten, and there were children in the street. In those days you could play games in the street because there was no traffic." Besides being with friends, Fry began to amuse himself by reading after his kindergarten teacher revealed to him the magic of words. "As vividly as if it were yesterday, I remember the morning when Miss Spence opened my ears to the life of words," he writes in *Can You Find Me.* "What stories she read to us as we sat at her feet I don't remember . . . , but suddenly words were not only sentences but individuals. She gave each word so exactly its proper weight and meaning, yet so lightly, I felt I could hold the words like coloured stones in my hand." One of his favorite books was Aunt Ada's illustrated copy of John Bunyan's *Pilgrim's Progress,* a classic tale of how one man finds God after resisting the temptations and pitfalls of life. "First of all I feasted on the illustrations, 102 of them, and then the serious matter of reading began," Fry recalled in his *SATA* interview. This book, along with the poetry of writers like William Wordsworth and Alfred Tennyson, opened the world of reading to him.

In addition to being an avid reader, Fry's childhood visions also played a key role in his development as a writer. Not long after his father's death, for example, Fry saw an image of his father. "It must have been fairly late at night, for my mother was in bed and asleep," he remembers in *Can You Find Me.* "I woke to the feeling of approach, of the darkness bringing something to me. I think the door was shut, and yet the place where the door was seemed very deep, like a tunnel, and it was bringing something to me with a kind of taut deliberation or slow emphasis. Then I saw my father standing beside the bed, faintly lit by the tiny paraffin lamp or night-light. I called out to my mother 'Daddy's here, daddy's here,' but my mother, barely awake, simply murmured to me to go back to sleep. I remember feeling puzzled and sorry that she wouldn't wake up properly or believe me, and by then I had lost sight of my father." Later he saw other things as well. Once he believed he saw an elf in his yard. Another time, while in bed but not asleep, he saw an underwater scene as if he were looking through the eyes of a fish. This early ability to see more into life than the simple, physical reality was later reflected in his verse plays that celebrate the mysterious side of life.

But Fry was aware of the grim aspects of life as well. As a child he lived through World War I. In *Can You Find Me* he recalls how the war changed his life. One day, when he was six years old, he went to "the park to play, but there was no playing, no hide-and-seek in the two round areas of grass surrounded by shrubbery, which we called the Pancake and the Frying Pan; no rolling down the steep bank below the

Bowling Green. The park was full of soldiers, horses, and mules. Mules were a new animal to me, and not pleasant. One kicked out a soldier's eye. . . . Within a month the military had taken over the corner of the field where the cricket-nets had been, over the hedge at the bottom of our backyard, and built a brick rifle-range." Growing up during the war years had an influence on his plays: many of them include soldiers or take place during wartime.

Though World War I gave Fry plenty of memories of pain, fear, and sorrow, the end of the war was a joyous time. In *Can You Find Me,* Fry recounts the day in 1918 when the fighting stopped. "On the morning of 11 November, a Monday, the fifth form of the junior school was being taught by a little clergyman called Shepherd-Smith, known to us as 'Smuts.' We were restless and excited, knowing already the importance of the day. We cheered and thumped our desks, bouncing up and down in our seats, quite prepared to run out of the building and into the street. We could hardly believe that Shepherd-Smith meant us to go on with our work, as though the world had not been completely transformed. The world was at peace, a state of affairs I could hardly remember, and at peace perhaps for ever. There would be bonfires, and flags, and fireworks, and no more death until the time for death."

After the war Fry continued his schooling at Bedford Modern School, developing along the way his interest in drawing, reading, and writing. When he finished school in 1926, Fry was uncertain about his future. "I didn't know what I was going to do," he told Courtney. "I was rescued by the headmistress of the Froebel training college. There'd been talk about my going to art school, but we had no money and the local Bedford council wouldn't give me a grant, so that was that. Then the headmistress of the Froebel suggested that I should go on to the staff at the training college. This was pure charity. The headmaster of Bedford Modern had helped me a bit because he had got me to go back there to take some art classes with some of the school forms. I think he thought it would be good for my character to learn how to deal with these younger boys. There I was, at the age of eighteen, having to take care of fourteen and fifteen year olds. Still, we got on all right."

Though he was working, Fry had not yet decided what career he really wanted. He had seen plays as a child and thought the theater might interest him. So in 1927 he began working with a theater group at Citizen House in Bath, England. "I was both office boy and occasional actor," Fry recollected in his *SATA* interview with Courtney. "I was hurled into the first part I played. The head of the whole place was a woman called Consuelo de Reyes, who had red hair and was a very tough lady. Just as I arrived she had a terrible row with Hubert Cross, the leading character of the verse play they were doing. She sacked him and said to me, 'You will play this part tomorrow night.' I didn't even get a rehearsal. She took me down onto the stage, I can still remember, with the script and said, 'When you say this, move here and then here.' I stayed up all night learning these terrible lines. Luckily I was young and I could nearly keep it in my head. I remember the awful first performance with the other actors helping me if they could, here and there. This was the first thing I did there. I was too scared to notice whether I was good, I just did it."

Fry stayed with Citizen House for one year. He returned to teaching in 1928, becoming a schoolmaster at Hazelwood Preparatory School until 1931. The work pleased him for a while, he told Courtney, but he still thought of returning to the theater. "I quite enjoyed teaching for a time, then it got a bit boring. I was always teaching the same age group. I taught English right through the school, and my own form I took in everything except mathematics. They were eight and nine year olds. I always thought—I don't know why—that eventually I'd be writing plays."

Fry moved back to the theater in 1932, when he became founding director of the Tunbridge Wells Repertory Players. "The Tunbridge Wells Theatre was three parts amateur," Fry related to Courtney. "One extraordinary thing that happened while I was there was that I heard that George Bernard Shaw had written a new play, *Village Wooing,* and I had the great impertinence to write to him to see if I could direct it first? To my great astonishment—he knew absolutely nothing about me at all—he just wrote back and said, 'yes,' and promptly went off to New Zealand. We did it, and it seemed to go happily."

Though he would later return to Tunbridge Theatre, Fry left in 1935 to pursue his writing. The following year he married Phyllis Marjorie Hart, and shortly after he had his first play produced. "When I was married we went down to live in Ashdown Forest," Fry said in his *SATA* interview. "The vicar asked if I would write a play for the Jubilee of the church, and he suggested the story of Cuthman from a book called *The Worthies of Sussex.* That was really the beginning because that was seen by Gerard Hopkins, who worked for the Oxford University Press, and through him I was introduced to Charles Williams, who was also at the Oxford University Press. Charles introduced me to T. S. Eliot and E. Martin Browne. All these things came about through the first production of *The Boy with a Cart.*" After being produced in 1938, *The Boy with a Cart* became Fry's first published play when Oxford University Press printed it the following year.

Since that time, Fry has written and directed many plays. Some of his best known dramas include *A Phoenix Too Frequent, The Lady's Not for Burning, Venus Observed, A Sleep of Prisoners, The Dark Is Light Enough,* and *One Thing More; or, Caedmon Construed.* He has also translated and adapted plays written by such notable playwrights as Jean Anouilh and Henrik Ibsen. Among his television dramas for the British Broadcasting Corporation are *The Brontes of Haworth* and *Sister Dora.* In addition, Fry is known for his lectures and essays on topics ranging from comedy to death. Though most of his writings are for adults, he is the author of the librettos for *Seven at a Stroke* and *Robert of Sicily,* two operas for children. He also wrote a juvenile tale entitled *The Boat That Mooed.* Fry's writings, moreover, have earned him several awards, including the New York Critics Circle Award and the Queen's Gold Medal for Poetry.

For all his success in the literary world, Fry still finds it a chore to write. "It would be nice to be the kind of writer that enjoyed sitting down in a room and working all day, a sort of Anthony Trollope," Fry confessed to Courtney. "What pleasure that would be. I've never been the sort of writer that had to write. There are some people who can't live without writing. I have to bring myself to the point where it's my bounden duty to get on with it. I'd much rather not be writing. I'm lazy in the sense that I find it so good just to 'be,' to walk about the village or to do some gardening or write some letters. When I've got to write I'm not lazy. I go on and get it done on time, however many hours that means. I wish I liked writing better."

Better known for his religious dramas, Christopher Fry is also the translator of a French fairy tale by Colette. (From *The Boy and the Magic*, illustrated by Gerard Hoffnung.)

Fry has continued his involvement in the theater world in recent years, though his plays are no longer as widely produced as they were in the 1950s. In a 1986 article written by Courtney in *Observer Colour Magazine,* Michael Bakewell attributed Fry's decline in popularity to the type of poetic verse contained in his plays. The verse in Fry's plays is very different from the kind found in plays by writers like Samuel Beckett, whose works show life to be bleak and absurd. Bakewell said the two different approaches "ought to be able to live together. The theatregoers underestimate the extraordinary impact his plays had when they first appeared. I saw 'The Lady's Not For Burning' on a television set in an RAF hut in 1949, and the effect was tremendous. It was very, very exciting. This is one of Christopher's great qualities—he makes you enjoy things. He also makes you see things in a different way."

WORKS CITED:

Courtney, Cathy, "Fry's Saxon Delight," *Observer Colour Magazine,* November 2, 1986.

Fry, Christopher, *Can You Find Me: A Family History,* Oxford University Press, 1978.

Fry, Christopher, interview with Cathy Courtney for *Something about the Author.*

Hobson, Harold, *Drama,* spring, 1979.

FOR MORE INFORMATION SEE:

BOOKS

Contemporary Literary Criticism, Gale, Volume 2, 1974, Volume 10, 1979, Volume 14, 1980.

(From Colette's *The Boy and the Magic*, translated by Christopher Fry, illustrated by Gerard Hoffnung.)

Dictionary of Literary Biography, Volume 13: *British Drama-tists since World War II,* Gale, 1982.
Kirkpatrick, D. L., editor, *Contemporary Dramatists,* 4th edition, St. James Press, 1988.
Leeming, Glenda, *Poetic Drama,* Macmillan, 1989.
Leeming, Glenda, *Christopher Fry,* Twayne, 1990.
Roy, Emil, *Christopher Fry,* Southern Illinois University Press, 1968.
Stanford, Derek, *Christopher Fry: An Appreciation,* Peter Nevill, 1951.
Wiersma, Stanley, *More Than the Ear Discovers: God in the Plays of Christopher Fry,* Loyola University Press, 1983.

PERIODICALS

Ariel, October, 1975.
Literary Half-Yearly, July, 1971.
New Republic, August 20, 1951; March 3, 1952; December 2, 1978.
Newsweek, July 27, 1970.

New York Times Book Review, January 21, 1979.
New York Times Magazine, March 12, 1950.
Plays and Players, December, 1987.
Saturday Review, March 1, 1952; March 21, 1953.
Theatre Arts, September, 1950.
Times Literary Supplement, April 2, 1949; August 21, 1970; October 20, 1978.

*   *   *

GALDONE, Paul 1907(?)-1986

PERSONAL: Born in Budapest, Hungary, c. 1907; immigrated to United States, 1928; died November 7, 1986; married; wife's name, Jannelise; children: Joanna, Paul Ferencz. *Education:* Studied art at the Art Student's League and New York School for Industrial Design. *Hobbies and other interests:* Hiking, forestry, and gardening.

PAUL GALDONE

CAREER: Painter, sculptor, and illustrator of books for children. Worked variously as a bus boy, electrician's helper, fur dyer, and staff illustrator in the art department at Doubleday & Company (publisher). *Military service:* U.S. Army Engineers, World War II.

AWARDS, HONORS: Runner-up for the Caldecott Medal, 1957, for *Anatole,* and 1958, for *Anatole and the Cat* (both written by Eve Titus).

WRITINGS:

SELF-ILLUSTRATED

(With Eve Titus) *Basil of Baker Street,* McGraw, 1958.
Paddy the Penguin, Crowell, 1959.
Old Woman and Her Pig, Whittlesey House, 1960.
The House That Jack Built, Whittlesey House, 1961.
The Three Wishes, Whittlesey House, 1961.
(With Titus) *Anatole over Paris,* McGraw, 1961.
Hare and the Tortoise, McGraw, 1962.
(With Feenie Ziner) *Counting Carnival,* Coward, 1962.
Little Tuppen, Seabury, 1967.
The Horse, the Fox, and the Lion, Seabury, 1968.
Life of Jack Sprat, His Wife, and Cat, McGraw, 1969.
The Monkey and the Crocodile, Seabury, 1969.
(With Richard W. Armour) *All Sizes and Shapes of Monkeys and Apes,* McGraw, 1970.
(With daughter, Joanna Galdone) *Honeybee's Party,* F. Watts, 1972.

The Moving Adventures of Old Dame Trot and Her Comical Cat, McGraw, 1973.
(With J. Galdone) *Gertrude, the Goose Who Forgot,* F. Watts, 1975.
The Magic Porridge Pot, Seabury, 1976.
Cinderella, McGraw, 1978.
The Amazing Pig, Houghton Mifflin, 1981.
Hansel and Gretel, McGraw, 1982.
The Monster and the Tailor, Ticknor & Fields, 1982.
Jack and the Beanstalk, Ticknor & Fields, 1982.
The Greedy Old Fat Man, Houghton Mifflin, 1983.
The Elves and the Shoemaker, Ticknor & Fields, 1984.
Cat Goes Fiddle-i-Fee, Ticknor & Fields, 1985.
Little Bo-Peep, Ticknor & Fields, 1986.
Over in the Meadow, Simon & Shuster, 1989.

ILLUSTRATOR

Ellen MacGregor, *Miss Pickerell Goes to Mars,* Whittlesey House, 1951.
Edward Fenton, *Nine Lives,* Pantheon, 1951.
Ruthven Todd, *Space Cat,* Scribner, 1952, reprinted, 1971.
MacGregor, *Miss Pickerell and the Geiger Counter,* McGraw, 1953.
Doris T. Plenn, *Green Song,* McKay, 1954.
MacGregor, *Miss Pickerell Goes to the Arctic,* McGraw, 1954, reprinted, 1967.
Mary Mapes Dodge, *Hans Brinker,* Doubleday, 1954.
Miriam Schlein, *How Do You Travel?,* Abingdon, 1954.
William O. Steele, *Winter Danger,* Harcourt, 1954.

MacGregor, *Theodore Turtle*, Whittlesey House, 1955.
Steele, *Tomahawks and Trouble*, Harcourt, 1955.
Edward M. Eager, *Playing Possum*, Putnam, 1955.
MacGregor, *Mr. Ferguson and the Fire Department*, Whittlesey House, 1956.
Steele, *Lone Hunt*, Harcourt, 1956.
Titus, *Anatole*, Whittlesey House, 1956.
Margaret T. Burroughs, *Did You Feed My Cow?*, Crowell, 1956.
Amy Hogeboom, *Audubon and His Sons*, Lothrop, 1956.
Clyde T. Bulla, *Sword in the Tree*, Crowell, 1956.
Titus, *Anatole and the Cat*, McGraw, 1957.
Farley Mowat, *The Dog Who Wouldn't Be*, Little, 1957.
Todd, *Space Cat Meets Mars*, Scribner, 1957.
Steele, *Flaming Arrows*, Harcourt, 1957.
Bulla, *Old Charlie*, F. Watts, 1957.
M. Franklin and Eleanor K. Vaughan, *Rusty Rings a Bell*, Crowell, 1957.
Steele, *Perilous Road*, Harcourt, 1958.
Steele, *Far Frontier*, Harcourt, 1959.
Nathaniel Hawthorne, *The Golden Touch*, McGraw, 1959.
Franklin and Vaughan, *Timmy and the Tin-Can Telephone*, Crowell, 1959.
Mother Goose, *Old Mother Hubbard and Her Dog*, McGraw, 1960.
Scott Corbett, *The Lemonade Trick*, Little, Brown, 1960.
Eve Merriam, *A Gaggle of Geese*, Knopf, 1960.
Alfred Steinburg, *Woodrow Wilson*, Putnam, 1961.
Corbett, *The Mailbox Trick*, Little, Brown, 1961.
Cora Cheney and Ben Partridge, *Rendezvous in Singapore*, Knopf, 1961.
Karin Anckarsvärd, *Robber Ghost*, translated from the Swedish by Annabelle Macmillan, Harcourt, 1961.
Esther M. Meeks, *Jeff and Mr. James' Pond*, Lothrop, 1962.
Edward Lear, *The Two Old Bachelors*, McGraw, 1962.
Anckarsvärd, *Madcap Mystery*, translated from the Swedish by A. MacMillan, Harcourt, 1962.
The First Seven Days (adapted from the Bible), Crowell, 1962.
Alice E. Goudey, *Sunnyvale Fair*, Scribner, 1962.
John G. Saxe, *The Blind Men and the Elephant*, McGraw, 1963.
Henry Wadsworth Longfellow, *Paul Revere's Ride*, Crowell, 1963.
Corbett, *The Disappearing Dog Trick*, Little, Brown, 1963.
Wilson Gage, *Miss Osborne-the-Mop*, World Publishing, 1963.
Robert Barry, *Mister Willowby's Christmas Tree*, McGraw, 1963.
Rhoda Bacmeister, *People Downstairs, and Other City Stories*, Coward-McCann, 1964.
Vitali Bianki, *Peek the Piper*, Braziller, 1964.
Johnston, *Edie Changes Her Mind*, Putnam, 1964.
Corbett, *The Limerick Trick*, Little, Brown, 1964.
Francis Hopkinson, *The Battle of the Kegs*, Crowell, 1964.
Mother Goose, *Tom, Tom, the Piper's Son*, McGraw, 1964.
Mary O'Neill, *People I'd Like to Keep*, Doubleday, 1964.
Titus, *Anatole and the Poodle*, Whittlesey House, 1965.
John Greenleaf Whittier, *Barbara Frietchie*, Crowell, 1965.
Richard W. Armour, *The Adventures of Egbert the Easter Egg*, McGraw, 1965.
Oliver Wendell Holmes, *The Deacon's Masterpiece*, McGraw, 1965.
Shadrach, Meshach and Abednego, Whittlesey House, 1965.
Helen E. Buckley, *The Little Boy and the Birthdays*, Lothrop, 1965.
Corbett, *The Baseball Trick*, Little, Brown, 1965.
Anckarsvärd, *Mysterious Schoolmaster*, translated from the Swedish by A. MacMillan, Harcourt, 1965.

Hans Peterson, *Brownie*, Lothrop, 1965.
Dale Fife, *Who's in Charge of Lincoln?*, Coward-McCann, 1965.
Titus, *Anatole and the Piano*, McGraw, 1966.
Johnston, *That's Right, Edie*, Putnam, 1966.
The History of Simple Simon, McGraw, 1966.
Francis Scott Key, *The Star-Spangled Banner*, Crowell, 1966.
Ivan Kusan, *Koko and the Ghosts*, Harcourt, 1966.
Lear, *Two Laughable Lyrics*, Putnam, 1966.
Armour, *Animals on the Ceiling*, McGraw, 1966.
Wilson Gage, *The Ghost of Five Owl Farm*, World Publishing, 1966.
Lee G. Goetz, *A Camel in the Sea*, McGraw, 1966.
Sidney Offit, *The Adventures of Homer Fink*, St. Martin, 1966.
Edgar Allan Poe, *Three Poems of Edgar Allan Poe*, McGraw, 1966.
Wylly Folk St. John, *The Secrets of Hidden Creek*, Viking, 1966.
Armour, *A Dozen Dinosaurs*, McGraw, 1967.
Guy Daniels, *The Tsar's Riddles*, McGraw, 1967.
Corbett, *The Turnabout Trick*, Little, Brown, 1967.
Barbara Rinkoff, *Elbert, the Mind Reader*, Lothrop, 1967.
Hawthorne, *Pandora's Box: The Paradise of Children*, McGraw, 1967.
Patricia M. Martin, *Woody's Big Trouble*, Putnam, 1967.
Letta Schatz, *Whiskers, My Cat*, McGraw, 1967.
Judy Van der Veer, *Wallace the Wandering Pig*, Harcourt, 1967.
Armour, *Who's in Holes*, McGraw, 1967.
Paul Showers, *Your Skin and Mine*, Black, 1967.
Franklyn M. Branley, *High Sounds, Low Sounds*, Crowell, 1967.
Armour, *Odd Old Mammals*, McGraw-Hill, 1968.
Steele, *The Buffalo Knife*, Harcourt, 1968.
Richard Shaw, *Budd's Noisy Wagon*, F. Warne, 1968.
Augusta R. Goldin, *Sunlit Sea*, Crowell, 1968.
Grimm Brothers, *The Bremen Town Musicians*, McGraw, 1968.
Clement C. Moore, *A Visit from St. Nicholas*, McGraw, 1968.
Francois Rabelais, *The Wise Fool*, Random, 1968.
Henny Penny, Seabury, 1968.
Peggy Mann, *The Boy with a Billion Pets*, Coward-McCann, 1968.
Corbett, *The Hairy Horror Trick*, Little, Brown, 1969.
H. E. Buckley, *Grandmother and I*, Lothrop, 1969.
Jean Fritz, *George Washington's Breakfast*, Coward-McCann, 1969.
Carol Iden, *Sidney's Ghost*, World Publishing, 1969.
Van der Veer, *To the Rescue*, Harcourt, 1969.
Pura Belpre, *Ote*, Pantheon, 1969.
Titus, *Anatole and the Thirty Thieves*, McGraw, 1969.
Androcles and the Lion, McGraw, 1970.
Three Little Pigs, Seabury, 1970.
History of Little Tom Tucker, McGraw, 1970.
Fife, *What's New, Lincoln?*, Coward-McCann, 1970.
Roberta Greene, *Two and Me Makes Three*, Coward-McCann, 1970.
Titus, *Anatole and the Toyshop*, McGraw, 1970.
Judith Viorst, *Try It Again, Sam: Safety When You Walk*, Lothrop, 1970.
Fife, *What's the Prize, Lincoln?*, Coward-McCann, 1971.
Obedient Jack, F. Watts, 1971.
The Town Mouse and the Country Mouse, McGraw, 1971.
Aesop, *Three Aesop Fox Fables*, Seabury, 1971.
John Knoepfle, *Dogs and Cats and Things Like That* (poems), McGraw, 1971.
Corbett, *The Hateful Plateful Trick*, Little, Brown, 1971.
Titus, *Basil and the Pygmy Cats*, McGraw, 1971.

Goldilocks was so frightened that
she tumbled out of bed and ran to the open window.

Out she jumped!

(From *The Three Bears*, written and illustrated by Paul Galdone.)

Beatrice S. de Regniers, *It Does Not Say Meow*, Seabury, 1972.

Mary L. Solot, *100 Hamburgers: The Getting Thin Book*, Lothrop, 1972.

Belpre, *Dance of the Animals: A Puetro Rican Folk Tale*, F. Warne, 1972.

Zibby Oneal, *The Improbable Adventures of Marvelous O'Hara Soapstone*, Viking, 1972.

The Three Bears, Seabury, 1972.

Corbett, *The Home Run Trick*, Little, Brown, 1973.

F. N. Monjo, *Clarence and the Burglar*, Coward-McCann, 1973.

Diane Wolkstein, *The Cool Ride in the Sky*, Knopf, 1973.

Titus, *Anatole in Italy*, McGraw, 1973.

Peter C. Asbjornsen, *The Three Billy Goats Gruff*, Seabury, 1973.

Joseph Jacobs, *Hereafterthis*, McGraw, 1973.

The Little Red Hen, Seabury, 1973.

Edna Barth, *Jack O'Lantern*, Seabury, 1974.

Armour, *Sea Full of Whales*, McGraw, 1974.

The History of Mother Twaddle and the Marvelous Achievements of Her Son Jack, Seabury, 1974.

Johnston, *Speak Up, Edie!*, Putnam, 1974.

Corbett, *The Hockey Trick*, Little, Brown, 1974.

Grimm Brothers, *Little Red Riding Hood*, McGraw, 1974.

Grimm Brothers, *The Frog Prince*, McGraw, 1974.

Dorothy Van Woerkom, *The Queen Who Couldn't Bake Gingerbread*, Random House, 1975.

Mary Q. Steele, *Because of the Sand Witches There*, Greenwillow Books, 1975.

Fife, *Who Goes There, Lincoln?*, Coward-McCann 1975.

Showers, *Follow Your Nose*, Crowell, 1975.

Titus, *Basil in Mexico*, McGraw, 1975.

The Gingerbread Boy, Seabury, 1975.

Pat D. Tapio, *The Lady Who Saw the Good Side of Everything*, Seabury, 1975.

Patricia Lauber, *Clarence and the Burglar*, Worlds Work 1975.

Showers, *Look at Your Eyes*, Black, 1969, Crowell, 1976.

Showers, *How Many Teeth?*, Crowell, 1976.

Corbett, *The Black Mask Trick*, Little, Brown, 1976.

Charles Perrault, *Puss in Boots*, Seabury, 1976.

Grimm Brothers, *The Table, the Donkey, and the Stick*, McGraw, 1976.

Joanna Galdone, *Amber Day*, McGraw, 1978.

Hans Christian Andersen, *The Princess and the Pea*, Seabury, 1978.

Kathleen Leverich, *The Hungry Fox and the Foxy Duck*, Parents, 1979.

de Regniers, *It Does Not Say Meow*, Houghton Mifflin, 1979.

Joanna Galdone, *The Little Girl and the Big Bear*, Houghton Mifflin, 1980.

Joseph Jacobs, *King of Cats*, Houghton Mifflin, 1980.

Titus, *Basil in the Old West*, McGraw, 1981.

Charles Keller, *Norma Lee, I Don't Knock on Doors: Knock Knock Jokes*, Prentice-Hall, 1983.

Corbett, *The Disappearing Dog Trick*, Scholastic, 1983.

Jean Fritz, *George Washington's Breakfast*, Putnam, 1984.

John W. Ivimey, *The Complete Story of the Three Blind Mice*, Ticknor & Fields, 1989.

SIDELIGHTS: The late Paul Galdone was an accomplished artist in a variety of media. He was best known as a writer and illustrator of children's books. Galdone usually used pen, ink, and wash in his drawings, and he often looked to nature for inspiration. Galdone especially enjoyed sketching animals (cats being a particular favorite). Inspired by artists such as Arthur Rackham and Walter Crane, Galdone also created critically acclaimed picture book adaptations of classic fairy tales and fables.

In an interview with Lee Bennett Hopkins for *Books Are by People: Interviews with 104 Authors and Illustrators of Books for Young Children*, Paul Galdone discussed his sometimes difficult childhood. He told Bennett: "When I was about fourteen my family and I left Budapest. On arrival in New Jersey I was promptly enrolled in high school. The Hungarian language did not prove very useful in the United States.... I had to attend three English classes every day in addition to biology class." Because he could not express himself very well in English, Galdone found it difficult to speak in front of his classmates. He found an escape in biology, where he "felt more successful; when it was discovered that I was proficient in the drawing of grasshoppers I was soon drawing them for all the pupils."

While still a teenager, Galdone took a number of jobs to help support his family. He was a busboy, electrician's helper, and fur-dyer. At night, Galdone attended art school at the Art Student's League and the New York School of Industrial Design. After working in the art department of Doubleday & Company for four years, Galdone had the opportunity to design a book jacket. The design project was such a big success that Galdone decided to leave the company and become a freelance artist.

Galdone got an apartment in Greenwich Village and began working on book cover ideas. "I kept up my interest in fine arts by drawing and painting and by long sketching vacations in Vermont," he related to Hopkins. At the same time, Galdone was experimenting with book illustration. After a slow start, Galdone began to sell his work. Eventually, he was successful enough to satisfy his long-term dream of moving to the country. The realization of Galdone's dream was made all the more special when Galdone's brother-in-law designed a home for the artist and his family in rural Rockland County, New York. Because his new house was in the country, Galdone was able to engage in two of his favorite hobbies: gardening and enjoying the outdoors. "I love the outdoors. I love everything about nature. Look at these trees. Trees give you such permanence," Galdone commented to Hopkins.

Many of Galdone's works have been adaptations of classic fairy tales and fables. Critics have praised his ability to breathe new life into the old tales with colorful images and intricate details. A *Library Journal* critic lauded Galdone's work for managing to "capture the mood of the moment, and, through subtle touches, [add] much to the story." The *School Library Journal* cited *The Gingerbread Boy* as "broadly humorous" and the "most delectable" version of the story currently available. "Big bold, uncluttered pictures that are just right for using with a group of children at story hour.... Galdone at his vigorous best," noted the *Bulletin of the Center for Children's Books* about *The Three Billy Goats Gruff*. And a reviewer for *Publishers Weekly* was equally laudatory about Galdone's adaptation of *Puss in Boots*. The reviewer noted that Galdone's "interpretation of the ancient French tale, accompanied by richly colored and detailed pictures, glows with satiric wit."

Galdone attributed part of his success in writing and illustrating children's books to the "freedom of their naturally whimsical nature." He also found that taking his time when working on a new project made a big difference. "One of the

(From *The Elves and the Shoemaker,* written and illustrated by Paul Galdone.)

most valuable things in life to me is time," Galdone told Hopkins, "Time to work, to live, to be out under the sky, and to be with my family."

WORKS CITED:

Hopkins, Lee Bennett, *Books Are by People: Interviews with 104 Authors and Illustrators of Books for Young Children,* Citation Press, 1969.
Something about the Author, Volume 17, Gale, 1979, pp. 69-75.

FOR MORE INFORMATION SEE:

PERIODICALS

Book World, November 9, 1969.

Bulletin of the Center for Children's Books, February, 1982; October, 1982; December, 1982; June, 1983; December, 1986.
Hornbook, February, 1978; August, 1981.
Junior Bookshelf, October, 1978; April, 1979; December, 1979; June, 1980; October, 1980; December, 1980; June, 1981; December, 1981.
Junior Literary Guild, September, 1962; September, 1965; March, 1980; March, 1987.
New York Times Book Review, February 24, 1985.
Publishers Weekly, February 23, 1976; November 20, 1978; March 12, 1982; June 3, 1982; July 23, 1982; October 28, 1983; July 27, 1984; August 9, 1985; February 21, 1986; August 22, 1986.
Time, July 7, 1986.
Times Literary Supplement, September 17, 1982.
Young Wings, December, 1955.

GALLOWAY, Priscilla 1930-
(Anne Peebles)

PERSONAL: Born July 22, 1930, in Montreal, Quebec, Canada; daughter of Allon (an economist) and Noeline (a social worker and printmaker; maiden name, Bruce) Peebles; married Bev Galloway, September 17, 1949 (died October 25, 1985); children: Noel, Walt, Glenn. *Education:* Queen's University, Kingston, Ontario, B.A., 1951; University of Toronto, M.A., 1959, Ph.D., 1977.

ADDRESSES: Home and office—12 Didrickson Dr., North York, Ontario, Canada M2P 1J6.

CAREER: English teacher at public school in Toronto, Ontario, 1954-56; Board of Education for the City of North York, North York, Ontario, 1956-86, began as English teacher, became reading and language arts consultant. Scholar-in-residence at Queen's University, Kingston, Ontario, 1978; instructor at University of Toronto, 1979—, University of British Columbia, summer, 1980, Christchurch Teachers' College, Christchurch, New Zealand, 1985-86, and Acadia University, 1991; writer-in-residence in the libraries of Cobalt, Haileybury, and New Liskeard, northern Ontario, 1987-88; member of Council of Queen's University.

MEMBER: Writers' Union of Canada (chairman of curriculum committee, 1983-84), Canadian Society of Children's Authors, Illustrators, and Performers (vice-president, 1988-89; president, 1989-91), Ontario Council of Teachers of English (president, 1973-75), Canadian Council of Teachers of English, Children's Literature Association.

AWARDS, HONORS: Teacher of the year award from Ontario Council of Teachers of English, 1975; Marty Memorial Scholarship from Queen's University, 1976-77.

WRITINGS:

FOR CHILDREN

Good Times, Bad Times, Mummy and Me (illustrated by Lissa Calvert), Women's Press, 1980.
When You Were Little and I Was Big (illustrated by Heather Collins), Annick Press, 1984.
Jennifer Has Two Daddies (illustrated by Ana Auml), Women's Press, 1985.
Seal Is Lost (illustrated by Karen Patkau), Annick Press, 1988.

TRANSLATOR OF "ANNA, PAUL AND TOMMYCAT" SERIES; ALL BY NICOLE GIRARD AND PAUL DANHEUX

Anna, Paul and Tommycat Say Hello, Lorimer, 1987.
Looking for Tommycat, Lorimer, 1987.
Where Is Tommycat?, Lorimer, 1988.
A Letter from the Moon, Lorimer, 1988.
Tommycat Comes Back at Last, Lorimer, 1988.
Tommycat Is Gone Again, Lorimer, 1988.

OTHER

What's Wrong With High School English?: It's Sexist, Un-Canadian, Outdated, Ontario Institute for Studies in Education Press, 1980.
(Editor) *Timely and Timeless: Contemporary Prose,* Clarke, Irwin, 1983.
(Contributor) Joy Parr, editor, *Personal Stories by Queen's Women to Celebrate the Fiftieth Anniversary of the Mary*

PRISCILLA GALLOWAY

Memorial Scholarship, Queen's Alumnae Association, 1987.
(Editor) *The Tri-Town Writers' Anthology,* Cobalt Public Library, 1988.

Also author of more than twenty teaching guides and student activities for *Books about You* kits published by Annick Educational (series 1: primary, series 2: junior, and series 3: pattern books), 1987—. Contributor of stories, poems and articles to education journals and popular magazines, including *Chatelaine, Canadian Forum, Waves,* and *Atlantis,* and to newspapers, sometimes under pseudonym Anne Peebles.

WORK IN PROGRESS: Mum and Me and Ms. T. and *Monster Lunch,* children's books; a book of adult fairy tales; further "Anna, Paul and Tommycat" adaptations from the French; further study guides for Annick Educational.

SIDELIGHTS: Priscilla Galloway was born in Montreal. She lived as a child in western Canada, learning to swim in the icy waters of the Pacific Ocean. She moved to Central Canada with her family during World War II, attending secondary school in Ottawa. "I began writing poetry almost as soon as I could form words on a page," she told *Something about the Author.* "My father had literary ambitions for me. When I came home at age fourteen, thrilled with my first summer job offer as half-time sales clerk in a shoe store, Dad was indignant at this proposed waste of my time. He matched the shoe store's offer of $7.00 per week, paying me to spend

A little girl trades roles with her mother in Priscilla Galloway's 1984 picture book, *When You Were Little and I Was Big.* (Cover illustration by Heather Collins.)

the same amount of time at home, writing. My first paid publication was a story in a Sunday school paper when I was twelve; it earned three dollars.

"I have been a compulsive reader since before starting school, but for a long time thought I could not become a 'real' writer, one of those literary people I loved and revered. As a teenager, I intended to go into journalism. The height of my ambition was to do graduate work in journalism at Columbia, where my parents had met and my father had done his Ph.D., but there seemed no way to finance such a venture. My father had his first heart attack in my final year of high school; that was my loss of innocence time; my father's support, both emotional and financial, was gone for ever.

For the rest of his life, he would be increasingly dependent on other people.

"When I began undergraduate studies in 1947, universities were full of men (and some women) back from war, often many years in the armed forces or in prisoner of war camps. I was a very naive civilian, just turned seventeen. I began my apprenticeship in journalism on the university paper, where I had the library beat. Ours was a professional paper, edited by men with years of pre-war and wartime experience. Because I had to support myself, I was not able to continue this unpaid work after my first year, and the journalism dream began to fade.

"I married and had a baby before completing my undergraduate degree, taking my final courses extramurally. Our first two children were born eighteen months apart in northern Quebec, where my husband worked underground as a geological engineer, first for a small gold mine, then for a large base metal mine. I couldn't get a job of any kind at that time there. Mining was (and is) a precarious business, and my husband was outspoken and independent. It was frightening to be dependent on him, especially as we were still repaying money we had borrowed for university.

"When we moved to Ontario and I was offered some part-time teaching, I was quick to accept. Bev lost the new job after a few months and went as a field geologist to northern Manitoba, leaving me to keep the home fires (in the form of a coal furnace) burning. Teaching gave me the opportunity to leave my babies in other hands for a few hours, while I had rational converse with people who could speak. It was energy-intensive work, but I am convinced it saved my sanity through the drifts of that long winter. In early spring Bev was injured and sent for rehabilitation therapy to hospital in Toronto, where I could qualify as a secondary school English teacher. Journalism was abandoned, and I began a thirty-one year career in education.

"From the beginning, however, I wrote articles for other teachers. I also wrote poetry with my students. I worked with associations of English teachers and began to know the important people in the academic literary establishment in Canada. I also ran the office, did the payroll, and kept the books for Bev's various business enterprises, managing an apartment building and a trailer park as well as producing a third child.

"Tillie Olson writes about how women's writing voice has been silenced, often with household drudgery and babies, with lack of personal time and space. I had a professional career and live-in housekeepers to care for my children, but no time, space or energy for myself and my own needs. In my mid-forties, I took stock and began to act out some of my fantasies. I wrote short stories, and made sales to two of the three most prestigious markets in Canada, the Canadian Broadcasting Corporation's literary program, *Anthology,* and *Chatelaine.* Some poetry was published. I took up scuba and did a Ph.D. My first two books were published within a month of each other: *Good Times, Bad Times, Mummy and Me,* a children's picture book, and *What's Wrong with High School English?: It's Sexist, UnCanadian, Outdated,* based on my doctoral research. I arranged a teaching exchange and went to New Zealand as an instructor at Christchurch Teacher's College.

"Bev and I had moved a long way apart, and he did not come with me when I left, although he was to come for the long vacation in December. He died, totally unexpectedly, at the end of October. I have since then retired from my full-time position in education; these days I smile and say 'author' when required to state my occupation, although I continue part-time university teaching, mainly in the graduate faculty of education at the University of Toronto. My children are all married; there are eight grandchildren in the three families.

"For a year, I was writer-in-residence in libraries in three small communities in Northern Ontario, returning to the mining region where I began to teach. With a car, an office, a position of prestige, and neither coal furnace nor babies, I had a marvelous year working with local writers and aspiring writers. (Would that there had been somebody to give me that kind of help ten or twelve years ago!) The local libraries received a grant from the provincial government for the residency. It was a delight to encourage and help the talented and enthusiastic people who came, some from many miles, for courses, workshops, and individual sessions. I edited an anthology of their work, and the Cobalt Public Library published it. As CANSCAIP president in 1989-91, I worked with other authors, illustrators and performers on behalf of Canadian children's culture.

"Life is rich and full. As I write this, I have many books in print. Larger projects are forming in my mind and notebooks are filling. Is a novel next? Or two?"

*   *   *

GERROLD, David 1944-

PERSONAL: Born January 24, 1944, in Chicago, IL; son of Lewis (a photographer) and Johanna (Fleischer) Friedman. *Education:* Attended University of Southern California; received B.A. from California State University at Northridge.

ADDRESSES: Home and office—Box 1190, Hollywood, CA 90078. *Agent:* Richard Curtis, 164 East 64th St., New York, NY 10021.

CAREER: Science-fiction writer, 1967—.

AWARDS, HONORS: Hugo Award nomination, 1968, for *The Trouble with Tribbles;* Nebula Award nomination, 1972, for *In the Deadlands,* and 1977, for *Moonstar Odyssey;* Hugo and Nebula Award nominations, 1972, for *When Harlie Was One,* 1973, for *The Man Who Folded Himself,* and 1977, for *Moonstar Odyssey;* Skylark Award, 1979.

WRITINGS:

(With Larry Niven) *The Flying Sorcerers* (novel), Ballantine, 1971.
(Editor with Stephen Goldin) *Protostars,* Ballantine, 1971.
(Editor with Goldin) *Generation,* Dell, 1972.
Space Skimmer (novel), Ballantine, 1972.
When Harlie Was One (Science Fiction Book Club selection), Doubleday, 1972.
With a Finger in My Eye (short stories), Ballantine, 1972.
Yesterday's Children (novel), Dell, 1972.
Battle for the Planet of the Apes (novel; adapted from the screenplay by John William Corrington and Joyce Hooper Corrington), Universal Publishing & Distributing, 1973.
The Man Who Folded Himself (Science Fiction Book Club selection), Random House, 1973.
The World of Star Trek, Ballantine, 1973, revised edition, Bluejay Books, 1984.
(Editor) *Alternities* (anthology), Dell, 1974.
(Editor) *Emphasis* (anthology), Ballantine, 1974.
(Contributor) Alan Dean Foster, editor, *Star Trek Log,* Corgi, 1976.
(Editor) *Ascents of Wonder* (anthology), Popular Library, 1977.
Moonstar Odyssey (novel), New American Library, 1977.
Deathbeast (novel), Popular Library, 1978.
When Harlie Was Two, Bantam, 1987.
Star Trek—The Next Generation: Encounter at Farpoint (also see below; adapted from the teleplay of same title), Pocket Books, 1987.
Chess with a Dragon, illustrated by Daniel Torres, Walker & Co., 1988.

555

David Gerrold's 1967 "Star Trek" script, "The Trouble with Tribbles," addresses the havoc wreaked by harmless-looking furry creatures.

A Matter for Men, Bantam, 1989.
A Day for Damnation, Bantam, 1989.
A Rage for Revenge, Bantam, 1989.
War against Chtorr, Books: 1-3, Bantam, 1989.

TELEPLAYS

The Trouble with Tribbles (first produced as episode of "Star Trek" television series, broadcast on NBC-TV, December 29, 1967), Ballantine, 1973.

Also author of a revision of *I, Mudd,* produced in 1967, and *The Cloud Minders,* produced in 1968, both as episodes for "Star Trek" series, and of *More Troubles, More Tribbles* and *BEM,* both for the animated "Star Trek" series. Author of *A Day in Beaumont* for "Twilight Zone" series and contributed to screenplay *Encounter at Farpoint* for "Star Trek: The Next Generation" series. Author of adaptation of Ted Sturgeon's *A Saucer of Loneliness.*

OTHER

Columnist in *Starlog* and *Galileo.* Story editor for "Land of the Lost" series, 1974, and "Buck Rogers" series.

WORK IN PROGRESS: "It's bad luck to talk about them prior to completion."

SIDELIGHTS: David Gerrold is a respected writer of a variety of works of science-fiction, including short stories, books, screenplays, and television scripts. While his various works are very popular with the general public, the majority of his writings have received little attention from reviewers and critics.

Gerrold's professional writing career began in 1967 when his script *The Trouble with Tribbles* was produced as an episode on the popular "Star Trek" series. This entertaining episode concerns the havoc and danger little fury creatures produce on the Starship Enterprise. This script was nominated for the prestigious Hugo Award. Since this first contribution, Gerrold has regularly written quality material for such successful network television series as "Star Trek," "Twilight Zone," and "Star Trek: The Next Generation."

In 1971, Gerrold collaborated with fellow science fiction fan and writer, Larry Niven, to write *The Flying Sorcerers.* This novel amusingly recounts a planet's transfer of it's reliance on magic to science and it's emergence toward industrialization. "The shrewd and practical protagonist and the character of the humor reveal Niven's touch, but the word play, sympathy for women, and general humanity seem to be Gerrold's," remarks Edra Bogle in the *Dictionary of Literary Biography,* Volume 8: *Twentieth-Century American Science Fiction Writers.*

Another of Gerrold's science fiction novels is *Yesterday's Children.* The *Times Literary Supplement* calls this book a "rare thing in the genre: a study of character." Aboard the starship *Burlingame,* a weak and tired captain contends with his mutinous crew, gives reluctant chase to an enemy space craft, and struggles with an ambitious, power-usurping officer for control of the ship. *Yesterday's Children* has been compared to the *Caine Mutiny,* because both books examine the emotional and moral conflicts generated by the shifting balance of military authority. The *Times Literary Supplement* concluded: "*Yesterday's Children* remains a solidly worked-out SF novel with unusually good characterization."

WORKS CITED:

Edra Bogle, "David Gerrold," *Dictionary of Literary Biography,* Volume 8: *Twentieth-Century American Science Fiction Writers,* Part 1, Gale, 1981, pp. 189-191.
Times Literary Supplement, June 14, 1974, p. 644.

David Gerrold's science-fiction novel, *When Harlie Was One,* was nominated for both the Hugo and Nebula awards. (Cover art by Frank Riley.)

FOR MORE INFORMATION SEE:

PERIODICALS

Book World, March 30, 1975.
Publishers Weekly, February 4, 1974; May 13, 1974; January 3, 1977; June 5, 1978.
Times Literary Supplement, February 15, 1974.
Village Voice, June 13, 1974.

*   *   *

GIBSON, William 1914-

PERSONAL: Born November 13, 1914, in New York, NY; son of George Irving (a bank clerk) and Florence (Dore) Gibson; married first wife, c. 1935 (divorced); married Margaret Brenman (a psychoanalyst), September 6, 1940; children: Thomas, Daniel. *Education:* Attended City College (now City College of the City University of New York), 1930-32. *Politics:* Democrat. *Religion:* None.

ADDRESSES: Home—Stockbridge, MA. *Agent*—Flora Roberts, 157 West 57th St., New York, NY 10022.

CAREER: Author and playwright. Piano teacher and player at intervals in early writing days to supplement income. President and cofounder of Berkshire Theatre Festival, Stockbridge, MA, 1966—.

MEMBER: PEN, Authors League of America, Dramatists Guild.

AWARDS, HONORS: Harriet Monroe Memorial Prize, 1945, for group of poems published in *Poetry;* Topeka Civic Theatre award, 1947, for *A Cry of Players;* Sylvania Award, 1957, for television play *The Miracle Worker.*

WRITINGS:

PLAYS

I Lay in Zion (one-act; first produced in Topeka, KS, at the Topeka Civic Theatre, 1943), Samuel French, 1947.
The Ruby (one-act lyrical drama based on Lord Dunsany's *A Night at an Inn;* music by Norman Dello Joio), Ricordi, 1955.
The Miracle Worker (three-act; originally written as a television drama; produced by Columbia Broadcasting System for *Playhouse 90* in 1957 and by National Broadcasting Company in 1979; rewritten for stage and first produced on Broadway at the Playhouse Theatre, October 19, 1959; rewritten for screen and produced by United Artists in 1962; also see below), Knopf, 1957.
Two for the Seesaw (three-act comedy; copyrighted in 1956 as *After the Verb to Love;* first produced on Broadway at the Booth Theatre, January 16, 1958; also see below), Samuel French, 1960.
Dinny and the Witches [and] *The Miracle Worker* (the former first produced in Topeka at the Topeka Civic Theatre, 1948; produced Off-Broadway at the Cherry Lane Theatre, December 9, 1959; also see below), Atheneum, 1960.
Dinny and the Witches: A Frolic on Grave Matters Dramatists Play Service, 1961.
(With Clifford Odets) *Golden Boy* (musical adaptation of Odets's original drama; lyrics by Lee Adams and music

WILLIAM GIBSON

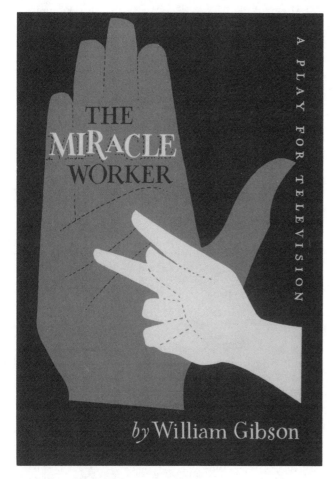

William Gibson's award-winning play recounts how a deaf, dumb, and blind Helen Keller learned to communicate. (*The Miracle Worker* jacket design by Guy Fleming.)

by Charles Strouse; first produced on Broadway at the Majestic Theatre, October 20, 1964), Atheneum, 1965.

A Cry of Players (three-act; first produced in Topeka at the Topeka Civic Theatre, February, 1948; produced on Broadway at the Vivian Beaumont Theatre, November 14, 1968), Atheneum, 1969.

John and Abigail (three-act; first produced in Stockbridge, MA, at the Berkshire Theatre Festival, summer, 1969, produced in Washington, DC, at Ford's Theatre, January 9, 1970), published as *American Primitive: The Words of John and Abigail Adams Put into a Sequence for the Theatre, with Addenda in Rhyme,* Atheneum, 1972.

The Body and the Wheel (first produced in Lenox, MA, at the Pierce Chapel, April 5, 1974), Dramatists Play Service, 1975.

The Butterfingers Angel, Mary and Joseph, Herod the Nut, and the Slaughter of Twelve Hit Carols in a Pear Tree (first produced in Lenox at the Pierce Chapel, December, 1974), Dramatists Play Service, 1975.

Golda (first produced on Broadway at the Morosco Theatre, November 14, 1977), Samuel French, 1977.

Monday after the Miracle (first produced in Charleston, SC, at the Dock Street Theatre, May, 1982, produced on Broadway at the Eugene O'Neill Theatre, December 14, 1982), Atheneum, 1983.

Raggedy Ann (musical), first produced in Albany, NY, at the Egg Theatre, December 7, 1985.

Goodly Creatures (first produced in Washington, DC, at the Round House Theatre, January, 1980), Dramatists Play Service, 1986.

Handy Dandy (first produced in Syracuse, NY, at the Syracuse Stage Theatre, October 12, 1984), Dramatists Play Service, 1986.

OTHER

Winter Crook (poems), Oxford University Press, 1948.

The Cobweb (novel), Knopf, 1954.

The Seesaw Log (a chronicle of the stage production, including the text of *Two for the Seesaw*), Knopf, 1959.

A Mass for the Dead (chronicle and poems), Atheneum, 1968.

A Season in Heaven (chronicle), Atheneum, 1974.

Shakespeare's Game (criticism), Atheneum, 1978.

Notes on How to Turn a Phoenix into Ashes: The Story of the Stage Production, with the Text of "Golda," Atheneum, 1978.

Contributor to periodicals, including *Poetry.*

ADAPTATIONS: The Cobweb was made into a motion picture starring Lauren Bacall, Charles Boyer, and Richard Widmark, Metro-Goldwyn-Mayer, 1955; *Two for the Seesaw* was made into a motion picture starring Robert Mitchum and Shirley MacLaine, United Artists, 1962.

SIDELIGHTS: Eager to rise above poor beginnings, William Gibson's family moved frequently, resettling Gibson and his younger sister throughout the Bronx and Queens where he attended public school, primarily because his mother believed that Catholic schooling, by concentrating too heavily on religion, would produce illiterates. For years, however, she would force her son to walk to church services and Sunday school every week, regardless of the weather. When he was finally old enough to act on his own he left the church, creating a gulf between himself and his mother.

As a child Gibson was more advanced in his studies than his older schoolmates—and much smaller. So he took refuge in books. He relished pulp magazines featuring western, science fiction, and "amazing" stories, and he would become so engrossed in these adventures that he would not hear a houseful of people when he was reading. His favorite Christmas gift was the complete works of his favorite sports biographer.

In addition to reading stories, Gibson found solace in writing them, often imitating the style of the author he was interested in at the time. He burrowed so deeply into his world of letters, in fact, that his parents became concerned and urged him to play outside with other children. Eager to please them, Gibson would overdo it, often landing in the doctor's office with various injuries, including a lollipop stick impaled in his palate, knocked-out teeth, and a broken wrist.

But during his teen years Gibson struggled with his parents' high expectations of him. He rebelled against school, his mother's religion, and his parents' politics, but he could not deny his love for the piano, a passion he shared with his father. Still, when the two played jazz duets, the son would always try to outplay his father.

As high school graduation approached, Gibson toyed with the idea of becoming a writer. He never worked for the school newspaper—he hated deadlines—but he continued to compose his own stories, one of which, about a former boxer, won first prize in the school magazine contest. As an added reward, for a graduation gift his parents bought him his own typewriter.

Gibson entered City College of the City University of New York to study science. He was an average student, but he soon became bored with his classes. He again sought refuge in writing, and submitted poetry and short stories to magazines, which were rejected. Nonetheless, he continued to write. After two years of study, Gibson quit school and set out on a course of self education, concentrating first on criminology and then biographies of U.S. presidents.

As his stories continued to be turned down by magazines and he grew more concerned with his future, Gibson decided to return to college to become an English teacher. He blossomed in his writing classes and ignored all others; this resulted in his expulsion, but not before he had made the decision to become a writer.

At twenty-one, Gibson moved out of his parents' house and married, informing his parents after the event. The marriage lasted a year. Soon after his father suffered a hemorrhage. It was during his father's convalescence that Gibson sold his first story for $150 to a magazine. His father prophesied, sadly, that although one day his son would be famous, he would not live long enough to see it. When his father was diagnosed as having abdominal cancer, Gibson returned to his parents' home to help care for his dying father and rented a storeroom nearby to use as his writing office.

After his father's death at Christmastime, Gibson stayed with his mother and sister through the winter, and in spring moved back to a flat with Margaret Brenman, whom he met in Queens. After two years of work on a play—whose mediocrity proved to Gibson that he knew nothing about playwriting—Gibson took an acting job with the Barter Theatre in Arbingdon, Virginia, and played jazz piano in bars to supplement his income. When Brenman secured a position working in the Menninger Clinic in Topeka, Kansas, Gibson and she headed West. They married in 1940.

Gibson first enjoyed literary success in 1943, when his one-act verse play *I Lay in Zion* was produced at the Topeka Civic Theatre. In 1948 *A Cry of Players,* which chronicles the early life of William Shakespeare, and *Dinny and the Witches* were also produced at the Topeka Civic Theatre. Gibson then published a novel, *The Cobweb,* in 1954; three years later Metro-Goldwyn-Mayer filmed the story, with Lauren Bacall, Charles Boyer, and Richard Widmark.

The lifelong distance between Gibson and his mother was finally mended when Gibson himself became a parent. Financially strapped and with his wife in her ninth month, Gibson wrote a television script to pay the bills. Although the script earned Gibson a great amount of money, the newborn returned to Gibson a greater joy, his mother, who took care of the household while Gibson's wife was in the hospital.

That successful television script, written in the summer of 1956, was *The Miracle Worker,* the story of a young tutor who teaches a blind and deaf girl to speak. "Three years earlier I had first read Annie Sullivan's letters recounting her work with the child Helen Keller," Gibson recalled in a *Theatre Arts* article, "and [had] been so smitten with love that I turned them into a narrative intended to accompany a solo dancer. The dance evaporated, and I was left with twelve pages of narration on my hands." Gibson subsequently sent the pages to his friend, the director Arthur Penn, who sold the television rights in forty-eight hours. After Gibson and Penn outlined the action, Gibson spent nearly two months perfecting the script. When the program aired in February, 1957, directed by Penn, it was critically acclaimed and Gibson, as he stated in *Theatre Arts,* has "been referred to ever since as a graduate of the television industry."

The Miracle Worker was produced by CBS for *Playhouse 90* and won the Sylvania Award for television. Gibson next enjoyed Broadway success with his stage version of *The Miracle Worker,* starring Anne Bancroft and Patty Duke. The play ran seven hundred performances, until July 1, 1961, and in 1962 United Artists released the movie version with the same cast.

WORKS CITED:

Gibson, William, "Second Wind," *Theatre Arts,* October, 1959.

FOR MORE INFORMATION SEE:

BOOKS

Contemporary Literary Criticism, Volume 23, Gale, 1983.
Dictionary of Literary Biography, Volume 7: *Twentieth-Century American Dramatists,* Gale, 1981.
Duprey, Richard A., *Just off the Aisle: The Ramblings of a Catholic Critic,* Newman Press, 1962.

PERIODICALS

Boston Sunday Globe, July 6, 1969.
Cosmopolitan, August, 1958.
Dramatists Guild Quarterly, spring, 1981.
Los Angeles Times, October 19, 1982.
Nation, December 2, 1968.
New England Theatre, spring, 1970.
New Leader, December 16, 1968.
Newsweek, March 16, 1959; July 27, 1970.
New Yorker, February 15, 1958; November 23, 1968.
New York Post, November 4, 1959.

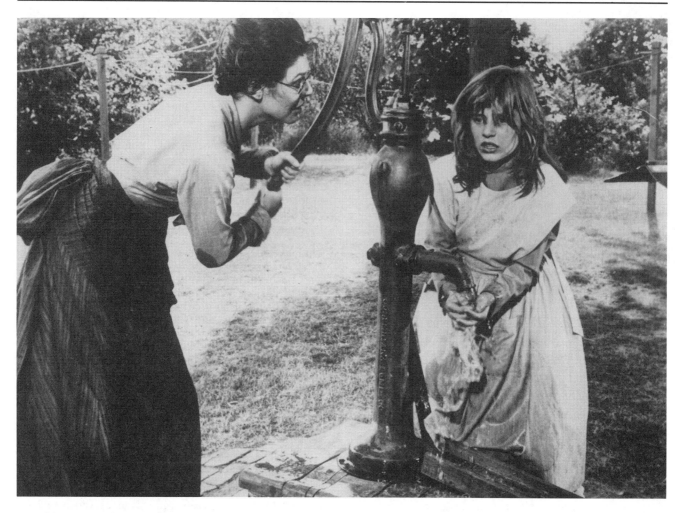

Anne Bancroft and Patty Duke won Oscars for their performances in the 1962 United Artists movie, *The Miracle Worker.*

New York Times, March 7, 1954; January 27, 1958; October 18, 1959; October 26, 1959; May 24, 1962; May 27, 1962; June 3, 1962; May 31, 1964; October 21, 1964; May 23, 1965; March 27, 1966; June 18, 1967; December 10, 1967; April 6, 1968; November 15, 1968; November 24, 1968; April 15, 1977; November 16, 1977; December 9, 1980; May 26, 1982; December 15, 1982.

New York Times Book Review, April 14, 1968.

New York Times Magazine, March 15, 1959.

People, October 14, 1985.

Saturday Review, March 14, 1959; March 23, 1968.

Time, December 21, 1959.

Tulane Drama Review, May, 1960.

Variety, February 21, 1971; December 29, 1982.

Village Voice, November 18, 1959.

Vogue, March, 1985.

Washington Post, October 13, 1979; January 20, 1980; January 26, 1980; November 27, 1981; December 3, 1981; October 3, 1982; October 14, 1982.

*   *   *

GODKIN, Celia (Marilyn) 1948-

PERSONAL: Born April 15, 1948, in London, England; daughter of Geoffrey Maxwell (a pharmacist) and Olive Mary (a teacher; maiden name, Oakey) Godkin. *Education:* University of London, B.Sc. (with honors), 1969; Ontario College of Art, A.O.C.A., 1983; University of Toronto, M.Sc., 1983. *Hobbies and other interests:* Gardening, wilderness camping, cycling, reading, classical music.

ADDRESSES: Home—1155A Dundas St. W., Toronto, Ontario, Canada M6J 1X3.

CAREER: Worked as biologist and teacher, 1969-76; University of Toronto, Toronto, Ontario, instructor in natural science illustration, 1981-82; Wilfrid Laurier University, Waterloo, Ontario, presented weekend workshops in biological illustration, 1983-85; University of Toronto, assistant professor of art as applied to medicine, 1987—, department program supervisor, 1988-89, instructor for school of continuing studies, 1988—. Arts and crafts instructor, Riverdale Community Action Centre, 1973-74; instructor, Network for Learning, 1985, and Royal Ontario Museum, 1985-90. Herpetologist, Reptile Breeding Foundation, 1974-76; fisheries biologist, Glenora Fisheries Station, Ontario Ministry of Natural Resources, summers, 1976-81; biological consultant, Ministry of the Environment, 1985-86. Illustrator, Assiniboine Park Zoo, 1983; work exhibited at Gallery 76, Slusser Gallery, Royal Ontario Museum, and Taiwan Museum.

MEMBER: Guild of Natural Science Illustrators, Canadian Wildlife Federation.

AWARDS, HONORS: Information Book Award, Children's Literature Roundtables of Canada, 1990, for *Wolf Island*.

WRITINGS:

(Illustrator) Clive Roots, *Endangered Species: Canada's Disappearing Wildlife*, Fitzhenry & Whiteside, 1987.
Wolf Island (for children), self-illustrated, Fitzhenry & Whiteside, 1989.

Illustrator of about twenty high school textbooks; contributor of articles and illustrations to scientific journals. Newsletter editor, Guild of Natural Science Illustrators.

WORK IN PROGRESS: Writing and illustrating *Ladybug Garden*, a children's book, for Fitzhenry & Whiteside; planning the children's book *Sea Otter Bay*, also for Fitzhenry & Whiteside.

SIDELIGHTS: In the 1970s Celia Godkin began writing nature texts for children. However, she was unable to find a publisher for such writings until the late 1980s, when a series of camping trips in the Canadian wilderness inspired her to write and illustrate *Wolf Island*. This book is about the animals of Wolf Island and their relationship to the natural environment. Godkin's forthcoming works, *Ladybug Garden* and *Sea Otter Bay*, will be about similar topics.

Godkin commented: "Writing has always been for me a means of communicating an idea, and I think of myself as an educator or as an illustrator rather than a writer. Most important ideas are fundamentally simple, though in many cases their ramifications are not. For this reason, I like to present the idea in its simplest form and suggest some of the ramifications, without laboring over them, so that the reader is encouraged to think through the implications themselves. One advantage of being a Jill-of-all-trades is that there is complete agreement between the scientist, writer, designer, and artist, since they are all housed in the same person. As a result, my text can be purposely spare because I know any embellishment required will be picked up by the illustrations."

FOR MORE INFORMATION SEE:

BOOKS

Science Explorations 10, Wiley, 1987.

PERIODICALS

Toronto Star, December 9, 1989.

*   *   *

GOODALL, John S(trickland) 1908-

PERSONAL: Born June 7, 1908, in Heacham, Norfolk, England; son of Joseph Strickland (a physician and surgeon) and Amelia (Hunt) Goodall; married Margaret Alison Nicol, March 25, 1933; children: Sarah Strickland Stead-Ellis. *Education:* Attended Harrow School, 1922-24, and Royal Academy School of Art, 1925-29; studied under J. Watson Nicol, Sir Arthur Cope, and Harold Speed. *Politics:* Conservative. *Religion:* Church of England.

JOHN S. GOODALL

ADDRESSES: Home and office—Lawn Cottage, Tisbury, Wiltshire, SP3 6SG England.

CAREER: Painter. Illustrator for books, periodicals, and advertising; draughtsman. *Exhibitions:* Work has been shown in Delhi and Calcutta, India, and London and Canterbury, England. *Military service:* British Army, Royal Norfolk Regiment, 1939-45; served in India and Burma.

MEMBER: Royal Society of British Artists, National Society of British Artists, Royal Institute of Water Colour Painters.

AWARDS, HONORS: Boston Globe/Horn Book award for excellence in authorship and illustration of a children's book, 1969, for *The Adventures of Paddy Pork;* Children's Book Showcase awards, 1973, for *Jacko*, 1974, for *Paddy's Evening Out*, 1976, for *Creepy Castle*, and 1977, for *Paddy Pork's Holiday;* Spring Book Festival younger honor, 1973, for *The Midnight Adventures of Kelly, Dot, and Esmerelda;* New York Times best illustrated book citation, 1977, for *The Surprise Picnic*, and 1982, for *Paddy Goes Traveling;* Parents' Choice best illustration award, 1980, for *Paddy's New Hat; The Ballooning Adventures of Paddy Pork* was named an American Library Association notable book and received a *Horn Book* honor listing.

WRITINGS:

PICTURE BOOKS

Field Mouse House, Blackie & Son, 1954.
Dr. Owl's Party, Blackie & Son, 1954.
The Adventures of Paddy Pork, Harcourt, 1968.
The Ballooning Adventures of Paddy Pork, Harcourt, 1969.
Shrewbettina's Birthday, Harcourt, 1971.

Jacko, Macmillan, 1971.
Kelly, Atheneum, 1971.
Kelly, Dot, and Esmerelda, Macmillan, 1972.
Paddy's Evening Out, Macmillan, 1974.
The Surprise Picnic, Macmillan, 1974.
Creepy Castle, Macmillan, 1975.
Naughty Nancy the Bad Bridesmaid, Macmillan, 1975.
An Edwardian Summer, Macmillan, 1976.
Paddy Pork's Holiday, Macmillan, 1976.
An Edwardian Christmas, Macmillan, 1977.
An Edwardian Holiday, Macmillan, 1978.
Story of an English Village, Macmillan, 1978.
An Edwardian Season, Macmillan, 1979.
Escapade, Macmillan, 1980.
Paddy's New Hat, Macmillan, 1980.
Victorians Abroad, Macmillan, 1980.
Before the War, 1908-1939: An Autobiography in Pictures, Macmillan, 1981.
Edwardian Entertainments, Macmillan, 1981.
Paddy Finds a Job, Macmillan, 1981.
Shrewbettina Goes to Work, Macmillan, 1981.
Above and below Stairs, Macmillan, 1982.
Lavinia's Cottage, Macmillan, 1982.
Paddy Goes Traveling, Macmillan, 1982.
Paddy Pork: Odd Jobs, Macmillan, 1982.
Paddy under the Water, Macmillan, 1983.
The Midnight Adventures of Kelly, Dot, and Esmerelda, Macmillan, 1984.
Naughty Nancy Goes to School, Deutsch, 1985.

Children playing on a beach in nineteenth-century England. (Watercolor from *The Story of the Seashore* by John S. Goodall.)

Paddy to the Rescue, Deutsch, 1985.
Story of a Castle, Deutsch, 1986.
Story of a High Street, Deutsch, 1987.
(Adapter) *Little Red Riding Hood,* Deutsch, 1988.
Story of a Farm, Deutsch, 1989.
Story of a Seashore, Deutsch, 1990.
(Adapter) *Puss in Boots,* Deutsch, 1990.

ILLUSTRATOR

Anthony Robertson, *How to Do and Say in England,* Dickson, 1936.
Susan Dorritt, *Jason's Lucky Day,* Abelard, 1958.
Edith N. Bland, *Five Children and It,* Looking Glass Library, 1959.
Bland, *Story of the Amulet,* Looking Glass Library, 1960.
Bland, *Phoenix and the Carpet,* Looking Glass Library, 1960.
Barbara Ker Wilson, *Fairy Tales of England,* Dutton, 1960.
Lewis Carroll, *Alice in Wonderland,* Blackie & Son, 1965.

Also illustrated *No Holly for Miss Quinn,* M. Joseph, 1976, *All the Village School,* M. Joseph, the "Thrush Green" series, M. Joseph, and the "Fairacre" series, all by Miss Read; *Suffolk Childhood,* Hutchinson, *Essex Schooldays,* Hutchinson, and *When All the World Was Young,* Hutchinson, all by Simon Dewes; *Trumpets over Merriford,* M. Joseph, and *The Round House,* M. Joseph, both by R. Arkell; Garrick Play Books, Blackie & Son; two books by Chenvix Trench, Basil Blackwood; a number of "Seekers and Finders" books, by Anabel Williams-Ellis, Blackie & Son; and others.

Contributor to periodicals, including *Connoisseur* and *Radio Times.*

WORK IN PROGRESS: The Great Day of a Country House, for John Murray.

SIDELIGHTS: John S. Goodall is a noted watercolorist renowned for his unique picture books. Distinguished by their alternating half and whole pages of full-color illustration, his wordless books charm children by allowing them to formulate their own narratives. The inventive use of half pages has been hailed for heightening the action of the stories, as the drama is alternately hidden and revealed by these smaller pages.

Born in 1908 in Heacham, England, Goodall grew up in his family's country home. His father was a doctor who, having descended from a long line of medical professionals, was surprised that his son showed no interest in the medical field. Displaying talent in painting, Goodall was introduced by his father to prominent English artists who advised him on how to proceed with a career in art. He studied painting under private instruction and later attended the Royal Academy School of Art. Working mostly with oil paints, Goodall was trained to paint in the Victorian tradition.

Upon completion of his schooling, Goodall began illustrating in order to earn a living. When World War II began, Goodall served in the Far East and India, where he first began painting in watercolors. His works were exhibited successfully in India, and when Goodall returned to England he was enlisted to paint portraits of members of the royal family.

Goodall also continued his career as an illustrator, drawing for other people's books. Soon he decided to produce books of his own—informally for his daughter and granddaughter. Small with alternating whole and half pages, the books

Paddy Pork is one of John Goodall's most popular characters. (Cover illustration from *Paddy to the Rescue* by John Goodall.)

proved difficult to mass produce. An English publisher eventually devised a way to print the books and, since their introduction to the public, have been admired by children and adults alike for their ingenious design, adventurous drama, and artistic expertise. Among the most popular of Goodall's works are a number of books set in Edwardian England as well as his books featuring the character Paddy Pork.

FOR MORE INFORMATION SEE:

PERIODICALS

Connoisseur, July, 1968; November, 1971.
Globe and Mail (Toronto), March 10, 1990.
Graphis 155, Volume 27, Graphis Press, 1971/72.
Horn Book, December, 1969; June, 1971; May, 1989.
Library Journal, March 15, 1970.
Life, December 17, 1971.
New York Times Book Review, April 24, 1983; November 8, 1987.
Times Literary Supplement, April 16, 1970.
Washington Post Book World, October 20, 1968; January 10, 1982.

GREENE, Carol 19(?)-

PERSONAL: Education: Park College, B.A. in English literature; Indiana University, M.A. in musicology. *Hobbies and other interests:* Reading, travel, singing, volunteer work at church.

ADDRESSES: Home—St. Louis, MO.

CAREER: Author of books for children. Former editor of children's books; taught adult classes in writing for children.

AWARDS, HONORS: Hinny Winny Bunco was selected as one of American Library Association's notable children's books, 1982; *Robin Hill* was selected one of Child Study Association of America's Children's Books of the Year, 1986.

WRITINGS:

FOR CHILDREN

Kiri and the First Easter, Concordia, 1972.
The Dancing Bear and Other Stories, illustrated by Joe Szeghy, Concordia, 1973.
God's My Friend, illustrated by Jack Glover, Concordia, 1973.

The Truly Remarkable Day, illustrated by Gordon Willman, Concordia, 1974.
The Super Snoops and the Missing Sleepers, illustrated by Gene Sharp, Childrens Press, 1976.
Seven Baths for Naaman: The Healing of Naaman for Beginning Readers: 2 Kings 5:1-15 for Children, illustrated by Aline Cunningham, Concordia, 1977.
No More Than a Mustard Seed, Concordia, 1980.
Give Us This Day: 365 Daily Devotions for Today's Child, illustrated by Ted Bolte, Concordia, 1980.
Proverbs: Important Things to Know, Concordia, 1980.
Hinny Winny Bunco, illustrated by Jeanette Winter, Harper, 1982.
Each One Specially, Concordia, 1982.
Christmas on the Street: The Secret of the Second Basement, illustrated with photographs by Herb Halpern and David Boyanchek, Concordia, 1984.
Welcome the Stranger, illustrated with photographs by Halpern and Boyanchek, Concordia, 1984.
The Insignificant Elephant, illustrated by Susan Gantner, Harcourt, 1985.
I Am One: Prayers for Singles, Augsburg, 1985.
Robin Hill, illustrated by Ellen Eagle, Harper, 1986.
The Easter Women: The Resurrection as Seen by the Women with Jesus, Concordia, 1987.
Wendy and the While, Concordia, 1987.
Waiting for Christmas: Stories and Activities for Advent, illustrated by Elizabeth Swisher, Augsburg, 1987.
The Jenny Summer, illustrated by Eagle, Harper, 1988.

Also author of *Why Boys and Girls Are Different.*

PICTURE-STORY BIOGRAPHIES

Sandra Day O'Connor: First Woman on the Supreme Court, Childrens Press, 1982.
Mother Teresa: Friend of the Friendless, Children Press, 1983.
Diana, Princess of Wales, Childrens Press, 1985.
Indira Nehru Gandhi: Ruler of India, Childrens Press, 1985.
Desmond Tutu: Bishop of Peace, Childrens Press, 1986.
Elie Wiesel: Messenger from the Holocaust, Childrens Press, 1987.

"ROOKIE READER" SERIES

Rain! Rain!, illustrated by Larry Frederick, Childrens Press, 1982.
Please, Wind?, illustrated by G. Sharp, Childrens Press, 1982.
Snow Joe, illustrated by Paul Sharp, Childrens Press, 1983.
Hi, Clouds, illustrated by G. Sharp, Childrens Press, 1983.
Ice Is . . . Whee!, illustrated by P. Sharp, Childrens Press, 1983.
Shine, Sun!, illustrated by G. Sharp, Childrens Press, 1983.

"ENCHANTMENT OF THE WORLD" SERIES

England, Childrens Press, 1982.
Poland, Childrens Press, 1983.
Japan, Childrens Press, 1983.
Yugoslavia, Childrens Press, 1984.
Austria, Childrens Press, 1986.

"NEW TRUE BOOKS" SERIES

Holidays around the World, Childrens Press, 1982.
Language, Childrens Press, 1983.
Music, Childrens Press, 1983.
The United Nations, Childrens Press, 1983.
Robots, Childrens Press, 1983.
Astronauts, Childrens Press, 1984.
Presidents, Childrens Press, 1984.
Congress, Children Press, 1985.
The Supreme Court, Childrens Press, 1985.

How a Book Is Made, Childrens Press, 1988.

"SING-ALONG HOLIDAY STORIES" SERIES

A Computer Went A-Courting: A Love Song for Valentine's Day, illustrated by Tom Dunnington, Childrens Press, 1983.
The Thirteen Days of Halloween, illustrated by Dunnington, Childrens Press, 1983.
The World's Biggest Birthday Cake, illustrated by Dunnington, Childrens Press, 1985.
The Pilgrims Are Marching, Childrens Press, 1988.
Columbus and Frankie the Cat, Childrens Press, 1989.

"I CAN BE" SERIES

I Can Be a Football Player, Childrens Press, 1984.
I Can Be a Baseball Player, Childrens Press, 1985.
I Can Be a Model, Childrens Press, 1985.
I Can Be a Librarian, Childrens Press, 1988.
I Can Be a Forest Ranger, Childrens Press, 1989.
I Can Be a Salesperson, Childrens Press, 1989.

"PEOPLE OF DISTINCTION" SERIES

Marie Curie: Pioneer Physicist, Childrens Press, 1984.
Louisa May Alcott: Author, Nurse, Suffragette, Childrens Press, 1984.
Thomas Alva Edison: Bringer of Life, Childrens Press, 1985.
Hans Christian Andersen: Teller of Tales, Childrens Press, 1986.
Marco Polo: Voyager to the Orient, Childrens Press, 1987.
Wolfgang Amadeus Mozart: Musician, Childrens Press, 1987.
Simon Bolivar: South American Liberator, Childrens Press, 1989.

"READING WELL" SERIES

Blue Ben, illustrated by Joe Boddy, Milliken, 1987.
Miss Apple's Hats, Milliken, 1988.

"ROOKIE BIOGRAPHIES" SERIES

Benjamin Franklin: A Man with Many Jobs, Childrens Press, 1988.
Pocahontas: Daughter of a Chief, Childrens Press, 1988.
Abraham Lincoln: President of a Divided Country, Childrens Press, 1989.
Christopher Columbus: A Great Explorer, Childrens Press, 1989.
Ludwig Van Beethoven: Musical Pioneer, Childrens Press, 1989.
Robert E. Lee: Leader in War and Peace. Childrens Press, 1989.
Martin Luther King: A Man Who Changed Things, Childrens Press, 1989.
Daniel Boone: Man of the Forests, Childrens Press, 1990.
Jackie Robinson: Baseball's First Black Major Leaguer, Childrens Press, 1990.
Laura Ingalls Wilder: Author of the Little House Books, Childrens Press, 1990.

EDITOR

Sarah Fletcher, *My Bible Story Book: Bible Stories for Small Children,* illustrated by Don Kueker, Concordia, 1974.
(With Daniel Burow) *The Little Christian's Songbook,* illustrated by Art Kirchoff, Concordia, 1975.
S. Fletcher, *Bible Story Book, New Testament,* illustrated by Edward Ostendorf, Concordia, 1983.
S. Fletcher, *Bible Story Book, Old Testament,* illustrated by Ostendorf, Concordia, 1983.
S. Fletcher, *The Christian Babysitter's Handbook,* Concordia, 1985.

OTHER

Also author of poems, songs, and filmstrips.

*   *   *

GREGORICH, Barbara 1943-

PERSONAL: Born December 10, 1943, in Sharon, PA; daughter of Joseph (a millwright) and Mary (a homemaker; maiden name, Detelich) Gregorich; married Philip Passen. *Education:* Kent State University, B.A., 1964; University of Wisconsin—Madison, M.A., 1965; attended Harvard University, 1966-67.

ADDRESSES: Home—Chicago, IL. *Agent*—Jane Jordan Browne, Multimedia Product Development, Inc., 410 South Michigan, Suite 724, Chicago, IL 60605-1465.

CAREER: Educator and writer. Kent State University, Kent, OH, instructor in English, 1965-66; Cleveland State University, Cleveland, OH, instructor in English, 1966; Cuyahoga Community College, Cleveland, instructor in English, 1967-71; *Boston Globe,* Boston, MA, typesetter, 1971-73; *Gary Post-Tribune,* Gary, IN, typesetter, 1973; *Chicago Tribune,* Chicago, IL, typesetter, 1973-76; U.S. Postal Service, Matteson, IL, letter carrier, 1976-77; Society for Visual Education, Chicago, IL, writer and producer, 1977-78; writer and editor, 1978—. Lecturer to writers' groups.

MEMBER: International Association of Crime Writers, Mystery Writers of America, Private Eye Writers of America, Society for American Baseball Research, National Writers Club, Authors Guild, Society of Children's Book Writers, Children's Reading Round Table, Sisters in Crime.

WRITINGS:

FOR CHILDREN; FROM SCHOOL ZONE PUBLISHING

The Gum on the Drum, 1984.
My Friend Goes Left, 1984.
Up Went the Goat, 1984.
The Fox on the Box, 1984.
Jog, Frog, Jog, 1984.
Sue Likes Blue, 1984.
Say Good Night, 1984.
I Want a Pet, 1984.
Beep, Beep, 1984.
Nine Men Chase a Hen, 1984.
Jace, Mace, and the Big Race, 1985.
Elephant and Envelope, 1985.
Nicole Digs a Hole, 1987.
The Great Ape Trick, 1987.
It's Magic, 1987.
The Fox, the Goose, and the Corn, 1988.
Trouble Again, 1988.

Author of additional educational materials, including the "Read and Think," "Fast Forward," and "Get Ready" workbook series. Also free-lance editor for School Zone, 1983-90.

OTHER; FOR CHILDREN

Author of additional educational materials, including workbooks for Macdonald Publishing, Learning Works, J. Weston Walch, and Scott, Foresman; filmstrips for Encyclopaedia Britannica Education Corp. and Society for

BARBARA GREGORICH

Visual Education; and computer software series for Wicat. Several books available in Spanish translation.

FOR ADULTS

She's on First (novel), Contemporary Books, 1987.
Dirty Proof (novel), Pageant/Crown, 1988.
Writing for the Educational Market (nonfiction), J. Weston Walch, 1990.

WORK IN PROGRESS: A book on women in baseball from 1866 to the present; further titles in the *Dirty Proof* series of detective novels, including *Child-Proof* and *Waterproof.*

SIDELIGHTS: "When I was little it never occurred to me that one could be a writer as a job," said Barbara Gregorich in an interview with *Something about the Author (SATA).* "I always wanted to be a baseball player." Eventually sports gave place to literature and Gregorich went on to a successful career as an educational writer, creating everything from high school workbooks to preschool readers. She never lost her interest in baseball, though, and in 1987 published *She's on First*—a fictional account of the first woman to play in baseball's major leagues.

Gregorich grew up in rural Masury, Ohio, just across the border from Pennsylvania. "It was an extended-family situation," she recalled, in which grandparents, cousins, aunts, and uncles lived nearby; as with much of the family, she helped out several days a week on her uncle's dairy farm. Growing up in the country "helped make me a patient person," Gregorich said, "and I think that in order to be a writer you need both drive and patience." She also learned about baseball. "My uncle plowed up a regulation Little League diamond on the farm—bases, everything—and I played with all my cousins, boys and girls."

But for a little girl in the 1950s, baseball seemed a hopelessly male-dominated sport. "It finally dawned on me when I was eleven," Gregorich said, "that there was no way I could be a major leaguer because the major leagues discriminated against women. So I decided the next best thing was to be a writer." By the late 1960s Gregorich had finished her schooling and was a college English teacher in Cleveland, but at the same time "I did do a tremendous amount of writing—all of it for free. I was writing for causes, things I believed in very deeply," she explained, including "civil rights and women's liberation." In the early 1970s, as job markets tightened, Gregorich went with her husband to Boston and then Chicago as he searched for work. Teaching jobs were in short supply, so she became a typesetter for a series of newspapers. By 1976, as such work became increasingly automated, Gregorich found herself laid off from the *Chicago Tribune* and possibly out of a livelihood.

But she put the setback to good use. In the columns of the *Tribune*—the very paper that had laid her off—she found an ad for educational writers. "I felt confident I could do that," she told *SATA*, "because I could write and I had taught." Soon she was creating filmstrips for the Society for Visual Education. "I thought up the creative situation, wrote the filmstrip, hired the actors and photographers and narrators and produced the entire thing," she recalled. She went on to

The Gum on the Drum **is one of Barbara Gregorich's most popular children's educational books**. (Cover illustration by John Sanford.)

write dozens of workbooks for a variety of companies, and even branched out into educational computer software.

At first Gregorich wrote mostly for high school students, but in the early 1980s a new audience emerged in the educational market: children of the post-World War II "baby boom" were having children of their own, and publishers were increasingly interested in teaching materials for the very young. "I had never thought of writing a children's book," Gregorich said, "but School Zone Publishing asked me to do one, I did it, and we both loved it. I enjoyed the experience and the next thing you know that's what I was writing." In the mid-1980s she wrote a dozen stories for School Zone's "Start-to-Read" series. Among the most popular with reviewers was *The Gum on the Drum,* in which a drum-playing bear takes the chewing gum from his mouth and becomes a tangled mess of sticky fur. "I was playing with rhyming words," Gregorich recalled. "I came up with 'gum' and 'drum' and boy, was it tough." The book "went through eighteen drafts, and it's what—ten sentences long?"

Meanwhile Gregorich was also writing for the grown-up audience. Her layoff from the *Tribune* gave her time to begin her baseball novel, *She's on First.* Set largely in Chicago, the book focuses on Linda Sunshine, who receives her chance to play pro ball at the whim of a maverick teamowner. Against the gritty background of daily life in the world of baseball, Linda battles sexism and gradually realizes her debt to the pioneering feminists of earlier years. "The baseball scenes are crackerjack," declared a reviewer for *Publishers Weekly,* "and readers should end up wondering, 'Why not?' or 'Why not before now?'" The theme of overcoming barriers, Gregorich believes, accounts for the "tremendous appeal" that the novel has to teenagers. "I wasn't reading such books when I was thirteen years old," she observed, "so I'm constantly surprised, in a very pleasant way, at how young people read certain books meant for adults."

Getting the first novel published was hard work. "I read sixty nonfiction baseball books before sitting down to write *She's on First* just so that I could get through research what I may have missed through observation," Gregorich told *SATA*. She completed the first version of the book in 1978 and sent the manuscript to dozens of publishers. "I got many personal replies from editors, which is a very good sign, but they all said that sports fiction was not taken seriously—baseball fiction least seriously of all. They saw no market for the book, and they were very sorry. Now this is ironic because, as you probably know, baseball literature is now booming." Gregorich rewrote the book four times, submitted it twice to Chicago's Contemporary Books—the second time through her agent—and finally saw it published in 1987. Her second novel, the mystery *Dirty Proof,* was published a year later.

Now a successful author, Gregorich speaks regularly to writers' groups—people who "have a secret burning desire to write and want to know that it can be done. They want professional hints; they want to know what happened to you, the published writer. They need hope." Gregorich offered some of her professional hints to *SATA*. "I may spend two or three hours in the morning writing for adults and then two or three hours in the afternoon writing for children," she noted. "People often ask me, 'How can you do that?—they're so different!' First of all, I never think about it because children are *people*—they just happen to be very young people, like any group with special interests and special needs. You simply ask yourself, what kind of story do you think this person would like? Beyond that, every single writer who has ever lived has been a child. Writing for children you can

AGES 4-7
06009

NINE MEN CHASE A HEN

A **SCHOOL ZONE®** START TO READ BOOK

Barbara Gregorich has written a dozen stories for the School Zone Publishing "Start to Read" series, including the rhyming book *Nine Men Chase a Hen*. (Cover illustration by John Sanford.)

always go back to what you liked, to what excited you, to what you thought was funny, and if you still have those feelings alive in you, you can write about them." Also, she added, "If you still have those feelings you're a very lucky person because that means that the child in you has never died."

Writing, Gregorich suggested, should be both thought-provoking and entertaining, whether it's for a novel or a textbook, for an adult or for a child. "I see many books submitted for children, textbooks especially, that are really dull. No adult is interested in them, why should a child be? There is no lesser criterion for children—'well, this is really boring for adults, but kids will love it.' I don't think that's true. I think a book has to be interesting in itself for any age level." Similarly, an exciting novel should still have something to teach. "I always try to write the kind of story that I like to read," she said. "When I finish it I might forget the characters' names, but I'll remember situations and what they may have meant, and I'll think about questions raised by the book."

For young would-be writers, Gregorich recommends the basics, beginning with reading. "Read, enjoy reading, read all you can," she advised. "When you're young read the things you *don't* like as well as the things you like. Read what is assigned in literature classes, listen, talk about what you've read with your friends and your teachers." To write well, students should learn the mechanics of writing. "Even in writing children's books, you must know what a conflict is,

what an antagonist is, who a protagonist is, what a denouement is. You have to know what foreshadowing is, and it's essential you know point of view. There—I've just thrown out six *technological* writing terms, but they are critical. Unless you study writing, you won't know what those mean, and if you don't know what those mean, you can't re-write to improve what you have originally written."

Is being a writer worth all that work? "When I was a typesetter I typed 102 words a minute, I loved the job, but I can't really say I found it fulfilling," Gregorich recalled. "Whereas as a writer, I *do* find self-fulfillment." She's continued to pursue her love of baseball by preparing yet another book—a history of the unsung women who have been playing the game since the nineteenth century. "I just had the great fortune of interviewing an eighty-eight-year-old who from 1915 to 1921 played hardball on her factory team," she told *SATA*. "I didn't know anyone like Linda Sunshine when I was writing *She's on First*, but I probably know many people like her now."

WORKS CITED:

Gregorich, Barbara, telephone interview with Thomas Kozikowski for *Something about the Author*, February 28, 1991.
Review of *She's on First, Publishers Weekly*, February 27, 1987, p. 150.

FOR MORE INFORMATION SEE:

PERIODICALS

Library Journal, May 1, 1987.
Publishers Weekly, March 16, 1984; August 12, 1988.
School Library Journal, May, 1984; December, 1985.
Tribune Chronicle (Warren, OH), April 19, 1987.

Sketch by Thomas Kozikowski

*   *   *

GRIFALCONI, Ann 1929-

PERSONAL: Surname is pronounced "*Gree*-fal-koh-nee"; born September 22, 1929, in New York, NY; daughter of Joseph and Mary Hays (a writer; maiden name, Weik) Grifalconi. *Education:* Cooper Union Art School, certificate in advertising art, 1950; attended University of Cincinnati, 1951; New York University, B.S., 1954; postgraduate studies at Hunter College, one year, and New School for Social Research, two years. *Hobbies and other interests:* Writing music, photography, archaeology, travel to Africa, Europe and Central America.

ADDRESSES: Home and office—124 Waverly Pl., New York, NY 10011.

CAREER: Artist and designer in advertising and display, 1950-54; High School of Fashion Industry, New York City, teacher of art and display, 1954-65; full-time free-lance artist and illustrator, largely in children's book field, 1965—; Media Plus, Inc., New York City, president, beginning 1968; producer, Greyfalcon House, New York City. *Exhibitions:* Several one-woman shows, including at Vassar Library, 1989, Muscarelli Museum, 1990, and Kimberly Gallery, New York City, 1991; contributor of artwork to collections, including the Kerlan Collection, and traveling exhibits, including "And Peace Attend Thee."

AWARDS, HONORS: New York Times Best Illustrated Book of 1968 and Newbery Honor Book, 1968, both for *The Jazz Man; New York Times* citation and Ad Club Best Designed Book award, both for *The Ballad of the Burglar of Babylon;* Coretta Scott King Award, 1985, for *Everett Anderson's Goodbye;* Caldecott Honor Award, American Library Association, 1987, for *The Village of Round and Square Houses.*

WRITINGS:

JUVENILES; SELF-ILLUSTRATED

City Rhythms, Bobbs-Merrill, 1965.
The Toy Trumpet: Story and Pictures, Bobbs-Merrill, 1968.
The Matter with Lucy: An Album, Bobbs-Merrill, 1973.
The Village of Round and Square Houses, Little, Brown, 1986.
Darkness and the Butterfly, Little, Brown, 1987.
Osa's Pride, Little, Brown, 1990.
The Flyaway Girl, Little, Brown, 1991.
Kinda Blue, Little, Brown, 1991.

ILLUSTRATOR

Rhoda Bacmeister, *Voices in the Night,* Bobbs-Merrill, 1965.
Ina B. Forbus, *Tawny's Trick,* Viking, 1965.
Gladys Tabor, *Still Meadow Cookbook,* Lippincott, 1965.
O. Arnold, *Hidden Treasures of the Wild West,* Abelard, 1966.
Margaret Embry, *Peg-Leg-Willy,* Holiday House, 1966.
Edwin Palmer Hoyt, *American Steamboat Stories,* Abelard, 1966.
De Luca, editor, *Italian Poetry Selections,* Harvey House, 1966.

ANN GRIFALCONI

Mary Hays Weik (Grifalconi's mother), *The Jazz Man,* Atheneum, 1966.
N. Zimmelman, *Pepito,* Reilly & Lee, 1967.
Tillie S. Pine and Joseph Levine, *The Africans Knew,* McGraw, 1967.
Johanna Johnston, *A Special Bravery,* Dodd, 1967.
E. S. Lampman, *Half-Breed,* Doubleday, 1967.
Louise A. Steintorf, *The Treasure of Tolmec,* John Day, 1967.
Barbara Reid, *Carlo's Cricket,* McGraw, 1967.
Pine and Levine, *The Incas Knew,* McGraw, 1968.
Pine and Levine, *The Maya Knew,* McGraw, 1968.
Betsy Byars, *Midnight Fox,* Viking, 1968.
John and Sara Westbrook Brewton, compilers, *America Forever New,* Crowell, 1968.
Bronson Potter, *Antonio,* Atheneum, 1968.
Anton Chekov, *Shadows and Light,* translated by M. Morton, Doubleday, 1968.
Elizabeth Bishop, *The Ballad of the Burglar of Babylon,* Farrar, Straus, 1968.
Anne Norris Baldwin, *Sunflowers for Tina,* Doubleday, 1969.
Ruby Zagoren, *Venture for Freedom,* World Publishing, 1969.
Lois Kalb Bouchard, *The Boy Who Wouldn't Talk,* Doubleday, 1969.
Langston Hughes, *Don't You Turn Back: Poems,* edited by Lee Bennett Hopkins, Knopf, 1969.
Hopkins, *This Street's for Me!,* Crown, 1970.
Lorenz B. Graham, *David He No Fear,* Crowell, 1971.
Walter Dean Myers, *The Dragon Takes a Wife,* Bobbs-Merrill, 1972.
Toby Talbot, *The Night of the Radishes,* Putnam, 1972.
Weik, *A House on Liberty Street,* Atheneum, 1972.
John Lonzo Anderson, *The Day the Hurricane Happened,* Scribner, 1974.
Lucille Clifton, *Everett Anderson's Year,* Holt, 1974.
Ann McGovern, *The Secret Soldier,* Four Winds Press, 1975.
Letta Schatz, *Banji's Magic Wheel,* Follett, 1975.
Clifton, *Everett Anderson's Friend,* Holt, 1976.
Clifton, *Everett Anderson's 1 2 3,* Holt, 1977.
Giovanni Boccaccio, *Stories from the Decameron,* limited edition, Franklin Library, 1977.
Clifton, *Everett Anderson's Nine Month Long,* Holt, 1978.
Genevieve S. Gray, *How Far, Felipe?,* Harper, 1978.
William Styron, *The Confessions of Nat Turner,* limited edition, Franklin Library, 1979.
Clifton, *Everett Anderson's Goodbye,* Holt, 1983.

OTHER

(With Ruth Jacobsen) *Camping through Europe by Car, with Maximum Fun at Minimum Cost* (travelogue), Crown, 1963.

Also author of screenplays for *The House on Liberty Street* series (based on her mother's book, *A House on Liberty Street,* which Grifalconi illustrated), *The Jazz Man* (based on her mother's book of the same title, which Grifalconi illustrated), and for television series, "Quinta Raza." Also illustrator of other books and texts.

ADAPTATIONS: The Village of Round and Square Houses has been recorded on cassette, video, and filmstrip; *The Toy Trumpet* and *City Rhythms* are available as bilingual filmstrip/cassette sets.

WORK IN PROGRESS: The Lion and the Jaguar, a novel on Columbus' actual meeting with a Mayan pilot, awaiting publication; writing and illustrating books; a musical based on *The Jazz Man.*

In *Everett Anderson's Goodbye*, by Lucille Clifton, illustrator Ann Grifalconi uses large, dark pencil drawings to convey a boy's grief at the loss of his father.

SIDELIGHTS: Since the mid-1960s, Ann Grifalconi has expanded children's literature by presenting realistic characters from other cultures. Her Caldecott Honor Book *The Village of Round and Square Houses* is just one of her books that tell of African village life and traditions. Grifalconi has also written about the Mexican and Mayan peoples, and has been a pioneer in the portrayal of African-American children with both her own books and her illustrations for others. Since books played a major part in her own childhood, Grifalconi wants to create works that expand her readers' horizons. "Among other things, my goal is to illuminate either the heart or the spirit or the mind of a child, and hopefully, to bring them something new," Grifalconi said in an interview with *Something about the Author (SATA).*

Grifalconi was born during the Depression. Since her parents were divorced, she and her brother were raised by her mother, the writer Mary Hays Weik. Although it was difficult for a single parent to raise two children during trying times, Grifalconi's mother worked hard to secure a good education for her children. "Basically as a survivor my mother had to move with her two children wherever the jobs were and wherever the schools were," Grifalconi told *SATA.* "She believed in public schools; her father was a Lincoln historian and she had a very strong belief in the common man and the purpose of the public institution to be universally equal—but she picked very carefully. She moved wherever a good school happened to be."

Gran'ma fixed me with a stare

And began to rock with the tale...

For she was the best storyteller in the whole village!

Ann Grifalconi's visit to the isolated African village of Tos inspired her Caldecott Honor book, *The Village of Round and Square Houses*.

Because Grifalconi rarely spent long in any one neighborhood, books became her companions. "They were portable and I could always walk into the library and take out four books a day, so I always had an opportunity to read," she said in her interview. Grifalconi was an avid reader throughout her youth: "The reading I did expanded my world view. I was reading historical romances, adventures around the world. A lot of those things were introduced to me through Mother because she also had been a reader." She also began reading the *National Geographic* and other magazines, which gave her a feeling for the rest of the world.

Grifalconi was also interested in the wonderful pictures that accompanied her favorite books, such as the "Red," "White," and "Violet" storybooks, with illustrations by Howard Pyle and others. "When I was a little girl my Mother gave me Arthur Rackham's beautiful book of illustrations for *A Midsummer Night's Dream*—that thrilled me!"

Grifalconi was also a comic book reader at an early age—"not that my mother approved!"—with her favorites being "very realistic, such as *Tarzan* and *Flash Gordon,* all of which were done by very good illustrators of their period." Another source of excellent artwork was the *Saturday Evening Post,* which her brother sold. "Because I didn't have the money to buy it myself," the author related in her interview, "I used to read it the day before he gave it out to the people—without bending the paper! There were a lot of very, very fine illustrators in there at that period whose work was painted, atmospheric, full of character. They simply don't have that sort of work in magazines anymore."

When she was young, Grifalconi didn't consider herself a good artist; she only drew doodles once in a while. But when she was about ten, her mother moved the family back to her hometown in Indiana. In school there, Grifalconi had an art teacher who noticed she had talent. "He sort of picked me

Gran'ma smiled down at me: "And so you see it has been to this day!

For the women have decided they *enjoy* getting together

To talk and to laugh and to sing

And the men have become *used* to being together,

And relaxing in their own place.

(From *The Village of Round and Square Houses,* written and illustrated by Ann Grifalconi.)

from the group and said 'I think you can draw. Why don't you work on it a little bit?'" The family returned to New York City after the school year finished, and during that summer vacation Grifalconi practiced drawing and painting. She spent her time "looking out the window and doing water colors of the scene as well as reading a tremendous number of books," she continued in her interview. "That was also the year I broke through to the adult library—having read through the junior one down the street."

Grifalconi's mother moved one more time before her kids started high school, so that they could attend the special New York City public schools that had majors in art and architecture. Grifalconi's art school "was a perfect school for me because it had a creative writing class straight through, which was non-graded." In particular, Grifalconi remembered "a very gifted teacher, Miss Estelle Stiles, who taught us in a pleasant classroom where we all contributed to the school magazine. I also had another very gifted art teacher, Mrs.

Julia Winston, who encouraged us all to write and illustrate our own short stories and poems. So we had a continuous art and writing experience straight through high school." She also continued expanding her imagination by reading and by going to movies—"everything from reading *Scaramouche,* a famous historical book recommended by my mother, to seeing Olivia de Havilland and Errol Flynn in *Robin Hood.*"

As a teenager, Grifalconi didn't really consider writing and illustrating children's books as a career. "I thought at one time I would become a fashion illustrator, because that was a field that one could earn a living in," the artist said in her *SATA* interview. "The idea of becoming a writer and illustrator of children's books hadn't fully entered my head, because I also started thinking in terms of careers available in New York City. Art is a field which is a very practical one, and so your mind begins to turn to practical things—not to a career as a writer of children's books. That didn't appear to be a career, it appeared to be more of a wonderful thought."

Testing with one thousand other high school graduates, Grifalconi won one of ninety competitive scholarships to attend Cooper Union in New York City, a specialized free college. "Cooper Union was one of the better opportunities for a person without money who wanted to expand their horizons, and study art, architecture, or engineering," she told *SATA* in her interview. "That was a wonderful experience: we had very small classes, we were right in New York, so all sorts of famous people, artists, writer, thinkers, would visit our school, such as Dylan Thomas, the poet who was in America then, or Buckminster Fuller. We really had contact with them: we listened to their voices and were inspired by their ideas, and even became students for short individual class sessions, as I did with 'Bucky' Fuller. So I think I had a great education." Also interested in printmaking and painting, Grifalconi graduated after three years with a certificate in advertising, and began looking for her first job.

By that time, she remarked in her interview, "I had somewhat given up the idea of fashion illustration although I had a few samples in my portfolio. My first job in advertising was depressing, mainly because I just did little ads and little thumb nail sketches." Grifalconi didn't enjoy her next job, either, because of her boss's negative attitude. "He was mean to the people who didn't deliver on time. I also didn't like the idea that you would sell your soul for a bar of soap, so I moved away from advertising and moved out to Cincinnati." She joined her mother and brother, who had moved there previously. "I thought, 'I'm going to have to rethink this thing.'"

But Grifalconi couldn't get a job in Cincinnati to suit her art background. "There was a small amount of prejudice there in terms of a woman doing anything professional, or earning enough to live on her own as an artist. I really couldn't get a job that was worth my skills out in Cincinnati, so I had to come back to New York," she said. Because her studies at Cooper Union didn't give her a bachelor's degree, Grifalconi decided to go to school again. She won a scholarship to attend New York University. She completed her degree in art history, but also earned a minor in history, one of her long-time interests.

Grifalconi also had a great desire to teach. "That's the reason that I came back to New York, to get that college degree, to teach," she said. "I had a 'calling' at the time, to make people ask questions, engender questions in people's minds. My favorite high school history teacher, Mr. Tortarella, used to make us ask questions, being a fine history teacher." After earning her degree, Grifalconi joined the staff at the High School of Fashion Industry in New York City, where she taught "display, merchandising, interior design, fashion art, and a number of other things which included a sense of the world as it really was."

"Meanwhile," the artist continued in her interview, "I was also moving into writing and illustrating my own books. It began by example. I had been doing some woodcuts and my mother, who was a writer, liked a woodcut I had done of a jazz musician. When mother had said, 'Oh, I like that,' she made me realize that what I was doing might turn into something. That's how I started my first children's book called *City Rhythms,* about the sound of music and the pulse of the city." Two years later Grifalconi's mother sent her a manuscript about a jazz player, which turned out to be *The Jazz Man,* the Newbery Honor Book which Grifalconi would illustrate. Even though she had almost finished her own book, "when Mother's *Jazz Man* manuscript came back, I thought her story was such a beauty that I put my own project

aside," the author continued. "Of course mother had always been a very fine writer—she started as a poet."

After she finished the woodcut illustrations for *The Jazz Man,* Grifalconi concluded work on her own book, *City Rhythms.* But it was difficult finding the time to take her work around to publishers, especially since she was still teaching. "But, I started realizing around a certain age that if I was going to carry out my art thing I'd better do it now, so, even though I was teaching full time, I would make appointments and take my portfolio around." A knowledgeable friend told Grifalconi she should make a "dummy" book, complete with illustrations, and show it around. The author did, and *City Rhythms* was accepted by Bobbs-Merrill and published in 1965.

Grifalconi's success in finding a publisher was due to her persistence in showing her work around, and adjusting to the reactions her work got. "One really learns by going out there and facing the public," she said, "which in this case happened to be editors." Her effort paid off, for Joan Lear Sher praised *City Rhythms,* the story of how a little boy finds music in the city life around him. "The impressionistic, brightly-colored illustrations have visual movement and make Jimmy's Harlem block seem like a wonderland," Sher said in the *New York Times Book Review.*

Meanwhile, Grifalconi's mother, Mary Hays Weik, was having trouble finding a publisher for her own book. "*The Jazz Man* was sent to a number of people and often it was regretfully rejected and turned back. Sometimes editors literally had tears in their eyes because they liked it so much, but it was a bit controversial—it was not entirely upbeat," Grifalconi explained in her interview. "Finally Mother said, 'Would you please take it with you while you're taking your portfolio around?'" Grifalconi took the book to Atheneum, who accepted it. "So Mother and I got to work on this project together, which was one of the great satisfactions in both of our lives."

While Grifalconi was putting in long hours creating illustrations and looking for publishers, she was also teaching. "Teaching is like running a marathon everyday, it's the hardest job I've ever done in my life," Grifalconi said. "By comparison, publishing seemed easy, fun, simple and lyric." And while she was working on *The Jazz Man,* she continued, "I realized it was a work of love and I think it was then that I began to realize that I liked doing this more than teaching." Grifalconi decided to leave her job at school. "I felt I was short-changing the kids," she explained in her interview. "So I just felt that I had to make a decision where I was going to go. When *The Jazz Man* got a Newbery Honor, then of course I got honors along with it, to some extent. I also had more opportunities by this time. My footwork, going around with my heavy portfolio to every publisher, had begun to pay off and I was doing one or two books a year. I realized that the quality of my work wouldn't necessarily improve unless I could devote more time to it."

In addition, Grifalconi saw a need in children's books that she could fill. "I was aware that there were no really attractive black children or black families. It seemed they would make little white faces and smear them black," she remarked. Unhappy with this situation, Grifalconi decided to start making her own contributions. "I had a very good background in life drawing and figure drawing, so I felt that I could do it. I also thought that black people were truly beautiful. Many of my friends were black and I saw them as real people and I hated these sort of imitation white people drawings. So when I left I had finally decided, 'Now!' I just did it.''

Grifalconi had maintained a longtime interest in political issues such as the civil rights movement. "We had a very vigorous family interest in politics and in integration," the author explained in her interview, "and when we were out in Cincinnati we were members of the C.O.R.E. group that started integration of the music schools in Cincinnati. Many of my best friends in Cincinnati happened to be black simply because they were some of the best and brightest people that I'd ever met. When I got back to New York I was still very interested in the civil rights movement, so much of my spare time was involved in that. The idea of exercising your rights to debate and to discuss and to help make the world a better place to live was always a very deep part of our family life."

Grifalconi traced her concern for civil rights and racial harmony back to her childhood. "Mother believed very much in living with people of different races and getting used to the real world," the author stated in her *SATA* interview. "For many generations, my family has always very strongly been anti-prejudicial, has always talked to us and explained away any prejudice that might have come from other sources, so I think that is a very very deep part of my life."

Grifalconi still had a desire to educate people, even though she no longer worked at a New York school. "I was feeling a little guilty: 'Once a teacher always a teacher.' My 'mission' was to teach." So when she left teaching, Grifalconi and an editor friend, a black woman who "also wanted to correct some impressions about black students and black history," formed the company Media Plus to create interracial multi-media materials. "Since I was already used to doing two things at once, taking on a company seemed perfectly right. I had a lot of energy, so with two people to share this thing we turned out a number of fine programs that we were very proud of." These included films and sound filmstrips on black and white history, women's rights, black and white living poets, and bilingual programs in Spanish and English. There was even a filmstrip version of her book, *The Toy Trumpet*, in both languages. Grifalconi and her partner later sold the company to Doubleday/Random House, but Grifalconi continued to work on educational multi-media projects.

In 1968 Grifalconi had come out with *The Toy Trumpet*, a book about a Mexican boy who wants an instrument of his own to play. Next came a book illustrated with collages, *The Matter with Lucy*. This book tells the story of a little girl around the turn of the century who is ignored by her elders and told to be "seen and not heard." That story, the author recalled in her interview, "came from stories my mother told me about after her own mother died. Her father's sister, a more rigid Germanic person, came over to run the household. She told mother that 'little girls should be seen and not heard.' She believed that boys were more important and had to be educated and that girls had no need of things like books! So Mother actually had to hide her reading—she actually hid under the bed to read (good books, too)! The aunt favored Mother's brother to such an extreme degree that my grandfather finally woke up from his grief over the loss of his wife and asked her kindly to leave. 'We'll take care of ourselves from now on, thank you!' Mother never forgot this act of her father's."

In addition to her first three books and her work with Media Plus, Grifalconi also spent her time illustrating the books of other writers. She remembered one collaboration in particu-

lar, with poet Elizabeth Bishop: "When I was doing *The Ballad of the Burglar of Babylon* the poet came all the way up from Brazil," the artist related in her interview. The poem, which is set in Brazil, tells the story of a thief who is chased and killed by police. "She came up and we sat and talked, and she showed me where the sun rose, say from a certain side, and that the beaches would be a certain color, the parasols would be striped or wavy lined, that the kites would be made in the shapes of birds, all these little details. These are pieces of warm, important information, so that even though you can't always see them, I know they're there. Bishop helped to make the landscape real."

Grifalconi illustrated that landscape with three colors of woodcuts, a medium she thought would suit the story best. "When full color wasn't available and the story was powerful, such as *The Ballad of the Burglar of Babylon,* I felt woodcut to be a very strong medium and should be used when the story had a lot of depth to it," she explained. In illustrating other writers' work, Grifalconi tries to match the style of her artwork to the style of the story. She added, "I try to sympathetically feel what the poet or writer is trying to say. I try to follow the *word*. I think the word is very important."

Grifalconi is also noted for her illustrations for several of Lucille Clifton's books about Everett Anderson, a young African-American. The publisher of Clifton's book only allowed one or two colors for the illustrations, so in this case Grifalconi decided that pencil would best relate the mood of the stories. "Because it had to be delicate and yet warm while it was also black," *Everett Anderson's Nine Month Long* "was a delicate pencil tone because it's about waiting for a baby," Grifalconi remarked in her interview. "When I was working with *Everett Anderson's Goodbye,*" she continued, "where the boy is remembering the death of his father and trying to adjust to it, it seemed to me that a deeper black and white was called for. I used a much darker, bigger pencil and worked very large with *Everett Anderson's Goodbye*. I felt there was deep grief there and I wanted to express that, so I had to go large and dark."

Grifalconi studies and explores her subject thoroughly when she prepares to write and illustrate a book. "It's the old idea of gathering, gathering, gathering, and over-gathering," she said in her *SATA* interview. "I love history and I love research. I either go to the place or I get it together here and I do immense amounts of research—immense!" That research can include using the large library she keeps in her New York home, or visiting local libraries, or traveling around the world. "I went to Africa," she continued. "I've been going back and forth to Central America. I love it; it's one of my special places! I've been to Haiti many times, because it seems almost identical to Africa—even the earth, the plants, everything. I can see why Africans who found themselves in Haiti felt at home, it's just exactly like Equatorial West Africa."

While Grifalconi was visiting a village in Cameroon, Africa, a young woman there explained that in her own hometown, the women of the village lived in round huts, while the men lived in square ones. Her trip to that village gave Grifalconi the idea for her book *The Village of Round and Square Houses*, which was later given a Caldecott Honor. The author told *SATA* how that project came about: "During the time I had the media company I developed a skill with photography, so I'd take pictures of things that catch my eye. I still take pretty good pictures, but I don't use them much now except as research. Well the odd thing was, on that trip something was wrong with my camera, and of course all my pictures in Africa didn't come out! I thought, 'What a shame, to lose that

In *Darkness and the Butterfly*, a young girl dreams she is following a butterfly and then feels herself flying. (Written and illustrated by Ann Grifalconi.)

experience!'" To replace the pictures, Grifalconi decided to write a book—*The Village of Round and Square Houses*—about her travels there.

Luckily for her, Grifalconi has a good memory. "I had developed this photographic memory, because it is not always possible, especially in a foreign country, to take pictures of things you see," she said to *SATA*. "You can be badly treated if you are in the wrong place at the wrong time—so I've learned to remember. My mind is very trained and I can remember very well, with just a tiny sketch, or by making some note of things. So then, aided with research, it all comes back to me. Then I can draw from this imaginary place in my head." After all her research is done, Grifalconi added, "eventually I'm like a little bird. I can fly anywhere in my imagination in the landscape, in writing about it or in painting it and drawing it. I can actually see it, like a real place. That's basically what I use in my work."

Grifalconi re-creates the village of Tos in *The Village of Round and Square Houses*. After helping prepare dinner for her elders, young Osa, a village girl, hears a story from her grandmother. Osa's grandmother tells her the legend of how the men and women of the village came to live in different houses after a volcano had destroyed all but "one round and one square house in the village." "Grifalconi effortlessly embroiders the customs of the village into her melodious narration," a *Publishers Weekly* reviewer commented.

Grifalconi uses paints and chalks to draw the village in her book. "I picked the medium to suit the message with *Village of Round and Square Houses*," she said in her interview. "I felt there was a lot of warmth, I remembered the sunlight, the intensity of the color, the laughter of the children, the richness of the sunlight on the trees and I wanted to depict as much as I could that magical richness. It ended up a mixed technique. I started with watercolor and I realized that I wanted to enhance the textures so it became a mixed media thing."

Grifalconi's artwork earned praise from critics as well as a Caldecott Honor citation. Her "bold, dramatic illustrations echo the rhythm of African life," Lisa Lane remarked in the *Christian Science Monitor*. The *Publishers Weekly* writer also found that the village and its people "are all captured beautifully by Grifalconi's art." "What Grifalconi has brought to these pages is master storytelling, a melding of words and pictures to communicate an imaginative piece of folklore," Bonita Brodt concluded in Chicago *Tribune Books*.

In *Darkness and Butterfly* Grifalconi returned to Tos to tell of Osa's struggle to overcome her fear of the dark. Osa is brave during the day, when she will climb the highest trees in the village, but after sundown she is frightened by the gloom of night. Osa visits a village wise woman, who encourages Osa and inspires the girl to dream. Osa dreams she is following a butterfly, and then feels herself flying higher, near the moon and stars. She discovers that the nighttime is filled with beauty and brilliance, and awakens to find her fear gone. Grifalconi uses watercolor paints to picture Osa's journey. "In *Darkness of the Butterfly* it was a lyric thing and I thought it needed watercolor, because watercolors flow," she said in her interview. "I wanted to show air, and flying."

School Library Journal contributor Patricia Dooley complimented the book's illustrations. "The artwork is gorgeous: its colors are as radiant as stained glass, and a change in technique signals the dream-sequence," the critic wrote. "[Like] *The Village of Round and Square Houses,* this is a beautifully evocative tale of childhood in an African tribal setting," a *Publishers Weekly* reviewer said, adding that "the story and paintings are suffused with love and warmth; they reassure with their universal appeal." *Darkness and the Butterfly* also earned praise for having "warm, realistic illustrations of African village life," as Beryl Graham Kalisa stated in another *School Library Journal.*

Grifalconi's third book set in the village of Tos, *Osa's Pride,* shows Osa making up tall stories about her soldier father, who has never returned from war. Osa is so busy telling tales about how wonderful her father was that she has no time to listen to her friends' stories about their own parents. Her grandmother, seeing that Osa is losing her friends, tells Osa the tale of a vain girl who sees people staring at her. The girl is losing eggs out of the basket she carries, but she is too proud to look down and notice them falling. Osa's grandmother leaves the story unfinished, and Osa comes up with her own answer to the girl's problem. At the same time she sees how her foolish pride is bothering her friends and how she can change.

Although a *Publishers Weekly* reviewer thought that the story of *Osa's Pride* was a bit too preachy, the critic admitted that "artistically, the book is superb; the pictures capture the community life and Osa's personal struggle with vivid images and rich, vibrant colors." "The strengths of the book are the details of village life, the warm relationship depicted between Osa and her grandmother, and the richness of the illustrations," a writer for the *Bulletin of the Center for Children's Books* said. And Kay E. Vandergrift believed that "there is a luminous quality to these pastels that seem to leap from the page to capture the heat of the land and the colors of village life." Vandergrift added in the *School Library Journal* that "unlike many stories in the folk tradition, this one does not distance readers; rather, the characters and the pace of the telling invite them into this satisfying book."

Grifalconi uses Africa as a backdrop for so many of her books because she believes its cultures have had a great influence on American culture. "I present Africa because it's an originating culture," she said in her *SATA* interview. "Many of us have come from that culture, and for many others, even if we're not black ourselves, nevertheless our music, our clothing, the idea of being cool, the jazz music—a lot of our originating art has come from Africa. Why did they come, where did they come, what was the atmosphere like, you want to know the answers to those questions. How do people live in different places in the world? Why do they live differently? You want to know how, and why. So you start creating stories that present the life there and yet you also give them human characteristics that are true of all human beings."

"And of course, another thing that attracts me to more traditional cultures is because I am an urban child, and I have

often been an outsider," Grifalconi went on to say. "I begun to wonder how this all started: what are the basics that are true of all human beings; can I present them before all these cultures have disappeared? Are there some truths that these cultures have to offer us, before we get hopelessly complicated in our urban, second-hand culture? I am trying to find and present originating cultures to our more complex civilization so that we could choose that which is good, that which is valuable, and warm and living."

Grifalconi's upcoming children's book will also use Africa as its setting, she revealed to *SATA.* "The book I'm working on now, *The Flyaway Girl,* focuses on the fact that the Africans believe in the ancestral spirits, that they are all around and they help you. They're not frightening, they're not like ghosts, the way we think of ghosts: rising from graveyards. The Africans think of ancestors as continuously supportive around you, always there, helping you in your daily life. All you have to do is stop and listen and they'll be there."

Grifalconi also tried a different style of illustration for this book. "Because Africa is such a rich continent," the artist continued, she wanted to use the rich images of collage in a book about Africa. "I wanted to make a magic landscape that was Africa intensified, where you have these stark contrasts," she explained. "So I started cutting out paper dolls and cutting out figures here and there from the collection that I had developed since I was sixteen, different kinds of African figures, children and people, and I started redressing them in a basic clothing." Grifalconi also chose collage for *Flyaway Girl* because "I thought collage was the right message for a girl that is being protected by ancestor spirits," she said in her interview. "How better could I show them than to show African masks themselves, and to show this girl walking through a magic landscape made up of bright red poppies or a forest of inverted trees? It's magic realism but it brings out the mystery that runs throughout Africa. This book of collages marks a very stark difference from much of the work I've done before, but I think it is very very dramatic."

"There is no limit to what a modern artist can do," Grifalconi said. In *Flyaway Girl,* she explained, "I'm using the full resources of the color xerox to develop images that are tiny into large, and the reverse. I'm using whatever technological advance is out there. And so should anybody who's interested in illustrating—I mean we may look traditional, but we consider everything."

For the past several years, Grifalconi has been working on a novel, now finished, in between her illustrating assignments. Tentatively titled *The Lion and the Jaguar,* the book takes place during the time of Christopher Columbus's final voyage to America, from 1502 to 1504. During Columbus's fourth journey to the New World, he actually met and brought aboard a Mayan pilot to help him explore the coast of Central America. To create a parallel structure, Grifalconi invented a grandson of the Mayan pilot to accompany them. "I use him and Ferdinand, Columbus's son also traveling with him for this voyage (and who later became his father's biographer), to tell the story of this experience so that you can see this first meeting of the two high civilizations from both points of view, the native and the European."

In coming up with ideas for her books, Grifalconi said in her interview, a focus comes to her gradually. "It's like the way a musician might walk around listening to this and that and finally a theme presents itself to him, becomes a persistent theme. Then you want to pin it down, so you try to find a story—or a character. When a character walks through that

NOT TOO LONG AGO, nor far away,

Where spirits live in the trees and rocks

And in the animals that roam at night,

There was a bright and pretty girl named Osa

Who was *so* afraid of the dark . . .

Darkness and the Butterfly uses flowing watercolors to convey the brilliance and beauty of the night. (Written and illustrated by Ann Grifalconi.)

maze of new information with a story, it begins to come to life." The author added that "if you're doing a children's book, you might want a child protagonist. Then you want to see what she seeks in that landscape, what kind of problems present themselves to her or him in that particular country, and how solving those problems would help you to understand human nature."

"Finally, my goal is to reflect the spirit of that particular story in the most appropriate way," Grifalconi commented. "In the background as well as in the story, I try to choose words carefully so that there will be just a few new words, or I try to use words the readers can easily understand. I try to present ideas on each page, so they have time to look them over. Children ought to have the satisfaction of being presented with an idea and then being presented with an accompanying image, which is also rich enough for them to go over further anytime they want to. For example, in the background they might find little discoveries, they might find things that illustrate the word or they might find additional information, especially when I'm doing work about Africa or something historical. I want rich information in the picture, as well as in the word!"

"The audience, the person I feel I address in my mind's eye, is the child who's beginning to *feel*—like the boy who's concerned about the death of his father and is beginning to have to deal with it on his own. The child who's beginning to

wonder, the child who's beginning to deal with the world—just his or her first tiny, little mental and emotional steps into the world, I think that's the moment that I find quite wonderful," Grifalconi told *SATA.* "I think that's one of the reasons that I like this adventure story about Columbus and his son, because that was his son's first voyage into a strange world, away from the Spanish Court. That's very similar to that moment which you go out and explore this different world and see how you feel about it, how and if you do understand it.

"Possibly that relates to the fact that I was often a child who was going from one school to another," the author explained. "I was always in a new school, finding out a new situation, trying to figure it all out. I think I'm very interested in that process. I think that's perhaps my deepest underlining theme, exploring that with a child and with young persons." Her goal, Grifalconi stated, is "to bring the mind and the soul in contact with new information or consideration. I think it is also to try to remain very human in that process, and to have the child come to love and understand others and himself. I hope," she concluded, that "I give a loving, living interpretation of life as I've seen, or imagined it."

WORKS CITED:

Brodt, Bonita, "Just for Children," *Tribune Books* (Chicago), January 25, 1987, p. 4.

Review of *Darkness and the Butterfly, Publishers Weekly,* November 13, 1987, p. 69.

Dooley, Patricia, review of *Darkness and the Butterfly, School Library Journal,* January, 1988, p. 65.

Grifalconi, Ann, telephone interview for *Something about the Author* conducted by Diane Telgen, February 11, 1991.

Kalisa, Beryl Graham, "Africa in Picture Books: Portrait or Preconception," *School Library Journal,* February, 1990, pp. 36-37.

Lane, Lisa, "Choices for Children," *Christian Science Monitor,* May 2, 1986, p. B7.

Review of *Osa's Pride, Bulletin of the Center for Children's Books,* June, 1990, p, 240.

Review of *Osa's Pride, Publishers Weekly,* April 13, 1990, p. 63.

Sher, Joan Lear, review of *City Rhythms, New York Times Book Review,* March 27, 1966, p. 34.

Vandergrift, Kay E., review of *Osa's Pride, School Library Journal,* April, 1990, p. 90.

Review of *The Village of Round and Square Houses, Publishers Weekly,* April 25, 1986, p. 72.

FOR MORE INFORMATION SEE:

BOOKS

Hopkins, Lee Bennett, *Books Are by People,* Citation Press, 1969.

PERIODICALS

Bulletin of the Center for Children's Books, June, 1986; February, 1988.
Christian Science Monitor, May 1, 1969.
Horn Book, January, 1987.
New York Times Book Review, June 22, 1986.
School Library Journal, August, 1986; June-July, 1988.

Sketch by Diane Telgen

*   *   *

GRUBER, Terry (deRoy) 1953-

PERSONAL: Born January 27, 1953, in Pittsburgh, PA, son of Irving Bernard (an industrial broker) and Aaronel (an artist, painter, and sculptor; maiden name, deRoy) Gruber. *Education:* Vassar College, A.B., 1975; Columbia University Film School, M.F.A., 1988.

ADDRESSES: Home and office—885 West End Ave., No. 9-A, New York, NY 10025.

CAREER: Independent filmmaker and producer in Los Angeles, CA, 1976-77; self-employed photographer in New York City, 1977—. Producer, Workshop for Women, American Film Institute, 1976-77. Assistant teacher, Master Director's Workshop, Maine International Film and Television Workshops, 1988-90. Film work includes: co-producer of *Number One,* directed by Dyan Cannon, 1976-77; producer of *The Wedding Journey,* directed by Judith Rascoe, 1976-77; assistant director of *The August,* directed by Anne Bancroft. Worked on productions of *Kramer vs. Kramer* and *The Last Tenant,* 1978-79. Director of film shorts, including *Not Just Any Flower* and *Dating Your Mom.*

MEMBER: American Society of Magazine Photographers.

AWARDS, HONORS: Working Cats was included on the New York Public Library's Books for the Teenager List, 1980; *Not Just Any Flower* has been featured in the international film festivals held in the cities of Cleveland, Chicago, and Ft. Lauderdale, and in Suffolk County, and at the Brooklyn Academy of Arts and the U.S. Film Festival.

WRITINGS:

Working Cats, illustrated with own photographs, Lippincott, 1980.
Fat Cats, illustrated with own photographs, Harper, 1982.
Cat High: The Yearbook, Congdon & Weed, 1984, Prima Publishers, 1988.

Also author and director of film scripts, *Just My Style, Epic, Not Just Any Flower,* and *Marvin.* Contributor of photographs to newspapers and magazines, including *People, Scholastic, Esquire, New York Post,* and *Ambience.*

SIDELIGHTS: Terry Gruber told *SATA:* "As a child, I was very independent. For example, I was never scared to be alone in the house and I was self-sufficient if it came to cooking for myself. I was given freedom and responsibility.

"My mother influenced my writing, sense of composition, and photography. When I was young she used to take me to her studio, above a neighbor's garage, to show me her art and get my opinion. Somehow I always had an opinion and suggestions of neat things to do. As different trends in art evolved, I watched the transitions in her work. This was very educational.

"She was very meticulous. A perfectionist. I've always felt the importance of well-designed, clean work. I never liked to hand in sloppy work in school—like a graph or paper. My dad was a goal-oriented businessman and a great sales person. His influence built my confidence to go out into the world and represent myself as a photographer/filmmaker/writer. He helped me achieve long term goals through good planning.

"My senior year in high school, I spent nine months alone in Florida and made a children's movie, *Hey Look at Me,* in cooperation with a psychiatrist. I was in charge of all the technical work, which I learned from professionals as I made the film. At times I didn't believe that I was actually doing a *job* because I was doing something creative with my time and effort, which didn't feel like schoolwork, yet it was for high school credit. The experience of working on the film was a maturing one. It taught me that I had a calling: film.

"*Hey Look at Me* was about attention seeking and showed how children sometimes act like clowns, which is fine when they're happy, but sometimes when they're sad, they act like clowns as well. The film tried to teach children (ages four to ten) about themselves, and was meant as a discussion-provoking tool to get children to talk about their emotions. It was this film that stimulated my interest in children's psychology and literature, which I then studied in college.

"When I moved to New York City, I shared an apartment with my sister and two cats. Shortly thereafter she got a kitten (an Abyssinian), we called him Talese. Talese adopted me as his playmate, since my sister was playing with the other two. One day he brought in about six feet of string, jumped up on the bed and dropped it in my hand. We played with the string, and I was able to lead him all around the room with the string.

"Through exploring all these string games, I developed an understanding of how patient I had to be when working with a cat and how I had to constantly entertain a cat to keep his interest. If you keep a cat's interest, you can get good expressions and poses.

"When I was putting together *Working Cats* I wanted something off beat, not just studio images of cats in baskets. I wanted to show how human we are in our relationship to animals. I wanted humorous images, like juxtaposing objects with funny cat expressions. I wanted something both humorous and touching.

"Through the text, I tried to illuminate the relationship between cats and their owners. I loved Talese because he was so sensitive to me and shared my moods and traits. Talese reflected my sociability (he always hung out at parties). He was calm, easygoing, finicky (he loved gourmet food) and very vocal about what he wanted—usually by getting on the windowsill and screaming. In my books, I tried to show this human aspect of cats.

"Creativity is being daring enough to trust your instincts. I was very mischievous as a kid. I still am. I used to play practical jokes, like 'getting the teacher,' which were never too nasty. Once my classmates and I poured disappearing ink all over the teacher's desk, which to our satisfaction, sent her running out of the room. Of course, we played innocent to it. Part of being creative is being daring in that same way. Maybe you do come close to getting someone mad, but you have an affect on them—perhaps an affect of change in a person; perhaps making them aware of their own shortsightedness.

"I think it's important to allow the mind to play games. As a kid I always felt I saw things other people didn't. Sharing these thoughts with my friends shaped my personality and affected my friend's perception of me.

"The biggest thrill I can get is when someone looks at *Cat High* and cracks up. I know I've communicated a feeling of happiness with that person. I've communicated something I've observed, and they are agreeing with me by laughing. The importance of making someone laugh, when appropriate, is making them feel good."

*   *   *

HAERTLING, Peter 1933-

PERSONAL: Born November 13, 1933, in Chemnitz (now Karl-Marx-Stadt), Germany; son of Rudolf (a lawyer) and Erika (Haentzschel) Haertling; married Mechthild Maier, July 3, 1959; children: Fabian, Friederike, Clemens, Sophie. *Education:* Educated in Germany. *Religion:* "Evangelic." *Hobbies and other interests:* Reading, conversing with wife, children, and friends.

ADDRESSES: Home—Finkenweg 1, 6082 Moerfelden-Walldorf, Germany.

CAREER: Writer. *Deutsche Zeitung und Wirtschaftzeitung* (newspaper), Stuttgart and Cologne, West Germany (now Germany), literary editor, 1955-62; *Der Monat* (magazine), West Berlin, West Germany (now Berlin, Germany), editor and copublisher, 1962-70; S. Fischer Verlag (publisher), Frankfurt am Main, West Germany (now Germany), editor and managing director, 1967-74; free-lance writer, 1974—.

Raised by his grandmother after his parents died, Peter Haertling writes about relationships between the young and old in children's books like *Old John*. (Jacket illustration by Ted Lewin.)

MEMBER: P.E.N., Akademie der Kuenste, Akademie der Wissenschaften und der Literatur, Deutsche Akademie fuer Sprache und Dichtung.

AWARDS, HONORS: Literaturpreis des deutschen Kritikerverbandes, 1964, for *Niembsch; oder, Der Stillstand;* Literaturpreis des Kulturkreises der deutschen Industrie, 1965; Literarischer Foerderungspreis des landes Niedersachen, 1965; Prix du meilleur livre etranger, 1966, for *Niembsch; oder, Der Stillstand;* Gerhart Hauptmann Preis, 1971; Schubart Prize of the City of Aalen, 1973; Deutscher Jugendbuchpreis (German Children's Book Award), 1976; Wilhelmine Luebke Prize, 1978; Stadtschreiber von Bergen-Enkheim, 1978-79; Poetik-Dozentur, Universitaet Frankfurt, 1983-84; Hermann Sinsheimer Prize of the City of Freinsheim and Hoelderlin Prize of the City of Bad Homburg, both 1987; Batchelder Award, 1989, for *Crutches;* Andreas-Gryphius Preis, 1990.

WRITINGS:

IN ENGLISH TRANSLATION; JUVENILE

Oma, translation by Anthea Bell, Harper, 1977, published in England as *Granny: The Story of Karl, Who Loses His Parents and Goes to Live with His Grandmother,* Hutchinson, 1977 (originally published in German as *Oma: Die*

Geschichte von Kalle, der seine Eltern verliert und von seiner Grossmutter aufgenommen wird, Beltz & Gelberg, 1975).

Theo Runs Away, translation by Anthea Bell, Andersen Press, 1978 (originally published in German as *Theo haut ab,* Beltz & Gelberg, 1977).

Crutches, translation by Elizabeth D. Crawford, Lothrop, 1988 (originally published in German as *Krucke,* Beltz & Gelberg, 1986).

Ben Loves Anna, Overlook Press, 1990 (originally published in German as *Ben liebt Anna,* Beltz & Gelberg, 1979).

Old John, translation by Elizabeth D. Crawford, Lothrop, 1990 (originally published in German as *Alter John,* Beltz & Gelberg, 1981).

NOVELS

Im Schein des Kometen (title means "By the Light of the Comet,"), H. Goverts (Stuttgart), 1959.

Niembsch; oder, Der Stillstand: Eine Suite, H. Goverts, 1964.

Janek: Portraet einer Erinnerung (title means "Janek: A Portrait of Remembrance"), H. Goverts, 1966.

Das Familienfest; oder, Das Ende der Geschichte (title means "The Family Festival; or, The End of the Story"), H. Goverts, 1969.

Ein Abend, eine Nacht, ein Morgen: Eine Geschichte (title means "An Evening, a Night, a Morning"), Luchterhand, 1971.

Zwettl: Nachpruefung einer Erinnerung (title means "Zwettl: Checking the Remembrance"), Luchterhand, 1973.

Eine Frau, Luchterhand, 1974, translation by Joachim Neugroschel published as *A Woman,* Holmes & Meier, 1988.

Hoelderlin, Luchterhand, 1976.

Hubert; oder Die Rueckkehr nach Casablanca (title means "Hubert; or, The Return to Casablanca"), Luchterhand, 1978.

Nachgetragene Liebe (title means "A Supplement of Love"), Luchterhand, 1980.

Die dreifache Maria, Luchterhand, 1982.

Das Windrad (title means "The Windmill"), Luchterhand, 1983.

Felix Guttmann, Luchterhand, 1985.

Waiblingers Augen (biographical novel; title means "With the Eyes of the Poet Waiblinger," Luchterhand, 1987.

Herzwand (title means "The Side of My Heart"), Luchterhand, 1990.

POETRY

Poems and Songs, Bechtle, 1953.

Yamins Stationen (title means "Yamin's Way"), Bechtle, 1955.

Unter den Brunnen: Neue Gedichte, 1959-61 (title means "Below the Wells: New Poems"), Bechtle, 1958.

Spielgeist, Spiegelgeist: Gedichte, 1959-1961 (title means "The Spirit of Play, the Spirit of Mirrors: Poems, 1959-1961"), H. Goverts, 1962.

Neue Gedichte (title means "New Poems"), J. G. Blaschke, 1972.

Zum laut und leise lesen (juvenile; title means "To Read for Oneself and for All"), Luchterhand, 1975.

Anreden: Gedichten aus die Jahren, 1972-1977 (title means "Addresses: Poems from 1972 to 1977"), Luchterhand, 1977.

Ausgewaehlte Gedichte, 1953-1979 (title means "Collected Poems"), Luchterhand, 1979.

Vorwarnung, Luchterhand, 1983.

Ich rufe die Woerter zusammen: Gedichte, 1983-84, Luchterhand, 1984.

Die Moersinger Pappel (poems; title means "The Poplar-Tree of Moersingen"), Luchterhand, 1987.

Die Gedichte, Luchterhand, 1989.

OTHER

In Zeilen zuhaus (essays; title means "To Be at Home in Sentences"), Neske, 1957.

Palmstroem gruesst Anna Blume: Essay und Anthologie der Geister aus Poetia (essays: title means "Palmstroem Greets Anna Blume"), H. Goverts, 1961.

Vergessene Buecher: Hinweise und Beispiele (essays; main title means "Forgotten Books"), H. Goverts, 1961.

(Editor) Nicolaus Lenau, *Briefe an Sophie von Loewenthal, 1834-1845* (title means "Lenau's Letters to Sophie von Loewenthal"), Koesel, 1968.

(Editor) Christian Friedrich Damiel Schubart, *Gedichte* (title means "Poems"), Fischer Buecherei, 1968.

(Compiler) *Die Vaeter: Berichte und Geschichten* (title means "The Fathers: Reports and Stories"), S. Fischer, 1968.

. . . und das ist die ganze Familie: Tageslaeufe mit Kindern (title means "This Is the Whole Family: Everyday with Children"), Bitter, 1970.

Gilles: Ein Kostuemstueck aus der Revolution (twenty-two act play; title means "Gilles: A Play on the French Revolution"; first produced in Hamburg, Germany, at Ernst-Deutsch-Theatre, September 26, 1973), H. Goverts, 1970.

Winner of the 1989 Batchelder Award for most outstanding translated children's book, *Crutches* focuses on a boy's struggle for survival after losing his family in World War II. (Jacket illustration by Wendell Minor.)

(Compiler) *Leporello faellt aus der Rolle: Zeitgenossische Autoren erzaehlen das Leben von Figuren der Weltliteratur weiter* (title means "Leporello Forgets Himself: The Life of Famous Figures of Literature"), S. Fischer, 1971.

Das war der Hirbel: Wie Hirbel ins Heim kam, warum er anders ist als andere und ob ihm zu helfen ist (children's novel; main title means "This Was a Poor Boy Called Hirbel"), Beltz & Gelberg, 1973.

(Contributor) Willy Michel, *Die Aktualitaet des Interpretierens* (title means "The Acute Problem of Interpretation"), Quelle & Meyer, 1978.

Sophie macht Geschichten (juvenile; title means "Stories on Sophie"), Beltz & Gelberg, 1980.

Der wiederholte Unfall (stories; title means "The Repeated Accident"), Reclam, 1980.

Mein Lektuere: Literatur als Widerstand (essays; title means "My Reading: Literature as Resistance"), edited by Klaus Siblewski, Luchterhand, 1981.

(Editor and author of afterword) Eduard Friedrich Morike, *Du bist Orplid, mein Land,* Luchterhand, 1982.

Ueber Heimat (essay; title means "My Country"), Verlag der Buchhandlung Aigner, 1982.

Jakob hinter der blauen Tuer (juvenile; title means "Jacob behind the Blue Door"), Beltz & Gelberg, 1983.

Der spanische Soldat oder Finden und Erfinden-Frankfurter Poetik-Vorlesungen, Luchterhand, 1984.

Fuer Ottla (story; title means "For Ottla"), Radius, 1984.

(Compiler) *Helft den Buechern, helft den Kindern!* (essays; title means "Help the Books! Help the Children!"), Hanser (Munich), 1985.

Zueignung (essays; title means "Dedication"), Radius, 1985.

Briefe an meine Kinder (title means "Letters to My Children"), Radius, 1986.

Die kleine Welle (stories; title means "The Little Wave"), Radius, 1987.

Der Wanderer (stories and essays; title means "The Wanderer"), Luchterhand, 1988.

Author of introduction for *Die Kopfkissen-Gans und andere Geschichten von grossen Dichtern fuer kleine Leute* ("The Goose under the Coverlet: Stories for Children"), Huber, 1978. Contributor to periodicals.

ADAPTATIONS: Adapted for television were *Oma,* 1976, and *Ben liebt Anna,* 1982; *Jakob hinter der blauen Tuer* was adapted for film, 1987.

WORK IN PROGRESS: A children's novel, *Mit Clara sind wir sechs* (title means "With Clara We Are Six"); a novel about composer Franz Schubert.

SIDELIGHTS: Peter Haertling is a versatile German author of poetry, novels, and most recently, children's books. In his novels Haertling explores the ways that people remember and seeks to show that it is impossible to truly understand the past. His children's books often relate in some way to his own childhood experiences.

Haertling was born in 1933 in Chemnitz, Germany. While he was growing up he was deeply affected by the turmoil of Nazi Germany. His father died in a Russian prisoner of war camp in 1945, when the author was twelve years old. At this time his mother moved the family to Zwettl, Austria, and then to Nuertingen in southwest Germany. A year later, overcome by grief, she took her own life. From then on Haertling was raised by his grandmother. He attended high school in

Nuertingen but did not graduate. Instead he worked for a short time in a factory, then began a career in journalism that would last for more than twenty years. During his career he held positions as literary editor of *Deutsche Zeitung,* a national paper of West Germany, from 1955 to 1962, editor of the monthly magazine *Der Monat,* in West Berlin, from 1962 to 1970, and editor for the prestigious publisher S. Fischer, from 1967 to 1974.

Throughout these years Haertling also published a great deal of poetry and fiction. His first poetry collection appeared in 1953, when he was only twenty years old. He published several other highly regarded poetry collections and essays on the subject during the 1950s and early 1960s. In 1959 two major events occurred in Haertling's life: He married his wife, Mechthild Maier, and published his first novel, *Im Schein des Kometen* ("By the Light of the Comet"), which states for the first time his ideas about memory. Continuing this theme in his second novel, *Niembsch oder der Stillstand* in 1964, "Haertling proved he had mastered the novel," wrote Egbert Krispyn in the *Dictionary of Literary Biography.* Both *Niembsch* and a later novel, *Hoelderlin,* describe the lives of German writers of the 1800s and demonstrate that a biographer can not completely reconstruct a person's life, even with the aid of documents.

Among his other novels for adults, *Janek: Portraet einer Erinnerung* ("Janek: A Portrait of Remembrance") and *Zwettl: Nachpruefung einer Erinnerung* ("Zwettl: Checking the Remembrance") draw directly from the author's life. The main character is a young boy whose father, like Haertling's, died in Russia at the end of World War II. The story relates the boy's obsessive desire to know about his father and to find his grave.

Some of the author's books for children—begun after deciding to devote himself to writing full-time in 1974—are set in Germany in the aftermath of the war, reflecting the author's early years and the troubles of this period. Families during this time were sometimes separated and food and shelter were scarce. Several of Haertling's children's books have been published in English translation, including *Oma, Crutches,* and *Old John.*

Oma, also translated as *Granny,* is the tale of a young boy named Kalle, who lives with his grandmother after his parents die in a car crash. The book describes how the two relatives adapt to this major change in their lives, cope with poverty, and grow in their relationship with each other. Oma is a hearty, courageous person but far from perfect, and she sometimes embarrasses and angers Kalle by talking to herself, wearing funny clothes, or making unkind remarks about his mother. After five years together, Oma has a heart attack, forcing them both to face fears about the possibility of Oma dying. Oma's reflections about Kalle at chapter ends are considered a highlight of the book. Marilyn Sachs asserted in the *New York Times Book Review* that the story "manages to make a warm human statement about ordinary people who love each other." And Elinor Lyon wrote in the *Times Literary Supplement* that the book "should give its readers or hearers new ideas about their relations with old people." For his first children's book, Haertling was awarded the German Children's Book Award in 1976.

Haertling's second book for children, *Crutches (Krucke),* is set in Vienna, Austria, in 1945. The book describes the adventures of thirteen-year-old Thomas Schramm, whose father has been killed and who has been separated from his mother. He succeeds, eventually, in gaining the help of a one-legged man called Crutches who travels with him until they find the boy's mother. In the *Bulletin of Children's Books* Betsy Hearne praised the author's portrayal of the two characters as well as the tension of the war-torn country. Hearne was most impressed with the author's depiction of Crutches, "an embittered, anti-Hitlerian ex-soldier who tries to protect his battered heart . . . but who cannot resist getting involved" in aiding the boy. During their journey, Thomas learns from Crutches a new view of Nazism, which he had been taught to admire. Their parting, when Thomas is at last reunited with his mother, makes the book's ending "bittersweet" and "tinged with sadness," noted Mary M. Burns in *Horn Book*.

Like *Oma, Old John (Alter John)*, describes a relationship between young and old. In this story, though, it is Jacob's lively, independent-minded, and cranky grandfather who comes to live with the family, causing them quite a bit of excitement. Old John finds entertainment in town with his friends and announces that he has fallen in love with a local schoolteacher. While filling the book with humorous episodes, Haertling portrays Old John with affection and sympathy. John's illness and death are strongly felt by not only the family, but the reader as well, a reviewer for *Horn Book* noted.

Haertling has received numerous honors for his writings, including the Gerhart Hauptmann Prize for *Gilles*, his twenty-two act play about the French Revolution. He lives with his wife and four children in Moerfelden-Walldorf, Germany.

WORKS CITED:

Burns, Mary M., review of *Crutches, Horn Book,* November/ December, 1988, pp. 787-88.
Dictionary of Literary Biography, Volume 75: *Contemporary German Fiction Writers,* Second Series, Gale, 1988, pp. 92-96.
Hearne, Betsy, review of *Crutches, Bulletin of the Center for Children's Books,* November, 1988, p. 74.
Lyon, Elinor, review of *Granny, Times Literary Supplement,* December 2, 1977, p. 1412.
Sachs, Marilyn, review of *Oma, New York Times Book Review,* November 20, 1977, p. 30.

FOR MORE INFORMATION SEE:

PERIODICALS

Booklist, February 1, 1989.
Books Abroad, autumn, 1967; spring, 1970.
Horn Book, July/August, 1990.
New York Times Book Review, March 12, 1967.
Times Literary Supplement, October 14, 1983.
World Literature Today, autumn, 1983; winter, 1984; spring, 1986; autumn, 1989.

*   *   *

HALE, Glenn
See WALKER, Robert W(ayne)

*   *   *

HALE, Kathleen 1898-

PERSONAL: Born May 24, 1898, in Broughton, Biggar, Lanarkshire, Scotland, to English citizens; daughter of

KATHLEEN HALE

Charles Edward Hale and Ethel Alice (Hughes) Aylmer; married Douglas McClean (a bacteriologist), 1926 (died, 1967); children: Simon Peregrine, Andrew Nicolas. *Education:* Attended Manchester School of Art, Reading University, Central School of Arts and Crafts, London, and East Anglican School of Painting and Drawing.

ADDRESSES: Home—Oxfordshire, England.

CAREER: Author and illustrator. Worked for the Ministry of Food, England, 1918; after World War I, held various small jobs such as minding babies, collecting bad debts for a window cleaner, mending, and darning; worked as a secretary for painter Augustus John; later began designing book jackets and posters; wrote and illustrated stories for *Child Education;* started writing the "Orlando" books for her children. Her works have been exhibited at numerous galleries, including New English Arts Club, Grosvenor Galleries, Vermont Gallery, Gallery Edward Harvane, New Grafton Gallery, Parkin Gallery, Lefevre Galleries, and Leicester Galleries; designed mural for Festival of Britain schools section, London, 1951.

MEMBER: Society of Industrial Arts and Designers (fellow), Society of Authors, Chelsea Arts Club.

AWARDS, HONORS: Officer of the Order of the British Empire, 1976.

WRITINGS:

ALL SELF-ILLUSTRATED

Henrietta the Faithful Hen, Transatlantic, 1943.
Manda the Jersey Calf, J. Murray, 1952, Coward-McCann, 1953.
Henrietta's Magic Egg, Allen & Unwin, 1973.

"ORLANDO" SERIES; AUTHOR, ILLUSTRATOR, AND LITHOGRAPHER

Orlando the Marmalade Cat: A Camping Holiday, Scribner, 1938.
Orlando the Marmalade Cat: A Trip Abroad, Country Life, 1939.
Orlando's Evening Out, Penguin, 1941.
Orlando's Home Life, Penguin, 1942.
Orlando the Marmalade Cat Buys a Farm, Transatlantic, 1942.
Orlando the Marmalade Cat Becomes a Doctor, Transatlantic, 1944.
Orlando the Marmalade Cat: His Silver Wedding, Transatlantic, 1944.
Orlando's Invisible Pyjamas, Transatlantic, 1947, new edition, J. Murray, 1964.
Orlando the Marmalade Cat Keeps a Dog, Transatlantic, 1949.
Orlando the Judge, J. Murray, 1950.
Orlando's Country Peep Show, Chatto & Windus, 1950.
Orlando the Marmalade Cat: A Seaside Holiday, Country Life, 1952.
Orlando's Zoo, J. Murray, 1954.
Orlando the Marmalade Cat: The Frisky Housewife, Country Life, 1956.
Orlando's Magic Carpet, J. Murray, 1958.
Orlando the Marmalade Cat Buys a Cottage, Country Life, 1963.
Orlando and the Three Graces, J. Murray, 1965.
Orlando the Marmalade Cat Goes to the Moon, J. Murray, 1968.
Orlando the Marmalade Cat and the Water Cats, J. Cape, 1972.

ILLUSTRATOR

Mary Rachel Harrower, *I Don't Mix Much with Fairies,* Eyre & Spottiswode, 1928.
Harrower, *Plain Jane,* Coward-McCann, 1929.
Charles Perrault, *Puss-in-Boots: A Peep-Show Book,* Houghton, 1951.

Designer of frontispiece and cover picture of Evelyn Waugh's *Basil Seal Rides Again,* Chapman & Hall, 1963.

OTHER

Contributor to periodicals, including *Home and Garden* and *Propaganda.*

WORK IN PROGRESS: An autobiography.

ADAPTATIONS: Numerous exploits of Orlando the Marmalade Cat—as a judge, a doctor, an astronaut, a circus star—were narrated by David Davis on BBC radio's *Children's Hour* during the late 1940s and early 1950s; an out-of-doors ballet based on *Orlando's Silver Wedding* was choreographed by Andre Howard for the Festival of Britain in 1951.

SIDELIGHTS: Kathleen Hale told Cathy Courtney in an interview for *Something about the Author (SATA)* that she

was born on May 24, 1898, at her English parents' summer home in Broughton, Scotland, the youngest of three children. Her father was a very successful sales agent for Chappell's pianos, and, until his death in 1903, the Hales lived quite comfortably. "We had a house in Didsbury, near Manchester, England, as well as a house in Scotland where we spent holidays. Our Scottish house was lovely. Across the road was a little hill called the Hill of Man, where my father used to go grouse shooting with his friends. We had a tennis court with a tiny railroad chugging along the bottom of it twice a day. Although it was transporting goods and was not a passenger train, I always enjoyed watching it go by. It was great fun.

"My father died when I was five. For the next several years I had a particular nightmare in which my father and I are running together hand in hand, through a very dark landscape in stormy weather. We didn't know where we were going or why but the feeling was one of fright and urgency. I do not remember my father well but for me to have had such a dream he must have meant a lot. I do remember, however, that when he played tennis I was terribly jealous of the other players—I tried stopping the game by hanging on to his white flannel trousers, screaming. I also remember seeing him in a nursing home just before he died.

"After my father's death, money stopped coming in and the family split up. My brother and I were put with our grandparents in Yorkshire, while my sister was sent to live with an aunt. My grandfather was a dear old man who didn't make much of an impression on me; my grandmother was practically moribund, and my aunt, their youngest daughter, was very cruel and insensitive to us. Leaving home at five was quite traumatic. I did what most children would have done given the circumstances: I wetted my drawers. My aunt hung a big placard around my neck saying, 'I wet my drawers.' I was forced to wear that sign all day, and distinctly recalled

Hale as a child.

inching backward up the stairs, trying to hide it from the curate who had came to visit.

"My grandfather was the vicar of the local church and my brother and I were not permitted to play on Sundays. Instead, we were allowed to look at a very big Bible with the most gloomy illustrations. I was put right off. After prayers at home, we went to church for the morning service; we attended Sunday school in the afternoon; we returned to church for the six o'clock service; and we knelt down together to pray before we went to bed. Every morning the whole household, including the maids and the gardener, knelt down with us to pray. It was such a silly boring business—I loathed it. I don't remember ever going outside the large garden except to go to church.

"When I was nine my mother bought a house in Manchester and we all lived together again. Although my mother was a marvelous woman who showed great courage raising us on her own, she never expressed affection. I had a rather cold upbringing. I never sat on her knee nor do I remember ever being kissed by her. I'm certain our mother loved me, but she rarely acknowledged me in any way and nagged me. If ever I picked up a book she would say, 'Haven't you got something better to do? Darn your brother's socks.' She used to chase me to the lavatory where she knew I'd lock myself in with a book. Her greatest punishment was to take away my beloved drawing materials—sometimes for a whole week. Many years later, when she was dying, the last thing she said to me was, 'You were such a dear little girl and I did go on at you.'

"In a dutiful way, my sister, who was five years older than I, did all the things for me that my mother ought to have done. She read me stories, she took me into the country for walks, and, when I was older, she took me twice with her to the opera. As a child, I was regularly sick and used to be plagued with what were called 'bilious attacks'; my sister was always the one who rushed to my assistance. Although when we were older she confessed feeling guilty for not having been more loving toward me, I don't know where I'd have been without her help.

"It was not a happy childhood but I made mine happy by running wild and neglecting my homework. I absolutely refused to learn anything at all, but I was very good at writing stories, and was eventually allowed to drop everything at school except English literature, French, and drawing. Because I didn't conform and flouted the conventions, the headmistress said that I was the naughtiest girl in the school. And there were six hundred of us. Virtually the whole of my schooldays were spent outside the classroom in the corridor in disgrace for making the other girls and teachers laugh. On the whole my classmates were conformist and swallowed it whole about 'esprit de corps' and loyalty to the school. It was accepted so unquestioningly that it made me rebel. But then, I thought, I'm too peculiar—I must have a friend. So I chose three, which was a mistake as they ganged up against me and laughed at me behind my back. But I kept two, though I decided friendship with girls of my own age was not for me.

"I did much better with middle-age gentlemen. They usually liked me because I was an original and lively child. There was a humpbacked doctor whom I used to visit. He had reproductions of Giotto all around his waiting room; I had never seen pictures like those and loved them. There was another friend who introduced me to good illustrations by giving me the Edmund Dulac and Arthur Rackham books. I was also good friends with an uncle who was very attached to me."

When Hale was fifteen her headmistress, who had become aware of Hale's drawing talent, gave her permission to attend life-drawing classes two days a week at the Manchester School of Art. Special dispensation was required because some of the models were naked men and Hale was considered too young. Hale told *SATA,* "It rather shattered me to see a naked man, even though he was wearing long shorts down to his knees. Going to art school among adult students was my first taste of freedom . . . it was bliss."

Following high school graduation, Hale won a two year art scholarship to Reading University College. "I lived in St. Andrews hostel, where, for the first time, I had a room to myself," she recalled in her *SATA* interview. "I was delighted. Until then I had shared my mother's bed and, although I was comfy when a child, I disliked it intensely as I was growing up.

"Art education at Reading was a tiny little part of the university. We were surrounded by the agricultural students, and the musicians and scientists. I was eager to learn everything and attended lectures on every possible subject. To me the most interesting place of all was the college farm. I used to get up very early in the morning and somehow sneaked out of St. Andrews with my bicycle, although the doors were still bolted. I rode to the farm to milk the cows and helped with various chores like spudding thistles for sixpence an hour. Herbicide was not used in those days, everything had to be done by hand.

"Because of World War I most of the men were in the army and the art department was short of staff. Outside of wood engraving I didn't learn much. Mr. Seaby, the principal, was very keen on Chinese woodcutting, and, although it was not my cup of tea, I could not escape it. The process of engraving is quite tedious. You have to cut away everything on a hard wood block except fine lines. If you do one little nip that you are not supposed to do, that meant starting all over again on a new block. Nevertheless, I still managed to achieve one very good woodcut. Unfortunately, we didn't have life classes: the school used male models and it was impossible to get any during the war. I never understood why we couldn't have female models. But I went around the back streets of Manchester and drew the open markets and the people.

"I also got very interested in music, particularly Bach, because one of the students at the hostel played his work beautifully. Dr. Allen, who was quite famous in the musical world at the time, ran a Bach choir. I was dying to take part in it and decided to attend an audition, even though I couldn't sing a note. For the audition we were played a chord of three notes and we were supposed to pick out the middle one. Well, I don't know how, but I did it and was accepted. Later we rehearsed 'St. Matthew's Passion' and I was just mouthing the words—not making a sound—when Dr. Allen suddenly told me, 'You, just sing the last bit.' I turned purple and silent. He very kindly passed me over and I remained in the choir. He understood that I deeply wanted to be there. After that I started to take singing lessons with a friend and developed the most extraordinary little voice—a little peep like a young nestling.

"After I finished the course at Reading I was offered a scholarship to stay on for another two years, mainly because I had worked so hard. I often had to be shoved out of the school at closing time. Otherwise, I would still have been there in the night working on my own drawings.

A spotlight was turned on Orlando, who I'm afraid wasn't listening. He was dealing with an overexcited flea which, tired of circus life on a tiger, wished for domestic peace on Orlando. (From *Orlando's Evening Out*, written and illustrated by Kathleen Hale.)

"My mother wanted me to come home to learn typing and shorthand. I, on the other hand, was determined to go to London and be an artist. One of my teachers guaranteed any students of his a job at the Ministry of Food and so I arrived in London and stepped straight into earning my living. Since I had absolutely no qualifications, the job was a disaster. My first assignment was to add up how many people in the British Isles were eating how much meat a week. I could neither add nor subtract and when the results were published in the public food report, I was of course found out. I was then transferred to the department of coloring maps, but was unable to keep the colors inside the lines and was taken off that job as well. The Ministry of Food did not know what to do with me but, because I was very lively and amusing, they decided to keep me on. I was considered to be helping the war effort by keeping other workers' morale up! I eventually got bored with doing nothing other than making people laugh. I decided to become a land girl in a very large market garden at Barnes, in charge of a huge horse-drawn wagon and a plow.

"Though without experience, I bluffed my way as a carter because I loved horses. Even so, I didn't know how to take care of them. I managed to work the old hand plow, though it was so heavy that it sent me spinning sideways at each end of the furrow. Also I had to drive a huge wagon to Covent Garden Market at night, sleeping while my horse plodded on his well-known way.

"It was a wonderful job. I could nip up to London to dances in my land army uniform and back again driving lorries full of manure from pub stables for our farm. It was a wonderful summer and when armistice came in November I decided to stay on until March. I wanted to see it through the winter.

"London was a magical city then. There were fewer people than now and wherever you went, whether it was on Hampstead Heath, Primrose Hill, or Picadilly, you always ran into somebody you knew. I joined the Studio Club, a contemporary artists' meeting-place in a basement in Lower Regent Street. A pianist endlessly played dance music and every evening we danced. The bar was run by a fierce cockney lady who was drunk half of the time but who cooked wonderful piping-hot steaks and chips and puddings. She was the first really belligerent person I'd ever met and I thought, 'I'm going to tame you. I'm going to make you like me.' And I did. She used to give me double quantities of food.

"Though the Club was depleted because of the war it was still frequented by interesting people such as the artists C. R. W. Nevinson and Ethelbert White, the well-known war correspondent Ward Muir, and the theatrical producer Leon M. Lyons, who commissioned me to do a poster for a play called *The Chinese Poster.*

"It was a very simple poster that was considered avant garde. I drew a big black circle with, inside, a Chinese mandarin. It was displayed on every tube railway station, and sandwichmen were walking the streets of London wearing it. It was plastered all over the place—it was incredible. I didn't realize what a wonderful opportunity it was, but it didn't immediately lead to more work for me.

"One evening, after the war was over, the painter Augustus John appeared at the Studio Club. I had just won a prize of twenty-five pounds in a poster competition and knew he had been one of the judges. I thought, I'll have a bit of fun, so I went up and said, 'Thank you very much for the twenty-five pounds.' He looked horrified. I could see him thinking, 'Who is this girl? I never paid for "it" before!' I let him simmer for a bit then told him who I was. He asked me what I was doing and upon learning that I was collecting unpaid bills for a window-cleaner, doing family darning for sixteen shillings a week, and taking babies for walks, he asked me to become his secretary for two pounds a week, including a midday meal. After sixteen months I gave up the job.

"It was a very interesting experience. I thought it would open the whole world of art to me; in fact, it consisted of answering the telephone, which rang all day and into the early morning, and trying to make Augustus answer his letters, which was difficult as he was often in the pub. He used to call me 'p.p.' because I just signed p.p. [per personal] and my name at the bottom of all the letters I knew that didn't need his signature. I was very clever with him and got the best results by humoring him. One day, Lady Tredegar, whose portrait he had been commissioned to do, arrived for her appointment in her Rolls Royce. Augustus was in a pub in Chelsea and I went to fetch him. It wouldn't have worked to have gone to him and say, 'You must come back, the old girl's here.' I sat down next to him and he said, 'Have a drink.' I said, 'I don't mind if I do.' So, we had a gin. When I judged that the timing was right I said, 'By the way, Augustus, do you remember Lady Tredegar?' 'Yes, what about her?' 'Well she is waiting for you.' Only then did he agree to come home. There were piles of his drawings spread out on the grand piano in his studio, and not only were cigarette ashes and cups of tea and beer being slopped on them, they were being stolen by people. I could never make him do anything about it, he just thought I had a nasty character. After I left he used to say about me, 'She was a bloody good cook but a rotten secretary.' It was a wonderful compliment. I was expected to cook lunch for him and I didn't know how to cook, but I learned from his wife how to roast pheasant in wine with good ingredients.

"I was a live-in secretary until I decided to rent a room nearby because the job gave me no time off at all. But while I was still living at Mallard Street, Augustus's wife, Dorelia, who lived in their country house, came up to look me over. She knew all about her husband's infidelities, but at that time I was besotted with my first love—an etcher just out of the army—and was proof against Augustus's wiles. I realized very quickly that the best thing to do to keep him aloof was either to laugh merrily or to look stonily indifferent. The whole of that society was just as promiscuous then as it is now. Everybody was living with everybody and nobody ever got married. Or if they did get married, they had mistresses or got divorced. It was most interesting.

"Dorelia John became the most important person in my life. She influenced me more than anybody in the matter of taste and living. She was awfully kind to me and I loved her dearly. It would take a whole book to describe her. Though Augustus always drew her as very tall and slim, she was a small woman and quite dumpy, but exquisitely beautiful with dark hair in loops, wide cheekbones with a small chin and mouth, and a domed forehead, like a Jan Vermeer painting of a Dutch woman. She was very monosyllabic with the kindest, tired-looking eyes. She never moved her face, she never laughed aloud, she chuckled like a hen, too deep in her throat with amusement. She was infinitely tolerant and always with a hint of humor. She wore dresses that she made herself of an individual style that all the Slade students used to copy.

"I did a pen drawing of Augustus asleep and one of Dorelia sewing. They are part of my better work and have been

exhibited, but I shall never sell them because they have too much sentimental value.

"After I quit my job at Augustus's, my first love and I went to live in Etaples, Normandy, France, for four months. I had just received about fifteen dust-jacket commissions from W. H. Smith at two guineas a week and living was very cheap in Normandy after the war.

"Etaples had been a thriving fishing village but was badly bombed during the war, reducing a lot of it to rubble. Looking back it was tragic, but to me everything was new and interesting. I did hundreds and hundreds of drawings and sold nearly all when I showed them at galleries. My works were reproduced in many art journals, such as *The Studio* and *Drawing and Design.* We employed models morning and afternoon from the village, the old and young women, children and babies. It was an incredibly productive time. I have never lived in such a state of ecstasy in my life, before or since; we thought of nothing but work. We ate exactly the same meal every day: black french coffee with french bread in the morning, poached eggs, black coffee, and french bread for lunch and supper. At night we went to the local dances with the fisher people, and I was constantly being seized without a word by the fisher girls to dance their very, very, very fast waltz. The men were never so bold as to ask me—there was a lot of etiquette.

"When I returned to England I exhibited my work in several galleries and sold most of it. At the same time, Augustus got me a job with an interior decorator. I designed a couple of nurseries in which I painted the furniture from nursery rhymes. I also worked for an advertising firm doing commercial black-and-white pictures of motor cars and sewing machines—none of which I could do. I had to be sacked. Eventually I found work in my own field after I met Charles Kay Ogden, who invented Basic English. He introduced me to *Child Education* magazine, for which I wrote and illustrated stories. Ogden was incidental to my books being published."

In 1926 Hale married Douglas McClean, a bacteriologist at the Lister Institute for Preventive Medicine. They were married for forty-one years until his death in 1967. "I met my husband through his father, Dr. McClean, who ran the London Fever Hospital," Hale explained in her *SATA* interview. "I had spent one Christmas in the hospital with a bad throat infection and Dr. McClean and I became friends. He was sixty-five. I had been looking for a father all my life, and I loved him because he was a lovely, intelligent man—I felt he was my father. He had two sons and a daughter. His daughter was two years older than I and terrified that I was going to marry her father. Then Dr. McClean decided that I ought to marry his son. I was interested because I thought, that's wonderful! I've got a father, now I'm going to have a brother. We met and he fell in love with me—though I could only regard him as a brother.

"Douglas was tall and frail looking. Years later it was found that he had tuberculosis in both lungs, and he was a rather gloomy young man, which was not surprising. He wooed me with quotations from sad poems and a postcard with a reproduction of Albrecht Durer's drawing of a skeleton, 'Father Time.' He was an intellectual and a great reader. I used to tease him, telling him that printer's ink ran in his veins. He took me to highbrow plays, concerts, and Labor Party meetings, way out of my element. I couldn't even make him laugh and actually stopped seeing him for some time because he depressed me. Then one evening I went to the

Orlando taught them how to play "Cat's Cradle" with pieces of string. (From *Orlando the Marmalade Cat: A Camping Holiday*, written and illustrated by Kathleen Hale.)

Cave of Harmony, a club for theater and the arts, and there was a tall young stranger with a beard who I thought looked marvelous. It was Douglas. So I married a beard really. His father died six months after we were married, which devastated us both.

"Though Douglas and I were very different, we complemented each other. He had a kind of wit but no sense of fun; I was low on the scale of wit but I had a terrific sense of fun. When I started to do my books, *Orlando the Marmalade Cat*, Douglas said seriously, 'Kathleen, cats don't *do* these things.' I though it was an absolutely delicious remark.

"Unlike Douglas, I was a great party-goer. The evening of our first married day he settled down in an armchair with the *New Statesman*. I had hardly ever stayed at home for evenings. I thought, 'God Almighty, is this what I'm expected to do? Heavens!' I stuck it out, but the next day, I dragged Douglas to a party at the studio of the painters Cedric Morris and Arthur Lett Haines—they gave the most amusing and interesting parties—and there he sat, in a corner of this huge studio, reading his *New Statesman*. I have pulled his leg many times about the *New Statesman* and even pictured him with it in my books.

"By the time I got married I was making a nice living for myself, but not exactly the sort of work I wanted to do. So, I decided to learn oil painting, which I had never tackled because I hadn't been able to afford the cost of canvas, paint, and brushes. I went to the Central School of Arts and Crafts, where I was taught oil painting by Fred Porter and life drawing by Bernard Meninsky, a remarkable man and an outstanding teacher. About a drawing he would never correct the drawing but would insist, 'The space is just as important as the model,' which showed the way to play a composition around the figure.

"I was commissioned to paint a certain amount of children's portraits. I hated this, partly because children never sit still. Also parents have wonderful ideas of how lovely their children are; they were horrified not to recognize the reality in my finished paintings. I once drew a beloved Siamese cat for someone and he tore the painting in pieces in front of me. It was before the marked squint had been bred out of their eyes."

After the birth of her first son Peregrine in 1930, Hale moved to the rural surroundings of Hertfordshire in order to raise her family. "A neighbor congratulated us on buying the most hideous house in the district," she told *SATA*. "It was a raw, red-brick Victorian house with yellow bricks round the windows and a featureless slate roof. It was a pretty dreary-looking place, but after we improved it with white paint covering the walls, it turned out to be very attractive. Though we were only thirteen miles as the crow flies to Picadilly Circus, we had four miles of sheer country and farms around us.

"I continued doing what I liked doing, including making assemblages out of metal, wire, and gauze, which turned out to be a great success. *Vogue* photographed them, they were exhibited at Liberty's, Fortnum and Masons, and the Lefevre Galleries, and Gaumont British made a documentary film of me at work. With the outbreak of World War II, metal was no longer available and I had to stop making this kind of work.

"By the time my second son, Nicolas, was born in 1933, I was already getting tired of rereading the same children's stories,

night after night, no matter how lovely they were. Children's books tended to be awfully bad in those days; the only good ones were those of Beatrix Potter and Edward Ardizzone and Jean de Brunoff's *Babar the Elephant*. I didn't want books like those of Enid Blyton to come into the house so I started to make up stories about our cat. He was given to us as a kitten when Peregrine was six months old; they were the same age and the cat was very important to him.

"But it was not until I ran into Ogden again that I began to think seriously about writing for children. As I was discussing the lack of interesting children's books and that I made up my own about our cat, Ogden suggested that I write the stories and illustrate it in black and white. He would then have them translated into Basic English and sell them to the Japanese. I went home excited and used seven colors and made books the same large size as *Babar the Elephant*. I put them into the hands of an agent, but they went the rounds for two years without finding a publisher. Eventually they were shown to Noel Carrington, the juveniles editor of *Country Life*. He was much impressed but knew the drawings were too expensive to reproduce. Geoffrey Smith, an Ipswich printer, convinced him that he could lower the cost by reducing the colors to four and by having me make the illustrations into lithographs. Unlike today, lithography was the cheapest method of reproducing illustrations, only done by the artist to save expense.

"I worked very long hours drawing straight onto the printer's plates, one for each color. It took me seven hours a day, seven days a week for four-and-a-half months to do one book. And I was not even paid for that labor; I was bearing the brunt of most of the expense. Though at the time I did not mind: I was utterly obsessed by writing the books and was so pleased to be published."

The first Orlando book, *Orlando the Marmalade Cat: A Camping Holiday,* was published in 1938, and its sequel *Orlando the Marmalade Cat: A Trip Abroad,* in 1939. "Both were a complete flop and *Country Life* decided to remainder them," Hale revealed in her *SATA* interview. "I had just enough business sense then to remind them that my contract agreement stipulated they could not do that for another two years. John Lane, the creator of the Puffin books, asked me to do a small Orlando, which I agreed to do if they mentioned the other two on the jacket."

As soon as the *Orlando* published by Puffin came out, all three *Country Life* books became instant best-sellers, selling thousands of copies and challenging *Babar the Elephant* books by Jean de Brunoff, another pioneer of color offset lithography. Between 1938 and 1972 Hale published eighteen *Orlandos*. They have appeared and reappeared under many different imprints and many different formats—folio, oblong octavo, quarto, and pop-up. By the early 1950s, Orlando the Cat had become a well-known personality. His numerous exploits as a judge, a doctor, an astronaut, a star of the circus were narrated by David Davis on BBC radio's *Children's Hour*. An Orlando ballet—for which Hale designed the costumes, scenery, and props—was choreographed by Andre Howard for the Festival of Britain in 1951. It turned out to be a fiasco, however, because "the rain ruined it," Hale told *SATA*. "The stage was not properly leveled; it was quickly covered with puddles making it impossible for the dancers to dance. It only ran for two performances and was canceled, like all the 'high-brow' entertainment, to save money."

Orlando's first adventures were accounts Hale gave her children of vacations she took with her husband. The author

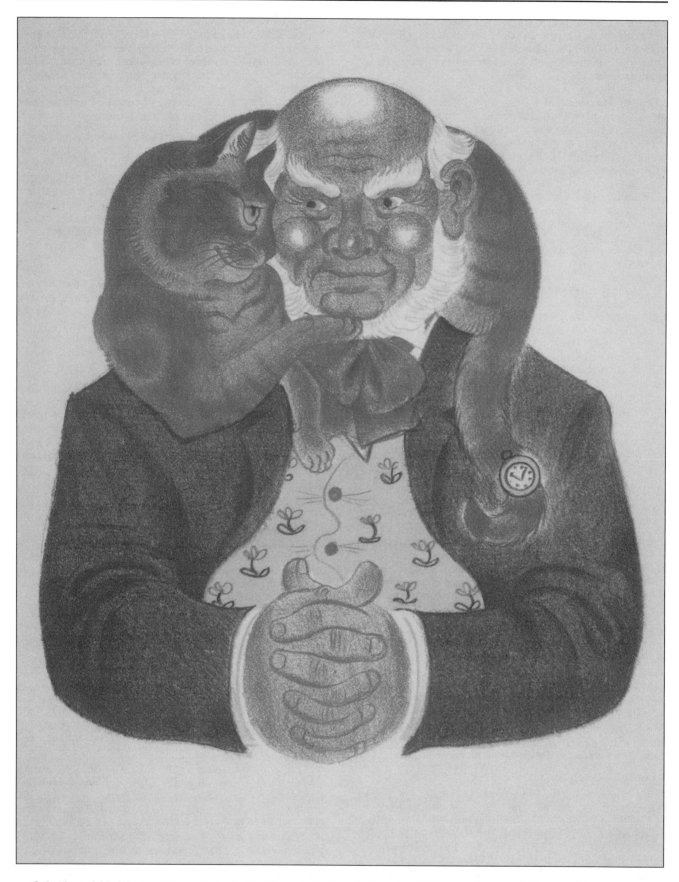

Orlando and his Master. (From *Orlando the Marmalade Cat: A Camping Holiday,* written and illustrated by Kathleen Hale.)

explained to *SATA* that "*A Camping Holiday* was my way to describe to my children the camping trips that Douglas and I took together. We used to go camping a lot and the children always wanted to know—down to the smallest details—what we had done. In the village shop that is drawn in that book, there is a glass door separating the shop from the living quarters. And through the lace curtains are two little children looking into the shop. I have had a long correspondence with those two little children, who are now grandmothers. They wrote how they remembered me and how pleased they were to recognize themselves in my book looking through the glass door. *A Trip Abroad* was inspired by my first visit to Paris.

"*Buys a Farm* is a combination of the farm next door to our home and my experience as a land-girl during World War I. *Buys a Cottage* is based on our own house, or at least began with it. It's a three-hundred-year-old house and my husband went to the Bodleian Library to find out what he could about it. Unfortunately the archives only went back a hundred years.

"I have often been asked how I worked. Well, first I chose a topic for the book, then the text and the illustrations always grew side by side. I had to decide how much of the page was going to be taken up by words and how much would be left for the picture. If I wanted more room for the pictures I shortened the text, or vice versa. Some people prefer the text, others the illustrations, but as far as I am concerned they are interwoven—it's impossible to do without either.

"The characters in the books are distillations of familiar people. Orlando was my husband. He has his integrity and his feelings of responsibility. Orlando's wife, Grace, was the sort of woman I would have liked to have been: infinitely sweet and feminine but slightly dotty. I would have loved to have been more dotty than overly practical. Tinkle, who is a little bit of a rebel, was based on me, though he had to be softened not to appear too subversive from the parents' point of view. Through Tinkle I wanted to convey a message of tolerance and understanding, that if a child is being difficult it may not be because he is 'naughty' but because something creative inside of him is steaming up. When writing my books I kept in mind children who were deprived of family love and always tried to portray a warm happy family life. Pansy and Blanche were nice little, well-behaved girls with maternal instincts towards Tinkle.

"My theories about life are inevitably expressed in my books. For instance, one of my beliefs is that we should not be killing animals for fur coats. I also realize the terrible power of too much money. In the story about a shop, Grace says, 'Money doesn't smell nice and you can't eat it.' So, instead buying and selling she sets up an exchange system.

I had to disguise Master because of possible libel. Our friend wore the same pince-nez in real life and had the same extraordinary angularity as Master, but he was blond and never wore a straw hat. I don't think he would ever have libeled me, but I became very libel conscious after I did *Seaside Holiday.* I did realistic drawings of those enchanting and absurd houses with turrets that were built along the sea front. I turned one of them into Mr. Curmudgeon's home. *Country Life* told me I could not do that as I was liable to be libeled by the owner for putting such an unpleasant character in his house. I think *Country Life* was being a bit overcautious. Nevertheless, I had to alter the drawing of that house.

"After we acquired a dog called Bill, I introduced him in the story. It amused me to have to confront the bumbling, well-meaning personality of a dog with the extreme fastidiousness of cats. I liked the clash of personalities. The other animals in the books came from the sketchbooks I still had from the time when I used to go drawing at the zoo.

"As the children grew older I had to invent new ideas until I found that the books were getting too grown-up. By the time I had written ten of them I wanted to stop. I thought it was a bit vulgar to have written so many. I would have liked, like Lewis Carroll, to have been famous for only one book.

"But *Country Life* offered me such a whacking advance royalty—four hundred pounds—to do another book that I could not refuse. I had two friends living in Lebanon whom I had always wanted to visit. It seemed like a good opportunity and out of that experience I wrote *Orlando's Magic Carpet.* Then, just before the astronauts went up to the moon, I was asked to do *Orlando the Marmalade Cat Goes to the Moon.* I spent eighteen months reading about space and airplanes and stratospheres. Not only was I bored with the subject but I could not understand a word of it. I ended up making up a lot of the information, which terribly annoyed *Country Life,* who was expecting a sensible and probable story. When they asked me to do Orlando buying a car I flatly refused. I dislike machines and don't understand them. They are not of my world. The last of the series, *Orlando the Marmalade Cat and the Water Cats* was published in 1972."

When the "Orlando" series went out of print in the late 1980s, Kathleen Hale, according to James McClure in *Limited Edition,* exclaimed, "The books are dead—*now* I'm going to live." However, in 1990 Warne publishers decided to reissue the series and asked Hale to correct mistakes and adjust drawings for the new edition. "I didn't alter much," Hale remarked in her *SATA* interview. "Although the books are dated, the idea was to reissue them as they had been done originally. I took out one joke I thought was facetious. I made a pattern with white paint on a red kite which looked a bit flat, and I lightened a few things that were too dark, including a kitten in a tree that had become hardly visible."

In addition to the Orlando series, Hale was commissioned to create the frontispiece and cover picture for Evelyn Waugh's *Basil Seal Rides Again,* which was published in a limited edition of 750 signed and numbered copies. She also wrote *Henrietta the Faithful Hen, Henrietta's Magic Egg,* and *Manda the Jersey Calf.* Hale told *SATA* that "the idea of *The Jersey Calf* was born during a trip to Ireland. I loved Ireland. On the way home, I decided to write a book on the adventures of a Jersey calf in Ireland. We didn't fly in those days, we traveled by boat. I was always seasick and before returning to England I took some anti-seasickness pills. That got me across all right but made me terribly sleepy. To wake me up my husband gave me some Dexedrine. I wrote *The Jersey Calf* under the influence of Dexedrine, in the car during the journey back."

Although she stopped writing children's books, Hale continues to paint and is planning to write her autobiography. "Tom Maschler asked me years ago to write my memoirs," she recounted to her *SATA* interviewer. "I said, 'I can't. I have no philosophy about life. I've never learnt anything from my mistakes and I keep on making the same one.' Maschler didn't give up and I eventually agreed to give it a try.

"I did not like writing about myself. I wrestled with it for about eighteen months and abandoned the project. Then, a neighbor's son died in a motor car accident. She had often offered to take dictation and do typing for me, and I thought it might help her get through the immediate winter if she worked on the book with me. The collaboration worked quite well and lasted six years. It was a desultory kind of thing: we worked two hours a day when one of us was not away or ill or too busy. When the first draft was finished I made the most terrible mistake. I sent it to the publisher omitting to mention that it was a first draft. They found the book too scattered and too long. So, I sent it to Noel Carrington, my original publisher, who was ninety by then, and asked him to reduce the manuscript to a manageable size. He cut out all the best bits and sent it to the people at Virago Press, who said that there was not enough to make a book. Fortunately, I had kept a copy of my original first draft. Since then, I really got interested in writing an autobiography and, though it will take time and research, I am confident that it will be done."

WORKS CITED:

Hale, Kathleen, in an interview with Cathy Courtney for *Something about the Author*, in London, England.
McClure, James, "Orlando's Other Mother," *Limited Edition: The Magazine of Oxfordshire*, April, 1990.

FOR MORE INFORMATION SEE:

PERIODICALS

Book Collector, November, 1988.
Christian Science Monitor, December 12, 1947.
New York Herald Tribune, July 15, 1971.
New York Times, November 30, 1947.
Sunday Telegraph, April 15, 1990.
Times Educational Supplement, June, 1990.

*   *   *

HALL, Willis 1929-

PERSONAL: Born April 6, 1929, in Leeds, England; son of Walter (a fitter) and Gladys (Gomersal) Hall; married Valerie Shute, 1973; children: Peter, Macer, Daniel, James. *Education:* Educated in Leeds, England.

ADDRESSES: Home—64 Clarence Rd., St. Albans, Hertfordshire, England. *Agent*—London Management, 235-241 Regent St., London WlA 2JT, England.

CAREER: Writer. Served as radio playwright for Chinese Schools Department of Radio Malaya. *Military service:* British Regular Army, 1947-52.

MEMBER: Garrick Club, Savage Club, Lansdowne Club.

AWARDS, HONORS: Drama award for play of the year from *Evening Standard*, 1959, for *The Long and the Short and the Tall*.

WRITINGS:

JUVENILE

(With I. O. Evans) *They Found the World*, Warne, 1959.

The Royal Astrologers: Adventures of Father Molecricket; or, The Malayan Legends, Heinemann, 1960, Coward, 1962.
Editor (with Peter Waterhouse) *Writer's Theatre*, Heineman, 1967.
(With Michael Parkinson) *The A to Z of Soccer*, Pelham, 1970.
(With Bob Monkhouse) *The A to Z of Television*, Pelham, 1971.
(With Parkinson) *Football Report: An Anthology of Soccer*, Pelham, 1973.
Football Classified: An Anthology of Soccer, Luscombe, 1975.
Football Final, Pelham, 1975.
Incredible Kidnapping, Heinemann, 1975.
The Last Vampire, Bodley Head, 1982.
The Irish Adventures of Worzel Gummidge, Severn House, 1984.
Dragon Days, illustrated by Alison Claire Darke, Bodley Head, 1985.

Also author of *The Summer of the Dinosaur*, 1977; *The Inflatable Shop*, 1984; *The Return of the Antelope*, 1985; *Spooky Rhymes*, 1987; *The Antelope Company at Large*, 1987; *Dr. Jekyll and Mr. Hollins*, 1988; and *Henry Hollins and the Dinosaur*, 1989.

PUBLISHED PLAYS
Final at Furnell (radio play; broadcast in 1954), M. Evans, 1956.
(With Lewis Jones) *Poet and Peasant* (radio play; first broadcast in 1955), Deane, 1959.
The Long and the Short and the Tall (produced in Edinburgh, Scotland, 1958, later London, England, 1959, then New York City, 1962), Heinemann, 1959, Theatre Arts, 1961.
A Glimpse of the Sea: Three Short Plays (contains *A Glimpse of the Sea*, one-act, produced in London, 1959; *The Last Day in Dreamland*, one-act, produced in London, 1959; *Return to the Sea*, television play, first broadcast in 1959), M. Evans, 1960.
The Play of the Royal Astrologers (produced in Birmingham, England, 1958, London, 1968), Heinemann, 1960.
The Day's Beginning: An Easter Play, Heinemann, 1963.
The Gentle Knight (radio play; first broadcast in 1964), Blackie, 1966.
The Railwayman's New Clothes (television play; first broadcast in 1971), S. French, 1974.
Kidnapped at Christmas (produced in London, 1975), Heinemann, 1975.
My Sporting Life, Luscombe, l975.
Walk On, Walk On (produced in Liverpool, England, 1975), S. French, 1976.
A Right Christmas Caper (produced in 1977), S. French, 1978.
Treasure Island (musical; based on novel by Robert Louis Stevenson; first produced in London, 1985), S. French, 1986.
Wind in the Willows (musical; based on story by Kenneth Grahame; first produced in London, 1985), S. French, 1986.

PUBLISHED PLAYS; WITH PETER WATERHOUSE
Billy Liar (adaptation of novel by Waterhouse; produced in London, 1960, produced in New York City, 1963), Norton, 1960.
Celebration: The Wedding and the Funeral (produced in Nottingham, England, 1961, produced in London, 1961), M. Joseph, 1961.
England, Our England (musical; first produced in London, 1962), M. Evans, 1964.

The Sponge Room (first produced in Nottingham, 1962), M. Evans, 1963.

Squat Betty (first produced in London, 1962), M. Evans, 1963.

All Things Bright and Beautiful (first produced in Bristol, England, 1962, produced in London, 1962), M. Joseph, 1963.

Come Laughing Home (first produced as *They Called the Bastard Stephen* in Bristol, 1964; produced as *Come Laughing Home* in Wimbledon, England, 1965), M. Evans, 1965.

Say Who You Are (first produced in London, 1965), M. Evans, 1967, also published as *Help Stamp Out Marriage* (first produced in New York City, 1966), S. French, 1966.

Children's Day (produced in Edinburgh, 1969, produced in London, 1969), S. French, 1975.

Who's Who (produced in Coventry, England, 1971, produced in London, 1973), S. French, 1974.

(Also translators) *Saturday, Sunday, Monday* (adaptation of a play by Eduardo de Filippo; first produced in London, 1973, produced in New York City, 1973), Heinemann, 1974.

Worzel Gummidge (musical; adaptation of television series based on characters created by Barbara Euphan Todd; first produced in London, 1981), S. French, 1984.

UNPUBLISHED PLAYS

Chin-Chin (adaptation of play, *Tchin-Tchin,* by Francois Billetdoux), first produced in London, 1960.

(With Robin Maugham) *Azouk* (adaptation of play by Alexandre Rivemale), first produced in Newcastle-Upon-Tyne, England, 1962.

(Co-author) *Yer What?* (revue), first produced in Nottingham, 1962.

The Love Game (adaptation of play by Marcel Archard), first produced in London, 1964.

(With Waterhouse) *Joey, Joey* (musical), first produced in London, 1966.

(With Waterhouse) *Whoops-a-Daisy,* first produced in Nottingham, 1968.

(With Waterhouse) *The Card* (musical; adaptation of novel by Arnold Bennett), first produced in Bristol, 1973, produced in London, 1973.

Christmas Crackers, first produced in London, 1976.

Stag-Night, first produced in London, 1976.

Filumena (adaptation of work by de Filippo), first produced in 1977.

The Water Babies (musical; based on work by Charles Kingsley), first produced in London, 1987.

(With Waterhouse) *Budgie* (musical), first produced in London, 1989.

Author of screenplays, including *The Long and the Short and the Tall,* 1961; (with Waterhouse) *Whistle Down the Wind,* 1961; (with Waterhouse) *A Kind of Loving,* 1961; *The Valiant,* 1962; (with Waterhouse) *Billy Liar* (adapted from novel by Waterhouse), 1963; *West Eleven,* 1963; (with Waterhouse) *Man in the Middle,* 1964; (with Waterhouse) *Pretty Polly,* 1968; *Lock Up Your Daughters,* 1969.

Author of television plays, including *Air Mail from Cyprus,* 1958; *On the Night of the Murder,* 1962; *By Endeavour Alone,* 1963; (with Waterhouse) *Happy Moorings,* 1963; *How Many Angels,* 1964; *The Ticket,* 1969; *They Don't All Open Men's Boutiques,* 1972; *The Villa Maroc,* 1972; *Song at Twilight,* 1973; *Friendly Encounter,* 1974; *The Piano-Smashers of the Golden Sun,* 1974; *Illegal Approach,* 1974; *Midgley,* 1975; *MatchFit,* 1976; *The Road to 1984.*

Author of radio plays, including *The Nightingale,* 1954; *Furore at Furnell,* 1955; *Frenzy at Furnell,* 1955; *Friendly at Furnell,* 1955; *Fluster at Furnell,* 1955; *One Man Absent,* 1955; *A Run for the Money,* 1956; *Afternoon for Antigone,* 1956; *The Long Years,* 1956; *Any Dark Morning,* 1956; *Feodor's Bride,* 1956; *One Man Returns,* 1956; *A Ride on the Donkeys,* 1957; *The Calverdon Road Job,* 1957; *Harvest the Sea,* 1957; *Monday at Seven,* 1957; *Annual Outing,* 1958; *The Larford Lad,* 1958; (with Leslie Halward) *The Case of Walter Grimshaw,* 1958.

Writer for television shows, including *Inside George Webley,* 1968; *Queenie's Castle,* 1970; *Budgie,* 1971-72; *The Upper Crusts,* 1973; *Three's Company,* 1973; *Billy Liar,* 1973-74; *The Fuzz,* 1977; *Worzel Gummidge,* 1979; *The Danedyke Mystery,* 1979; *Stan's Last Game,* 1983; *The Bright Side,* 1985; *The Return of the Antelope,* 1986.

Work represented in anthologies, including: *The Television Playwright: Ten Plays for BBC Television,* edited by Michael Barry, Hill & Wang, 1960; *Modern Short Plays from Broadway and London,* edited by Stanley Richards, Random House, 1969; *Drama Study Units,* edited by John Foster, Heinemann, 1975.

* * *

HAMILTON, (John) Alan 1943-

PERSONAL: Born April 22, 1943, in Edinburgh, Scotland. *Education:* Attended University of Edinburgh, 1961-66.

ADDRESSES: Office—Times Newspapers Ltd., P.O. Box 481, Virginia St., London E1 9BD, England.

CAREER: Reporter and correspondent for the *Times,* London, England; radio broadcaster for the British Broadcasting Corp., London; writer.

WRITINGS:

Essential Edinburgh, Deutsch, 1978.

Paul McCartney, illustrated by Karen Heywood, Hamish Hamilton, 1983.

Queen Elizabeth II, illustrated by Heywood, Hamish Hamilton, 1983.

Queen Elizabeth, the Queen Mother, illustrated by Stephen Gulbis, Hamish Hamilton, 1984.

(With W. S. Lacey) *Britain's National Parks,* Windward, 1984.

Prince Philip, Hamish Hamilton, 1984.

The First One Hundred People in Line of Succession to the Throne of Britain, M. Joseph, 1985.

The Real Charles, Collins, 1988.

* * *

HAUGEN, Tormod 1945-

PERSONAL: Born May 12, 1945, in Trysil, Norway.

ADDRESSES: Home—Oslo, Norway. *Agent*—c/o Gyldendal Norsk Forlag, Postboks 6860, St. Olavs Plass, 0130 Oslo 1, Norway.

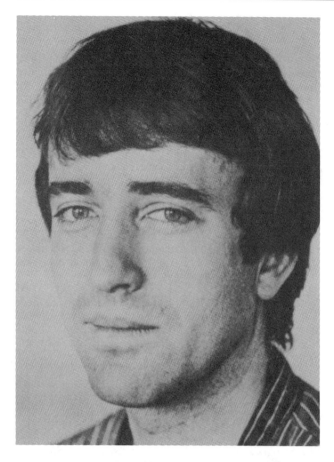

TORMOD HAUGEN

CAREER: Author of books for children, 1973—; translator.

AWARDS, HONORS: Prizes from Norwegian Ministry of Culture, 1976, for *Nattfuglene,* and 1977, for *Zeppelin;* Deutscher Jugendbuchpreis, Norwegian Children's Book Prize, and Hans Christian Andersen Honors List, all 1979, for *Nattfuglene;* Norwegian Literary Critics' Prize, c. 1979, for *Joakim;* Nordic Council Literature Prize, nomination, 1984, for *Dagen som forsvant,* and prize, 1986; Pier Paolo Vergerio European Prize for Children's Literature, University of Padova—Sector for Research on Reading and Children's Literature, 1987, for *Romanen om Merkel Hanssen og Donna Winter og den store flukten;* International Hans Christian Andersen Medal, International Board on Books for Young People, 1990.

WRITINGS:

NOVELS IN ENGLISH TRANSLATION

The Night Birds, translation by Sheila La Farge, Delacorte, 1982 (published in Norwegian as *Nattfuglene,* Gyldendal, 1975).
Zeppelin, translation by David Jacobs, Turton & Chambers, 1991 (published in Norwegian by Gyldendal, 1976).

NOVELS IN NORWEGIAN

Ikke som i fjor (title means "Not Like Last Year"), Gyldendal (Oslo, Norway), 1973.
Til sommeren—kanskje (title means "Next Summer, Perhaps"), Gyldendal, 1974.
Synnadroem (title means "Southerly Dreams"), Gyldendal, 1977.

Joakim, Gyldendal, 1979.
Slottet det hvite (title means "The White Castle"), Gyldendal, 1980.
Dagen som forsvant (for children; title means "The Day That Disappeared"), Gyldendal, 1983.
Vinterstedet (title means "The Winter Place"), Gyldendal, 1984.
Romanen om Merkel Hanssen og Donna Winter og den store flukten (title means "The Story of Merkel Hanssen and Donna Winter and the Great Escape"), Gyldendal, 1986.
Farlig ferd (title means "Perilous Journey"), Gyldendal, 1988.
Skriket fra jungelen (title means "The Scream from the Jungle"), Gyldendal, 1989.

OTHER

Also translator of works by other authors. Haugen's works have been translated into seventeen languages.

ADAPTATIONS: Zeppelin was adapted as a feature film, Marcus Film, 1980.

SIDELIGHTS: Tormod Haugen has won a number of awards, notably the 1990 International Hans Christian Andersen Medal, for his sensitive, reflective books for children. "His writing erases age categories," said a writer in *Bookbird.* "He takes the children's point of view, and the poetic strength

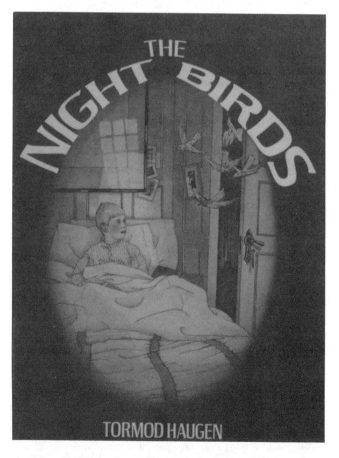

Tormod Haugen's award-winning children's book, *The Night Birds,* originally published in Norwegian, has been translated into eight languages. (Jacket illustration by Stan Skardinski.)

and intensity with which he approaches his literary material has become a trademark of all of his fiction."

Haugen's books deal with the real pain, joy, and growth of childhood as well as with fantasy and imagination. His first book is a realistic view of one summer in the lives of a timid boy and a bold girl. The prize-winning novel *The Night Birds* is a blend of reality and fantasy. The story shows how a boy's troubled home life, his imagination, and the lies of another child work together to make him fearful and fill his bedroom with shadows and the rustlings of mysterious birds. Gradually the boy overcomes some of his fears and makes new friends. Haugen's other books with strong fantasy elements include *Dagen som forsvant* ("The Day That Disappeared"), whose young hero wakes up one morning to discover he is invisible because he is not loved, and *Skriket fra jungelen* ("The Scream from the Jungle"), in which an evil scientist invents a way to steal the imaginations of children.

In the acceptance speech he gave when he won the Andersen Medal, Haugen said he "never thought about becoming a writer. It was far from my background, when I grew up in a small village in the vast forests of Norway." His early writing, done in small notebooks, was simply his own versions of stories he read in his mother's weekly magazines.

Haugen went on to say that he does not always find writing easy. "In periods, when my mind and heart are willing to guide my imagination and a plot is near and words arise from the deep inner oceans of my mind, but my hands fail to co-operate, then I feel more than awful. In those moments, the pain that fills my heart is stronger than my heart. And I think, 'I can never write another word in my life', and I want my inner oceans to dry up and disappear forever.... Writing means fighting and struggling to make one's vision come true—but it never *really* does. I can only hope to get close to it." He does not see himself as "bearing the shining armour of the noble, fighting knight, mounted on his proud steed." Still, he added, "I now and then sharpen my sword when I feel that I have something to contribute, and then I start trying to climb rose-covered walls of impregnable castles, hoping to save a damsel in distress or a young distressed man who cannot find his way out of the sleep-struck castle."

"I have written 12 books," he added. "It has taken me most of my adult life, and I know I have always been as honest as I can in my writing. But I do not pretend to know THE truth or how life really is.... I can only write a book that I believe in, hoping it gets around to one reader."

Haugen has commented: "When I am going to start writing a book, I never think about who will read it. That is not meant as an expression of arrogance, but rather of exactly the opposite. I feel that it is impossible to write a book for a specific audience of readers, for people I do not even know. No two ten-year-olds are alike. They are individual persons, with different personalities, interests, different lives, experiences and insight. And it sounds so strange and oppressive, therefore, to talk of people as if they are all alike.

"There are so many adults/parents who do not see a child as the child really is. They see their hopes, their own picture of the child, and that picture may not actually compare with the real child at all. We grown-ups have so many conscious and unconscious dreams and hopes for our children. And then is it not true that the child becomes a continuation of the adult, whereas the truth is that the adult is the continuation of the child?

"The greatest difference between a child and an adult is the fact that the adult has lived longer and can draw on lifelong experience. The children have lived such a short time that they are living right in the middle of their experiences without a chance to defend/help themselves by using experience, such as a grown-up can. But common to us all, to children and adults, is that we all have the same fundamental needs: food, sleep, love, affection, etc. ...

"I think it is much more difficult to write a so-called children's book than it is to write an adult novel. If one writes about a child using the established norms and values, the challenge will be minimal. But the moment one questions the conventional, the accepted, and finds that other possibilities are lurking behind the established, one is challenged. The very simplest word in a 'children's book' can be a shattering challenge, because writing about a child means having very close contact with one's own platform and daring to accept the challenges and discoveries that writing about childhood can lead one to. It is worth it."

WORKS CITED:

"Acceptance Speech by Tormod Haugen (Norway): Upon receiving the 1990 Hans Christian Andersen Award for Writing," *Focus IBBY,* Number 4, 1990, pp. 3-5.
"1990 Hans Christian Andersen Awards," *Bookbird,* September, 1990, p. 3.

FOR MORE INFORMATION SEE:

PERIODICALS

News of Norway, October, 1990.

[Sketch verified by Eva Lie-Nielsen, Gyldendal foreign rights agent]

*   *   *

HELLER, Ruth M. 1924-

PERSONAL: Born April 2, 1924, in Winnipeg, Manitoba, Canada; daughter of Henry (a merchant) and Leah (a homemaker; maiden name, Serkau) Rosenblat; married Henry Heller, December 22, 1951 (died, 1965); married Richard Gross (an investment broker), March 21, 1987; children: Paul Garson, Philip Heller. *Education:* University of California, Berkeley, B.A., 1946; attended California College of Arts and Crafts, 1963-65. *Politics:* Democrat. *Religion:* Jewish. *Hobbies and other interests:* Tennis, swimming, cooking.

ADDRESSES: Home—999 Green St., San Francisco, CA 94133. *Office*—150 Lombard St., San Francisco, CA 94111.

CAREER: Mount Zion Hospital, San Francisco, CA, medical secretary, 1949-53; free-lance designer and illustrator, 1967-81; writer, 1981—. Art consultant for Physicians Art Service, 1975-76.

MEMBER: Artists in Print, National Women's Book Association, Authors Guild, Society of Children's Book Writers, San Francisco Society of Illustrators, New York Society of Illustrators, Guild of Natural Science Illustrators (honorary member).

RUTH M. HELLER

AWARDS, HONORS: Honorable mention, New York Academy of Science's Children's Book Award competition, 1983, for *Chickens Aren't the Only Ones;* illustrations from *Animals Born Alive and Well* were exhibited at the Bologna International Children's Book Fair, 1983.

WRITINGS:

SELF-ILLUSTRATED CHILDREN'S BOOKS

Chickens Aren't the Only Ones, Grosset, 1981.
Animals Born Alive and Well, Grosset, 1982.
The Reason for a Flower, Grosset, 1983.
Plants That Never Ever Bloom, Grosset, 1984.
Natural Camouflage of Animals, Grosset, 1985.
A Cache of Jewels and Other Collective Nouns, Grosset, 1987.
Kites Sail High: A Book about Verbs, Grosset, 1988.
Many Luscious Lollipops: A Book about Adjectives, Grosset, 1989.
Merry-Go-Round: A Book about Nouns, Grosset, 1990.

"HOW TO HIDE" SERIES; ALL SELF-ILLUSTRATED

How To Hide a Polar Bear and Other Mammals, Grosset, 1985.
How to Hide a Butterfly and Other Insects, Grosset, 1985.
How to Hide an Octopus and Other Sea Creatures, Grosset, 1985.
How to Hide a Crocodile and Other Reptiles, Grosset, 1986.
How to Hide a Whip-Poor-Will and Other Birds, Grosset, 1986.
How to Hide a Grey Tree Frog and Other Amphibians, Grosset, 1986.

ILLUSTRATOR

Color and Puzzle, Troubador Press, 1968.
Color and Stitch, Troubador Press, 1971.
Maze Craze, Troubador Press, 1971.
The Butterfly Coloring Book, Price, Stern, 1971.
The Butterfly Coloring Book, Number 2, Price, Stern, 1972.
The Tropical Fish Coloring Book, Price, Stern, 1972.
The World's Largest Maze, Series Number 1, Price, Stern, 1972.
The Endangered Species Coloring Book, Price, Stern, 1973.
The Oriental Rug Coloring Book, Price, Stern, 1973.
The Shell Coloring Book, Price, Stern, 1973.
The Tropical Bird Coloring Book, Price, Stern, 1974.
The World's Largest Maze, Series Number 2, Price, Stern, 1974.
Color Puzzles, Golden Press, 1974.
Designs for Coloring, Grosset, 1976.
More Designs for Coloring, Grosset, 1976.
Designs for Coloring 3, Grosset, 1977.
Designs for Coloring 4, Grosset, 1977.
Opt-Iddle, Golden Press, 1977.
Chroma-Schema, Golden Press, 1977.
Designs for Coloring 5, Grosset, 1978.
Designs for Coloring 6, Grosset, 1978.
Designs for Coloring 7: Sea Shells, Grosset, 1978.
Designs for Coloring 8: Alphabet and Numbers, Grosset, 1978.
Designs for Coloring 9: Birds, Grosset, 1979.
Designs for Coloring 10: Butterflies and Moths, Grosset, 1979.
Animal Designs for Coloring 11: Cats, Grosset, 1979.
Animal Designs for Coloring 12: Owls, Grosset, 1979.
Deluxe Designs for Coloring I, Grosset, 1981.
Deluxe Designs for Coloring II, Grosset, 1981.
Miriam Schlein, *Purim,* Behrman House, 1982.
Shirley Climo, *King of the Birds,* Harper, 1987.
Climo, *The Egyptian Cinderella,* Crowell, 1989.

Also author of *Up, up and Away: A Book about Adverbs,* 1991. Illustrator of "Ponder Posters," for Creative Playthings; "Puzzle Posters" and *Aftermath I-IV,* for Creative Publications; a "Barbie Talk" graphic puzzle for Mattel; and *Contact Lenses* for Physicians Art Service.

Heller's illustrations have been exhibited at Pasadena Art and Cal Expo, Sacramento, 1968; Master Eagle Gallery, 1985 and 1986; and Palo Alto Cultural Center, 1985.

SIDELIGHTS: Ruth Heller commented: "I began my career designing wrapping paper, cocktail napkins, kites, mugs, greeting cards, posters, and then coloring books. While researching at Steinhart Aquarium for a coloring book on tropical fish, I became intrigued with a strange looking shape floating in one of the tanks, and found that it was the egg sac of a dogfish shark. This led me to read about other egg-laying (oviparous) animals. My reading stimulated visions of colors and shapes and compositions. In addition to this visual wealth, I felt I had found enough information to convince me that I wanted to write and illustrate a book. *Chickens Aren't the Only Ones* is the title I chose.

"It proved to be successful enough to warrant a sequel which I called *Animals Born Alive and Well.* As seeds (in the plant kingdom) are comparable to eggs, I titled the third book in the series, *The Reason for a Flower,* and the fourth, *Plants That Never Ever Bloom.* I also have a series of six science books for very young children. The subject of these is camouflage. The titles include *How to Hide a Butterfly and Other Insects, How to Hide an Octopus and Other Sea Crea-*

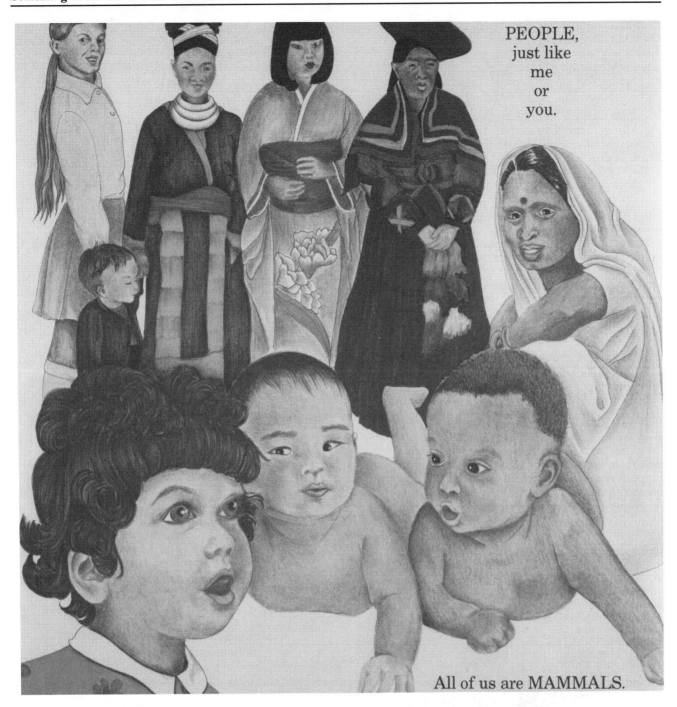

PEOPLE,
just like
me
or
you.

All of us are MAMMALS.

(From *Animals Born Alive and Well,* written and illustrated by Ruth M. Heller.)

tures, and *How to Hide a Polar Bear and Other Mammals.* My science background is minimal, so I must depend on meticulous research and professional approval.

"I find writing in rhyme enjoyable and think it is an easy way for the reader or listener to remember new facts and vocabulary. I try to be succinct, to decide what it is I wish to say, to say it simply and directly allowing the illustration to convey as much information as possible. I am delighted to find that my books appeal to teachers and librarians as well as to the public. There is never a lack of ideas. As I am working on one project, ideas for others keep arising. Creativity begets creativity."

FOR MORE INFORMATION SEE:

PERIODICALS

San Francisco Chronicle, September 2, 1971.

* * *

HILL, Eric 1927-

PERSONAL: Born September 7, 1927, in London, England; son of Roden Basil (a sportsman) and Alice M. (Ellis) Hill; married Barbara Hobson, March 25, 1950 (divorced, 1972); married Gillian McCarthy (an artist), February 23, 1973;

children: Jane, Christopher. *Hobbies and other interests:* Collecting metal toys.

ADDRESSES: c/o Putnam Publishing, 200 Madison Ave., New York, NY 10016.

CAREER: Graphic designer, author and illustrator of books for children. Cooper Studio (art studio), London, England, messenger and sweeper, 1943-45; free-lance cartoonist, 1948; Erwin Wasey (advertising agency), London, art director, 1955-58; free-lance artist, 1958-80; author, 1980—. *Military service:* Royal Air Force, 1945-48.

AWARDS, HONORS: Notable Children's Book citations, American Library Association, in 1980 for *Where's Spot?,* in 1981 for *Spot's First Walk,* and in 1982 for *Spot's Birthday Party;* Mother Goose Award runner-up, 1981, for *Where's Spot?; Spot's First Words* was named a Children's Book of the Year by the Child Study Association of America, 1987.

WRITINGS:

"SPOT" SERIES; SELF-ILLUSTRATED

Where's Spot?, Putnam, 1980.
Spot's First Walk, Putnam, 1981.
Spot's Birthday Party, Putnam, 1982.
Puppy Love, Putnam, 1982.
Spot's Busy Year, Putnam, 1983.
Spot's First Christmas, Putnam, 1983.
Spot Learns to Count, Putnam, 1983.
Spot Tells the Time, Putnam, 1983.
Spot's Alphabet, Putnam, 1983.
Sweet Dreams, Spot!, Putnam, 1984.
Spot's Friends, Putnam, 1984.
Spot's Toys, Putnam, 1984.

ERIC HILL

Here's Spot, Putnam, 1984.
Spot Goes Splash!, Putnam, 1984.
Spot Goes to School, Putnam, 1984.
Spot on the Farm, Putnam, 1985.
Spot Goes to the Beach (Junior Literary Guild selection), Putnam, 1985.
Spot at Play, Putnam, 1985.
Spot at the Fair, Putnam, 1985.
Spot Goes to the Circus (Junior Literary Guild selection), Putnam, 1986.
Spot's First Words, Putnam, 1986.
Spot's Doghouse, Putnam, 1986.
Spot Looks at Colors, Putnam, 1986.
Spot Looks at Shapes, Putnam, 1986.
Spot Goes to the Farm, Putnam, 1987.
Spot's First Picnic, Putnam, 1987.
Spot Visits the Hospital, Putnam, 1987.
Spot's Big Book of Words, Putnam, 1988.
Spot's First Easter, Putnam, 1988.
Spot Counts from One to Ten, Putnam, 1989.
Spot Looks at Opposites, Putnam, 1989.
Spot Looks at the Weather, Putnam, 1989.
Spot's Baby Sister, Putnam, 1989.
Spot Sleeps Over, Putnam, 1990.
Spot Goes to the Park, Putnam, 1991.
Spot in the Garden, Putnam, 1991.
Spot's Toy Box, Putnam, 1991.
Spot at Home, Putnam, 1991.

"PEEK-A-BOOK" SERIES; SELF-ILLUSTRATED

Nursery Rhymes, Price Stern, 1982.
Opposites, Price Stern, 1982.
Animals, Price Stern, 1982.
Who Does What?, Price Stern, 1982.
Baby Animals, Price Stern, 1984.
More Opposites, Price Stern, 1985.
Fairy Tales, Price Stern, 1985.
What's Inside?, Price Stern, 1985.

"BABY BEAR STORYBOOK" SERIES; SELF-ILLUSTRATED

At Home, Random House, 1983.
My Pets, Random House, 1983.
The Park, Random House, 1983.
Up There, Random House, 1983.
Baby Bear's Bedtime, Random House, 1984.
Good Morning, Baby Bear, Random House, 1984.

ILLUSTRATOR

June Dutton, *Smorgasbord,* Determined Productions, 1970.
Helen Hoke, *Hoke's Jokes, Cartoons and Funny Things,* F. Watts, 1973.
Dutton, *The First Adventure of the S.S. Happiness Crew: Cap'n Joshua's Dangerous Dilemma,* Determined Productions, 1980.
Dutton, *The Second Adventure of the S.S. Happiness Crew: Mystery in the Middle of the Ocean,* Determined Productions, 1981.
Dutton, *The Third Adventure of the S.S. Happiness Crew: Cap'n Joshua's Super Secret,* Determined Productions, 1982.
Allan Ahlberg, *Poorly Pig,* Granada, 1982.
Ahlberg, *Bad Bear,* Granada, 1982.
Ahlberg, *Silly Sheep,* Granada, 1982.
Ahlberg, *Fast Frog,* Granada, 1982.
Ahlberg, *Rubber Rabbit,* Granada, 1982.
Ahlberg, *Double Ducks,* Granada, 1982.
Dutton, *The Fourth Adventure of the S.S. Happiness Crew: Visit to a Magic Mountain,* Determined Productions, 1983.

What is the opposite of closed?

Open. (From *More Opposites,* written and illustrated by Eric Hill.)

OTHER; SELF-ILLUSTRATED

S.S. Happiness Crew Book of Numbers, Determined Productions, 1983.
Book of Colors, Determined Productions, 1984.
Book of Shapes, Determined Productions, 1984.
Eric Hill's Crazy Mix or Match: Funny Picture Stories for Preschoolers, Random House, 1984.
Eric Hill's Crazy Crazy Wheels Mix or Match, Random House, 1984.

Hill's works have been translated into more than sixty languages, including American Sign Language.

ADAPTATIONS: Stories about Spot were adapted for an animated television series, *Adventures of Spot,* British Broadcasting Corporation (BBC), 1987.

WORK IN PROGRESS: Continuing titles in the Spot flap-book series; second series of television stories for BBC.

SIDELIGHTS: Eric Hill is the creator of the beloved puppy Spot, hero of many popular children's books and a television cartoon. He has also written and illustrated fairy-tale books, books about other animals, and "mix and match" books that let beginning readers make their own pictures with different combinations of page sections. Hill got his start in drawing when he was fifteen, after he left school for a job in an art studio. One of the artists at the studio taught him basic cartooning in his spare time. Some writers say this simple style of drawing is part of why Hill's books are so popular with young readers, because it is similar to the way children draw. Another important feature of Hill's art is his use of bright colors, humor, and surprise. When a child lifts the flap of a closet door in a Hill book, for example, he is less likely to find coats, hats, and shoes than a smiling wild animal.

Hill's first Spot book, *Where's Spot?,* was actually written for his son, Christopher. Hill was making movable flaps for an advertising project, and when he saw that Christopher liked lifting the flaps to see what was underneath, he made up a children's story using them. Later, the daughter of a friend of Hill's took the little handmade book to the Frankfurt Book Fair, where she found Hill a publisher. *Where's Spot?* quickly became a best-seller, and demand grew for more books like it. Since the publication of *Where's Spot?* in 1980, Hill has produced more than thirty other books about Spot. Together the Spot books have sold over eighteen million copies.

Hill told Margaret Frith in *Horn Book* that he chose a puppy for Christopher's book because "I love dogs, and it seemed that the easiest thing for me to do was to draw something I loved." Even though Spot does some things a real dog cannot, such as draw or fly a kite, Hill tries to keep him "as near to a puppy as possible." Hill added, "I've gotten to a place where I don't know what he can do and what he can't do. I rely on my instincts." Asked why he thinks Spot is so popular, Hill answered: "I was not doing the book for profit or publicity but for entertainment for my own little boy. I kept the story line familiar and simple and always fun. All of the things Spot is doing a young child might do, so one can assume a young child will understand the story—without taking away some of the mischief or excitement."

Hill told *SATA:* "I consider myself very fortunate indeed to have created a character which has captured the imagination and enthusiasm of so many children worldwide. They are my family, and Spot belongs to them all."

In the sign language edition of *Where's Spot?*, young readers help Spot's mother find Spot. (Written and illustrated by Eric Hill.)

WORKS CITED:

Frith, Margaret, "Interview with Eric Hill," *Horn Book,* September/October, 1987, pp. 557-85.

FOR MORE INFORMATION SEE:

BOOKS

Children's Literature Review, Volume 13, Gale, 1987.

PERIODICALS

Publishers Weekly, July 25, 1986.

*   *   *

HITZ, Demi 1942-
(Demi)

PERSONAL: Born September 2, 1942, in Cambridge, MA; daughter of William Morris (an architect, actor, and entrepreneur) and Rosamond (an artist; maiden name, Pier) Hunt; married John Rawlins Hitz (a teacher and writer), December 18, 1965; children: John. *Education:* Attended Instituto Allende and Rhode Island School of Design; Immaculate Heart College, B.A., 1962; University of Baroda, M.S., 1963; additional graduate study at China Institute. *Hobbies and other interests:* Travel (has been to Mexico, Guatemala, Brazil, Chile, England, and Japan).

ADDRESSES: Home and office—325 Riverside Dr., New York, NY 10025. *Agent*—Julian Bach, Inc., 747 Third Ave., New York, NY 10017.

CAREER: Artist and writer. Speaker at colleges, universities, libraries, and children's events.

MEMBER: China Institute.

AWARDS, HONORS: Fulbright fellow, 1962; awards from Boston Globe scholastic competitions, 1961, California State Fair, California Arts and Science Fair, Los Angeles County Museum, and Los Angeles Outdoor Art Festival, all 1962.

WRITINGS:

The Book of Moving Pictures, Knopf, 1979.
Under the Shade of the Mulberry Tree, Prentice-Hall, 1979.
Where Is It?, Doubleday, 1980.
Liang and the Magic Paint Brush, Holt, 1980.
The Leaky Umbrella, Prentice-Hall, 1980.
The Adventures of Marco Polo, Holt, 1981.
The Elephant Book, Random House, 1981.
Follow the Line (wordless story), Holt, 1981.
Where's Willie Worm?, Random House, 1981.
Cinderella on Wheels, Holt, 1982.
Peek-A-Boo, Random House, 1982.
Demi's Find the Animals A B C, Putnam, 1985.
Demi's Count the Animals One-Two-Three, Putnam, 1986.
Dragon Kites & Dragonflies: A Collection of Chinese Nursery Rhymes, Harcourt, 1986.
So Soft Kitty, Putnam, 1986.
Chen Ping and His Magic Axe, Dodd, 1987.
Cuddly Chick, Putnam, 1987.
Demi's Opposites, Grosset, 1987.
Downy Duckling, Putnam, 1987.
Fleecy Lamb, Putnam, 1987.
Fuzzy Wuzzy Puppy, Putnam, 1987.
The Hallowed Horse: A Folktale from India, Putnam, 1987.
A Chinese Zoo: Fables and Proverbs, Harcourt, 1988.
Demi's Reflective Fables, Putnam, 1988.
Find Demi's Dinosaurs: An Animal Game Book, Putnam, 1989.
Jolly Koala Bear, Putnam, 1989.
Roly Poly Panda, Putnam, 1989.
Demi's Christmas Surprise, Putnam, 1990.
The Empty Pot, Holt, 1990.
Find Demi's Baby Animals, Putnam, 1990.
The Magic Boat, Holt, 1990.

"I admire Ping's great courage to appear before me with the empty truth, and now I reward him with my entire kingdom and make him Emperor of all the land!"

(From *The Empty Pot,* written and illustrated by Demi Hitz.)

(From *Demi's Count the Animals One-Two-Three*, written and illustrated by Demi Hitz.)

ILLUSTRATOR

Partap Sharma, *The Surangini Tales*, Harcourt, 1973.
Lu Yu, *The Classic of Tea*, translation by Francis Ross Carpenter, Little, Brown, 1974.
Smith and Wardhough, *Feelings*, Macmillan, 1975.
Tom Glazer, *The Tom Glazer Guitar Book*, Warner Brothers, 1976.

ILLUSTRATOR, UNDER NAME DEMI

Augusta Goldin, *The Shape of Water*, Doubleday, 1979.
Yushin Yoo, *Bong Nam and the Pheasants*, Prentice-Hall, 1979.
Jane Yolan, *Dragon Night and Other Lullabies*, Methuen, 1980.
Ann S. McGrath, *Tone's Tunnel*, Prentice-Hall, 1981.
Miriam Chaikin, *Light Another Candle: The Story and Meaning of Hanukkah*, Clarion Books, 1981.
Chaikin, *Make Noise, Make Merry: The Story and Meaning of Purim*, Ticknor & Fields, 1986.
Han Christian Andersen, *The Nightengale*, Harcourt, 1988.
Andersen, *Thumbelina*, Putnam, 1989.

OTHER

Illustrator of *The Wild, Wild World of Animals: The Cats*, Vineyard Books, 1976, and *Lu Pan*, Prentice-Hall, 1978. Also illustrator of selected titles in "All about Your Name" series by Tom Glazer, Doubleday, 1978. Contributor of illustrations and stories to periodicals, including *New Yorker, Young Children, New York Times, Christian Science Monitor, Art News, China Trade Journal,* and *House and Garden.*

SIDELIGHTS: Demi Hitz was born into a family of artists and craftsmen. She has been praised for her ability to mesh text and illustration in numerous children's books. The *Bulletin of the Center for Children's Books* lauded *Demi's Count the Animals One-Two-Three* as "a counting book that is an effective teaching tool, with clear correlation between words, digits, pictures, and attractive illustrations of animals." Similarly, the *Bulletin* described *A Chinese Zoo* as "impressive but gracefully restrained."

Demi Hitz has painted murals in Mexico, walls for modern homes, and the dome of St. Peter & Paul Church in Wilmington, CA. There have been exibitions of her work all over the United States and in India. A filmstrip about Demi's work entitled "Making Mosaics" was shown in Boston on CBS-TV.

WORKS CITED:

Bulletin of the Center for Children's Books, February, 1988, p. 48.

FOR MORE INFORMATION SEE:

PERIODICALS

Bulletin of the Center For Children's Books, July-August, 1987; January, 1988.
New York Times Book Review, April 25, 1982.
Time, December 23, 1985.

*   *   *

HOLME, Bryan 1913-1990 (Charles Francis)

OBITUARY NOTICE—See index for *SATA* sketch: Born June 25, 1913, in Church Crookham, England; immigrated to United States, 1932, naturalized citizen, 1946; died of kidney failure, August 8, 1990, in Round Pond, ME. Publisher, editor, and author. Holme, who came from a family of publishers, went to the United States as a young man and founded Studio Publications, which specialized in art books and other illustrated works. There he presided as publisher and edited some volumes on his own, including *The Classical Figure* and *Masterpieces in Color at the Metropolitan Museum of Art, New York.* He remained head of the organization after it became the Studio Books division of Viking Press in 1959. After retiring in 1976, Holme wrote such works as *Advertising, Princely Feasts and Festivals,* and *A Clowder of Cats.* Holme also wrote *Make Your Own Greeting Cards* under the pseudonym Charles Francis.

OBITUARIES AND OTHER SOURCES:

PERIODICALS

New York Times, August 11, 1990.

*   *   *

JAFFEE, Al(lan) 1921-

PERSONAL: Born March 13, 1921, in Savannah, GA. *Education:* Attended High School of Music and Art, New York.

ADDRESSES: Office—c/o *Mad* magazine, E. C. Publications, Inc., 485 Madison Ave., New York, NY 10022.

CAREER: Quality Comics, writer and artist of *Inferior Man,* 1941; Marvel Comics, humor feature writer, 1942-55; *Trump* and *Humbug* (magazines), writer and artist, 1955-58; *Mad* magazine, writer and artist, 1955, 1958—; free-lance advertising illustrator, 1958—; illustrator of children's books, 1960—. Author and illustrator of syndicated comic strips, "Tall Tales," 1958-65, and "Debbie Deere," 1966; contribut-

(From *Snappy Answers to Stupid Questions, No. 7,* written and illustrated by Al Jaffe.)

ing artist and writer to *Playboy* magazine's comic strip, "Little Annie Fanny," 1964-66.

AWARDS, HONORS: Best special features award, 1971, for *Mad* magazine's "Fold-in," best advertising and illustration artist award, 1973, best special features award, 1975, and best humor book award, 1979, all from the National Cartoonist Society.

WRITINGS:

AUTHOR AND ILLUSTRATOR

Tall Tales, Doubleday, 1960.
"Mad's" Al Jaffee Spews Out Snappy Answers to Stupid Questions, New American Library, 1968.
Funny Jokes and Foxy Riddles, Western Publishing, 1968.
Witty Jokes and Wild Riddles, Western Publishing, 1968.
Al Jaffee's Mad (Yecch!) Monstrosities, Warner Books, 1974.
Al Jaffee Gags, New American Library, 1974.
Al Jaffee Gags Again, New American Library, 1975.
Al Jaffee Blows His Mind, New American Library, 1975.

"Mad's" Al Jaffee Spews Out Still More Snappy Answers to Stupid Questions, Warner Books, 1976.
Ghastly Jokes, New American Library, 1976.
(Written with Frank Jacobs) *Sing Along with Mad,* Warner Books, 1977.
Al Jaffee Draws a Crowd, New American Library, 1978.
(Written with Nick Meglin) *Rotten Rhymes and Other Crimes,* New American Library, 1978.
Al Jaffee Bombs Again, New American Library, 1978.
Al Jaffee Sinks to a New Low, New American Library, 1978.
Al Jaffee's Mad Inventions, Warner Books, 1978.
Al Jaffee Meets His End, New American Library, 1979.
The Ghoulish Book of Weird Records, New American Library, 1979.
More Snappy Answers to Stupid Questions, Warner Books, 1979.
Good Lord! Not Another Book of Snappy Answers to Stupid Questions, Warner Books, 1980.
Al Jaffee Gets His Just Desserts, New American Library, 1980.
Al Jaffee: Dead or Alive, New American Library, 1980.
Al Jaffee Fowls His Nest, New American Library, 1981.
Al Jaffee Meets Willie Weirdie, New American Library, 1981.

Al Jaffee Hogs the Show, New American Library, 1981.

Al Jaffee Goes Bananas, New American Library, 1982.

Al Jaffee Shoots His Mouth Off, New American Library, 1982.

"Mad's" Al Jaffee Freaks Out, Warner Books, 1982.

Willie Weirdie Zaps Al Jaffee, New American Library, 1983.

"Mad's" Vastly Overrated Al Jaffee, Warner Books, 1983.

Snappy Answers to Stupid Questions, No. 5, Warner Books, 1984.

A Pretentious Compendium of "Mad's" Very Best Snappy Answers to Stupid Questions, E. C. Publications, 1986.

"Mad" Book of Puzzles, Games, and Lousy Jokes, Warner Books, 1986.

Once Again "Mad's" Al Jaffee Spews Out Snappy Answers to Stupid Questions, Warner Books, 1987.

Al Jaffee's "Mad" Book of Magic and Other Dirty Tricks, Warner Books, 1988.

Snappy Answers to Stupid Questions, No.7, Warner Books, 1989.

Al Jaffee's Mad Rejects, Warner Books, 1990.

An Overblown Collection: MORE Mad Snappy Answers to Stupid Questions, E. C. Publications, 1990.

(From *Snappy Answers to Stupid Questions, No. 7,* written and illustrated by Al Jaffe.)

ILLUSTRATOR

Editors of *Mad* magazine, *Clods' Letters to Mad,* Warner Books, 1981.

Daniel Goleman and Jonathan Freedman, *What Psychology Knows that Everyone Should,* Lewis, 1981.

SIDELIGHTS: Al Jaffee began cartooning professionally in 1941 when he became author and illustrator of Quality Comics' "Inferior Man" series. From there, Jaffee moved on to work as a humor feature writer and artist for Marvel Comics until he met *Mad* magazine editor Harvey Kurtzman in 1955. Jaffee quit his Marvel post and took a substantial pay cut in favor of the artistic freedom that *Mad* offered. His initial career at *Mad,* however, was short-lived. Kurtzman and Jaffee left that publication for two new humor projects, the *Playboy*-published *Trump* magazine, and the artist-owned *Humbug.* Though the two series lasted a combined total of only thirteen issues, they were critically acclaimed; and Jaffee became known among his peers as one of the most inventive and skillful satirists in the field. During this period, he developed his stylistic trademarks: sharp, clear drawing that emphasizes humorous effect over anatomical proportion.

After *Humbug* folded in 1958, Jaffee returned to *Mad* and supplemented his income through advertising work and the syndicated "Tall Tales" panel. His advertising illustrations were particularly respected, earning Jaffee the 1973 National Cartoonist Society award for best advertising and illustrations artist of the year. In 1964, he introduced one of his most innovative cartoon concepts, the *Mad* "Fold-in." This back-cover feature involved an intricately written and drawn illustration that, when folded in thirds, produced a satire of the first illustration. That same year, Jaffee resumed his occasional collaborations with Harvey Kurtzman on another *Playboy* project, "Little Annie Fanny." This cartoon was distinctive because of its extensive production process. Every panel in the strip was rendered in full color and then reproduced in the same four-color separation process as the rest of the magazine; each illustration therefore had the detail of a full-color painting.

In 1965, "Tall Tales" was discontinued. Jaffee followed that cartoon feature as writer of the short-lived comic strip, "Debbie Deere" (1966). Meanwhile, he began illustrating and writing more frequently for *Mad,* making him one of its most popular and respected contributors. The artist began publishing collections of his *Mad* work, often preempting potential detractors with titles that read like bad reviews: *Al Jaffee Shoots His Mouth Off, "Mad's" Vastly Overrated Al Jaffee, A Pretentious Compendium of Mad's Very Best Snappy Answers to Stupid Questions,* and others. Jaffee also contributed cartoons to a textbook entitled *What Psychology Knows that Everyone Should* (1981), which received high marks for its entertaining presentation style.

FOR MORE INFORMATION SEE:

BOOKS

Maurice Horn, editor, *The World Encyclopedia of Comics,* Chelsea House, 1976.

Nick Meglin, *Art of Humorous Illustration,* Watson-Guptill, 1973.

PERIODICALS

Book Review Digest, May, 1983.

Los Angeles Times, December 11, 1980.

* * *

JANGER, Kathleen N. 1940-

PERSONAL: Born January 21, 1940, in Davenport, IA; daughter of Leo J. and Eileen (Martens) Nugent; married Stephen A. Janger (a foundation president), March 8, 1970; children: Margaret Michelle, Jay Adam, Andrea Lee. *Education:* Attended William Smith College.

ADDRESSES: Home—1502 Mintwood Dr., McLean, VA 22101. *Office*—Young Writer's Contest Foundation, P.O. Box 6092, McLean, VA 22106.

CAREER: AIMS-International, Washington, DC, co-founder and administrative assistant, 1966-70; Close Up Foundation, Arlington, VA, co-founder and administrative coordinator, 1970-75; writer and editor, 1975—; Young Writer's Contest Foundation, McLean, VA, co-founder and executive director, 1984—.

WRITINGS:

(With Michael Korenblit) *Until We Meet Again: A True Story of Love and War,* Putnam, 1983.
(With Joan Korenblit) *Knowing Beans about Coffee,* WRC Publishing, 1985.

Also editor with J. Korenblit of an annually published anthology titled *Rainbow Collection: Stories and Poetry by Young People,* Young Writer's Contest Foundation, 1985—. Contributor to newspapers. Editor of computer software programs.

WORK IN PROGRESS: Quest for the Perfect Hairdo—and Other Dead Ends; a collection of essays.

SIDELIGHTS: Kathleen N. Janger commented: "*Until We Meet Again* is a true story that takes place during World War II. It is about my co-author's parents as teenagers in Poland and their separation. After internment in thirteen concentration camps between them, they found each other after the war. While we were writing the book, our research led us on a trail that resulted in the discovery of my co-author's uncle (long thought dead) alive and well in Newcastle, England. Writing the book was an extraordinary experience—a very personal one. When we began, we thought we had one miracle; we ended up with two miracles. We wrote it to record two people's experiences under the Nazis and to offer testimony to refute the *Historical Review* people's claims that the Holocaust never took place. The book is not a discussion of military offensives or the like, because the characters were not aware of such information. They knew only what was happening to themselves.

"While I continue to write for and about myself, most of my attention is focused on the Young Writer's Contest Foundation, a national writing competition for first through eighth graders. Through this activity, we hope to encourage youngsters to care about their native tongue and to use it to express themselves, not only creatively, but also in a manner suitable to practical applications."

JENNINGS, Elizabeth (Joan) 1926-

PERSONAL: Born July 18, 1926, in Boston, Lincolnshire, England; daughter of Henry Cecil Jennings (a physician). *Education:* St. Anne's College, Oxford, M.A. (with honors), 1949. *Religion:* Roman Catholic. *Hobbies and other interests:* Travel, art, the theater, conversation.

ADDRESSES: Home—11 Winchester Rd., Oxford OX2 6NA, England. *Agent*—David Higham Associates Ltd., 5-8 Lower John St., Golden Square, London W1R 4HA, England.

CAREER: Oxford City Library, Oxford, England, assistant, 1950-58; Chatto & Windus (publishing firm), London, England, reader, 1958-60; poet and free-lance writer, 1961—. Guildersleeve Lecturer, Barnard College, Columbia University, 1974.

MEMBER: Society of Authors.

AWARDS, HONORS: Arts Council award, 1953, for *Poems;* Somerset Maugham Award, 1956, for *A Way of Looking;* Arts Council bursary, 1965 and 1968; Richard Hillary Memorial Prize, 1966, for *The Mind Has Mountains;* Arts Council grant, 1972; W. H. Smith award, 1987, for *Collected Poems.*

WRITINGS:

Poems, Fantasy Press, 1953.
A Way of Looking: Poems, Deutsch, 1955, Rinehart, 1956.
(Editor with Dannie Abse and Stephen Spender) *New Poems 1956: A P.E.N. Anthology,* M. Joseph, 1956.
A Child and the Seashell, Feathered Serpent Press, 1957.
(Editor) *The Batsford Book of Children's Verse,* Batsford, 1958.
A Sense of the World: Poems, Deutsch, 1958, Rinehart, 1959.
Let's Have Some Poetry! (prose; for young readers), Museum Press, 1960.
Song for a Birth or a Death and Other Poems, Deutsch, 1961, Dufour (Pennsylvania), 1962.
(Editor) *An Anthology of Modern Verse, 1940-60,* Methuen, 1961.
Every Changing Shape, Deutsch, 1961.
Poetry Today, Longmans, Green, 1961.
(Translator) *The Sonnets of Michaelangelo,* Folio Society, 1961, revised edition, Allison & Busby, 1969, Doubleday, 1970, reprinted, Carcanet Press, 1989.
(With Lawrence Durrell and R. S. Thomas) *Penguin Modern Poets I,* Penguin, 1962.
Recoveries: Poems, Dufour, 1964.
Frost, Oliver & Boyd, 1964, Barnes & Noble, 1965.
Christian Poetry, Hawthorn, 1965 (published in England as *Christianity and Poetry,* Burns & Oates, 1965).
The Mind Has Mountains, St. Martin's, 1966.
The Secret Brother and Other Poems for Children, St. Martin's, 1966.
Collected Poems, 1967, Dufour, 1967.
The Animals' Arrival, Dufour, 1969.
Lucidities, Macmillan, 1970.
(Editor) *A Choice of Christina Rossetti's Verse,* Faber, 1970.
Hurt, Poem-of-the-Month Club, 1970.
(With others) *Folio,* Sceptre Press, 1971.
Relationships, Macmillan, 1972.
Growing Points: New Poems, (poems), Carcanet Press, 1975.

Seven Men of Vision: An Appreciation (literary criticism), Harper, 1977.
Consequently I Rejoice (poems), Carcanet Press, 1977.
After the Ark (children's poems), Oxford University Press, 1978.
Winter Wind (poems), Janus Press, 1979.
A Dream of Spring (poems), Celandine, 1980.
Selected Poems, Carcanet Press, 1980.
Moments of Grace (poems), Carcanet Press, 1980.
Italian Light and Other Poems, Snake River Press, 1981.
(Editor) *The Batsford Book of Religious Verse,* Batsford, 1981.
Celebrations and Elegies (poems), Carcanet Press, 1982.
(Editor) *In Praise of Our Lady,* Batsford, 1982.
Extending the Territory (poems), Carcanet Press, 1985.
In Shakespeare's Company, Celandine, 1985.
(With others) *Poets in Hand: A Puffin Quintet,* Penguin, 1985.
Collected Poems, 1953-86, Carcanet Press, 1986.
Tributes (poems), Carcanet, 1989.

Contributor of poems and articles to numerous periodicals, including *Agenda, London Magazine, Poetry Review, New Yorker, Scotsman, Vogue,* and *Encounter.* Jennings's manuscripts are in the collections of the Oxford City Library and the University of Washington, Seattle, and Georgetown University Library, Washington, D.C.

SIDELIGHTS: British poet Elizabeth Jennings established her literary reputation during the 1950s. She was associated with The Movement, a group of writers including Kingsley Amis, Thom Gunn, and Philip Larkin, who used literature as a means of social protest. Often called the "angry young men," the group's works bitterly attacked attitudes that they felt were outdated and senseless. Jennings "brought the 'sensitive' dimension to the no-nonsense Movement," Alan Brownjohn writes in the *New Statesman.* She wrote quietly and effectively about topics that did not interest other writers of The Movement, including love, childhood, religion, and travel. In the years since her debut, Brownjohn notes, Jennings has "impressively increased the scope and richness, and the technical variety and command, of her writing."

"A poet's childhood," Jennings writes in her *Contemporary Authors Autobiography Series* entry, "is usually a great storehouse of exciting events, passions, throngs of touchings and handlings." Jennings was born into a Catholic doctor's family in the town of Boston, in the Lincolnshire region of England. When she was six, her family moved to Oxford, where the children could get a better education. Since she and her family were Catholics—and, at that time, England denied Catholics the right to attend public schools without special permission—Jennings had to attend a private Catholic school. Jennings did poorly there; she comments, "In fact, I was on the way to becoming a classic case of juvenile delinquency." Her father decided to remove his children from the private Catholic school and place them in the Oxford High School, a public school not associated with the Catholic church. It was there that Jennings began to develop an interest in literature in general and in poetry in particular.

"I began to love poetry when I was thirteen," Jennings writes. "One day in an English literature class we read G. K. Chesterton's great battle poem 'Lepanto'; I was gathered up and carried away. I felt a strange new excitement and I went home and wrote a very enthusiastic essay. In my Term Report our wonderful English teacher wrote, 'Latterly she has developed a taste for poetry.'

"I had developed more than a taste; I was experiencing a new passion. We soon went on to study [William] Wordsworth, [Samuel Taylor] Coleridge, [John] Keats, and [Percy Bysshe] Shelley. When I read Keats's 'Ode on a Grecian Urn,' 'Thou still unravished bride of quietness,' or Coleridge's *Ancient Mariner,* 'And ice, mast-high, came floating by,/As green as emerald,' or Wordsworth's sonnet written on Westminster Bridge, 'Earth hath not anything to show more fair,' my spirit and senses were quickened." She had, Jennings felt, discovered her vocation.

"By the time I was fifteen," Jennings continues, ". . . I had begun to send out my verses in long brown envelopes. Back they came relentlessly through the letterbox. They deserved to be rejected but I was greatly warmed one day when a rejection slip from the *New English Weekly* (long since dead) contained the hand-written words, 'These poems show talent.'

Jennings went on to attend St. Anne's College, at Oxford. There she made the acquaintance of the people who would later form The Movement, including Kingsley Amis, Philip Larkin, and Thom Gunn. In the year Jennings graduated from St. Anne's, several of her poems were collected in *Oxford Poetry 1949,* a periodical edited by Kingsley Amis. Her work appealed to them. While sharing a "love of simplicity" and a "willing acceptance of rhyme and metrical regularity" with the other members of The Movement, states William Blisset in the *Dictionary of Literary Biography,* Jennings differed from the others in teaching at the University and in her devout Catholic Christianity.

In addition to her own poetry, Jennings has edited the *Batsford Book of Children's Verse,* and written *Let's Have Some Poetry,* a book for young readers. "My fourteenth book of poems, *Extending the Territory,*" writes Jennings, ". . . contains many poems about my childhood because recently my Lincolnshire childhood has become more and more vivid to me. Maybe this is a sign of old age, but I somehow don't think so."

WORKS CITED:

Blisset, William, "Elizabeth Jennings," *Dictionary of Literary Biography,* Volume 27: *Poets of Great Britain and Ireland, 1945-1960,* Gale, 1984, pp. 163-70.
Brownjohn, Alan, "Hymenoptera," *New Statesman,* May 30, 1975, pp. 732-33.
Jennings, Elizabeth, *Contemporary Authors Autobiography Series,* Volume 5, Gale, 1987, pp. 103-15.

FOR MORE INFORMATION SEE:

BOOKS

Contemporary Literary Criticism, Gale, Volume 5, 1976; Volume 14, 1980.
Schmidt, Michael, and Grevel Lindop, editors, *British Poetry since 1960,* Carcanet Press, 1972.

PERIODICALS

Books and Bookmen, December, 1972; February, 1980.
Listener, July 23, 1964; January 31, 1980.
New Statesman, October 13, 1967; November 2, 1979.
Poetry, March, 1977.
Spectator, December 1, 1979.
Times (London), January 16, 1986; February 11, 1989.

Times Literary Supplement, December 30, 1977; February 1, 1980; July 16, 1982; May 30, 1986; November 28, 1986; May 5, 1989.

*   *   *

JORDAN, Lee
See SCHOLEFIELD, Alan

*   *   *

KESEY, Ken (Elton) 1935-

PERSONAL: Born September 17, 1935, in La Junta, CO; son of Fred A. and Geneva (Smith) Kesey; married Faye Haxby, May 20, 1956; children: Shannon, Zane, Jed (deceased), Sunshine. *Education:* University of Oregon, B.A., 1957; Stanford University, graduate study, 1958-59, 1960-61, 1963.

ADDRESSES: Home—85829 Ridgeway Rd., Pleasant Hill, OR 97455. *Agent*—Sterling Lord Agency, Inc., One Madison Ave., New York, NY 10010.

CAREER: Multi-media artist and farmer. Instructor at University of Oregon, Eugene. Night attendant in psychiatric ward, Veterans Administration Hospital, Menlo Park, CA, 1961; president, Intrepid Trips, Inc. (motion picture company), 1964.

AWARDS, HONORS: Woodrow Wilson fellowship; Saxton Fund fellowship, 1959; Oregon Distinguished Service Award, 1978.

WRITINGS:

One Flew over the Cuckoo's Nest (novel), Viking, 1962, new edition with criticism, edited by John C. Pratt, 1973.
Sometimes a Great Notion (novel), Viking, 1964.
(Editor with Paul Krassner and contributor) *The Last Supplement to the Whole Earth Catalog,* Portola Institute, 1971.
Kesey's Garage Sale (collection of interviews, articles, and screenplay "Over the Border"), introduction by Arthur Miller, Viking, 1973.
(Author of introduction) Krassner, editor, *Best of "The Realist": The Sixties' Most Outrageously Irreverent Magazine,* Running Press, 1984.
Demon Box (collection of essays, poetry, and stories, including "The Day Superman Died"), Viking, 1986.
Little Tickler the Squirrel Meets Big Double the Bear (for children), illustrations by Barry Moser, Viking, 1990.
(With others) *Caverns* (mystery novel), Penguin, 1989.
The Further Inquiry, Viking, 1990.
The Sea Lion (for children), illustrated by Neil Waldman, Viking, 1991.

Also author of two unpublished novels, "End of Autumn" and "Zoo." Work included in anthologies, including *Stanford Short Stories 1962,* edited by Wallace Stegner and Richard Scowcroft, Stanford University Press, 1962. Editor and publisher of *Spit in the Ocean,* beginning 1974. A collection of Kesey's manuscripts is housed at the University of Oregon.

ADAPTATIONS: One Flew over the Cuckoo's Nest was adapted for the stage and produced on Broadway at the Cort

KEN KESEY

Theatre on November 13, 1963, and adapted for film by United Artists in 1975; *Sometimes a Great Notion* was adapted for film by Universal in 1972. *Little Tricker the Squirrel Meets Big Double the Bear* was adapted to be performed with the San Francisco Symphony in 1987 and has been performed by other major U.S. orchestras; *Little Tricker the Squirrel Meets Big Double the Bear* has also been adapted and performed as a ballet in 1990.

WORK IN PROGRESS: Sailor Song, a novel.

SIDELIGHTS: Ken Kesey is a multi-media artist and author who achieved world-wide fame writing for adults before he wrote his first book for children, *Little Tickler the Squirrel Meets Big Double the Bear.* Many adult readers have greatly enjoyed his first two popular novels, *One Flew over the Cuckoo's Nest* and *Sometimes a Great Notion.* Kesey has also penned a critically well-received collection of writings, *Demon Box* and *Kesey's Garage Sale* and has contributed to the widely read *The Last Supplement to the Whole Earth Catalog.* Kesey frequently sets his stories in what is referred to as "the great Northwest" area of America—in the picturesque states of Washington and Oregon. Individualism, personal strength, and freedom are recurring themes in Kesey's writings, especially in his works of fiction.

Kesey grew up in Colorado and in Oregon. His father, Fred Kesey, taught young Ken to value courage, strength, resourcefulness, and self-sufficiency. Under his father's influence, Kesey developed a love for the out-of-doors and a respect for nature at a very early age.

In high school, Kesey was involved in a variety of activities. With equal zest, he attended to his classroom studies, became an accomplished athlete, and enthusiastically pursued his love of acting and writing. Kesey was voted "most talented" by his fellow classmates and was awarded a wrestling scholarship to the University of Oregon. As a high school and college student, Kesey turned his love of illusions into a part-time career and performed at numerous magic shows. During this time, he also worked as a ventriloquist and became interested in acting and the theater. While still in college, Kesey married his high school sweetheart, Faye Haxby. Although very busy with his many activities, Kesey earned high grades and was awarded a Woodrow Wilson fellowship in his junior year at the university.

After his college graduation, Kesey decided to pursue his love of writing and enrolled in the creative writing program at Stanford University. Accepted into the program, Kesey moved with Faye to the San Francisco Bay area in the fall of 1958 and Kesey began studying under such talented writers and critics as Wallace Stegner, Malcolm Cowley, Frank O'Connor, and Richard Scowcroft. Not only did these years at Stanford shape and refine Kesey's literary style, they also appear to have dramatically influenced Kesey's life in other ways. It was while living in the San Francisco Bay area that Kesey began to embrace the Bohemian counterculture experience of the 1960s.

Considered one of the early pioneers and leaders of the hippie movement, Kesey adopted a free-wheeling life-style that seemed to reflect the decade's search for inner peace and personal fulfillment, in addition to the unbridled need to creatively express oneself. Kesey and his ban of "merry pranksters," as those who followed him were called, purchased a used school bus, painted it red, white, and blue and Day-Glo florescent colors, and embarked on a cross-country tour to various mid-60s "events." Their exploits during this fascinating time in history have been recorded by writer Tom Wolfe in the bestselling *The Electric Kool-Aid Acid Test.*

Many people see Kesey's life as a contradiction. While traditional family values were very important to him, he wholeheartedly chose to live for several years an extremely unconventional lifestyle. While he admired personal strength, courage, and the laws of nature, Kesey, who once volunteered for drug experiments at the Veteran's Administration Hospital, later spent years experimenting with dangerous and illegal substances. And finally, while he loved and felt at peace in the back country of Oregon and Washington, he lived in the San Francisco Bay area for a time and embraced its culture. The hows and whys behind Kesey's transformation from intelligent, well-liked, personable, sports-minded young man from a traditional and close-knit family to a forerunner of the rebellious "Psychedelic Sixties" generation is an intriguing mystery. As Stephen Tanner writes in *Contemporary Authors New Revision Series:* "In [Kesey's] life as well as his fiction, there exist tensions between country and city; between family roots and individual discovery; between traditional Christian values and those of a new counterculture; between the straight and the drug cultures; and between respectability and outlawry."

In 1965, Kesey was arrested for possession of marijuana. He was tried and convicted of the crime but fled to Mexico to avoid prosecution. He returned six months later and served

about five months in the San Mateo County Jail and later at the San Mateo County Sheriff's Honor Camp.

In 1967, Kesey moved his family to Pleasant Hill, Oregon and bought a farm. His quiet lifestyle no longer grabs the nation's attention. Busy farming his land, raising his family, working on community projects, and teaching, Kesey has also continued to write. Recently, Kesey has published a mystery novel, *Caverns,* written with thirteen members of his graduate writing seminar, composed an intriguing book that he originally wrote as a screenplay, *The Further Inquiry,* as well as producing two books for children, *Little Tickler the Squirrel Meets Big Double the Bear* and *The Sea Lion.*

Kesey's children's writings unite his love of nature with his respect of courage, inner strength, and traditional values. In his lively tale *Little Tickler the Squirrel Meets Big Double the Bear,* good triumphs over evil. Set in the picturesque Ozark Mountains, this book is the story of a little squirrel's plot to put an end to the bullying of Big Double the Bear. As a result of the squirrel's planning and resourcefulness the offensive bear's reign of terror is stopped and this area of the mountains is once again peaceful and safe for the animals who call it home. "This tall tale from the Ozarks serves as a fine vehicle for Kesey," writes a reviewer for *Publishers Weekly,* "proving ample enough for his quirky vision and his freewheeling use of language—his dialogue crackles, his forceful images and metaphors tumble one after another in an inexorable rush."

WORKS CITED:

Contemporary Authors New Revision Series, Volume 22, Gale, 1988, pp. 237-243.
Publishers Weekly, September 28, 1990, p. 99.

FOR MORE INFORMATION SEE:

BOOKS

Billingsley, Ronald G., *The Artistry of Ken Kesey,* University of Oregon, 1971.
Carnes, Bruce, *Ken Kesey,* Boise State University, 1974.
Contemporary Literary Criticism, Gale, Volume 1, 1973, Volume 3, 1975, Volume 6, 1976, Volume 11, 1979, Volume 46, 1988.
Dictionary of Literary Biography, Gale, Volume 2: *American Novelists since World War II,* 1978, Volume 16: *The Beats: Literary Bohemians in Postwar America,* 1983.
Kassner, Paul, *How a Satirical Editor Became a Yippie Conspirator in Ten Easy Years,* Putnam, 1971.
Leeds, Barry H., *Ken Kesey,* Ungar, 1981.
Perry, Paul, and Ken Babbs, *On the Bus: The Complete Guide to the Legendary Trip of Ken Kesey and The Merry Pranksters and the Birth of the Counterculture,* Thunder's Mouth, 1990.
Wolfe, Tom, *The Electric Kool-Aid Acid Test,* Farrar, Straus, 1968.

PERIODICALS

Chicago Tribune, February 4, 1962.
Chicago Tribune Book World, July 27, 1986.
Crawdaddy, Volume 29, 1972.
Library Journal, June 1, 1964; November 1, 1973; January 15, 1974.
Los Angeles Times, September 24, 1986.
Los Angeles Times Book Review, August 31, 1986.
Nation, February 23, 1974.

Newsweek, August 3, 1964.
New York Times Book Review, February 4, 1962; August 2, 1964; August 18, 1968; October 7, 1973; August 4, 1986; September 14, 1986.
People, March 22, 1976.
Rolling Stone, March 7, 1970; September 27, 1973; July 18, 1974.
Time, February 16, 1962; July 24, 1964; February 12, 1965; September 8, 1986.
Times Literary Review, February 24, 1966; February 25, 1972.

*   *   *

KING, Larry L. 1929-

PERSONAL: Born January 1, 1929, in Putnam, TX; son of Clyde Clayton (a farmer and blacksmith) and Cora Lee (Clark) King; married second wife, Rosemarie Coumarias (a photographer), February 20, 1965 (died, 1972); married Barbara S. Blaine (an attorney), May 6, 1979; children: (first marriage) Cheryl Ann, Kerri Lee, Bradley Clayton; (third marriage) Lindsay, Blaine. *Education:* Attended Texas Technological College (now Texas Tech University), 1949-50. *Politics:* Liberal-Internationalist-Democrat. *Hobbies and other interests:* Breeding show dogs, singing opera, ballet dancing.

ADDRESSES: Agent—Barbara S. Blaine, 1015 Fifteenth St. N.W., Suite 1000, Washington, DC 20005.

CAREER: Oil field worker in Texas, 1944-46; newspaper reporter in Hobbs, NM, 1949, Midland, TX, 1950-51, and Odessa, TX, 1952-54; radio station KCRS, Midland, news director, 1951-52; administrative assistant to U.S. Congressman J. T. Rutherford, Washington, DC, 1955-62, and James C. Wright, Jr., 1962-64; *Capitol Hill* (magazine), Washington, DC, editor, 1965; free-lance writer, 1964—. President, Texhouse Corp., 1979—. Member of Kennedy-Johnson campaign team, traveling in Southwest, 1960. Ferris Professor of Journalism, Princeton University, 1973-75. *Military Service:* U.S. Army, Signal Corps, writer, 1946-48; became staff sergeant.

MEMBER: PEN International, National Writers Union, National Academy of Television Arts and Sciences, Authors Guild, Authors League of America, Dramatists Guild, Screenwriters Guild East, Actors' Equity.

AWARDS, HONORS: Neiman fellow at Harvard University, 1969-70; National Book Award nomination, 1971, for *Confessions of a White Racist;* Stanley Walker Journalism Award, Texas Institute of Letters, 1973, for *The Lost Frontier;* Duke Fellow of Communications at Duke University, 1976; Tony Award nomination for best book of a musical, 1979, for *The Best Little Whorehouse in Texas;* Emmy award, 1981, for *CBS Reports* (documentary on statehouse politics); Helen Hayes and Mary Goldwater awards for best new play, 1988, for *The Night Hank Williams Died;* Children's Choice Award, 1989, for *Because of Lozo Brown;* elected to Texas Institute of Letters, 1970, and Texas Walk of Stars, 1987.

WRITINGS:

CHILDREN'S BOOK

Because of Lozo Brown, illustrated by Amy Schwartz, Viking, 1989.

OTHER

The One-Eyed Man (novel; Literary Guild selection), New American Library, 1966.
. . . And Other Dirty Stories (collected articles), World, 1968.
Confessions of a White Racist (nonfiction), Viking, 1971.
The Old Man and Lesser Mortals (collected articles), Viking, 1974.
(With Peter Masterson and Carol Hall) *The Best Little Whorehouse in Texas* (musical; also see below), first produced in New York at Actors Studio, October, 1977, produced on Broadway at 46th Street Theater, June 19, 1978.
(With Bobby Baker) *Wheeling and Dealing,* Norton, 1978.
(With Ben Z. Grant) *The Kingfish* (play), first produced in Washington, DC, at New Playwrights' Theater, August 9, 1979; produced Off-Broadway, March 24, 1991.
Of Outlaws, Con Men, Whores, Politicians and Other Artists (collected articles), Viking, 1980.
That Terrible Night Santa Got Lost in the Woods (also see below), with drawings by Pat Oliphant, Encino Press, 1981.
(With Masterson and Colin Higgins) *The Best Little Whorehouse in Texas* (screenplay; based on his musical of the same title), Universal Pictures, 1982.
The Whorehouse Papers (nonfiction), Viking, 1982.
None But a Blockhead: On Being a Writer (nonfiction), Viking, 1986.
Warning: Writer at Work (nonfiction), Texas Christian University Press, 1986.
Christmas: 1933 (play based on the book *That Terrible Night Santa Got Lost in the Woods;* first produced in Memphis, TN, at Circuit Playhouse, 1986), Samuel French, 1987.
The Golden Shadows Old West Museum (play), first produced in Little Rock, AR, at Arkansas Repertory Theater, c. 1988, produced in Washington, DC, at American Playwrights Theater, 1989.
The Night Hank Williams Died (play; first produced at Memphis State University, 1985, new version produced in Washington, DC, at New Playwrights' Theater, February 3, 1988, produced Off-Broadway at WPA Theater, January 23, 1989), Southern Methodist University Press, 1989.

Also author of unpublished book *The Blue Chip Prospect,* 1989. Contributing editor, *Texas Observer,* 1964-76, *Harper's,* 1967-71, *New Times,* 1974-77, *Texas Monthly,* beginning in 1973, and *Parade* magazine, beginning in 1983.

FOR MORE INFORMATION SEE:

BOOKS

King, Larry L., *. . . And Other Dirty Stories,* World, 1968.
King, *Confessions of a White Racist,* Viking, 1971.
King, *The Old Man and Lesser Mortals,* Viking, 1974.
King, *The Whorehouse Papers,* Viking, 1982.
King, *None But a Blockhead: On Being a Writer,* Viking, 1986.

PERIODICALS

Book World, July 4, 1971.
Chicago Tribune, May 23, 1980; July 26, 1982.
Detroit News, May 16, 1982.
Life, June 11, 1971.
New Republic, March 16, 1974.
Newsweek, June 7, 1971.
New York Review of Books, September 2, 1971.

New York Times, August 27, 1968; May 24, 1971; January 31, 1974; July 21, 1982; February 6, 1986; April 10, 1988; January 22, 1989; January 25, 1989; July 2, 1989.
New York Times Book Review, November 3, 1968; June 27, 1971; April 29, 1980; April 25, 1982; February 23, 1986.
Time, May 24, 1982.
Washington Post, June 8, 1979; August 11, 1979; January 25, 1980; April 28, 1982.
Washington Post Book World, February 17, 1974; April 7, 1980; February 12, 1986.

*   *   *

KLIBAN, B(ernard) 1935-1990

OBITUARY NOTICE—See index for *SATA* sketch: Born January 1, 1935, in Norwalk, CT; died following heart surgery, August 12, 1990, in San Francisco, CA. Artist and author. Kliban was a well-known cartoonist whose humorous portraits of plump, striped cats with human capabilities adorned tee-shirts, greeting cards, and calendars. An artschool dropout who worked variously drawing for advertisements and *Playboy* magazine, Kliban burst into fame when he specialized in cat illustrations, producing the book *Cat* in 1975. The figures in the book, hailed for embodying the uninhibited and often hilarious essence of felines, soon decorated numerous products that burgeoned into a fifty-million-dollar industry in the mid-1980s. Among Kliban's other successful publications are *Never Eat Anything Bigger Than Your Head and Other Drawings, Whack Your Porcupine and Other Drawings, Playboy's Kliban, Two Guys Fooling around with the Moon,* and *Luminous Animals and Other Drawings.*

OBITUARIES AND OTHER SOURCES:

BOOKS

Who's Who in America, 45th edition, Marquis, 1988.

PERIODICALS

Chicago Tribune, August 14, 1990.
Los Angeles Times, August 14, 1990.
New York Times, August 14, 1990.
Washington Post, August 15, 1990.

*   *   *

KNOEPFLE, John (Ignatius) 1923-

PERSONAL: Surname pronounced "Know-full"; born February 4, 1923, in Cincinnati, OH; son of Rudolph (in sales) and Catherine (Brickley) Knoepfle; married Margaret Godfrey Sower, December 26, 1956; children: John Michael, Mary Catherine, David Edmund, James Girard (deceased), Christopher Brickley. *Education:* Xavier University, Ph.B., 1947, M.A., 1949; St. Louis University, Ph.D., 1967. *Politics:* Democrat. *Religion:* Catholic.

ADDRESSES: Home—Auburn, IL. *Office*—Brookens 390, Sangamon State University, Springfield, IL 62708.

CAREER: WCET (educational television), Cincinnati, OH, producer-director, 1953-55; Ohio State University, Columbus, assistant instructor, 1956-57; Southern Illinois University, East St. Louis, IL, lecturer, 1957-61; St. Louis University High School, St. Louis, MO, lecturer in English, 1961-62; Maryville College of the Sacred Heart, St. Louis, MO, assistant professor of English, 1962-66; St. Louis University, St.

Louis, MO, associate professor and director of creative writing, 1967-71; Sangamon State University, Springfield, IL, professor of literature, 1972—. Affiliated with Mark Twain Summer Institute, 1962-64, Washington University College, 1963-66, and State University of New York at Buffalo, summer, 1969. Collector of "The Knoepfle Collection," fifty one-hour recordings of steamboat men of the inland rivers, Division of Inland Rivers, Public Library of Cincinnati and Hamilton County, 1954-60. Consultant to Project Upward Bound, 1965-70. *Military service:* U.S. Navy, 1942-46; became lieutenant junior grade; received Purple Heart.

MEMBER: Associated Writers Programs, American Studies Association.

AWARDS, HONORS: Rockefeller Foundation fellowship, 1967; National Endowment for the Arts fellowship, 1980; Mark Twain Award, Society for the Study of Midwestern Literature, 1986, for distinguished contributions to midwestern literature; Illinois Author of the Year, Illinois Association of Teachers of English, 1986; Illinois Arts Council fellowship, 1986.

WRITINGS:

(Translator with James Wright and Robert Bly) *Twenty Poems of Cesar Vallejo,* Sixties Press, 1961, published as *Neruda and Vallejo: Selected Poems,* Beacon Press, 1971.
Rivers into Islands (poems), University of Chicago Press, 1965.
An Affair of Culture, and Other Poems, Northeast/Juniper, 1969.

JOHN KNOEPFLE

After Gray Days, and Other Poems, Crabgrass Press, 1969.
Songs for Gail Guidry's Guitar, New Rivers Press, 1969.
The Intricate Land (poems), New Rivers Press, 1970.
*Dogs and Cats and Things Like That: A Book of Poems for
    Children,* illustrations by Paul Galdone, McGraw, 1971.
The 10:15 Community Poems, Back Door, 1971.
Our Street Feels Good: A Book of Poems for Children,
    photographs by Bonnie Unsworth, McGraw, 1972.
Whetstone: A Book of Poems, Bk Mk Press (University of
    Missouri at Kansas City), 1972.
Deep Winter Poems, Three Sheets, 1972.
Thinking of Offerings: Poems 1970-1973, Juniper, 1975.
A Box of Sandalwood: Love Poems, Juniper, 1978.
A Gathering of Voices, Rook, 1978.
(Editor with Dan Jaffe) *Frontier Literature: Images of the
    American West,* McGraw, 1979.
Poems for the Hours, Uzzano, 1979.
Selected Poems, Bk Mk Press, 1985.
Poems from the Sangamon, University of Illinois Press, 1985.
(Selector and translator with Wang Shouyi) *T'ang Dynasty
    Poems* (text in Chinese and English), Spoon River Po-
    etry Press, 1985.
(Selector and translator with Wang Shouyi) *Song Dynasty
    Poems* (text in Chinese and English), Spoon River Po-
    etry Press, 1985.
Dim Tales, Stormline Press, 1989.

Work represented in anthologies, including *Poems at the
Gate,* 1964; *Heartland: Poets of the Midwest,* edited by Lucien
Stryk, Northern Illinois University Press, 1967; *From the
Hungarian Revolution,* edited by David Ray, Cornell Univer-
sity Press, 1967; *Voyages to the Inland Sea,* edited by John
Judson, Juniper, 1971; *Messages,* Little, Brown, 1972;
Regional Perspectives: America's Literary Heritage, edited by
John Gordon Blake, American Library, 1973; *Late Harvest:
Plains and Prairie Poets,* Bk Mk, 1977; *Five Missouri Poets,*
edited by Jim Barnes, Chariton Press, 1979; *Prairie Voices: A
Collection of Illinois Poets,* edited by Lucien Stryk, Illinois
Arts Council Foundation, 1980; and *A Reader's Guide to
Illinois Literature,* Read Illinois Program, 1985. Contributor
to periodicals, including *Minnesota Review, Illinois Writers
Review, River Styx, ACM,* and *New Letters.*

SIDELIGHTS: "I wanted to write about the area where I
grew up, the Ohio River valley, especially in and around
Cincinnati," John Knoepfle told *SATA.* "And then, by
happenstance, I came to teach in East St. Louis at Southern
Illinois University from 1957 to 1961, so I just extended my
interest in the inland rivers to the Mississippi. And later
teaching in the St. Louis, Missouri, area, I just continued
writing so that my book *Rivers into Islands* has as its locale the
Ohio and Mississippi river valleys. There's a poem about
Marietta, Ohio, in there, as well as some about Cincinnati,
southern Illinois, East St. Louis, and the greater St. Louis
area. East St. Louis and the surrounding environment is very
rich in folklore."

From 1954 until 1960 Knoepfle interviewed steamboat men
of these inland rivers and transcribed fifty one-hour recordings, known as "The Knoepfle Collection." "I had a knowledge of the Ohio Valley and the steamboat men who worked
in it, and I wanted to write about that," Knoepfle explained
to *SATA.* "I could not find a statement about the place I
came from in any of the literature I grew up with. The river
tapes enabled me to say something about where I came from,
in terms of its geography and its social history.

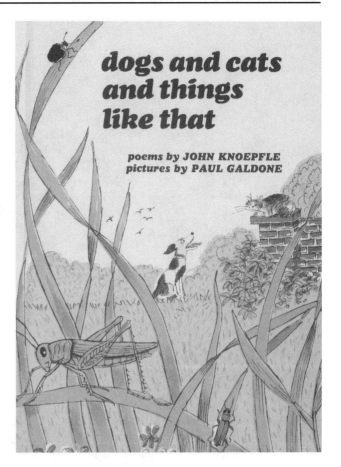

Though most of his poetry is for adults, John
Knoepfle also writes poems for children. (Cover illus-
tration from *Dogs and Cats and Things Like That* by
Paul Galdone.)

"My taping the river men made a lot of difference as to how I
was going to write because it made me very conscious of the
spoken voice. There's a difference between the way people
speak and written language. The taping of the old timers also
encouraged me to not shy away from narrative poems or
dramatic poems, and my poems ever since then have been
multivoiced poems. A reader will just expect that there will be
more than one voice floating around in a poem, even if only
one voice is speaking on the top level of the poem. But there's
usually a voice or two quoted in there also."

In 1969 Knoepfle and his family spent the summer in Buffalo,
New York, where he was teaching at the state university.
While there Knoepfle began to compose poetry to amuse his
children, John, Molly, Dave, and Chris, who were ages eleven
to four at the time. "The children were coming to a place
where they had no companions," Knoepfle told *SATA.* "So
that threw them back on themselves and on us in terms of this
little society. And I began to listen very closely to them,
especially the two younger boys, and to concoct small poems
for their enjoyment. And I would put Molly and John in too.
So the poems do have the flavor of the child's voice in them.

"But there was another strategy for my writing the children's
poems. David had gone to a preschool. And at that time the
teachers would try to teach relationships to children, but they
didn't have a lot of materials to work with. So a lot of my
poems are just about that: things within things, or directions,
or how the sun works going down behind the roof of the
store, the idea of 'here' and 'there.'

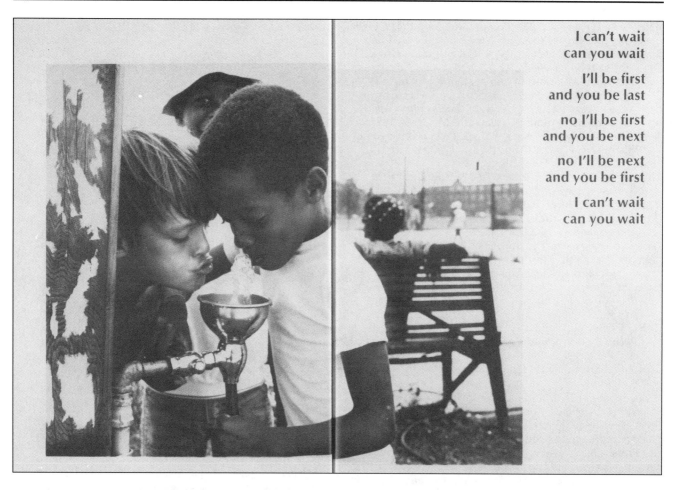

I can't wait
can you wait

I'll be first
and you be last

no I'll be first
and you be next

no I'll be next
and you be first

I can't wait
can you wait

(From *Our Street Feels Good,* by John Knoepfle, photographs by Bonnie Unsworth.)

"The poems were deliberately concocted to aid people who wanted to help children with directions and relationships. But of course *Sesame Street* came on the air after that, and the *Electric Company,* and they did that beautifully with repetitions and visuals. But that's what was on my mind.

"I ended up with a big batch of poems, so I made a little book of these poems and sent them to McGraw-Hill publishers. One of their editors sent it to Paul Galdone, one of their main illustrators. Galdone said there were two books here: one about the animals and birds, another about the children on the street. So it ended up there were two books published, *Dogs and Cats and Things Like That* and *Our Street Feels Good."*

In 1972 Knoepfle joined the English faculty at Sangamon State University in Springfield, Illinois. "As part of my contribution to Sangamon State University's Sangamon Valley Project I wrote a book of place poems, *Poems from the Sangamon,"* Knoepfle recounted to *SATA.* "I started the poems in 1980; it took me about four years to finish them.

"A big event in 1980," Knoepfle continued, "was that we purchased our first air-conditioned car. An air-conditioned car! We drove all over the valley in it and saw almost every little town from here to Ellsworth. And by doing that I was able to discover some of the natural images that would go through the book, such as turtles and trumpet vines and spiders and wolves.

"I put a lot of work into *Poems from the Sangamon.* I read all of the issues of the Illinois Historical Society journal, going back to the 1890s, culling through them for any ideas, letters, whatever. And I read all of the extant literature—like Cullom Bryant's prairie poems, which were inspired by a visit to his brother in Jacksonville. Bryant wrote perhaps the best account of travels in the Sangamon valley during the pioneer days. I read Francis Grierson's *Valley of the Shadows* and Edgar Lee Master's *The Sangamon*—anything to get the historical and literary underpinning. And I signatured much of that stuff into the book. There are a lot of references to Masters; there's a half line from Dave Etter's 'Night in August' in my poem on Clinton, Illinois; there's a little bit of Carl Sandburg—by accident—because we were using the same source, *Old Times in McLean County.*

"There are also poems about mid-sized cities in the valley—Decatur and Springfield, about farms, about the river itself, about winners and losers. There is also a sub-theme of male and female relationships in the volume.

"The cover of the book is taken from a photograph by Larry Kanfer of a farm with Islamic-looking architecture near the town of Mohamet, Illinois. Mohamet is mentioned in *Poems from the Sangamon* in 'Lines for the Tribe of Ben Ishmael,' a poem that's based on an essay by Hugo P. Leaming in *Ethnic Frontier,* a collection of essays about ethnic history in Illinois. Leaming writes about a pretty large group of people who were made up of escaped English bond servants, fugitive African slaves, and remnant Indian peoples who had come together in the mountains of Kentucky and formed a hunting and gathering society. This society had a Muslim cast—Ben Ishmael. The Muslim influence may have come from the escaped slaves.

"The Ben Ishmaelites came to Cincinnati and then settled in Indianapolis, building their shanties on the White River mud flats. American Indian tribal chief Tecumseh gave them his permission to hunt on that territory, and they had an annual migration. They went up north toward Chicago, past Morocco, and then they cut down southwest to Mahomet and then cut back east, past Mecca, to Indianapolis. The names on Mahomet's early town lists—such as Ahmid—are very suggestive of Islamic rather than Anglo-Saxon names as well.

"These people never made it in terms of mainstream American society. They never settled down; they became beggars and launderers and baby sitters. At the turn of the century Indiana passed a law providing for sterilization of certain undesirables on the advice of a surgeon. The law didn't mention Ben Ishmaelites specifically, but it talked about idiots and other people who were transient. The law was declared unconstitutional very quickly, but the Ben Ishmaelites kind of disappeared from Indiana. They may be one of the sources of the Muslim movement that grew up later among African-Americans living in Chicago and other big cities.

poems from the sangamon

POEMS BY JOHN KNOEPFLE

John Knoepfle read back issues of the Illinois Historical Society from the 1890s in preparation for writing *Poems from the Sangamon.* (Cover photograph by Larry Kanfer.)

" 'Lines for the Tribe of Ben Ishmael' jars people," Knoepfle explained to *SATA,* because of its "linking of an old Indiana law with the Holocaust." From reading this poem about what happened to the Ben-Ishmaelites, Knoepfle suggests, "suddenly you can talk about the death of Biafrans and the death of Russians and the death of Greeks and Jews and gypsies. Indeed, much of the poetry in *Poems from the Sangamon* is a commentary on the country and the world too. And so we have 'The Last Things'—poems about nuclear war. Some people like to read *Poems from the Sangamon* and see it as a lot of folksy poems. That isn't what it's about.

"After *Poems from the Sangamon* was published in 1985 I started composing 'Dim stories.' Dim is a character I made up. He was the famous central Illinois proverbist who coined the proverb 'Suck an egg today, scramble one tomorrow.' After having 'discovered' some of Dim's journals at a garage sale, I deciphered some of his stories—they are all set in Illinois. I actually used to make these up driving back and forth to school, and then I would tell them to friends.

"There's a big range in these stories. I teach folk literature, and we cover all kinds and varieties of folk tales, so one of the Dim stories is an Arthurian tale, another is just a tall tale, and one of them is a riddle tale. Then I have one that involves Henry Allison's ancestor, Revelations Dim, in a great hunt.

"There is also a big range in subject matter. One of the stories is about a five-mile-long worm. That's possible because of our horrifying situation, with what we know of genetics and all kinds of chemicals and things. Then there's one about a flying saucer, in which Dim saves the world. There's a cycle of Dim tales about Lake Springfield. Not to mention the tiny tarts and the mouse king and the frogs of Hannibal.

"There are about fifty or sixty Dim stories; I used to tell them over WSSU, the university radio station, on its program 'Folk Festival,' and had them printed regularly in a southern Illinois magazine called *Springhouse.*" Stormline Press published a collection, *Dim Tales,* in 1989.

"I was kind of downcast after 1985 because I had had such a big year: My *Selected Poems* and *Poems from the Sangamon* were published, as were two books of translations I had done with Wang Shouyi—*T'ang Dynasty Poems* and *Song Dynasty Poems,*" Knoepfle told *SATA.* "I was written out, and I didn't write any poems for three years. In May of 1988 I began to write again.

"I recently finished something I call a free form. It's a book in sort of a concrete poetry using material from seventeenth-century Jesuit manuscripts of the language of the Peoria and Miami Indians, plus some church records and treaty signatures, and manuscripts from nineteenth- and early-twentieth-century linguists who talked to the remnant speakers of Miami and Peoria at about the turn of the century. I made this twenty-page poem using materials from the Jesuit account of Genesis as rendered into the Peoria. Thus you have statements like 'After the first broken up,' which describes God's creation of the universe. Creation begins after 'the first broken up,' which, to my mind, is a lot better than talking about the Big Bang. There's something about the tenses there that puts it into another kind of perspective.

"Right now I'm doing two vastly different things: I'm working on a book of poems called *Sacred Places,* based on what I've seen and heard and thought about as I travel the length and breadth of the country. Some of those poems have been published in *River Styx, ACM, New Letters,* and other magazines. At the same time I've been writing a series called *The Green Snake Interviews.* These are fun to write because the poet doesn't like the interviewer, and the interviewer wishes that his poet was famous. The combination allows me to say almost anything I want to. I think these two projects will keep me busy for quite a while."

FOR MORE INFORMATION SEE:

PERIODICALS

Focus Midwest, Number 14, 1980.
Great Lakes Review, Number 3, 1976.
Minnesota Review, Number 3, 1968.

*   *   *

KRASNE, Betty
See LEVINE, Betty K(rasne)

*   *   *

KROLL, Steven 1941-

PERSONAL: Born August 11, 1941, in New York, NY; son of Julius (a diamond merchant) and Anita (a business executive; maiden name, Berger) Kroll; married Edite Niedringhaus (a children's book editor), April 18, 1964 (divorced, 1978); married Abigail Aldridge (a milliner), June 3, 1989. *Education:* Harvard University, B.A., 1962. *Politics:* "Committed to change." *Religion:* Jewish. *Hobbies and other interests:* Walking, traveling, and playing squash and tennis.

ADDRESSES: Home and office—64 West Eleventh St., New York, NY 10011.

CAREER: Transatlantic Review, London, England, associate editor, 1962-65; Chatto & Windus Ltd., London, reader and editor, 1962-65; Holt, Rinehart & Winston, New York City, acquiring editor, adult trade department, 1965-69; freelance writer, 1969—. Instructor in English, University of Maine at Augusta, 1970-71.

MEMBER: PEN American Center (chairman of children's book committee and member of executive board), Authors Guild, Authors League of America, Harvard Club (New York).

WRITINGS:

FOR CHILDREN

Is Milton Missing? (Junior Literary Guild selection), illustrated by Dick Gackenbach, Holiday House, 1975.
That Makes Me Mad!, illustrated by Hilary Knight, Pantheon, 1976.
The Tyrannosaurus Game, illustrated by Tomie de Paola, Holiday House, 1976.
Gobbledygook, illustrated by Kelly Oechsli, Holiday House, 1977.
If I Could Be My Grandmother, illustrated by Lady McCrady, Pantheon, 1977.
Sleepy Ida and Other Nonsense Poems, illustrated by Seymour Chwast, Pantheon, 1977.
Fat Magic, illustrated by Tomie de Paola, Holiday House, 1978.
Santa's Crash-Bang Christmas, illustrated by Tomie de Paola, Holiday House, 1978.

STEVEN KROLL

T. J. Folger, Thief, illustrated by Bill Morrison, Holiday House, 1978.
The Candy Witch, illustrated by Marylin Hafner, Holiday House, 1979.
Space Cats, illustrated by Friso Henstra, Holiday House, 1979.
Amanda and the Giggling Ghost, illustrated by Dick Gackenbach, Holiday House, 1980.
Dirty Feet, illustrated by Toni Hormann, Parents Magazine Press, 1980.
Monster Birthday, illustrated by Dennis Kendrick, Holiday House, 1980.
Friday the 13th, illustrated by Dick Gackenbach, Holiday House, 1981.
Giant Journey, illustrated by Kay Chorao, Holiday House, 1981.
Are You Pirates?, illustrated by Marylin Hafner, Pantheon, 1982.
Banana Bits, illustrated by Maxie Chambliss, Avon, 1982.
Bathrooms, illustrated by Maxie Chambliss, Avon, 1982.
The Big Bunny and the Easter Eggs, illustrated by Janet Stevens, Holiday House, 1982.
The Goat Parade, illustrated by Tim Kirk, Parents Magazine Press, 1982.
One Tough Turkey, illustrated by John Wallner, Holiday House, 1982.
The Hand-Me-Down Doll, illustrated by Evaline Ness, Holiday House, 1983.
Otto, illustrated by Ned Delaney, Parents Magazine Press, 1983.
Pigs in the House, illustrated by Tim Kirk, Parents Magazine Press, 1983.
Toot! Toot!, illustrated by Anne Rockwell, Holiday House, 1983.
Woof, Woof!, illustrated by Nicole Rubel, Dial, 1983.
The Biggest Pumpkin Ever (Junior Literary Guild selection), illustrated by Jeni Bassett, Holiday House, 1984.

Loose Tooth, illustrated by Tricia Tusa, Holiday House, 1984.

Happy Mother's Day, illustrated by Marylin Hafner, Holiday House, 1985.

Mrs. Claus's Crazy Christmas, illustrated by John Wallner, Holiday House, 1985.

Annie's Four Grannies, illustrated by Eileen Christelow, Holiday House, 1986.

The Big Bunny and the Magic Show, illustrated by Janet Stevens, Holiday House, 1986.

Don't Get Me in Trouble!, illustrated by Marvin Glass, Crown, 1987.

I'd Like to Be, illustrated by Ellen Appleby, Parents Magazine Press, 1987.

I Love Spring, illustrated by Kathryn E. Shoemaker, Holiday House, 1987.

It's Groundhog Day!, illustrated by Jeni Bassett, Holiday House, 1987.

Happy Father's Day, illustrated by Marylin Hafner, Holiday House, 1988.

Looking for Daniela: A Romantic Adventure, illustrated by Anita Lobel, Holiday House, 1988.

Newsman Ned Meets the New Family, illustrated by Denise Brunkus, Scholastic Inc., 1988.

Oh, What a Thanksgiving!, illustrated by S. D. Schindler, Scholastic Inc., 1988.

Big Jeremy, illustrated by Donald Carrick, Holiday House, 1989.

The Hokey-Pokey Man, illustrated by Deborah Kogan Ray, Holiday House, 1989.

In books such as *Gone Fishing,* Steven Kroll aims to recapture the wonder of being a child. (Cover illustration by Harvey Stevenson.)

"I'd like other adults to let down the barriers and feel the wonder in their own lives that I feel in these books," Steven Kroll remarked to *Something about the Author.* (Cover from *Branigan's Cat and the Halloween Ghost,* by Steven Kroll, illustrated by Carolyn Ewing.)

Newsman Ned and the Broken Rules, illustrated by Denise Brunkus, Scholastic Inc., 1989.

Branigan's Cat and the Halloween Ghost, Holiday House, 1990.

Gone Fishing, illustrated by Harvey Stevenson, Crown, 1990.

It's April Fools' Day!, Holiday House, 1990.

Annabelle's Un-Birthday, Macmillan, 1991.

Howard and Gracie's Luncheonette, illustrated by Michael Sours, Holt, 1991.

Mary McLean and the St. Patrick's Day Parade, illustrated by Michael Dooling, Scholastic Inc., 1991.

Princess Abigail and the Wonderful Hat, illustrated by Patience Brewster, Holiday House, 1991.

The Squirrels' Thanksgiving, Holiday House, 1991.

YOUNG ADULT BOOKS

Take It Easy, Four Winds, 1983.
Breaking Camp, Macmillan, 1985.
Multiple Choice, Macmillan, 1987.

OTHER

Contributor of book reviews to *Book World, Commonweal, Village Voice, Listener, New York Times Book Review, Spectator, Times Literary Supplement,* and *London Magazine.* Some of Kroll's works have been translated into French, Spanish, and Japanese.

ADAPTATIONS: The Biggest Pumpkin Ever and Other Stories (includes *The Biggest Pumpkin Ever; Sleepy Ida and Other Nonsense Poems; T. J. Folger, Thief;* and *Woof, Woof!*) recorded onto audiocassette, Caedmon, 1986.

WORK IN PROGRESS: A Young Camelot baseball series, publication of first four books by Avon expected in 1992; *The Magic Rocket,* publication by Holiday House, *Will You Be My Valentine?,* publication by Holiday House, *By the Dawn's Early Light: The Story of the Star-Spangled Banner,* publication by Scholastic, Inc., and *Andrew Wants a Dog,* publication by Hyperion Press, all expected in 1992; *Queen of the May,* publication by Holiday House expected in 1993.

SIDELIGHTS: Children's author Steven Kroll possesses a unique ability to view his stories as a child would, so he understands what interests and entertains his young audience. Even though he fell into writing by chance, and into children's writing by an off-hand suggestion, the author has never regretted his career choice. Writing for children affords Kroll a special connection with his own youth—something he values. "What is most important is the feeling that I am somehow in touch with my own childhood," Kroll told *SATA.* "To be in touch with your own childhood is to be, in some way, touched with wonder, and when I write for children, that is what I feel."

As a child in New York City, the author entertained himself with imaginative games, baseball, and trips to the local candy store. When he was older school occupied his time, as did studying sculpture at the Museum of Modern Art on Tuesday afternoons. Naturally, people thought Kroll would become a sculptor. "But I turned to writing instead," the author admitted in the *Junior Literary Guild* magazine. "It happened quite by accident." Appointed editor of *Panorama,* his secondary school literary journal, Kroll discovered "there wasn't much to publish. Someone had to fill the gap. I sat

PRINCESS ABIGAIL
AND THE WONDERFUL HAT

BY STEVEN KROLL
ILLUSTRATED BY PATIENCE BREWSTER

Steven Kroll, with the publication of such 1991 books as *Princess Abigail and the Wonderful Hat,* has more than fifty books to his credit. (Cover illustration by Patience Brewster.)

down and wrote two stories and I've been hooked on writing ever since."

Kroll never set out to write children's stories. Following his graduation from Harvard University in 1962, he worked as an editor of adult trade books in both London, England, and in New York City. In 1969 he moved to Maine so he could write full time. He was contributing book reviews to magazines and writing adult short stories and novels during the early 1970s when his former wife, a children's book editor, and other friends in children's book publishing suggested he try writing for children. "I said, 'Oh, no. I couldn't possibly. I don't know how to do that,'" Kroll recalled in *Behind the Covers.* But "one night at a dinner party I got an idea for a children's story. I wrote it and it was bad. But I discovered an important thing: I liked doing it."

After spending a few years writing unsuccessful children's picture-book stories, Kroll moved back to New York City, where he met Margery Cuyler. She became his editor at Holiday House and published his first book, *Is Milton Missing?,* in 1975. Since then Kroll has steadily produced at least two books per year, sometimes as many as six, for Holiday House and other publishers. As a result, with his spring, 1991, publication of three additional stories, including *Princess Abigail and the Wonderful Hat,* the prolific author has written more than fifty children's books.

For his story ideas and settings Kroll often recalls places and instances from his own childhood. "When I write about a child's room, that room is often my own—the one in the Manhattan apartment house where I grew up," Kroll told *SATA.* "When I write about an urban street or an urban school, it is often my street or my school, taken out of time into a situation I have invented. And sometimes," the author continued, "if I'm writing about a suburb or a small town, that place will resemble the home of a summer camp friend I visited once, and longed to see again."

Kroll's stories appeal greatly to young readers, evidenced by the great number of letters the author constantly receives. His favorites are those from children who particularly enjoyed one of his books, but "the best letter I ever got was from a first grader in Connecticut where I was going to speak the following week," Kroll recollected in *Behind the Covers.* "This one read, 'Dear Mr. Kroll, My heart is beating because it's so anxious to see what you look like.' The little girl was wonderful! She signed everything she wrote with her name and 'Made in U.S.A.'"

Kroll never regrets leaving his full-time job to become a children's author. "I really love writing for children," he told *SATA.* "I love starting the fireworks, love that explosion of emotion, of excitement, terror, and enthusiasm that comes with putting those words on paper and sometimes, if the mood is right, doing a draft of a whole picture-book story in one sitting. I've been doing a lot more picture books, but I've also become much more involved in writing chapter books for middle grade readers." Writing for children is what Kroll feels most content doing. "It's part of me now," the author concluded, "and I'd like other adults to let down the barriers and feel the wonder in their own lives that I feel in these books."

WORKS CITED:

Review of *Is Milton Missing?, Junior Literary Guild,* September, 1975, p. 7.

Roginski, Jim, *Behind the Covers: Interviews with Authors and Illustrators of Books for Children and Young Adults,* Libraries Unlimited, 1985, pp. 130-137.

FOR MORE INFORMATION SEE:

BOOKS

Something about the Author Autobiography Series, Volume 7, Gale, 1989.

PERIODICALS

Wilson Library Bulletin, January, 1985.

Sketch by Denise E. Kasinec

*   *   *

LAVERTY, Donald
See BLISH, James (Benjamin)

*   *   *

LEBRUN, Claude 1929-

PERSONAL: Born August 13, 1929, in Saint Paterne, France; daughter of Gabriel Hodbert and Victorine Lepron; married Francois Lebrun (a teacher), April 6, 1956; children: Pierre-Francois, Jerome. *Education:* Universite de Poitiers, secondary teaching certificate, 1956. *Hobbies and other interests:* Cooking.

CLAUDE LEBRUN

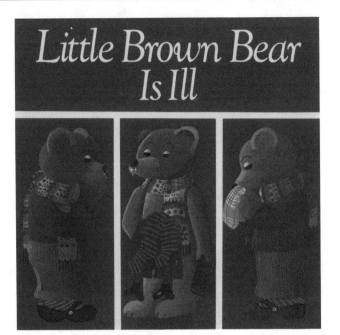

Author Claude Lebrun teamed up with illustrator Daniele Bour for the "Little Brown Bear" series, which includes *Little Brown Bear Is Ill.*

ADDRESSES: Home—Allee Cassandre, 41800 Couture-sur-Loir, France.

CAREER: Teacher of literature in France, 1956-1989; writer.

WRITINGS:

"LITTLE BROWN BEAR" SERIES; ILLUSTRATED BY DANIELE BOUR

Little Brown Bear's Cold, Methuen, 1982.
Little Brown Bear Gets Dressed (originally published in French as *Petit Ours Brun s'habille,* Bayard, 1979), Barron's, 1982.
Little Brown Bear Is Cross, Methuen, 1982.
Little Brown Bear Is Ill (originally published in French as *Petit Ours Brun est malade,* Bayard, 1979), Barron's, 1982.
Little Brown Bear Says No (originally published in French as *Petit Ours Brun dit non,* Bayard, 1979), Barron's, 1982.
Little Brown Bear's Story, Methuen, 1982.
Little Brown Bear Takes a Bath (originally published in French as *Petit Ours Brun se lave,* Bayard, 1979), Barron's, 1982.
Little Brown Bear's Tricycle, Methuen, 1982.
Little Brown Bear Wakes Up (originally published in French as *Petit Ours Brun se reveille,* Bayard, 1982), Barron's, 1982.
Little Brown Bear's Walk, Methuen, 1982.
Little Brown Bear Wants a Kiss (originally published in French as *Petit Ours Brun veut un baiser,* 1980), Barron's, 1982.
Little Brown Bear Won't Eat!, Methuen, 1982.
Little Brown Bear's Bad Day, Methuen Children's, 1983.
Little Brown Bear's Breakfast Egg, Methuen Children's, 1983.
Little Brown Bear Can Cook!, Methuen Children's, 1983.

Little Brown Bear Is Big!, Methuen Children's, 1983.
Little Brown Bear's Playtime, Methuen Children's, 1983.
Little Brown Bear's Snowball, Methuen Children's, 1983.

OTHER

Invitation a Jean Sulivan, Editions du Cerf, 1981.
1000 mots francais pour reussir, Belin, 1986.

The "Little Brown Bear" series has also been translated into Japanese.

WORK IN PROGRESS: Vocabulaire specialise pour la preparation de l'examen de francais au baccalaureat (title means "*Specialized Vocabulary for French Examination of Baccalaureat*"), publication expected in 1991; a book of French cooking, publication expected in 1992.

SIDELIGHTS: Claude Lebrun told *SATA* that she created the character of the Little Brown Bear so she could tell stories to her own children when they were young. The author also pointed out that *Invitation a Jean Sulivan* is about a priest she knew and is a "presentation and analysis of Jean Sulivan's books" so that others will wish to read them. She wrote the book because she felt it of great importance to Christianity that his thoughts and works be known.

Lebrun noted that *1000 mots francais pour reussir* involves educational research that focuses on learning words at the high school level. She said that the first published volume contains general terms. The second volume is in progress. Lebrun also indicated that she feels it is quite important that students have the opportunity to learn the exact meanings of the words they need and that the book was written to help "improve French students' vocabulary."

FOR MORE INFORMATION SEE:

PERIODICALS

Growing Point, January, 1984.
Junior Bookshelf, February, 1984.
Publishers Weekly, July 23, 1982; December 24, 1982.

* * *

LEVIN, Ira 1929-

PERSONAL: Born August 27, 1929, in New York City; son of Charles (a toy importer) and Beatrice (maiden name, Schlansky) Levin; married Gabrielle Aronsohn, August 20, 1960 (divorced January, 1968); married Phyllis Finkel, 1979 (divorced, 1981); children: (first marriage) Adam, Jared, Nicholas. *Education:* Attended Drake University, 1946-48; New York University, A.B., 1950.

ADDRESSES: Agent—Harold Ober Associates, 425 Madison Ave., New York, NY 10017.

CAREER: Novelist and playwright. *Military service:* U.S. Army, Signal Corps., 1953-55.

MEMBER: Dramatists Guild, Authors Guild, Authors League of America, American Society of Composers, Authors and Publishers.

IRA LEVIN

AWARDS, HONORS: Edgar Allan Poe Award, 1953, for *A Kiss before Dying,* and 1980, for *Deathtrap; The Boys from Brazil* was named a New York Public Library "Book for the Teen Age," 1980, 1981, and 1982.

WRITINGS:

NOVELS

A Kiss before Dying, Simon & Shuster, 1953.
Rosemary's Baby, Random House, 1967.
This Perfect Day (Literary Guild selection), Random House, 1970.
The Stepford Wives, Random House, 1972.
The Boys from Brazil, Random House, 1976.
Three By Ira Levin (contains *Rosemary's Baby, The Stepford Wives,* and *This Perfect Day*), Random House, 1985.
Sliver, Bantam, 1991.

PLAYS

No Time for Sergeants (adapted from the novel by Mac Hyman; produced on Broadway at the Alvin Theatre, October 20, 1955, produced on the West End at Her Majesty's Theatre, August 23, 1956), Random House, 1956.
Interlock (produced on Broadway at the ANTA Theatre, February 6, 1958), Dramatists Play Service, 1958.
Critic's Choice (produced on Broadway at the Ethel Barrymore Theatre, February 14, 1960), Random House, 1961.

General Seeger (produced on Broadway at the Lyceum Theatre, February 28, 1962), Dramatists Play Service, 1962.

(With music by Milton Schaefer) *Drat! The Cat!,* produced on Broadway at the Martin Beck Theatre, October 10, 1965.

Dr. Cook's Garden, produced on Broadway at the Belasco Theatre, September 26, 1967.

Veronica's Room (produced on Broadway at the Music Box Theatre, 1973), Random House, 1974.

Deathtrap (produced on Broadway at the Music Box Theatre, February 26, 1978), Random House, 1979.

Break a Leg (produced on Broadway at the Palace Theatre, April 29, 1979), S. French, 1981.

Cantorial, produced Off-Broadway at the Jewish Repertory Theatre, 1984.

Author of *Footsteps,* 1983. Also author of scripts for the television series *Clock, Lights Out,* and *U.S. Steel Hour.*

ADAPTATIONS:

MOTION PICTURES

A Kiss before Dying, United Artists, 1956.

Ira Levin has been frightening readers with his novels since 1953. (Dustjacket from the 1990 paperback edition of *Rosemary's Baby.*)

All of Levin's books have been bestsellers. (Dustjacket from the 1990 paperback edition of *The Boys from Brazil.*)

No Time for Sergeants, Twentieth Century-Fox, 1959.
Critic's Choice, Warner Brothers, 1962.
Rosemary's Baby, Paramount, 1968.
Dr. Cook's Garden, ABC Circle Films, 1970.
The Stepford Wives, Columbia, 1975.
The Boys from Brazil, Twentieth Century-Fox, 1978.
Deathtrap, Warner Brothers, 1982.
A Kiss before Dying, Universal, 1991.

OTHER

Rosemary's Baby was recorded on audio cassette and released by Random Audiobooks, 1986.

SIDELIGHTS: Ira Levin has been frightening people with his novels and plays since 1953. The author of such works as *Rosemary's Baby, The Boys from Brazil,* and *Deathtrap,* Levin is a genial, family man who delights in combining thrills with black humor. He is particularly adept at weaving sinister plots out of the more mundane aspects of everyday life. The mix of horror, humor, and the commonplace found in Levin's writings has served him well. All of Levin's books have been bestsellers, and *Deathtrap* was the longest-running thriller in Broadway history.

Ira Levin was born and raised in New York City. His father was a successful toy importer who introduced his family to the many cultural highlights of the city. As a boy, Levin loved to read, especially Edgar Allan Poe and mystery writers such as Agatha Christie and Ellery Queen. He also liked magic and became a regular at Tannen's magic shop on Times Square. In an interview with *People* magazine, Levin admitted to Alfred Gillespie that the "tricks didn't work as well once [I] was at home."

Levin fell in love with the theater after seeing his first play, *Charley's Aunt.* In fact, his initial thoughts about a writing career centered on being a playwright. "I looked up at a theater marquee on day," Levin told the *Daily Mirror,* "And saw the playwright's name, and told myself 'Oh boy! One of these days . . . .'"

Levin did not start writing in earnest, however, until he began college at Drake University in Des Moines, Iowa. While at Drake, Levin received critical assistance from poet E. L. Mayo, who advised the fledgling writer to both clarify his prose and avoid superfluous adverbs. After spending a couple of years honing his skills at Drake, Levin transferred to New York University (NYU) in order to be closer to his family.

As Levin approached graduation from NYU, his father suggested he consider joining the family import business. The younger Levin had another plan. He told Gillespie that he asked his father to support his writing efforts for one year, promising, "If the writing doesn't work out, *then* I'll come in with you." Levin's father agreed. Within months, Levin wrote a half-hour thriller entitled *The Old Woman* that was a runner-up in a CBS writing contest. The story of a 103-year-old-woman who foils a murder plot, *The Old Woman* became Levin's first literary sale when NBC bought it for a segment

Mia Farrow starred in the movie version of *Rosemary's Baby,* released by Paramount in 1968.

of *Lights Out.* Two more script sales followed, and their success encouraged Levin to begin work on his first novel, *A Kiss before Dying.*

A Kiss before Dying is considered by many critics to be Levin's masterpiece. Published when Levin was only twenty-three, the novel concerns the deadly get-rich-quick schemes of an amoral college student. The book was an immediate bestseller. It became a Mystery Guild selection and won the Edgar Allan Poe Award from the Mystery Writers of America for best mystery novel of the year. *New York Times* critic James Sandoe called *A Kiss before Dying* the "most striking debut of the year." He added: "Mr. Levin's considerable strength is the steady pull of his narrative, set down economically and with compulsive breathlessness. . . . You'll read it straight through and then fidget intermittently for his second novel since this first one warrants so much more richly than usual the word 'promising.'"

Levin had little time to enjoy his new celebrity status. In late 1953, he was drafted into the Army and sent to radar school. After his writing background was brought to the attention of his superiors, Levin was transferred to the Pictorial Center where he helped write and produce training films. During this time, *A Kiss before Dying* was sold to Twentieth Century-Fox. While happy about the sale, Levin was frustrated by his inability to supervise the screen adaptation. In an interview with the *New York Times,* he recalled: "I felt as though I had sold a particularly plump daughter into the household of a sadist. What were they doing to my book out there? Strange reports sifted back to my post at the Signal Corps Pictorial Center. . . . These extra-military frettings detracted lamentably from the brilliance of the training film scenarios that were my assigned duty."

A few days before his discharge from the Army, Levin received a call from actor-producer Maurice Evans. Evans asked Levin if he would be interested in writing a stage adaptation of the novel *No Time for Sergeants.* According to the *New York Times* interview, Levin thought the phone call was a prank; in a British accent, he told Evans to "drop dead, old chap." Happily, Evans was able to convince Levin that the offer was sincere. Levin's adaptation of *No Time for Sergeants* went on to become a huge popular and critical success both as a stage play and film starring Andy Griffith.

After the success of *No Time for Sergeants,* Levin continued to work at playwriting with mixed results. *Interlock* was a critical and commercial failure, while *Critic's Choice* enjoyed a three-month Broadway run. Levin's only musical, *Drat! The Cat!,* took three years to produce and closed in one week. Levin told *People* that the failure of *Drat! The Cat!* was particularly difficult to accept: "I still love *Drat!,* almost in its entirety . . . and money would have saved it. We came to New York penniless. It succeeded only in sending me back to novels."

Inspired by a human life-cycle lecture, Levin began work on *Rosemary's Baby. Rosemary's Baby* is the tale of a young New York housewife who is chosen by a coven to be the mother of Satan's son. Levin disclosed the idea for his second novel to *Playbill:* "I was intrigued by the idea of a woman who is pregnant with a fetus that the reader knows is very different from what she expects. I figured either witchcraft or something from outer space had to be responsible. Since a science fiction writer named John Wyndham had already done outer space in the *Midwich Cuckoos,* I opted for witchcraft."

In *The Stepford Wives,* **a group of upper-middle class husbands replace their wives with docile robot replicas.** (From the Columbia Pictures movie, released in 1975.)

While writing *Rosemary's Baby,* Levin attempted to balance the fantasy element of the novel with factual background details. Levin told Barbara A. Bannon of *Publisher's Weekly* that he kept a pile of newspapers on hand while working on the final draft, fitting references from daily papers into the text. At times, even Levin was disturbed by the novel's theme. He stated that he didn't "think any pregnant women should read it." (In fact, Levin's wife was pregnant while he worked on the book, and he would not let her see the manuscript.)

Critical response to *Rosemary's Baby* was generally favorable. Peter Corodimas, writing in *Bestsellers,* termed the book "superb." He added that the book is "an exercise in sheer terror and tight craftsmanship." In a review for the *New York Times,* Thomas J. Fleming was equally laudatory: "Mr. Levin's suspense is beautifully intertwined with everyday incidents; the delicate line between belief and disbelief is faultlessly drawn. . . . Up to [the denouement], we are with him entirely, admiring his skill and simultaneously searching out possible, probable and improbable explanations of how he is going to extricate the heroine." A movie adaptation filmed by Roman Polanski was also well received.

Levin followed *Rosemary's Baby* with another play entitled *Dr. Cook's Garden.* Although the melodrama contained many of the suspense elements found in Levin's novels, *Dr. Cook's Garden* received poor reviews and closed after four-teen performances. At the time, Levin related to *Playbill* that

while he was "having disaster after disaster in the theater, I always managed to do well on my books."

Both of Levin's next two novels had futuristic themes. *This Perfect Day* is about a society where human behavior is controlled by computer, while *The Stepford Wives* concerns an upper-middle class neighborhood where husbands get rid of undesirable wives and replace them with docile robot replicas. *This Perfect Day* was a moderate popular and critical success. "For enthusiasts of the genre, *This Perfect Day* offers a good deal less sci than fi, and a good deal more derivative than *deja vu,*" wrote Alex Keneas of *Newsweek.* He added: "But Levin shows, as he did with *Rosemary's Baby,* that he knows how to handle plot . . . so that his story breezes along." *The Stepford Wives* was a much bigger hit, appearing on numerous bestseller lists despite many negative reviews. Webster Schott of *Saturday Review* summed up critical reaction to the book when he wrote that "the most serious short-coming is the lack of density or complexity. Levin doesn't probe his plot or explore his conceit, robot women . . . ." Despite such criticism, a film version of the book was success-fully made by Columbia in 1975.

After Levin's next theatrical effort, *Veronica's Room,* met with mixed reviews and a short run, he returned to writing novels and produced another bestseller—*The Boys from Brazil.* Levin got the idea for *The Boys from Brazil* from an article on cloning. Levin told Andy Port of *Women's Wear*

Daily that the *New York Times* "had this article on cloning with a picture of Mozart and a picture of Hitler. Well, of course I ignored Mozart and started thinking about Hitler. Nazis make terrific villains." The premise of *The Boys from Brazil* concerns a bizarre plot by Nazi doctor Josef Mengele to create Hitler clones. Christopher Lehmann-Haupt of the *New York Times* reacted to the book by writing: "Ira Levin has come up with a wild one, certainly his most appallingly inventive plot since *Rosemary's Baby."* In 1978, Lawrence Olivier and Gregory Peck starred in a well-received film version of the novel.

Despite his previous bad luck with theatrical productions, Levin followed *The Boys from Brazil* with a stage thriller entitled *Deathtrap.* He was pleasantly surprised when his play about the machinations of a conniving, burned-out mystery writer became a huge hit on Broadway. Levin explained his love for writing thrillers, especially for the stage, in an interview with David Sterritt of the *Christian Science Monitor:* "I think [thrillers] touch deep emotional chords. . . . They touch our fears, anxieties, guilts. It's a way of exorcising them. It gives the emotions a workout." Like many of Levin's earlier works, *Deathtrap* was effectively adapted as a movie.

Levin's next two plays, *Break a Leg* and *Cantorial,* did not match the success of *Deathtrap.* Discouraged, Levin returned to novel writing and produced *Sliver,* a thriller about a sinister New York City apartment building. In his interview with Sterritt, Levin attempted to explain why he found the mystery genre so appealing: "When I started, my ambitions were much higher. . . . I was going to write serious plays and tragedies and the great American novel. But so far, all I've been doing is purely entertainment. . . . When I got out of college, I stopped reading things that weren't fun to read—I don't care what it is, if I'm not having a good time I put it aside. In the long run, I think Agatha Christie's body of work will be respected more than the books of many people who were considered literary lights at the time she was writing."

Although Levin's works do not share a common theme, he does admit that some of his writings have an autobiographical slant. "More than half of the things I've done concern a father-son relationship which obviously was very crucial to me," Levin told Mervyn Rothstein of the *New York Times.* He added: "I finally did work out a very good relationship with my father, but it was rough growing up. We had a lot of conflict, and I think it surfaced in many of my works. Even in *Rosemary's Baby,* which is about paternity, and *The Boys from Brazil,* which is really about paternity." Ultimately, Levin sees writing as a way of dealing with certain personal problems. In an interview with Douglas Fowler for the *Starmont Reader's Guide,* Levin mused: "I write, as I believe all artists perform their art, to exorcise internal conflicts and supplant reality with something more shapely and gratifying."

WORKS CITED:

Bannon, Barbara A., "Authors and Editors," *Publisher's Weekly,* May 22, 1967, p. 19.
Fowler, Douglas, "Ira Levin," *Starmont Reader's Guide,* Volume 34, Starmont House, 1988, p. 3.
Fields, Sidney, "Only Human," *Daily Mirror,* September 21, 1954, p. 24.
Gillespie, Alfred, "When the Audience Screams in Fright, It's Music (And Money) to Ira Levin," *People,* May 15, 1978, p. 56.

"Ira Levin: The Author of *Rosemary's Baby* and *The Boys from Brazil* Takes a Chance on Broadway with a New Thriller," *Playbill,* March, 1978.
Keneas, Alex, "Post-U," *Newsweek,* March 16, 1970, p. 108,
Lehmann-Haupt, Christopher, "Great Experiments in Living," *New York Times,* March 10, 1976, p. 34.
Levin, Ira, "Agent Adaptation without Representation," *New York Times,* June 24, 1956, p. 43.
Port, Andy, "Ira Levin's Eye for Evil," *Women's Wear Daily,* December 27, 1977, p. 12.
Rothstein, Mervyn, "It's a Compelling Ghost, and It Sings in Hebrew," *New York Times,* February 12, 1989, p. 28.
Sandoe, James, "Mystery and Suspense," *New York Herald Tribune,* October 18, 1953.
Schott, Webster, "Daughter of *Rosemary's Baby,"* *Saturday Review,* October 7 1972, p. 98.
Sterritt, David, "What's Involved in Concocting a Thriller," *Christian Science Monitor,* September 14, 1978.

FOR MORE INFORMATION SEE:

PERIODICALS

English Journal, May, 1969.
Fairpress, February 15, 1984.
Look, June 25, 1968.
Nation, April 3, 1983.
New Yorker, February 15, 1958; December 24, 1960; October 7, 1967; May 7, 1979; August 28, 1979; December 3, 1982; November 5, 1983.
New York Post, September 30, 1967.
New York Times, September 27, 1967; August 17, 1981.
New York Times Book Review, April 30, 1967.
Saturday Review, February 6, 1954.
Theater Arts, December, 1955.
Village Voice, November 8, 1973.

*   *   *

LEVINE, Betty K(rasne) 1933-
(Betty Krasne)

PERSONAL: Born May 25, 1933, in New York, NY; daughter of Israel (in wholesale grocery business) and Hannah (Goldstein) Krasne; married Robert Phillip Levine (an attorney), May 4, 1958; children: Thomas Krasne, Jonathan Newman, Kate Israel. *Education:* Mount Holyoke College, B.A. (cum laude), 1955; Columbia University, M.A. (with highest honors), 1957; Union Graduate School, Yellow Springs, Ohio, Ph.D., 1979.

ADDRESSES: Home—42 Eastern Dr., Ardsley, NY 10502. *Office*—Department of English and Humanities, Mercy College, 555 Broadway, Dobbs Ferry, NY 10522.

CAREER: Equitable Life Assurance Co., New York City, editorial assistant, 1955-56; Gimbel's (department store), New York City, assistant director of public relations, 1957-58, advertising copywriter, 1958-59; Mercy College, Dobbs Ferry, NY, lecturer, 1967-68, instructor, 1968-70, assistant professor, 1970-78, associate professor, 1979-82, professor of English and humanities, 1983—, director of honors programs, 1980—. Aspen Writer's Conference, member, 1978.

MEMBER: Modern Language Association of America, American Association of University Professors, National Collegiate Honors Council (northeast region president,

1990), Mercy College Faculty Association (president, 1979), Phi Beta Kappa, Kappa Delta Phi, Lamba Iota Tau.

AWARDS, HONORS: First prize, Greenburgh Poetry Competition, 1977, for "The Good Daughter"; faculty development grants, 1984, 1987, and 1990.

WRITINGS:

Hex House (novel), illustrated by Dan Marshall, Harper, 1973.
Hawk High (novel), illustrated by Louise Jefferson, Atheneum, 1980.
The Great Burgerland Disaster (novel), Atheneum, 1980.

Contributor of stories, poems, and articles to newspapers and magazines, including *Anima, New York Times, Scarsdale Inquirer, The Quarterly, Greenburgh Inquirer,* and *Litchfield County Times.*

The Great Burgerland Disaster was translated into Swedish in 1986.

WORK IN PROGRESS: Dog Days, a novel for young readers; *Playing the Part,* poems; *Another Time in the Same Place,* a novel; and, under name Betty Krasne, *Beware of Death by Water: A Thematic Study of Women in Myth and Fiction.*

SIDELIGHTS: Betty K. Levine told *SATA:* "All my writings reflect an interest in exploring the role of women in society and in examining the way literature, interacting with life, reflects traditional roles and expresses new models. In addition, my fiction always seems to involve places where I have lived. A sense of place plays a significant part in each work of fiction.

"My writing has also tended to change in direct relation to the ages of our children. As the three of them grow older, so do the characters in the novels, whose concerns thus become more sophisticated and complex.

"My present interest in fiction is short stories, and the audience I am writing for is adults. On a sabbatical, which I spent living in France, I wrote four stories, which I have since added to and tinkered with. My novels for young readers were largely tales of empowerment, of new female heroes, of people who take the existing conditions of their lives and somehow break through the status quo; my short stories, however, are about adults who, though they care very much for each other, are destined to be on slightly different wavelengths. The elements common throughout most of the writing—both the long fiction for children and the shorter works for adults—are humor and a strong sense of place."

*   *   *

LIFTON, Robert Jay 1926-

PERSONAL: Born May 16, 1926, in Brooklyn, NY; son of Harold A. (in business) and Ciel (a homemaker; maiden name, Roth) Lifton; married Betty Jean Kirschner (a writer), March 1, 1952; children: Kenneth Jay, Natasha Karen. *Education:* Attended Cornell University, 1942-44; New York Medical College, M.D., 1948. *Religion:* Jewish. *Hobbies and other interests:* Tennis, films.

ROBERT JAY LIFTON

ADDRESSES: Home—New York, NY. *Agent*—Lynn Nesbit, Janklow and Nesbit Associates, 598 Madison Ave., New York, NY 10022. *Office*—John Jay College of Criminal Justice of the City University of New York, 899 Tenth Ave., New York, NY 10019.

CAREER: Licensed to practice medicine in New York and Connecticut; certified by National Board of Medical Examiners, 1949. Jewish Hospital of Brooklyn, New York City, intern, 1948-49; State University Medical Center, Veterans Administration Program, Northport and Brooklyn, NY, resident in psychiatry, 1949-51; Washington School of Psychiatry, Washington, DC, member of faculty, 1954-55; Massachusetts General Hospital, Boston, MA, associate in psychiatry, 1956-60; Harvard University, Cambridge, MA, associate in East Asian studies, 1956-61; Yale University, New Haven, CT, Foundations' Fund for Research Associate Professor, 1961-67, Foundations' Fund for Research Professor of Psychiatry, 1967-85; Yale-New Haven Hospital, New Haven, associate in psychiatry, 1961—; City University of New York, John Jay College of Criminal Justice and Graduate School and University Center, New York City, distinguished professor of psychiatry and psychology, 1985—, director of the Center on Violence and Human Survival, 1986—. Walter Reed Army Institute of Research, research psychiatrist, 1956; research associate in psychiatry, Massachusetts General Hospital, 1956-61, and Tokyo University, 1960-61; Boston Psychoanalytic Institute, candidate, 1957-60; Wellfleet Psychohistory Group, organizer and coordinator, 1966—; Max Planck Institute for Psychiatry and Psychotherapy, visiting fellow, 1978-79; Harvard Medical School Nuclear Psychology Program, senior research associate, 1985. Visiting lecturer at various colleges and universities, including University of Michigan and Tulane, Duquesne, and Duke universities; lecturer at Harvard and Cornell universities.

Member of Yale University Council on East Asian Studies, 1964-75, and American Psychiatric Association Task Force to Monitor Nuclear Developments, 1982-85. Consultant to New York Bar Association Committee on the Invasion of Privacy, 1963-64, to Columbia University seminars on modern Japan and Oriental thought and religion, 1965—, to U.S. Senate Committee on Veterans, 1971, to Williams & Connolly, 1973-74, and to Arnold & Porter, 1977-78, both on 1972 Buffalo Flood Creek disaster, to Harmon & Weiss and David Berger on psychological effects of 1979 Three Mile Island nuclear accident, 1980-81, and to U.S. House Select Committee on Children, Youth, and Families on children's fear of war, 1984; behavioral studies consultant to National Institutes of Mental Health, 1962-64; consultant on films *Home: A Documentary about Four Families* and *Threads*. *Military service:* U.S. Air Force, 1951-53; became captain.

MEMBER: International Society of Political Psychology, International Physicians for the Prevention of Nuclear War, American Academy of Arts and Sciences (fellow), American Academy of Psychoanalysis, American Psychiatric Association (fellow), American Anthropological Association, Association for Asian Studies, Physicians for Social Responsibility (member of board of directors, 1981—).

AWARDS, HONORS: Asia Foundation fellow (Hong Kong), 1954; Washington School of Psychiatry research fellow, 1954-55; Walter Reed Army Institute of Research fellow in psychiatry, 1956; Ford Foundation and Foundations' Fund for Research in Psychiatry fellowship, 1956-61; National Book Award for science and Van Wyck Brooks Award for nonfiction, both 1969, for *Death in Life: Survivors of Hiroshima;* New York Medical College alumni medal, 1970; public service award, New York Society of Clinical Psychologists, 1970; William V. Silverberg Memorial Lecture Award, American Academy of Psychoanalysis, 1971; St. Peter's College Centennial Award, 1972; Karen Horney Lecture Award, Association for the Advancement of Psychoanalysis, 1972; distinguished service award, Society for Adolescent Psychology, 1972; Mount Airy Foundation Gold Medal for excellence in psychiatry, 1973; Hofstra University faculty distinguished scholar award, 1973; Nobel lectureship, Gustavus Adolphus College, 1974; National Book Award nomination, 1974, for *Home from the War;* Hiroshima Gold Medal, 1975; *Living and Dying* was named a New York Public Library Book for the Teen Age, 1980; Yad Vashem Medal, 1980; New Jersey SANE Peace Award, 1982; John Simon Guggenheim Memorial Foundation fellow, 1983-84; Gandhi Peace Award, 1984; Martin Luther King Memorial Prize, 1985, for *In a Dark Time;* Bertrand Russell Society Award, 1985; Holocaust Memorial Award, New York Society of Clinical Psychologists, 1986; Nuclear Psychology Research Award, Nuclear Psychology Program of Harvard University, 1986; Oskar Pfister Award, American Psychiatric Association, 1987; Brit HaDorot Covenant of the Generations Award, Shalom Center, 1987; *Los Angeles Times* Book Award for history, and National Jewish Book Award for work on the Holocaust, both 1987, for *The Nazi Doctors: Medical Killing and the Psychology of Genocide;* Lisl and Leo Eitinger Award, University of Oslo, Norway, 1988, for

scholarly work on the Holocaust and genocide. Honorary degrees from Lawrence University, 1971, Merrimack College, 1973, Wilmington College, 1975, New York Medical College, 1977, Maryville College, 1983, Marlboro College, 1983, University of Vermont, 1984, University of New Haven, 1987, and Universitaet Muenchen, Munich, Germany, 1988.

WRITINGS:

Thought Reform and the Psychology of Totalism: A Study of "Brainwashing" in China, Norton, 1961.
Death in Life: Survivors of Hiroshima, Random House, 1968.
Revolutionary Immortality: Mao Tse-Tung and the Chinese Cultural Revolution, Random House, 1968.
Birds (cartoons), Random House, 1969.
Boundaries: Psychological Man in Revolution, Random House, 1970.
History and Human Survival: Essays on the Young and the Old, Survivors and the Dead, Peace and War, and on Contemporary Psychohistory, Random House, 1970.
Home from the War: Vietnam Veterans—Neither Victims nor Executioners, Simon & Schuster, 1973.
(And illustrator; with Eric Olson) *Living and Dying,* Praeger, 1974.
The Life of the Self: Toward a New Psychology, Simon & Schuster, 1976.
Closing the Circle (film), Harcourt, 1976.
PsychoBirds (cartoons), Countryman, 1978.
(With Shuichi Kato and Michael Reich) *Six Lives/Six Deaths: Portraits from Modern Japan,* Yale University Press, 1979.
The Broken Connection: On Death and the Continuity of Life, Simon & Schuster, 1979.
(With Richard A. Falk) *Indefensible Weapons: The Political and Psychological Case against Nuclearism,* Basic Books, 1982.
The Nazi Doctors: Medical Killing and the Psychology of Genocide, Basic Books, 1986.
The Future of Immortality, and Other Essays for a Nuclear Age, Basic Books, 1987.
(With Eric Markusen) *The Genocidal Mentality: Nazi Holocaust and Nuclear Threat,* Basic Books, 1990.

EDITOR

The Woman in America, Houghton, 1965.
America and the Asian Revolutions, Transaction Books, 1966.
(With Falk and Gabriel Kolko) *Crimes of War,* Random House, 1971.
(With Olson) *Explorations in Psychohistory: The Wellfleet Papers of Erik Erikson, Robert Jay Lifton, and Kenneth Kenniston,* Simon & Schuster, 1975.
(With Eric Chivian, Susanna Chivian, and John E. Mack) *Last Aid: Medical Dimensions of Nuclear War,* Freeman Press, 1982.
(With Nicholas Humphrey) *In a Dark Time,* Harvard University Press, 1984.

Contributor to *New York Times, New York Review of Books, Guardian, Dagens Nyheter, Daedalus, American Scholar, New Republic, Partisan Review, Journal of Asian Studies, Psychology Today, American Journal of Psychiatry,* and other professional journals in the fields of psychiatry, psychology, history, and Asian studies. Consulting editor, *Suicide and Life-Threatening Behavior,* 1974—; member of editorial board, *American Journal of Drug and Alcohol Abuse,* 1975—; member of editorial advisory board, *International Encyclopedia of Psychiatry, Psychoanalysis, and Psychology,* 1975—; member of board of editors, *Psychohistory Review,* 1977—; mem-

(From *Living and Dying,* by Robert Jay Lifton and Eric Olson, illustration by Lifton.)

ber of editorial board, *Journal of Political Psychology,* 1981—; member of advisory board, *Zygon: Journal of Religion and Science,* 1981—.

ADAPTATIONS: Death in Life: Survivors of Hiroshima was adapted by Robert Vas for the film *To Die, To Live—The Survivors of Hiroshima,* British Broadcasting Corporation, 1975.

WORK IN PROGRESS: Continued study of the survivor theme; the psychology of death and the continuity of life; the relationship between death imagery and violence, especially in American society. Specific studies on how individual, social, and historic change affect Japanese youth and innovative young professionals.

SIDELIGHTS: Robert Jay Lifton is a psychiatrist and author who examines the ways in which human beings cope with stress and tragedy. He has written more than twenty books on his studies of people who have lived through the bombing of Hiroshima, the Holocaust, and the Vietnam War. While his writings deal with complex social, historical, and psychological subjects, they have taken on a special significance for a generation of young readers who live in fear of the destruction of the world by nuclear war.

Death in Life: Survivors of Hiroshima is among Lifton's early books on the impact of history on the individual. The book is a study of the survivors of the atom bomb that was dropped on the city of Hiroshima, Japan, at the end of World War II. In many cases, the survivors experienced feelings of guilt and sadness at living through the bombing that killed so many of their friends and family members. Similarly, as noted in Lifton's other works, survivors of the Holocaust and veterans of the Vietnam War frequently show signs of severe psychological stress.

Lifton believes that historical tragedies occur because people allow themselves to commit horrible acts. During the Holocaust of World War II, for instance, Jewish people were tortured and killed by Nazis under the direction of German leader Adolf Hitler. When writing his 1986 book *The Nazi Doctors,* Lifton interviewed doctors who participated in the Holocaust. The doctors had experimented on and murdered Jewish people who were imprisoned in concentration camps. As a Jew, Lifton found his conversations with these physicians particularly difficult. "I experienced waves of pain, agitation and resentment at hearing their experiences," he told William Goldstein in a *Publishers Weekly* interview.

Lifton suggests that we can begin to comprehend what makes ordinary people capable of performing gruesome, evil actions through an understanding of the concept of "doubling," the ability of a highly stressed individual to psychologically split himself into two selves. "Convinced of the rightness and urgency of their mission," explained Sheila Tobias in the *New York Times Book Review,* these other selves then feel that it is their duty to carry out even the most inhumane tasks, such as torture and murder. In an interview with Walter W. Ross, Lifton used the example of Nazi doctors to clarify the meaning of "doubling": "A Nazi doctor at [the concentration camp] Auschwitz would adjust to the Auschwitz environment and form an Auschwitz self while at the same time he would retain his prior self when he went back and visited his family outside and was again a father and a husband."

In *The Genocidal Mentality*, Lifton compares the reality of the Holocaust with the threat of nuclear disaster. The author claims that our reliance on nuclear weapons as a symbol of national power is dangerous. He further suggests that the same thought processes that allowed Nazi doctors to experiment on and kill Jews during World War II allows nuclear scientists to engineer the destruction of the world.

For nearly thirty years, Lifton has been concerned about the effects of the threat of nuclear war on young people. In *Living and Dying*, first published in 1974, he encourages people to view death as a normal part of life. Lifton suggests that if today's adolescents become more comfortable with the concept of death, they can achieve a sense of well-being—even in the face of nuclear disaster. A more recent book, *The Future of Immortality*, deals with the uncertainties all people have about the future of the world and the human race. In an article for *Newsweek*, David Gates summarized Lifton's main worry: that "the threat of nuclear holocaust . . . has done unique psychic damage" to human beings.

Although the possibility of nuclear warfare may have already caused psychological injury in people, Lifton sees reason to believe that there is a growing opposition to an unrestricted arms race: "Even though our nuclear policies haven't changed as much as one would have hoped, it has been recorded by various surveys and polls that there's been a significant and gratifying increase in awareness of nuclear danger, and an increasing conviction on the part of Americans in general that something should be done," he remarked to Ross.

In his conversation with Ross, Lifton said that he takes "a psychological approach to historical questions." *New York Times* writer Christopher Lehmann-Haupt noted that Lifton's conclusions are important because they show "that even in contemporary situations, history and psychology cannot be separated, and that therefore psychiatrists must . . . take history into account when treating their patients."

WORKS CITED:

Gates, David, review of *The Future of Immortality*, *Newsweek*, March 2, 1987, p. 76.
Goldstein, William, "PW Interviews: Robert Jay Lifton," *Publishers Weekly*, November 7, 1986, pp. 50-51.
Lehmann-Haupt, Christopher, review of *Home from the War*, *New York Times*, August 6, 1973, p. 29.
Ross, Walter, interview with Robert Jay Lifton, *Contemporary Authors New Revision Series*, Volume 27, Gale, 1989, pp. 298-301.
Tobias, Sheila, "The Seeds of Our Own Destruction?," *New York Times Book Review*, May 27, 1990, p. 19.

FOR MORE INFORMATION SEE:

PERIODICALS

Chicago Tribune Book World, October 24, 1982; December 12, 1982.
Globe and Mail (Toronto), November 1, 1986.
Harper's, February, 1983.

Los Angeles Times Book Review, January 24, 1980; September 9, 1984; October 12, 1986; October 18, 1987; November 8, 1987; March 20, 1988.
Nation, May 6, 1968; November 9, 1970.
Newsweek, February 19, 1968; October 7, 1968; June 18, 1973.
New York Review of Books, March 25, 1968; January 16, 1969; June 28, 1973; October 31, 1974; May 28, 1987.
New York Times, September 30, 1968; February 6, 1970; July 26, 1979; November 4, 1979, March 1, 1981; March 28, 1981; April 13, 1981; March 15, 1982; September 25, 1986.
New York Times Book Review, March 31, 1968; August 2, 1970; December 6, 1970; June 24, 1973; December 2, 1973; March 10, 1974; July 21, 1974; November 4, 1979; November 25, 1979; July 27, 1980; March 1, 1981; October 10, 1982; December 26, 1982; January 16, 1983; December 18, 1983; February 17, 1985; October 5, 1986; April 5, 1987; March 20, 1988.
Saturday Review, February 3, 1968; March 15, 1969; February 21, 1970; February 20, 1971; September 25, 1971.
Time, February 16, 1968; October 18, 1968; July 9, 1973; June 25, 1979.
Times Literary Supplement, April 10, 1969; July 18, 1975; December 7, 1979; June 12, 1987.
Village Voice, August 15, 1974; October 14, 1986.
Washington Post Book World, March 24, 1968; October 20, 1968; January 25, 1970; June 24, 1973; May 16, 1976; April 1, 1979; November 5, 1979; December 23, 1979; February 20, 1983; October 5, 1986.

* * *

LYONS, Marcus
See BLISH, James (Benjamin)

* * *

MacDOUGAL, John
See BLISH, James (Benjamin)

* * *

MAETERLINCK, Maurice 1862-1949

PERSONAL: Given name sometimes transliterated Mauritius or Mooris; born August 29, 1862, in Ghent, Belgium; died of a heart attack, May 6, 1949, in Nice, France; son of Polydore-Jacques-Marie-Bernard (a notary, land owner, and horticulturist) and Mathilde-Colette-Francoise (Van den Bossche) Maeterlinck; companion of Georgette Leblanc (an opera singer and actress), c. 1895-1918; married Renee Dahon (an actress), February 15, 1919. *Education:* University of Ghent, doctor of law and registered as barrister, both 1885.

CAREER: Playwright, poet, short story writer, and essayist. Practiced law in Ghent, Belgium, 1886-89.

MEMBER: Belgian Royal Academy.

AWARDS, HONORS: Triennial Prize for Dramatic Literature, Belgian Government, 1891 (Maeterlinck declined award), 1903, for *Monna Vanna*, and 1910, for *The Blue Bird;* Nobel Prize for Literature, 1911; Grand Officier, 1912, and Grand Croix, 1920, de l'Ordre de Leopold; named Count of the Kingdom of Belgium, 1932; elected to the French Academy, 1937; Medal of the French Language, 1948; honorary degrees from Glasgow University, 1919, University of Brussels, 1920, and Rollins Park College, 1941.

WRITINGS:

PLAYS

The Princess Maleine (five-act), translated by Richard Hovey, Dodd, 1913 (published in French as *La Princesse Maleine,* Vanmelle [Ghent, Belgium], 1889).

The Blind [and] *The Intruder,* translated by Mary Viele, W. H. Morrison, 1891 (published in French as *Les Aveugles* [contains *L'Intruse* and *Les Aveugles; L'Intruse* produced in Paris at Theatre d'Art, 1892], P. Lacomblez [Brussels], 1890).

The Seven Princesses, translated by Charlotte Porter and Helen A. Clarke, published in *Poet Lore,* 1894 (published in French as *Les Sept Princesses,* P. Lacomblez, 1891).

Pelleas and Melisande (five-act), translated by Erving Winslow, Crowell, 1894 (published in French as *Pelleas et Melisande* [produced at Theatre des Bouffes-Parisiens, 1893], P. Lacomblez, 1892).

"*Alladine and Palomides,*" "*Interior,*" *and* "*The Death of Tintagiles,*" translated by William Archer and Alfred Sutro, Duckworth, 1899, published as *Three Little Dramas:* "*Alladine and Palomides,*" "*Interior,*" *and* "*The Death of Tintagiles,*" Brentano's, 1915 (published in French as "*Alladine et Palomides,*" "*Interieur,*" *et* "*La Mort de Tintagiles*": *Trois Petits Drames pour marionnettes,* Ed. Deman [Brussels], 1894; the three plays have also been published separately).

(Translator into French) John Ford, *Annabella: 'Tis Pity She's a Whore* (five-act), P. Ollendorff (Paris), 1895.

MAURICE MAETERLINCK

Aglavaine and Selysette (five-act), translated by Alfred Sutro, Grant Richards (London), 1897, Dodd, 1911 (published in French as *Aglavaine et Selysette,* Mercure de France [Paris], 1896).

Sister Beatrice [and] *Ariadne and Barbe-Bleue,* translated by Bernard Miall, G. Allen (London), 1901, Dodd, 1902 (both published in French as *Soeur Beatrice* and *Ariane et Barbe-Bleue* in *Theatre* [also see below], Volume 3, Ed. Deman, 1902; the former produced in Paris in 1915; the latter produced in Paris at Opera-Comique, 1907; music by Paul Dukas).

Theatre (collection), three volumes, Ed. Deman, 1901-02.

Monna Vanna (three-act), translated by A. I. Du Pont Coleman, Harper, 1903 (published in French under same title by E. Fasquelle [Paris] and produced at Theatre de l'Oevre, both 1902).

Joyzelle (five-act), translated by Clarence Stratton, published in *Poet Lore,* 1905 (published in French under same title by E. Fasquelle and produced in Paris at Theatre du Gymnase, both 1903).

The Miracle of Saint Anthony (two-act), translated by Ralph Roeder, published in New York, 1916 (published in German as *Das Wunder des heiligen Antonius,* E. Diederichs, 1904; published in French as *Le Miracle de Saint Antoine,* Edouard-Joseph, 1919).

The Blue Bird (six-act), translated by Alexander Teixeira de Mattos, Dodd, 1909 (published in French as *L'Oiseau bleu* [produced in Moscow in 1908], E. Fasquelle, 1909).

(Translator into French) William Shakespeare, *Macbeth* (produced in 1909), Illustration (Paris), 1909.

Mary Magdalene (three-act), translated by Alexander Teixeira de Mattos, Dodd, 1910 (published in French as *Marie-Magdeleine* [produced at Theatre du Chatelet, 1913], Charpentier et Fasquelle, 1913).

The Burgomaster of Stilemonde (three-act), translated by Alexander Teixeira de Mattos, Dodd, 1918 (published in French as *Le Bourgmestre de Stilmonde* [produced in Buenes Aires in 1918], Edouard-Joseph, 1919; also published as *Le Bourgmestre de Stilmonde* [suivi de] *Le Sel de la vie* [the latter, two-act; title means "The Salt of the Earth"], E. Fasquelle, 1920).

The Betrothal: A Sequel to "The Blue Bird" (five-act; produced in New York City at Shubert Theatre, 1918), translated by Alexander Teixeira de Mattos, Dodd, 1918 (published in French as *Les Fiancailles,* E. Fasquelle, 1922), children's edition published as *The Blue Bird Chooses: Being the Story of Maurice Maeterlinck's Play "The Betrothal,"* translated by de Mattos, Dodd, 1919, another children's edition published as *Tyltyl: Being the Story of Maurice Maeterlinck's Play "The Betrothal,"* translated by de Mattos, illustrated by Herbert Paus, Dodd, 1920.

The Cloud That Lifted [and] *The Power of the Dead* (the former, three-act; the latter, four-act), translated by F. M. Atkinson, Century, 1923 (the former published in French as *Le Malheur passe,* A. Fayard [Paris], 1925; the latter published in French as *La Puissance des morts,* A. Fayard, 1926).

Berniquel, published in *Candide,* 1926, Editions des Cahiers Libre (Paris), 1929.

Marie-Victoire (four-act), A. Fayard, 1927.

Juda de Kerioth, A. Fayard, 1929.

La Princesse Isabelle (produced in Paris at Theatre de la Renaissance, 1935), E. Fasquelle, 1935.

Jeanne d'Arc, Editions du Rocher (Monaco), 1948.

Theatre inedit (collection; contains *L'Abbe Setubal* [two-act], *Les Tro Justiciers,* and *Le Jugement dernier* [three-act]), Del Duca (Paris), 1959.

Maeterlinck as a schoolboy at the College Sainte-Barbe.

Plays have been published in various combinations, in collections, in periodicals, and in many languages.

OTHER

Serres chaudes (poems; title means "Hothouses"), L. Vanier (Paris), 1889, published as *Serres chaudes* [suivies de] *Quinze Chansons,* Calmann-Levy (Paris), 1900.

(Translator into French) Jan van Ruysbroek, *L'Ornement des noces spirituelles de Ruysbroek l'Admirable,* P. Lacomblez, 1891 (published in English as *Ruysbroek and the Mystics,* translated by Jane T. Stoddart, Hodder & Stoughton, 1894).

(Translator into French) Novalis, *Les Disciples a Sais et les Fragments de Novalis,* P. Lacomblez, 1895.

Twelve Songs (poems), translated by Martin Schuetze, illustrated by Charles Doudelet, Ralph Fletcher Seymore Co., 1912, published as *Poems,* translated by Bernard Miall, Dodd, 1915 (published in French as *Douze Chansons,* P. V. Stock [Paris], 1896).

The Treasure of the Humble (essays), translated by Alfred Sutro, Dodd, 1897, published as *The Inner Beauty,* Holt, 1911, published as *On Emerson and Other Essays,* translated by Montrose J. Moses, Dodd, 1912 (published in French as *Le Tresor des humbles,* Societe du Mercure de France [Paris], 1896, 76th edition, 1912).

Wisdom and Destiny (essays), translated by Alfred Sutro, Dodd, 1898 (published in French as *La Sagesse et la destinee,* E. Fasquelle, 1898).

The Life of the Bee (essays; also see below), translated by Alfred Sutro, Dodd, 1901 (published in French as *La Vie des abeilles,* E. Fasquelle, 1901), children's edition published as *The Children's Life of the Bee,* selected and

arranged by Sutro and Herschel Williams, illustrated by Edward J. Detmold, Dodd, 1919.

The Buried Temple (essays), translated by Alfred Sutro, Dodd, 1902 (published in French as *Le Temple enseveli,* E. Fasquelle, 1902).

Thoughts from Maeterlinck, chosen and arranged by Esther Stella Sutro, Dodd, 1903.

The Double Garden (essays; also see below), translated by Alexander Teixeira de Mattos, Dodd, 1904 (published in French as *Le Double Jardin,* E. Fasquelle, 1904).

Our Friend the Dog, illustrated by Paul J. Meylan, decorations by Charles B. Falls, Dodd, 1904, published in England as *My Dog,* translated by Alexander Teixeira de Mattos, illustrated by G. Vernon Stokes, G. Allen, 1906.

Old Fashioned Flowers and Other Out-of-Door Studies (includes portions of *The Double Garden*), illustrated by Falls, Dodd, 1905.

The Swarm (excerpt from *The Life of the Bee*), Dodd, 1906.

Chrysanthemums and Other Essays (includes portions of *The Double Garden*), translated by Alexander Teixeira de Mattos, Dodd, 1907.

The Intelligence of Flowers (essays; also see below), translated by Alexander Teixeira de Mattos, Dodd, 1907 (also published under title *The Measure of the Hours;* published in French as *L'Intelligence des fleurs,* E. Fasquelle, 1907).

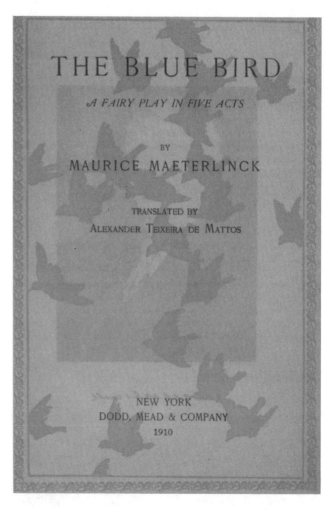

THE BLUE BIRD

A FAIRY PLAY IN FIVE ACTS

BY

MAURICE MAETERLINCK

TRANSLATED BY

ALEXANDER TEIXEIRA DE MATTOS

NEW YORK
DODD, MEAD & COMPANY
1910

Title page from an early American edition of Maurice Maeterlinck's acclaimed "fairy play" *The Blue Bird*.

The Leaf of Olive (includes portions of *The Double Garden*), translated by Alexander Teixeira de Mattos, Dodd, 1908.

Morceaux choisis, introduction by Georgette Leblanc, Nelson (Paris), 1910.

Death (essays), translated by Alexander Teixeira de Mattos, Methuen, 1911, Dodd, 1912, published as *Our Eternity,* 1913 (published in French as *La Mort,* E. Fasquelle, 1913).

Hours of Gladness (contains *The Double Garden* and *The Intelligence of Flowers*), translated by Alexander Teixeira de Mattos, illustrated by Edward J. Detmold, Dodd, 1912.

News of Spring and Other Nature Studies (excerpts from *The Double Garden* and *The Intelligence of Flowers*), translated by Alexander Teixeira de Mattos, illustrated by Edward J. Detmold, Dodd, 1913.

The Massacre of the Innocents, translated by Alfred Allinson, Allen & Unwin, 1914 (title in French is *Le Massacre des innocents;* also see below).

The Unknown Guest (also see below), translated by Alexander Teixeira de Mattos, Dodd, 1914 (published in French as *L'Hote inconnu,* E. Fasquelle, 1917).

The Wrack of the Storm (essays; also see below), translated by Alexander Teixeira de Mattos, Dodd, 1916 (published in French as *Les Debris de la guerre,* E. Fasquelle, 1916).

The Light Beyond (excerpts from *The Unknown Guest* and *The Wrack of the Storm*), translated by Alexander Teixeira de Mattos, Dodd, 1917.

Deux contes: Le Massacre des innocents, Onirologie (stories), G. Cres (Paris), 1918.

(With Cyriel Buysse and L. Dumont-Wilden) *La Belgique en guerre* (title means "Belgium at War"), E. Van Hammee (Brussels), 1918, translated into English, 1918.

Mountain Paths (essays), translated by Alexander Teixeira de Mattos, Dodd, 1919 (published in French as *Les Sentiers dans la montagne,* E. Fasquelle, 1919).

The Great Secret (essays), translated by Bernard Miall, Century, 1922 (published in French as *Le Grand Secret,* E. Fasquelle, 1921).

Ancient Egypt, translated by Alfred Sutro, Allen & Unwin, 1925 (published in French as *En Egypte,* Aux Horizons de France, 1928).

The Life of the White Ant (essays), translated by Alfred Sutro, Allen & Unwin, 1927 (published in French as *La Vie des termites,* E. Fasquelle, 1926).

En Sicile et en Calabre, S. Kra (Paris), 1927.

The Life of Space (essays), translated by Bernard Miall, Dodd, 1928 (published in French as *La Vie de l'espace,* E. Fasquelle, 1928).

The Magic of the Stars, translated by Alfred Sutro, Dodd, 1930 (published in French as *La Grande Feerie: Immensite de l'univers, notre terre, influences siderales,* E. Fasquelle, 1929).

The Life of the Ant (essays), translated by Bernard Miall, John Day, 1930 (published in French as *La Vie des fourmis,* E. Fasquelle, 1930).

Pigeons [and] *Spiders (The Water Spider),* translated by Bernard Miall, Allen & Unwin, 1934, Norton, 1936 (published in French as *L'Araignee de verre,* E. Fasquelle, 1932).

The Supreme Law (essays), translated by K. S. Shelvankar, Dutton, 1935 (published in French as *La Grande Loi,* E. Fasquelle, 1933).

Before the Great Silence, translated by Bernard Miall, Allen & Unwin, 1935 (published in French as *Avant le grand silence,* E. Fasquelle, 1934).

The Hour-Glass, translated by Bernard Miall, Frederick A. Stokes, 1936 (published in French as *Le Sablier,* E. Fasquelle, 1936).

L'Ombre des ailes (essays), E. Fasquelle, 1936.

Devant Dieu (essays), E. Fasquelle, 1937.

La Grande Porte (essays), E. Fasquelle, 1939.

The Great Beyond, translated by Marta K. Neufeld and Renee Spodhem, Philosophical Library, 1947 (published in French as *L'Autre Monde; ou, Le Cadran stellaire,* Editions de la Maison Francaise [New York], 1942).

Bulles bleues: Souvenirs heureux, Editions du Rocher, 1948.

Also author of *Le Mystere de la justice,* 1900. Author of numerous prefaces to other books. Works have been published in various combinations; in collections, including *Insectes et fleurs,* 1954; in periodicals; and in many languages.

ADAPTATIONS: The Blue Bird has been adapted into books for children, including *The Children's Blue Bird,* by Georgette Leblanc, translated by Alexander Teixeira de Mattos, illustrated by Herbert Paus, Dodd, 1913; and *The Bluebird for Children: The Wonderful Adventures of Tyltyl and Mytyl in Search of Happiness,* by Leblanc, edited and arranged for schools by Frederick Orville Perkins, translated by de Mattos, Silver, Burdett & Co., 1913. *The Blue Bird* also has been adapted as motion pictures of the same title, including a silent film, produced by Paramount, 1918; a movie starring Shirley Temple, produced by Twentieth Century-Fox, 1940; a film featuring Elizabeth Taylor and Jane Fonda, produced by Twentieth Century-Fox, 1976; and an animated cartoon. Some of Maeterlinck's plays have been adapted as sound recordings.

SIDELIGHTS: Recipient of the Nobel Prize for literature in 1911, Maurice Maeterlinck was a dramatist, poet, and essayist renowned for his highly symbolic works contemplating the mysteries of human existence. He is best known among young readers for *The Blue Bird* (*L'Oiseau bleu*), his acclaimed play exhibiting fairy tale qualities. Immensely popular, the play spawned the common phrase "The blue bird of happiness" and has been adapted into illustrated books and popular films for children.

Born in Ghent, Belgium, in 1862, Maeterlinck descended from a prosperous Flemish family whose name dated back to the fourteenth century. In Flemish, Maeterlinck means "the measurer," in honor of an ancestor who during a famine in 1395 measured out a few ladles of grain to each citizen in his town. Maeterlinck was adventurous and active as a boy, frequently engaging in vigorous physical exercise. Though generally content while growing up, the author often recounted feeling like "the black sheep" in his conservative, Catholic family, and he once stated that his parents never finished reading any work he wrote.

Maeterlinck began his formal education at a primary school run by local nuns. After the age of seven, though, boys were no longer welcome at the school, for the nuns wished to educate only girls of upper-class families. Maeterlinck subsequently was taught at home by a succession of tutors from England and Germany, and he learned to speak several languages. His father later sent him to the highly reputed Jesuit College de Sainte-Barbe, where two Nobel Prize nominees in literature had been educated. There Maeterlinck became close friends with aspiring writers Gregoire Le Roy and Charles Van Lerberghe. The three formed a literary trio, inspiring, encouraging, and critiquing each other's writings.

Shirley Temple starred in the first Twentieth Century-Fox version of Maurice Maeterlinck's *The Blue Bird*, released in 1940.

Maeterlinck's first literary endeavors exhibited themes of medievalism, a preoccupation with death, and a yearning to escape reality, motifs that would dominate his writing career.

One of Maeterlinck's early poems appeared in the November, 1883, issue of the periodical *Jeune Belgique*. His second submission of poetry, however, met with harsh rejection. A letter from the magazine's editor, according to W. D. Halls in *Maurice Maeterlinck: A Study of His Life and Thought,* read: "M. Maeter.—bad, your verses to your friend Charles V[an] L[erberghe], supremely bad."

Maeterlinck's parents strongly disapproved of their son devoting himself full-time to poetry, and they sent him to law school. On the pretext of preparing for the French bar exam, he convinced his father to support him for a year in Paris. Maeterlinck spent virtually all of his time writing. In addition, he and his friends Le Roy and Van Lerberghe spent

much time associating with the symbolists, a group of artists who abandoned realism and instead used symbols to convey their concern with the puzzle of human existence and destiny.

Maeterlinck was described by a fellow poet in the mid-1880s as "beardless, with short hair, protruding forehead, clear, distinct eyes, with a straightforward gaze, his face harshly set, the whole denoting will-power, decision, stubbornness, a real Flemish face, with undertones of reverie and colourful sensibility," the description was quoted by Halls. "At heart a taciturn person, who is very reserved, but whose friendship must be reliable." In Paris Maeterlinck's nickname was "*le taiseux,*" which means the silent one.

Despite literary distractions, Maeterlinck earned his law degree. In 1886 he returned to Ghent and began, halfheartedly, to practice litigation. He found the job especially distasteful, and he later admitted that courtroom procedures were so traumatic that all his life he retained a dread of public speaking. He divided his time between Ghent and his family's country home in Oostacker, Belgium, where he wrote, gardened, cycled, rowed, and kept bees. His poems written during this period were published in anthologies and quarterlies.

In 1888, with money from his family and help from several friends, Maeterlinck published a poetry collection, *Serres chaudes* (title means "Hothouses"). He and his friends produced the book themselves on a small hand machine, working at night because the borrowed type machine was needed in the print shop during the day. Though the volume resulted neither in income nor critical notice, *Serres chaudes* is nonetheless significant. Death-obsessed, the poems are full of spiritual angst and bleak imagery. In a letter to poet Emile Verhaeren, Maeterlinck, as quoted by Halls, wrote: "I think that illness, sleep, and death are feasts of the flesh, profound, mysterious, and not understood; I think there is much to seek and find in this domain . . . and that the hospital is perhaps the temple of Isis."

In 1889 Maeterlinck wrote his first play, *The Princess Maleine* (*La Princesse Maleine*), which would catapult him to international fame. After its publication in a Belgian literary review, Maeterlinck sent a copy to the pioneering symbolist poet Stephane Mallarme in Paris. Mallarme was so impressed that he sent the play to the influential French dramatist and critic Octave Mirbeau. "Maeterlinck," according to Mirbeau as quoted by Halls, "has written a masterpiece, . . . an admirable and pure and eternal masterpiece, a masterpiece that suffices to render a name immortal and to cause that name to be blessed by all those that hunger after the beautiful and the great; a masterpiece such as honourable, tormented artists have sometimes dreamed, in moments of enthusiasm, of writing, and as they have never written hitherto. In short, . . . Maeterlinck has given us the work of this age most full of genius, and the most extraordinary and most simple as well, comparable and—shall I dare say it?—superior in beauty to what is most beautiful in Shakespeare."

From 1890 to 1900 Maeterlinck produced a succession of major plays; among the more well-known are *The Intruder* (*L'Intruse*), *The Blind* (*Les Aveugle*) and *Pelleas and Melisande* (*Pelleas et Melisande*), the latter of which is often considered his masterpiece. He also created three plays designed to be acted by marionettes. Liberally employing ritual, myth, and dream-like imagery in his plays, Maeterlinck made extensive use of symbols. According to Bettina Knapp in *Maurice Maeterlinck*, "symbols are the chief vehicles used in his dramas to arouse sensation, to breathe life into the ephemeral essences which people Maeterlinck's stage."

Maeterlinck quickly earned a reputation for shunning conventionality, and a *Fortnightly Review* writer commented in 1897: "Maeterlinck aspires after nothing less than a complete reconstruction of the modern drama. . . . He hopes to see life in its material manifestations strictly subordinated to its spiritual sub-consciousness. Plot and action are to be relegated to an entirely secondary position, the stage is to be swept clear of cheap trickery and superficial effects, and the eternal mystery of life is to rise up in an almost palpable sense before the spectator."

During an interview with Jane T. Stoddart, published in a 1895 issue of the *Bookman*, Maeterlinck was asked to explain his interest in mysticism. He responded: "I think . . . that we are living in one of the ages when the human soul awakes.

In 1976 Twentieth Century-Fox released its second film version of *The Blue Bird*, featuring Cicely Tyson as "Cat."

There are such times, and they are to me the only really interesting periods of history. A new inspiration, a new activity becomes felt, not in one country, but all over the world. The ancient Egyptians had such awakenings; the mystics of the fourteenth century had their part in another and not less marvellous revival. In dull and self-conscious times the soul seems small, poor, and limited, but in the great ages of mysticism its powers and its resources are felt to be inexhaustible. Truths after which humanity was dimly groping are expressed by the mystics with unerring certainty."

While the decade before the turn of the century established Maeterlinck as a relatively brooding and pessimistic figure, the dramatist had made some positive changes in his life that lightened his outlook. In the mid-1890s he met and fell in love with opera singer Georgette Leblanc, who would be his close companion for the next two decades. Also, in 1897 Maeterlinck left Belgium, where he had been living discontentedly with his parents, to reside permanently in France.

In France Maeterlinck continued to write plays as well as acclaimed works of nonfiction. One of his most important books is *The Life of the Bee* (*La Vie des abeilles*), published in 1901. The highly structured society of the bee, in which each member has a well-defined role and works in close cooperation with his fellows, represented an ideal to Maeterlinck. Katharine De Forest in *Harper's Bazaar* wrote of her visit to the author shortly before the publication of *The Life of the Bee*. "The proof-sheets . . . lay scattered over his work table. . . . Maeterlinck's study with its light, its austerity, its simple tones, seems a place for clear, lofty thought. The exquisite neatness of a Dutch interior reigns there. . . . Just outside the window Maeterlinck places his beehive, made with glass sides, where he watches . . . that marvellous world from which he has drawn his latest book, reflections of such a lofty philosophy that one volume alone would reveal him one of the greatest minds of this earth.

"No one could know, without talking with its author," De Forest continued, "what endless detail of observation, for one thing, the book has involved. 'I knew that bees could communicate with each other,' Maeterlinck said to me. 'I knew that one bee could say to another, "In such and such a place I have found honey. Come with me and I will take you there." But what I wanted to find out was whether one bee could relate a connected story to another, could say, "In such and such a place there is honey; to reach it you must first go to the right, then the left, then go along the corridor." *Eh bien!* I have found two or three bees who could do that!' " *The Life of the Bee* has been adapted into *The Children's Life of the Bee.* Additional works presenting Maeterlinck's fascination with nature, science, and extreme discipline include *The Life of Space* (*La Vie de l'espace*) and *The Life of the Ant* (*La Vie des fourmis*).

As his career progressed, Maeterlinck steadily turned away from the somberness prominent in his early works and produced plays rooted in realism and more hopeful topics. Such dramas include the popular *Monna Vanna,* produced in 1902. And, at the height of his optimism, Maeterlinck wrote *The Blue Bird,* his 1909 play that, while reverting to his early fixation with dreams and mysticism, expresses quite cheerful themes. Considered one of Maeterlinck's finest artistic and commercial achievements, *The Blue Bird* centers on the dream of two poor children, Tyltyl and Mytyl. One night, after they are put to bed, a fairy visits their room. Named Berylune, the fairy resembles the children's neighbor, Berlingnot, whose daughter is quite ill. Beseeching the children to go out the window to find the Blue Bird for her daughter who longs to be happy, Berylune gives them a hat adorned with a diamond. When Tyltyl puts on the hat and turns the diamond, everything in the room glows with beauty. The children begin their search, discovering such joyful places as the Land of Memory, the Garden of Happiness, and the Kingdom of the Future. Though they fail to find the Blue Bird by journey's end, they awake from their dream the next morning to find their surroundings appear more bright and cheerful. Tyltyl discovers his pet turtledove has turned blue during the night; he gives the bird to Berlingnot's daughter, who is so happy her illness seems to disappear. The bird escapes, though, and Tyltyl turns to ask the audience for their help in finding the Blue Bird.

Conveying the message that happiness is always within one's reach, *The Blue Bird* was hugely successful. It has been adapted as the book *The Children's Blue Bird* as well as two Twentieth Century-Fox films, one in 1940 starring Shirley Temple, the other in 1976 starring Elizabeth Taylor and Jane Fonda. Maeterlinck wrote the play's sequel, *The Betrothal* (*Les Fiancailles*), several years later.

The playwright earned the Nobel Prize in 1911, though several years before he had begun suffering from depression, poor eyesight, and lack of inspiration. His plays published after World War I are generally considered inferior to previous works. In addition, some of his later writings returned to a preoccupation with death. Maeterlinck moved to the United States in 1940 but, experiencing deteriorating health, moved back to France seven years later. Maeterlinck lived his last years in virtual seclusion with his wife, Renee Dahon, in their villa near Nice, on the French Riviera. He did practically no writing, devoting his time to rigorous study of science, gardening, beekeeping, long walks and bicycle rides, lavish meals, and other domestic pleasures.

Despite his failing physical condition and diminished success, Maeterlinck's last book, *Bulles bleues: Souvenirs heureux* (subtitle means "Happy Memories"), is decidedly upbeat, speaking fondly of his youth and zest for living. The author is generally remembered for his fascination with life's mysteries and his intense interest in the wonders of science. "There are so many things of which we still know nothing!," Maeterlinck told Juan Jose de Soiza Reilly in *Living Age.* "Little by little, however, science is changing our idea of the Universe. Everything that happens in the infinitely great is identical with what happens in the infinitely small. Astronomers have become chemists and physicists. Chemists and physicists are to-day the astronomers of the molecule. It is they who are proving that there is an eternal, omniscient being in the cosmos, that there is a God. What difference does it make what we call Him? The important thing is that God is the Universe—space and time without limit—eternity.

"Are there other worlds more perfect than our own?," Maeterlinck continued. "Possibly, but they should not frighten us. We should seek to improve our own world until it is the equal of the others. I am almost certain that we are being observed from other planets and perhaps they are listening to us, too. We transmit ideas and feelings to each other by wireless through the ether and since the ether is exactly the same in any part of the cosmos, why can't there be communication between different worlds? Every time we think or feel, we set molecules in motion, and these molecules give off waves and electrons which travel for great distances through the ether. The study of light has taught us that space is no obstacle to its waves. And as far as death is concerned, there is no such thing! No! Nothingness does not follow after death. Science affirms that nothing dies. There is nothing mortal in the Universe."

WORKS CITED:

De Forest, Katharine, "Recent Happenings in Paris," *Harper's Bazaar,* May, 1901, pp. 49-50.
de Soiza Reilly, Juan Jose, "Maurice Maeterlinck at Home," *Living Age,* September, 1929-February, 1930, p. 155.
Fortnightly Review, July-December 1897, p. 184.
Halls, W. D., *Maurice Maeterlinck: A Study of His Life and Thought,* Greenwood Press Publishers, 1978, pp. 13-23.
Knapp, Bettina, *Maurice Maeterlinck,* G. K. Hall & Co., 1975, p. 9.
Stoddart, Jane T., "An Interview with M. Maurice Maeterlinck," *Bookman,* May, 1895, p. 247.

FOR MORE INFORMATION SEE:

BOOKS

Brucher, Roger, *Maurice Maeterlinck: L'Oevre et son audience,* Palais des Academies (Brussels), 1972.
European Writers, Volume 8: *The Twentieth Century,* edited by George Stade, Scribner, 1989.
Harris, Frank, *Contemporary Portraits,* Mitchell Kennerley, 1915.
Hind, C. Lewis, *Authors and I,* Books for Libraries Press, 1921.
Konrad, Linn Bratteteig, *Modern Drama as Crisis: The Case of Maurice Maeterlinck,* Peter Lang, 1986.
Leblanc, Georgette, *Souvenirs: My Life with Maeterlinck,* translated by Janet Flanner, Dutton, 1932.
Twentieth-Century Literary Criticism, Volume 3, Gale, 1980.

PERIODICALS

Baum Bugle, autumn, 1990.
Bookman, August/September, 1895-February, 1896.
Harper's Weekly, July 5, 1902.
Ladies' Home Journal, April, 1930.

Best known for his dramas, Maeterlinck also published highly acclaimed works of natural science. This photo of termite nests in Africa is taken from *The Life of the White Ant.* (Photo by Victor Wolfgang von Hagen.)

Living Age, October 16, 1897; December 24, 1910.
Outlook, September-December, 1901.
Review of Reviews, February, 1930.

*   *   *

MARSDEN, John 1950-

PERSONAL: Born September 27, 1950, in Melbourne, Australia; son of Eustace Cullen Hudson (a banker) and Jeanne Lawler (a homemaker; maiden name, Ray) Marsden. *Education:* Mitchell College, diploma in teaching, 1978; University of New England, B.A., 1981. *Politics:* "!!!"

ADDRESSES: Home—Roadside Delivery 438, Sandon, Victoria, Australia 3462.

CAREER: Geelong Grammar School, Geelong, Victoria, Australia, English teacher, 1982-90; full-time writer, 1991—.

AWARDS, HONORS: Children's Book of the Year (Australia), 1988, Premier's Award (Victoria), 1988, Young Adult Book Award (New South Wales), 1988, Christopher Medal, 1989, ALA Notable Book, 1989, all for *So Much to Tell You . . .*

WRITINGS:

So Much to Tell You . . . , Walter McVitty, 1988, Joy Street/ Little, Brown, 1989.
The Journey, Pan Australia, 1988.
The Great Gatenby, Pan Australia, 1989.
Staying Alive in Year 5, Pan Australia, 1989.
Out of Time, Pan Australia, 1990.
Letters from the Inside, Pan Australia, 1991.

SIDELIGHTS: John Marsden writes, "I'm interested in the sub-culture of young people: their values, behaviours, attitudes, language. I write for them and about them. I try to make my books realistic and truthful, though sometimes I use elements of fantasy.

"My school career was so exasperating and boring on the academic level and so fascinating on the human level, that I guess that's when I started to get interested in sub-cultures. The only thing I liked about school was the underground life.

"After I left school I drifted through many jobs, from selling pizzas to working in a hospital mortuary. In my late twenties I discovered teaching as a career, and found it wonderfully fulfilling. I like the variety and the busy-ness, and I like proving that the way I was taught was not the best way at all! I plan to go back to teaching in 1992.

"Writing has given me a whole new range of experiences, especially travelling round the world, taking workshops, meeting people, seeing places. I'm very grateful to it!"

Marsden's Christopher Award-winning novel *So Much to Tell You . . .* is based on a true incident. It tells the story of a disfigured, silent, fourteen-year-old girl living at a boarding school in Australia. The book, the girl's diary, slowly reveals the circumstances which led to her disfigurement: her father had accidentally attacked her with acid, instead of his unfaithful wife. Marsden details the slow process of the girl's healing in a volume that Libby K. White, writing in the *School Library Journal,* calls "an intelligent work of literature which is satisfying both intellectually and emotionally."

WORKS CITED:

White, Libby K., *School Library Journal,* May, 1989, p. 127.

FOR MORE INFORMATION SEE:

PERIODICALS

Booklist, July, 1989.
Bulletin of the Center for Children's Books, April, 1989.
Horn Book, September/October, 1989.

*   *   *

MARSH, Dave 1950-

PERSONAL: Born March 1, 1950, in Pontiac, MI; son of O. K. (a railroad worker) and Mary (Evon) Marsh; married Barbara Carr (a recording executive), July 21, 1979; stepchildren: Sasha, Kristen. *Education:* Attended Wayne State University, 1968-69.

ADDRESSES: Office—*Rock and Roll Confidential,* P.O. Box 1073, Maywood, NJ 07607.

DAVE MARSH

CAREER: Creem (magazine), Birmingham, MI, editor, 1969-73; *Real Paper,* Boston, MA, music editor, 1974; *Newsday,* Garden City, NY, staff member, 1974-75; *Rolling Stone,* New York City, record reviews editor and writer, 1975-78; free-lance writer, 1978—; *Rock and Roll Confidential,* Maywood, NJ, editor and publisher, 1983—.

AWARDS, HONORS: Born to Run: The Bruce Springsteen Story was included on the "Best Books for Young Adults 1979" list, compiled by the American Library Association, 1979.

WRITINGS:

Born to Run: The Bruce Springsteen Story, Doubleday, 1979.
(Editor with John Swenson) *Rolling Stone Record Guide: Reviews and Ratings of Almost Ten Thousand Currently Available Pop, Rock, Soul, Country, Blues, Jazz, and Gospel Albums,* Random House, 1980, revised edition published as *The New Rolling Stone Record Guide,* 1983.
(With Kevin Stein) *The Book of Rock Lists,* Dell, 1980.
Elvis, Times Books, 1981.
Before I Get Old: The Story of the Who, St. Martin's, 1982.
(With Sandra Charon and Deborah Geller) *Rocktopicon,* Contemporary, 1984.
Fortunate Son: The Best of Dave Marsh, Random House, 1985.
The First Rock and Roll Confidential Report: Inside the World of Rock and Roll, Pantheon, 1985.
Trapped: Michael Jackson and the Crossover Dream, Bantam, 1985.
Sun City: The Struggle for Freedom in South Africa, Penguin Books, 1985.
Glory Days: The Bruce Springsteen Story Continues, Pantheon, 1987.
The Heart of Rock and Soul: The 1001 Greatest Singles Ever Made, New American Library, 1989.
(Editor with Harold Leventhal) Woody Guthrie, *Pastures of Plenty: The Unpublished Writings of an American Folk Hero,* Harper, 1990.

Also author of "American Grandstand," a column in *Rolling Stone,* 1976-79. Contributor to magazines and newspapers, including *New York Daily News, Los Angeles Times, Look, Film Comment, Boston Phoenix,* and *Village Voice.* Critic for *Playboy* magazine, 1985—.

SIDELIGHTS: Dave Marsh is a critic of popular music who is most noted for his profiles on rock and roll singer Bruce Springsteen. Author of the acclaimed book *Born to Run: The Bruce Springsteen Story,* he has also written such works as *Before I Get Old: The Story of the Who* and *The Heart of Rock and Soul.* Marsh, according to Wendy Smith in *Publishers Weekly,* possesses a "fierce belief in rock's importance as both a cultural and political phenomenon, a conviction he expresses in intensely personal language that also articulates the experience and emotions of a generation."

Born in the Detroit suburb of Pontiac, Michigan, Marsh grew up in a working-class environment. "It was pretty grim," Marsh told Smith. "You were surrounded. If you walked a block and a half, you were at Assembly Line 16, where thy made Bonnevilles and later GTOs. It was just a fact of life; they were going to get you one way or another. Everybody was on the same track: you were going to go to work at the plant or, maybe, for the phone company." At a young age Marsh exhibited interest in writing. The author told *SATA:* "My mother says that the from the time I was seven years old, the only thing I ever talked about being was a writer. Maybe I didn't talk about the other things, but I know that life would have been very satisfactory as a member of the Detroit Tigers or as a singer (even a backup singer) in a group like Smokey Robinson and the Miracles.

"But if I didn't talk about those dreams out loud," continued Marsh, "that was because I had this other thing, one that I seemed to be good at. When I wrote, people displayed their emotions. Sometimes they even laughed when I wanted them, too. Just as important, my own confused thoughts and feelings seemed clear. Writing for me has always been a way of disentangling the conflicting impressions of events and people and experiences, the basic circumstances of living in the world.

"So, in a sense, it didn't matter very much what one wrote about. Some people would insist that that must be the case, to have focused for twenty years on something as trivial as the world of rock and roll music. But I'd say the opposite. Where I came from, there were no writers. People in my neighborhood labored on the railroad, like my dad, or worked at the auto assembly plant up the block. Nothing and nobody that I knew about told their stories. Except for the songs on the radio. If I was blessed early with a calling to write, it came about very much as a response to this gap in our culture. And for me, that's why it was worthwhile to write about rock and roll music, which is made and listened to by all sorts of people but especially by the kind of people who didn't have writers to tell their stories. It seemed to me that if you could get close to the source of the music and what it was trying to say, then that was a good thing to do in the world. It might help some other kid like me, who is mystified by that TV world where everyone—everyone!—went to work in a jacket and tie, no one ever came home dirty and exhausted, and all the houses were airy and bright and had big backyards."

After Marsh graduated from high school he wrote for a variety of small publications while attending Wayne State University. At the age of nineteen he dropped out of college and began editing *Creem,* a rock and roll magazine. He left that post in 1973 and moved to the East Coast, where he was music writer for *Newsday* and Boston's *Real Paper.* While in Boston, he became friendly with Jon Landau, another rock and roll critic, and the pair eventually became quite close to Bruce Springsteen (Landau eventually became Springsteen's manager and producer). Working closely with Springsteen, Marsh produced not only *Born to Run* but *Glory Days: The Bruce Springsteen Story Continues* in 1987. His books on other popular singers include *Elvis* and *Trapped: Michael Jackson and the Crossover Dream.* A music editor and writer for *Rolling Stone* magazine during the late 1970s, Marsh has also earned acclaim for his *Rolling Stone Record Guide.* In addition to writing books, Marsh is the publisher of *Rock and Roll Confidential,* a newsletter whose goal, as quoted by Smith, "is to create the most committed and aware group of readers and rock fans in America."

Marsh continued to relate to *SATA* why he enjoys writing about rock and roll for a living: "Thanks to people like Southern author Bobbie Ann Mason and, in his own weird way, horror writer Stephen King, today working-class people have their stories told much more frequently (though still in nothing like the proportion which they inhabit our world). So I don't think I'd necessarily do the same things starting out as I did then. But I don't think I've wasted a minute of my time, either. The things we do in our daily lives—listening to the radio, shopping for clothes and dinner, driving to work—matter enough to bear down and focus in on their

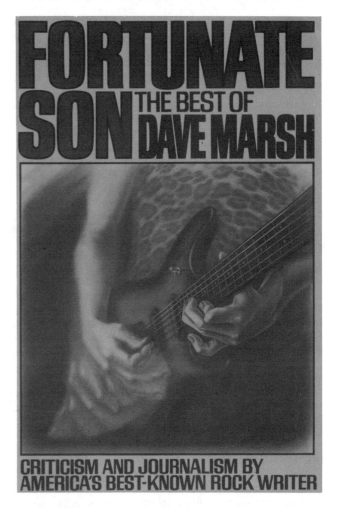

Fortunate Son **is a collection of Dave Marsh's music writing between 1970 and 1985.** (Cover art by John Sposato.)

meaning. The everyday heroes we produce, whether named Elvis, Michael, Bruce, Cyndi, or Madonna, deserve serious consideration. It can be strange to tell such a story when you're far from being a teenager yourself, when you have kids in high school and college. It's always odd to explain—in some 'grown up' situation—exactly what you do for a living. But I don't think I'd trade with anyone. (Except maybe baseball player Alan Trammell. And eventually I'll write my book about Detroit and the Tigers and get that out of my system, too.)

"The first thing that people always want to know about being a music critic is how often you listen to the records. The answer is, as many times as it takes to understand them. Often, that's appallingly few, but there are other records—like those of Aretha Franklin or Roy Orbison or even the Beatles—whose depths I don't think I'll ever entirely finish exploring. And there are others, like Madonna's, that seem incredibly shallow at first but keep drawing you back. I grew up in a household of incredibly angry people, and Madonna's song 'Live to Tell' has more to say about that experience than any other song or poem or story or play that I know about.

"The other question I'm frequently asked is, 'What is (fill in the blank) really like?' Mostly, it's not something that I can answer in conversation. If I could, I probably wouldn't feel the need to write it down. That has something to do with the fact that celebrities are people, and people are just plain complicated. Think of how many years it took you to understand yourself, or your family, and how limited your understanding is, and you'll see that it's not so easy to summarize anyone—much less someone you're meeting in a highly artificial interview setting, and much much less when that person is, by training and inclination, trained to wear masks and look natural doing it, as all entertainers are.

"I often work on several books at once," Marsh continued to relate to *SATA*. "I always seem to want to know what my next project is when I'm in the middle of the current one, which may have something to do with my journalistic background or may be just pure insecurity. I've wanted to write about the campaign to censor rock music. For the past few years, I've been a ferocious opponent of the well-connected women in Washington, D.C., who want to label and restrict access to a variety of records, including such innocuous stuff as Springsteen's 'I'm on Fire' and the Jacksons' 'Torture.' It's a complicated subject, and the movement to repress this kind of music has deep roots. (They go all the way back to Cotton Mather, who lectured his congregation about their cacophonous hymn singing in the seventeenth century!) But I also think it's important to talk about the parts of rock and roll that those of us who love it try to defend or explain away—things like Altamont or Woodstock. Today, who can believe that half a million people in a muddy field without adequate food or sanitation or shelter would seem like a wave of the future—much less a desirable wave of the future! In the late 1980s Woodstock sounds like a rehearsal for the national plague of homelessness. And so I wanted to write a book that ties these things together.

"Another of my projects concerns the story of 'Louie Louie,' the most legendary of all censored hit singles. It was originally written in 1955, had a very brief and obscure life as a California rhythm and blues hit, disappeared for half a dozen years, got picked up by some bands in the Pacific Northwest, and became a huge hit in 1963 when performed by the Portland, Oregon, band, the Kingsmen. They didn't know the words very well, so they mumbled them. This made some people think that the words must be dirty. Kids loved the idea of sharing such a secret; parents and teachers and politicians and preachers hated it just as much. The Governor of Indiana banned the song from the airwaves of his state, and the FBI and the Federal Communications Commission were called in to investigate. Their ultimate conclusion was that the lyrics were 'unintelligible at any speed.' 'Louie Louie' was revived by actor John Belushi in the film *Animal House*, and since then it's become increasingly popular. A couple of California radio stations have yearly 'Louie Louie' marathons that last several days each, where they play nothing but different versions of the song. And each spring, the American Leukemia Society sponsors 'Louie Louie' parades to raise money to cure that disease. (That makes the song sound almost too respectable for my taste. Too bad the words aren't really dirty, I guess.) Anyway, I think that the story of that record is the social history of rock and roll in microcosm. And that's the story I try to tell. Sounds like fun, which is the best part of the job."

WORKS CITED:

Smith, Wendy, "Dave Marsh," *Publishers Weekly,* October 21, 1983, pp. 69-70.

FOR MORE INFORMATION SEE:

PERIODICALS

Choice, June, 1980.
Detroit News, May 17, 1987.
Los Angeles Times, May 15, 1983; December 11, 1983; February 5, 1984.
Los Angeles Times Book Review, December 2, 1990.
New Statesman, September 24, 1982.
Newsweek, October 31, 1983; April 13, 1987.
New York Times, November 16, 1979.
New York Times Book Review, December 30, 1979; November 28, 1982; July 28, 1985; July 5, 1987.
People, July 13, 1987.
Time, January 7, 1980.
Times Educational Supplement, December 24, 1982.
Tribune Books (Chicago), November 5, 1989.
Washington Post, April 26, 1987; June 15, 1987.
Washington Post Book World, September 11, 1982.

* * *

McGRATH, Thomas (Matthew) 1916-1990

OBITUARY NOTICE—See index for *SATA* sketch: Born November 20, 1916, near Sheldon, ND; died September 19, 1990, in Minneapolis, MN. Educator, novelist, and poet. McGrath was known for his accomplished poetry and his leftist politics. His debut verse collection, *First Manifesto,* appeared in 1940, and subsequent volumes included *A Sound of One Hand, Waiting for the Angel,* and the prize-winning *Figures from a Double World* and *McGrath's Selected Poems, 1938-1988.* He also wrote film scripts and the novel *The Gates of Horn.* McGrath often supported himself by teaching at institutions including Colby College, North Dakota State University, and Moorhead State University. He lost one teaching job during the 1950s, when he was subpoenaed to appear before a government committee investigating alleged communists; he refused to testify. Some writers have argued that McGrath's politics caused him to receive less recognition than he deserved.

OBITUARIES AND OTHER SOURCES:

BOOKS

Contemporary Literary Criticism, Volume 28, Gale, 1984.
Who's Who in U.S. Writers, Editors, and Poets, 1988, December Press, 1988.

PERIODICALS

Washington Post, September 22, 1990.

* * *

MENDEZ, Raymond A. 1947-

PERSONAL: Born July 2, 1947, in New York, NY; son of Raymond and Dulce (Quinzan) Mendez; married Kate Bennett (a music director). *Education:* Attended New York University and Queensboro College, 1966-71, and School of Visual Arts, 1971-76.

ADDRESSES: Home—220 West 98th St., Apt. 12-B, New York, NY 10025.

CAREER: Nature photographer and model maker. American Museum of Natural History, New York City, assistant preparator in museum training program, 1966-69, scientific assistant in department of entomology, 1969-70, preparator in exhibition department, 1970-72, senior preparator, 1972-76, principal preparator, 1976-79, field research associate, 1980. Co-leader of Junior Etonomological Society seminars in Arizona, Florida, Virgin Islands, and Trinidad, 1969-76; lecturer in natural history and photography, 1970—; leader for seminar on tropical entomology for Wonder Bird Tours, 1977—; instructor in macro-photography at School of Visual Arts, 1978-80. Has done special effects, exhibit construction, animation, model making, and animal wrangling for motion pictures and television, including creating the egg for the motion picture *Alien.* Scientific adviser for *On the Wing.* Consulting entomologist for the Department of Parks, New York City. Constructed various living habitats for Manhattan Laboratory Museum. Designer and consultant for Museum of the Hudson Highlands and Smithsonian Institution, and for Alan Sunfist, a kinetic artist. Member of board of trustees, Asa Wright Nature Center, 1980—. *Exhibitions:* Work has been exhibited at Audubon Center, Greenwich, CT.

MEMBER: Mac Club.

AWARDS, HONORS: National Science Foundation grant, 1966.

ILLUSTRATOR:

(With Jerome Wexler) Joanna Cole, *An Insect's Body* (illustrated with photographs), Morrow, 1984.

Dustjacket from the 1984 edition of a nature book on crickets, photographed by Raymond A. Mendez and Jerome Wexler. (Cover photo by Mendez.)

Photographs have appeared in *Natural History, Successful Farming, Discover, Science 84, Smithsonian, Audubon,* and *BBC Wildlife.*

*　　*　　*

MERLIN, Arthur
See BLISH, James (Benjamin)

*　　*　　*

MITTON, Jacqueline 1948-

PERSONAL: Born July 10, 1948, in Stoke-on-Trent, England; daughter of Charles (a teacher) and Gertrude (Bridgewood) Pardoe; married Simon Mitton (a publisher), June 27, 1970; children: Lavinia, Veronica. *Education:* Oxford University, B.A., 1969; Cambridge University, Ph.D., 1975.

ADDRESSES: Home—8A Canterbury Close, Cambridge CB4 3QQ, England. *Agent*—Murray Pollinger, 4 Garrick St., London WC2E 9BH, England.

CAREER: Teacher at convent school in Cambridge, England, 1972-74; Cambridge University, Cambridge, researcher in astronomy, 1975-78; writer and researcher, 1978—.

MEMBER: British Astronomical Association, Royal Astronomical Society (fellow), Royal College of Music (associate member), Astronomical Society of the Pacific.

WRITINGS:

Astronomy: An Introduction for the Amateur Astronomer, Scribner, 1978.
(With husband, Simon Mitton) *The Prentice-Hall Concise Book of Astronomy,* Prentice-Hall, 1979.
(With S. Mitton) *Star Atlas,* Crown, 1979.
(Translator from French with S. Mitton) Jean Heidmann, *An Introduction to Cosmology,* Springer-Verlag, 1980.
Feeding Your Baby: From Birth to Three Years, Granada, 1980.
A Language of Its Own: Astronomy, Frederick Muller, 1981.
(With S. Mitton) *Invitation to Astronomy,* Basil Blackwell, 1986.

WORK IN PROGRESS: Looking at the Night Sky, an astronomy book for children.

SIDELIGHTS: Jacqueline Mitton once commented: "I doubt whether I would have ever written anything at all if my husband, Simon, had not started writing when we were both graduate students. At the time I thought, 'If he can do it, I can do it.' My first book, in fact, which was created from an astronomy course I had been teaching, has since become a standard text for that course in the United Kingdom."

Mitton and her husband have since collaborated on four books. "Our joint efforts have been particularly fruitful since we specialize in separate fields," she explained. "The criticism we offer each other seems to result in something better than we might have produced individually. We have no problems in working together.

"Being the mother of two young children severely restricts my output of writings, but the things my children have taught me have also been useful to me as a writer. I am now particularly interested in children's books, and I am thinking about writing a book on astronomy for primary school-aged children. Although people imagine writing for children is easy, there is a real challenge in choosing the few words and ideas carefully."

* * *

MITTON, Simon 1946-

PERSONAL: Born December 18, 1946, in Bristol, England; son of Francis (an accountant) and Margaret (Schlaphoff) Mitton; married Jacqueline Pardoe (a writer), June 27, 1970; children: Lavinia, Veronica. *Education:* Oxford University, B.A., 1968; Cambridge University, Ph.D., 1971.

ADDRESSES: Home—8A Canterbury Close, Cambridge CB4 3QQ, England. *Agent*—Murray Pollinger, 4 Garrick St., London WC2E 9BH, England. *Office*—Cambridge University Press, Pitt Building, Trumpington St., Cambridge CB2 3RL, England.

CAREER: Cambridge University, Cambridge, England, secretary of Institute of Astronomy, 1972-78; Cambridge University Press, science publisher, 1978—. Guest on television and radio programs.

MEMBER: Royal Astronomical Society (fellow; member of council, 1975-78).

AWARDS, HONORS: Honorable mention for best older children's book, New York Academy of Sciences, 1979, for *The Crab Nebula.*

WRITINGS:

Exploring the Galaxies, Scribner, 1976.
(With Peter P. Eggleton and John A. J. Whelan) *Close Binary Systems* (monograph), J. Reidel, 1977.
(Editor) *The Cambridge Encyclopaedia of Astronomy,* Crown, 1978.
The Crab Nebula, Scribner, 1979.
(With wife, Jacqueline Mitton) *Star Atlas,* Crown, 1979.
(With J. Mitton) *The Prentice-Hall Concise Book of Astronomy,* Prentice-Hall, 1979.
(Editor, with Cyril Hazard) *Active Galactic Nuclei* (monograph), Cambridge University Press, 1979.
(Translator from French with J. Mitton) Jean Heidmann, *An Introduction to Cosmology,* Springer-Verlag, 1980.
Daytime Star: The Story of Our Sun, Scribner, 1981.
Beyond the Moon, Cambridge University Press, 1981.
(With J. Mitton) *Invitation to Astronomy,* Basil Blackwell, 1986.
(Translator) Jean Heidmann, *Cosmic Odyssey,* Cambridge University Press, 1989.

Writer and presenter for *Beyond the Moon,* a series on British independent television, 1979. Contributor to scholarly journals and popular magazines in Britain and the United States, including *New Scientist, Nature,* and *Astronomy Now;* contributor to encyclopedias and dictionaries, including *Children's Britannica,* and *Chamber's Dictionary of Science and Technology,* Cambridge University Press, 1988. Editor of

Quarterly Journal of the Royal Astronomical Society, 1975-80.

SIDELIGHTS: Simon Mitton commented: "I am motivated by a desire to explain modern astronomy in the simplest terms, using clear text and excellent illustrations. I began with magazine articles, then progressed to books. I have visited major observatories in Europe, the United States, and Australia, and this travel has given me numerous valuable contacts with professional astronomers.

"My training as a physicist has enabled me to follow the complex reasoning used by theorists to explain modern astronomical discoveries. In writing I can present material at any level from ten-year-old children to graduate students, and I have tried never to write things that are plain wrong just because the readers may not have the knowledge to see the error. Always I try to find photographs that have not been used before, and I think this makes my books look fresh.

"Like most writers I write for selfish reasons: I like to do it and I enjoy the challenge of understanding a new field well enough to write a definitive book. Before I wrote *The Crab Nebula* and *Daytime Star* I knew almost nothing about these subjects. Although I am the physical science publisher at Cambridge University Press, I welcome the opportunity to write for our competitors; it broadens my experience of publishing and stops me from feeling that I work all hours for the same employer. Significantly I create more ideas for books as a publisher than I could as a full-time writer. In fact, most of my writing now takes place after an approach from a publisher, and I much prefer to work with an editor who already has a reasonable idea of what the book should look like. I liked writing *Invitation to Astronomy,* which explains to older school children what astronomers actually do and how you can become an astronomer yourself.

"Surprisingly, perhaps, I read very little myself. Much of what is published seems poorly written, and yet there is also much that is superb. The one author who had the greatest influence on my writing is Professor Sir Fred Hoyle, the giant among Cambridge astronomers. In fiction I like Mark Twain, Joyce Carol Oates, Henry James, and David Lodge. To aspiring science writers I would advise a good stint at the discipline of magazine and newspaper writing. Far too much popular science is written by professional journalists, too little by scientists themselves. I have long thought that scientists, in comparison to economists and politicians for example, do not make sufficient effort to communicate with ordinary people, and it is this that motivates me the most in my own work.

"Recently I have contributed to children's reference books, including the British revision of *Children's Britannica.* Astronomy and space are fascinating to children, and these subjects can stimulate a life-long interest in science and the universe around us."

* * *

MORRIS, Chris(topher Crosby) 1946-
(Casey Prescott, Daniel Stryker)

PERSONAL: Born March 15, 1946, in New York City; son of John G. (a photo-journalist), and Mary Adele Crosby Morris; married Janet Freeman (a writer), October 31, 1971. *Religion:* "Cosmic."

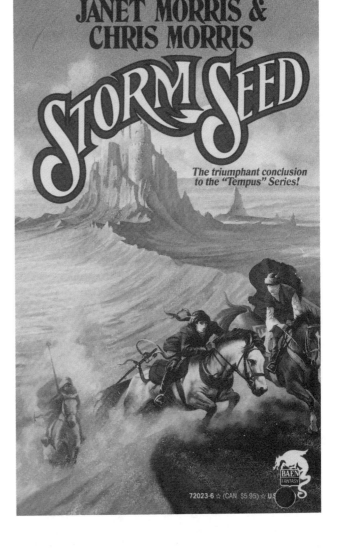

The Little Helliad and *Storm Seed* are just two of several fantasy adventures co-written by husband and wife, Chris and Janet Morris.

ADDRESSES: Home—West Hyannisport, MA. *Agent*—Perry Knowlton, Curtis Brown Ltd., 10 Astor Pl., New York, NY 10003.

CAREER: Author and musical composer. United States Global Strategy Council, currently research director.

MEMBER: Science Fiction Writers of America, Center for Strategic and International Studies, Amnesty International.

WRITINGS:

WITH WIFE, JANET MORRIS

40 Minute War, Baen Books, 1984.
M.E.D.U.S.A., Baen Books, 1986.
Outpassage, Crown, 1988.
The Little Helliad, Baen Books, 1988.
City at the Edge of Time, Baen Books, 1988.
Storm Seed, Baen Books, 1990.
Threshold, New American Library, 1990.

OTHER

(Under pseudonym Casey Prescott) *Asset in Black,* Arbor House, 1985.
(Under pseudonym Daniel Stryker) *Hawkeye,* Jove, 1991.

Songwriter with wife, Janet Morris, on record *Christopher Morris Band* (contains: "Do You Want to be Loved," "I Feel Like I Never Felt Before," "What's Gone Wrong?," "Go Down Believin'," "Train in My Heart," "Down This Road Forever," "Amazing Ways," and "What Kinda Song"), MCA Records, 1977.

SIDELIGHTS: Christopher Morris told *SATA:* "I think of writing as a musical form. Before [my wife] Janet or I attempted storytelling for the commercial market, we wrote songs together. We still do.

"When Janet first started pounding out *High Couch of Silistra* on our antiquated Royal, I became addicted to reading the day's output—the Sheherazade syndrome. At first I would only fix the occasional typos and express my expectations as a reader. This sort of input can have momentous repercussive potential and, in our case, resulted in near emotional calamity more than once. Luckily, I learned the Editor's Caveat: the writer and the work are never more vulnerable to misleading input than at the moment between having produced and being read for the first time; therefore, it shall behoove all first readers to say only those things about the work that they genuinely feel, *and* can support. That goes double for works in progress.

"Once you know the rules of this game, you're a player. We have collaborated happily ever since. We decided to keep my name off the literary stuff and Janet's off the music, so as not to 'confuse' would-be buyers who are often skittish of people who are capable in more than one area.

"Our standard operating procedure is to read aloud every night the pages created that day, make whatever corrections seem appropriate, discuss if need be, and insert the changes the following morning before drafting the next chapters. Sometimes we change roles but this is more or less our routine today. The reading aloud part is what is unique.

"A few writers we know read their work aloud; none so far have told us they're read *to*. By reading aloud together the way we do, we *voice* our prose—we consciously let what we hear influence our punctuation, phrasing, pacing—even the way the words lie on the page.

"Just as in singing, a trained prose voice has more range, articulative skill, flexibility and depth. Each of our characters has his or her own voice and our readers recognize them by their individual sounds, the way their words come out of them when they speak, the usage level during their ruminative viewpoint scenes.

"I think writers should constantly strive to refine an ear for the way language identifies and conveys their characters' personalities, not to mention the writers'. The average reader has a profound understanding of nuance that goes begging in today's fiction.

"So listen up, writers! There's a sonic stage out there and your auditory skills are needed to fill it with prosaic music. Your audience is waiting."

*   *   *

MORRIS, Janet (Ellen) 1946-

PERSONAL: Born May 25, 1946, in Boston, MA; daughter of Cecil R. (in real estate) and Anne H. (a businesswoman) Freeman; married Christopher Crosby Morris (a musician), October 31, 1971. *Education:* Attended New York University, 1965-66.

ADDRESSES: Home—West Hyannisport, MA. *Agent*—Perry Knowlton, Curtis Brown Ltd., 575 Madison Ave., New York, NY 10022.

CAREER: Writer. Songwriter and recording artist, 1967—; Record Plant, night manager, 1970; Christopher Morris Band, bass player, 1975, 1977; U.S. Global Strategy Council, project director, 1989; Non-Lethal Programs, research director, 1990—; Institute for Geopolitical Studies, associate, 1990—.

MEMBER: Science Fiction Writers of America, Costeau Society, Musicians Union, Broadcast Music, National Intelligence Study Center, National Space Society, New York Academy of Science, Association of Old Crows.

WRITINGS:

NOVELS

High Couch of Silistra, Bantam, 1977.
The Golden Sword, Bantam, 1977.

Janet Morris, who frequently co-authors books with her husband, also publishes novels on her own.

Wind from the Abyss, Bantam, 1978.
The Carnelian Throne, Bantam, 1978.
Dream Dancer, Berkley Publishing, 1980.
Cruiser Dreams, Berkley Publishing, 1981.
Earth Dreams, Berkley Publishing, 1982.
I, the Sun, Dell, 1983.
(With husband, Chris Morris) *40 Minute War,* Baen Books, 1984.
Returning Creation, Baen Books, 1984.
(With David Drake) *Active Measures,* Baen Books, 1985.
(Editor) *Afterwar,* Baen Books, 1985.
(With C. Morris) *M.E.D.U.S.A,* Baen Books, 1986.
Beyond Sanctuary (book 1 in "Thieves' World Series"), Baen Books, 1986.
Beyond the Veil (book 2 in "Thieves' World Series"), Baen Books, 1987.
Tempus, Baen Books, 1987.
(With D. Drake) *Kill Ratio,* Berkley Publishing, 1987.
Warlord!, Pocket Books, 1987.
(With C. Morris) *Outpassage,* Crown, 1988.
(With C. Morris) *City at the Edge of Time,* Baen Books, 1988.
Beyond Wizardwall (book 3 in "Thieves' World Series"), Baen Books, 1988.
Target, Ace Books, 1989.
Tempus Unbound, Simon & Schuster, 1989.

(With C. Morris) *Storm Seed,* Baen Books, 1990.
(With C. Morris) *Threshold,* New American Library, 1990.

Also author of novels under two undisclosed pseudonyms.

"HEROES IN HELL" SERIES; PUBLISHED BY BAEN BOOKS

(Editor, with others) *Heroes in Hell,* 1986.
Rebels in Hell, 1986.
(With C. J. Cherryh) *Gates of Hell,* 1986.
(With C. J. Cherryh) *Kings in Hell,* 1987.
Angels in Hell, 1987.
Masters in Hell, 1987.
Crusaders in Hell, 1987.
(With C. Morris) *The Little Helliad,* 1988.
War in Hell, 1988.
Prophets in Hell, 1989.
Explorers in Hell, 1989.

OTHER

Songwriter with husband, Chris Morris, on record *Christopher Morris Band* (contains: "Do You Want to be Loved," "I Feel Like I Never Felt Before," "What's Gone Wrong?," "Go Down Believin'," "Train in My Heart," "Down This Road Forever," "Amazing Ways," and "What Kinda Song"), MCA Records, 1977.

Also author of more than 50 short stories and articles, and a concept paper, "Nonlethality," for U.S. Global Strategy Council, 1990. Editor and contributor to *Window of Opportunity,* by Newt Gingrich. Contributor to *Tales from the Vulgar Unicorn,* Ace Books, 1980; *Shadows of Sanctuary,* Ace Books, 1981; *Berkley Showcase,* Berkley Publishing, 1981; *Storm Season,* Ace Books, 1982; and *Face of Chaos,* Ace Books, 1983. Contributor to continuing series, "Thieves' World," "The Fleet," and "Merovingen."

WORK IN PROGRESS: A nonfiction book with Colonel John Alexander and Captain Richard Groller, *The Warrior's Edge,* to be published by Morrow; and a short story for *Yacht* magazine.

SIDELIGHTS: Janet Morris told *SATA:* "Much of my inspiration is drawn from history, and from life, from study and from that mystical place where art and scholarship mix. When I write about something, I've researched it until the research is no longer book-learned, but part of my psyche."

FOR MORE INFORMATION SEE:

PERIODICALS

Analog, January, 1983.
Chicago Tribune Book World, June 14, 1981.
New York Times Book Review, June 26, 1977.
Science Fiction Review, summer, 1982; summer, 1983.

*   *   *

MORRISON, Bill 1935-

PERSONAL: Born in 1935; married; wife's name, Patty; children: David, Robb, Julie. *Hobbies and other interests:* Archaeology.

ADDRESSES: Home—68 Glandore Rd., Westwood, MA 02090.

CAREER: Instructor of children's illustration at Massachusetts College of Art, Boston; illustrator and author. *Exhibitions:* Has exhibited art work nationally.

MEMBER: Society of Illustrators (New York), Graphic Artists Guild.

AWARDS, HONORS: Awards from Society of Illustrators for works in national exhibitions.

WRITINGS:

SELF-ILLUSTRATED CHILDREN'S BOOKS

Squeeze a Sneeze, Houghton, 1977.
Louis James Hates School, Houghton, 1978.
Simon Says, Little, Brown, 1983.

ILLUSTRATOR

Mae Freeman, *Finding Out about Shapes,* McGraw-Hill, 1969.
John E. Maher, *Ideas about Money,* F. Watts, 1970.
Margaret O. Hyde and Bruce G. Hyde, *Know about Drugs,* McGraw-Hill, 1971, 2nd edition, 1979.
Jeannette McNeely, *Where's Izzy?,* Follett, 1972.
Laurence B. White, *So You Want to Be a Magician?,* Addison-Wesley, 1972.
Peggy Mann, *William the Watchcat,* Rand McNally, 1972.
Adelaide Holl, *Too Fat to Fly,* Garrard, 1973.
Adelaide Holl, *Gus Gets the Message,* Garrard, 1974.
Donna L. Pape, *A Bone for Breakfast,* Garrard, 1974.
Kenneth Truse, *Benny's Magic Baking Pan,* Garrard, 1974.
Donna L. Pape, *The Big White Thing,* Garrard, 1975.
(With Cynthia Crowley) Douglas Morse, *The Brook Book,* Storyfold (Newburyport, MA), 1975.
Jonah Kelb, *The Easy Hockey Book,* Houghton, 1977.
Margaret O. Hyde, *Know about Alcohol,* McGraw-Hill, 1978.
Steven Kroll, *T. J. Folger, Thief,* Holiday House, 1978.
Ray Broekel and Laurence B. White, Jr., *Now You See It: Easy Magic for Beginners,* Little, Brown, 1979.
Carol R. Law, *The Case of the Weird Street Firebug,* Knopf, 1980.
L. Frank Baum's Over the Rainbow, adapted by C. J. Naden, Troll Associates, 1980.
L. Frank Baum's Dorothy and the Wicked Witch, adapted by C. J. Naden, Troll Associates, 1980.
L. Frank Baum's Dorothy and the Wizard, adapted by C. J. Naden, Troll Associates, 1980.
L. Frank Baum's Off to See the Wizard, adapted by C. J. Naden, Troll Associates, 1980.
Patty Wolcott, *The Dragon and the Wild Fandango,* Addison-Wesley, 1980.
Audrey Wood, *Tickleoctopus,* Houghton, 1980.
Ellen Weiss, *Fix It, Please: Featuring Jim Henson's Sesame Street Muppets,* Western Publishing Co./Children's Theatre Workshop, 1980.
Sid Fleischman, *The Bloodhound Gang in the Case of Princess Tomorrow,* Random House, 1981.
Vicki Cobb, *The Secret Life of School Supplies,* Harper, 1981.
Patty Wolcott, *Pirates, Pirates over the Salt, Salt Sea,* Addison-Wesley, 1981.
Sid Fleischman, *The Bloodhound Gang in the Case of the 264-Pound Burglar,* Random House, 1982.
Seymour Simon, *How to Be a Space Scientist in Your Own Home,* Lippincott, 1982.
Vicki Cobb, *The Secret Life of Hardware: A Science Experiment Book,* Lippincott, 1982.
Maria Polushkin, *Morning,* Four Winds, 1983.

Louis James discovers a world of limited job opportunities when he leaves school. (Cover from *Louis James Hates School,* written and illustrated by Bill Morrison.)

Sid Fleischman, *The Bloodhound Gang's Secret Code Book: With Five Stories,* Random House/Children's Television Workshop, 1983.

SIDELIGHTS: A teacher of illustration, Morrison has illustrated more than thirty children's books by various authors and has also written and illustrated three books of his own: *Squeeze a Sneeze, Louis James Hates School,* and *Simon Says.* A picture book of nonsense rhyme, *Squeeze a Sneeze,* encourages children to enjoy words and create their own rhymes. In *Louis James Hates School,* the title character quits school and works briefly as a pea picker, pickle packer, and prune peeler, but returns to school when he discovers that he could get better jobs if he knew how to read and write. Morrison's third book, *Simon Says,* features a group of animals playing that familiar children's game. The turtle—teased because he cannot do what the others do—earns

the thanks and respect of the other players when he warns them to hide from a hungry tiger. Morrison's work has been praised as light-hearted, exuberant, and joyous. The Society of Illustrators honored him with several awards for his art.

*   *   *

NAYLOR, Phyllis
See NAYLOR, Phyllis Reynolds

*   *   *

NAYLOR, Phyllis Reynolds 1933-
(Phyllis Naylor)

PERSONAL: Born January 4, 1933, in Anderson, IN; daughter of Eugene S. (in sales) and Lura (a teacher; maiden name, Schield) Reynolds; married second husband, Rex V. Naylor (a speech pathologist), May 26, 1960; children: Jeffrey Alan, Michael Scott. *Education:* Joliet Junior College, diploma, 1953; American University, B.A., 1963. *Politics:* Independent. *Religion:* Unitarian Universalist. *Hobbies and other interests:* Music, drama, hiking, swimming.

ADDRESSES: Home and office—9910 Holmhurst Rd., Bethesda, MD 20817. *Agent*—John Hawkins & Associates, Inc., 71 West 23rd St., Suite 1600, New York, NY 10010.

CAREER: Billings Hospital, Chicago, IL, clinical secretary, 1953-56; elementary school teacher in Hazelcrest, IL, 1956; Montgomery County Education Association, Rockville, MD, assistant executive secretary, 1958-59; National Education Association, Washington, DC, editorial assistant with *NEA Journal,* 1959-60; full-time writer, 1960—. Active in civil rights and peace organizations.

MEMBER: P.E.N., Society of Children's Book Writers, Authors Guild, Authors League of America, Children's Book Guild (Washington, DC; president, 1974-75 and 1983-84).

AWARDS, HONORS: Children's Books of the Year from Child Study Association of America, 1971, for *Wrestle the Mountain,* 1979, for *How Lazy Can You Get?,* and 1986, for *The Agony of Alice; Wrestle the Mountain* was a Junior Literary Guild selection, 1971; *To Walk the Sky Path* was a Weekly Reader Book Club selection, 1973; *Walking through the Dark* was a Junior Literary Guild selection, 1976; *Crazy Love: An Autobiographical Account of Marriage and Madness* was a Literary Guild selection, 1977; Golden Kite Award for Nonfiction from Society of Children's Book Writers, 1978, and Children's Choice from International Reading Association and Children's Book Council, 1979, both for *How I Came to Be a Writer; How Lazy Can You Get?* was a Weekly Reader Book Club selection, 1979; Children's Choice, 1980, for *How Lazy Can You Get?,* and 1986, for *The Agony of Alice;* Best Book for Young Adults from Young Adult Services Division of American Library Association, and Notable Children's Book in the Field of Social Studies from National Council for Social Studies and Children's Book Council, both 1982, and South Carolina Young Adult Book Award, 1985-86, all for *A String of Chances;* Child Study Award from Bank Street of College of Education, 1983, for *The Solomon System;* Edgar Allan Poe Award from Mystery Writers of America, 1985, for *Night Cry; The Agony of Alice* was an American Library Association (ALA) Notable book, 1985; Notable Children's Book in the Field of Social Studies, 1985, for *The Dark of the Tunnel,* 1985; *The Keeper* was a Junior Literary Guild selection, 1986; Best Book for Young Adults from Young Adult Services Division of the American Library Association, 1986, for *The Keeper,* and 1987, for *The Year of the Gopher;* Creative Writing Fellowship Grant from National Endowment for the Arts, 1987; Society of School Librarians International Book Award, 1988, for *Maudie in the Middle;* Best Young Adult Book of the Year from Michigan Library Association, 1988, for *The Year of the Gopher;* Christopher Award from the Christophers, 1989, for *Keeping a Christmas Secret; Send No Blessings* was an ALA Notable Book for Young Adults, 1990.

WRITINGS:

FOR CHILDREN AND YOUNG ADULTS; FICTION

The Galloping Goat and Other Stories, Abingdon, 1965.
Grasshoppers in the Soup: Short Stories for Teen-agers, Fortress, 1965.
Knee Deep in Ice Cream and Other Stories, Fortress, 1967.
What the Gulls Were Singing, Follett, 1967.
(Under name Phyllis Naylor) *Jennifer Jean, the Cross-Eyed Queen,* Lerner, 1967.
To Shake a Shadow, Abingdon, 1967.
(Under name Phyllis Naylor) *The New Schoolmaster,* Silver Burdett, 1967.
(Under name Phyllis Naylor) *A New Year's Surprise,* Silver Burdett, 1967.
When Rivers Meet, Friendship, 1968.
The Dark Side of the Moon (short stories), Fortress, 1969.
Meet Murdock, Follett, 1969.
To Make a Wee Moon, illustrated by Beth Krush and Joe Krush, Follett, 1969.
The Private I and Other Stories, Fortress, 1969.
Making It Happen, Follett, 1970.
Ships in the Night (short stories), Fortress, 1970.
Wrestle the Mountain, Follett, 1971.
No Easy Circle, Follett, 1972.
To Walk the Sky Path, Follett, 1973.
Witch's Sister (first volume of "Witch" trilogy), illustrated by Gail Owens, Atheneum, 1975.
Walking through the Dark, Atheneum, 1976.
Witch Water (second volume of "Witch" trilogy), illustrated by G. Owens, Atheneum, 1977.
The Witch Herself (third volume of "Witch" trilogy), illustrated by G. Owens, Atheneum, 1978.
How Lazy Can You Get?, illustrated by Alan Daniel, Atheneum, 1979.

PHYLLIS REYNOLDS NAYLOR

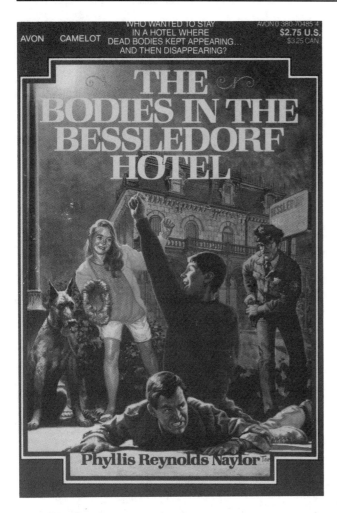

The Bodies in the Besseldorf Hotel is the second volume in Phyllis Naylor's ongoing comic murder mystery series.

A Change in the Wind (short stories), Augsburg Press, 1980.

Eddie, Incorporated, illustrated by Blanche Sims, Atheneum, 1980.

Shadows on the Wall (first volume of "York" trilogy), Atheneum, 1980.

All Because I'm Older, illustrated by Leslie Morrill, Atheneum, 1981.

Faces in the Water (second volume of "York" trilogy), Atheneum, 1981.

Footprints at the Window (third volume of "York" trilogy), Atheneum, 1981.

The Boy with the Helium Head, illustrated by Kay Chorao, Atheneum, 1982.

A String of Chances, Atheneum, 1982.

Never Born a Hero (short stories), Augsburg Press, 1982.

The Solomon System, Atheneum, 1983.

The Mad Gasser of Bessledorf Street (first volume in "Bessledorf" series), Atheneum, 1983.

A Triangle Has Four Sides (short stories), Augsburg Press, 1984.

Night Cry, Atheneum, 1984.

Old Sadie and the Christmas Bear, illustrated by Patricia Montgomery Newton, Atheneum, 1984.

The Dark of the Tunnel, Atheneum, 1985.

The Agony of Alice (first volume in "Alice" series), Atheneum, 1985.

The Keeper, Atheneum, 1986.

The Bodies in the Bessledorf Hotel (second volume in "Bessledorf" series), Atheneum, 1986.

The Baby, the Bed, and the Rose, illustrated by Mary Szilagyi, Clarion, 1987.

The Year of the Gopher, Atheneum, 1987.

Beetles, Lightly Toasted, Atheneum, 1987.

One of the Third Grade Thonkers, illustrated by Walter Gaffney Kessell, Atheneum, 1988.

(With mother, Lura Schield Reynolds) *Maudie in the Middle,* illustrated by Judith Gwyn Brown, Atheneum, 1988.

Alice in Rapture, Sort of (second volume in "Alice" series), Atheneum, 1989.

Keeping a Christmas Secret, illustrated by Lena Shiffman, Atheneum, 1989.

Bernie and the Bessledorf Ghost (third volume in "Bessledorf" series), Atheneum, 1990.

Witch's Eye (first volume in second "Witch" trilogy), Delacorte, 1990.

Send No Blessings, Atheneum, 1990.

Reluctantly Alice (third volume in "Alice" series), Atheneum, 1991.

Shiloh, Atheneum, 1991.

King of the Playground, Atheneum, 1991.

Witch Weed (second volume in second "Witch" trilogy), Delacorte, 1991.

Josie's Troubles, Atheneum, in press.

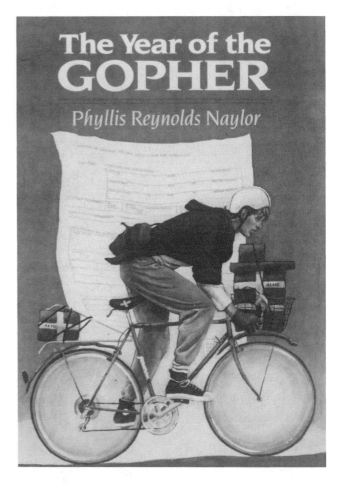

Phyllis Reynolds Naylor has won several awards, including the 1987 Best Book for Young Adults award from the American Library Association for *The Year of the Gopher*.

A preacher's daughter questions her religious beliefs after her cousin's baby suffers crib death. (Cover from *A String of Chances,* written by Phyllis Reynolds Naylor.)

The Witch Returns (third volume in second "Witch" trilogy), Delacorte, in press.
All But Alice, (fourth volume in "Alice" series), Atheneum, in press.

FOR CHILDREN AND YOUNG ADULTS; NONFICTION

How to Find Your Wonderful Someone, How to Keep Him/Her If You Do, How to Survive If You Don't, Fortress, 1972.
An Amish Family, illustrated by George Armstrong, J. Philip O'Hara, 1974.
Getting Along in Your Family, illustrated by Rick Cooley, Abingdon, 1976.
How I Came to Be a Writer, Atheneum, 1978, revised edition, Aladdin Books, 1987.
Getting Along with Your Friends, illustrated by R. Cooley, Abingdon, 1980.
Getting Along with Your Teachers, Abingdon, 1981.

FOR ADULTS

(Under name Phyllis Naylor) *Crazy Love: An Autobiographical Account of Marriage and Madness* (nonfiction), Morrow, 1977.

(Under name Phyllis Naylor) *In Small Doses* (humorous fiction), Atheneum, 1979.
(Under name Phyllis Naylor) *Revelations* (novel), St. Martin's, 1979.
(Under name Phyllis Naylor) *Unexpected Pleasures* (fiction), Putnam, 1986.
The Craft of Writing the Novel (nonfiction), Writer, 1989.

OTHER

Contributor of stories and articles to periodicals.

ADAPTATIONS: The Keeper was the basis for "My Dad Can't Be Crazy, Can He?," an "Afterschool Special" aired September 14, 1989, on American Broadcasting Companies (ABC-TV).

WORK IN PROGRESS: The Grand Escape and *Being Danny's Dog,* both for Atheneum, 1993; *The Boys Start the War,* for Delacorte; *The Face in the Bessledorf Funeral Parlor,* for Atheneum; *Carrying On,* a novel for adults; *Heather and the Horrible Baby; Girls against Boys;* and *Alice in April.*

SIDELIGHTS: Phyllis Naylor is a prolific author of fiction and nonfiction for children, adolescents, and adults. In writing about young adults she displays strong empathy for their concerns and understanding of their feelings. Critics hail her ability to create believable, appealing characters and to write from a young person's point of view. Taken as a whole, Naylor's writings are notable for their great diversity, ranging from books about her own life to advice about ways to

In this comic novel a boy tries to win a conservation contest by using bugs in recipes, which he tests on unsuspecting friends. (Cover from *Beetles, Lightly Toasted,* written by Phyllis Reynolds Naylor.)

maintain family communication and friendships to fiction exploring contemporary problems facing young people. Naylor enjoys the change of pace that comes with varying her subjects and writing for different audiences. "I can never imagine myself writing only for children or only for adults," she commented. "I like to follow up a mystery story for the nine-to-twelve set with a contemporary novel for adults; after that perhaps I will do a picture book, or a realistic novel for teens, or possibly a humorous book for children. The marvelous thing about writing is that I may play the part of so many different people—an old grandmother on one page, a young boy the next; a middle-aged man or a girl of fifteen. I feel most whole when I can look at a scene through the eyes of several different people."

The author was born January 4, 1933, in Anderson, Indiana, to a strongly religious family with conservative, midwestern values. Because her father was a traveling salesman, Naylor moved frequently and considered no one place "home." During the summers, her family vacationed either in Iowa, where her mother's parents lived, or in Maryland, where her father's parents lived. Though both sets of grandparents lived on farms, their personalities and environments were very different. Her grandparents in Iowa were isolated from any other neighbors and were staid and reserved by temperament. "Hugs were reserved for arrivals and departures, and in between was the practical, no-nonsense business of the day to attend to, without emotion or fuss," Naylor wrote in *How I Came to Be a Writer.* In contrast, her other grandparents were outgoing and lived within walking distance of neighbors in the town of Marbury, Maryland, where her grandfather was a church pastor and her grandmother a midwife. Consequently, during her visits there she came into contact with many more people and had a more lively time. In *How I Came to Be a Writer* Naylor related how this grandmother, called "Mammaw," gathered children for Sunday school: "On Sundays, my southern grandmother would pile us all in the car early and go traveling about the back roads of Charles County with a trunk full of donated clothes. At every home along her circuit, she would stop and see if the children were ready for Sunday School. If they were, they would climb aboard. If the excuse was no clothes to wear, Mammaw would simply open the trunk, find something the right size, and another child would be crammed in the backseat."

Naylor's summertime experiences made a great impression upon her and she drew on memories of Iowa in writing *To Make a Wee Moon* and *Beetles, Lightly Toasted,* and on those of Maryland to write the books *Revelations, A String of Chances,* and *Unexpected Pleasures.* "I never once thought of Maryland as my home, any more than I thought of all the other places we had lived as home but, quite without knowing it, I was soaking up the setting for future books," Naylor commented in *How I Came to Be a Writer.* She added, "By the time I placed a second novel . . . in Marbury, and then a third . . . , I realized this small southern Maryland town had worked its way into my blood."

One constant in Naylor's early life was storytelling and reading. Though she grew up during the Depression and her family did not have a lot of money, Naylor stated that she never felt poor because her family owned good books. Her parents enjoyed reading stories to the children—her father would imitate the characters in *Huckleberry Finn* and *Tom Sawyer*—and her mother read to them every evening, "almost until we were old enough to go out on dates, though we never would have admitted this to anyone," Naylor wrote in *How I Came to Be a Writer.*

Two brothers struggle to understand and adjust to their parents' divorce. (Cover from *The Solomon System,* written by Phyllis Reynolds Naylor.)

During grade school Naylor eagerly began writing her own stories, as she relates in *How I Came to Be a Writer:* "Each day I would rush home from school to see if the wastebasket held any discarded paper that had one side blank. We were not allowed to use new sheets of paper for our writing and drawing, so books had to be done on used paper. I would staple these sheets together and sometimes paste a strip of colored paper over the staples to give it the appearance of a bound book. Then I would grandly begin my story, writing the words at the top of each page and drawing an accompanying picture on the bottom. Sometimes I typed the story before stapling the pages. And sometimes I even cut old envelopes in half and pasted them on the inside covers as pockets, slipping an index card in each one, like a library book, so I could check it out to friends and neighbors. I was the author, illustrator, printer, binder, and librarian, all in one."

When Naylor was sixteen she began writing stories and poems for a church paper at the invitation of a former Sunday school teacher. Encouraged, she decided to send short stories to widely read magazines such as *Jack and Jill* and *Highlights for Children.* She came to realize, though, that her writing was not yet professional when her stories were returned with rejection slips. "My dreams of fame and fortune had vanished," she related in *How I Came to Be a Writer.* "They were replaced with a new respect for the business of writing."

In 1951, at the age of eighteen, she got married, and after graduating from Joliet Junior College she moved with her husband to Chicago, where he worked on an advanced degree. She found a job as a clinical secretary at the university hospital, and then taught third grade for six months.

When she was twenty-three, her husband began to display symptoms of mental illness. She felt great pressure to write stories in order to pay for her husband's treatment, her rent, and other expenses, as she later related in her nonfiction book, *How I Came to Be a Writer:* "One day, while we were living in Chicago, my husband suddenly showed signs of severe mental illness; he believed that the professors at the University were trying to kill him. For the next three years, while we moved from state to state, hospital to hospital, I wrote in earnest and in panic to support us. Sometimes I would take a whole afternoon and go off to a remote spot just to brainstorm—writing down ideas however they occurred to me until finally I had a list of plots to see me through the next few months." She was finally hired as a typist by the Board of Education's psychology office in Rockville, Maryland, and then worked a year for the Montgomery County Education Association. Eventually she lost hope that her husband would recover from his disease—diagnosed as paranoid schizophrenia—and decided to divorce him. The laws at that time made this a difficult procedure, because they required that her husband be declared incurable. Meanwhile, she fell in love, and when she succeeded in divorcing her first husband, she married Rex Naylor, a speech pathologist, on May 26, 1960.

Returning to school to become a clinical psychologist, Naylor earned a bachelor's degree in psychology from American University. At this point, though, she knew that she wanted to be a full-time writer and canceled plans for graduate school. Instead she began a family and wrote a column about family life that was published in church magazines. She also began a column for teenagers that would continue for twenty-five years. In 1965 she published her first book, a short story collection called *The Galloping Goat and Other Stories.* Her first children's novel, *What the Gulls Were Singing,* appeared two years later. Since then she has published one or more books each year.

In 1977, enough time had passed that Naylor could write about the painful experience of having a loved one become mentally ill. She discussed her book *Crazy Love: An Autobiographical Account of Marriage and Madness* in an interview for the American Audio Prose Library: "I knew that was a good story, beginning with the first insinuations that something was wrong and going through all the hell that you go through living with a paranoid schizophrenic. . . . The big problem was how to write this without making it sound like violins were in the background, and had I written it before I'm sure it would have been a horrible book. . . . But when you get fifteen years down the road and you look back, there were funny parts of it. . . . They weren't at the time, but there were things that he did which you could just sit back and laugh and say 'My god, that must have looked ridiculous,' or 'What on earth did that salesclerk at Sears think?' And so those were in the book in a sort of sardonic way to give me relief as the writer and give the reader relief from this heavy, heavy material. . . . I probably got more fan mail for *Crazy Love* than any other book I wrote. . . . And I began to think, hey, if I couldn't cope with this so well as a twenty-three-year-old woman, how would a thirteen-year-old boy handle it? And, of course, that's how fiction begins: 'What if, what if?' "

In her 1987 young adult novel *The Keeper,* she imagines a teen-age boy's reactions to his father's psychological illness. Nick sees his father become paranoid and distrustful and attempts to help him, but finally struggles to convince authorities that his father needs to be admitted to an institution. The book was well-regarded for its insightful and believable portrayal of Nick's responses and emotions.

Several of Naylor's other novels for young adults grapple with sensitive issues and problems. In *A String of Chances,* Evie, the daughter of a Maryland preacher, faces her doubts about her religious faith when her cousin's baby suffers crib death. Because it questions religious beliefs, the book caused some controversy among religious fundamentalists. *The Solomon System* describes how two adolescent brothers cope with their parents' divorce. Gayle Berge of *School Library Journal* judged *The Solomon System* "a very realistic look at the heartache and loneliness that divorce causes children to bear." In her 1985 novel *The Dark of the Tunnel,* Naylor addressed the subject of a parent's death, describing an eighteen-year old boy whose mother is dying from cancer. John R. Lord in *Voice of Youth Advocates* considered it "one of the best adolescent novels" on the subject of death,

"A valuable book for kids who may be living with a mentally ill loved one, or for teens who need to understand the circumstance under which a friend lives."—The Washington Post

A boy copes with his father's mental illness in Phyllis Reynolds Naylor's *The Keeper,* which was made into the ABC Afterschool Special *My Dad Can't Be Crazy.*

primarily because the book "concerns itself with the dying process and the recognition of the two young people and their mother."

Not all of Naylor's books are so serious, though. Well-known among her novels are trilogies noted for their Gothic suspense and mystery. Her first "Witch" trilogy, published during the 1970s, includes *Witch's Sister, Witch Water,* and *The Witch Herself,* and concerns a young girl who suspects her sister and a neighbor of witchcraft. The "York" trilogy, which appeared during the 1980s, features the character Dan Roberts in *Shadows on the Wall, Faces in the Water,* and *Footprints at the Window.* The teenager confronts the present worry that he might inherit a disease and encounters the supernatural when he travels back in time to fourth-century England. Naylor also has many humorous novels to her credit, including *How Lazy Can You Get,* a comedy about kids who outwit their baby-sitter, and *Beetles, Lightly Toasted,* about a boy who wants to win a conservation contest at school. This prompts him to devise recipes using bugs as ingredients, which he tests on unsuspecting class-mates. Naylor continues to sympathize with the young, as her 1980s novels *Alice in Agony* and *Maudie in the Middle* illustrate. Alice, a teen-age girl, searches for a female role model after her mother's death, and Maudie longs to find special recognition in a large family.

"I am not very interested in writing about the wealthy, probably because I was never one of them," Naylor commented. "While the rich, too, suffer disappointment and loss, money does help. But when a person with little education, money, or social skills faces the same problem, that, to me, is more of a challenge. 'How on earth is he going to solve *this?*' I wonder, and so I begin."

Never at a loss for ideas, Naylor once commented that her "biggest problem is that there are always four or five books waiting in the wings. Scarcely am I halfway through one book than another begins to intrude. I'm happy, of course, that ideas come so easily, but it is like having a monkey on my back. I am never quite free of it. Almost everything that happens to me or to the people I know ends up in a book at some time, all mixed up, of course, with imaginings. I can't think of anything else in the world I would rather do than write." Similarly, in *How I Came to Be a Writer* she declared, "On my deathbed, I am sure, I will gasp, 'But I still have five more books to write!' . . . I will go on writing, because an idea in the head is like a rock in the shoe; I just can't wait to get it out."

WORKS CITED:

Berge, Gayle, review of *The Solomon System, School Library Journal,* October, 1983, p. 161.
Bonetti, Kay, "Interview with Phyllis Naylor," American Audio Prose Library #7036, February, 1987.
Lord, John R., review of *The Dark of the Tunnel, Voice of Youth Advocates,* August, 1985, p. 188.
Naylor, Phyllis, *Crazy Love: An Autobiographical Account of Marriage and Madness,* Morrow, 1977.
Naylor, Phyllis Reynolds, *How I Came to Be a Writer,* Atheneum, 1978, revised edition, Aladdin Books, 1987.

FOR MORE INFORMATION SEE:

BOOKS

Children's Literature Review, Volume 17, Gale, 1989.

Something about the Author Autobiography Series, Volume 10, Gale, 1990.

PERIODICALS

Chicago Tribune Book World, March 2, 1986.
Christian Science Monitor, March 14, 1988.
Horn Book, September/October, 1986.
Lion and the Unicorn, fall, 1977.
Los Angeles Times, November 1, 1986.
New York Times Book Review, December 2, 1979; November 2, 1986.
School Library Journal, April, 1984.
Voice of Youth Advocates, April, 1983; June, 1987.
Washington Post Book World, September 12, 1982; November 6, 1983; November 8, 1983; June 9, 1985; March 9, 1986; May 11, 1986; November 25, 1986; December 14, 1986; May 10, 1987.

*　　*　　*

NICHOL, B(arrie) P(hillip) 1944-1988

PERSONAL: Name is often cited as bpNichol; born September 30, 1944, in Vancouver, British Columbia, Canada; died following surgery for a spinal tumor, September 25, 1988, in Toronto, Ontario, Canada; son of G. F. and Avis Aileen (Workman) Nichol; married Eleanor Hiebert, 1980; children: Sarah Katherine. *Education:* University of British Columbia, Elementary Basic Teaching Certificate, 1963.

ADDRESSES: Home—114 Lauder Ave., Toronto, Ontario M6H 3E5, Canada.

CAREER: Port Coquitlam, British Columbia, Canada, elementary school teacher, 1963; worked briefly at University of Toronto Library, Toronto, Ontario, Canada; Therafields Environmental Centre Ltd., "theradramist," 1966-88; York University, Toronto, one-time teacher in creative writing. Co-founder, Toronto Research Group, 1972. Member of The Four Horsemen (a collaborative sound poem group), 1970-88.

AWARDS, HONORS: Governor General's Award, 1971, for *Beach Head, The True Eventual Story of Billy the Kid, The Cosmic Chef,* and *Still Water;* three grants from Canada Council.

WRITINGS:

JUVENILE POETRY

Moosequakes & Other Disasters, Black Moss, 1981.
The Man Who Loved His Knees, Black Moss, 1983.
To the End of the Block, Black Moss, 1984.
Giants, Moosequakes & Other Disasters, Black Moss, 1985.
ONCE: a lullaby (illustrated by Anita Lobel), Greenwillow, 1986.

POETRY

bp (includes audio recording and packet of concrete poem objects), Coach House Press, 1967.
JOURNEYING & the returns, Coach House Press, 1967.
(Editor) *The Cosmic Chef: An Evening of Concrete,* Oberon Press, 1970.
Still Water, Talonbooks, 1970.
ABC: the aleph beth book, Oberon Press, 1971.
Monotones, Talonbooks, 1971.

The Martyrology Book I & II, Coach House Press, 1972, revised edition, 1977.

(Editor with Jiri Valoch) *The Pipe: An Anthology of Recent Czech Concrete*, Coach House Press, 1973.

Love: a book of remembrances, Talonbooks, 1974.

(Editor with Steve McCaffery) *The Story So Four*, Coach House Press, 1975.

The Martyrology Book III & IV, Coach House Press, 1976.

(Editor with S. McCaffery) *Sound Poetry: A Catalogue*, Underwhich, 1978.

(Editor) *The Arches: Selected Poetry of Frank Davey*, Talonbooks, 1980.

The Martyrology Book V, Coach House Press, 1982.

The Martyrology Book VI, Coach House Press, 1987.

POETRY ON AUDIO RECORDINGS

"Motherlove," Allied Records, 1968.

(With Rafael Barreto-Rivera, S. McCaffery and Paul Dutton, known as The Four Horsemen) "Canadada," Griffin House, 1972.

"bpNichol," High Barnet, 1973.

(With The Four Horsemen) "Live in the West," Starborne, 1977.

"Ear Rational," Membrane Press, 1982.

PROSE

Two Novels (contains *Andy* and *For Jesus Lunatick*), Coach House Press, 1969, 2nd edition, 1971.

Nights on Prose Mountain (short prose), grOnk, 1969.

The True Eventual Story of Billy the Kid, Weed/Flower Press, 1970.

Craft Dinner: Stories and Texts 1966-1976, Longwood, 1976.

(With S. McCaffery) *In England Now That Spring: Polaroid Poems, Found Texts, Visions and Collaborations; Records of a Journey through Scotland and England*, Longwood, 1978.

Journal (novel), Coach House Press, 1978.

Extreme Positions (novel), Longspoon Press, 1981.

Briefly: The Birthdeath Cycle from "The Book of Hours" (novel), Island Writing Series, 1981.

Continental Trance (novella), Oolichan Books, 1982.

Still (novella), Pulp Press, 1983.

Zygal: A Book of Mysteries and Translations, Coach House Press, 1985.

Art Facts: A Book of Contexts, Chax Press, 1990.

PAMPHLETS

Cycles Etc., 7 Flowers Press, 1965.

Scraptures: 2nd Sequence, Ganglia Press, 1965.

Calendar, Openings Press, 1966, 2nd edition published as *A New Calendar*, Ganglia Press, 1969.

(With David Aylward) *Strange Grey Town*, Ganglia Press, 1966.

Scraptures: 3rd Sequence, Ganglia Press, 1966.

Scraptures: 4th Sequence, Press Today, 1966.

Fodder Folder, Ganglia Press, 1966.

Portrait of David, Ganglia Press, 1966.

A Vision in the U of T Stacks, Ganglia Press, 1966.

A Little Pome for Yur Fingertips, Ganglia Press, 1966.

Langwedge, Ganglia Press, 1966.

Alphabit, Ganglia Press, 1966.

Stan's Ikon, Ganglia Press, 1966.

The Birth of O, Ganglia Press, 1966.

Chocolate Poem, privately printed, 1966.

Last Poem with You in Mind, Ganglia Press, 1967.

Scraptures: 10th Sequence, Ganglia Press, 1967.

Scraptures: 11th Sequence, Fleye Press, 1967.

Ruth, Fleye Press, 1967.

The Year of the Frog, Ganglia Press, 1967.

Konfessions of an Elizabethan Fan Dancer, Writers Forum, 1967, revised edition, Weed/Flower Press, 1973.

Ballads of the Restless Are, Runcible Spoon, 1968.

Dada Lama, Cavan McCarthy, 1968.

D. A. Dead (a lament), grOnk, 1968.

Kon 66 & 67, grOnk, 1968.

The Complete Works, Ganglia Press, 1968.

3rd Fragment from a Poem Continually in the Process of Being Written, Ganglia Press, 1969.

Astronomical Observations: July 69, Ganglia Press, 1969.

Sail, Ganglia Press, 1969.

A Condensed History of Nothing, Ganglia Press, 1970.

Lament, Ganglia Press, 1970, 2nd edition, Writers Forum, 1970.

Beach Head, Runcible Spoon, 1970.

The Captain Poetry Poems, Blewointment Press, 1972.

(With S. McCaffery) *Collbrations*, grOnk, 1972.

The Other Side of the Room, Weed/Flower Press, 1972.

(With others) *Six Fillious*, Membrane Press, 1978.

Translating Translating Apollinaire: A Preliminary Report from a Book of Research, Membrane Press, 1979.

(Editor with Jack David) *As Elected: Selected Writing 1962-1979*, Talonbooks, 1980.

Sharp Facts: Selections from TTA, Membrane Press, 1981.

(With The Four Horsemen) *The Prose Tattoo: Selected Performance Scores*, Membrane Press, 1983.

OTHER

Work represented in anthologies, including *Concrete Poetry: Britain, Canada, United States*, Hansjorg Mayer (Stuttgart), 1966; *Anthology of Concrete Poetry*, edited by Emmett Williams, Something Else Press, 1967; *Concrete Poetry: A World View*, edited by M. E. Solt and Willis Barnstone, Indiana University Press, 1969; *The Long Poem Anthology*, edited by Michael Ondaatje, Coach House Press, 1979; and *An Anthology of Canadian Literature in English*, edited by Donna Bennett and Russell Brown, Oxford University Press, 1983.

Collaborator with Barbara Caruso on volume of prints, *The Adventures of Milt the Morph in Colour*, Seripress, 1973. Author of six-episode radio serial, "Little Boy Lost Meets Mother Tongue," broadcast by Canadian Broadcasting Corp., 1969. Author of songs and scripts for television series *Fraggle Rock* and *The Raccoons*. Contributor to periodicals, including *Open Letter*, *Essays on Canadian Writing*, *White Pelican*, and *Line*. Editor, *Ganglia*, 1965-66, *grOnk*, 1967-88, and *Synapsis*, 1969-71; contributing editor, *Open Letter* (second series), 1970-75.

FOR MORE INFORMATION SEE:

BOOKS

Davey, Frank, *From There to Here*, Press Porcepic, 1974.

Dictionary of Literary Biography, Volume 53: *Canadian Writers since 1960*, Gale, 1986.

Scobie, Stephen, *bpNichol: What History Teaches*, Talonbooks, 1984.

PERIODICALS

Alphabet, June, 1971.

Boundary, fall, 1974.

Capilano Review, fall, 1975; spring, 1976.

Essays in Canadian Criticism, Volume 1, number 1, 1974.

Essays on Canadian Writing, winter, 1974; spring, 1976; winter, 1977-78.

Varsity, February, 1975.

[Date of death provided by wife, Eleanor Nichol]

NICKLESS, Will 1902-1979(?)

PERSONAL: Born April 4, 1902, in Brentwood, Essex, England; died c. 1979; son of William Thomas and Ada (Baylis) Nickless; married Nellie Agnes Carter, 1927; children: Will. *Education:* Attended St. Martin's School of Art, London, England. *Hobbies and other interests:* Handicrafts; novelist Charles Dickens and the illustrators of Dickens's books.

ADDRESSES: Home—Heathfield Hall, Town Row Green, Rotherfield, Sussex, England.

CAREER: Painter, illustrator, and author. Illustrator for technical periodicals, including *Motor* and *Aeroplane,* 1920-25; free-lance illustrator of books, periodicals, and advertisements, beginning in 1925. Advertising consultant to Enfield Rolling Mills, 1942-45.

AWARDS, HONORS: Owlglass was placed on *Horn Book*'s honor list, 1967.

WRITINGS:

The Little Fly and Other Verses, Virgin Press (London), 1957.
(Compiler) Aesop, Jean de la Fontaine, and others, *Book of Fables,* self-illustrated, Warne, 1963.
Owlglass, self-illustrated, John Baker (London), 1964, John Day (New York), 1966.
The Nitehood, self-illustrated, Oliver & Boyd (Edinburgh), 1966.
Molepie, self-illustrated, John Baker, 1967.
Dotted Lines, self-illustrated, John Baker, 1968.

Also author of the poetry collection *A Guide to the Tower.*

ILLUSTRATOR

Hans Christian Andersen, *The Ugly Duckling,* Houghton, 1948.
Thomas Hughes, *Tom Brown's Schooldays,* Collins, 1953.
H. Rider Haggard, *Allan Quatermain,* Collins, 1955.
Haggard, *King Solomon's Mines,* Collins, 1955.
Haggard, *She: A History of Adventure,* Collins, 1957.
Haggard, *Ayesha: The Return of She,* Collins, 1957.
Haggard, *Nada the Lily,* Collins, 1957.
Henry Treece, *Further Adventures of Robinson Crusoe,* S. G. Phillips, 1958.
Frank Knight, *Stories of Famous Ships,* Oliver & Boyd, 1963, Westminster Press (Philadelphia), 1966.
Knight, *Stories of Famous Sea Fights,* Oliver & Boyd, 1963, Westminster Press, 1967.
Aesop, *Fables,* Ward, Lock, 1964.
Knight, *Stories of Famous Explorers by Sea,* Oliver & Boyd, 1964, Westminster Press, 1966.
Knight, *Stories of Famous Sea Adventures,* Oliver & Boyd, 1966, Westminster Press, 1967.
Knight, *Stories of Famous Adventurers,* Oliver & Boyd, 1966.
Knight, *Stories of Famous Explorers by Land,* Westminster Press, 1966.
Girls' Adventure Stories of Long Ago, Hamlyn (Feltham, England), 1968.
Aubrey Feist, *The Field of Waterloo, June 18, 1815,* Lutterworth (London), 1969.
Edward Fox, *The Battle of Britain, August-September, 1940,* Lutterworth, 1969.
(With George Thompson) Alan Cooper, *Fishes of the World,* Hamlyn, 1969, Grosset & Dunlap, 1971.

WILL NICKLESS

Rivers and River Life, Macdonald Educational (London), 1971.
Fred J. Schonell, *Happy Venture,* Oliver & Boyd, 1971.
Neil Grant, *David Livingstone,* F. Watts (London), 1974.

Illustrator of additional works, including *Heidi, A History of the Catholic Church,* Jane Austen's *Pride and Prejudice,* Charles Dickens's *A Christmas Carol,* and Mark Twain's *Tom Sawyer.*

SIDELIGHTS: At the age of twenty-three Will Nickless began a lifelong career in the demanding field of free-lance illustrating. "Fear of not earning a living," he told Howard Cooley in the *Times Educational Supplement,* "made me keep going." Nickless illustrated children's books for years before he wrote one of his own: in the winter of 1963, he was out of work and snowbound in his country house when he decided to write *Owlglass.* This book and its sequels—*The Nitehood, Molepie,* and *Dotted Lines*—are set among the animals of "Rotherside," a thinly-disguised version of his home village of Rotherfield. In the Rotherside books, Nickless uses animals with human traits to poke fun at the foolish behavior he sees in everyday life. Older children and even grown-ups, he told Cooley, will probably enjoy these books the most.

When he was not busy as an illustrator, Nickless had several side interests that kept him working with his hands. He painted, holding an exhibition every few years when he had enough works to show. His portrait of English Chief Justice Lord Goddard was purchased to hang in London's Middle Temple, a center for the study of English law. Nickless used a hand press to print his own poems and bound the sheets himself into book form. He also built everything from violins to model trains.

This line drawing from the _Further Adventures of Robinson Crusoe_ is one of many Will Nickless created during a lifelong career of free-lance illustrating.

WORKS CITED:

Cooley, Howard, "Literary Host by Instinct," _Times Educational Supplement,_ February 16, 1968.

FOR MORE INFORMATION SEE:

PERIODICALS

Horn Book, June, 1966.
New York Times Book Review, November 10, 1963.
Times Literary Supplement, April 3, 1969.

*   *   *

OLDS, Elizabeth 1896-1991

OBITUARY NOTICE—See index for _SATA_ sketch: Born December 10, 1896, in Minneapolis, MN; died March 4, 1991, in Sarasota, FL. Artist and author. Olds was a painter and printmaker whose art was displayed in major museums and purchased for private collections. She was the first woman artist to receive a Guggenheim fellowship for her work, and some of her prints are kept in the permanent collections of the National Museum of American Art, the Library of Congress, New York's Metropolitan Museum, and the Museum of Modern Art. On the suggestion of a

museum dean, she developed a children's book called _The Big Fire_ from one of her prints. This work, along with such later books as _Riding the Rails, Deep Treasure,_ and _Plop Plop Ploppie,_ was chosen as a Junior Literary Guild selection.

OBITUARIES AND OTHER SOURCES:

BOOKS

Who's Who in America, 45th edition, Marquis, 1988.
Who's Who in American Art, 18th edition, Bowker, 1989.

PERIODICALS

New York Times, March 7, 1991.

*   *   *

PEEBLES, Anne
See GALLOWAY, Priscilla

*   *   *

PENROSE, Gordon 1925-
(Dr. Zed)

PERSONAL: Also known as "Dr. Zed"; born July 24, 1925, in Hamilton, Ontario, Canada; son of Thomas William (an electrical engineer) and Marion Gertrude (a homemaker; maiden name, Middleton) Penrose; married Marion Seymour (a teacher), August 21, 1948; children: Lynda, Donna, Sandra. _Education:_ University of Western Ontario, B.A., 1956; University of Toronto, B.Ed., 1958, M.E., 1964. _Hobbies and other interests:_ Lapidary work (cutting, grinding, and polishing semiprecious stones), photography, baking—especially experimenting with breads.

ADDRESSES: Home and office—14 Abbeville Rd., Scarborough, Ontario, Canada M1H 1Y3.

CAREER: Public schoolteacher in Hamilton, Ontario, 1948-59; Toronto Teachers' College, Toronto, Ontario, teaching master, 1960-69; York Regional Board of Education, master teacher in Stouffville, Richmond Hill, and Thornhill, Ontario, 1969-81; writer, 1981—. Fellow of the Ontario Institute for Studies in Education, 1981. Consultant to the Canadian Broadcasting Corp. (CBC) series _The Wonderful World of Science,_ 1980; appeared as Dr. Zed on TV-Ontario, the Canadian TV program _Romper Room,_ and _OWL-TV,_ CBC, 1985-1990, Canadian Television Network (CTV), 1990-91; gives readings in schools, libraries, bookstores, and at teachers' conferences; honorary chairman of Ontario fund-raising campaign for United Nations Children's Fund (UNICEF), 1982-83.

MEMBER: Canadian Society of Children's Authors, Illustrators, and Performers, Writers Union of Canada.

WRITINGS:

Dr. Zed's Zany Brilliant Book of Science Experiments (juvenile; illustrated by Linda Bucholtz-Ross), Barron, 1977, published in Canada as _It's Dr. Zed's Brilliant Book of Science Experiments,_ Greey de Pencier Books, 1977.
Dr. Zed's Dazzling Book of Science Activities (juvenile; illustrated by Bucholtz-Ross), Greey de Pencier Books, 1982.

Gordon Penrose, known to children as Dr. Zed.

Fooling around with Science: The Best of Dr. Zed's Brilliant Experiments, (juvenile; illustrated by Tina Holdcroft), Greey de Pencier Books, 1986.
Magic Mud and Other Great Experiments (juvenile; illustrated by Holdcroft), Greey de Pencier Books, 1987, Simon & Schuster, 1988.
Dr. Zed's Science Surprises (juvenile; illustrated by Holdcroft; photographs by Ray Boudreau), Greey de Pencier Books, 1989, Simon & Schuster, 1990.
Sensational Science Activities with Dr. Zed (juvenile), Simon & Schuster, 1990.

Contributor to "Dr. Zed" feature in *OWL* magazine, 1977—, and in *Chickadee* magazine, 1986—.

WORK IN PROGRESS: A new book of science experiments, publication expected in 1992.

SIDELIGHTS: A retired teacher of science, Gordon Penrose continues teaching in the role of madcap scientist "Dr. Zed." Dr. Zed was originally a cartoon figure in *OWL* magazine, but since Penrose began making appearances as the character—demonstrating experiments to children's groups and on Canadian television—he has undeniably become Dr. Zed. To transform himself into the character he enlists the aid of children, who help him apply his eyebrow makeup, put on his glasses, and get into his white lab coat. Penrose then invites them to participate in the activities. His experiments have been published in several children's books, including *Magic Mud and Other Great Experiments* and *Dr. Zed's Science Surprises.*

Penrose commented: "Annabel Slaight, the president of the Young Naturalists Foundation, knocked on my resource room door and asked me if I would like to try out to be Dr.

Zed in February, 1977. What a marvelous surprise! Dr. Zed experiments are developed from readily available household materials; they work every time; they are safe; they have often surprising results; they are based on scientific principles; and they can be extended when the children choose to change one variable at a time.

"I encourage participation rather than merely watching or reading how to do the experiments. Many children write and offer suggestions as to how I can improve, as well as telling me the experiments they have tried and changed. Children also send pictures, which I paste on the outside of my suitcases that hold Dr. Zed equipment and supplies. The most delightful words for me are 'Wow! It really works.'"

*　　*　　*

PRELUTSKY, Jack 1940-

PERSONAL: Born September 8, 1940, in Brooklyn, NY; son of Charles (an electrician) and Dorothea (a housewife; maiden name, Weiss) Prelutsky; married wife, Carolynn, 1979. *Education:* Attended Hunter College (now of the City University of New York); has studied voice at several music schools. *Hobbies and other interests:* Making plastic and

JACK PRELUTSKY

metal sculptures, bicycling, inventing word games, collecting books and model frogs.

ADDRESSES: Home—Olympia, WA; and c/o Greenwillow Books, 1350 Avenue of the Americas, New York, NY 10019.

CAREER: Poet and singer. Has worked as a cab driver, busboy, actor, photographer, furniture mover, potter, sculptor, day laborer, waiter, carpenter, clerk, bookseller, and door-to-door salesman.

AWARDS, HONORS: Nightmares: Poems to Trouble Your Sleep was selected for the Children's Book Showcase of the Children's Book Council, and was included in the American Institute of Graphic Arts Book Show, both 1977, and one of *School Library Journal*'s Best of the Best Books, 1979; Children's Choice, International Reading Association/Children's Book Council, 1978, for *The Mean Old Mean Hyena; The Headless Horseman Rides Tonight: More Poems to Trouble Your Sleep* was selected one of the *New York Times*'s Outstanding Books of the Year and one of the Best Illustrated Books of the Year, both 1980; *School Library Journal*'s Best Books selections, 1980, for *The Headless Horseman Rides Tonight*, 1981, for *The Wild Baby*, 1983, for *The Random House Book of Poetry for Children* and *The Wild Baby Goes to Sea*, and 1986, for *Read-Aloud Rhymes for the Very Young; Booklist* Children's Reviewers' Choice, 1980, for *The Headless Horseman Rides Tonight; The Random House Book of Poetry for Children* was a Child Study Association Children's Book of the Year and Library of Congress Book of the Year, 1983; Parents' Choice Award, Parents' Choice Foundation, and Garden State Children's Book Award, New Jersey Library Association, both 1986, both for *The New Kid on the Block;* Notable Children's Recording, American Library Association, 1987, for *The New Kid on the Block; Something Big Has Been Here* was an Association for Library Services to Children Notable Book and *Booklist* Editor's Choice, both 1990.

WRITINGS:

(Translator) Rudolf Neumann, *The Bad Bear,* illustrated by Eva Johanna Rubin, Macmillan, 1967.
(Translator) Heinrich Hoffman, *The Mountain Bounder,* Macmillan, 1967.
A Gopher in the Garden and Other Animal Poems (also see below), illustrated by Robert Leydenfrost, Macmillan, 1967.
(Translator) *No End of Nonsense: Humorous Verses,* illustrated by Wilfried Blecher, Macmillan, 1968.
Lazy Blackbird and Other Verses, illustrated by Janosch, Macmillan, 1969.
(Translator) *Three Saxon Nobles and Other Verses,* illustrated by Rubin, Macmillan, 1969.
(Translator) James Kruess, *The Proud Wooden Drummer,* illustrated by Rubin, Doubleday, 1969.
The Terrible Tiger, illustrated by Arnold Lobel, Macmillan, 1970.
Toucans Two and Other Poems (also see below), illustrated by Jose Aruego, Macmillan, 1970 (published in England as *Zoo Doings and Other Poems,* Hamish Hamilton, 1971).
Circus!, illustrated by Lobel, Macmillan, 1974.
The Pack Rat's Day and Other Poems (also see below), illustrated by Margaret Bloy Graham, Macmillan, 1974.
Nightmares: Poems to Trouble Your Sleep (American Library Association [ALA] Notable Book), illustrated by Lobel, Greenwillow, 1976.

A leading children's poet, Jack Prelutsky recognizes that an occasional fright can be fun and exciting. (Cover illustration from *Nightmares: Poems to Trouble Your Sleep* by Arnold Lobel.)

It's Halloween, illustrated by Marylin Hafner, Greenwillow, 1977.
The Snopp on the Sidewalk and Other Poems (ALA Notable Book; also see below), illustrated by Byron Barton, Greenwillow, 1977.
The Mean Old Mean Hyena, illustrated by Lobel, Greenwillow, 1978.
The Queen of Eene (ALA Notable Book; also see below), illustrated by Victoria Chess, Greenwillow, 1978.
Rolling Harvey down the Hill (also see below), illustrated by Chess, Greenwillow, 1980.
The Headless Horseman Rides Tonight: More Poems to Trouble Your Sleep, illustrated by Lobel, Greenwillow, 1980.
Rainy, Rainy Saturday, illustrated by Hafner, Greenwillow, 1980.
(Adapter) Barbro Lindgren, *The Wild Baby,* illustrated by Eva Eriksson, Greenwillow, 1981.
It's Christmas, illustrated by Hafner, Greenwillow, 1981.
The Sheriff of Rottenshot: Poems by Jack Prelutsky, illustrated by Chess, Greenwillow, 1982.
Kermit's Garden of Verses, illustrated by Bruce McNally, Random House, 1982.
It's Thanksgiving, illustrated by Hafner, Greenwillow, 1982.
The Baby Uggs Are Hatching, illustrated by James Stevenson, Greenwillow, 1982.
Zoo Doings: Animal Poems (includes *A Gopher in the Garden and Other Animal Poems, Toucans Two and Other*

Poems, and *The Pack Rat's Day and Other Poems*), illustrated by Paul O. Zelinsky, Greenwillow, 1983.

It's Valentine's Day, illustrated by Yossi Abolafia, Greenwillow, 1983.

(Adapter) Lindgren, *The Wild Baby Goes to Sea,* illustrated by Eriksson, Greenwillow, 1983.

(Compiler and editor) *The Random House Book of Poetry for Children* (ALA Notable Book), illustrated by Lobel, Random House, 1983.

It's Snowing! It's Snowing!, illustrated by Jeanne Titherington, Greenwillow, 1984.

What I Did Last Summer, illustrated by Abolafia, Greenwillow, 1984.

The New Kid on the Block (ALA Notable Book), illustrated by Stevenson, Greenwillow, 1984.

My Parents Think I'm Sleeping, illustrated by Abolafia, Greenwillow, 1985.

(Adapter) Lindgren, *The Wild Baby Gets a Puppy,* illustrated by Eriksson, Greenwillow, 1985.

Ride a Purple Pelican, illustrated by Garth Williams, Greenwillow, 1986.

(Adapter) Rose Lagercrantz and Samuel Lagercrantz, *Brave Little Pete of Geranium Street,* illustrated by Eriksson, Greenwillow, 1986.

(Compiler and editor) *Read-Aloud Rhymes for the Very Young,* illustrated by Marc Brown, Knopf, 1986.

Tyrannosaurus Was a Beast: Dinosaur Poems, illustrated by Lobel, Greenwillow, 1988.

(Collector and editor) *Poems of A. Nonny Mouse,* illustrated by Henrik Drescher, Knopf, 1989.

Beneath a Blue Umbrella, illustrated by Williams, Greenwillow, 1990.

Something Big Has Been Here (ALA Notable Book), illustrated by Stevenson, Greenwillow, 1990.

(Compiler and editor) *For Laughing Out Loud,* illustrated by Marjorie Priceman, Knopf, 1991.

Twickham Tweer (from *The Sheriff of Rottenshot*), illustrated by Eldon Doty, DLM, 1991.

Archives of Prelutsky's work are kept in the University of Southern Mississippi's De Grummond Collection and the University of Minnesota's Kerlan Collection.

ADAPTATIONS:

Nightmares and Other Poems to Trouble Your Sleep (record; cassette), Children's Books and Music, 1985.

It's Thanksgiving (cassette), Listening Library, 1985.

The New Kid on the Block (cassette), Listening Library, 1986.

It's Halloween (cassette), Scholastic, 1987.

It's Christmas (cassette), Scholastic, 1987.

Ride a Purple Pelican (cassette), Listening Library, 1988.

Read-Aloud Rhymes for the Very Young (cassette), Knopf, 1988.

It's Valentine's Day (cassette), Scholastic, 1988.

Something Big Has Been Here (cassette), Listening Library, 1991.

An audio recording has also been produced for *Rainy, Rainy Saturday* (cassette), Random House. Prelutsky's poems have been included in *Graveyard Tales* (record), NAPPS; and *People, Animals and Other Monsters* (record; cassette; includes poems from *The Snopp on the Sidewalk, The Queen of Eene, Rolling Harvey Down the Hill, The Pack-Rat's Day, A Gopher in the Garden,* and *Toucans Two and Other Poems*), Caedmon.

SIDELIGHTS: Born in Brooklyn, New York, Jack Prelutsky was a gifted and restless child whose intelligence made it difficult for him to conform to the undemanding expectations of public school. His overactive mind also made it hard for his mother and teachers to manage him. "In those days," Prelutsky recalls in *Early Years,* ". . . schools and parents didn't have the knowledge, the machinery or the experience to handle kids like me." However, it soon became clear that this boy with behavior problems also had a rare talent: a magnificent singing voice.

At the age of ten, Prelutsky's abilities were already recognized by many people. Some considered him a prodigy and paid the boy to sing at weddings and other special occasions. The Choir Master of New York's Metropolitan Opera considered the boy so gifted that he willingly gave Prelutsky free singing lessons. As a teenager, the promising opera student attended the High School of Music and Art in New York City, where he also studied piano. He graduated from the school in 1958.

It seemed like Prelutsky was on his way to an operatic career. But then one day his determination was shattered when he heard the world renowned Luciano Pavarotti perform. After that, Prelutsky abandoned the idea of becoming a famous opera singer. "I knew I could never compete with him. . . . I didn't have the fire in the belly," he comments in *Early Years.* Prelutsky experimented with numerous other professions. He became an excellent photographer, good enough to earn a living and even exhibit some of his work, but not—in his opinion—the best. He undertook a number of manual labor jobs, such as carpentry and furniture moving, as well as other occupations like cab driver, bookseller, and clerk. During the late 1950s and early 1960s, Prelutsky tried the life of the beatnik, bumming around the country and earning a living by playing his guitar and singing. He also made pottery and tried his hand at sculpting and collage. One day, while working in a coffeehouse in Greenwich Village, New York, Prelutsky met and became friends with musician Bob Dylan. They shared a common love of folk music and admired each other's performing abilities. According to Allen Raymond in *Early Years,* Dylan once observed that Prelutsky's voice sounded "like a cross between Woody Guthrie and Enrico Caruso."

Prelutsky had always felt that he was meant to be an artist, but he was not sure if being a folk singer was what he wanted to be for the rest of his life. One day he decided to try drawing. Using ink and watercolors, he labored for six months to create two dozen imaginary animals. The animals were fanciful creations that he made up himself, and had no basis in mythology or literature whatsoever. On an impulse, Prelutsky composed short poems to go with each of the drawings and then put his finished work away and forgot about it. One of his friends, who happened to be an author of children's books, saw the drawings and poems on Prelutsky's desk and persuaded him to get them published.

The first publisher Prelutsky went to turned him down, but the second, Macmillan, was very enthusiastic about his poetry. Susan Hirschman, the children's editor there, did not like the new poet's drawings very much, but Raymond writes that Hirschman believed the new author had "the talent to be one of the best poets in the world for children." Prelutsky credits Hirschman for inspiring him to become the successful poet he is today: "She saw something in my poems. I can't imagine what. I found those original ones recently and if I'd been an editor I'd have suggested to me that I go learn a

THE BOGEYMAN

In the desolate depths of a perilous place
the bogeyman lurks, with a snarl on his face.
Never dare, never dare to approach his dark lair
for he's waiting . . . just waiting . . . to get you.

He skulks in the shadows, relentless and wild
in his search for a tender, delectable child.
With his steely sharp claws and his slavering jaws
oh he's waiting . . . just waiting . . . to get you.

Many have entered his dreary domain
but not even one has been heard from again.
They no doubt made a feast for the butchering beast
and he's waiting . . . just waiting . . . to get you.

In that sulphurous, sunless and sinister place
he'll crumple your bones in his bogey embrace.
Never never go near if you hold your life dear,
for oh! . . . what he'll do . . . when he gets you!

12

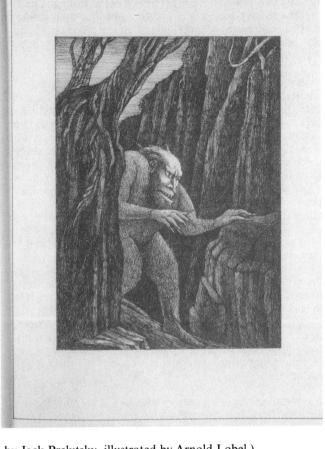

(From *Nightmares: Poems to Trouble Your Sleep,* by Jack Prelutsky, illustrated by Arnold Lobel.)

trade—the poems were a little above average for a 12-year-old."

After his first meeting with Hirschman, Prelutsky was convinced he had found a career in which he could be the best because he resolved to approach his verse in a way that would excite children. He remembered that when he was a boy poetry seemed like terribly dull reading that had no relevance to the real world. His childhood friends, Raymond reports, "used to think poets had to be either boring, . . . siss[ies,] or dead." But in his introduction to *The Random House Book of Poetry for Children* the author asserts that children don't have a natural aversion to verse. "For very young children, responding to poetry is as natural as breathing. Even before they can speak, most babies delight in the playful cadences of nursery rhymes and the soothing rhythms of lullabies. . . . Poetry is as delightful and surprising as being tickled or catching a snowflake on a mitten. . . . But then something happens to this early love affair with poetry. At some point during their school careers, many children seem to lose their interest and enthusiasm for poetry and their easygoing pleasure in its sounds and images. They begin to find poetry boring and irrelevant, too difficult or too dull to bother with."

Prelutsky was determined never to talk down to children, nor turn them off by creating lifeless, uninvolving poetry. The key, he discovered, was to write verses that children could relate to while also presenting them in an interesting manner. Regarding the content of his verses, *Dictionary of Literary Biography* contributor Anita Trout comments, "Prelutsky's

poetry features animals and fantastic beasts which behave in inventive ways. He also writes of people and problems familiar to youngsters: dealing with the neighborhood bully, going to school, and being afraid of the dark. Writing in traditional poetic forms, he employs puns, alliteration, and word play in ways which have caused him to be ranked among the masters of contemporary verse for children." His "primary fascination for children, however," Trout later notes, "seems to be his macabre delight in the darker side of fantasy and human nature." Of his more than thirty poetry collections, many are about monsters and other frightening creatures that often turn out to be friendly, or are presented with such exaggeration that they become humorous. But Prelutsky also recognizes that an occasional fright can be fun and exciting. In books like *Nightmares: Poems to Trouble Your Sleep* and *The Headless Horseman Rides Tonight: More Poems to Trouble Your Sleep* the poems are designed to cause a "shivery delight for the young reader," says Trout.

As for presentation, Prelutsky improved his approach by taking a lesson from his childhood. In *Through the Eyes of a Child: An Introduction to Children's Literature,* he recites a parable about two teachers who display the right and wrong ways to nurture the natural love that children have for poetry. The first teacher would take out a book of poems, read one of the verses to her students, put the book away, and proceed to teach another subject like history or geography. The poems she selected were about bees, flowers, hills, and other topics that failed to capture the student's imaginations. But the second teacher turned poetry into a game. She proclaimed a "silly monster week," and started the celebration by reciting a poem about a silly monster. "She shared a number of other poems during 'silly monster week,'" writes Prelutsky, "always showing her honest enthusiasm and finding imaginative methods of presentation. She used masks, musical instruments, dance, sound effects recordings, and clay sculpture. The children grew so involved that she soon was able to recite poems with no props at all."

In his own poetry, Prelutsky has sought to engage and entertain his audience the same way that this second teacher did. "I realized poetry was a means of communication," he says in *Early Years*, "that it could be as exciting or as boring as that person or that experience." The author does not try to write moralistic poetry, or poetry that contains some deep, inner truth. Instead, he indulges in nonsense verses that aim to delight the audience with their wordplay. The poems in *The Sheriff of Rottenshot* and *Ride a Purple Pelican* offer good examples of verse in which the poet uses repetition, alliteration, rhythm and other devices to entertain children.

Because of Prelutsky's emphasis on the sounds words make, his verses are often most effective when read aloud, or, as he does, performed with guitar accompaniment. Every year, Prelutsky spends a few weeks travelling and visiting schools, where he tells stories, performs songs, and recites poetry. He remarks in *Children's Literature in Education:* "Until I started visiting schools, I tended to work in a sort of vacuum, never really knowing how my books were received by the only really important audience—the children. Book reviews are, of course, important. . . . [But] it's the children that really matter."

It was during one of his yearly excursions that Prelutsky met his wife, Carolynn. She was a children's librarian in Albuquerque, New Mexico. On the first day they met, Carolynn was assigned to give Prelutsky a tour of the city. The poet

realized almost immediately that they made a perfect pair and proposed marriage to her. The next day, Carolynn accepted and they were soon married. Prelutsky settled down in Albuquerque, where he and his wife remained until their move to Washington state in 1990.

Today, Prelutsky continues to entertain children in schools and to lecture and give seminars to educators throughout the country. In addition to his many books of poetry, he has adapted German and Swedish verses and edited several other collections. The combination of writing and performing has made Prelutsky one of the most popular entertainers for young audiences in the United States. "Contemporary poets such as Jack Prelutsky," Trout concludes, "restore the fun and fascination in the study of the English language and its rhythmic patterns."

WORKS CITED:

Dictionary of Literary Biography, Volume 61: *American Writers for Children since 1960: Poets, Illustrators, and Nonfiction Authors,* Gale, 1987, pp. 242-247.
Miles, Betty, editor, "When Writers Visit Schools: A Symposium," *Children's Literature in Education,* Volume 11, number 3, 1980, pp. 133, 135-136.
Prelutsky, Jack, "Introduction," *The Random House Book of Poetry for Children,* Random House, 1983, pp. 18-19.
Prelutsky, Jack, "Through the Eyes of a Poet: Poetry Doesn't Have to Be Boring," *Through the Eyes of a Child: An Introduction to Children's Literature,* by Donna E. Norton, Merrill, 1983, pp. 322-323.
Raymond, Allen, "Jack Prelutsky . . . Man of Many Talents," *Early Years,* November-December, 1986, pp. 38, 40-42.

FOR MORE INFORMATION SEE:

BOOKS

Children's Literature Review, Volume 13, Gale, 1987.
Holtze, Sally Holmes, editor, *Fifth Book of Junior Authors and Illustrators,* H. W. Wilson, 1983.
Kirkpatrick, D. L., editor, *Twentieth-Century Children's Writers,* 2nd edition, St. Martin's, 1983.
Shaw, John Mackay, *Childhood in Poetry,* Gale, 1967.

PERIODICALS

Horn Book, December, 1967; August, 1970; April, 1971; August, 1974; December, 1974; October, 1976; October, 1977; April, 1978; June, 1978, October, 1980; October, 1982; September-October, 1984; January-February, 1986; January-February, 1987; September-October, 1988; January-February, 1990.
Juvenile Miscellany, summer, 1985.
Lion and the Unicorn, winter, 1980-81.
Publishers Weekly, July 29, 1988.
Wilson Library Bulletin, May, 1987; May, 1988; June, 1989.

*   *   *

PRESCOTT, Casey
See MORRIS, Chris(topher Crosby)

*   *   *

PRICHARD, Katharine Susannah 1883-1969

PERSONAL: Born December 4, 1883, in Levuka, Ovalau, Fiji; immigrated to Australia; died October 2, 1969; daughter of Tom Henry (editor of *Fiji Times*) and Edith Isabel (Fraser)

Alligators Are Unfriendly

Alligators are unfriendly,
they are easily upset,
I suspect that I would never
care to have one for a pet.
Oh, I know they do not bellow,
and I think they do not shed,
but I'd probably be nervous
if I had one in my bed.

Alligators are not clever,
they are something of a bore,
they can't heel or catch a Frisbee,
they don't greet you at the door,
for their courtesy is lacking,
and their tempers are not sweet,
they won't even fetch your slippers
. . . though they just might eat your feet.

(From *The New Kid on the Block,* by Jack Prelutsky, illustrated by James Stevenson.)

KATHARINE SUSANNAH PRICHARD

Prichard; married Hugo Throssell (an army captain), 1919 (committed suicide, 1933); children: Ric Prichard. *Politics:* Communist. *Education:* Educated in Australian schools.

ADDRESSES: Home—Greenmount, Australia.

CAREER: Journalist, editor, novelist, short story writer, poet, dramatist, autobiographer, and nonfiction writer. Journalist for newspapers in Melbourne and Sydney and for other Australian publications, and free-lance journalist in London, England, 1908 and 1912-16; full-time writer in Australia, 1916-69. Founding member of the Communist party of Australia.

MEMBER: Australian Writers' League (founding member and federal president), Modern Women's Club (founder), Unemployed Women and Girls' Association (Perth; founding member).

AWARDS, HONORS: Prize of one thousand pounds from Hodder & Stoughton, 1924, for *The Pioneers; Art in Australia* Prize, 1924, for short story "The Grey Horse"; *Triad* Award for a three-act Australian play, 1927, for *Brumby Innes;* prize of five hundred pounds from *Bulletin* (Sydney), 1928, for *Coonardoo.*

WRITINGS:

The Pioneers, Hodder & Stoughton, 1915, revised edition, Angus & Robertson, 1963.
Windlestraws, Holden & Hardingham, 1917.
The Black Opal, Heinemann, 1921.
Working Bullocks, Viking, 1927.
The Wild Oats of Han (juvenile), Angus & Robertson, 1928, revised edition, Lansdowne Press, 1968.

Coonardoo, the Well in the Shadow, J. Cape, 1929, Norton, 1930.
Haxby's Circus: The Lightest, Brightest Little Show on Earth, J. Cape, 1930, published as *Fay's Circus,* Norton, 1931.
Earth Lover (poems), Sunnybrook Press, 1930.
Kiss on the Lips, and Other Stories, J. Cape, 1932.
The Real Russia (political nonfiction), Modern Publishers, 1934.
(Contributor) *Best Australian One-Act Plays,* edited by William Moore and T. I. Moore, Angus & Robertson, 1937.
Intimate Strangers, J. Cape, 1937.
Brumby Innes (three-act play), Paterson's Printing Press, 1940.
Moon of Desire, J. Cape, 1941.
(Editor with others) *Australian New Writing: 1943-1945,* Current Books, 1943-1945.
Potch and Colour (short stories), Angus & Robertson, 1944.
The Roaring Nineties: A Story of the Goldfields of Western Australia, J. Cape, 1946.
Golden Miles, J. Cape, 1948.
Winged Seeds, J. Cape, 1950.
N'goola, and Other Stories, Australasian Book Society, 1959.
Child of the Hurricane (autobiography), Angus & Robertson, 1963.
On Strenuous Wings: A Half-Century of Selected Writings from the Works of Katharine Susannah Prichard, edited with an introduction by Joan Williams, Seven Seas Publishers, 1965.
Happiness: Selected Short Stories, Angus & Robertson, 1967.
Subtle Flame, Australasian Book Society, 1967.
Moggie and Her Circus Pony (juvenile), illustrated by Elaine Haxton, F. W. Cheshire, 1967.
Straight Left: Articles and Addresses on Politics, Literature, and Women's Affairs over Almost Sixty Years from 1910-1968, collected and introduced by son, Ric Throssell, Wild & Woolley, 1982.

Also author of poetry collection *Clovelly Verses,* a play titled *Bid Me to Love,* and a short story volume titled *The Grey Horse.* Work anthologized in *The World's Greatest Short Stories,* Crown.

Prichard's books have been translated into twelve languages, including Russian, Latvian, Hungarian, Slovak, Afrikaans, Armenian, and Chinese.

ADAPTATIONS: The Pioneers was adapted for two Australian films, released in 1916 and 1926.

SIDELIGHTS: Katharine Susannah Prichard was born in 1883 on Ovalau, one of the Fiji Islands of the Pacific Ocean, and moved with her family to Australia when she was a young girl. She began her writing career as a journalist in the early 1900s and went on to become one of Australia's most important authors. Prichard wrote both fiction and nonfiction, but she is probably best remembered for her poetic, realistic novels that deal with Australia and its people. In addition to her writings for adults, Prichard published two books for young people: *The Wild Oats of Han,* a novel based largely on her own childhood in Australia, and a picture book for children titled *Moggie and Her Circus Pony.* She also wrote a full-length autobiography, *Child of the Hurricane,* in 1963.

FOR MORE INFORMATION SEE:

BOOKS

Contemporary Literary Criticism, Volume 46, Gale, 1988.
Drake-Brockman, Henrietta, *Katharine Susannah Prichard,* Oxford University Press, 1967.
Prichard, Katharine Susannah, *Child of the Hurricane,* Angus & Robertson, 1963.
Throssell, Ric, *Wild Weeds and Windflowers: The Life and Letters of Katharine Susannah Prichard,* Angus & Robertson, 1975.

* * *

PROVOST, Gary (Richard) 1944-

PERSONAL: Surname is pronounced "*pro*-vo"; born November 14, 1944, in Boston, MA; son of Rosario Francis and Evelyn Mary Provost; married Elearnor Mears, October 22, 1975 (divorced, December, 1983); married Gail Levine-Freidus (an artist and writer), December 29, 1984. *Education:* Graduated from high school. *Religion:* Unitarian-Universalist.

ADDRESSES: P.O. Box 139, South Lancaster, MA 01561. *Agent*—Sterling Lord Literistic, Inc., One Madison Ave., New York, NY 10010.

CAREER: Worked variously as computer operator, bellboy, desk clerk, dispatcher, truck driver, and telephone operator, 1962-75; *Unitarian-Universalist World,* editor, 1978-81; writer, 1981—. Member of board of directors of Women's Health Service, Marlboro, MA, 1982.

MEMBER: International P.E.N., Authors Guild, American Film Institute.

AWARDS, HONORS: National Jewish Book Award for children's literature, 1985, for *Good If It Goes.*

WRITINGS:

Make Every Word Count, Writer's Digest, 1980.
The Freelance Writer's Handbook, New American Library, 1982.
The Pork Chop War (juvenile), Bradbury, 1982.
(With wife, Gail Levine-Freidus) *Good If It Goes* (juvenile), Bradbury, 1984.
(With wife, Gail Levine-Provost) *Popcorn* (juvenile), Bradbury, 1985.
Doctor's Orders, Bantam, 1985.
One Hundred Ways to Improve Your Writing, New American Library, 1985.
Beyond Style: Mastering the Finer Points of Writing, Writer's Digest, 1987.
(With Levine-Provost) *David and Max* (juvenile), Jewish Publication Society, 1988.
(With Marilyn Greene) *Finder: The True Story of a Private Investigator,* Crown, 1988.
Across the Border: The True Story of the Satanic Cult Killings in Matamoros, Mexico, Pocket Books, 1989.
Make Your Words Work, Writer's Digest, 1990.
Without Mercy: Obsession and Murder under the Influence, Pocket Books, 1990.

Contributor of more than one thousand articles and stories to national, regional, and local magazines and newspapers. Contributing editor and columnist, *Writer's Digest.*

WORK IN PROGRESS: The Moon and New York City, a novel about male liberation.

SIDELIGHTS: Gary Provost commented: "Writing about writing is only one facet of my career. I have written everything from hardware catalogs to radio scripts. I am capable of writing a love story or a sports how-to book.

"My first children's book, *The Pork Chop War,* was based on my own childhood in the slums of Boston. *Doctor's Orders* is the true story of nurse Anne Capute, who was tried for first degree murder as the result of an alleged mercy killing at a Massachusetts hospital."

* * *

PURDY, Carol 1943-

PERSONAL: Born January 5, 1943, in Long Beach, CA; daughter of Melvin Boyce (a machinist) and Kathryn (a homemaker; maiden name, Wilbur) Slaughter; married John Purdy (a teacher), June 8, 1963; children: Laura, Mark, Sarah. *Education:* California State University, Long Beach, B.A., 1964; California State University, Sacramento, M.S.W., 1990. *Religion:* Church of Christ. *Hobbies and other*

CAROL PURDY

interests: Music, gardening, aerobics, drawing, water-skiing, traveling.

ADDRESSES: Home—25310 68th Ave., Los Molinos, CA 96055. *Office*—Tehama County Mental Health, 1860 Walnut, Red Bluff, CA 96080. *Agent*—Faith Hamlin, Sanford J. Greenburger Associates, Inc., 55 Fifth Ave., New York, NY 10003.

CAREER: Orange Unified School District, Orange, CA, elementary school teacher, 1964-67; Kid Power Program, Red Bluff, CA, founder, 1988—; Tehama County Mental Health, Red Bluff, social worker, 1989—; writer.

MEMBER: Society of Children's Book Writers, National Association of Social Workers, American Art Therapy Association.

WRITINGS:

Iva Dunnit and the Big Wind, illustrated by Steven Kellogg, Dial, 1985.
Least of All, illustrated by Tim Arnold, Macmillan, 1987.
Kid Power: Groups for High Risk Children, Mill Creek Publishers, 1989.
Mrs. Merriwether's Musical Cat, Putnam, in press.

WORK IN PROGRESS: Research on native Americans of California.

SIDELIGHTS: Carol Purdy told *SATA:* "I was not one of those children who took a flashlight to bed in order to write in my journal and knew from age three that my destiny was to be an author. While growing up in the big city of Long Beach, California, I had no idea I would some day be a writer. My greatest interests as a child were art and music. I sang in the school choir, played several instruments, and took art classes.

"While in college I married a fellow student, and we both decided to become elementary school teachers. When we were expecting our first child, we wanted to find a country environment in which to raise a family. We moved to a seventy-five year old farmhouse near Red Bluff, California, and tried everything from raising pigs, horses, cattle and chickens to doing our own butchering, cheesemaking, and butter churning.

"After the birth of my third child, I thought of the advice of my high school English teacher who said I should become a writer. Six years later, after wearing out three typewriters, my book *Iva Dunnit and the Big Wind* was accepted for publication.

"The evolution of this first book was a slow and lengthy process. Originally it was entitled *Tales of Iva Dunnit,* and consisted of two short stories based on true incidents passed down in the oral traditions of my family. I rewrote this manuscript several times for editors at various publishing houses over a period of five years. At one point, I was asked if there were any more Iva Dunnit stories. I responded by writing *Iva Dunnit and the Big Wind* in a two hour sitting. However, *Tales of Iva Dunnit,* which had now grown to three stories, was rejected by that editor with the explanation, 'Collections are hard to sell.'

"The next time out, Amy Ehrlich, then editor at Dial, asked me to combine the three stories into one for the same reason—collections don't sell well. I did, and was told that the resulting tale was not as good as the third story standing alone, *Iva Dunnit and the Big Wind.* Dial made the decision to publish it as a picture book, and Steven Kellogg agreed to do the illustrations. I learned a great deal about writing picture books from the process of revising this tale and leaving room for the illustrator to tell part of the story.

"In writing my second book, *Least of All,* I utilized everything I had learned during the development of the Iva Dunnit story. This story sold immediately and required no revision. As with my first book, the plot is based on a true event. I chose the setting of the state of Vermont after visiting my sister who lived there for many years. The changing seasons and old fashioned customs were the perfect backdrop for a story based on my mother-in-law's childhood on a farm overrun with big brothers where her only contribution was hours at the butter churn.

"*Mrs. Merriwether's Musical Cat* was fun to write because of my family's involvement with music, music lessons, and cats. The idea of a cat who can magically inspire young music student to produce heavenly sounds is appealing when your home attracts budding musicians playing everything from pianos and electric guitars to clarinets and drums. In actuality, our cats flee rather than assist in improving the quality of the music.

"With the wealth of family stories and ever changing events of my life, there are always ideas for children's books. Finding time to write is the continual problem. I have never been a writer who devotes a certain portion of each day to the written word. Rather, I have only written when an idea became enticing to the point that I couldn't keep from developing it into a story.

"My keen interest in the problems facing children today led me learn skills to help with those problems. My primary activities today center around my work as a psychotherapist and counselor with children and families. In addition, I lecture and train on the subjects of high-risk children, art therapy, and the Kid Power Program, which I developed early in my career, to help children from troubled families.

"My enthusiasm for writing children's books has not dimmed, and one of the most delightful aspects of my life is doing author visits at elementary schools. I also continue to be alert for that compelling idea which will start me writing the next book."

*   *   *

PYLE, Katharine 1863-1938

PERSONAL: Some sources spell given name Katherine; born in 1863, in Wilmington, DE; died February 19, 1938, in Wilmington, DE; daughter of William and Margaret C. Pyle. *Education:* Studied with brother, Howard Pyle, at Drexel Institute; attended Philadelphia School of Design and New York Art Students' League.

ADDRESSES: Home—1616 Rodney St., Wilmington, DE.

CAREER: Author and illustrator of children's books; artist. *Exhibitions:* Columbian Expo, Chicago, IL, 1893.

MBER: Wilmington Society.

RITINGS:

SELF-ILLUSTRATED

The Counterpane Fairy, Dutton, 1898, reissued, 1928.
Prose and Verse for Children, American Book Co., 1899.
The Christmas Angel, Little, Brown, 1900.
As the Goose Flies, Little, Brown, 1901.
Stories of Humble Friends, American Book Co.,1902.
In the Green Forest, Little, Brown, 1902.
Nancy Rutledge (based on author's childhood), Little, Brown, 1906.
Fairy Tales from Many Lands, Dutton, 1911.
Six Little Ducklings, Dodd, 1915.
Wonder Tales Retold, Little, Brown, 1916.
Two Little Mice, and Others, Dodd, 1917.
Mother's Nursery Tales, Dutton, 1918.
Tales of Folk and Fairies, Little, Brown, 1919.
Tales of Wonder and Magic, Little, Brown, 1920.
Three Little Kittens, Dodd, 1920.
Fairy Tales from Far and Near, Little, Brown, 1922.
The Black-eyed Puppy, Dutton, 1923.
(Compiler) *The Katharine Pyle Book of Fairy Tales,* Dutton, 1925.
(Reteller) *Tales from Greek Mythology,* Lippincott, 1928.
(Reteller) *Tales from Norse Mythology,* Lippincott, 1930.
Charlemagne and His Knights, Lippincott, 1932.
(Reteller) *Heroic Tales from Greek Mythology,* Lippincott, 1934.
(Reteller) *Heroic Tales from the Norse,* Lippincott, 1934.

OTHER

The Rabbit Witch, and Other Tales, Dutton, 1895.
(Illustrator) Edith M. Thomas, *In Sunshine Land,* Houghton, 1895.
(Reteller) *When the Wind Blows: Being Ten Fairy Tales from Ten Nations,* illustrated by Bertha Corson Day, R. H. Russell, 1902, Dutton, 1910.
Careless Jane, and Other Tales, Dutton, 1902.
Childhood Poems, illustrated by Sarah S. Stilwell, Dutton, 1904.
(With Laura Spencer Portor) *Theodora,* illustrated by William A. McCullough, Little, Brown, 1907.
Once Upon a Time in Delaware, edited by Emily P. Bissell, illustrated by Ethel Pennewill Brown, Mercantile, 1911.
Tales of Two Bunnies, Dutton, 1913.
Once Upon a Time in Rhode Island, illustrated by Helen B. Mason, Doubleday, Page, 1914.
Lazy Matilda, and Other Tales, Dutton, 1921.
(Editor and illustrator) Mary Eliza Isabella Frere, *Fairy Tales from India,* Lippincott, 1926.

Illustrator of Anna Sewell's *Black Beauty,* Dodd. Contributor to *The Wonder Clock; or, Four and Twenty Marvelous Tales, Being One for Each Hour of the Day,* written and illustrated by Howard Pyle, Harper, 1888, reissued, Dover, 1965.

Work represented in numerous anthologies, including *Dolls: An Anthology,* compiled by Julia A. Robinson, Whitman, 1938; *Beastly Boys and Ghastly Girls,* collected by William Cole, World Publishing Co., 1964; and *Poems for the Children's Hour,* compiled by Josephine Bouton, Platt & Munk. Contributor to periodicals, including *St. Nicholas Magazine, Wide Awake,* and *Harper's.*

FOR MORE INFORMATION SEE:

BOOKS

Pyle, Katharine, *Nancy Rutledge,* Little, Brown, 1906.

*   *   *

REEDER, Carolyn 1937-

PERSONAL: Born November 16, 1937, in Washington, DC; daughter of Raymond and Pauline Owens; married Jack Reeder; children: David, Linda. *Education:* American University, B.A. and M.Ed.

ADDRESSES: Home—7314 University Ave., Glen Echo, MD 20812. *Office*—Georgetown Day School, 4500 MacArthur Blvd., N.W., Washington, DC 20007.

CAREER: Writer. Elementary school teacher.

AWARDS, HONORS: Scott O'Dell Award for historical fiction, 1989, for *Shades of Grey;* Child Study Children's Book Committee Award, 1989; Jefferson Cup Award from Virginia Library Association, 1990; *Shenandoah Secrets: The Story of the Park's Hidden Past* was named to the American Library Association's notable book list.

WRITINGS:

NONFICTION FOR ADULTS; WITH HUSBAND, JACK REEDER

Shenandoah Heritage: The Story of the People before the Park, Potomac Appalachian Trail Club, 1978.
Shenandoah Vestiges: What the Mountain People Left Behind, Potomac Appalachian Trail Club, 1980.
Shenandoah Secrets: The Story of the Park's Hidden Past, Potomac Appalachian Trail Club, 1991.

NOVELS FOR CHILDREN

Shades of Grey, Macmillan, 1989.
Grandpa's Mountain, Macmillan, 1991.

*   *   *

RENAUD, Bernadette 1945-

PERSONAL: Born April 18, 1945, in Ascot Corner, Quebec, Canada; daughter of Albert and Aline (Audet) Renaud; married Pierre La Brosse (a computer scientist), May, 1976. *Education:* Ecole Presentation de Marie, Granby, Quebec, teaching diploma, 1964; College de Maisonneuve, Montreal, Quebec, diplome enseignement collegial, 1972. *Hobbies and other interests:* "I have a love of travel and have travelled to Brazil, France, Italy, the Virgin Islands, Mexico, Peru, Bolivia, Greece, Israel, Egypt, U.S.S.R., United States, and all across Canada. My new hobby? Painting watercolor! It could be my next creating way.... Why not ... ?"

ADDRESSES: Home—Contrecoeur, Quebec, Canada.

CAREER: Writer and scriptwriter. Elementary school teacher and assistant librarian in Waterloo, Quebec, 1964-67; administrative secretary in Montreal, Quebec, 1972-76; free-lance writer, 1976—; free-lance scriptwriter, 1981—. Member of board of directors, Communication-Jeunesse, Quebec,

BERNADETTE RENAUD

1977-82, 1984-86, and Conseil Culturel de la Monteregie, Quebec, 1987-90.

MEMBER: Union des Ecrivains Quebecois, Societe des Auteurs, Recherchistes, Documentalistes et Compositeurs.

AWARDS, HONORS: Children Literature's Award, Canada Council of Arts, and Alvine Belisle Award, Association des Sciences et des Techniques de la Documentation, both 1977, both for *Emilie, la baignoire a pattes;* honorable mention, Association Canadienne d'Education en Langue Francaise, 1979, for *La Revolte de la Courtepointe; The Cat in the Cathedral* was named an Our Choice/Your Choice Canadian Children's Book, 1985-86; awards from Fifth Festival de cinema international en Abitibi-Temiscamingue (Canada), 1986, Fifth Festival du Cinema Jeune Public de Laon (France), First Festival International d'Alger du film pour l'Enfance et la Jeunesse (Algeria), Le Caroussel du film pour enfants (Rimouski, Canada), First Festival International d'Alger du film, Fifteenth Moscow International Film Festival, First Festival du Cinema Francophone (Martinique), 22nd Rencontres Internationales Film et Jeunesse de Cannes (France), and Felix Award, all 1987, all for film *Bach et bottine; Bach et bottine* was named the best record/album for children, 1987, Association du Disque et du Spectacle Quebecois (Canada).

WRITINGS:

Emilie, la baignoire a pattes (title means "Emily, the Four-Footed Bathtub"), illustrated by France Bedard, Heritage, 1976.
Le Petit Pompier, Le Sablier, 1976.
L'Autobus en colere, Le Sablier, 1978.
La Fete de la citrouille, Le Sablier, 1978.
Le Carte de Noel, Le Sablier, 1978.
Le Menage de samedi, Le Sablier, 1978.
Oscar a disparu, Le Sablier, 1978.
Le Dentiste, Le Sablier, 1978.
Le Matins de Martin, Le Sablier, 1978.
Sophie a l'epicerie, Le Sablier, 1978.
Le Chat de l'oratoire, illustrated by Josette Michaud, Fides, 1978, translation by Frances Morgan published as *The Cat in the Cathedral,* Press Porcepic, 1983.
La Tempete de neige, Le Sablier, 1979.
Les 4 Saisons de Branchu, Le Sablier, 1979.
Le Gateau d'anniversaire, Le Sablier, 1979.
Les Jouets, Le Sablier, 1979.
Ca ira mieux demain, Le Sablier, 1979.
La Maison tete de pioche (title means "The Stubborn House"), Heritage, 1979.
La Revolte de la Courtepointe (title means "The Runaway Quilt"), Fides, 1979.
C'est maman qui travaille, Le Sablier, 1979.
Sur le chemin de l'ecole, Le Sablier, 1980.
Un chat . . . jamais, Le Sablier, 1980.
Marie-Jo a la grippe, Le Sablier, 1980.
Papa vient dimanche, Le Sablier, 1980.
Les Maneges, Le Sablier, 1980.
La Depression de l'ordinateur, Fides, 1981, translation by Morgan published as *The Computer Revolts,* Press Porcepic, 1984.
Une boite magique tres embetante (title means "A Bothering Magic Box"; play; produced in Ottawa at the National Center of Arts of Canada, 1982), Lemeac, 1981.
La grande question de Tomatelle (title means "The Tomato's Odd Quest"), Lemeac, 1982.
Comment on fait un livre? (title means "The Making of Books"), illustrated by Christine Dufour, Meridien, 1983.
Bach et bottine (film; also see below), Productions La Fete, 1986.
Bach et bottine, Quebec-Amerique, 1986, translation published as *Bach and Broccoli,* Montreal Press, 1987.
Quand l'accent devient grave (short film), National Film Board of Canada, 1989.

Also author of scripts for Radio-Canada television series *Klimbo,* 1981-82, and *Michou et Pilo,* 1984-85.

ADAPTATIONS: Bach et bottine was released as a recording; three of Renaud's books have been released in Braille editions.

WORK IN PROGRESS: An experimental television script for youth; a novel for adults.

SIDELIGHTS: "I decided to become a writer when I was eight years old," Bernadette Renaud told *SATA.* "Of course, my early writings that I created in primary schools were done with care and pleasure and it became clear that this would be my career some day.

"As I grew up, I was not sure that writing was what I wanted to do and so I worked for some years at other occupations ssistant school librarian, teacher, and administrative y.

day I decided to write my first book, which was oured with two awards. It was the beginning of the most xciting time of my life. Since 1976 I have worked as a professional writer producing scripts for television and movies; and books: short stories, plays, science fiction, documentaries, tales and novels.

"From where do my ideas come? From nowhere and everywhere. My book, *La Maison tete de pioche,* was done when we bought an old house and repaired it; *The Cat in the Cathedral,* when we went to a concert by a friend who was a musician; *La grande question de Tomatelle,* when I visited a greenhouse and found that, unfortunately, all tomatoes grow like all the others; so I decided to write a story with a special tomato which wanted to be personal and have a special life too.

"I was born under the sign of Aries with ascendance to Leo. Therefore, I enjoy experimenting with many types of writing.

"I have had the occasion to meet thousands of school children and their teachers throughout Canada, including Indians and Inuit. Recently, I have expanded my reading public to include the United States, France and Belgium. Although I do not receive many new ideas from children, I feel it is important for me to be in contact with my reading public.

"Why did I begin to write for youth? I believe it was during my involvement as a cub scout chief, teacher, and librarian in schools as well as the fact that I have forty or so nieces and nephews. As an idea begins and takes shape in my mind, I immediately know what age group it is for.

"Meanwhile, I have many things to say to adults. As well, my first movie, *Bach and Broccoli,* was talking about man and child. Two worlds, two ways of living. In my mind, I have, of course, many projects for adults. One of them is now done and will be published in 1991."

*   *   *

RHYNE, Nancy 1926-

PERSONAL: Born June 16, 1926, in Mount Holly, NC; daughter of Benjamin A. (a power company employee) and Ella (a homemaker; maiden name, Henson) Garrison; married Sidney S. Rhyne, December 15, 1950; children: Garrison. *Education:* Attended Lenoir-Rhyne College and University of North Carolina. *Politics:* Democrat. *Religion:* United Methodist.

ADDRESSES: Home and office—3194 LaBruce Lane, Murrells Inlet, SC 29576.

CAREER: Mecklenburg County Courthouse, Charlotte, NC, deputy clerk of Superior Court; Kennedy, Covington, Lobdell & Hickman (attorneys), Charlotte, secretary to the senior partner; Davidson College, Davidson, NC, secretary to the vice-president; writer.

AWARDS, HONORS: National Federation of Media Women, third place award, 1982, for *Tales of the South Carolina Low Country,* second place award, 1984, for *More Tales of the South Carolina Low Country;* South Carolina Federation of Media Women, first place awards, 1982, for

Tales of the South Carolina Low Country, and 1984, for *More Tales of the South Carolina Low Country.*

WRITINGS:

The Grand Strand: An Uncommon Guide to Myrtle Beach and Its Surroundings, East Woods Press, 1981.
Carolina Seashells, East Woods Press, 1982.
Tales of the South Carolina Low Country, John Blair, 1982.
More Tales of the South Carolina Low Country, John Blair, 1984.
Coastal Ghosts, East Woods Press, 1985.
Murder in the Carolinas, John Blair, 1988.
Once upon a Time on a Plantation (juvenile), Pelican Publishing, 1988.
Plantation Tales, Sandlapper, 1989.
More Murder in the Carolinas, John Blair, 1990.
Alice Flagg: The Ghost of the Hermitage, Pelican Publishing, 1990.

WORK IN PROGRESS: South Carolina Lizard Man, a children's book; *Huntington, Baruch, Vanderbilt: Plantation Neighbors.*

*   *   *

RIQ
See ATWATER, Richard (Tupper)

*   *   *

ROBERTSON, Stephen
See WALKER, Robert W(ayne)

*   *   *

SANDERSON, Irma 1912-

PERSONAL: Born January 30, 1912, in Tehkummah, Canada; daughter of Alexander and Dorothy Anne (Conley) Russell; married Howard Sanderson, July 19, 1933 (died June 23, 1984); children: Gerald, Allan, David. *Education:* Attended Sault Business College, 1929. *Hobbies and other interests:* Wildlife, amateur photography, seashells, fossils.

ADDRESSES: Home—Pioneer Park, R.R.2, Box 49, Sault Ste. Marie, Ontario, Canada P6A 5K7.

CAREER: Writer. Secretary; file clerk; receptionist. Sault Ste. Marie PTA, secretary, 1957-58, president, 1959-61, treasurer, 1962-63. Cubmaster in Sault Ste. Marie, 1950-55, district cubmaster, 1956-60; member of Gilwell staff, Blue Springs, Ontario, 1956.

MEMBER: Canadian Society of Children's Authors, Illustrators and Peformers, Canadian Children's Book Centre.

AWARDS, HONORS: First Prize for Best Poem of the Year, *Other Voices,* 1971.

WRITINGS:

The Naughty Billy Goat, illustrated by Juliette Mayhew Daley, Lyndon House, 1981.
(Contributor) *The Dancing Sun* (anthology), Press Porcepic, 1981.

Also author of *Jeremy and the Peanut That Grew and Grew, The Three Squirrels, Ralphy, Elfy and Alfy, Puzzles and Quizzes: The Animal Kingdom* (with son, David Sanderson), *Knock Knocks to Read at Night,* all 1988, and *The Silver Slippers, Flowers Are for the Living* (adult poems), and *The Things I Saw Today* (juvenile poems), all 1989. Contributor of poems and stories to several magazines, including *Jabberwocky, Canadian Children's Magazine, Discover, Highlights for Children, Young Miss, Poetry Parade, Encore,* and *Home Life.*

WORK IN PROGRESS: Fun and Games with Words and Names, a play on words and names; four sequels to *Knock Knocks to Read at Night; The Gift of Love,* a story of a girl who died on Christmas Eve and went to Heaven; *The Bear That Came to Our House,* a children's story in verse; *The Timid Ghost,* a story book in verse; *Crooked Foot,* a story of an Indian boy; *King Gundar;* two or three other books in verse.

SIDELIGHTS: "I was born on January 30, 1912, in Tehkummah on the Manitoulin Island, the largest fresh water island in the world, which nestles in Georgian Bay and Lake Huron," Irma Sanderson told *SATA.* "I subsequently lived in mill and mining towns on the mainland and moved to Sault Ste. Marie in 1928.

"I learned to read at an early age—when I was seven I was reading Charles Dickens' books, beginning with *The Cricket on the Hearth.* My parents were avid readers, and my mother read books to us and told us stories. I believed these stories to be of personal experiences, but later learned that they were stories of great writers—Guy de Maupaussant, Honore de Balzac, and Gustave Flaubert.

IRMA SANDERSON

"Ours was also a writing family. My maternal grandmother, my mother, my sisters and brothers all wrote poetry and short stories—the lack of a typewriter and markets prevented them from being published. I wanted to write from the time I could read. To entertain, to inform, to make people feel deeply, as I felt, was my aim. Particularly I was interested in writing for children. Why, then, haven't I at least several books to my credit? That is a rather long story.

"At the age of seven, just after my father returned from World War I, and influenza swept the country, the flu left me with a suppurating gathering in my throat—quinsy. There were no antibiotics at that time, and it was a matter of whether I would choke to death, or the gathering would break. I was in a coma, and when it broke all of the poison was swallowed and was absorbed throughout my entire system. I was in bed for months—when I was up and getting around I began to fall and soon was unable to walk. Later I crawled on the floor and pulled myself up, and eventually was able to walk. I was never to fully recover from that illness, was never able to run again, or play as other children did. It was, I believe, to be the start of another illness that was diagnosed many years later.

"It was nearly three years before I was able to go back to school—when I was nine years old I weighed only thirty pounds. Does that sound tragic? It wasn't so with me. I took it for granted, just as I took for granted that one day I would be a writer. I did very well in writing essays in school and my teacher read what I wrote to every grade in the school. My education was scant and almost nonexistent. I learned from reading."

Sanderson eventually married and started a family. Her activities with the local school parent association and Cub Scouts left her little time for writing. Then she had to give those up when she again became ill. "My speech was affected—sentences became a jumble of sounds," she wrote. "I walked backwards and in circles. I couldn't enjoy the luxury of laughing—the effort was too costly to my strength. I was sent to a hospital in Ottawa, Ontario, and a neurologist diagnosed the symptoms as multiple sclerosis [MS]." Sanderson kept writing, but her first article, about her MS, was left unpublished when the magazine that accepted it went out of business.

"I was becoming weaker and my neighbors expected any day to hear that I had died," the author continued. "Anything I would write had to be short. One of my grandsons who wished to have, first, an elephant, then a camel, and when he could have neither he said, 'I'd like to have a tiny, tiny, tiny, little elephant.'

"That was the nucleus for one of my first poems for children. It sold, and I wrote many more. Each one was written from the point of view of a child, and almost all included animals—anything from elephants to bumble bees. And they, too, sold." Many of Sanderson's early poems have been reprinted, once in a Braille magazine for the blind. "These reprints meant a great deal to me," the author said, because "more children were reached, and, I hope, touched in some special way."

In 1967 Sanderson had an operation to take out an infected gall bladder, even though there was a possibility she would be paralyzed by it. "You can imagine, when I came out of the anesthetic, how wonderful it was, first, to be alive, and second to find that I could move," she wrote. But "what was more wonderful than being alive was the fact that my health

d considerably. I branched out into writing more
ories, children's and adult's, into writing literary
for adults. The latter was difficult—I had been
ht up in a world of rhyme. I worked at it, though, and
the help of my youngest son who is a writer, I mastered
e rhythm necessary." One of these efforts won a prize from
the Canadian magazine *Other Voices.*

"I went from Montreal to Vermont to do research for a book, a mystery for adults, and did a rough draft as well . . . for another mystery. I hope one day to finish those books and write many others—only my health and time will tell if this will be accomplished. My muscles are irreparably damaged.

"My greater interest, however, is in writing for children. If my writing can bring a smile to the face of a child, if it can make a child cry, make a child love animals and feel for them, if a child can be a more understanding person because of it, then I shall have accomplished something.

"I felt that if some of the children's stories I wrote could be published in book form they might reach a larger audience. Then, in 1981 (almost at exactly the same time that a story was included in an anthology *The Dancing Sun*), *The Naughty Billy Goat* was published by Lyndon House. I have read it to a great many school children, as has the publisher, and it caught the imagination of children even in grade eight. If I can fill a child's mind with laughter, wonder, and fantasy, even with one book, I shall feel rewarded. I have a number of story books—and longer books—under way and it is a matter of finding the right editor with the right book, at the right time.

"A recent heart attack has not diminished my interest in writing. I mention illnesses not as an excuse, nor for sympathy, but to encourage children who want to write, that if they want to badly enough they won't give up. Children today have more help available to them and much more opportunity. And those with good health can conquer almost anything."

*   *   *

SARAH, DUCHESS OF YORK
See FERGUSON, Sarah (Margaret)

*   *   *

SCHAEFER, Jack (Warner) 1907-1991

PERSONAL: Born November 19, 1907, in Cleveland, OH; died of congestive heart failure, January 24, 1991, in Santa Fe, NM; son of Carl Walter (a lawyer) and Minnie Luella (Hively) Schaefer; married Eugenia Hammond Ives, August 26, 1931 (divorced December, 1948); married Louise Wilhide Deans, June, 1949; children: (first marriage) Carl, Christopher, Emily Susann, Jonathan; stepchildren: Sharon, Stephani, Claudia. *Education:* Oberlin College, A.B., 1929; Columbia University, graduate study, 1929-30.

CAREER: United Press, New Haven, CT, reporter and office man, 1930-31; Connecticut State Reformatory, Cheshire, assistant director of education, 1931-38; *Journal-Courier,* New Haven, associate editor, 1932-39, editor, 1939-42; *Theatre News,* New Haven, editor and publisher, 1935-40; *Movies,* New Haven, editor and publisher, 1939-41; *Sun,* Baltimore, MD, editorial writer, 1942-44; *Virginian-Pilot,* Norfolk, VA, associate editor, 1944-48; *Shoreliner,* New

JACK SCHAEFER

Haven, editor, 1949; Lindsay Advertising Co., New Haven, associate, 1949; free-lance writer, 1949-91.

AWARDS, HONORS: New York Herald Tribune's Spring Book Festival Honor Book, 1960, for *Old Ramon,* and 1963, for *The Plainsmen;* American Library Association, Newbery honor book, 1961, and Aurianne Award, 1962, both for *Old Ramon;* Notable Book citations for *Old Ramon* and *Mavericks;* Ohioana Award, Ohioana Library Association, 1961, for *Old Ramon;* Distinguished Achievement Award, Western Literature Association, 1975; Western Writers of America, Golden Spur Award for best western novel ever written, 1985, and Levi-Strauss Saddleman Award, 1986, both for *Shane.*

WRITINGS:

FOR CHILDREN; PUBLISHED BY HOUGHTON, EXCEPT AS NOTED

Shane (first published serially as "Rider from Nowhere" in *Argosy,* 1946), illustrated by John McCormack, 1949.
First Blood, 1953.
The Canyon, 1953, published in England as *The Canyon and Other Stories,* Deutsch, 1955.
Old Ramon, illustrated by Harold West, 1960.
The Plainsmen, illustrated by Lorence Bjorklund, 1963.
Stubby Pringle's Christmas, illustrated by Bjorklund, 1964.
New Mexico, Coward-McCann, 1967.
Mavericks, illustrated by Bjorklund, 1967.

FOR ADULTS; PUBLISHED BY HOUGHTON, EXCEPT AS NOTED

The Big Range (short stories), 1953.
The Pioneers (short stories), 1954.

(Editor) *Out West: An Anthology of Stories,* 1955, published
     in England as *Out West: A Western Omnibus,* Deutsch,
     1959.
Company of Cowards, 1957.
The Kean Land, and Other Stories, 1959.
Tales from the West (short stories), Hamish Hamilton, 1961.
Incident on the Trail (short stories), Corgi, 1962.
Monte Walsh, 1963.
*The Great Endurance Horse Race: Six Hundred Miles on a
     Single Mount, 1908, from Evanston, Wyoming, to
     Denver,* Stagecoach Press, 1963.
Heroes without Glory: Some Goodmen of the Old West, 1965.
The Collected Stories of Jack Schaefer, 1966.
Adolphe Francis Alphonse Bandelier, Press of the Territorian,
     1966.
The Short Novels of Jack Schaefer, 1967.
Hal West: Western Gallery, Museum of New Mexico Press,
     1971.
An American Bestiary, illustrated by Linda K. Powell, 1975.
Jack Schaefer and the American West: Eight Stories, edited
     by C. E. J. Smith, Longman, 1978.
*Conversations with a Pocket Gopher and Other Outspoken
     Neighbors* (short stories), Capra Press, 1978.

Also author of screenplay, *Jinglebob,* and special material on
which the film *The Great Cowboy Race* is based. Contributor
of short stories and articles to magazines, including *Collier's,
Holiday, Boy's Life, Bluebook, Fresco, Gunsmoke,* and
Saturday Evening Post.

**Praised as one of the best westerns ever written, Jack
Schaefer's *Shane* is also a story about growing up.**
(Illustration from *Shane* by John McCormack.)

Schaefer's manuscript collection is at the Western History
Research Center at the University of Wyoming in Laramie.

ADAPTATIONS: Shane was adapted for a film starring
Alan Ladd, Paramount, 1953, as a filmstrip with cassette,
book, and teacher's guide, Center for Literary Review, 1978,
and as a cassette, Listen for Pleasure, 1982; *The Big Range*
was adapted for film as *The Silver Whip,* Twentieth Century-
Fox, 1953; *Company of Cowards* was adapted for film as
Advance to the Rear, starring Glenn Ford, Stella Stevens, and
Melvin Douglas, Metro Goldwyn-Mayer, 1964; *Monte
Walsh* was adapted for a film starring Jack Palance and Lee
Marvin, National General/Cinema Centre, c. 1969; *Old
Ramon* was adapted as a record, cassette, and filmstrip,
Miller-Brody, 1975.

SIDELIGHTS: Jack Schaefer, the author of *Shane,* had
never been west of his home state of Ohio when he wrote his
classic western novel. He had not read much western fiction,
either. Instead he came to the genre of western writing
through his strong interest in American history. Research
and his conviction that serious literature about the West
could be created were his primary tools.

Before publishing his first novel, Schaefer spent almost
twenty years in the newspaper business. Mainly he wrote
editorial essays, not strict reportage. According to the study
Jack Schaefer by Gerald Haslam, Schaefer once said, "I'm
reasonably certain that if I had done much reporting, I would
have ruined myself as a writer." Academic writing did not
appeal to him either. Schaefer felt that scholars paid too little
attention to discovering the writer's intention and too much
to their own theories. He also disliked their jargon. Schaefer's
stated intent was always "to write well, be literate and direct
and concise, express firm conviction based on thorough
research and honest reasoning and supported by sound argu-
ments." Reviewers called his a storyteller's style: clear, realistic, focused on its subject, and powerfully written.

Shane, praised in 1985 as the best western ever written, is a
classic example. It is the story of a mysterious former gunman
who hires on to help with a farmer's work and is ultimately
drawn into a conflict between farmers and cattlemen. The
narrator is the farmer's son, who was a young boy when
Shane arrived but is now grown up. Schaefer made it more
than just a tale of good guys versus bad guys; he showed that
the roles of cattleman and gunfighter were becoming things
of the past. The frontier and the freedom it represented were
giving way to civilization and law. He also showed that on
both sides of the conflict were complex individuals with both
good and bad points. Woven into the novel is the idea of
growing up; at first the boy idolizes Shane, and later he begins
to realize that his hero is not entirely flawless.

At about the time *Shane* was published Schaefer left journalism and began writing books full time. Over the next two
decades he produced a number of well-regarded novels and
short stories about the West. Their themes include growing
up, the passing of the frontier, and the need to balance
independence and responsibility. Although the books sold
well, won awards, and were occasionally made into movies,
Schaefer gradually became unhappy with his work. As he
wrote in his introduction to *An American Bestiary,* "I had
become ashamed of my species and myself." He felt that
civilization was destroying the natural world and that he was
part of that destruction. After 1967 Schaefer began to write
more about animals and the land itself.

Straight towards Young Jake he came and he reared on hind legs up in the terrifying stance of the fighting stallion. (From *Mavericks*, by Jack Schaefer, illustrated by Lorence Bjorklund.)

Attempting to present a true picture of the American West, Schaefer produced books of both critical and popular interest. His characters went beyond stereotypes such as the cool gunslinger and the greedy cattleman. Schaefer portrayed individuals "conditioned by the wide open spaces of the old West," he wrote in his preface to *The Big Range*, "in which the energies and capabilities of men and women, for good or for evil, were unleashed . . . as they had rarely been before or elsewhere in human history." His books appeal to both young and old. As Schaefer noted in Haslam's book, "They seem to be rather durable."

WORKS CITED:

Haslam, Gerald, *Jack Schaefer,* Boise State University, 1975, pp. 7 and 43.
Schaefer, Jack, preface to *The Big Range,* Houghton, 1953, p. I.
Schaefer, introduction to *An American Bestiary,* Houghton, 1975.

FOR MORE INFORMATION SEE:

BOOKS

Twentieth-Century Children's Writers, St. Martin's, 1978, 2nd edition, 1983.

PERIODICALS

Top of the News, May, 1962.
Wilson Library Bulletin, February, 1961.

OBITUARIES:

PERIODICALS

Chicago Tribune, January 27, 1991.
Los Angeles Times, January 27, 1991.
New York Times, January 27, 1991.
Washington Post, January 27, 1991.

*   *   *

SCHATELL, Brian

PERSONAL: Education: Attended Parsons School of Design. *Hobbies and other interests:* Collecting rare and obscure record albums.

ADDRESSES: Home—Hoboken, NJ. *Office*—Parsons School of Design, 66 West 12th St., New York, NY 10011.

CAREER: Parsons School of Design, New York, NY, teacher of children's book illustration; author and illustrator of children's books.

AWARDS, HONORS: Lots of Rot was selected an Outstanding Science and Trade Book by the National Council of Science, 1981.

WRITINGS:

FOR CHILDREN; SELF-ILLUSTRATED

Farmer Goff and His Turkey Sam, Lippincott, 1982.
Midge and Fred, Lippincott, 1983.
Sam's No Dummy, Farmer Goff (sequel to *Farmer Goff and His Turkey Sam*), Lippincott, 1984.
The McGoonys Have a Party, Lippincott, 1985.

ILLUSTRATOR

Vicki Cobb, *Lots of Rot,* Lippincott, 1981.
Cobb, *Fuzz Does It!,* Lippincott, 1982.
Cobb, *Gobs of Goo,* Lippincott, 1983.
Juli Barbato, *From Bed to Bus,* Macmillan, 1985.
Barbato, *Mom's Night Out,* Macmillan, 1985.

*   *   *

SCHOENHERR, John (Carl) 1935-

PERSONAL: Born July 5, 1935, in New York, NY; son of John F. and Frances (Braun) Schoenherr; married Judith Gray, September 17, 1960; children: Jennifer Lauren, Ian Gray. *Education:* Studied under Will Barnett and Frank Reilly at Art Students League; Pratt Institute, B.F.A., 1956.

ADDRESSES: Home—135 Upper Creek Rd., Stockton, NJ 08559.

CAREER: Free-lance illustrator and painter. South Hunterdon Juvenile Conference Committee, member, 1968. *Exhibitions:* Paintings exhibited at various locations, including Bronx Zoo, New York, 1968, Carson Gallery of Western American Art, Denver, 1983, Kent State University, 1983,

Colorado Historical Society, 1984-87, 1990, and most recently in a number of private collections.

MEMBER: Society of Illustrators, Society of Animal Artists, American Society of Mammalogists, Graphic Artists Guild.

AWARDS, HONORS: First prize, National Speleological Society Salon, 1963; recipient of citations, Society of Illustrators, 1964, 1966, 1967, 1968, 1969, 1970, 1972, 1973, 1974, 1976, 1979, 1980, 1981; Science Fiction Achievement Award (Hugo) for best artist, World Science Fiction Society, 1965; author award, New Jersey Council of Teachers of English, 1969, for *The Barn;* Society of Animal Artists Medal, 1979, 1984; Silver Medal, Philadelphia Academy of Natural Science, 1984; Caldecott Award, American Library Association, 1988, for *Owl Moon.*

WRITINGS:

(And illustrator) *The Barn* (ALA Notable Book), Little, Brown, 1968.
(And illustrator) *Art of Painting Wild Animals,* Grumbacher, 1974.
(And illustrator) *Bear,* Philomel, 1991.

ILLUSTRATOR

Sterling North, *Rascal: A Memoir of a Better Era* (Newbery honor book), Dutton, 1963.

JOHN SCHOENHERR

G. W. Moore and G. Nicholas, *Speleology: The Study of Caves,* Heath, 1964.
Walter Morey, *Gentle Ben,* Dutton, 1965.
Robert William Murphy, *The Golden Eagle,* Dutton, 1965.
R. W. Murphy, *The Phantom Setter,* Dutton, 1966.
Bernice Freschet, *Kangaroo Red,* Scribner, 1966.
Daniel P. Mannix, *The Fox and the Hound,* Dutton, 1967.
Era Zistel, *The Dangerous Year,* Random House, 1967.
Adrien Stoutenburg, *A Vanishing Thunder: Extinct and Threatened American Birds,* Natural History Press, 1967.
Arthur Catherall, *A Zebra Came to Drink,* Dutton, 1967.
A. Stoutenburg, *Animals at Bay: Rare and Rescued American Wildlife,* Doubleday, 1968.
Jean Craighead George, *The Moon of the Chickarees,* Crowell, 1968.
Julian May, *The Big Island,* Follett, 1968.
S. North, *The Wolfling: A Documentary Novel of the 1870s,* Dutton, 1969.
Allan W. Eckert, *Incident at Hawk's Hill* (Newbery honor book), Little, Brown, 1971.
Ferdinand N. Monjo, *The Jezebel Wolf,* Simon & Schuster, 1971.
J. C. George, *Julie of the Wolves* (Newbery Medal winner), Harper, 1971.
Theodore Clymer, *Travels of Atunga,* Little, Brown, 1973.
Harold Keith, *Susie's Scoundrel,* Crowell, 1974.
Allison Morgan, *River Song,* Harper, 1975.
Vincent Abraitys, *The Backyard Wilderness,* Columbia Publishing, 1975.
John A. Giegling, *Black Lightning: Three Years in the Life of a Fisher,* Coward, 1975.
Faith McNulty, *Whales: Their Life in the Sea,* Harper, 1975.
Joanne Ryder, *Simon Underground* (Children's Book Showcase selection), Harper, 1976.
Jane Annixter and Paul Annixter, *Wapootin,* Coward, 1976.
Nathaniel Benchley, *Kilroy and the Gull,* Harper, 1977.
Frank Herbert, *Dune,* Berkley, 1977.
Randall Jarrell, *A Bat Is Born* (poetry; excerpted from Jarrell's *The Bat-Poet*), Doubleday, 1977.
J. C. George, *The Wounded Wolf,* Harper, 1978.
Colin Thiel, *Storm Boy,* Harper, 1978.
Robert F. Leslie, *Miracle on Squaretop Mountain,* Dutton, 1979.
(With son, Ian Schoenherr) Lee Harding, *The Fallen Spaceman,* Harper, 1980.
Jane Yolen, *Owl Moon,* Philomel, 1987.

ILLUSTRATOR; BY MISKA MYLES

Mississippi Possum, Little, Brown, 1965.
The Fox and the Fire (*Horn Book* honor book; ALA Notable Book), Little, Brown, 1966.
Rabbit Garden, Little, Brown, 1967.
Nobody's Cat (ALA Notable Book), Little, Brown, 1969.
Eddie's Bear, Little, Brown, 1970.
Hoagie's Rifle-Gun (Junior Literary Guild selection), Little, Brown, 1970.
Wharf Rat, Little, Brown, 1972.
Somebody's Dog, Little, Brown, 1973.
Otter in the Cove, Little, Brown, 1974.
Beaver Moon, Little, Brown, 1978.

Also illustrator of more than three hundred science fiction book covers; contributor of illustrations to *Astounding Science Fiction* magazine.

WORK IN PROGRESS: Paintings and graphics.

OWL MOON

by Jane Yolen
illustrated by John Schoenherr

After taking a hiatus from illustrating, John Schoenherr returned in 1987 to illustrate the widely acclaimed *Owl Moon*, a Caldecott Medal winner written by Jane Yolen.

SIDELIGHTS: In addition to producing a substantial body of paintings that has been exhibited nationwide, John Schoenherr has illustrated more than forty children's books and hundreds of science fiction book covers. His illustrations for children's books—which are often sentimental depictions of wild animals and their surroundings—have earned the prolific artist a measure of recognition. His watercolor drawings for Jane Yolen's book *Owl Moon,* for example, won the 1988 Caldecott Medal. "I think I identify with wild animals, sometimes even more than with people," Schoenherr remarked in a *U.S. Art* article. "A friend of mine likes to say that I'm a bear disguised as a human being."

For a wildlife artist, Schoenherr certainly had an unlikely childhood—he was born and raised in New York City. "When I was four years old . . . I made the unsettling discovery that nobody out in the street where we lived in Queens could understand a word I said," he told Frances Traher in an interview for *Artists of the Rockies and the Golden West.* "My parents had come into the country in 1914—my mother from Hungary and my father from Germany—and German was what they'd taught me. A couple of houses down from us lived a little boy my own age who chattered away in Chinese, and around the corner Italian prevailed. I was a virtual mute in that polyglot precinct until the day I got so desperate to communicate that I grabbed up a pencil and *drew.* Later I learned English from the comic strips, but I still kept drawing all the time."

Schoenherr's interest in illustration developed steadily. At the age of eight, he was given his first set of oil paints; and by the time he reached thirteen, he was taking Saturday classes at the Art Students League in New York City. Besides art,

Schoenherr was fascinated with stone as a young boy, exploring caves and climbing the Long Island rock formations. "Climbing made me aware of the tactility of stone," he told Traher. "You almost climb with the feel of each hold to your fingers. Of late years, I've become aware again of the influence that Edward Weston had as a photographer, with his monumental stones and simplicity and elegance and strength of composition, the way he would reduce things to the minimum that would work and thereby produce a significant image that would move some people."

While he was in high school, Schoenherr developed a competing interest in biology, but his love for art prevailed when he was asked to dissect a frog in biology class. He chose to study at Pratt Institute in Brooklyn after high school. During the summers, Schoenherr would return to the Art Students League to study under Frank Reilly, an illustrator closely devoted to the old French Academy style. "I appreciated certain skills that style engendered," Schoenherr said in *Artists of the Rockies and the Golden West,* "and the perception it produced for seeing values and colors and changes in your subject—but I learned that I had to work out my organization on the painting itself. A too-rigid method wasn't for me. Organization itself, though, I liked; and early on, strong shapes and strong colors—those qualities, and going for the overall look instead of the detailed thing."

At the age of twenty-one, Schoenherr was becoming recognized as a successful science fiction illustrator. He worked extensively for *Astounding Science Fiction* (since renamed *Analog*). Schoenherr credits the publisher of that magazine, John Campbell, for providing the young artist with the opportunities to develop his personal brand of realism. "I'll always be proud of the 'genuine aliens' I designed for the stories Campbell published," Schoenherr told Traher. "Never were they humans with insect antennae. For beings from a heavy planet, I always managed to work out the structural support that logically their existence would have required."

While working as a magazine illustrator, Schoenherr had moved his family onto a farm in rural New Jersey. The woods and meadows surrounding the 1865 farmhouse gave Schoenherr an interest in animals and nature that gradually led him almost exclusively into wildlife illustration. To pursue his interest in the out-of-doors and in larger and more exotic animals, Schoenherr began travelling throughout the United States and abroad. He told Traher: "It was my travels back and forth through northern Arizona and around Albuquerque, and exploring caves in the non-developed areas of the Black Hills, Yellowstone and Montana, that taught me what my great love really is: it's structure. Back East, everything is covered with trees, whereas it's stone and dirt that I love. Deep down, I probably want to be a desert dweller. And yet, our New Jersey place is a tree farm—not for growing them, but for enjoying them. And I have made so much preparation for painting animals. I like raccoons with their robber or carnival masks. I never can decide which it is they wear. And bears! I tend to be more sympathetic with the larger monochromatic animals that I can use a big brush on. Bears, as I say, have a nice form. It's solid. And moose, I like. They look so awkward in an artificial situation; but I've seen a moose go through a cedar swamp over fallen, twisted tree trunks and matted growth without wrestling anything. A moose can be a dynamic, controlled, solid mass in movement."

Schoenherr has illustrated more than forty children's books, many of which have been acclaimed for their knowledgeable

We reached the line of pine trees, black and pointy against the sky, and Pa held up his hand. . . . Then he called: "*Whoo-whoo-who-who-who-whooooooo,*" the sound of the Great Horned Owl. (From *Owl Moon,* by Jane Yolen, illustrated by John Schoenherr.)

handling of animals and nature themes. His greatest achievement in that medium came in 1987, after a five-year pause from book illustration to concentrate on painting. In that year, Schoenherr returned to the children's book scene to illustrate Jane Yolen's *Owl Moon.* His watercolor pictures for the book earned him the American Library Association's Caldecott Award, presented yearly to the best-illustrated children's book. In a reprint of his acceptance speech in *Horn Book Magazine,* Schoenherr describes the satisfaction he receives from drawing animals: "I know the feeling of meeting a wild animal on its own ground. I've been face to face with field mice and Kodiak bears, bull moose and wild geese, wild boar and mountain goats, and, of course, owls. Large or small, I feel awe and wonder and respect. They are all presences and personalities, alien and largely unfathomable, but worth acceptance and contemplation for what they are. This is what I've found worth trying to express in my work. I was glad to discover I was not alone."

WORKS CITED:

Roberts, Nancy, "John Schoenherr: Bearable Endeavors," *U.S. Art,* December, 1988.
Schoenherr, John, "Caldecott Medal Acceptance," *Horn Book Magazine,* July/August, 1988.

King gingerly raised himself to a sitting position, and Ben tipped his big head forward, looking at him intently. Mark said, "You can pet him, Mr. King . . . ." (From *Gentle Ben,* by Walter Morey, illustrated by John Schoenherr.)

Once only he stopped—having heard some tiny squeaks among the tree roots—long enough to catch a woodmouse, which eased his long hunger. (From *Red Fox,* by Charles G. D. Roberts, illustrated by John Schoenherr.)

Traher, Frances, "John Schoenherr," *Artists of the Rockies and the Golden West,* summer, 1983.

FOR MORE INFORMATION SEE:

BOOKS

Contemporary American Illustrators of Children's Books, Rutgers University Art Gallery, 1974.
De Montreville, Doris, and Elizabeth D. Crawford, editors, *Fourth Book of Junior Authors and Illustrators,* H. W. Wilson, 1978.
Kingman, Lee, and others, compilers, *Illustrators of Children's Books,* Horn Book, *1957-1966,* 1968, *1967-1976,* 1978.
Klemin, Diana, *The Illustrated Book,* Clarkson Potter, 1970.

SCHOLEFIELD, A. T.
See SCHOLEFIELD, Alan

*   *   *

SCHOLEFIELD, Alan 1931-
(Lee Jordan, A. T. Scholefield)

PERSONAL: Born January 15, 1931, in Cape Town, South Africa; son of William Edward (a civil engineer) and Margaret Elizabeth (Tweedie) Scholefield; married Anthea Goddard (a novelist); children: Nicola, Lynn, Catherine. *Education:* University of Cape Town, B.A., 1951.

ADDRESSES: Home—Vinnells, Froxfield, Petersfield, Hampshire, England. *Agent*—Elaine Greene Ltd., 37 Goldhawk Rd., London W8 8QQ, England.

CAREER: Cape Argus, Cape Town, South Africa, member of staff, 1952-53; *Sydney Morning Herald,* Sydney, Australia, member of London staff, 1954-55, 1959-60; *Cape Times,* Cape Town, member of staff, 1957-59; *Scotsman,* Edinburgh, Scotland, defense correspondent, 1960-61; writer, 1961—.

AWARDS, HONORS: Venom was selected as a New York Public Library Book for the Teen-Age, 1980.

ALAN SCHOLEFIELD

WRITINGS:

NOVELS

A View of Vultures, Morrow, 1966.
Great Elephant, Morrow, 1967.
The Eagles of Malice, Morrow, 1968.
Wild Dog Running, Morrow, 1970.
The Young Masters, Morrow, 1971.
The Hammer of God, Morrow, 1973.
Lion in the Evening, Morrow, 1974.
The Alpha Raid, Morrow, 1976.
Venom, Morrow, 1978.
Point of Honor, Morrow, 1979.
Berlin Blind, Morrow, 1980.
The Stone Flower, Morrow, 1982.
The Sea Cave, Congdon & Weed, 1983.
Fire in the Ice, St. Martin's, 1984.
King of the Golden Valley, St. Martin's, 1985.
The Last Safari, St. Martin's, 1987.
The Lost Giants, St. Martin's, 1989.
(Under name A. T. Scholefield) *Dirty Weekend,* Macmillan (London), 1990, St. Martin's, 1991.

THRILLER NOVELS UNDER PSEUDONYM LEE JORDAN

Cat's Eyes, Hodder & Stoughton, 1981.
Criss-Cross, Coronet, 1984.
The Deadly Side of the Square, Macmillan (London), 1988.
The Toy Cupboard, Macmillan (London), 1989, Walker & Co., 1990.
Chain Reaction, Macmillan (London), 1989.

OTHER

(Under pseudonym Lee Jordan) *The Dark Kingdoms* (history), Morrow, 1975.

Also author of screenplay entitled "Chaka"; author of two television mini-series, "River Horse Lake" and "The Sea Tiger," and of the television movie, "My Friend Angelo"; author of a stage adaptation of Robert Louis Stevenson's *Treasure Island.* Contributor to magazines in England, Europe, the United States, and Canada. Scholefield's books have been translated into fourteen languages, including Japanese and Serbo-Croatian.

ADAPTATIONS: A movie adaptation of *Venom* was produced by Paramount Pictures, 1982.

WORK IN PROGRESS: A book entitled *Loyalties.*

SIDELIGHTS: A native of South Africa, Alan Scholefield moved to England because of his objection to the apartheid system in his homeland. He still visits South Africa frequently, however, and many of his books offer nostalgic views of Africa and its history.

FOR MORE INFORMATION SEE:

PERIODICALS

Los Angeles Times, August 14, 1984.
New York Times Book Review, January 7, 1968; September 29, 1968; January 3, 1971; January 30, 1972; May 27, 1973; March 31, 1974; March 26, 1978; August 16, 1979; September 28, 1980; October 14, 1984; February 10, 1991.
Spectator, February 16, 1974.

While maid Susan George watches, Cornelia Sharpe leans down to bid farewell to her son Lance Holcomb, not knowing during her trip an attempt will be made to kidnap the young boy and hold him for ransom in the 1982 Paramount Pictures release *Venom*, based on Alan Scholefield's 1978 book.

Times Literary Supplement, April 23, 1971; March 30, 1973; September 5, 1980; September 22, 1989.
Washington Post Book World, January 23, 1972; May 6, 1973; July 8, 1973; September 2, 1984.

*   *   *

SCHROEDER, Alan 1961-

PERSONAL: Born January 18, 1961, in Alameda, CA; son of Walter R. (a draftsman) and Hilda (Henningsen) Schroeder. *Education:* Received degree (with honors) from University of California, Santa Cruz, 1982.

ADDRESSES: Home—1225 College Ave., Alameda, CA 94501.

CAREER: Writer.

AWARDS, HONORS: Ragtime Tumpie was named a Notable Book of the Year by American Library Association, 1989, and received a teachers award from International Reading Association.

WRITINGS:

Ragtime Tumpie (juvenile biography), Little, Brown, 1989.
Josephine Baker (juvenile biography), Chelsea House, 1991.

Jack London (young adult biography), Chelsea House, 1991.

WORK IN PROGRESS: A picture book adaptation of a Japanese folktale; a young adult biography of Booker T. Washington, a former slave who became a leader in education.

SIDELIGHTS: Alan Schroeder commented: "People find it unusual that I've written two books for children about nightclub dancer and humanitarian Josephine Baker. I like the challenge of taking an unlikely subject—Baker, for instance—and turning it into something that's both inspirational and meaningful for young people."

FOR MORE INFORMATION SEE:

PERIODICALS

New York Times Book Review, February 25, 1990.

*   *   *

SEGAL, Lore (Groszmann) 1928-

PERSONAL: Born March 8, 1928, in Vienna, Austria; daughter of Ignatz (an accountant) and Franzi (Stern) Groszmann; married David Isaac Segal (an editor), November 3, 1961 (died, 1970); children: Beatrice, Jacob. *Education:*

LORE SEGAL

Bedford College, London, B.A. (with honors), 1948. *Religion:* Jewish.

ADDRESSES: Home—280 Riverside Dr., New York, NY 10025. *Agent*—Lynn Nesbit, International Creative Management, 40 West 57th St., New York, NY 10019.

CAREER: Writer. Teacher in Dominican Republic, 1948-51; Columbia University, New York City, professor of creative writing, 1969-78; University of Illinois at Chicago Circle, Chicago, professor of English, 1978—. Visiting professor, Bennington College, spring, 1973, Princeton University, spring, 1974, and Sarah Lawrence College, 1975-76.

AWARDS, HONORS: Guggenheim fellowship in creative writing, 1965-66; National Council of the Arts and Humanities grant, 1967-68; Creative Artists Public Service Program grant, 1972-73; Children's Spring Book Festival first prize, *Book World,* and American Library Association Notable Book Award, both 1970, both for *Tell Me a Mitzi; All the Way Home* and *The Juniper Tree and Other Tales from Grimm* were included in Children's Book Showcase, 1974; *New York Times* Notable Books List, 1985, for *The Story of Mrs. Lovewright and Purrless, Her Cat,* and 1987, for *The Book of Adam to Moses.*

WRITINGS:

Other People's Houses (autobiographical novel), Harcourt, 1964.
(Translator with W. D. Snodgrass) Christian Morgenstern, *Gallows Songs,* University of Michigan Press, 1967.
Tell Me a Mitzi, Farrar, Straus, 1970.
All the Way Home, Farrar, Straus, 1973.
(Translator with Randall Jarrell) Wilhelm Grimm and Jacob Grimm, *The Juniper Tree and Other Tales from Grimm,* Farrar, Straus, 1973.
The Church Mice Adrift, Macmillan, 1976.
Tell Me a Trudy, Farrar, Straus, 1978.
Lucinella (novel), Farrar, Straus, 1978.

(Translator) W. Grimm and J. Grimm, *The Bear and the Kingbird,* Farrar, Straus, 1979.
The Story of Old Mrs. Brubeck and How She Looked for Trouble and Where She Found Him, Pantheon, 1981.
The Story of Mrs. Lovewright and Purrless, Her Cat, Knopf, 1985.
Her First American (novel), Knopf, 1985.
The Book of Adam to Moses, Knopf, 1987.

Contributor of stories to *New Yorker, Saturday Evening Post, New Republic, Epoch, Commentary, New American Review, Story Quarterly,* and other periodicals. Contributor of reviews to *New York Times Book Review* and *New Republic.* Contributor of translations of poetry to *Mademoiselle, Atlantic, Hudson Review, Poetry,* and *Tri-Quarterly.*

ADAPTATIONS: The Story of Mrs. Lovewright and Purrless, Her Cat was recorded on cassette by Random House/ Miller-Brody Productions, 1986, *Tell Me a Mitzi* was recorded on cassette by Scholastic, 1986, and *Her First American* was recorded on cassette by New Letters, 1990.

SIDELIGHTS: Lore Segal was born in Vienna, Austria, in 1928: "I lived the first ten comfortable years," Segal writes in her article for *Something about the Author Autobiography Series (SAAS),* "as my parents' only child, my grandparents' only grandchild, my father's and my mother's brothers' only niece—the center of attention, admiration, and the focus of great expectations."

All that changed in 1938 when Adolf Hitler and the Nazis annexed Austria, and the German army occupied Vienna. "One day," Segal writes in *Other People's Houses,* "the first German regiment moved in. By noon, the square outside our windows was black with tanks, armored cars, radio trucks. Our yard was requisitioned for the paymaster's headquarters. The soldiers borrowed one of our kitchen chairs and the card table. . . . Two helmeted guards stood on either side of the table while the German soldiers in the gray-green uniforms filed past to collect their money."

The Nazis insisted that Jewish children attend a separate school from the other children. Segal and the other Jewish children found themselves separated from their old classmates. Her father lost his job at a bank because the Nazis did not want Jews working in non-Jewish organizations. Her uncle Paul had to leave the university after a fist fight with Nazi students.

Segal's family moved from Vienna to live in the country with her grandparents. But even in the country, Segal writes in *SAAS,* the family was still persecuted: "They wrote 'DON'T BUY FROM THE JEW' in red paint on the walls outside my grandfather's store. . . . At night they threw stones through the bedroom windows. One evening they brought ladders and stepped right through the living-room windows and carried away whatever they felt like taking."

The family left Austria and went to live in England where, because they were now poor, Segal's parents could not support her. She went to live with English families who were taking in the children of refugees. "From the time I arrived in England till I went to the University of London at eighteen years of age, I lived with five different English families," Segal writes in *SAAS.*

Segal lived in England until after the end of World War II. At that time, she and her mother moved to the Dominican

So Mitzi . . . took the top off Jacob's bottle and poured in the milk. (From *Tell Me a Mitzi,* by Lore Segal, illustrated by Harriet Pincus.)

Republic to join her grandparents. "It was at the beginning of my third year in college," Segal writes in *SAAS,* "that my grandfather became ill. My mother packed herself up and went to the Dominican Republic to help look after him. It was our understanding that after my final examination I would follow her. When the time came I went, but unwillingly."

For several years Segal taught English at a Dominican Republic business school. She also tutored members of the diplomatic corps who wanted to learn English. In 1951, she and her mother immigrated to the United States, living in New York City. Segal worked as a filing clerk in a shoe factory, as a receptionist, and for a textile-design studio. In 1961 she married David Segal, then a partner in his father's yarn business, but later a book editor. Her husband passed away in 1970.

Segal first began writing during the 1950s, selling stories to such magazines as *Commentary* and the *New Yorker.* In 1964, her novel *Other People's Houses* was published. The book is a fictional version of Segal's own life from her childhood in Austria to her life in the United States. Richard Gilman of the

New Republic calls the book "an extraordinarily subtle rendering of the self," while Elizabeth Thalman of *Library Journal* describes it as a "story of courage, endurance and humor."

In two later books Segal draws from her own life to create stories for children. *Tell Me a Mitzi* is a collection of stories about a little girl named Mitzi who gets into trouble with her baby brother Jacob. Each story is written as if it is being told by parents to their children, the children saying "tell me a Mitzi" when they want to hear another story. The same style is used in *Tell Me a Trudy.* The stories in both books are based on bedtime stories Segal told her own children. "All I can tell you about the writing of *Mitzi,*" Segal explained to *SATA,* "is that I told these stories to my children and then spent a couple of years writing them over and over until all the sentences sounded right."

Besides her books set in the modern world, Segal has also translated and adapted two books of fairy tales from the brothers Grimm, *The Juniper Tree and Other Tales from Grimm* and *The Bear and the Kingbird,* and she has written books in the style of traditional fairy tales, *The Story of Old*

TELL ME A TRUDY

LORE SEGAL

PICTURES BY

ROSEMARY WELLS

Lore Segal first told the stories contained in *Tell Me a Trudy* to her own children, who would say, "Tell me a Trudy" when they wanted to hear another tale. (Cover illustration by Rosemary Wells.)

Mrs. Brubeck and How She Looked for Trouble and Where She Found Him, and *The Story of Mrs. Lovewright and Purrless, Her Cat.*

WORKS CITED:

Gilman, Richard, review of *Other People's Houses, New Republic,* December 12, 1964.

Segal, Lore, *Other People's Houses,* Harcourt, 1964.

Something about the Author Autobiography Series, Volume 11, Gale, 1991.

Thalman, Elizabeth, review of *Other People's Houses, Library Journal,* November 15, 1964.

FOR MORE INFORMATION SEE:

BOOKS

Lanes, Selma G., *Down the Rabbit Hole,* Atheneum, 1971.

PERIODICALS

Book Week, November 29, 1964.
Commonweal, March, 1965.
New Statesman, March 19, 1965.
Newsweek, July 8, 1985.
New York Review of Books, November 19, 1964.
New York Times Book Review, May 17, 1970; October 24, 1976; May 19, 1985.
Reporter, November 19, 1964.
Saturday Review, July 25, 1970; October 16, 1976.
Time, April 24, 1972.

SETON, Anya 1904(?)-1990

OBITUARY NOTICE—See index for SATA sketch: Born c. 1904 in New York, NY; died of heart failure after a heart attack, November 8, 1990, in Greenwich, CT (one source says California). Author. Seton became internationally popular for her carefully researched historical novels, generally considered Gothic romances. Some of them, such as Dragonwyck and Foxfire, were made into films. Among her other books were Katherine and Devil Water, which some critics consider her best novel. Seton also wrote books for children, such as Mistletoe and Sword: A Story of Roman Britain and Washington Irving.

OBITUARIES AND OTHER SOURCES:

BOOKS

Who's Who, 143rd edition, St. Martin's, 1991.
The Writers Directory: 1988-1990, St. James Press, 1988.

PERIODICALS

Chicago Tribune, November 11, 1990.
Los Angeles Times, November 11, 1990.
Times (London), November 12, 1990.
Washington Post, November 11, 1990.

*   *   *

SPILLANE, Frank Morrison 1918-
(Mickey Spillane)

PERSONAL: Born March 9, 1918, in Brooklyn, NY; son of John Joseph (a bartender) and Catherine Anne Spillane; married Mary Ann Pearce, 1945 (divorced); married Sherri Malinou, November, 1965 (divorced); married Jane Rodgers Johnson, October, 1983; children: (first marriage) Kathy, Mark, Mike, Carolyn; (third marriage; stepdaughters) Britt, Lisa. Education: Attended Kansas State College (now University). Religion: Converted to Jehovah's Witnesses in 1952.

ADDRESSES: Home—Murrells Inlet, Myrtle Beach, SC. Agent—c/o E. P. Dutton, 375 Hudson St., New York, NY 10014.

CAREER: Writer of mystery and detective novels, short stories, books for children, comic books, and scripts for television and films. Spillane, with producer Robert Fellows, formed an independent film company in Nashville, TN, called Spillane-Fellows Productions, which filmed features and television productions, 1969. Creator of television series Mike Hammer, 1984-87. Actor; has appeared in commercials for Miller Lite Beer. Military service: U.S. Army Air Forces; taught cadets and flew fighter missions during World War II; became captain.

AWARDS, HONORS: Junior Literary Guild Award, 1979, for The Day the Sea Rolled Back.

WRITINGS:

UNDER NAME MICKEY SPILLANE; MYSTERY NOVELS

I, the Jury (also see below), Dutton, 1947, reprinted, New American Library, 1973.
Vengeance Is Mine! (also see below), Dutton, 1950.

My Gun Is Quick (also see below), Dutton, 1950, reprinted, Signet, 1988.
The Big Kill (also see below), Dutton, 1951, reprinted, New English Library, 1984.
One Lonely Night, Dutton, 1951, reprinted, New American Library, 1989.
The Long Wait, Dutton, 1951, reprinted, New American Library, 1972.
Kiss Me, Deadly (also see below), Dutton, 1952.
The Deep, Dutton, 1961.
The Girl Hunters (also see below), Dutton, 1962.
Day of the Guns, Dutton, 1964, reprinted, New American Library, 1981.
The Snake, Dutton, 1964.
Bloody Sunrise, Dutton, 1965.
The Death Dealers, Dutton, 1965, reprinted, New American Library, 1981.
The Twisted Thing, Dutton, 1966, published as For Whom the Gods Would Destroy, New American Library, 1971.
The By-Pass Control, Dutton, 1967.
The Delta Factor, Dutton, 1967.
Body Lovers, New American Library, 1967.
Killer Mine, New American Library, 1968.
Me, Hood!, New American Library, 1969.
Survival: Zero, Dutton, 1970.
Tough Guys, New American Library, 1970.
The Erection Set, Dutton, 1972.
The Last Cop Out, New American Library, 1973.
The Flier, Corgi, 1973.
Mickey Spillane: Five Complete Mike Hammer Novels (contains I, the Jury, Vengeance Is Mine!, My Gun Is Quick, The Big Kill, and Kiss Me, Deadly), Avenel Books, 1987.
The Killing Man, Dutton, 1989.

Also author of Return of the Hood.

OTHER

The Girl Hunters (screenplay; based on Spillane's novel of the same title and starring Spillane in role of Mike Hammer), Colorama Features, 1963.
The Day the Sea Rolled Back (for children), Windmill Books, 1979.
The Ship That Never Was (for children), Bantam, 1982.
Tomorrow I Die (stories), Mysterious Press, 1984.

Also author of The Shrinking Island. Creator and writer of comic books. Author of several television and movie screenplays. Contributor of short stories to magazines.

ADAPTATIONS: I, the Jury was filmed in 1953, The Long Wait in 1954, Kiss Me, Deadly in 1955, and My Gun Is Quick in 1957, all by United Artists; The Delta Factor was filmed in 1970 by Colorama Features; a remake of I, the Jury was filmed in 1981 by Twentieth Century-Fox. Mickey Spillane's Mike Hammer, a television series based on Spillane's mystery novels and his character, Mike Hammer, was produced by Revue Productions, distributed by MCA-TV Ltd., and premiered in 1958; another television series based on Spillane's writings, Mike Hammer, starring Stacey Keach, was produced and broadcasted from 1984-87.

SIDELIGHTS: Mickey Spillane is most noted for his mystery novels featuring the hard-boiled detective Mike Hammer. "From ever since I can remember," the author commented in the Junior Literary Guild, "I've been telling yarns, then writing them whenever I could get near a typewriter." He started his writing career in the early 1940s scripting comic books for Funnies, Inc. He made the switch from comic books to novels in 1946 when, needing one thousand dollars to buy a parcel of land, he decided the easiest and quickest way to earn the money was to write a novel. Three weeks later, he sent the finished manuscript of his first book, *I, the Jury,* to Dutton publishers. The editorial committee at Dutton questioned its good taste and literary merit, but they felt the book would sell. *I, the Jury* did indeed sell—well over twelve million copies have been sold since its first publication. In addition to buying the property, Spillane was able to construct a house on the site as well. This book would be the start of a long and prolific career that would make Spillane famous, wealthy, and a personality in his own right.

Spillane described himself to Margaret Kirk in the *Chicago Tribune* in this manner: "I'm a money writer, I write when I need money. And I'm not writing for the critics. I'm writing for the public. An author would never do that. They write one book, they think they're set. I'll tell you when you're a good writer. When you're successful. I'd write like [American novelist] Thomas Wolfe if I thought it would sell."

Not only did *I, the Jury* introduce Spillane to the book buying public, it also gave birth to the character Mike Hammer, a 6-foot, 190-pound, rough and tough private investigator. Spillane's next several novels recorded the action-packed adventures of Hammer as he drank, fought, and killed his way through solving mystery after mystery. While Hammer is not featured in all of Spillane's mysteries, he is undoubtedly the most popular of Spillane's leading men.

Spillane's audience has been very loyal to his Hammer character and his other mystery novels. During his more than forty-year career, more than 180 million copies of his books have been sold in more than sixteen languages. Seven of his books are still listed among the top fifteen all-time fiction best-sellers published in the last fifty years. "I'm the most translated writer in the world, behind Lenin, Tolstoy, Gorki, and Jules Verne," Spillane said to Art Harris in the *Washington Post.* "And they're all dead." Spillane went on to declare: "I have no fans. You know what I got? Customers. And customers are your friends."

In 1952 Spillane began a nine year break from writing mystery novels. Some people have attributed this break to his religious conversion to the sect of Jehovah's Witnesses, while others feel that Spillane earned enough money from his writings and by selling the film rights to several of his books to live comfortably, enjoying life in his new beach home on Murrells Inlet, located in Myrtle Beach, South Carolina. Although he stopped writing mysteries, Spillane wrote short stories for magazines and scripts for television and films. He also appeared on a number of television programs, often performing in parodies of his tough detective characters.

Spillane reappeared on the publishing scene in 1961 with his murder mystery *The Deep.* In the following year Mike Hammer returned to fight crime in *The Girl Hunter.* The public was ecstatic, buying copies of the novel as soon as they were placed on the shelf.

In 1979 Spillane's publisher dared him to write a book for children. A number of editors at the company felt he could never change his style of writing in order to appeal to a much younger audience. Not one to back down from a challenge, Spillane produced *The Day the Sea Rolled Back,* about two boys' search for a sunken ship containing treasures. Three years later Spillane wrote another children's book concern-

ing the sea, *The Ship that Never Was.* Generally, reviewers have praised the books for their suspense and high adventure. "As for my kids' books," Spillane maintained in the *Junior Literary Guild,* "I'm sure not new to boys-around-the-ocean stories, because I grew up on the Atlantic coastline, . . . and the stories I tell are things I've always thought about."

WORKS CITED:

Harris, Art, article about Spillane, *Washington Post,* October 24, 1984.
Junior Literary Guild, review of *The Day the Sea Rolled Back,* March, 1979.
Kirk, Margaret, article about Spillane, *Chicago Tribune,* April 18, 1986.

FOR MORE INFORMATION SEE:

BOOKS

Contemporary Literary Criticism, Gale, Volume 3, 1975, Volume 13, 1980.
Major Twentieth-Century Writers, Gale, 1990.

PERIODICALS

Books and Bookmen, September, 1967; June, 1969.
Chicago Tribune, April 18, 1986.
Chicago Tribune Magazine, April 8, 1984.
Christian Century, January 29, 1969.
Detroit Free Press, June 11, 1967; March 23, 1969.
Detroit News, September 14, 1967.
Globe and Mail (Toronto), December 23, 1989.
Los Angeles Times, March 26, 1989.
Los Angeles Times Book Review, January 14, 1990.
New York Times, November 11, 1951; October 26, 1952; June 14, 1989.
New York Times Book Review, October 14, 1962; February 27, 1966; August 13, 1967; February 27, 1972; May 20, 1973; October 15, 1989.
People, July 28, 1986.
Publishers Weekly, May 15, 1967.
Saturday Review, May 29, 1965; September 27, 1970; March 25, 1972; April 7, 1973.
Times Literary Supplement, November 10, 1961; September 19, 1980.
Tribune Books (Chicago), November 26, 1989.
Voice Literary Supplement, July, 1988.
Washington Post, October 24, 1984.
Washington Post Book World, May 10, 1981.
Writer's Digest, September, 1976.

*   *   *

SPILLANE, Mickey
See SPILLANE, Frank Morrison

*   *   *

STEEL, Danielle (Fernande) 1947-

PERSONAL: Born August 14, 1947, in New York, NY; daughter of John and Norma (Stone) Schuelein-Steel; married second husband, 1977 (divorced); married third husband, John Traina (a businessman); children: (first marriage) one daughter; (second marriage) one son; (third marriage) two stepsons, four daughters, one son. *Education:* Educated in France; attended Parsons School of Design, 1963, and New York University, 1963-67. *Religion:* Christian Scientist.

DANIELLE STEEL

ADDRESSES: Home—California. *Agent*—Morton L. Janklow Associates, Inc., 598 Madison Ave., New York, NY 10022.

CAREER: Supergirls, Ltd. (public relations firm), vice-president of public relations, 1968-71; Grey Advertising, San Francisco, CA, copywriter, 1973-74; has worked at other positions in public relations and advertising; writer.

WRITINGS:

JUVENILE

Martha's Best Friend, Delacorte, 1989.
Martha's New Daddy, Delacorte, 1989.
Martha's New School, Delacorte, 1989.
Max and the Baby-Sitter, Delacorte, 1989.
Max's Daddy Goes to the Hospital, Delacorte, 1989.
Max's New Baby, Delacorte, 1989.
Martha's New Puppy, Delacorte, 1989.
Max Runs Away, Delacorte, 1990.

NOVELS

Going Home, Pocket Books, 1973.
Passion's Promise, Dell, 1977.
The Promise (based on a screenplay by Garry Michael White), Dell, 1978.
Now and Forever, Dell, 1978.
Season of Passion, Dell, 1979.
Summer's End, Dell, 1979.
The Ring, Delacorte, 1980.
Loving, Dell, 1980.
Remembrance, Delacorte, 1981.
Palomino, Dell, 1981.
To Love Again, Dell, 1981.
Crossings, Delacorte, 1982.
Once in a Lifetime, Dell, 1982.

A Perfect Stranger, Dell, 1982.
Changes, Delacorte, 1983.
Thurston House, Dell, 1983.
Full Circle, Delacorte, 1984.
Secrets, Delacorte, 1985.
Family Album, Delacorte, 1985.
Wanderlust, Delacorte, 1986.
Fine Things, Delacorte, 1987.
Kaleidoscope, Delacorte, 1987.
Zoya, Delacorte, 1988.
Star, Delacorte, 1989.
Daddy, Delacorte, 1989.
Message from Nam, Delacorte, 1990.
Heartbeat, Delacorte, 1991.

OTHER

Love Poems: Danielle Steel (poetry), Dell, 1981, abridged edition, Delacorte, 1984.
(Co-author) *Having a Baby* (nonfiction), Dell, 1984.

Contributor of articles and poetry to numerous periodicals, including *Good Housekeeping, McCall's, Ladies' Home Journal,* and *Cosmopolitan.*

ADAPTATIONS: Now and Forever was adapted into a movie and released by Inter Planetary Pictures in 1983; *Crossings* was made into an ABC-TV miniseries in 1986; NBC made television movies of *Kaleidoscope* and *Fine Things* in 1990, and of *Changes* in 1991; several of Steel's other novels, including *Wanderlust* and *Daddy,* have been optioned for television films and miniseries.

WORK IN PROGRESS: More novels and children's books.

SIDELIGHTS: Although Danielle Steel is best known as the author of best-selling adult novels, with reportedly over 125 million of her books in print, she has also written several books for children. The mother of nine, Steel wrote her first children's book for her own kids. "I was looking for a book about saying good-bye and couldn't find one," Steel told Ellen Creager of the *Detroit Free Press.* "Then, my husband went into a hospital and I couldn't find a book about the grownup going into the hospital, so I ended up writing one. I wrote strictly for my own kids, the home team. But then I mentioned to my editor and agent I had written them, and they wanted to see them." The result was the "Max and Martha" series, with titles such as *Max's Daddy Goes to the Hospital* and *Martha's New School.*

Although she is continuing her "Max and Martha" series, Steel is also planning another children's series for the future, called the "Freddie" books. "While the 'Max and Martha' books are problem oriented and deal with things like going to a new school and having a grandparent die, the 'Freddie' books will talk about everyday kinds of events—taking a vacation, going to the doctor and things like that," the author explained in *Preferred Reader Guide.* Her adult novels may be popular with millions, but Steel believes that her juvenile books have a more important audience: "Writing the children's books has been great, because my children love them, so they feel like I've done something important."

Before their mother began writing picturebooks, in fact, Steel's younger children were unaware of her fame as writer, leading to some interesting situations. As the author once

Though her novels for adults have sold millions worldwide, Danielle Steel takes special pride in writing books for her children. She is pictured here with one of her nine children.

related: "Some [of my kids] are too little to care [about my being a famous writer]. But it can be very funny. We were in Aspen, and my little boy—he was then about five—had found another kid at the pool and wanted to go to his condo to play with him. I wasn't around at the time, but my husband said OK. I went to pick him up later, and apparently the boy's mother must have been reading one of my books. My son said, 'She had this book with your picture on the back of it, and I said that was my mommy but she didn't believe it.' Then I appeared, and she was so startled!"

Steel has been immensely successful with her adult romance novels; her popularity has also spilled over into television, where film versions of her books appear regularly, receiving good ratings each time. Steel's novels are peopled by women in powerful or glamorous positions; often they are forced to choose the priorities in their lives. Thus in *Changes* a New York anchorwoman who weds a Beverly Hills surgeon must decide whether her career means more to her than her long-distance marriage does. This reflects the author's own life, for she too has had to balance the demands of a high-profile job with taking care of her family. As a result, she tries to limit publicity tours that would take her away from her children. As she once commented, "I guess I'm a contemporary woman in that my family is very important and my work is, too. I manage to do both."

WORKS CITED:

"Author Talk," *Preferred Reader Guide*, Volume 2, issue 1, 1990, p. 3.

Creager, Ellen, "Best-seller Seeks Smaller Audience," *Detroit Free Press*, December 1, 1989, p. 1C.

FOR MORE INFORMATION SEE:

BOOKS

Bestsellers 89, Issue 1, Gale, 1989.
Bestsellers 90, Issue 4, Gale, 1991.

PERIODICALS

Chicago Tribune Book World, August 28, 1983.
Detroit News, September 11, 1983.
Globe & Mail (Toronto), July 9, 1988.
Los Angeles Times, January 6, 1988.
Los Angeles Times Book Review, April 14, 1985.
New York Times Book Review, September 11, 1983; August 19, 1984; March 3, 1985.
Time, November 25, 1985.
Washington Post Book World, July 3, 1983; March 3, 1985.

*   *   *

STEPHENS, Alice Barber 1858-1932

PERSONAL: Born July 1, 1858, near Salem, NJ; died July 13, 1932 (one source says July 14), in Rose Valley, PA; daughter of Samuel C. and Mary Owen Barber; married Charles H. Stephens (an instructor at Pennsylvania Academy), June, 1890; children: one son. *Education:* Attended Philadelphia School of Design for Women (now Moore College of Art), and Pennsylvania Academy of Fine Arts, 1876; attended Academie Julian and Colarossi Academy, Paris, 1886-87.

CAREER: Freelance engraver and illustrator; Philadelphia School of Design for Women, Philadelphia, PA, instructor. *Exhibitions:* Artwork has been exhibited at the Paris Salon, 1887, Plastic Club, Philadelphia, 1890, Columbian Exposition, Chicago, IL, 1893, Atlanta Exposition, 1895, and in London, England, 1902.

MEMBER: Plastic Club (Philadelphia; cofounder).

AWARDS, HONORS: Mary Smith Prize, Pennsylvania Academy of Fine Arts, 1890, for "Portrait of a Boy"; Bronze Medal, Paris Exposition Universelle, 1890, for illustrations for Nathaniel Hawthorne's *The Marble Faun;* Cotton States and International Exposition medal, Atlanta Exposition, 1895; Gold Medal, Exposition of Women's Work, 1899, for her illustrations for George Eliot's *Middlemarch* and her paintings for Maria Mulock Craik's *John Halifax, Gentlemen.*

ILLUSTRATOR:

Maria Mulock Craik, *John Halifax, Gentlemen*, Crowell, 1897.
Annie Trumball Slosson, *Fishin' Jimmy*, Scribner's, 1898.
Nathaniel Hawthorne, *The Marble Faun*, Houghton, 1900.
Louisa May Alcott, *Little Women; or, Meg, Jo, Beth, and Amy*, Little, Brown, 1902.
Alcott, *Under the Lilacs*, Little, Brown, 1905.
Kate Douglas Wiggin, *The Old Peabody Pew: A Christmas Romance of a Country Church*, Houghton, 1907.
Margaret Wade Deland, *An Encore*, Harper & Brothers, 1907.

She talked away all the time the man clipped, and diverted my mind nicely. (From *Little Women,* by Louisa May Alcott, illustrated by Alice Barber Stephens.)

Wiggin, *Susanna and Sue,* Houghton, 1909.
Deland, *Where the Laborers Are Few,* Harper & Brothers, 1909.
Deland, *The Way to Peace,* Harper & Brothers, 1910.

Also illustrator for numerous other books, including editions of *The Courtship of Miles Standish* by Henry Wadsworth Longfellow; *Middlemarch* by George Eliot; *Blindfolded* by Earle Ashley Walcott; *A Son of the Middle Border* by Hamlin Garland; *Why I Remained a Bachelor* by Julien Gordon; *The Stark Monroe Letters* by Arthur Conan Doyle; and more than thirty other fictional works by authors such as Bret Harte and Lucie Lillie. Contributor of illustrations to periodicals, including *Scribner's Monthly, Harper's Young People, Harper's Weekly, Woman's Words, Century, Frank Leslie's Weekly, Cosmopolitan, Collier's, Women's Home Companion,* and *Ladies' Home Journal.*

SIDELIGHTS: One of the most famous American women artists of the late nineteenth and early twentieth centuries, Alice Barber Stephens produced illustrations for books, magazines, and advertisements. She was also a talented photographer, although few of her photographs exist today. Stephens began her career as a wood engraver, reproducing other artists' work. However, her desire to create her own original illustrations and paintings led her to the Pennsylvania Academy of Fine Arts, where she studied under the

Here are the peacocks, coming to be fed. . . . (From *Under the Lilacs,* by Louisa May Alcott, illustrated by Alice Barber Stephens.)

renowned artist, Thomas Eakins. Eakins, impressed by her talent, introduced her to the art editor of *Scribner's Monthly,* Alexander Drake, for whom she did several engravings. Her first published illustration came several years later, in 1885, and appeared in *Harper's Young People* magazine. From that time until about 1895 Stephens's illustrations were influenced by Eakins's highly realistic style. However, new advancements in printing techniques that made possible the reproduction of illustrations done in oils, watercolors, and other mediums, and the rise of Impressionism, gave her the opportunity for freer artistic expression.

These influences helped Stephens to mature as an artist, and her ability to adapt to change made her unique among her peers. Art historian Helen Goodman commented in *American Artist:* "What set Alice Barber Stephens apart from other women illustrators of her generation was her great versatility and her dramatic sense. Like them, the majority of her work was directed at an audience made up of women and children, and she illustrated many romances, melodramas, and children's stories. But she also appealed to a male audience because she had learned . . . how to 'capture the significant visual moment.' This ability enabled her, unlike most other women illustrators of the day, to illustrate mysteries as well as adventure tales. She was even dubbed 'Mistress of Mysteries' by *Reader Magazine* in 1909."

A cofounder of the Plastic Club, a women's art club that was established in Philadelphia in 1897, Stephens was an ardent supporter of other women artists. She wanted women to have the same opportunities as men to expand their artistic talents. Towards this end, she taught for a short time at the Philadelphia School of Design for Women, establishing the first life-drawing class for women, a considerable achievement at a time when the idea of women studying nude models was a highly objectionable pursuit to Victorian moral standards. Goodman concludes that Stephens "was by all accounts an extremely gifted, generous, and caring teacher. She encouraged her students and opened her studio to them for chats concerning not just the specifics of art, but its ideals."

WORKS CITED:

Goodman, Helen, "Alice Barber Stephens," *American Artist,* April, 1984, pp. 47-48, 98-100.

*   *   *

STRYKER, Daniel
See MORRIS, Chris(topher Crosby)

*   *   *

TAMMINGA, Frederick William 1934-
(T. F. Willius)

PERSONAL: Born June 30, 1934, in the Netherlands; son of Willem (a farmer) and Jantje (a homemaker; maiden name, Zuiderveen) Tamminga; married Margaret Heerema, December 30, 1959 (divorced, 1975); married Wendy Jill Caddick (an adult care worker), July 7, 1984; children: (first marriage) Anna Jane Hart, Roland William, Philip Eduard, Doris Melinda, Theresa Louis, Patrick John. *Education:* Calvin College, Grand Rapids, MI, B.A., 1965; Simon Fraser University, Burnaby, British Columbia, Canada, graduate work, 1966-68. *Politics:* "Save-the-World Party."

FREDERICK WILLIAM TAMMINGA

ADDRESSES: Home—c/o Wedge Publishing Foundation, P.O. Box 1000, Jordan Station, Ontario L0OR 1SO, Canada.

CAREER: Poet, author, reflexologist and drug abuse counselor. Police constable, Calgary, Alberta, Canada, 1959-61; high school teacher, Surrey, British Columbia, Canada, 1968-73; probation, parole officer and bail supervisor, Coquitlam, British Columbia, 1975-84.

MEMBER: Victoria Life Enrichment Society.

AWARDS, HONORS: Honourable mention from *The Horror Show* (magazine), 1983, for horror story "Olga's Fur Farm and the Crow."

WRITINGS:

Signals against the Sky (poetry translations), privately printed, 1969.
Believe It Or . . . (poetic meditations), Shalom Productions, 1972.
Bunk among Dragons: Poems and Translinguistic Adaptations, illustrated by Matthew Cupido, Wedge Publishing, 1973.
Prescription Z (children's fantasy), illustrated by Robert Goheen, Scholastic-TAB, 1975.
On the Edge of Edgewood (translinguistic adaptations), privately printed, 1981.
On Your Way Rejoicing, Baker Book House, 1987.

Also author of *The Whispering Parchment* (juvenile novel).

CONTRIBUTOR TO ANTHOLOGIES

Six Days, Wedge Publishing, 1971.
Making Eden Grow, Scripture Union, 1974.
Country of the Risen King, Baker Book House, 1978.

PLAYS

The Great Hallel (adaptation of the first five Psalms of David), 1974.

OTHER

Contributor of short stories to *Fiddlehead, Canadian Fiction,* and *Credo.* Contributor of poems to *Antigonish Review, Malahat Review, Prism International, Mundus Artium,* and *Contemporary Literature Translation.* Editor of *Credo.*

ADAPTATIONS: The Great Hallel (recording), Iona Enterprises. "Believe It Or . . . ," slide show with music and mime performed by Tamminga.

WORK IN PROGRESS: Adaptations of the poetry of Jan H. De Groot, a Dutch poet; *The Witch of Endor and/or Daffodils,* a book of poetry; *Screech Tells a Story . . . ,* a children's booklet about a bird.

SIDELIGHTS: Frederick William Tamminga commented, "I was born when Europe was in political turmoil. I grew up in a polder, that is, land claimed from the sea—below sealevel. This was of course in Holland—the Wieringermeer Polder. When I was about nine or ten, the Germans exploded our dikes and we were literally washed out of our home and had to escape to what was formerly an island. I suppose all that is significant because in my imagery I often have the feeling or vision of rescuing, saving something from drowning, crawling up out of slime pits, looking for an island and so on. And, of course, I developed a healthy hatred for bombs and other toys grownups enjoyed playing with.

"I missed much of early family life since I was sickly. I looked up to my older brother and my two younger sisters used to look up to me. But I was sort of a stranger, being sickly and not home very much, being confined to various sanatoria in different parts of Holland.

"I read Dutch poems as a child and I didn't understand them but copied them down anyway in a scribbler. I was in love with arranging ordinary words—same words used for shopping lists, or for asking directions, or for talking, and make new arrangements with them. I learned early that there was a way of understanding things so strange that you couldn't talk about it. You just knew. But all around you were people who asked 'What does it mean?' I never could explain what a howling, ice-cold Dutch wind meant. But I knew that Rembrandt knew in some of his few-line sketches. Or what the sound of some poems meant. These things I knew with a part of my brain that was not for talking or thinking. So I became very secretive with grown-ups—except some artists I met in the sanitorium.

"Suddenly we were in Canada, my father having some pioneering spirit left in him. It was already quite something to move from a province where everything was the same as it always had been to a new polder where there was nothing but sea silt and everything had to be built up from nothing, including a way of getting the different Dutch clans to live and work together. But my mom and dad were pioneering souls. So Canada was a natural choice for them, especially since most Dutch people respected Canadians for liberating them. Sometimes I think it's only the Dutch who give the Canadian tenacious armies their proper credit.

"By this time I was not too eager to emigrate—but a boy of twelve has no choice. My schooling had been quite interrupted by the war and illnesses from the war, although I did meet some fine private tutors, poets and artists and I knew that someday I wanted to be a Dutch writer. Of course I wanted to write about rebuilding the world and about 'resisting' everything evil—which, at that time, was everything German. (It took me years to unlearn some hatreds. Now, of course, I have German friends, including one who sometimes helps me with my poetry.)

"We knew no English. We went to a one-room school (Sandwich School number something or other—actually went to a couple different ones). The teachers were, I thought, most wonderful. But they had never taught a foreigner English. This was in 1947. I learned all about Dick and Jane and Zeke, the latter a character I never met in real life since I never met anyone by that name. But I loved it. And I wanted to do well. The language was a problem though: when someone said policeman, I thought, for some time, they were talking about Polish men—and I had met some German soldiers

Frederick W. Tamminga, author of *Bunk among Dragons,* believes in the view popular during ancient times that poets and artists are prophets.

who were Poles. When they talked of desert, I thought of deserters from some army.

"At home we spoke some sort of Dutch dialect. But I continued to be sickly, mostly with asthma. I wanted so badly to be strong and become a good Canadian farmer raising black Aberdeen Angus cattle. I had lots of cowboy dreams.

"The Christian Reformed Church was a big factor in our life. Immigrant Dutch all together on Sundays. They were industrious and all wanted to do well for themselves in this new country. Many also wanted to contribute something . . . leave a mark of something good. And many Dutch immigrants did well and took derelict farms and turned them into profitable enterprises and so on. I, too, wanted to do something good for Canada. I still do.

"I secretly wrote. My first poems were very stilted and religious. They were printed in a Dutch-Canadian magazine which still exists, I think: *Calvinist-Contact.* And I wrote little mystery stories which I could not show to anyone because they were take-offs on comic book characters and comic books were something we were not allowed to read. 'They are not of God,' it was said. And for a while I thought that it was too bad that Dagwood and Blondie did not belong to our church—if they did, I could read them without guilt. And so I grew up and got a little healthier by secretly doing Charles Atlas exercises. And I sent away for weight bars. My mother was worried about these things but relaxed when I began to look stronger as a teenager.

"Then came a time when I was restless. I didn't only want to know Dutch immigrants. After high school I moved out west to Calgary, thinking maybe I could become a cowboy if I was healthy enough—but little Christian Reformed Dutch immigrant boys did not do wild west things so I knew I had to go off by myself so no one I knew could see me and forbid me. In Calgary, of course, I did what was expected: I joined the same church which had more Dutch immigrants, but, by this time, were more integrated in the community. So I still wasn't free. I also didn't know exactly how free I wanted to be.

"I married at twenty-four after having had a year at Calvin College in the United States. (A quality academic school—in fact, I haven't visited a university where they worked harder than at this denominational college.) Anyhow, I got married and was busy the next sixteen years raising a fine group of children, six of them.

"I have no regrets about these things. The point is that long ago in the old country while the bombs fell and the polder flooded and I saw people mistreated, I had made up my mind I was going to be an artist or writer or a musician with real meaningful songs or a combination of all these things because I thought that only through real honest expressions, honest 'seeing,' could something new come about in the world, could the men of greed and power and all sorts of dirtiness for profit be dethroned so that a sort of paradise could come on this earth. I still think all that. But I got involved mainly with church work, trying to make the church new and so on. It took a lot of energy. It was all okay but not okay. Something inside me said I wasn't dealing with an inner commandment.

"Eventually I wrote a children's book, *Prescription Z,* and then I knew it was that kind of business I should be doing all the time. Of course I couldn't. There were many financial obligations—all okay and not okay. I divorced. Remarried. Did some soul-searching; became professional in people's work. I had enough talent to do different things. I wasted time, was disatisfied with everything. Began to drink alcohol like everyone around me and found out I couldn't handle it like everyone around me. I knew I had to stop those things. Eventually I did. And now, of course, I am deeply involved with people who choose the same escapes.

"I was, of course, escaping from doing what my childhood dream said I was supposed to be doing: creating things with words or anything else. So now I do that as much as possible. It is my belief that this beautiful planet is being raped, destroyed, injured by smooth-talking people in power and that much of humanity has gone along with it (just as millions of Europeans went sort of along with Hitler . . . as if he wasn't serious) and that the world is in deep trouble. Some say it's too late, what's the use. I say, fight all the comfort-loving people, fight the shallow politicians and industrialists who take from this planet and give nothing back. I fight by using the arts. Art can be a thing of beauty. But a thing of beauty can also be a two-edged sword. In the ancient world, poets, troubadours and artists in general were more like prophets and priests who were listened to. I still believe in that role. An artist has a way of seeing reality that many scientists and other brainy folk can't afford to entertain. It would take some toys away. There is another way of knowing the truth about things besides the intellectual, scholarly, scientific, reasoning way. It's the artist's way—and the artist's way is never destructive—at least no more destructive than a torrentially cleansing rain. Basically that's what my writing is all about.

"I'm learning to go with the flow because my voice is very small and, being a proud person, I sometimes think it's up to me to save the world, which is as cocky as some scientists I know—and their record for good isn't that great."

FOR MORE INFORMATION SEE:

PERIODICALS

The News (Maple Ridge, Canada), February 6, 1985.

*   *   *

THOMPSON, Ruth Plumly 1891-1976
(L. Frank Baum)

PERSONAL: Born July 27, 1891 (some sources say 1893 or 1895), in Philadelphia, PA; died April 6, 1976; daughter of George Plumly and Amanda Elton (Shuff) Thompson. *Education:* High school graduate.

CAREER: Children's writer. *Public Ledger* (newspaper), Philadelphia, PA, began as free-lance editorial writer, became staff writer, 1912-14, editor of children's page, 1914-21; author of "Oz" books for Reilly & Lee, 1921-39.

AWARDS, HONORS: Silver Medal from the *Public Ledger*.

WRITINGS:

"OZ" BOOKS; PUBLISHED WITH CREDIT LINE "FOUNDED ON AND CONTINUING THE FAMOUS OZ STORIES BY L. FRANK BAUM"; ILLUSTRATED BY JOHN R. NEILL, EXCEPT AS NOTED; PUBLISHED BY REILLY & LEE, EXCEPT AS NOTED

(Under name L. Frank Baum) *The Royal Book of Oz,* 1921.
Kabumpo in Oz, 1922.

The Cowardly Lion of Oz, 1923.
Grampa in Oz, 1924.
The Lost King of Oz, 1925.
The Hungry Tiger in Oz, 1926.
The Gnome King of Oz, 1927.
The Giant Horse of Oz, 1928.
Jack Pumpkinhead of Oz, 1929.
The Yellow Knight of Oz, 1930.
Pirates in Oz, 1931.
The Purple Prince of Oz, 1932.
Ojo in Oz, 1933.
Speedy in Oz, 1934.
The Wishing Horse of Oz, 1935.
Captain Salt in Oz, 1936.
Handy Mandy in Oz, 1937.
The Silver Princess in Oz, 1938.
Ozoplaning with the Wizard of Oz, 1939.
Yankee in Oz, illustrated by Dick Martin, International Wizard of Oz Club, 1972.
The Enchanted Island of Oz, illustrated by Martin, International Wizard of Oz Club, 1976.

OTHER

The Perhappsy Chaps, illustrated by Arthur Henderson, Volland, 1918.
The Princess of Cozytown, illustrated by Janet Laura Scott, P. F. Volland, 1922.
The Curious Cruise of Captain Santa, illustrated by Neill, Reilly & Lee, 1926.
The Wonder Book: Stories, Pictures, Games, Puzzles, Hero Tales, Animal Lore, Plays, Fun and Fancy, Reilly & Lee, 1929.
King Kojo, illustrated by Marge, David McKay, 1938.
The Wizard of Way-Up and Other Wonders (collection of stories and poems), illustrations by Marge, Henderson, Chas J. Coll, Martin, and others, edited by James E. Haff and Douglas G. Greene, International Wizard of Oz Club, 1985.

Contributor to comic books, including *Ace, Magic,* and *King* comics. Author of radio plays for National Broadcasting Company (NBC), 1933. Also author of advertisements. Contributor of stories and verse to periodicals, including *Smart Set, Ladies' Home Journal, St. Nicholas, Saturday Evening Post,* and *Jack and Jill.* Author of monthly "Perky Puppet Page," *Jack and Jill,* 1965-70. Ghostwriter of Walt Disney books for David McKay.

SIDELIGHTS: Ruth Plumly Thompson was the author of twenty-one books about the fantasy land of Oz, continuing the series created by L. Frank Baum. With her strong imagination and fanciful wordplay, Thompson left her own distinctive mark on Oz. In addition to relating further adventures of Baum's characters Dorothy Gale, the Scarecrow, the Tin Woodman, and the Cowardly Lion of *The Wonderful Wizard of Oz,* as well as a host of other characters from the series, she created more stories and characters than had Baum, helping to preserve the popularity of the entire series of Oz books among young readers.

Thompson was born in Philadelphia, Pennsylvania, in 1891. The family moved to New York when her father became night editor of the *New York Times.* Due to overwork, her father died of a heart attack at age thirty-one, and her mother had to support herself and four small children. Mrs. Thompson returned to Philadelphia and began a highly successful career in hotel management. Ruth showed her storytelling abilities early on by making up fairy tales for her brother and sisters. Soon after high school, her stories and poems became published in newspapers and magazines. Though she had the opportunity to attend Swarthmore College on a scholarship, Thompson refused the offer in order to help her family financially as a full-time free-lance writer. Throughout her career she felt the necessity of working to support her mother, who also felt strained from overwork, a sister who was ill, and a brother who was gassed during World War I.

While in high school Thompson sold a fairy tale to the popular children's magazine, *St. Nicholas.* During her twenties her contributions to the magazine attracted the interest of the advertising manager, who obtained an interview for Thompson with the editor of the Philadelphia *Public Ledger.* Thompson boldly asked to write editorials for the paper, and the editor agreed to give her a chance. Thompson eventually became a member of the paper's staff, rising to editor of the Sunday children's page. Though the paper only expected her to adapt stories, Thompson came up with original material every week. Contributing to her success was her understanding of young readers. Douglas G. Greene, in the introduction to *Wizard of Way-Up,* a collection of the author's early work, noted that "Thompson's . . . stories usually have no moral; it was enough for her to make children laugh." Thompson's fondness of children led her to organize a Santa Claus Club that gave food and gifts to disadvantaged children in the holiday season. She also fostered the efforts of young writers and artists. One in particular, Marjorie Henderson, went on to serialize cartoons in the *Saturday Evening Post,* under the name Marge, and later contributed illustrations for Thompson's writings.

Thompson edited the children's page from 1914 to 1921. Much of her writing from this time was reprinted in *The Perhappsy Chaps, The Princess of Cozytown,* and *The Wonder Book* and later collected in *The Wizard of Way-Up.* These writings are noted for their cheerful, humorous attitude toward life and language. "Clearly Thompson loved words: she studs her prose with puns, slang, clever twists and turns of phrase that show a deftness and immediacy rare in other children's books of the time," asserted Michael Patrick Hearn in *Dictionary of Literary Biography.* For the most part her stories were just for fun, but she did occasionally include serious themes, as in the *Princess of Cozytown.* "Like some of her other stories and poems," remarked Greene "[this book's] theme is the tragedy of adults who have separated themselves from the joys of childhood—and have never realized what they have done." Hearn also noted the book's "understated poignancy: when Princess Poppsy is stolen by the Giant Grownupness, her subjects, toys all, abruptly fall dead."

An enthusiastic follower of Thompson's imaginative work, William F. Lee, was vice president of Reilly and Lee, the firm that published the Oz books. Upon Baum's death in 1919, Lee invited Thompson to become the second "Royal Historian of Oz." *The Wonderful Wizard of Oz,* on which the famous 1939 film was based, was only one of fourteen stories about the wondrous land of Oz. Thompson's first contribution to the series, *The Royal Book of Oz,* was published under Baum's name; Thompson received credit only for enlarging and editing the manuscript, though in fact she had written the entire book herself. In the Oz books Thompson continued to delight in her trademark puns. Daniel P. Mannix wrote in the *Baum Bugle* that Thompson "considered any page that did not have at least three jokes in it, usually puns—a page wasted." Her characters, christened with mischievous names like Sir Hokus of Pokes, Realbad, and Prince Pompadore, encounter distinctive, whimsically named kingdoms in their adventures throughout the realm. Hearn noted, for example,

that "numbers live in Rith Metic, candles in Illumi Nation, cats in Catty Corners, disembodied heads in Head Way. It seems that whenever Thompson came across some colorful phrase or bit of slang, she visualized it as if for the first time, as if through a child's eyes, and used it as the basis of its own distinctive culture."

Broadening the American perspective of Oz that Baum favored, Thompson added an international flavor by including Chinese and Turkish people, gypsies, and pirates, and by expanding its boundaries to include exotic eastern dominions, the desert kingdom of Rash, and numerous medieval territories. "In her experience, children were not fascinated by modern political issues (as Baum was in *The Marvelous Land of Oz . . .*) or in social utopias or in everyday things," wrote Greene. "Her . . . experience had persuaded her that children are drawn to the more distant realms of romance, to fairy tales with a 'once upon a time' remoteness, with monarchies and knights in shining armor, or with an oriental mysticism." Thompson also added elements of romance, which Baum had considered of no interest to children. She borrowed Baum's method of organizing the plot around a quest but, unlike Baum, often sent her characters in search of something important, often a princess suitable for marriage. In comparing Thompson's books to those written by Baum, Hearn decided that "while her books may lack the philosophical and imaginative depth of Baum's best stories, Thompson's tales possess a zest, a vitality noticeably wanting in Baum's more somber interludes in his Oz books."

While writing the Oz books, Thompson also engaged in a variety of other writing projects, including radio plays, ghostwritten books for another publisher, David McKay, and contributions to *Magic, King,* and *Ace* comic books. In order to earn more money she wrote stories that functioned as product advertisements. Admiring the author's wellspring of invention, Greene declared, "It is striking that she could create lively fairy tales around baking powder, and toothpaste, and shoe-heels, and gelatin." Reilly and Lee, however, did not always appreciate Thompson's other writing endeavors, particularly the publication of non-Oz books, considering them competition for the Oz series. Hearn noted that Thompson once declared, "Writing the Oz books . . . was one of the happiest experiences of my life," but her working relationship with her publisher was often strained. Problems also arose between Thompson and Baum's family. Frank J. Baum felt he should have been the person to continue his father's series, and he did write one Oz story—*The Laughing Dragon of Oz*—published by another firm. Thompson did not receive support for her ideas to market Oz in other media—records, films, comics—from either the Baums or Reilly and Lee, and after penning one book a year since 1920, she gave up the series in 1939. Thompson wrote one more book about Oz in 1961, but Reilly and Lee rejected it, saying they would end the series with a different author's book—*Merry Go Round in Oz.* Two of Thompson's earlier Oz adventures, *Yankee in Oz* and *The Enchanted Isle of Oz* were published for the first time by the International Wizard of Oz Club in the 1970s.

After resigning as Royal Historian of Oz, Thompson contributed some of her best stories to the children's magazine *Jack and Jill.* About these stories published in the 1940s and 1950s, Greene declared, "For a number of years, in the middle of a deadly desert of super-realistic stories pushed on children, it was a relief to come upon the oasis of Thompson's *Jack and Jill* fantasies." Nevertheless, it is for her additions to the Oz series that Thompson will probably be best remembered. "Although she never aspired to be another L. Frank Baum,"

Hearn concluded, "Thompson deserves more recognition as a writer than simply as a footnote in Baum's biography. She did not merely continue the Oz series; she transformed the Land of Oz into her own particular fairyland. . . . Her works should be considered a valid and substantial contribution to twentieth-century American juvenile fantasy."

WORKS CITED:

Baum Bugle, autumn, 1976.
Dictionary of Literary Biography, Volume 22: *American Writers for Children, 1900-1960,* Gale, 1983, pp. 307-14.
Thompson, Ruth Plumly, *The Wizard of Way-Up, and Other Stories,* edited by James E. Haff and Douglas G. Greene, International Wizard of Oz Club, 1985.

FOR MORE INFORMATION SEE:

PERIODICALS

Baum Bugle, April, 1961; autumn, 1965; autumn, 1970.

[Sketch verified by niece, Dorothy Curtiss Maryott.]

*   *   *

TIPPETT, James S(terling) 1885-1958

PERSONAL: Born September 7, 1885, in Memphis, MO; died February 20, 1958, in Chapel Hill, NC; son of Edward (a blacksmith) and Mary Olinda (Montgomery) Tippett; married Martha Louise Kelly (a teacher), August 3, 1929. *Education:* University of Missouri, B.S., 1915; graduate work, University of Chicago and Columbia University, 1923-27. *Politics:* Democrat. *Religion:* Presbyterian. *Hobbies and other interests:* Reading, gardening, and was a dog fancier.

CAREER: Writer; educator. Teacher at schools in Scotland County, MO, 1903-04, and Lancaster, MO, 1905-07; principal and superintendent of schools in Fayette, MO, 1914-17; principal of elementary school in Kansas City, MO, 1917-18; George Peabody College for Teachers, Nashville, TN, director, 1918-22; Lincoln School, Teachers College, Columbia University, New York City, teacher and special worker, 1922-28; assistant professor of elementary education at University of Pittsburgh and director of the Pittsburgh Community Schools, 1928-30; Avon Old Farms School, Avon, CT, dean of faculty, 1930-32; Parker School District, Greenville, SC, curriculum adviser, 1934-39. Visiting lecturer, University of North Carolina, 1939-58.

MEMBER: Association for Childhood Education, Phi Delta Kappa.

WRITINGS:

ILLUSTRATED BY ELIZABETH TYLER WOLCOTT

The Singing Farmer, World Book, 1927.
I Live in a City, Harper, 1927.
I Go a-Traveling, Harper, 1929.
Busy Carpenters, World Book, 1929.
I Spend the Summer, Harper, 1930.
A World to Know, Harper, 1933.
Counting the Days, Harper, 1940.

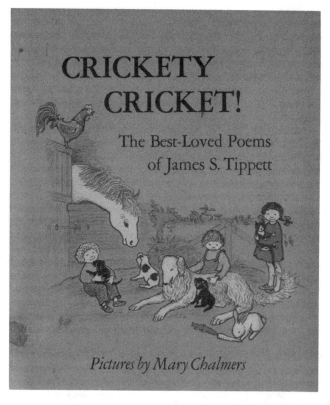

Nearly all of James S. Tippett's poems are based on memories from his childhood. (Cover from *Crickety Cricket!,* by James S. Tippett, illustrated by Mary Chalmers.)

ILLUSTRATED BY HELEN TORREY

Henry and the Garden, World Book, 1936, Grosset, 1938.
Stories about Henry, World Book, 1936, Grosset, 1938.
(And Melvern J. Barker) *Henry and His Friends,* World Book, 1939.
Here and There with Henry, World Book, 1943, published as *Here and There with Henry; With a Special Section, A Trip to Texas,* illustrated by Elise K. Wilkinson, World Book, 1947.

OTHER

Toys and Toy Makers, illustrated by Elizabeth Enright, Harper, 1931.
(Editor) *Schools for a Growing Democracy,* Ginn, 1936.
Paths to Conservation, Heath, 1937.
Shadow and the Stocking: A True Story, illustrated by Morgan Dennis, Harper, 1937.
(With wife, Martha Kelly Tippett) *Sniff,* illustrated by Morgan Dennis, Heath, 1937.
I Know Some Little Animals, illustrated by Flora Nash DeMuth, Harper, 1941.
Christmas Magic, illustrated by Helen Sewell, Grosset, 1942.
Tools for Andy, illustrated by Kay Draper, Abingdon-Cokesbury, 1951.
Abraham Lincoln, Humble and Great, illustrated by George D. Armstrong, Berkley Cardy, 1951.
Jesus Lights the Sabbath Lamp, illustrated by Doris Stolberg, Abingdon-Cokesbury, 1953.
A Search for Sammie, illustrated by Beth Krush, Abingdon, 1954.
Crickety-Cricket! The Best Loved Poems of James S. Tippett, illustrated by Mary Chalmers, introduction by Donald Bissett, Harper, 1973.

Also co-author with Charles W. Finley of pamphlet, *Field Work,* published by the Lincoln School of Teachers College, 1925. Co-author of "Understanding Science" series, grades one through six, published by Winston. Editor of *Curriculum Making in an Elementary School,* 1927. Author of *The Picnic,* 1938.

Tippett's works are contained in the Kerlan Collection at the University of Minnesota.

SIDELIGHTS: James S. Tippett was five years old when he moved from his birthplace of Memphis, Missouri, to an outlying farm. He returned to city life during his years as a student at the University of Missouri, and at the University of Chicago and Columbia University in Illinois.

He and his wife, Martha Louise, earned their living as teachers. Tippett became a school principal and school superintendent in Missouri. During the 1920s, he worked as a school administrator and associate professor of elementary education in New York City and Pittsburgh, Pennsylvania.

In 1927, he began writing, recapturing his childhood days in books based on his early experiences. *The Singing Farmer,* for example, recreates his explorations of the Missouri farm where he grew up. *I Spend the Summer* tells the story of a child's journey from Pennsylvania to North Carolina in 1929. *Here and There with Henry* and *I Know Some Little Animals* are based on a child's experiences in a small community in North Carolina, where the Tippetts settled in 1939.

Tippett was a respected leader in his field, a fact reflected in his books and pamphlets on the subject, including *Schools for a Growing Democracy,* a collection of essays which he edited, and *Field Work,* a pamphlet about problems in urban education published by the Lincoln School of Teachers College in New York City.

FOR MORE INFORMATION SEE:

BOOKS

Arbuthnot, May Hill, *Children and Books,* Scott, Foresman, 1947.
Cattell and Ross, *Leaders in Education,* Science Press, 1949.
The Ispescope, Methodist Publishing House, 1949.
North Carolina Authors, University of North Carolina Library, 1952.

OBITUARIES:

PERIODICALS

Wilson Library Bulletin, April, 1958.
Publishers Weekly, April 21, 1958.

*   *   *

TONG, Gary S. 1942-

PERSONAL: Born July 31, 1942, in Budapest, Hungary; immigrated to United States, 1957; son of Manny (in entertainment and business) and Magdolna (a mental hygiene therapist; maiden name, Schweitzer) Tong. *Education:* Queens College of the City University of New York, B.A., 1965; Harvard Graduate School of Arts and Sciences, M.A. 1969. *Hobbies and other interests:* Musical compositions,

synthesizers, computers, science, history, linguistics, ethics, and philosophy.

ADDRESSES: Home—156 East 37th St., New York, NY 10016.

CAREER: Free-lance illustrator, 1970—.

AWARDS, HONORS: Woodrow Wilson fellow, 1966; Lucky Book Club Four-Leaf Clover Award and Author of the Year award, both from Scholastic, 1982; Phi Beta Kappa.

WRITINGS:

SELF-ILLUSTRATED

Modeling with Self-Hardening Clay, Larousse, 1976.
Gary Tong's Crazy Cut-Outs, Scholastic, 1979.
Gary Tong's More Crazy Cut-Outs, Scholastic, 1980.
(With Murray F. Weisenfeld) *The Runners Repair Manual* (illustrated with Lori Weisenfeld), St. Martin's, 1981.
Gary Tong's Crazy Cut-Outs from Outer Space, Scholastic, 1982.
Gary Tong's Crazy Cut-Out Tricks and Puzzles, Scholastic, 1983.
Gary Tong's Crazy Pop-Ups, Scholastic, 1988.

Gary Tong's Crazy Cut-Outs has been published in Dutch, and *Gary Tong's Crazy Cut-Outs from Outer Space* and *Gary Tong's Crazy Pop-Ups* have been published in French.

ILLUSTRATOR

T. S. Bruner, *Processes of Cognitive Growth* (illustrated with photographs), Clark University Press, 1968.

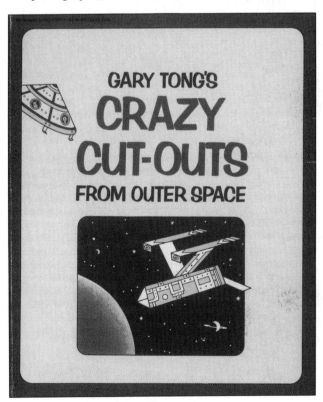

Kids fold, cut, and tape Gary Tong's illustrations into space toys. (Cover from *Crazy Cut-Outs from Outer Space,* by Gary Tong.)

T. B. Brazelton, *Infants and Mothers* (illustrated with photographs), Delacorte, 1969.

Malcolm E. Weiss and Doris E. Hadary, *Seeing through the Dark: Blind and Sighted—Vision Shared,* Harcourt, 1976.

WORK IN PROGRESS: The Illusions of Esthetics, art and visual psychology; *The Sayings of Manduke,* philosophy; *General Phonetics,* new interpretation of pronunciation and its evolution.

SIDELIGHTS: Gary S. Tong commented, "I was raised in Hungary and came to the United States at the age of fifteen. I received a B.A. in classical languages and a M.A. in Assyriology, and I have experience in photography. My father is Chinese, my mother is Hungarian Jewish."

* * *

TORLEY, Luke
 See BLISH, James (Benjamin)

* * *

TRAHERNE, Michael
 See WATKINS-PITCHFORD, Denys James

* * *

WALKER, Lou Ann 1952-

PERSONAL: Born December 9, 1952, in Hartford City, IN; daughter of Gale Freeman (a printer) and Doris Jean (a homemaker; maiden name, Wells) Walker; married Speed Vogel (a writer), September 8, 1986; children: Katherine. *Education:* Attended Ball State University, 1971-73; L'Universite de Besancon, degree in French language and literature, 1975; Harvard University, B.A., 1976.

ADDRESSES: Home and office—Sag Harbor, NY. *Agent*—Liz Darhansoff, 1220 Park Ave., New York, NY 10128.

CAREER: Indianapolis News, Indianapolis, IN, reporter, summer, 1975 and 1976; *New York* (magazine), New York City, assistant to executive editor, 1976; *Esquire* (magazine), New York City, assistant editor, 1977-78; *Cosmopolitan* (magazine), New York City, assistant to executive editor, 1978-79; *Diversion* (magazine), New York City, associate editor, 1979-80; *Direct* (magazine), New York City, editor, 1980-82; writer. Sign language interpreter in courts and hospitals in New York City, 1976—; Museum of Modern Art, New York City, consultant to Department of Special Education, 1980-85; Theatre Development Fund, New York City, sign language consultant for Broadway shows, 1984—.

MEMBER: Authors Guild, Registry of Interpreters for the Deaf.

AWARDS, HONORS: Rockefeller Foundation humanities grant, 1982-83; *Amy: The Story of a Deaf Child* was named one of year's ten best children's books by National Education Association, 1985; Christopher Award, 1987, for *A Loss for Words: The Story of Deafness in a Family;* National Endowment for the Arts creative writing grant, 1988.

LOU ANN WALKER

WRITINGS:

Amy: The Story of a Deaf Child, photographs by Michael Abramson, Lodestar, 1985.

A Loss for Words: The Story of Deafness in a Family (memoir; Book-of-the-Month Club editor's choice), Harper, 1986.

Contributor to periodicals, including *Harvard Magazine, New York Times Magazine, Parade,* and *People.* Contributing editor, *New York Woman.*

WORK IN PROGRESS: The Education of the Deaf in the United States, publication by Dial expected in 1992-93; a novel, *The Life Detector.*

SIDELIGHTS: Journalist and author Lou Ann Walker has written two books that deal with deafness. Her interest in the subject comes from her own life—both of her parents are deaf. Because she can hear, Walker has been a part of both the hearing and deaf cultures since she was a child. She writes about this experience in *A Loss for Words: The Story of Deafness in a Family.* Walker has also written *Amy: The Story of a Deaf Child,* a nonfiction book for children.

Walker's parents, Doris Jean and Gale, both became deaf when they were babies. When Doris Jean was six years old, she was sent to a school for the deaf. Because her parents couldn't communicate with her, they "had no way of telling her she was going away to school. And no way of letting her know she'd be able to come home again," Lou Ann Walker wrote in *A Loss for Words.* "It was several years before my mother understood why she was at the school. At first she wondered if she'd been exiled for misbehaving or if something terrible was about to happen to her own mother and father."

Walker's father went to the same school, though he was a few years older. The couple didn't meet until after they had completed school and were both living in Indianapolis, Indiana. They met, fell in love, and had their first child, Lou Ann. "My grandmother . . . had helped Mom and Dad choose that name. They'd needed words they could pronounce easily, a name with few syllables and one that didn't have any *t's* or *r's* or *p's.*" So that they could tell when Lou Ann was crying and needed something, the Walkers bought a special crib for her. They connected the crib to a lamp by their bed. When Lou Ann cried, the lamp flashed on and off. "Those times at night when I cried for no good reason, when I'd been fed and diapered and comforted and there was nothing left to do but wait out my tears, the flashing light strobed through the darkened house."

The Walkers communicated with each other and with their daughter by using sign language. But Lou Ann needed to learn spoken language as well, so her parents bought a television set. Through the TV, Walker was able to hear speech patterns and vocabulary. At a very young age, then, she knew two languages. "As soon as I began to sign and talk, I became my parents' guide," wrote Walker. "If a phone call had to be made, I was the one to make it. . . . [My parents] hated having to ask for so much to be done for them. But as practical people, they had no choice but to rely on me."

Because she can hear, Lou Ann Walker had to act as an interpreter for her deaf parents. (Cover from *A Loss for Words,* by Lou Ann Walker, jacket illustration by Judy Pedersen.)

Acting as interpreter for her parents was sometimes embarrassing and shameful for Walker. If an outsider insulted her parents or treated them rudely, Walker felt as though she had to hide the insult to protect her parents.

Walker's parents eventually had two other daughters, Kay and Jan, who could help Lou Ann interpret for them. When Lou Ann graduated from high school, she decided to attend Ball State, an Indiana college that was close to home. Dissatisfied, she transferred to Harvard University in Boston, Massachusetts, after two years. Though saddened that their daughter was so far from home, Walker's parents encouraged her because they wanted her to be independent and live her own life. Walker eventually graduated from Harvard and decided to move to New York City, where she found work as a magazine editor. She worked for such publications as *New York, Cosmopolitan, Diversion,* and *Esquire,* and she traveled to far-away places like the South Pacific and northern Africa.

In addition to her journalism duties, Walker worked as a sign-language teacher and as an interpreter for the deaf. "Mostly I interpreted in courtrooms, jail cells, hospital emergency rooms, welfare offices, mental institutions, and college classrooms, occasionally signing for press conferences and television programs," she recalled in her memoir. As an interpreter, Walker was forced to be like "a robot." She was not allowed to express her opinions or emotions. "If I felt a psychiatrist was coming to the conclusion that the deaf person was a raving loon, when he or she just happened to be exhibiting a deaf mannerism that was completely normal, I could not say anything to explain deafness or its educational limits. I was powerless to straighten out the misunderstandings." Such restrictions led her to become frustrated with her work as an interpreter.

At the same time, Walker began to experience troublesome feelings toward her parents. While she had always loved her parents, she felt guilty because she couldn't help them hear. From her early childhood on, she had tried to be good and dutiful so that she could fit in with others and make her parents fit in as well. But she realized that she could never change her parents' deafness. "There was ultimately nothing I could do—or can do—for them. . . . I could never make them hear. And I could never make the world hear them. So what had I accomplished? What could I ever accomplish?" Feeling worthless and bitter, Walker quit her magazine job and stopped interpreting.

It wasn't until she decided to write about her experiences that Walker began to feel better about her life. Writing *A Loss for Words,* though, was painful as well as healing. "Nothing is as difficult as writing about your family, nothing can tear your soul apart quicker, nothing can make you cry and ache and wish you'd never begun. Nothing is as dismal as the feeling that you may be deceiving them, or even that you may be overpraising them and thus leaving them without the dignity they had before." After she finished the book, Walker gave her parents a copy to read. She was worried that the bitterness in the book would upset her parents, but they responded with kindness. "They made only one substantive comment, . . . 'We hope no feelings hurt.'"

Critics liked the book. Writing in the *Washington Post,* Carol Eron called *A Loss for Words* a "delicate, carefully drawn memoir." She also praised the author's depiction of her childhood environment. "So clearly does the author evoke the private, glowing, almost otherworldly existence in their home that you can see and feel it, and even hear the cooing

Michael Abramson, Amy Rowley, and Lou Ann Walker—the photographer, the star, and the author of *Amy: The Story of a Deaf Child*.

sound that rises from her mother's throat when she hugs her children."

In *Amy: The Story of a Deaf Child,* Walker presents the true story of Amy Rowley, a fifth-grader who is deaf. Despite her deafness, Amy attends a regular school. She uses hearing aids and sign language to communicate with her friends, family, and teachers. Walker used Amy's own words to write the book. "In the mornings, my alarm clock has a flashing light to wake me up. I like it better when my mom comes to get me out of bed. Our house also has lights that flash when someone rings the doorbell," Amy comments. Of her hearing abilities, she states: "I can hear myself talking right now. I can hear some sounds, but I can't understand everything. Say I heard an ambulance go by. I wouldn't know what it was unless I saw it." The book contains many photographs that show Amy at home, at school, playing with friends, and demonstrating how to use sign language. Reviewers found *Amy: The Story of a Deaf Child* interesting and informative. "I recommend it highly," wrote *Appraisal* contributor Gwyneth E. Loud.

In addition to her books, Walker has written several articles for magazines. She has written about blind professionals and about families dealing with serious illness. She has also done celebrity interviews, including two with Marlee Matlin, a well-known actress who is deaf. Walker and her husband, writer Speed Vogel, live just outside New York City in Sag Harbor, New York.

WORKS CITED:

Eron, Carol, "The Trials of Silent Love," *Washington Post,* November 7, 1986, p. C6.

Loud, Gwyneth E., a review of *Amy: The Story of a Deaf Child, Appraisal,* winter, 1986, p. 37.
Walker, Lou Ann, *Amy: The Story of a Deaf Child,* Lodestar, 1985.
Walker, Lou Ann, *A Loss for Words: The Story of Deafness in a Family,* Harper, 1986.

FOR MORE INFORMATION SEE:

PERIODICALS

Los Angeles Times, March 30, 1987.
Newsweek, September 22, 1986.
New York Times Book Review, October 5, 1986.
New York Times Magazine, August 31, 1986.
People, December 15, 1986.

*   *   *

WALKER, Robert W(ayne) 1948-
(Geoffrey Caine, Glenn Hale, Stephen Robertson)

PERSONAL: Born November 17, 1948, in Corinth, MS; son of Richard Herman and Janie Elizabeth (McEachern) Walker; married Cheryl Anne Ernst (an accountant), September 8, 1967; children: Stephen Robert. *Education:* Northwestern University, B.S.Ed., 1971, M.S., 1972, additional study, 1975. *Politics:* "Nonpartisan."

ADDRESSES: Home and office—705 Lone Oak Dr., Port Orange, FL 32019. *Agent*—Adele Leone, 26 Nantucket Pl., Scarsdale, NY 10583.

ROBERT W. WALKER

CARFER: Free-lance writer of adult and children's books. English instructor at Bethune-Cookman College, Daytona Beach, FL.

MEMBER: Mystery Writers of America, Horror Writers of America.

WRITINGS:

CHILDREN'S BOOKS

Daniel Webster Jackson and the Wrongway Railway (novel), Oak Tree, 1982.
Spotty the Goat (storybook; originally published in booklet form), May Davenport, 1983.
Search for the Nile (novel in "Time Machine" series), illustrated by Jose Gonzalez Navaroo, Bantam, 1985.

ADULT NOVELS

Sub-Zero, Leisure Books, 1979.
Brain Watch, Leisure Books, 1985.
Aftershock, St. Martin's, 1987.
Salem's Child, Leisure Books, 1987.
Disembodied, St. Martin's, 1988.
(Under pseudonym Glenn Hale) *DR. O,* Zebra Books, 1991.

"DEAN GRANT MEDICAL EXAMINER" SERIES

Dead Man's Float, Pinnacle Books, 1989.
Razor's Edge, Pinnacle Books, 1989.
Burning Obsession, Pinnacle Books, 1990.
Dying Breath, Pinnacle Books, 1990.

UNDER PSEUDONYM STEPHEN ROBERTSON; "RYNE LANARK DECOY" SERIES

Decoy, Pinnacle Books, 1989.
Decoy Number Two: Blood Tells, Pinnacle Books, 1989.
Decoy Number Three: Blood Ties, Pinnacle Books, 1990.
The Handyman, Pinnacle Books, 1990.

UNDER PSEUDONYM GEOFFREY CAINE; "ABE STROUD" ARCHEOLOGY/HORROR SERIES

Curse of the Vampire, Berkley Publishing, 1991.
Wake of the Werewolf, Berkley Publishing, 1991.

WORK IN PROGRESS: Tort. 9 and *Tort. 6,* publication by Berkley Publishing expected in 1992; *Day of the Zombies,* third book in the "Abe Stroud" series, publication by Berkley Publishing expected in 1992, and *Flukes,* possible fourth book in the "Abe Stroud" series; a book titled *Random Violence* or *Millennium; Indian Brigades in the Civil War* (nonfiction); *Flashpoint; The Titanic Horror.*

SIDELIGHTS: Robert W. Walker told *SATA:* "I was born on November 17, 1948, in Corinth, Mississippi, and my parents moved the five children to Chicago, Illinois, when I was about five years old, my father following jobs and work. We had no say so in the decision and, like most children, would have preferred to stay in the country. However, as a writer, growing up in Chicago with its big city bustle and excitement and going to schools that were interracially mixed was a very important influence and learning experience. As a result, today I can draw on ethnic characters in my stories and, I feel, capture something real about people of other faiths, color, and background.

"I always loved stories and I read a great deal. I also listened to stories. Anyone who was willing to take the time to tell a story aloud, I was there to sit and listen, and SEE, in my mind,

DANIEL WEBSTER JACKSON AND THE WRONGWAY RAILWAY

A NOVEL BY ROBERT W. WALKER

"It was the manuscript for *Daniel* that got me into college, much more so than my grades," Robert W. Walker told *Something about the Author.* (Cover illustration from *Daniel Webster Jackson and the Wrongway Railway* by Neil K. Shigley.)

the story unfold. At age thirteen I tried my hand at song writing and failed miserably. I tried poetry, and it smelled bad. Finally I began to write short stories, sometimes borrowing my ideas from TV, or other stories I had read. I imitated Mark Twain's writing in *Huckleberry Finn* in order to write one page to see if I could do it—sound like Twain. I did, and one page became two, and soon I had a first chapter in a book I did go on to finish at 190 pages. It took a lot of rewriting and many years (seventeen) to sell the book, which was published as *Daniel Webster Jackson and the Wrongway Railway.* It was my first novel and it dealt with the Underground Railroad in 1850 Missouri. I finished it before I finished high school.

"It was the manuscript for *Daniel* that got me into college, much more so than my grades! I had a difficult time in college, too, just trying to keep up, so I had to cut back the time I spent writing fiction. Report writing just isn't the same. College did, however, teach me two most valuable lessons a writer needs to know: how to use time wisely (discipline) and how important research can be. The third most important thing is persistence, the stubborn mule-headedness that makes an Olympic athlete a winner makes a writer a winner.

"All my books are written only after I do some library work. All my fiction is built upon nonfiction, facts, information, interviews with people, letters, and telephone calls—even my ghost and horror stories. I sold my first six books without the help of an agent, and that's persistence.

"A valuable year for me was 1979, with the publication of my first suspense novel. It was a mix of mystery and science fiction, entitled *Sub-Zero,* about an ice age coming to claim Chicago. This was not the first novel I'd written, but the first I had sold! I made one thousand dollars on it, and at the time I knew I couldn't live on a writer's pay, so I kept my job and continued writing on the train, on weekends, *making* time for it. I rewrote *Daniel* after the success of *Sub-Zero,* knowing *Daniel* lacked an element of mystery-surprise. Now I always look for that mystery within the story that needs to be teased out of it. Every great story has an element of mystery, and young writers can learn more from writing a mystery than any other form. It teaches how to plot. You raise several or twenty questions in chapter one; to answer those questions, you then must build a plot around the questions and answers.

"Nineteen-eighty-two was a good year for me because *Daniel* sold to Oak Tree Publications on the same day that I decided to quit working a full-time job to write full time. My plan seemed to be 'blessed' by *Daniel* and Oak Tree since I got the contract only after I got home that night. My new plan was to write for one year to see if I could make a living at it. That year I wrote four historical novels on the order of *Daniel*—a young boy grows up amid a famous historical event, like the siege of Vicksburg, Mississippi, during the Civil War. None of these has been sold, but with each book I learned my craft. I put in my 'apprentice' year, and it turned into two, and three, and finally five years, and still I was managing to live and write, thanks a great deal to the patience and help of my family, my wife and son.

"*Brain Watch* was published in 1985, although I had written it originally in 1981, after *Sub-Zero.* Crazy as it may seem, it was turned down by every publisher of murder mysteries, including the publisher who, in 1985, seeing it for the second time around, published it. It was too short, however, and they wanted twenty thousand more words, but instead of letting them say no on the basis of this fact, I said, 'Give me a contract, and I'll give you the added twenty thousand words.' *Brain Watch* is the story of a genius who attempts to play god with other people's minds, both alive and 'dead.' It has elements of science fiction, horror, and police mystery. A lot of research involving how the brain works went into the writing of this novel.

"Also published in 1985 was *Search for the Nile,* a 'game-book' novel where you are the main character and get to decide which page to turn to next. Given a mission to accomplish, you return to the past through a time machine, are placed in uncharted Africa in the 1870s, and become a member of Henry M. Stanley's African expedition.

"Nineteen-eighty-seven was fun: it was my first year to see two titles published in the same year. *Salem's Child* revolves around the Salem, Massachusetts, witchcraft trials. Through the evil of a biblical creature, the convicted witches finally get their revenge in 1987, after three hundred years of waiting. *Aftershock* is the story of a Los Angeles, California, earthquake and what crawls up out of the rubble where a genetics lab had been. This book has sold more copies than any of my earlier titles.

"An exceptional year for me was 1988, and perhaps it meant the years of writing and getting little in return for all the work finally paid off. That year *Disembodied* saw print. It is the story of a psychic who goes on an astral journey, returns to his body, but cannot reenter it because someone has destroyed it. He must then investigate his own murder from another dimension, an ambitious project.

"Also in 1988 the first of a four-book series of my own creation, with the continuing character of Dean Grant, medical examiner for the city of Chicago, saw print under the title *Dead Man's Float,* followed by *Razor's Edge, Burning Obsession,* and *Dying Breath. Dead Man's Float* is both my best novel to date and my scariest—not for the faint of heart, even my agent could not read it all. Working with Zebra Books on the series, I was asked by them to do another series, this one about a policeman who specializes in decoy work. The series of four books is called 'Decoy' and is written under the pen name Stephen Robertson.

"Since the July, 1990, publication of *The Handyman,* the fourth in the 'Decoy' series, I have embarked on a major horror project with Berkley Publishing's new Diamond Books line. My first title is *Curse of the Vampire,* which follows the exploits of a police investigator turned archeologist who has a steel plate in his head from the Vietnam War. From time to time, this iron plate amplifies his natural extrasensory perception. Our archeologist, it seems, simply digs too deep and usually uncovers the supernatural along with relics and artifacts. Following are *Wake of the Werewolf,* also an 'Abe Stroud' horror/mystery, and *Day of the Zombies,* to be published in February, 1992. All the books in this series are written under the pen name Geoffrey Caine.

"Also in 1991 Zebra Books published *DR. O,* a Federal Bureau of Investigation/serial killer chase book that has been likened to Thomas Harris's *Silence of the Lambs,* a comparison my work has enjoyed on previous occasions—usually made by editors.

"Sometime in 1992 Berkley is expected to publish *Tort. 9,* to be followed by a sequel tentatively entitled *Tort. 6. Tort. 9* is the ultimate in terror, a true-life vampire being stalked by an FBI woman. The term 'tort. 9' is FBI lingo for the ninth level of torture endured by a victim of murder.

"Currently I am working on a possible fourth book in the 'Abe Stroud' archeologist series, following *Day of the Zombies,* tentatively titled *Flukes.* I am also working on a larger, more ambitious project that may or may not pose an explanation for random violence, tentatively titled either *Random Violence* or *Millennium.* I am attempting to sell two other titles, one dealing with the Titanic shipwreck and the second dealing with pyromania in the category of horror/suspense. Furthermore, I am desperately seeking a publisher for an ambitious nonfiction project on American Indians and the Civil War.

"It is a strange business, being a writer. In 1987 I had one book to work on and soon thereafter I had nine contracts for books that hadn't been printed yet. Ideas—where do they come from? They're all around us, in the news and in other books, in people and places. The careful writer just knows how to put those ideas to work for him. He rolls them up like a ball of twine, then the reader can unravel the story-twine to see what happens next.

"As for more young reader books, I have several, and, perhaps with the good fortune of my so-called adult books, these will be looked at with a fresh eye, as they have all been turned down by every publisher in New York. But so, too, had *Brain Watch.*"

"You ain't one of ours, child. Where'd you come from! Who is you?" "My name's Effram, ma'am," Daniel began.
(From *Daniel Webster Jackson and the Wrongway Railway,* by Robert W. Walker.)

FOR MORE INFORMATION SEE:

PERIODICALS

Chicago Reader, May 25, 1979.
Chicago Sun Times, May 15, 1979.
Courier & Freeman News, April 14, 1987.
Daytona News Journal, July 24, 1990.
Elgin Herald News, July 2, 1979.
Esprit, July, 1979.
Orlando Sentinel, December 27, 1987.
Publishers Weekly, May 28, 1979.
Watertown Daily Times, January 28, 1985; February 25, 1985; April 18, 1987.

*　　*　　*

WATKINS, Peter 1934-

PERSONAL: Born February 7, 1934, in London, England; son of Harry Gordon (a publisher) and Gladys (a home-maker; maiden name, Wood) Watkins; married Angela Berger (a teacher), August 20, 1966; children: Benjamin, Samuel, Jessica. *Education:* St. Peter's College, Oxford, M.A., 1957; attended Wycliffe Hall Theological College, 1957-59. *Politics:* Conservative. *Religion:* Church of England.

ADDRESSES: Home—7 North Common Rd., Ealing, London W5 2QA, England.

CAREER: Ordained Anglican priest, 1960; St. James's Episcopal Church, Birmingham, MI, assistant minister, 1963-65; vicar of St. Matthew's, Ealing Common, London, England, 1967—; writer. *Military service:* British Army, 1952-54, served in Korea; became second lieutenant.

WRITINGS:

(With Erica Hughes) *Here's the Church,* illustrated by Gill Tomblin, Julia MacRae, 1980.
(With E. Hughes), *Here's the Year,* illustrated by Gill Tomblin, F. Watts, 1981.
David and the Giant (juvenile), illustrated by Jan Martin, Julia MacRae, 1981, F. Watts, 1982.
(With E. Hughes) *A Book of Prayer,* Julia MacRae, 1982, F. Watts, 1983.
Eric Liddell: Born to Run, illustrated by G. Rowe, F. Watts, 1983.
(With E. Hughes) *Here Are the People,* illustrated by Susan Neale, Julia MacRae, 1984.
A Book of Animals, illustrated by William Geldart, Julia MacRae, 1985.
(With E. Hughes) *The Good Samaritan and Other Stories,* illustrated by Nigel Murray, Julia MacRae, 1987.

Contributor to magazines, including *Quarterly Review, Theology, Church Times, Harper's,* and *The Listener.*

WORK IN PROGRESS: "A history of the church in London—not parish by parish, but the great sweep of almost two thousand years. There was a Bishop of London long before there was a King of England or an Archbishop of Canterbury."

SIDELIGHTS: Peter Watkins commented: "I have concentrated on writing books on aspects of religion and Christianity for younger readers because most of the available literature of that kind seems to be either stuffy, shoddy, sentimental, or plain patronizing.

"*Here Are the People* explains the function of various official church figures like the dean, the bishop, the pope, etc. *A Book of Animals* describes some fifteen animals that have gripped man's imagination and really influenced man's life."

*   *   *

WATKINS-PITCHFORD, Denys James 1905-1990
(BB, Michael Traherne)

OBITUARY NOTICE—See index for *SATA* sketch: Born July 25, 1905, in Lamport, Northamptonshire, England; died September 8, 1990. Artist, educator, and author. Watkins-Pitchford, who generally published under the pseudonym BB, wrote and illustrated children's books such as *The Little Grey Men* and *Bill Badger's Voyage to the World's End.* An ardent naturalist, he also produced a variety of works inspired by his love of the outdoors and fishing and shooting, including *Confessions of a Carp Fisher, The Countryman's Bedside Book,* and, under the pseudonym Michael Traherne, *Be Quiet and Go A-Angling.* Watkins-Pitchford was an art teacher for fifteen years before he turned to writing and illustrating full time. In addition to designing his own books, he provided the artwork for the works of others. His 1979 autobiography, *A Child Alone,* was a best-seller.

OBITUARIES AND OTHER SOURCES:

BOOKS

International Authors and Writers Who's Who, 11th edition, International Biographical Centre, 1989.

PERIODICALS

Times (London), September 12, 1990.

*   *   *

WATTERSON, Bill 1958-

PERSONAL: Born in 1958, in Washington, DC; married; wife's name, Melissa (an artist). *Education:* Kenyon College, graduated, 1980.

ADDRESSES: Office—c/o Universal Press Syndicate, 4900 Main St., Kansas City, MO 64112.

CAREER: Cartoonist. *Cincinnati Post,* Cincinnati, OH, editorial cartoonist, 1980; creator of comic strip "Calvin and Hobbes," syndicated with Universal Press Syndicate, 1985—.

AWARDS, HONORS: Reuben Awards for Outstanding Cartoonist of the Year, National Cartoonists Society, 1986 and 1988; National Cartoonists Society award for outstanding humor strip, 1988.

WRITINGS:

COMIC STRIP COLLECTIONS; SELF-ILLUSTRATED

Calvin and Hobbes, Andrews & McMeel, 1987.
The Essential Calvin and Hobbes: A Calvin and Hobbes Treasury, Andrews & McMeel, 1988.
Something under the Bed Is Drooling: A Calvin and Hobbes Collection, Andrews & McMeel, 1988.
Yukon Ho!, Andrews & McMeel, 1989.
The Calvin & Hobbes Lazy Sunday Book, Andrews & McMeel, 1989.
The Authoritative Calvin and Hobbes, Andrews & McMeel, 1990.
Weirdos from Another Planet!, Andrews & McMeel, 1990.
The Revenge of the Baby-Sat, Andrews & McMeel, 1991.

Contributor of editorial cartoons to a chain of Cleveland newspapers. Cartoons have been published in *Target.*

SIDELIGHTS: Bill Watterson, creator of the very popular comic strip "Calvin and Hobbes," spent his childhood in Chagrin Falls, Ohio, where his family moved when he was six. As a child, he read the funny pages, particularly admiring Walt Kelly's "Pogo" and Charles Schulz's "Peanuts." He started his own cartooning for the Chagrin Falls high school newspaper and yearbook; he also did political drawings every week at Kenyon College in Gambier, Ohio, where he majored in political science.

"Right after I graduated from Kenyon, I was offered a job at the *Cincinnati Post* as their editorial cartoonist in a trial six-month arrangement," Watterson told Andrew Christie in *Honk!* "The agreement was that they could fire me or I could quit with no questions asked if things didn't work out during the first few months. Sure enough, things didn't work out."

The paper's editor, Watterson explained, "was going to publish only my very best work so that I wouldn't embarrass the newspaper while I learned the ropes. As sound as that idea may be from the management standpoint, it was disastrous for me because I was only getting a couple cartoons a week printed. I would turn out rough idea after rough idea, and he would veto eighty percent of them. As a result I lost all my self-confidence, and his intervention was really unhealthy, I think, as far as letting me experiment, and make mistakes, and become a stronger cartoonist for it. Obviously, if he wanted a more experienced cartoonist, he shouldn't have hired a kid just out of college. I pretty much prostituted myself for six months but I couldn't please him.

"I think the experience—now, in hindsight—was probably a good thing," the artist added. "It forced me to consider how interested I was in political cartooning. . . . I was never one of those people who reads the headlines and foams at the mouth with a rabid opinion that I've just got to get down on paper. I'm interested in the issues but . . . I just don't have the killer instinct that I think makes a great political cartoonist. I'd always enjoyed the comics more, and felt that as long as I was

(From *Calvin and Hobbes,* by Bill Watterson.)

unemployed it would be a good chance to pursue that and see what response I could get from a syndicate."

During the next five years Watterson continued to draw, submitting various strips to several syndicates, including "a sort of out-of-space parody" named "Spaceman Spiff," an animal comic, and a cartoon about a young man of his own age in his first job and apartment. "When each one was rejected, I would read into any comments the syndicates had written and try to figure out what they were looking for," the artist told David Astor in a 1986 *Editor & Publisher* article.

But trying to adapt his style to what the syndicates wanted didn't work for Watterson. "I don't think that's the way to draw your best material," he explained in his *Honk!* interview. "You should stick to what you're interested in and what you feel comfortable with, what you enjoy, what you find funny—that's the humor that will be the strongest, and that will transmit itself. Rather than trying to find out what the latest trend is, you should draw what is personally interesting."

One of the ideas Watterson submitted included the minor characters of Calvin and Hobbes, a little boy and his stuffed tiger playmate. Calvin and Hobbes caught the attention of United Features Syndicate, who proposed that Watterson build a series focusing on the duo. "I had thought they were the funniest characters myself, but I was unsure as to whether they could hold their own strip," Watterson said in *Honk!* But "their personalities expanded easily, and that takes a good 75 percent of the work out of it. If you have the

personalities down, you understand them and identify with them; you can stick them in any situation and have a pretty good idea of how they're going to respond. Then it's just a matter of sanding and polishing up the jokes. . . . These two characters clicked for me almost immediately and I [felt] very comfortable working with them."

Oddly enough, United Features turned down the new strip as Watterson had developed it. Instead, they offered syndication to Watterson only if he agreed to include the "Robotman" character, which had been created to merchandise a range of products. "Not knowing if 'Calvin and Hobbes' would ever go anywhere, it was difficult to turn down another chance at syndication. But I really recoiled at the idea of drawing somebody else's character. It's cartooning by committee, and I have a moral problem with that. It's not art then," Watterson declared in *Honk!*

Once again unemployed as a cartoonist, Watterson started sending "Calvin and Hobbes" around. Universal Press Syndicate eventually accepted it and "Calvin and Hobbes" was formally introduced on November 18, 1985. The title characters, an outrageously brash six-year-old and the cautious tiger that appears as a stuffed animal to everyone but Calvin, became an instant hit with readers. The popularity of the cartoon allowed Watterson to quit his advertising layout job to concentrate on his art. After less than three years in syndication, "Calvin and Hobbes" was appearing in more than six hundred newspapers, and its third anthology, *Something under the Bed Is Drooling,* stayed on bestseller lists for almost a year.

"Calvin and Hobbes" deals with the well-covered ground of family and relationships, but focuses mainly on the deep friendship between the hyperactive Calvin and the calmer Hobbes. Calvin "is the personification of kid-dom," as R. C. Harvey describes him in *Comics Journal*. "He's entirely self-centered, devoted wholly to his own self-gratification. In pursuit of this completely understandable childhood goal, Calvin acknowledges no obstacle, no restraint. His desire and its satisfaction are all that matter to him." On the other hand, Hobbes often warns Calvin against causing trouble, or competes against him in games. But even if the tiger seems to resist Calvin's schemes, he always remains the boy's best friend.

An extraordinary imagination isn't the only thing that distinguishes Calvin. "I've never sat down to spell it out," Watterson remarked to Paul Dean in a *Los Angeles Times* interview, ". . . but I guess [Calvin's] a little too intelligent for his age. The thing that I really enjoy about him is that he has no sense of restraint, he doesn't have the experience yet to know the things that you shouldn't do." Hobbes "is a little more restrained, a little more knowledgeable," the author continued, because he has "a little bit of that sense of consequence that Calvin lacks entirely." Together, Calvin and Hobbes "are more than the sum of their parts," the author told Richard West in *Comics Journal*. "Each ticks because the other is around to share in the little conspiracies, or to argue and fight with. . . . Each is funnier in contrast to the other than they would be by themselves."

Bright youngsters are common in the comics, and can lead to stale, overused storylines. "But rather than follow the easy formula of keeping Calvin an obnoxious but funny little kid, Watterson takes chances and explores other facets of his character," *Los Angeles Times Book Review* writer Charles Solomon says in an April, 1988 article. In one series, Calvin tries to save a baby raccoon that has been hurt, and doesn't know what to do when it dies. Another sequence shows a scared Calvin turning to his parents for help in finding Hobbes, who has been lost. "I'll have a slapstick joke one day, a fantasy another day, a friendship, a sadness," Watterson told West in *Comics Journal*. He added: "My main concern really is to keep the reader on his toes, or to keep the strip unpredictable. I try to achieve some sort of balance . . . that keeps the reader wondering what's going to happen next and be surprised."

Another unique feature of "Calvin and Hobbes" is the quality of Watterson's artwork. "Watterson draws comic strips the way they should be drawn," Harvey claims in *Comics Journal*. "Much of his humor lies in the pictures. And in many of the individual strips, the words alone make no sense at all without the pictures." In addition, says Harvey, "not only does the humor usually arise from the words and pictures in tandem, the pictures alone, without words, are funny. Their energy makes them funny. Watterson's action sequences, particularly, are comically imaginative and inventive. . . . With increasing mastery of his supple brush, Watterson makes credible even the most fantastic of Calvin's daydreams." Solomon agrees, noting that "'Calvin and Hobbes' continues the strongly pictorial tradition" of classic comics such as George Herriman's "Krazy Kat" and Watterson's childhood favorite, "Pogo." "Watterson's vivid drawings often don't require captions, as the characters' expressions and poses are all that's needed," Solomon declares.

Watterson's artistic achievement is remarkable, since he never attended art school. He is a self-taught artist who, over the years, has learned to use acrylics, watercolors, and do block prints. He enjoys different kinds of art, but is particularly fond of the German expressionists. Since he prefers drawing to writing, he works on the visual side of "Calvin and Hobbes" first.

"I enjoy the drawing more than the writing, so I try to think of ideas that will allow me to develop the visual side of the strip as fully as possible," Watterson commented in his *Comics Journal* interview with West. "Some ideas don't lend themselves to that. Even then, I try to make the drawings as interesting as I possibly can, given the very limited constraints of the format." "Sundays are the one day that I have a little more freedom with the visual aspects," Watterson told Christie in *Honk!*, explaining that "the fun of a Sunday is that I have more space."

Camera and publicity shy, Watterson lives with his wife Melissa and their three cats in an isolated century-old house somewhere in the Midwest. There, "Calvin and Hobbes" is born daily on a small drawing board in a 9x9 room overlooking a driveway. "Obviously the great thing about this job is the complete freedom of the schedule," he continued in his *Honk!* interview. "So long as I meet the deadline, they don't care when I work or how I work. Sometimes I work all day if I'm under a crunch; I take a day off here and there if I have something else pressing or if I'm just tired of what I'm doing. . . . The whole pleasure for me is having the opportunity to do a comic strip for a living, and now that I've finally got that I'm not going to give it away. It also gives me complete creative control."

Control over his work—and how it is sold—is important to Watterson. In 1987, when the first collection of "Calvin and Hobbes" was published, Watterson refused to take part in a national public appearance tour to promote the book. "They started out with three weeks in fifteen cities," Watterson remarked in the *Los Angeles Times*. "I said it would be no weeks in no cities." Watterson believes his comic's success should rely only on the quality of his writing and drawing. "Besides, if I had to spend two weeks shuttling between airports and shopping malls, my brain would be guacamole," the artist added.

Watterson also ended talks on licensing "Calvin and Hobbes" for T-shirts, greeting cards, toys and coloring books. "I'm happy that people enjoy the strip and have become devoted to it," Watterson told Harvey in *Comics Journal*. "But it seems that with a lot of the marketing stuff, the incentive is just to cash in. . . . Calvin and Hobbes will not exist intact if I do not exist intact; and I will not exist intact if I have to put up with all this stuff." As he further explained to West in another *Comics Journal* interview: "I'm not interested in removing all the subtlety from my work to condense it for a product. The strip is about more than jokes."

Protecting his privacy is also important to Watterson, who dislikes intrusions. "I enjoy the isolation, that's how I work. The motivation is the work itself and having a job I've aspired to since I was a kid. I wouldn't be doing this if I were just in it for the money," Watterson remarked in the *Los Angeles Times*. "I'd like to have the opportunity to draw this strip for years and see where it goes," Watterson said to Christie in *Honk!* "It's sort of a scary thing now to imagine; these cartoonists who've been drawing a strip for twenty years. I can't imagine coming up with that much material. If I just take it day by day, though, it's a lot of fun, and I do think I have a long way to go before I've exhausted the possibilities."

(From *The Calvin and Hobbes Lazy Sunday Book,* by Bill Watterson.)

Strips from two Calvin and Hobbes collections: (top and center) from *Something under the Bed Is Drooling* and (bottom) from *Yukon Ho!*

Solomon also believes that "Calvin and Hobbes" has the potential for a long run. In a *Los Angeles Times Book Review* of December, 1988, Solomon calls Watterson "among the most imaginative newspaper cartoonists working in America today." "His only interest is drawing a good comic strip," the critic concludes in his earlier *Los Angeles Times Book Review* article. "This dedication and integrity seem sadly out of place in an era that exalts hype over substance, but his readers and the art of the newspaper comic strip are richer for it." Watterson takes his position as a popular cartoonist seriously. As Astor quoted him in a 1989 *Editor & Publisher:* "I consider it a great privilege to be a cartoonist. Cartooning is an art."

WORKS CITED:

Astor, David, "An Overnight Success after Five Years," *Editor & Publisher,* February 8, 1986, p. 34.

Astor, David, "Watterson and Walker Differ on Comics," *Editor & Publisher,* November 4, 1989, pp. 42-44.

Christie, Andrew, "Bill Watterson," *Honk!,* January, 1987, pp. 28-33.

Dean, Paul, "Calvin and Hobbes Creator Draws on the Simple Life," *Los Angeles Times,* April 1, 1987, section V, p. 4.

Harvey, R. C., "Predestinations, Leviathan, and Plastic Man," *Comics Journal,* March, 1989, pp. 107-110.

Solomon, Charles, "Cartoon Art for Cartoon Art's Sake," *Los Angeles Times Book Review*, April 17, 1988, p. 15.
Solomon, Charles, "Santa Totes the Untouted as Well as the Heavily Promoted," *Los Angeles Times Book Review*, December 18, 1988, p. 6.
West, Richard, "Interview: Bill Watterson," *Comics Journal*, March, 1989, pp. 57-71.

FOR MORE INFORMATION SEE:

PERIODICALS

Booklist, June 15, 1988; December 15, 1988.
Editor & Publisher, December 3, 1988; May 27, 1989.
San Francisco Chronicle, April 13, 1987.
Wall Street Journal, November 3, 1988.

*   *   *

WESLEY, Mary 1912-
[A pseudonym]

PERSONAL: Born June 24, 1912, in Englefield Green, England; daughter of Mynors (a colonel) and Violet (Dalby) Farmar; married Charles Swinfen Eady (a baron), January, 1937 (divorced, 1944); married Eric Siepmann (a journalist), April 22, 1951 (died, 1970); children: (first marriage) Roger Mynors Swinfen Eady, Hugh Toby Eady; (second marriage) William. *Education:* Attended Queens College, London, 1928-30, and London School of Economics and Political Science, 1931-32. *Politics:* "Left-wing/Catholic." *Religion:* Roman Catholic.

ADDRESSES: Home—Cullaford, Buckfastleigh, Devon, England. *Agent*—Lekesche & Sayle, 11 Jubilee Place, London SW3, England.

MARY WESLEY

CAREER: Worked variously in an antique shop and as an instructor in French; War Office, London, England, staff member, 1939-41; writer, 1983—.

MEMBER: London Library.

AWARDS, HONORS: Carnegie Prize nomination for *Haphazard House;* runner-up for *Observer* Prize for children's fiction.

WRITINGS:

FOR CHILDREN

The Sixth Seal (fiction), MacDonald, 1969, revised edition, Dent, 1984.
Speaking Terms, Faber, 1969, Gambit, 1971.
Haphazard House (fiction), Dent, 1983.

NOVELS FOR ADULTS

Jumping the Queue, Macmillan (London), 1983, Penguin, 1988.
The Camomile Lawn, Macmillan, 1984.
Harnessing Peacocks, Macmillan, 1985.
The Vacillations of Poppy Carew, Macmillan, 1986, Penguin, 1988.
Not That Sort of Girl, Macmillan, 1987, Penguin, 1988.
Second Fiddle, Macmillan, 1988, Penguin, 1989.
A Sensible Life, Bantam, 1990.

ADAPTATIONS: Jumping the Queue was adapted as a two-part film by the British Broadcasting Corporation in 1988; *The Camomile Lawn, Harnessing Peacocks,* and *Not That Sort of Girl* were adapted for film.

SIDELIGHTS: Recently praised for her adult best-sellers, Mary Wesley began her writing career with children's novels. She had no background in literature. In fact, she had little formal education of any kind. "No Latin, maths, or history," Wesley recalled in a London *Sunday Times Magazine* interview with Keith Wheatley. "When I grew up I'd had governesses and been to four so-called schools and I was totally uneducated." Her father was a military officer, so the family moved from country to country as his military assignments changed, and Wesley and her sister often had foreign governesses. Wesley remembered them as "French, Italian or Swiss girls who did nothing whatsoever except talk their own language." When she started dating, men told her she was ignorant, so she took a few classes at London colleges.

Wesley was first married in 1937, to a baron. "I realised too late, of course, that I'd married him just to get out of family life," Wesley told Wheatley. World War II did nothing to bring them closer. She and their sons lived in Cornwall to escape the German bombing of London, and Wesley found herself a job working on secret documents for the War Office. She described the war to *Publishers Weekly* interviewer Clare Boylan as "frightening," "thrilling," and "very interesting. A lot of people were thought to have behaved badly during the war, but I think it was just that people felt free to be themselves because you never knew what was going to happen next." By 1944 she wanted a divorce. At that time divorce was still a rather shocking idea, but Wesley went ahead with it. Later she went to live with journalist Eric Siepmann, whom she married in 1951.

Wesley delighted in her second marriage, although she admits Siepmann was not perfect. Alternately very happy and very depressed, he moved from job to job and tended to spend money as soon as he earned it. But he developed other riches for Wesley, especially her writing talent. She had been writing stories and poems for years, but only for herself. Often Wesley tore up her manuscripts. "My husband used to tell me I could write but I thought it was just because he loved me," she told Jessica Baldwin in an Associated Press interview published in the *Ann Arbor News.* When he was stationed in France during the war he sent her poems to translate, and Wesley even wrote some newspaper articles for him in the late 1940s. Siepmann's editor did not notice the switch. Her first published books were the ones she wrote to read to him after he became seriously ill with Parkinson's disease.

Siepmann's death in 1970 devastated Wesley. She told Boylan that she wrote her first novel for adults, *Jumping the Queue,* "as a means of working out despair." Sorrow eventually gave way to fulfillment as first this novel and then several more were published and became successful. They have received praise from critics, and many have appeared on bestseller lists. Now content with her solitude, Wesley reserves her afternoons for writing. She also keeps active, swimming several times a week and tending her garden. "It isn't the first time in a longish life that she has been happy," wrote Wheatley, "but probably the first she's been able to do exactly what she wants, in her own way and with enough money."

WORKS CITED:

Baldwin, Jessica, "Best-selling Novelist Began Publishing Her Works at Age 70," *Ann Arbor News,* June 4, 1990, p. B11.
Boylan, Clare, "PW Interviews: Mary Wesley," *Publishers Weekly,* July 6, 1990, p. 51.
Wheatley, Keith, *Sunday Times Magazine* (London), September 25, 1988.

FOR MORE INFORMATION SEE:

PERIODICALS

Globe and Mail (Toronto), May 31, 1986.
Los Angeles Times, December 6, 1989.
New York Times, June 27, 1989.
New York Times Book Review, July 8, 1984; July 30, 1989.
Times (London), May 5, 1983; March 28, 1984; March 29, 1984; June 27, 1985; June 29, 1985; June 25, 1987; July 9, 1987.
Times Literary Supplement, June 17, 1983; September 30, 1983; March 28, 1984; April 13, 1984; June 28, 1985.
Washington Post, May 12, 1988.
Washington Post Book World, July 23, 1989.

*   *   *

WILLIAMS, Garth (Montgomery) 1912-

PERSONAL: Born April 16, 1912, in New York, NY, son of Hamilton (an artist) and Florence Stuart (an artist; maiden name, Davis) Williams; married first wife, Gunda V. Davidson (an interpreter; divorced); married second wife, Dorothea, 1945, (died, January, 1965); married third wife, Alicia (divorced); married fourth wife, Leticia (a dress designer); children: (first marriage) Fiona, Bettina, (second marriage) Jessica, Estyn, (third marriage) Dylan, (fourth

GARTH WILLIAMS

marriage) Dilys. *Education:* Attended the City of London School and Westminster Art School, 1929-31; Royal College of Art, A.R.C.A., 1934; graduate study at British School, Rome; has also studied in museums of many European countries, including France, Germany, Greece, and Holland.

ADDRESSES: c/o Richard M. Ticktin, Robinson, Brog, Leinwand, Reich, Genovese & Gluck, P.C., 1345 Avenue of the Americas, New York, NY 10105.

CAREER: Artist. Luton Art School, organizer, 1935-36; pursued an art career in varying capacities such as making portrait busts and working as an art editor of a proposed woman's magazine, 1938-39; *New Yorker,* New York City, artist, 1943-45; author and illustrator of children's books, 1944—. *Wartime service:* British Red Cross Civilian Defense, 1939-41.

AWARDS, HONORS: British Prix de Rome for sculpture, 1936; *The Rescuers* was selected one of the American Institute of Graphic Arts Children's Books, 1958-60; *Beneath a Blue Umbrella* was chosen as one of the ten best illustrated books of 1990 by the *New York Times.*

WRITINGS:

SELF-ILLUSTRATED

The Chicken Book: A Traditional Rhyme, Howell, Soskin, 1946.
The Adventures of Benjamin Pink, Harper, 1951.
Baby Animals, Simon & Schuster, 1952.
Baby Farm Animals, Simon & Schuster, 1953.
The Golden Animal ABC, Simon & Schuster, 1954, new edition published as *The Big Golden Animal ABC,* 1957

(published in England as *My Big Animal ABC,* Golden Pleasure Books, 1962).
Baby's First Book, Simon & Schuster, 1955.
The Rabbits' Wedding, Harper, 1958.

Also author of *Self-Portrait: Garth Williams,* Addison-Wesley.

ILLUSTRATOR

E. B. White, *Stuart Little,* Harper, 1945.
Ernest Poole, *The Great White Hills of New Hampshire,* Doubleday, 1946.
Damon Runyon, *In Our Town,* McClelland, 1946.
Margaret Wise Brown, *Little Fur Family,* Harper, 1946.
Evelyn S. Eaton, *Every Month Was May,* Harper, 1947.
Brown, *The Golden Sleepy Book,* Simon & Schuster, 1948.
Henry Gilbert, *Robin Hood,* Lippincott, 1948.
Dorothy Kunhardt, *Tiny Library,* Simon & Schuster, Volume 1: *A Dozen Animal Nonsense Tales,* 1948, Volume 2, 1949.
Brown, *Wait Till the Moon Is Full,* Harper, 1948.
Eva LeGallienne, *Flossie and Bossie,* Harper, 1948.
Jane Werner Watson, compiler, *The Tall Book of Make-Believe,* Harper, 1950.
Watson, editor, *Elves and Fairies* (anthology), Simon & Schuster, 1951.
White, *Charlotte's Web,* Harper, 1952.
Brown, *Mister Dog, the Dog Who Belonged to Himself,* Simon & Schuster, 1952.
Laura Ingalls Wilder, *Little House in the Big Woods,* Harper, 1953, new edition, 1983.
Wilder, *Little House on the Prairie,* Harper, 1953, revised edition, 1983.
Wilder, *Farmer Boy,* Harper, 1953, revised edition, 1983.
Wilder, *The Long Winter,* Harper, 1953, revised edition, 1983.
Wilder, *By the Shores of Silver Lake,* Harper, 1953.
Wilder, *Little Town on the Prairie,* Harper, 1953, revised edition, 1983.

Garth Williams's drawing in E. B. White's *Stuart Little,* a 1945 book that was so successful that Williams decided to become a full-time illustrator.

Wilder, *On the Banks of Plum Creek,* Harper, 1953, revised edition, 1983.
Wilder, *These Happy Golden Years,* Harper, 1953, revised edition, 1983.
Watson, *Animal Friends,* Simon & Schuster, 1953.
Brown and Watson, *My Bedtime Book,* Golden Press, 1953, new edition, 1964.
Brown, *The Sailor Dog,* Golden Press, 1953.
Brown, *The Friendly Book,* Western, 1954, new edition, Golden Press, 1974.
Miriam Norton, *The Kitten Who Thought He Was a Mouse,* Simon & Schuster, 1954.
Jennie D. Lindquist, *The Golden Name Day,* Harper, 1955.
Brown, *Home for a Bunny,* Simon & Schuster, 1956.
Lilian Moore, *My First Counting Book,* Simon & Schuster, 1956, published as *My Big Golden Counting Book,* 1957.
Brown, *Three Little Animals,* Harper, 1956.
Natalie Savage Carlson, *The Happy Orpheline,* Harper, 1957.
Charlotte Zolotow, *Over and Over,* Harper, 1957.
Zolotow, *Do You Know What I'll Do?,* Harper, 1958.
Carlson, *The Family under the Bridge,* Harper, 1958.
Three Bedtime Stories: The Three Little Kittens, The Three Bears, and The Three Little Pigs, Simon & Schuster, 1958.
Carlson, *A Brother for the Orphelines,* Harper, 1959.
Mary Stolz, *Emmett's Pig,* Harper, 1959.
Lindquist, *The Little Silver House,* Harper, 1959.
Margery Sharp, *The Rescuers,* Little, Brown, 1959.
Russell Hoban, *Bedtime for Frances,* Harper, 1960.
George Selden, *The Cricket in Times Square,* Farrar, Straus, 1960.
Sharp, *Miss Bianca,* Little, Brown, 1962.
Elizabeth H. MacPherson, *A Tale of Tails,* Golden Press, 1962.
Byrd Baylor Schweitzer, *Amigo,* Macmillan, 1963.
Else H. Minarik, *The Little Giant Girl and the Elf Boy,* Harper, 1963.
Zolotow, *The Sky Was Blue,* Harper, 1963.
Sharp, *The Turret,* Little, Brown, 1963.
Jane Werner, editor, *The Elves and Fairies Book,* Golden Press, 1963, published as *The Giant Golden Book of Elves and Fairies,* 1964.
Anne Colver, *Bread-and-Butter Indian,* Holt, 1964.
Randall Jarrell, *The Gingerbread Rabbit,* Macmillan, 1964.
Brown, *The Sailor Dog and Other Stories,* Golden Press, 1965.
(With Lillian Obligado) Brown, *The Whispering Rabbit and Other Stories,* Golden Press, 1965.
Sharp, *Miss Bianca in the Salt Mines,* Little, Brown, 1966.
A Horn Book Calendar in Honor of Laura Ingalls Wilder, Horn Book, 1968.
Eugenia Garson and Herbert Hanfrecht, editors, *The Laura Ingalls Wilder Songbook: Favorite Songs from the "Little House" Books,* Harper, 1968.
Jan Wahl, *Push Kitty,* Harper, 1968.
Selden, *Tucker's Countryside,* Farrar, Straus, 1969.
Colver, *Bread-and-Butter Journey,* Holt, 1970.
Wilder, *The First Four Years,* Harper, 1971.
(With J. P. Miller) D. Kunhardt, *Lucky Mrs. Ticklefeather and Other Funny Stories,* Western, 1973.
Selden, *Harry Cat's Pet Puppy,* Farrar, Straus, 1974.
Brown, *Fox Eyes,* Pantheon, 1977.
Barbara M. Walker, *The Little House Cookbook: Recipes for a Pioneer Kitchen,* Harper, 1979.
Walker, *The Little House Cookbook: Frontier Foods from Laura Ingalls Wilder's Classic Stories,* Harper, 1979.
Selden, *Chester Cricket's Pigeon Ride,* Farrar, Straus, 1981.
Selden, *Chester Cricket's New Home,* Farrar, Straus, 1983.
Wilder, *The Little House Diary,* Harper, 1985.

One morning he felt so ill he canceled Inspection. (From *Flossie and Bossie*, by Eva LeGalliene, illustrated by Garth Williams.)

Selden, *Harry Kitten and Tucker Mouse*, Farrar, Straus, 1986.

Jack Prelutsky, *Ride a Purple Pelican*, Greenwillow, 1986.

Selden, *The Old Meadow*, Farrar, Straus, 1987.

(With Maurice Sendak) Jerome Griswold, *The Children's Books of Randall Jarrell*, University of Georgia, 1988.

Prelutsky, *Beneath a Blue Umbrella*, Greenwillow, 1990.

OTHER

A collection of Williams's work is kept at the University of Missouri's Kerlan Collection.

ADAPTATIONS: Several books that Williams illustrated have been adapted as filmstrips, including *The Cricket in Times Square* (with cassette), Miller-Brody, 1975; *Tucker's Countryside* (with cassette), Random House; *Bedtime for Frances* (with record or cassette), BFA Educational Media; *Harry Cat's Pet Puppy* (with record or cassette), Random House; and *Fox Eyes* (with cassette), Random House.

WORK IN PROGRESS: A complete catalog of Williams's art work is being compiled by his wife, Leticia Williams, and others.

SIDELIGHTS: Garth Williams was born in New York City to parents who were both artists. His father had been a professional cartoonist since the age of seventeen and had published his work in London, Paris, and New York. His mother was a landscape painter who was also a pipe-smoking feminist. Although it is not surprising that Williams eventually became an artist himself, at one time he was interested in a profession as an architect. Circumstances discouraged him from this goal, however, and he was led to a career as an artist

and well known illustrator of books by such authors as E. B. White, Laura Ingalls Wilder, George Selden, and Margery Sharp.

In his *Something about the Author Autobiography Series* (*SAAS*) entry, Williams recalls his childhood years after his family moved from New York City to a farm near Caldwell, New Jersey: "I remember well most of those early years in New Jersey, especially when I was taken by the farmer, our landlord, on his lap to go harrowing or plowing. Or when we went driving out in his two-wheel buggy to Peterson or the Passaic River, crunching along a gravel road or splashing through puddles. I was a typical Huckleberry Finn, roaming barefoot around the farm, watching the farmer milk the cows by hand, or do his other chores.

"One day my father left his studio door open. I entered and found a pile of drawings he had ready to take to New York. I spent a long time looking at them and adding my art to them. I was not punished. 'I'm afraid he's going to be an artist,' my father said, and removed my additions."

"Everybody in my house was always either painting or drawing," Williams tells Leonard S. Marcus in *Publishers Weekly,* "so I thought there was nothing else to do in life but make pictures." Those first peaceful days on the New Jersey farm were interrupted by news of World War I. The artist writes in his autobiography, "I was aware of the war in Europe because I listened to my parents discussing the news, particularly when the German army was very close to Paris. I remember thinking the world was like a big flat dish, about twenty miles across. Where there had been a forest fire in Boonton, New Jersey, I was sure that was the war. If the Germans came to our house in Caldwell, I planned to run

At last Wilbur saw the creature that had spoken to him in such a kindly way. (From *Charlotte's Web,* by E. B. White, illustrated by Garth Williams.)

Laura and Mary helped Ma with the work.... (From *Little House in the Big Woods,* by Laura Ingalls Wilder, illustrated by Garth Williams.)

past the dairy, to the sea. I would look for a boat and row to England, a few miles out.... If the enemy followed, I would row to the edge of the world, where the water poured over. Fortunately the enemy didn't arrive."

Near the end of the war, Williams's mother took a job as the Art Mistress for an Ontario, Canada, finishing school for girls. The family lived in Canada until Williams was ten years old. At that time, his parents took him and his sister, Fiona, to England, where they felt their children could get the best education. They bought a house in Surrey and the young Williams attended a preparatory boarding school. The school had only eighteen students and six teachers, so Williams enjoyed personal instruction on an almost one-on-one level. He finished the three year course in only a single year.

Next, the future illustrator attended classes in a London school. He did not find the students there as likeable as those in the prep school, who, like him, had come from the distant outposts of the British Empire. He was happy to leave London for college. His original plan was to train as an architect. This decision was influenced by the six years he had spent assisting an old architect friend who taught him a great deal about mechanical drawing. When it was time for him to go to college, the Great Depression of the 1930s had begun and the prospects for finding gainful employment as an architect seemed dim. In his autobiographical entry, Williams remembers visiting two prominent architects with his mother: "They explained they had two fully trained architects helping in their office: one made tea, the other swept the floor. They only did redecoration and house-altering work."

Architecture school also required seven years of expensive training, and Williams's parents were not rich. Instead, he went to the Westminster School of Art and soon won a painting scholarship to the Royal College of Art. Many of his peers and instructors praised his portrait drawings, and this encouraged him to take his art in a new direction: sculpture. Williams's teacher, Eric Schilsky, quickly declared that his student had great promise and convinced Williams to exhibit his work. "I exhibited [a half figure sculpture] in London at the Royal Academy of Art annual show," the artist writes in his autobiography, "and stood next to it to hear what comments people would make. I was amused to hear several say I was an old-time, well-known sculptor who did excellent work. I was being confused with another Williams."

After receiving his degree in 1934, Williams became headmaster for a year at the Luton Art School outside of London. He lived in an apartment building in Chelsea that was across the hall from poet Dylan Thomas's apartment and above the living quarters of famous actress Eva LeGallienne. But the artist did not live there long because he hated the two hour daily commute by train. Also, the headmaster position took so much of the artist's time that he could not work on his own sculpting. He quit his job and asked his old sculpting instructor for advice on what to do next. Schilsky told Williams that he should enter the British Prix de Rome competition. Although he had only six weeks to prepare an entry for the judges, the artist managed to finish his sculpture and was amazed when it was announced that he had won.

With the scholarship that came with the prize, Williams had the means to travel throughout Europe. He went to Italy, where he marveled at the art and architecture of Rome and Florence, as well as to museums in France, Germany and other countries, where he studied art collections and architecture. It was while he was on his scholarship that the artist met Gunda V. Davidson, a German-born Englishwoman who spoke five languages. They married and returned to London in 1939. Gunda was quickly hired as an interpreter for an American firm and Williams landed a position at Pearson Publications, working on a new women's magazine. The beginning of World War II prevented the magazine from making its debut appearance.

Williams decided to become an ambulance dispatcher with the British Red Cross Civilian Defense and St. John's Ambulance Organization. For the first year the streets of London were quiet; then Hitler sent hundreds of airplanes to bomb the city. Williams felt it was safest to send his wife and daughter to safety in Canada. A few months later, Williams was wounded. "I was walking in a pleasant square in Chelsea," he writes in his autobiography, "... when a bomb landed by my side. There was no noise, just a blast of air and my eyes were squashed as though [by] someone's fingers." Not realizing the extent of his injuries, the Red Cross volunteer went home to bed. The next morning, Williams discovered that he could not sit up straight. He managed to pull himself out of bed and go to the head doctor of his Red Cross branch, but an examination revealed nothing wrong with him. Persuaded by the physician to sign resignation papers, Williams left the Red Cross. It was later established that the explosion had seriously injured his spine.

Williams was still eager to help in the war effort, however. He believed that with his knowledge of French and Italian he could be of service to the American Civil Defense, although America had not yet entered the war. He obtained a letter of introduction to President Roosevelt from Winston Churchill and sailed to New York City. Ten days after his arrival, Japan bombed Pearl Harbor and America was at war. Intending to pick up his commission at U.S. Army headquarters, Williams was surprised to find that the officer there had no records on him. He then took his letter of introduction to Eleanor Roosevelt's office, but was never allowed to meet the First Lady. "I felt that perhaps Winston Churchill's letter was considered a probable forgery," Williams writes in his *SAAS* essay. In an attempt to find out why he was being given the run around, the artist asked two of his friends in the Office of War Information to look in his F.B.I. file. They reported back that the F.B.I. had denied Williams a commission and had restricted him from returning to Europe. Confused and shocked by the F.B.I.'s suspicion of him, Williams gave up his efforts to join the military. Instead, for a short time he advised New York City companies on camoflage plans and worked in a war factory making lenses before returning to his artistic career.

"In 1943," Williams tells *Language Arts* interviewer Lee Bennett Hopkins, "I tried to become a *New Yorker* magazine cartoonist. Unfortunately my style was considered too wild and European." He eventually took his art portfolio to the publishing company, Harper and Row. "Ursula Nordstrom, the editor of children's books," he later writes, "said she had a manuscript coming in shortly which I could perhaps try to illustrate. When the manuscript arrived in her office, E. B. White had pinned a note on it saying, 'Try Garth Williams.' As it turned out it was a good omen because the manuscript was *Stuart Little.*"

The book was quickly established as a children's classic, and its success prompted Williams to commit himself permanently to book illustration. "I'd get into a bus and see three people reading *Stuart Little*," he relates to Marcus. "People everywhere were reading it, which made me feel very good. So I thought, 'Well, here's my profession.'" Seven years later, Williams also illustrated White's *Charlotte's Web.* "I found *Stuart Little* more fun to illustrate than *Charlotte's Web* as there were more moments of fantasy in it. . . . 'Stuart' and 'Charlotte,' of course, are among my own personal favorites. I feel extremely lucky to be able to share a little of the spotlight of these two books—books I love, admire, envy and emulate as an author."

In 1945, Williams married his second wife, Dorothea. (He had gotten a provisional divorce from Gunda during the war, fearing that he might be killed, taken prisoner, or be missing in action). He and his new bride moved to Connecticut, where Williams continued his artistic career. He created the illustrations for Henry Gilbert's *Robin Hood* and Eva LeGalliene's *Flossie and Bossie.* Next, the Williams family moved to a rented farm house in New York state. Williams found the farm to be the perfect setting on which to base his illustrations for *Charlotte's Web.* It was also a good background setting for the 1953 deluxe editions of Laura Ingalls Wilder's books. But Williams, who is a meticulous researcher, felt he needed more information before he could illustrate Wilder's stories about nineteenth-century frontier life. He visited Wilder's daughter, Rose Wilder Lane, and then studied cabins in North and South Carolina to make his drawings more accurate. Finally, Williams decided to go to the source and drove to Wilder's home in Missouri.

"[We] set out by car," Williams recalls in *Horn Book,* "drove through the Smokies and reached Mansfield, Missouri, ten days later. Mrs. Wilder was working in her garden when we arrived and was without any doubt the Laura of her books. She was small and nimble. Her eyes sparkled with good humor and she seemed a good twenty years younger than her age." After consulting with Wilder, Williams travelled to Oklahoma to study the site where the Ingalls family lived in *Little House on the Prairie,* and then to Walnut Grove, Plum Creek, Tracy, and De Smet, Minnesota, the town where Wilder's parents spent the last days of their lives.

Although the research was important, Williams stresses that attention to detail is not the only important aspect in his work. "Illustrating books is not just making pictures of the houses, the people and the articles mentioned by the author; the artist has to see everything with the same eyes. For example, an architect would have described the sod house on the bank of Plum Creek as extremely primitive, unhealthy and undesirable. . . . But to Laura's fresh young eyes it was a pleasant house, surrounded by flowers and with the music of a running stream and rustling leaves.

"She understood the meaning of hardship and struggle, of joy and work, of shyness and bravery. She was never overcome by drabness or squalor. She never glamorized anything; yet she saw the loveliness in everything. This was the way the illustrator had to follow—no glamorizing for him either; no giving everyone a permanent wave."

After the research was done, Williams completed the illustrations for all eight books in a few short weeks. To keep production costs down, he was required to make his drawings on tracing paper the same size as they were to appear in the books. Not long after making the approximately five hundred painstaking, small illustrations, Williams went to the optometrist to get his first pair of eyeglasses.

The 1950s were busy years for Williams. Not only did he illustrate the Wilder books, he also did the drawings for more than twenty other children's stories and wrote and illustrated six books of his own. One of the artist's books, *The Rabbits' Wedding,* "unexpectedly made international headlines when it was banned in some Southern libraries," according to Marcus. "In the inflamed atmosphere of the civil rights movement's early days, pro-segregationists were quick to find provocation in the artist's lilting tale about black and white rabbits who marry and 'live happily together in the big forest.'" Williams, however, never intended the story to be about racial integration. Rather, he made one rabbit white and the other black so that they could be told apart more easily. In the *New York Times,* Williams also defends, "I was only aware that a white horse next to a black horse looks very picturesque—and my rabbits were inspired by early Chinese paintings of black and white horses in misty landscapes." Despite the protests against it, *The Rabbits' Wedding* sold well and has remained in print since its original publication.

In the late 1950s, Williams and his wife, Dorothea, separated. She had been suffering from complications due to poor blood circulation and moved to England, where she underwent several operations. In the meantime, the illustrator bought some land in Guanajuato, Mexico, on which stood the remains of an old Spanish silver mine. Using what was left of the ruins, Williams spent the next ten years constructing a fortress-like home. Dorothea never came to visit her husband in Mexico, and in January, 1965, Williams received a telephone call from her doctor, who told him that his wife had passed away.

"I was sure Dorothea would come back to me," Williams writes in his *SAAS* entry, "and was heartbroken that she never came to see me in Mexico. I felt sure she would love the fascinating ruin which I made my home. I felt I had reached something like the end of my life. But a bright young girl came to work for me when another American couple left Mexico. Her name was Alicia and she was seventeen. She had a small baby boy. I married her, and life continued." Williams's marriage to Alicia did not work out, however, and they were later divorced. The artist then met a young Mexican woman named Leticia, who was a dress designer

Every morning they hopped out of bed and out into the early morning sunshine.

(From *The Rabbits' Wedding,* written and illustrated by Garth Williams.)

and also suffered from polio. They married, spent their honeymoon in France and Switzerland, and returned to Mexico. "She is the present, and last, Mrs. Garth Williams," Williams asserts in his autobiography.

Williams has not written any of his own books since *The Rabbits' Wedding,* but he has continued to successfully illustrate for other authors. Some of his best known work includes the drawings for George Selden's stories about the friendship of Chester Cricket, Tucker Mouse, and Harry Cat in *The Cricket in Times Square* and other books, and Margery Sharp's tales of Miss Bianca and the Mouse Prisoner's Aid Society, including *The Rescuers* and *Miss Bianca.* As with his other drawings, the illustrations for these books demonstrate Williams's ability to give animals human-like characteristics. In *Illustrators of Children's Books: 1957-1966,* Williams speaks of his art in general as a "highly personalized representation. . . . I start with the real animal, working over and over until I can get the effect of human qualities and expressions and poses. I redesign animals as it were."

"I believe that books given, or read, to children can have a profound influence on that child," Williams concludes in *Contemporary American Illustrators of Children's Books.* "For this reason I try to give the child something which will awaken something of importance . . . [such as] humor, responsibility, respect for others, interest in the world at large." Of his current plans, Williams writes in *SAAS,* "I am busy illustrating books until I strike a gold mine. I hope to retire and to be able to go back to serious art, painting and/or sculpting, some day soon."

WORKS CITED:

Contemporary American Illustrators of Children's Books, Rutgers University Art Gallery, 1974.
"Children's Book Stirs Alabama: White Rabbit Weds Black Rabbit," *New York Times,* May 22, 1959, p. 29.
Dictionary of Literary Biography, Volume 22: *American Writers for Children, 1900-1960,* Gale, 1983, pp. 367-375.
Kingman, Lee, and others, compilers, *Illustrators of Children's Books: 1957-1966,* Horn Book, 1968, p. 193.
Language Arts, October, 1976, pp. 806-809.
Marcus, Leonard S., "Garth Williams," *Publishers Weekly,* February 23, 1990, pp. 201-202.
Something about the Author Autobiography Series, Volume 7, Gale, 1989, pp. 313-327.
Williams, Garth, "Illustrating the Little House Books," *Horn Book,* December, 1953, pp. 414-422.

FOR MORE INFORMATION SEE:

BOOKS

Fuller, Muriel, editor, *More Junior Authors,* H. W. Wilson, 1963.
Huerlimann, Bettina, *Picture-Book World,* World Publishing, 1969.
The Illustrators Notebook, Horn Book, 1978.
Klemin, Diana, *The Art of Art for Children's Books,* Clarkson Potter, 1966.

From Jack Prelutsky's 1986 *Ride a Purple Pelican*, the 75th book Garth Williams illustrated for other authors.

Mahony, Bertha E., and others, compilers, *Illustrators of Children's Books, 1744-1945,* Horn Book, 1947.

Miller, B. E., and others, compilers, *Illustrators of Children's Books, 1946-1956,* Horn Book, 1958.

Ward, Martha E., and Dorothy A. Marquardt, *Authors of Books for Young People,* 2nd edition, Scarecrow, 1971.

PERIODICALS

Family Circle, December, 1968.
Graphis 155, Volume 27, 1971-72.
Horn Book, June, 1961.

*   *   *

WILLIAMS, Karen Lynn 1952-

PERSONAL: Born March 22, 1952, in New Haven, CT; daughter of Russell Drake (an optometrist) and Lenora Mary (a homemaker; maiden name, Yohans) Howard; married Steven Cranston Williams (a physician), June 18, 1978; children: Peter, Christopher, Rachel, Jonathan. *Education:* University of Connecticut, B.S., 1974; Southern Connecticut State University, M.S., 1977. *Religion:* Unitarian-Universalist. *Hobbies and other interests:* Reading, quilting, jogging, flea markets.

ADDRESSES: Home—6645 Northumberland St., Pittsburgh, PA 15217.

CAREER: Teacher of the deaf in North Haven, CT, 1977-80; U.S. Peace Corps, Washington, DC, teacher of English in Malawi, 1980-83; writer.

WRITINGS:

Galimoto (juvenile), illustrated by Catherine Stock, Lothrop, 1990.
Baseball and Butterflies (juvenile), Lothrop, 1990.
When Africa Was Home, Orchard Book, 1991.

Contributor of articles and stories to adult and children's magazines.

WORK IN PROGRESS: A sequel to *Baseball and Butterflies.*

SIDELIGHTS: Karen Lynn Williams commented: "Two of my books are drawn from experiences in Africa with my family. Most of my story ideas are based on my children's and my own childhood experiences. I have several more ideas for picture books and middle-age novels."

FOR MORE INFORMATION SEE:

PERIODICALS

New York Times Book Review, May 20, 1990.

*   *   *

WILLIUS, T. F.
See TAMMINGA, Frederick William

*   *   *

WOHLBERG, Meg 1905-1990

OBITUARY NOTICE—See index for *SATA* sketch: Born February 6, 1905, in New York, NY; died of pneumonia,

December 10, 1990, in Lexington, MA. Illustrator and author. Wohlberg worked in advertising during the 1930s, illustrating for manufacturers of baby-care and household products, and began drawing for children's books in the 1940s. She illustrated dozens of titles, including Clement C. Moore's *Night before Christmas* and Jane Thayer's books featuring a character named Andy. She also wrote and illustrated several volumes of her own, such as *Little Bimbo and the Lion, Toby's Trip* (which she wrote with M. Horn), and *Jody's Wonderful Day.*

OBITUARIES AND OTHER SOURCES:

PERIODICALS

New York Times, December 16, 1990.

*   *   *

WOODING, Sharon
See WOODING, Sharon L(ouise)

*   *   *

WOODING, Sharon L(ouise) 1943-
(Sharon Wooding)

PERSONAL: Born July 23, 1943, in Staten Island, NY; daughter of William Allen (an accountant) and Thelma (a nurse; maiden name, Fisher) Gilfillan; married Jerry Wooding (a chemistry teacher), August 14, 1965; children: Stephen, Hilary, Anson. *Education:* Bucknell University, B.S., 1965; attended Rutgers University, 1968-69, University of Colorado, 1974 and 1977, and Decordova Museum School, 1979-83. *Politics:* Democrat. *Religion:* Episcopalian.

SHARON L. WOODING

ADDRESSES: Home—Lawrence Academy Box 992, Groton, MA 01450. *Agent*—Kendra Marcus, Bookstop, 67 Meadow View Rd., Orinda, CA 94563.

CAREER: Painter, illustrator, portrait artist, author, and teacher. New York Public Schools, Staten Island, third grade teacher, 1965-66; Walter C. Black Elementary School, Hightstown, NJ, first grade teacher, 1966-69; Climbing Tower School, Carbondale, CO, preschool teacher, 1973-78; Colorado Rocky Mountain School, Carbondale, director of publications, 1978-79; Indian Hill Arts, Groton Center for the Arts, Groton, MA, art teacher, 1979-84; Groton Public Schools, Groton, elementary art teacher, 1987—. Member of Groton Arts Council (treasurer, 1983-88). *Exhibitions:* Cambridge Art Association, Cambridge, MA, 1985; Concord Art Association, Concord, MA, 1986 and 1988; Conant Gallery, Lawrence Academy, Groton, MA, 1987; New England Watercolor Society, Boston, MA, 1987 and 1990; Copley Society of Boston, 1989.

MEMBER: Society of Children's Book Writers, New England Watercolor Society, Cambridge Art Association, Concord Art Association, Indian Hill Arts, Acton Arts League (board member, 1984-85).

AWARDS, HONORS: Grumbacher Award for watercolor, Concord Art Association, 1983; Copley Artist Plaque, Copley Society of Boston, 1984; Juror's Award for painting, Cambridge Art Association, 1984; honorable mention, Winter Member's Show of New England Watercolor Society, 1986; *The Barrel in the Basement* was selected one of Child Study Association of America's Children's Books of the Year, 1986; Juror's Choice for watercolor, New England Watercolor Society, 1987; *I'll Meet You at the Cucumbers* was selected one of *School Library Journal*'s Best Books of 1988.

WRITINGS:

(And illustrator) *Arthur's Christmas Wish,* Atheneum, 1986.

ILLUSTRATOR

(Under name Sharon Wooding) Marjorie Stover, *Patrick and the Great Molasses Explosion,* Dillon, 1985.
(Under name Sharon Wooding) Barbara Brooks Wallace, *The Barrel in the Basement,* Atheneum, 1985.
(Under name Sharon Wooding) Lilian Moore, *I'll Meet You at the Cucumbers,* Atheneum, 1988.
(Under name Sharon Wooding) Lisa Westberg Peters, *Tania's Trolls,* Arcade, 1989.

Contributor to periodicals, including *Cricket* and *Young Children.*

WORK IN PROGRESS: Writing and illustrating *Micio, Cat of Venice,* for Putnam.

SIDELIGHTS: Sharon L. Wooding told *SATA:* "I was born and grew up on Staten Island, New York. We lived in a shady neighborhood of Victorian houses, where the sidewalks were of dirt and gravel and where a huge oak tree grew in the narrow paved street about a foot from the curb. I was the youngest of three children and the oldest of a batch of cousins who lived two houses away. None of us has ever been able to decide whether we grew up in rural America or in a major city. On one hand, most of us went barefoot all summer and played in the thick woods across the street. On the other, there was a New York City bus that stopped at the end of the road and connected us with other parts of the Island as well as with the ferry to Manhattan.

"I loved books when I was young, but I was more of a doer than a reader and spent many childhood hours playing the piano, writing stories, making up music, and drawing. There were many other children in the neighborhood, and together we produced plays—mostly musical comedies—ran around playing tag, and organized backyard fairs. We also built tree houses, and one night my cousin and I surreptitiously slept in one. We each tied a rope to our waists, just in case we were to roll out of bed during the night, and then we slept. Tolerance and good humor rather than the desire to supervise characterized the attitude of neighborhood parents towards our antics (except for the tree-house adventure, which no one knew about), and encouragement took the form of attendance at our performances and allowing us access to wood, nails, old fur pieces, and basement space. Our construction work and productions were, without question, children's projects.

"My favorite time of the year was summer, when I could do what I wanted to do when I wanted, and when I got to go with my family or cousins to a lake or to the ocean.

"I attended New York City public schools through high school, and although books and materials were in short supply in the fifties and sixties and the buildings were crowded, I came to know all kinds of children and some inspired teachers from many different backgrounds. During high school I did little with art but wrote for the school newspaper, mostly feature stories and poetry. I liked doing my 'Advice to the Lovelorn' column the best. I was also active in play production and received the drama award at graduation. I rarely became involved in theater as an adult, but the early experience has been invaluable to me as a teacher—directing children; as a writer—creating characters; and as an illustrator—setting up and pacing scenes that make up books.

"I went to Bucknell University, where I mostly took liberal arts courses, prepared to be an elementary school teacher, and was encouraged by a professor in the fine arts department to pursue further study in drawing and painting. It was there that I also fell in love with the biology major to whom I have been married for twenty-three years.

"While my husband, Jerry, began a career teaching secondary school science at the Peddie School in New Jersey, I continued to study painting through art associations and privately, and I taught in public school. In 1972, when our first child was almost two, we decided it was time for adventure and picked up and moved to Colorado Rocky Mountain School in Carbondale, where our daughter was born the following winter.

"Being a mother made me realize how completely fascinating young children were, and I took pages of notes on their development, especially in the area of language. For years observations on their unusual ways of looking at things (kitchen utensils that resembled rabbits), distortions in the way they heard words and phrases (a bee was a flasp and Johnny Appleseed was remembered as Peter Applegrower), and the emergence of imaginary friends were jotted down in profusion on papers tacked to the insides of kitchen cabinets. I began to see things through children's eyes, an ability I've been trying to cultivate ever since. I also became enamored of young children's literature during those years. All of this led

Arthur came out of his dream and looked up. Standing before his chair was a most peculiar looking mouse. (From *Arthur's Christmas Wish*, written and illustrated by Sharon L. Wooding.)

me into preschool teaching and classes and workshops in psychology, a subject that had fascinated me in college. I also continued to study life drawing and once spent a summer at the University of Colorado learning watermedia painting.

"In 1977, after our last child was born, I took on the position of director of publications at Colorado Rocky Mountain School, decided I really liked to write, and did an article about behaviors associated with hearing loss in children (our second child had a loss that had been difficult to detect). The article, my first, was accepted by *Young Children,* the journal of the National Association for the Education of Young Children. It was then that the notion crossed my mind that I might someday successfully write a children's book.

"When we moved back east to Massachusetts in 1979, Jerry and I made the decision that I would seriously pursue studies in visual arts, and I spent every spare moment away from the children—and sometimes with the children—working on assignments from classes I took at DeCordova and with a painter, George Dergalis of Wayland. This was a period of fast and steady growth artistically, and I began to enter my paintings in increasingly competitive shows in the Boston area, sometimes selling, winning prizes, occasionally accepting commissions, and finally beginning to see myself as a professional painter.

"One week, at the end of term, I wrote a story that I sent along with pictures to *Cricket* magazine, and after some good criticism from the editors there, a lot of rewriting, and some technical suggestions for the artwork, my first work of fiction, *Arthur's Christmas Wish,* was published. Confident now that I might be able to pass myself off as an author/illustrator, I began to build a children's illustration portfolio and set out for New York, where I saw eleven art directors and/or editors in five days. I got lots of advice and encouragement, but no work. The following spring I went to New York again, my portfolio slightly fatter, saw a few more publishers, and finally found myself in Jean Karl's office at Atheneum, being handed a manuscript. I would do a book this time.

"More writing and illustration work and now the teaching of elementary school art followed, and I try to get better and better at my crafts and more sensitive to what kids like to read. I'm up to fifty pages of manuscript now, my book designs are a bit more daring, and I'm still listening to children who thankfully still go barefoot sometimes, play in thick woods occasionally, and carry on, encouraged by adults' tolerance and good humor."

*   *   *

WRIGHTSON, (Alice) Patricia 1921-

PERSONAL: Born June 19, 1921, in Lismore, New South Wales, Australia; daughter of Charles Radcliff (a solicitor) and Alice (Dyer) Furlonger; married, 1943 (divorced, 1953); children: Jennifer Mary Wrightson Ireland, Peter Radcliff. *Education:* Attended St. Catherine's College, 1932, and State Correspondence School, 1933-34.

ADDRESSES: Home—Lohic, P.O. Box 91, Maclean, New South Wales 2463, Australia.

CAREER: Secretary and administrator with Bonalbo District Hospital, New South Wales, 1946-60, and Sydney District Nursing Association, New South Wales, 1960-64;

PATRICIA WRIGHTSON

Department of Education, New South Wales, assistant editor of *School Magazine,* 1964-70, editor, 1970-75; writer.

AWARDS, HONORS: Book of the Year Award from Children's Book Council of Australia, 1956, for *The Crooked Snake;* Notable Books of the Year Award from American Library Association, 1963, for *The Feather Star;* Book of the Year Award runner-up from Children's Book Council of Australia, and Children's Spring Book Festival Award from *Book World,* both 1968, and Hans Christian Andersen Honors List award of the International Board on Books for Young People (IBBY), 1970, all for *A Racecourse for Andy;* Book of the Year Honour List award from Children's Book Council of Australia, 1974, IBBY's Honor List for Text award, 1976, *Voice of Youth Advocate*'s Annual Selection of Best Science Fiction and Fantasy Titles for Young Adults, 1988, and Hans Christian Andersen Medal, all for *The Nargun and the Stars;* Officer, Order of the British Empire, 1978; Book of the Year award from Children's Book Council of Australia, and *Guardian* Award commendation, both 1978, IBBY's Books for Young People Honor List award, and Hans Christian Andersen Honors List award, both 1979, all for *The Ice Is Coming;* New South Wales Premier's Award for Ethnic Writing, 1979, selection as one of the Children's Books of the Year by Child Study Association of America, all 1979, all for *The Dark Bright Water;* Book of the Year Award high commendation from Children's Book Council of Australia, 1982, for *Behind the Wind;* Carnegie Medal Commendation, 1983, Book of the Year Award from the Children's

Book Council of Australia, *Boston Globe/Horn Book* Award for Fiction, Hans Christian Andersen Medal, and *Observer* Teenage Fiction Prize, all 1984, all for *A Little Fear;* Dromkeen Medal from the Dromkeen Children's Literature Foundation, 1984, for "a significant contribution to the appreciation and development of children's literature in Australia"; chosen to deliver sixteenth annual Arbuthnot Lecture, 1985; Golden Cat Award from the Sjoestrands Forlag AB, 1986, for "a contribution to children's and young adult literature"; Hans Christian Andersen Medal, 1986, for *Moon Dark;* Lady Cutler Award, 1986, New South Wales Premier's Special Occasional Award, 1988.

WRITINGS:

The Crooked Snake, illustrations by Margaret Horder, Angus & Robertson, 1955, reprinted, Hutchinson, 1972.
The Bunyip Hole, illustrations by Horder, Angus & Robertson, 1957, reprinted, Hutchinson, 1973.
The Rocks of Honey, illustrations by Horder, Angus & Robertson, 1960, reprinted, Penguin, 1977.
The Feather Star, illustrations by Noela Young, Hutchinson, 1962, Harcourt, 1963.
Down to Earth, illustrations by Horder, Harcourt, 1965.

Patricia Wrightson won the Children's Book Council of Australia's Book of the Year Honour for *The Nargun and the Stars.* (Cover illustration by Stephen Marchesi.)

I Own the Racecourse!, illustrations by Horder, Hutchinson, 1968, published in the United States as *A Racecourse for Andy,* Harcourt, 1968.
An Older Kind of Magic, illustrations by Young, Harcourt, 1972.
(Editor) *Beneath the Sun: An Australian Collection for Children,* Collins, 1972.
The Nargun and the Stars (fantasy), Hutchinson, 1973, Atheneum, 1974.
(Editor) *Emu Stew: An Illustrated Collection of Stories and Poems for Children,* Kestrel, 1976.
The Ice Is Coming (first book in fantasy trilogy), Atheneum, 1977.
The Dark Bright Water (second book in fantasy trilogy), Hutchinson, 1978, Atheneum, 1979.
Night Outside, illustrations by Jean Cooper-Brown, Rigby, 1979, illustrations by Beth Peck, Atheneum, 1985.
Behind the Wind (third book in fantasy trilogy), Hutchinson, 1981, published in the United States as *Journey behind the Wind,* Atheneum, 1981.
A Little Fear (fantasy), Atheneum, 1983.
Moon Dark, illustrated by Young, McElderry Books, 1988.
Balyet, McElderry Books, 1989.

Wrightson's books have been translated into nine languages, including German, Spanish, and Norwegian. Her papers are collected at the Lu Rees Archives, Canberra College of Advanced Education Library, Australia, and the Kerlan Collection at the University of Minnesota.

ADAPTATIONS: The Nargun and the Stars was adapted as a television series by ABC-TV in 1977. *I Own the Racecourse* was filmed by Barron Films in 1985.

SIDELIGHTS: Patricia Wrightson is one of Australia's best known writers for children and young adults. She has earned numerous awards and has gained an international following for her books, most of which are fantasies that draw upon ancient Australian myths. According to Zena Sutherland and May Hill Arbuthnot in their *Children and Books,* "Wrightson has been a channel through which children of her own and other countries have learned the beauty and dignity of the legendary creatures of Aborigine mythology."

Wrightson was born in 1921, in a small country town in New South Wales. She lived on a farm with her parents and older sisters until the age of four, and her memories of those early years are vivid and pleasant. With the exception of one year spent in a suburb of Sydney, she and her family remained in the coastal river country throughout her childhood. Culturally isolated, Wrightson became an avid reader and believes that her love of books originated in her father's nightly readings from Charles Dickens. As she indicates in her essay "Becoming an Australian" for *Something about the Author Autobiography Series:* "Our school was a good one, the central school for a large district and one of the biggest in the State; but it had no library. That's how things were in those days. . . . You had your own books, and lent them to friends and borrowed theirs. We were lucky; we had, between us, a lot of books, and my father bought lots that were 'family' books, mainly for adults but good for children to prowl in." However, as Wrightson continues, "Without knowing it, I began to feel dissatisfied about something, unsure about something; it was many years before I knew what, or why. . . . If you looked at all those books we had as children, and all the others that my friends had when they were children, you have to notice something strange: they were all fine books that I

Patricia Wrightson's *The Ice Is Coming* is a fantasy novel describing a journey through Australia, revealing the land and its creatures. (Cover illustration by Victor Mays.)

am glad to have known—but none of them were written by an Australian, or about Australia."

When she finished primary school, she spent one year in a boarding school before returning home to begin high school by a correspondence school for children who lived in isolated areas. She graduated when World War II began in 1939, and then went to Sydney with a friend to work in a munitions factory. By the time the war was over, she was married; however, when the marriage failed, she returned with her two children to live with her parents in the country. It was at that time that she began to think about writing books for her own children about the Australia they knew. She indicates in her autobiographical essay: "Before I had even finished typing each story, my father was reading to Jenny and Peter the part that was typed so far; and while he read I would sit quietly, watching the children's faces. . . . By watching their faces I knew what they really thought. I could see where something bothered them, and sort it out later." She sent the manuscript to a publisher and continued to work on other books; when *The Crooked Snake* was finally published, the Children's Book Council of Australia had granted it the Book of the Year Award. Together with its successors, *The Bunyip Hole, The Rocks of Honey, The Feather Star,* and *Down to Earth,* it recalls the author's own childhood in New South Wales, the country her grandfather helped pioneer.

"It was a surprising time," she relates in her autobiographical essay. "I had thought of my books as little, local things that hardly anyone would notice; I had never thought how far a book might travel. It was surprising to discover, by winning the award, a whole community of people who were deeply interested in books for children, who noticed every new one, and with whom you could talk seriously and deeply about them."

Wrightson was relatively unknown outside Australia until the publication of *A Racecourse for Andy,* when, according to John Rowe Townsend in *A Sounding of Storytellers: New and Revised Essays on Contemporary Writers for Children,* she "was suddenly recognized far beyond her own shores as a leading children's writer." The book centers on Andy, a mildly retarded boy who is convinced that he has "bought" the local racecourse from a derelict for three dollars. His conviction results in a conflict between the adults, who encourage the fantasy because they don't want to disappoint him, and his young friends, who realize the potential harm of deluding him. As Townsend writes: "One wonders what way out there can be that will not deal a fearful psychological blow to Andy. But the author finds one; and it is the perfect and satisfying answer."

Critics praised Wrightson's portrayal of Andy as realistic and sensitive; she "allows us to understand him and feel his frustration," remarks Christine McDonnell in *Horn Book.* "Wrightson marks Andy's difference from the other boys with subtle indications of his behaviour, his facial expressions, his mode of speech," notes Margery Fisher in her

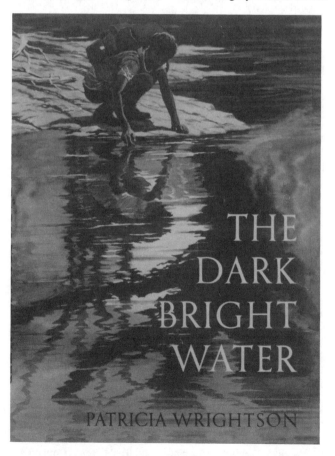

Dustjacket from *The Dark Bright Water,* the second book in Patricia Wrightson's fantasy trilogy. (Cover illustration by Victor Mays.)

Who's Who in Children's Books: A Treasury of the Familiar Characters of Childhood. Calling it "a refreshing, optimistic book," McDonnell adds: "It is about the best in people, their basic goodness. It is about friendship and the responsibility friends have for each other. . . . But most of all, it is about Andy, who sees life through the glass in the window, who trusts and smiles, who means well even in his most calamitous undertakings, who shares his laughter and his happiness. Andy is special, but his limitations can be seen as assets. Andy is innocent, and Patricia Wrightson shows us that innocence is a gift."

It would have been very easy for Wrightson to duplicate the success of her first book by writing a second book similar to it; because she felt she needed to learn her craft, she vowed to try to attempt something new each time. "I felt very much a beginner who needed to learn . . . ," she says in her *Top of the News* article, "Stones into Pools." "It might be a simple story, easy for other writers, but it should be new and difficult for me." Wanting to try fantasy, Wrightson was specific in the type of magic she was trying to write about. In her autobiographical essay, she explains, "I wanted real magic in my story, of the kind that people once believed: the dangerous kind that makes your fingers prickle." And, as she indicates in an essay in Townsend's *A Sounding of Storytellers,* "Each book at least from the second on was a move towards . . . fantasy. Not the escape from life that some people see as fantasy, nor the symbolism of life that is some fantasy, but that strangeness and fullness of life that spills out of the bucket of reality—the human experience of fantasy."

According to Wrightson, though, she had a difficult time achieving in words the kind of fantasy she had imagined. Fearful that Australia had no magic or fairies of its own, she stumbled upon a story about elfish spirits in the beliefs of the Aboriginal Australians: "They seemed to fit very naturally into Australian rock and forest," she recalls in her autobiographical essay. "At last I began to see. Of course there would be Australian fairies, because all people have fairies. Fairies explain the odd happenings that you don't understand, and the things that you very nearly see. . . . Magic belongs to simple people, and is shaped by the things that simple people know: the places where they live and the lives they lead."

After much reading, Wrightson collected a small number of "native Australian spirits and sprites and monsters," but was still having trouble. "The difficulty was such a problem that in the end it became a strength," she continues in her autobiographical essay. "No matter how much anthropology I read in my search for more spirits, I could not become Aboriginal. There was only one thing I shared with the Aboriginal people, and that was the land itself. Since I couldn't imagine myself forward into the people, I must imagine myself backward into the land—and, in some mysterious way, this worked. I could get the feel of these native spirits as long as I kept on seeing them as part of the land."

Wrightson's efforts proved successful with other people as well; and, as she concludes: "I was finding that fantasy was what I most wanted to write. More than that: in my struggle to see the folklore truly, in terms of the land out of which it grew, I myself seemed to have become truly Australian at last. I had gained a wider and truer vision of the strange old land; I was surely at home in it." Wrightson explains in a *Horn Book* interview: "It really was an accident that threw me into the folklore of Aboriginal Australia. I was just a writer with a need to explore, one who liked the kind of fantasy that draws on authentic experience in order to compel belief; and it

seemed a worthwhile challenge to try to produce a fantasy of that kind."

Wrightson's readers responded warmly to these spirit characters, especially the Nargun, an ancient mass of stone. "The Nargun, a being evoked from a boulder, never humanized, allowed limited movement but the merest semblance of limb and eye, must be accounted one of the most remarkable myth-beings ever created," states Fisher. Wrightson comments in *Horn Book* that after *The Nargun and the Stars* was published, she received many letters and calls from people who "all said the same thing: the Nargun identified something for them, gave them the country as they had known and felt it in an unspoken way."

The Nargun and the Stars, which tells the story of a boy and his aunt and uncle who try to protect their land from the Nargun, was equally well-received by critics. A *Times Literary Supplement* contributor, for example, comments that "the Nargun itself, described with passion, is a poetic creation, genuinely frightening and pitiful." C. S. Hannabuss, in *Children's Book Review,* indicates that "the landscape . . . is a reflection and extension of the imagination." Townsend suggests that "there is something more truly spine-chilling here than anywhere else" in her work. Though menacing, the Nargun is essentially amoral; thus the horror in the book "has its own origin not so much in the acts of an intrinsically evil being, but in a creature's natural response to threats to its own existence," observe Hugh and Maureen Crago in *Signal.* Ethel L. Heins indicates in a *Horn Book* review that the book's "essentially simple plot is worked into the rich fabric of a story that begins serenely, arches up to a great crescendo of suspense, and then falls away at the end to 'a whisper in the dark.'"

In *The Ice Is Coming,* Wrightson describes a journey from the interior of Australia down the eastern seaboard to the southwest coast of Victoria. Calling it "a magnificent heroic novel," a contributor to the *Junior Bookshelf,* details its plot: "It is the story of how the Ninya, manlike spirits of ice, broke out of their caves in the heart of Australia and set out to create a new ice age, and how their enterprise was challenged by a young Aborigine and a Mimi, a frail spirit of the rocks." Referring to the novel as a "tale of Australian beings," Margery Fisher continues in *Growing Point:* "The relation of the various beings to the land, the central element in the complex folk-beliefs of the aboriginals, is consistently felt through the book, not superimposed but an integral part of its argument and its setting." Rebecca Lukens, writing in the *World of Children's Books,* regards the novel as stylistically pleasing, as well. "Her keen appreciation of the land, of its sounds, its wild animals and birds, its insects and its climate is apparent in the imagery rich with connotative meaning." According to Jane Langton in the *New York Times Book Review,* "Wrightson gives a sentence a gentle shove and it seems to roll over the Australian landscape, echoing down the page in patterns of sound, transforming print into vistas of haunted cliffs." Believing that "Wrightson handles her extra-human characters with the utmost ease and confidence," Fisher concludes: "More diffused in narrative and less concentrated than *The Nargun and the Stars,* it is an inevitable sequel to it, taking us more deeply into a unique, serious, considered interpretation of nature."

Moon Dark is about a dog who lives with an old fisherman in a remote area by the sea. When the population grows and disturbs wildlife habitats, the animals intercede by tricking the humans. "Wrightson's prose has real fairytale qualities, and when the animals act to restore ecological balance, they

The new street was a quiet one, dimly lit. (From *Night Outside,* by Patricia Wrightson, illustrated by Beth Peck.)

do so through magic," writes Donald McCaig in the *Washington Post Book World.* "Their magic owes more to Australian Aboriginal beliefs than Hans Christian Andersen." Praising Wrightson for bringing an understanding of the ecology to children, Leonard H. Orr suggests, however, in the *New York Times Book Review* that this goal sometimes "seems to impede the flow of an otherwise accomplished tale," adding that "such objections may be the quibbles of a grown-up, for young readers have an appetite for this sort of animal tale."

Wrightson indicates in *Authors and Artists for Young Adults:* "I do think I've been lucky to work in Australia, for there we had no paths to follow. Most other countries had well-established paths. . . . We have all seen the field extending as the new paths opened it up, so that now the work of thirty years ago needs to be seen in the context of its time. But Australian writers, with so small a body of work behind them, could feel that the country's literature was immediately in their hands. Every story that anyone could conceive was his own new concept, not shaped or directed or limited by other people's thinking; to be worked out in his own way and for almost the first time." She indicates in her "Hans Christian Andersen Award Acceptance Speech" that even her failures were lucky: "It can't be common, in the twentieth century, for a writer to discover a hole in his nation's literature through the accident of falling into it; and then to

find the missing piece through sheer need, and to have it welcomed so warmly."

WORKS CITED:

Crago, Hugh and Maureen, "Patricia Wrightson," *Signal,* January, 1976, pp. 31-39.

Fisher, Margery, *Who's Who in Children's Books: A Treasury of Familiar Characters of Childhood,* Holt, 1975, pp. 21-22, 256.

Fisher, Margery, "Special Review," *Growing Point,* December, 1977, pp. 3217-18.

Hannabuss, C. S., review of *The Nargun and the Stars, Children's Book Review,* December, 1973, pp. 180-81.

Heins, Ethel L., review of *The Nargun and the Stars, Horn Book,* August, 1974, pp. 382-83.

Langton, Jane, review of *The Ice Is Coming, New York Times Book Review,* January 28, 1978, p. 26.

Lukens, Rebecca, review of *The Ice Is Coming, World of Children's Books,* fall, 1978, pp. 63-65.

McCaig, Donald, review of *Moon Dark, Washington Post Book World,* May 8, 1988, p. 23.

McDonnell, Christine, review of *A Racecourse for Andy, Horn Book,* April, 1980, pp. 196-99.

Orr, Leonard H., review of *Moon Dark, New York Times Book Review,* January 29, 1989, p. 39.

Review of *The Ice Is Coming, Junior Bookshelf,* February, 1978, pp. 52-53.

Dustjacket from *Journey behind the Wind,* a fantasy novel that won high commendation from the Children's Book Council of Australia in 1982.

Something about the Author Autobiography Series, Volume 4, Gale, 1987, pp. 335-46.

Sutherland, Zena, and May Hill Arbuthnot, *Children and Books,* 7th edition, Scott, Foresman, 1986, p. 232.

Times Literary Supplement, November 23, 1973, p. 1434.

Townsend, John Rowe, *A Sounding of Storytellers: New and Revised Essays on Contemporary Writers for Children,* Lippincott, 1971, pp. 194-206.

Wrightson, Patricia, "Ever Since My Accident: Aboriginal Folklore and Australian Fantasy," *Horn Book,* December, 1980, pp. 609-17.

Wrightson, Patricia, "Stones into Pools," *Top of the News,* spring, 1985.

Wrightson, Patricia, "Hans Christian Andersen Award Acceptance Speech," *Bookbird,* March/April, 1986.

Wrightson, Patricia, *Authors and Artists for Young Adults,* Volume 5, Gale, 1990, pp. 236-237.

FOR MORE INFORMATION SEE:

BOOKS

Author's Choice/2, Crowell, 1974.

Children's Literature in Education/15, APS Publications, 1974.

Children's Literature Review, Gale, Volume 4, 1982, Volume 14, 1988.

Contemporary Authors New Revision Series, Volume 19, Gale, 1987.

de Montreville, Doris, and Elizabeth D. Crawford, *Fourth Book of Junior Authors and Illustrators,* H. W. Wilson, 1978.

Kirkpatrick, D. L., *Twentieth-Century Children's Writers,* St. Martin's, 1978, 2nd edition, 1983.

Saxby, H. M., *A History of Australian Children's Literature,* Volume 2, Wentworth Books, 1971.

Something about the Author, Volume 8, Gale, 1976.

Townsend, John Rowe, *A Sense of Story,* Lippincott, 1971.

Townsend, *Written for Children: An Outline of English-Language Children's Literature,* 2nd revised edition, Lippincott, 1983.

Ward, Martha E., and Dorothy A. Marquardt, *Authors of Books for Young People,* Scarecrow, 1971.

PERIODICALS

Best Sellers, December, 1983.

Bookbird, Number 2, 1970; April, 1984; February, 1986; June 15, 1986.

Book World, May 5, 1968.

Books and Bookmen, July, 1968.

Bulletin of the Center for Children's Books, February, 1978; July/August, 1979; November, 1983; October, 1985; May, 1988.

Children's Book World, July/August, 1987.

Children's Literature in Education, September, 1974; spring, 1978.

Growing Point, October, 1977; September, 1979.

Horn Book, June, 1963; June, 1965; October, 1972; February, 1978; April, 1979; August, 1981; August, 1982; February, 1984; January/February, 1985; January/February, 1986; September/October, 1986; March/April, 1988.

Junior Bookshelf, August, 1979; December, 1981; October, 1983.

Kirkus Reviews, September 15, 1977.

National Observer, July 1, 1968.

Newsletter, May, 1970.

New York Public Library News Release, April, 1985.

New York Times Book Review, November 13, 1983.

Publishers Weekly, August 30, 1985; October 31, 1986; October 30, 1987; March 21, 1989.

Patricia Wrightson's *A Little Fear* garnered several awards, including a 1983 Carnegie Medal Commendation. (Cover illustration by Robert Roennfeldt.)

School Librarian, March, 1969; December, 1973.

School Library Journal, May, 1984; December, 1985.

Starship: The Magazine about Science Fiction, winter/spring, 1982-83.

Times Literary Supplement, March 25, 1977.

Voice of Youth Advocate, April, 1988.

Washington Post Book World, November 5, 1972.

Young Readers' Review, September, 1968.

*   *   *

ZAIDENBERG, Arthur 1908(?)-1990 (Azaid)

OBITUARY NOTICE—See index for *SATA* sketch: Born August 15, 1908 (one source indicates c. 1902), in New York, NY; died April 16, 1990, in San Miguel de Allende, Mexico. Artist, educator, editor, and author. Zaidenberg created murals for more than one hundred hotels throughout the Miami Beach area. In addition, he was a pioneering art instructor whose career spanned from the 1930s, when he taught at the Roerich Museum in New York City, to the 1970s, when he worked at the Institute of San Miguel in

Mexico. As a teacher, he developed various techniques—including one derived from alphabet shapes—to improve students' drawing skills. Among his many books are *Anyone Can Draw,* written with Jerome D. Engel; *Simple Cartooning: Self-Taught,* written under the pseudonym Azaid; *The Art of the Artist: Theories and Techniques of Art by The Artists Themselves,* which he edited; *The Art of Drawing Women: A Gallery of Life Figures;* and *The Painting of Pictures.* He also produced the "How to Draw" series for young people.

OBITUARIES AND OTHER SOURCES:

BOOKS

Who's Who in America, 43rd edition, Marquis, 1984.

PERIODICALS

Chicago Tribune, April 23, 1990.

*   *   *

ZED, Dr.
See PENROSE, Gordon

*   *   *

ZWERGER, Lisbeth 1954-

PERSONAL: Surname is pronounced "tsvair-ger"; born May 26, 1954, in Vienna, Austria; daughter of Reinhold (a designer) and Waltraut (a medical assistant; maiden name, Passler) Zwerger; married John Rowe (an artist), January 19, 1984. *Education:* Attended Hochschule fuer Angewandte Kunst in Wien (University of Applied Art in Vienna), 1971-74.

ADDRESSES: c/o Neugebauer Press, Bonauweg 11, A-5020 Salzburg, Austria.

CAREER: Illustrator. Worked part-time for an insurance company. *Exhibitions:* Illustrative work has been shown in Austria, Belgium, Czechoslovakia, Germany, Italy, Japan, and the United States.

AWARDS, HONORS: Honored for graphic excellence at the Bologna International Children's Book Fair, 1978, for *The Strange Child,* 1980, for *Hansel and Gretel,* 1982, for *The Swineherd,* 1986, for *The Deliverers of Their Country,* and 1987, for *The Canterville Ghost;* International Biennial of Illustration, Bratislava, Czechoslovakia, received honor diploma, 1979, for *Hansel and Gretel* and *The Legend of Rosepetal,* received gold plaquette, 1981, for *Thumbeline,* and 1983, for *The Seven Ravens* and *Little Red Cap,* and received a Golden Apple, 1985, for *Selfish Giant; New York Times* chose *Little Red Cap* and *The Gift of the Magi,* both 1983, as among the Best Illustrated Books of the year; Hans Christian Andersen Award for Illustration, 1990.

ILLUSTRATOR:

E. T. A. Hoffmann, *The Strange Child,* Picture Book Studio, 1984 (published in German as *Das fremde Kind,* Neugebauer, 1977).

Clemens Brentano, *The Legend of Rosepetal,* Picture Book Studio, 1985 (published in German as *Das Maerchen von Rosenblaettchen,* Neugebauer, 1978).

LISBETH ZWERGER

Jakob and Wilhelm K. Grimm, *Hansel and Gretel,* translated by Elizabeth D. Crawford, Morrow, 1979.

E. T. A. Hoffmann, *The Nutcracker,* adapted by Anthea Bell, Picture Book Studio, 1987 (published in German as *Nussknacker und Mausekoenig,* Neugebauer, 1979).

Hans Christian Andersen, *Thumbeline,* translated by Richard and Clara Winston, Morrow, 1980.

Jakob and Wilhelm K. Grimm, *The Seven Ravens,* translated by Crawford, Morrow, 1981.

Hans Christian Andersen, *The Swineherd,* translated by Bell, Morrow, 1982.

O. Henry, *The Gift of the Magi,* Picture Book Studio, 1982.

Jakob and Wilhelm K. Grimm, *Little Red Cap,* Morrow, 1983.

Oscar Wilde, *The Selfish Giant,* Picture Book Studio, 1984.

Hans Christian Andersen, *The Nightingale,* Picture Book Studio, 1984.

Edith Nesbit, *The Deliverers of Their Country,* Picture Book Studio, 1985.

Oscar Wilde, *The Canterville Ghost,* Picture Book Studio, 1986.

Charles Dickens, *A Christmas Carol,* Picture Book Studio, 1988.

Aesop, *Aesop's Fables,* Picture Book Studio, 1989.

Heinz Janisch, *Till Eulenspiegel's Merry Pranks,* translated by Bell, Picture Book Studio, 1990.

Zwerger's books have been published in many countries, including Australia, Belgium, Denmark, England, Finland, France, Greece, Holland, Hungary, Italy, Japan, South Africa, Spain, Sweden, and the United States.

WORK IN PROGRESS: Illustrating a book tentatively titled *Twelve Hans Christian Andersen Fairy Tales: Selected and Illustrated by Lisbeth Zwerger,* for Neugebauer Press, 1991, and for Picture Book Studio, 1992.

SIDELIGHTS: Lisbeth Zwerger is recognized internationally as one of the finest illustrators of children's literature. Providing the drawings for such classic narratives as O. Henry's *The Gift of the Magi* and Charles Dickens's *A Christmas Carol,* Zwerger is the 1990 recipient of the prestigious Hans Christian Andersen Award. "Zwerger's dreamy, delicately drawn ink-and-wash illustrations shine with humanity, and are often spiced with humor," Heather Frederick writes in *Publishers Weekly,* describing the illustrator's appeal. Her drawings are further celebrated for their ability to enhance and complement the literature they accompany. According to Frederick, "Zwerger is indisputably one of the most talented illustrators this century has produced."

Born in 1954 in Vienna, Austria, Zwerger grew up in a household attuned to artistic values: her father was a graphic artist, and her mother, a medical assistant, had a knack for fashion design. While Zwerger relished the emphasis on art in her childhood, she experienced many troubles in her schooling. "I wish I could say that by growing up in such 'colourful' surroundings my childhood was somehow different or exciting," Zwerger expressed in *Something about the Author Autobiography Series* (*SAAS*), "but sadly it was neither." She continued, "I had an awful time at school; I hated it. I was fat and wore thick-lensed glasses. I had troubles with my lessons, I hated sport, and I disliked all the teachers."

In addition to her public schooling, Zwerger took private lessons, a common practice in European education. She would begin her days practicing the piano, proceed by going to school, return home for lunch, and later attend private tutoring sessions where the teachers "would do their best in trying to turn us into young Einsteins," proclaimed Zwerger later in *SAAS.* "It was all a nightmare for me."

Zwerger, however, does hold some fond memories of her childhood. Having relatives on the opposite side of Austria in the mountains of East Tirol, Zwerger enjoyed spending summers on a farm with her sister, Christine. "The summers seemed endless then; and there, for a while at least, I could forget all about my problems at school," the illustrator related in *SAAS.*

Although Zwerger cannot remember exactly when she started drawing, she recalls being encouraged to sketch by her parents, who were talented in creating such works of art and craft as paintings, puppets, and photography. Zwerger and her sister engaged in many drawing projects, but Zwerger always exhibited a tendency toward illustration.

Meanwhile at school, Zwerger's distress persisted, and her parents took her to a child psychologist. "I was a problem child!," exclaimed Zwerger in *SAAS.* Recognizing Zwerger's talent in drawing, the psychologist suggested the young girl attend a less academically oriented school. Enrolling in 1970 in a cloister school, where she was extremely unhappy, Zwerger later enlisted in the Hochschule fuer Angewandte Kunst in Wien (University of Applied Art in Vienna). There, under less restrictive instruction, Zwerger at last felt at ease in school. She enjoyed her art classes as well as her freedom, but she was disappointed at the lack of classes focusing on illustration. The teachers at the school were "even anti-

illustration," Zwerger recalled in *SAAS,* "and did their best to squash any feelings for illustration that I might have had by telling me that it would be quite impossible to make a living or find work connected with it. Having said this they didn't then offer me any alternative ways of surviving; we were just left to wonder what it was all about.

"Even so," Zwerger continued, "I did manage to somehow illustrate a few things, but in general I felt a bit discouraged. The longer I attended college, the further away I seemed to drift from illustrating or drawing, until eventually things came to a sort of standstill and I lost interest all together."

During the spring of 1974 Zwerger met John Rowe, an English artist vacationing in Vienna who later became Zwerger's husband. The two became best friends and, when Rowe decided to remain in Vienna to study, they began looking for an apartment to rent together. "This did not please my parents one little bit," Zwerger maintained in *SAAS.* In addition, the illustrator dropped out of college, deciding her time there was not well spent. "Just when my parents had started to believe that I would be saved after all," Zwerger continued, "I brought their hopes and dreams crashing down with these two decisions. Once again I was a problem."

Financially desperate and seemingly without direction, Zwerger was inspired to illustrate again when Rowe brought home a book of illustrations by English artist Arthur Rackham; the book "was to change my whole outlook, if not my life!," declared Zwerger in *SAAS.* "I had never seen anything like them, and as I looked through the book, something inside of me seemed to come alive. My love for illustrating returned there and then. I felt so inspired that I wanted to start again straight away."

Accustomed to drawing in black and white, Zwerger tried to imitate Rackham's style of line and color. Rowe showed her how to use a two-color technique, at which Zwerger soon became adept. Only when Zwerger's mother offered to purchase some of her illustrations did Zwerger begin to earn money from her craft. The money helped immensely, for Zwerger and Rowe lived in a Vienna apartment with little furniture and limited funds for food.

Using the two-color technique to illustrate scenes from stories by such authors as E. T. A. Hoffmann and Hans Christian Andersen, Zwerger found modest success with her illustrations outside of her mother's purchases; when she showed several drawings at a private gallery in a joint exhibition with her father and Rowe, every one of her pieces was sold.

Following this taste of success, Zwerger and Rowe decided to move to England where they secured a tiny attic apartment; Rowe worked as a book packer, and Zwerger continued to illustrate. In the meantime, Zwerger's mother was showing her daughter's drawings to various publishers in and around Vienna—with little fortune. Eventually, though, Friedrich Neugebauer, the owner of a small publishing company, took an interest in Zwerger's work; when Zwerger and Rowe returned to Vienna to live, Zwerger met with Neugebauer. The publisher liked her drawings for Hoffmann's *The Strange Child* and decided to have Zwerger prepare illustrations for the entire book.

Zwerger, who was accustomed to drawing on a small scale, had some difficulty adjusting to producing larger illustrations. Persevering, she finished the drawings about one year later. Though surprised at the length of time Zwerger took on

The curtains of his bed were drawn aside; and Scrooge, starting up into a half-recumbent attitude, found himself face to face with the unearthly visitor who drew them. (From *A Christmas Carol,* by Charles Dickens, illustrated by Lisbeth Zwerger.)

The Spirit stood among the graves and pointed down to one. (From *A Christmas Carol,* by Charles Dickens, illustrated by Lisbeth Zwerger.)

the illustrations, Neugebauer was impressed by the work, bought the drawings, and enlisted Zwerger to illustrate three more books. Zwerger later produced illustrations for the Neugebauer's son, Michael, who had bought his father's publishing company.

Even though Zwerger has found success with her drawings, she contends that illustrating is never a simple process. "I slowly overcame many of the technical problems," she pointed out in *SAAS,* "but I have to admit that, as with so many 'artists,' I have to relearn everything at the start of each picture. It's never easy for me and I often have the feeling that I've never drawn before in my life as I sit looking at a blank sheet of paper, wondering how I'm going to manage with this one. . . . It always takes a few pictures before I can settle down and get into it, and I'm often a bit bad tempered at this stage. [My husband], who is my resident critic (the only one I trust), always looks through my 'roughs,' criticizing this or that, and we always end up shouting at each other. It's a touchy time and I think we're both relieved once it's over."

While she takes great pains to perfect the technical aspects of her craft, Zwerger points out that choosing the subject matter of her illustrations is just as important and, in fact, the most enjoyable part of her work. "When I design each illustra-

**Down rippled the brown cascade. "Twenty dollars,"
said Madame, lifting the mass with a practised hand.**
(From *The Gift of the Magi,* by O. Henry, illustrated by Lisbeth Zwerger.)

tion," Zwerger continued in *SAAS,* "I take particular pleasure in using objects, animals, and people that have some personal meaning to me. It might be a piece of furniture, or a cat, or even a picture hanging on the wall within my picture." Zwerger also includes in her works details associated with people she knows. For example, her husband has appeared as several characters in her illustrations. In addition, she conducts research in order to accurately portray certain objects, characters, and time periods in her pictures.

Another aspect that Zwerger deems important in her work is determining the proper story to illustrate. "At first I was quite content to carry on illustrating the sort of stories that I knew from my childhood, all the classics from Grimm or Andersen," she disclosed in *SAAS,* "but gradually I began to find the moral in some of them slightly degrading. The sort of stories that I mean are the ones where a beautiful, poor, but suffering girl, finally ends up marrying a prince, because deep down at heart she has been a good girl all along and in spite of all the suffering has managed to do all the right things. . . . What's more, it became increasingly boring to always illustrate the same sort of stories. It was very refreshing to later illustrate such stories as *The Gift of the Magi* and [Oscar Wilde's] *The Selfish Giant.*

"But it's a never-ending problem for me now," Zwerger continued. "When I look for a story, it has to contain all the right ingredients: for a start, it has to be the right length; I like it to have a main character who is both comical and touching; it has to interest me (of course); it has to be the sort of story that my type of illustrations fit; and, last but not least, it has to have no sexist morals."

Zwerger has considered writing her own stories but as yet has decided to stay with illustrating only. She feels fortunate that her publishers, both Friedrich and Michael Neugebauer, have given her extensive freedom to illustrate the stories of her choice. "I don't think I could have ever survived as an illustrator without it," Zwerger expressed in *SAAS.* "It's so important for me to really identify with the characters that if someone were to choose the stories, I might not be able to identify with any part of it."

Since Michael Neugebauer began publishing her work, Zwerger has become internationally recognized, particularly in the United States. She toured America in 1984 and, having won the Hans Christian Andersen Award, plans another tour of the country. The artist then expects to illustrate another book by Andersen. "Although she's eager to start work on it," Frederick asserted, "Zwerger notes that most likely some critics will say, 'Not Andersen again!' [Zwerger] smiles and shrugs. 'So what do you do? I want to do the stories I like. It's difficult.'"

WORKS CITED:

Frederick, Heather, "A Talk with Lisbeth Zwerger," *Publishers Weekly,* October 26, 1990, p. 42.
Zwerger, Lisbeth, *Something about the Author Autobiography Series,* Volume 13, Gale, 1991.